Reading and All That Jazz

Peter Mather

Rita McCarthy

Glendale Community College

Glendale, Arizona

McGraw Hill

Boston   Burr Ridge, IL   Dubuque, IA   Madison, WI
New York   San Francisco   St. Louis   Bangkok
Bogotá   Caracas   Lisbon   London   Madrid
Mexico City   Milan   New Delhi   Seoul   Singapore
Sydney   Taipei   Toronto

McGraw-Hill

A Division of The **McGraw·Hill** *Companies*

READING AND ALL THAT JAZZ: TUNING UP YOUR
READING, THINKING, AND STUDY SKILLS

Copyright © 1999 by The McGraw-Hill Companies, Inc.
All rights reserved. Printed in the United States of
America. Except as permitted under the United States
Copyright Act of 1976, no part of this publication may be
reproduced or distributed in any form or by any means,
or stored in a data base or retrieval system, without the
prior written permission of the publisher.

This book is printed on acid-free paper.

5 6 7 8 9 0 QPD/QPD 9 3 2 1

ISBN 0-07-041099-2

Editorial director: *Phillip A. Butcher*
Sponsoring editor: *Sarah Moyers*
Editorial assistant: *Bennett Morrison*
Marketing manager: *Lesley Denton*
Project manager: *Alisa Watson*
Senior production supervisor: *Melonie Salvati*
Freelance design coordinator: *Gino Cieslik*
Photo research coordinator: *Sharon Miller*
Photo freelancer: *Connie Gardner*
Supplement coordinator: *Rose M. Range*
Compositor: *GAC Shepard Poorman Communications*
Typeface: *10/13 Palatino*
Printer: *Quebecor Printing Book Group/Dubuque*

Library of Congress Cataloging-in-Publication Data
Mather, Peter.
    Reading and all that jazz: Tuning Up your reading, thinking, and
study skills/Peter Mather, Rita McCarthy.
        p.   cm.
    Includes index.
    ISBN 0-07-041099-2 (alk. paper)
    1. Reading (Higher education)—United States. 2. English
language—Rhetoric. 3. Critical thinking—Study and teaching
(Higher)—United States. 4. Study skills—United States.
I. McCarthy, Rita. II. Title.
LB2395.3.M28 1999
428.4'071'1—dc21   98-18568
                                                            CIP

http://www.mhhe.com

Peter dedicates this book to his late parents, Carl and Dorothy; and his brother and sister-in-law, John and Peggy.

Rita dedicates this book to her parents, Adolph and Bertha; her sons, Ryan and Steve; and especially her husband, Greg.

About the Authors

Peter Mather—Dr. Mather earned his B.A. in Government from the University of Redlands, an M.A. in African Studies from the University of California, Los Angeles, an M.A. in Reading from California State University, Los Angeles, and an Ed.D. in Curriculum and Instruction from the University of Southern California. He has taught reading at the secondary, adult-education, and community-college levels for over 20 years. For the past eight years, he has taught reading and American government at Glendale Community College. He has published articles in the *Journal of Reading*.

Rita Romero McCarthy—Ms. McCarthy earned a B.A. in Sociology and History from the University of California, Berkeley, and an M.A. in Education from Arizona State University. She has taught at the elementary, secondary, adult-education, and community-college levels. For the past 10 years, she has taught developmental reading and E.S.L. classes at Glendale Community College. Ms. McCarthy has published articles in professional journals and other media on the use of bibliotherapy. She has also published reading lists for beginning and remedial readers and is a reading specialist.

Brief Contents

Contents

Copyright © 1999 by The McGraw-Hill Companies, Inc.

Preface to the Instructor

Purpose of the Text

This book is based on the premise that learning to be a good reader requires the development of critical thinking skills. As the British philosopher John Locke said, "Reading furnishes the mind only with materials of knowledge; it is thinking that makes what we read ours."

The material presented in this book has a three-fold purpose: (1) to help students develop effective reading and studying skills, (2) to expose students to well-written contemporary material from eminent authors, and (3) to encourage the students to be personally involved in the reading process by providing them with information that they will find useful and interesting in developing themselves as persons and learners. A student who completes this book should be well-prepared to take college-level courses that emphasize reading and critical thinking skills.

Theme and Title

The theme of jazz loosely holds the book together. The theme and title were selected to emphasize a positive, exciting, personally involved approach to reading and learning. We want teachers to feel free to improvise in their use of this book so that it will become an effective learning tool for classes of differing skill levels and areas of interest. We also want students to have practice not just with multiple-choice and true-or-false questions but also with open-ended questions that require more analysis and personal involvement from them. Continuing our theme through the book, each part begins with a quote relating reading to jazz.

Reading Selections

The selections appearing in the book were chosen for excellence in writing, contemporary relevance and interest, and appeal to a diverse audience. Many of the authors are famous or award-winning. Though the predominant emphasis is on contemporary material, some "classics" have also been included. We made an effort to find selections that would be supportive, encouraging, and useful to the students. The selections enable the students to clarify their own values and experience events through another's eyes. Most of the reading selections have not previously appeared in a reading textbook. The selections come from a variety of sources, including textbooks, contemporary literature (fiction and nonfiction), magazines, and newspapers. Some of the selections come from essays; others from poetry, fables, and cartoons. The selections have all been classroom tested.

Organization of the Text

This book is organized along two dimensions. First, each successive part of the book focuses on different skills that an effective learner and reader must master. Second, the book begins with a narrow perspective focusing on the student as learner and then moves to increasingly broader perspectives focusing in turn on interpersonal, social, national, and then international issues. As the student progresses through the text, it becomes more difficult, until in the later parts the student is confronted with reading material such as is commonly found in college-level textbooks.

Part 1 of this book is designed to capture the attention and interest of the students by helping them discover more about themselves as learners. The goal in Part 1 is to explore the skills likely to lead to a successful college experience and to help students recognize the individual strengths and weaknesses they bring to the learning process. The mood of the selections is "upbeat" in the sense of being positive and encouraging. The Introduction in Part 1 is deliberately short and is meant to be completed in the first week of class. The Pretest and the short written paragraph assignments that follow the selections are designed so that the teacher can use them for quickly assessing the skills of individual students and classes as a whole. The theme of Part 1 is the student as learner.

Part 2 is directed at developing the basic skills needed to make reading easier and more productive. The focus is on the process and structure of reading. Skills emphasized include identifying the topic, main idea, supporting details, and determining the author's purpose. Also introduced in Part 2 are transition words and patterns of organization. Themes touched on in Part 2 are communication, anger, and work.

Part 3 emphasizes reading as an interpretive process. The goal of Part 3 is to enable students to become proficient at "reading between the lines." Topics introduced in Part 3 include inference, figurative language, and author's tone.

Part 4 focuses on modes of writing. This part introduces the student to the primary modes of narrative, descriptive, expository, and persuasive writing. It also familiarizes the student with the various modes of organization, including cause and effect, categories, and chronological order. The theme of Part 4 is relationships. Most of the selections in Part 4 approach the level of difficulty that students can be expected to encounter in college textbooks.

Part 5 concentrates on developing critical reading and thinking skills. Topics discussed include fact and opinion, bias, propaganda techniques, and evaluating the evidence. The theme of Part 5 concerns such social issues as substance abuse, and capital punishment, as well as others. A series of paired readings are included in this part.

Part 6 is devoted to improving classroom skills, including skimming and scanning, outlining and mapping. One theme of Part 6 is the environment.

The **Appendices** focus on the specific skills of using dictionaries and interpreting visual aids, such as charts and graphs. A section on tips for taking objective and subjective tests is also included.

Vocabulary Development

All parts of the book emphasize vocabulary development. Because students often have difficulty distinguishing homonyms, a section on homonyms is included in Part 1. How to use context clues to discover the meaning of words is also introduced in Part 1, and work continues on this topic through the rest of the book. Before each reading selection, there is a discussion of the meaning of unusual words that will appear in the selection. One purpose of the questions following the reading selections is to test knowledge of vocabulary used in the selection. Distributed throughout the book are seven independent vocabulary units. These units place an emphasis on Latin and Greek word parts, and each vocabulary unit has a crossword puzzle for practicing the new vocabulary. The Instructor's Manual contains a vocabulary quiz for each of the units.

Organization of the Chapters

Each chapter begins with an overview of the topic for the chapter and a discussion of the key terms needed for understanding the topic. Short exercises designed to help the student understand and master the topic follow. A "Bio-Sketch" of the author appears before most of the longer reading selections, followed by a section entitled "Notes on Vocabulary," which in turn is followed by a section entitled "Tuning In to Reading." "Tuning In to Reading" contains questions designed to actively engage the student with the subject of the upcoming selection. Following the selections will be different kinds of exercises.

At times, there will be directions for longer written assignments, some of which will call for research by the students. Each chapter concludes with a chapter test. The chapter tests are geared to preparing the students to take standardized reading tests, such as the CLAST and TASP. Review tests are interspersed throughout the text to reinforce skills and remind the students that while individual skills may be practiced in isolation, the reading process is cumulative.

The exercises in each chapter are sequential and progress from the relatively easy to the quite difficult. These exercises use many different formats in order to maintain student interest. The instructor should feel free to pick and choose among the exercises in accord with the needs of particular students or classes. The exercises are designed so that the instructor can have the students work either individually or in groups.

Reading Selection Questions

The questions following the reading selections require the students to engage in recalling, interpreting, and evaluating. These questions come in multiple formats, including multiple choice, true or false, fill-in-the-blank, matching, and discussion and written-response questions, which are called "In Your Own Words."

Open-ended questions are included to give the students practice in analyzing and synthesizing. These questions also give the students an opportunity to bring their personal experiences to bear on the selection.

The open-ended questions are organized in such a way as to progressively lead the student to a greater understanding of the selection. Many of these questions have no right or wrong answer and are meant to encourage classroom discussion and debate.

Instructor's Manual

The Instructor's Manual contains the answers to all of the various exercises in the Student Edition. It also contains the following: seven additional vocabulary exercises and quizzes; a unit test for each part of the Student Edition; midterm and final exams; Teaching Tips, which are classroom-tested suggestions for teaching the material; Making Connections, which relate some of the selections to further resources and events, such as books, poems, movies, and political or cultural persons or experiences; supplementary activities, such as materials for creating panel discussions or debates; and recommended alternative sequences for covering the material, a sample syllabus, and get-acquainted activities. Much of the material in the Instructor's Manual should be especially helpful to adjunct faculty.

Acknowledgements

We are grateful to the following instructors for their help in developing our book: Carole Shaw, Northeast State Technical Community College; Kevin Hayes, Essex Community College; Elizabeth Ragsdale, Darton College; Barbara Culhane, Nassau Community College; Aida Pavese, Suffolk Community College; Margaret McClain, Arkansas State University; Mitye Jo Richey, Community College of Allegheny County; Anne Willekens, Antelope Valley College; Dennis Gabriel, Cuyahoga Community College West; Keflyn Reed, Bishop State College; and Diane Starke, El Paso Community College.

Preface to the Student

"Reading furnishes the mind only with materials of knowledge; it is thinking that makes what we read ours."—John Locke

Our goal in this book is not only to improve your reading and study skills, but to encourage excitement about reading. With this in mind, we have chosen lively, varied, and thought-provoking selections. While several selections could be called "old classics," most are contemporary. This book contains both close-ended questions—such as multiple choice and true-or-false questions—and open-ended, discussion-type questions. The open-ended questions will require genuine thinking, interpretation, and even some improvisation on your part. We want your use of this book to be enjoyable, exciting, and active. Hence the title of our book, *Reading and All That Jazz.*

At the beginning of the text, we start with what you know best—you. Selections at the beginning of the book emphasize the individual. Then, as the book moves forward, the selections gradually broaden into interpersonal and social issues (anger, work, and relationships) before concluding with community and global issues.

Before many of the reading selections, you will find a section entitled "Tuning In to Reading." The purpose of these sections is to help you "tune in" to the upcoming reading selection by encouraging you to begin thinking about your own personal experiences as they relate to the topic. In other ways, too, we try to make connections between the reading selections and your own personal experiences. To further help you make connections, we have included background information about the author before each selection and quotes from the famous and not so famous in the margins. Also before each reading selection, you will find a section called "Notes on Vocabulary" that will introduce you to unusual words and phrases that will appear in the selection.

By the time you finish this book, you should be well-prepared to take college-level courses that place an emphasis on reading and critical thinking skills.

Jazz, the only essentially American music form, is a theme that loosely holds the textbook together. The word *jazz* or *jazzy* indicates a certain upbeat, positive style—an excitement. While most of us listen to music on a daily basis, all too few of us settle down with a good book. We hope that by the conclusion of this book, you will discover the joy of reading and make it, like music, a significant part of your daily life.

PART 1 Getting a Handle on College

In jazz, the essential quality is the right to be an individual.

Ornette Coleman

It is as if jazz were saying to us that not only is far greater individuality possible to man than he has so far allowed himself, but that such individuality, far from being a threat to a cooperative social structure, can actually enhance society.

Martin Williams
from Jazz Is *by Nat Hentoff*

Because musicians bring their individual backgrounds and talents to the music they play, each musician has a distinctive style of playing. A musician's style of playing is what works best for the musician and produces the kind of music the musician enjoys. So too with learning. Each of you brings your individual backgrounds and talents to learning. These backgrounds and talents determine your learning style, which is the method of learning that works best for you. No two of you will have the same learning style. The objective of Part 1 of this book is to help you discover your individual learning style so that you can do better in school and life.

Introduction

Your First Week in Class

Some of you just recently graduated from high school. Others have been out in the "real world" and now realize the importance of a college education. Each of you decides what is important in your life, and you have decided that going to college is important. Besides investing your time, you are also investing money, and so you want to get as much benefit as you can out of college. In high school, perhaps many of you did well in your classes without trying very hard. This won't happen in college because college is more demanding. Whether you succeed in college is up to you. It is your responsibility to attend class, study, and turn in your work on time. No one else can do it for you.

Reading and studying will be an important part of your college career. You can't expect to do well in college without having good reading and studying skills. In this book, we will provide you with techniques for improving these skills. Using these techniques will make the time you spend in college more enjoyable and productive.

Assignment Sheets

Success in college requires an organized and disciplined approach. So, one of the first things you need to think about is how to organize yourself as a serious student. Perhaps the easiest way to improve your college performance is to take charge of your assignments. Many of your assignments will be listed in the class syllabi, while other assignments will be announced in class. In some classes, late assignments will receive less credit, and in others they will not be accepted at all—no excuses! The best way to keep a record of your classroom assignments is by using assignment sheets.

As you begin taking this course and using this book, we would like you to try the assignment sheets provided on the following pages. Developing the habit of carefully recording your assignments is crucial not only in this class, but in your other classes as well.

On the next few pages are samples of different types of assignment sheets. The first sheet has a weekly format, the second has a monthly format, and the third has a "continuous log" format. Feel free to experiment with them and find the format that works best for you. We have provided you with a copy of each type of format. So that you can make copies to use in your other classes, additional copies can be found in the Appendix. When you find a format you like, be sure to save copies of it for future use.

Your First Assignment:

Now you can write down your first assignment for this class. This assignment will be due the next class session. You will find a crossword puzzle that will introduce you to the material covered in this book. Read the clues, find the answers in the book, and put the answers into the puzzle. Bring your completed puzzle back the next time class meets.

2

ASSIGNMENTS

MONDAY

TUESDAY

WEDNESDAY

THURSDAY

FRIDAY

OTHER ASSIGNMENTS, TESTS, ETC.

MONTH _____

Sunday	Monday	Tuesday	Wednesday	Thursday	Friday	Saturday

ASSIGNMENT SHEET

Subject(s) _____

Date	Assignments	Due	Finished

Introduction

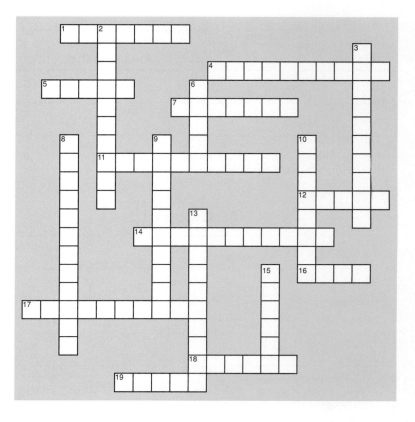

ACROSS CLUES

1. _____ are one type of figure of speech. They use words such as "like" and "as."

4. "Notes on _____" will introduce you to new words. (Preface to the Student)

5. A word part meaning "four." (Vocabulary: Word Structure and Unit 1 in Chapter 3)

7. One type of pattern of organization in Chapter 4 is the _____/contrast pattern.

11. Chapter 5 contains information about _____(s).

12. You will learn how to improve your reading and _____ skills. (Preface to the Student)

14. One type of learning style discussed in Chapter 1.

16. This book was published in nineteen ninety-_____.

17. Both authors of this textbook attended colleges in _____.

18. The author of "A Hanging" is George _____.

19. One selection in Chapter 4 is entitled "Police Power in _____."

DOWN CLUES

2. The publisher of this book is _____. (Don't use a hyphen.)

3. Chapter 12 discusses _____ techniques.

6. "It is thinking that makes reading ours" is a quote by John _____. (Preface to the Student)

8. The title of the reading selection by Pat Riley.

9. The first type of context clue discussed in "Vocabulary: Words in Context" in **Chapter 1**.

10. The "Q" in SQ3R stands for _____.

13. The table of contents lists one mode of writing in Chapter 8 as _____/argumentation.

15. The author of *My American Journey* is Colin _____.

Are You Ready for College?

College is not for everyone. Only 60 percent of those who begin a four-year degree program will later walk across the graduation stage and receive their diplomas. Half of the students who begin taking classes at a community college will drop out by the end of the first year. Notice how many cars there are in the parking lot now. As the days and weeks pass, you will see more empty parking spaces as gradually students drop out for one reason or another. You are the one who decides whether or not you are going to be a survivor. *Decide to be a survivor!*

Below is a short, informal test for assessing how difficult it may be for you to stay in college. This test is just for you and is *not* to be turned in. Place a check beside each statement that seems to apply to you.

Motivational Test

_____   1.   I have not yet really decided what my career objective is. Or, it is difficult for me to visualize what I will be doing in five years.

_____   2.   High school was easy for me and I never really had to study hard to get good grades. Or, I never really studied in high school and got average or below average grades.

_____   3.   My main reason for being here is athletics.

_____   4.   I have small children at home I must take care of.

_____   5.   I need to stay in school so that I can remain on my parents' health insurance.

_____   6.   My parents want me to go to college, and I want to please them.

_____   7.   I am working 30 to 40 hours a week and taking 12 to 15 units. (Consider unpaid activities such as athletics as part of this 30 to 40 hours.)

_____   8.   I am living with two or more roommates and plan to do most of my studying at home or in my dorm room.

_____   9.   I am at this college mostly because my boyfriend or girlfriend goes here.

_____   10. I need to work part-time to pay for my car, clothes, stereo, etc.

_____   11. This is the first time I have been away from home on my own.

_____   12. I plan to get married in the near future. Or, I am going through a divorce.

Now take a look at the number of statements you checked. The more you checked, the greater your chances of not making it. If you checked a lot, this does not mean that you will drop out. But it does mean that you need to do some thinking about your priorities and goals. Your chances of not making it are greater if you are here for the wrong reasons or if you have too many other commitments.

This Is the Week That Was

Assignment

Your next assignment is one that is going to take you a week to do. On the following page you will find a weekly calendar. We want you to keep track of how

THIS IS THE WEEK THAT WAS

Name _____   Date _____

	Monday	Tuesday	Wednesday	Thursday	Friday	Saturday	Sunday
6:00–7:00							
7:00–8:00							
8:00–9:00							
9:00–10:00							
10:00–11:00							
11:00–12:00							
12:00–1:00							
1:00–2:00							
2:00–3:00							
3:00–4:00							
4:00–5:00							
5:00–6:00							
6:00–7:00							
7:00–8:00							
8:00–9:00							
9:00–10:00							
10:00–11:00							
11:00–12:00							

you spend your time each day for a week. Each evening fill in the calendar as best you can showing how you spent your time that day. Also keep track of how much sleep you get each night. *Be honest, and work on your calendar each day— don't wait until several days have passed.* At the end of the week, determine the total number of hours you spent on each of the following activities. Fill in your totals on the lines below. You may find the results surprising. We hope you will also find them useful.

Sleep	_____	(You should sleep about 6–8 hours per night, or about 50 hours.)
Classes	_____	(This number will equal actual hours in class.)
Homework	_____	(We recommend that you spend two hours outside of class for every hour in class.)
Social Activities	_____	
Family Activities	_____	
Work	_____	
School Activities	_____	(For example, field trips, digs for archeology, painting for art class, softball practice, and games.)
Eating	_____	
Exercise	_____	(Don't overlook the need for this.)
Other	_____	(This may include church or other activities.)
TOTAL	_____	(This number should be 168 because there are 168 hours in a week.)

In a later chapter, we will show you how to make a study schedule to manage your time better. But for now, answer the following questions:

1. What categories did you spend too much time on?

2. What categories did you spend too little time on?

3. How much time did you spend on classes, homework, and school activities? How does this number compare with the time you spent on other activities, such as social activities and work?

4. What result surprises you the most?

Here is an excerpt from Colin Powell's autobiography, *My American Journey.* This excerpt may inspire you to take advantage of your opportunities in college. Powell succeeded in college and life, and so can you.

Bio-sketch

General Powell became the National Security Advisor to President Reagan and eventually served as Chairman of the Joint Chiefs of Staff during the conflict with Iraq in the early 1990s. Powell (1937–) was born to Jamaican parents in Harlem.

Colin Powell. (Bob Daemmrich/Sygma)

He graduated from City College of New York, and while attending that institution, joined the Army ROTC to be trained to become an Army officer. In 1961, he met Alma Vivian Johnson on a blind date and married her two years later.

Notes on Vocabulary

bumpkin—someone not very bright. The word *bumpkin* is borrowed from the Dutch *boomken*, meaning "small tree."

muckraker—a person who exposes corruption. President Theodore Roosevelt is thought to have created this term commonly used at the end of the nineteenth and the beginning of the twentieth centuries. The word is made by combining *muck* with *rake* and literally means "raking the muck." Upton Sinclair (1878–1968), who is mentioned in the essay below, was a socialist and activist whose most famous book, *The Jungle*, portrayed the wretched conditions in Chicago's meat-packing plants.

Gothic—a style of architecture that had its origins in the Middle Ages (12th to 16th centuries). Gothic architecture is characterized by pointed arches, high ceilings, and flying buttresses. Many famous cathedrals were built using this style, including Chartres and Notre Dame of Paris. The world's largest Gothic cathedral is St. John the Divine in New York City.

Pershing Rifles—This organization was named after General John Pershing (1860–1948), who was the commander of U.S. troops sent to fight in Europe during World War I. His book, *Experiences in the World War*, won the Pulitzer Prize for literature.

pretzel—This tasty snack dates from at least the middle of the nineteenth century. The word "pretzel" probably comes from the German word *brezel*, which itself came from the Latin word *bracchium*, meaning "arm." Pretzels were so named because they looked like folded or intertwining arms. German monks gave *brezels* to children for learning their prayers. Today the *brezel* is the symbol in Germany for bakers, just as the barber pole is the symbol in the United States for barbers.

Excerpt from **My American Journey**   *by Colin Powell*

READING

The Bronx can be a cold, harsh place in February, and it was frigid the day I set out for college. After two bus rides, I was finally deposited, shivering, at the corner of 156th Street and Convent Avenue in Harlem. I got out and craned my neck like a bumpkin in from the sticks, gazing at handsome brownstones and apartment houses. This was the best of Harlem, where blacks with educations and good jobs lived, the Gold Coast.

I stopped at the corner of Convent and 141st and looked into the campus of the City College of New York. I was about to enter a college established in the previous century "to provide higher education for the children of the working class." Ever since then, New York's poorest and brightest have seized that opportunity. Those who preceded me at CCNY include the polio vaccine discoverer, Dr. Jonas Salk, Supreme Court Justice Felix Frankfurter, the muckraker novelist Upton Sinclair, the actor Edward G. Robinson, the playwright Paddy Chayefsky, the *New York Times* editor Abe Rosenthal, the novelist Bernard Malamud, the labor leader A. Phillip Randolph, New York City mayors Abraham Beane and Edward Koch, U.S. Senator Robert Wagner, and eight Nobel Prize winners. As I took in the grand Gothic structures, a C-average student out of middling Morris High School, I felt overwhelmed. And then I heard a friendly voice: "Hey, kid, you new?"

He was a short, red-faced, weather-beaten man with gnarled hands, and he stood behind a steaming cart of those giant pretzels that New Yorkers are addicted to. I had met a CCNY fixture called, for some unaccountable reason, "Raymond the Bagel Man," though he sold pretzels. I bought a warm, salty pretzel from Raymond, and we shot the breeze for a few minutes. That broke the ice for me. CCNY was somehow less intimidating. I was to become a regular of Raymond's over the next four and a half years. And it either speaks well of his character or poorly of my scholarship that while my memory of most of my professors has faded, the memory of Raymond the Bagel Man remains undimmed.

As I headed toward the main building, Sheppard Hall, towering like a prop out of a horror movie, I passed by an undistinguished old building, I do not remember paying any attention to it at the time. It was, however, to become the focus of my life for the next four years, the ROTC drill hall.

5   My first semester as an engineering major went surprisingly well, mainly because I had not yet taken any engineering courses. I decided to prepare myself that summer with a course in mechanical drawing. One hot afternoon the instructor asked us to draw "a cone intersecting a plane in space." The other students went at it; I just sat there. After a while, the instructor came to my desk and looked over my shoulder at a blank page. For the life of me I could not visualize a cone intersecting a plane in space. If this was engineering, the game was over.

My parents were disappointed when I told them that I was changing my major. There goes Colin again, nice boy, but no direction. When I announced my new major, a hurried family council was held. Phone calls flew between aunts and uncles. Had anybody ever heard of anyone studying geology? What did you do with geology? Where did you go with it? Prospecting for oil? A novel pursuit for a black kid from the South Bronx. And, most critical to these security-haunted people, could geology lead to a pension? That was the magic word in our world. I remember coming home after I had been in the Army for five years and visiting my well-meaning, occasionally meddling Aunt Laurice. What kind of career was this Army? she asked, like a cross-examiner. What was I doing with my life? Snatching at the nearest defense, I mentioned that after 20 years I would get a half-pay pension. And I would only be 41. Her eyes widened. A pension? At 41? The discussion was over. I had made it.

During my first semester at CCNY, something had caught my eye—young guys on campus in uniform. CCNY was a hotbed of liberalism, radicalism, even some leftover communism from the 30s; it was not a place where you would expect much of a military presence. When I returned to school in the fall of 1954, I enquired about the Reserve Officers Training Corps, and I enrolled in ROTC. I am not sure why. Maybe it was growing up in World War II and coming of age during the Korean conflict: the little banners in windows with a blue star, meaning someone from the family was in the service, or a gold star, meaning someone was not coming back. *Back to Bataan, Thirty Seconds over Tokyo, Guadalcanal Diary,* Colin Kelly, Audie Murphy, the five Sullivan brothers who went down with the cruiser U.S.S. *Juneau, Pork Chop Hill,* and *The Bridges at Toko-Ri.* All these images were burned into my consciousness during my most impressionable years. Or maybe it was the common refrain of the era—you are going to be drafted anyway, you might as well go in as an officer. I was not alone. CCNY might not have been West Point, but during the 50s it had the largest voluntary ROTC contingent in America, 1,500 cadets at the height of the Korean War.

There came a day when I stood in line in the drill hall to be issued olive-drab pants and jacket, brown shirt, brown tie, brown shoes, a belt with a brass buckle, and an overseas cap. As soon as I got home, I put the uniform on and looked in the mirror. I liked what I saw. At this point not a single Kelly street friend of mine was going to college. I was 17. I felt cut off and lonely. The uniform gave me a sense of belonging, and something I had never experienced all the while I was growing up; I felt distinctive.

In class, I stumbled through math, fumbled through physics, and did reasonably well in, and even enjoyed, geology. All I ever looked forward to was ROTC. Colonel Harold C. Brookhart, Professor of Military Science and Tactics, was our commanding officer. The colonel was a West Pointer and regular Army to his fingertips. He was about 50 years old, with thinning hair, of only medium height, yet he seemed imposing because of his bearing, impeccable dress, and no-nonsense manner. His assignment could not have been a coveted one for a career officer. I am sure he would have preferred commanding a regiment to teaching ROTC to a bunch of smart-aleck city kids on a liberal New York campus. But the Korean War had ended the year before. The Army was overloaded with officers, and Brookhart was probably grateful to land anywhere. Whatever he felt, he never let us sense that what we were doing was anything less than deadly serious.

10   That fall, I experienced the novel pleasure of being courted by the three military societies on campus, the Webb Patrol, Scabbard and Blade, and the Pershing Rifles, ROTC counterparts of fraternities. Rushing consisted mostly of inviting potential pledges to smokers where we drank beer and watched pornographic movies. The movies, in the sexually repressed 50s, were supposed to be a draw. I hooted and hollered with the rest of the college boys through these grainy 8-millimeter films, in which the male star usually wore socks. But they were not what drew me to the Pershing Rifles. I pledged the PRs because they were the elite of the three groups.

The pledge period involved typical ritualistic bowing and scraping before upperclassman, and some hazing that aped West Point traditions. A junior would stand you at attention and demand the definition of certain words. To this day I can parrot the response for milk: "She walks, she talks, she's made of chalk, the lactile fluid extracted from the female of the bovine species . . . " and on and on. I can spout half a dozen similar daffy definitions. When we finished the pledge period, we were allowed to wear distinctive blue-and-white shoulder cords and enamel crests on our uniforms. I found that I was much attracted by forms and symbols.

One Pershing Rifles member impressed me from the start. Ronald Brooks was a young black man, tall, trim, handsome, the son of a Harlem Baptist preacher and possessed of a maturity beyond most college students. Ronnie was only two years older than I, but something in him commanded deference. And unlike me, Ronnie, a chemistry major, was a brilliant student. He was a cadet leader in the ROTC and an officer in the Pershing Rifles. He could drill men so that they moved like parts of a watch. Ronnie was sharp, quick, disciplined, organized—qualities then invisible in Colin Powell. I had found a model and a mentor. I set out to remake myself in the Ronnie Brooks mold.

My experience in high school, on basketball and track teams, and briefly in Boy Scouting had never produced a sense of belonging or many permanent friends. The Pershing Rifles did. For the first time in my life I was a member of a brotherhood. The PRs were in the CCNY tradition only in that we were ethnically diverse and so many of us were the sons of immigrants. Otherwise, we were out of sync with both the student radicals and the conservative engineering majors, the latter easy to spot by the slide rules hanging from their belts. PRs drilled together. We partied together. We cut classes together. We chased girls together. We had a fraternity office on campus from which we occasionally sortied out to class or, just as often, to the student lounge, where we tried to master the mambo. I served as an unlikely academic advisor, steering other Pershing Rifles into geology as an easy yet respectable route to a degree.

The discipline, the structure, the camaraderie, the sense of belonging were what I craved. I became a leader almost immediately. I found a selflessness within our ranks that reminded me of the caring atmosphere within my family. Race, color, background, income meant nothing. The PRs would go the limit for each other and for the group. If this was what soldiering was all about, then maybe I wanted to be a soldier.

From My American Journey *by Colin L. Powell. Copyright © 1995 by Colin L. Powell. Reprinted by permission of Random House, Inc.*

Now that you have read this article, answer the following questions.

Pretest

Multiple choice—For each question, circle the letter for the best answer.

1. Which of the following people was *not* involved with the ROTC or the military?
   a. Ronnie Brooks
   b. Harold Brookhart
   c. Abe Rosenthal
   d. Members of the Scabbard and Blade

2. In paragraph 9, *impeccable* dress means
   a. tattered
   b. too large
   c. flawless
   d. new

3. The best title for this selection would be
   a. "Why I Went to CCNY."
   b. "The Army ROTC."
   c. "My Activities with the Pershing Rifles."
   d. "I Found My Future by Joining the ROTC."

4. Which of the following can you infer from this selection?
   a. Powell knew he wanted to be in the ROTC before attending CCNY.
   b. Powell was on the basketball team at CCNY.
   c. Powell found discipline in the ROTC.
   d. The Pershing Rifles was a purely academic organization.

5. Which of the following careers would Powell probably have had the most difficulty in?
   a. commercial artist
   b. geologist
   c. computer programmer
   d. accountant

True or false—In the space provided, indicate whether each statement is true or false.

_____   6.   Powell decided he had a natural aptitude for studying engineering.

_____   7. Powell's introduction to Raymond the Pizza Man served to make college life less intimidating.

_____   8. The magic phrase in the Powell family was "job satisfaction."

_____   9. Powell disliked wearing a uniform because it set him apart from the crowd.

_____   10. Powell chose to join the most prestigious of the three ROTC societies.

_____   11. The sense of belonging within the Pershing Rifles was similar to what Powell had enjoyed as a child.

Vocabulary—Without using a dictionary, write the meanings of the following phrases.

12. craned his neck (paragraph 1) _____

13. shot the breeze (paragraph 3)_____

14. caught my eye (paragraph 7) _____

15. moved like parts of a watch (paragraph 12) _____

Written Assignment

Powell in this excerpt describes his early days on the CCNY campus when he was still struggling to find his place in college. Write a few paragraphs about your first days in college and the adjustments you had to make.

Understanding the Words in the Story

Directions: Choose one of the following words to complete the sentences below. Use each word only once.

harsh	frigid	intimidating	haunted	visualize
contingent	hazing	craved	impressionable	distinctive
elite	meddling			

1. Fraternity _____ is banned on many college campuses because too many pledges have been hurt or killed as a result of it.

2. Arriving at a new school for the first time can be _____.

3. The _____ weather in the Northeast has been responsible for power outages across New Hampshire and Maine.

4. The young man, a first-time offender, nevertheless received a _____ punishment from the judge.

5. The old man was _____ by the recent death of his only child. Some thought he would never get over the tragedy.

6. Many Olympic skaters try to _____ a perfect performance in their minds before actually going out onto the ice.

7. Getting into a top-10 college is _____ on outstanding grades and excellent recommendations.

8. Even though he was a vegetarian, he still _____ a juicy T-bone steak every once in a while.

9. Melinda believed that because young children are so _____, they need to be protected from violent images.

Copyright © 1999 by The McGraw-Hill Companies, Inc.

10. Now that she was married and on her own, she did not want her mother _____ in her affairs.

11. The young girl recognized her attacker by the _____ tattoos on his arms.

12. In baseball, only an _____ few have hit 60 home runs in a single season.

"Ode to the Present" *by Pablo Neruda*

READING

Pablo Neruda (1904–1973), widely regarded as the greatest Latin American poet of the 20th century, received the Nobel Prize for literature in 1971. Neruda, whose real name is Ricardo Eliezer Neftali Reyes y Basoalto, was born in Parral, Chile, the son of a railroad worker. He began to write poetry as a young teenager and later studied to be a teacher. At one point in his life, he was forced into exile because of his political beliefs. The movie, *Il Postino*, is based on this period of his life. In addition to being a poet, he served as a Chilean diplomat in various foreign countries, including Burma, Ceylon, Argentina, Mexico, and France. The following is the last stanza from one of Neruda's poems, which was translated from Spanish by Professor Maria Jacketti and appears in *Neruda's Garden: An Anthology of Odes.*

You	Tú
are	eres tu presente,
your present,	tu manzana:
your own apple.	tómala
Pick it from	de tu árbol,
your tree.	levántala
Raise it	en tu mano,
in your hand.	brilla
It's gleaming,	como una estrella,
rich with stars.	tócala,
Claim it.	híncale el diente y ándate
Take a luxurious bite	silbando en el camino.
out of the present,	
and whistle along the road	
of your destiny.	

"Oda al presente" from Nuevas Odas Elementales; *English translation "Ode to the Present" from* Neruda's Garden: An Anthology of Odes *by Pablo Neruda. Reprinted by permission of Agencia Literaria Carmen Balcells, S.A.*

Directions: Try to explain the meaning of the poem in your own words.

Vocabulary: Introduction

One purpose of this book is to help you improve your reading and writing skills by expanding your vocabulary. Vocabulary and reading are like the chicken and the egg—which comes first? Your reading is made easier if you know more words; and the more reading you do, the more words you will learn. Is there an easy "abracadabra" way to learn more words and become a more efficient reader? The answer is no. But there are techniques that can help. Some of the techniques we will be working with are the following:

Context: When you come across an unknown word in your reading, the first technique for discovering its meaning should be to look for context clues. The context of a word is what surrounds it, which includes the sentence it appears in, other nearby sentences, or even the whole essay or story. Try placing your finger over the unknown word, and see if you can supply another word that gives the sentence meaning, or at least enough meaning for your purposes. Remember that if you are reading a light novel for enjoyment, the exact meaning of a word may not be as important as when you are reading your psychology textbook.

Let's try a sentence with a word you may not know, and see if you can figure out the meaning of the word from the context of the sentence.

> Many airlines in the United States have been having financial difficulties in recent years. They are trying to become more *lucrative* businesses by cutting back on in-flight meals.

You could go to the dictionary to find the definition of *lucrative,* but you could probably guess from context clues that *lucrative* means "profitable."

We use context clues all the time when we read cartoons. The cartoon below uses the word "assertiveness." What do you think the Marines mean by assertiveness? Is this any different from its usual meaning?

Frank and Ernest

© 1995 Thaves / Reprinted with permission. Newspaper distribution by NEA, Inc.

Structure: Word structure gives you a way to discover the meaning of a word by breaking it down into its parts. Knowing the word parts should help you make an educated guess about its meaning. Let's try an example.

> The physical therapist used *abduction* in treating her patient's leg.

The word *abduction* has in it the word parts *ab* and *duc. Duc* means "lead" and *ab* means "away from." So, what was the physical therapist doing with her patient's leg? If you think she was stretching the leg outward, you are correct.

The seven vocabulary units inserted throughout the book will give you practice in using over 75 word parts. A complete list of these word parts is located at the end of Chapter 15.

❝The first book of the nation is the dictionary of its language.❞

Contanitin, Conte Volney

Dictionary: Often when you come across a word you don't know, your first thought is to look it up in the dictionary. But this should be your last way of determining the meaning of a word. It's best to first try to use context clues and word structure. If these methods don't give you an accurate enough definition, then go to the dictionary.

Before you grab the dictionary, it helps to know a little bit about the meaning of the word you are looking up. This is because the dictionary, which is a vast resource with much information (sometimes too much), may give several meanings, and you have to be able to select the appropriate one. For example, say that in your reading you come across the following sentence and you don't know what the word *annual* means.

> The man decided to buy *annual* plants for his front yard.

You look *annual* up in your dictionary and find two definitions. The first definition may be "something happening once every year," and the second definition may be "a plant that lasts for one season or year." You can see that the second definition is the one that fits this sentence. If the man buys annual plants, let's hope he doesn't expect them to bloom again.

We have placed the dictionary section in the Appendices. Your teacher may decide to have you work through that section as a class, or you can complete the exercises on your own. If nothing else, you should read the first part of that section before you purchase a dictionary.

Combination: In trying to determine the meaning of an unknown word, you can use all of these techniques in combination. Take the following example:

> David Letterman is a *contemporary* of many of your instructors.

You may be thinking that *contemporary* means "modern or recent," but that meaning doesn't make sense in this context. *Con* means "with" and *temp* means "time or moderate." Now you are getting closer to the meaning in this sentence. The word *contemporary* here means "with time." Now go to the dictionary. You will find the definition "modern," but you will also find the definition "same time period or age group." So, David Letterman is approximately the same age as many of your teachers.

Homonyms: As part of our vocabulary study, we will also be covering homonyms. Although homonyms are not a technique for discovering the meaning of an unknown word, we have included them because misuse of homonyms is a common mistake. *Homo* means "same" and *nym* means "name," so homonyms are words with the same "name," or pronunciation, but different spellings or meanings.

Look at the following sentence.

> Your grandfather *passed* away.

A common mistake when writing such a sentence is to use the word *past* instead of *passed*. Because "passing away" is an action, it is a verb, and you need to use the word *passed*. In the section on homonyms, you will learn how to use many homonyms correctly.

Names and Personalities

In the next couple of weeks, most of your teachers will be trying hard to learn the names of their students. They do this not only for convenience, but also for politeness because your name is important to your sense of identity. Think about how annoyed you become when your name is forgotten or mispronounced by someone who should know better. Many of you were given your name by a close relative who chose it because it had some personal significance. Perhaps it was the relative's name, or the name of a movie star or athlete the relative admired.

Some people are even named after special places or the day of the week on which they were born.

A long time ago, people were given names that had very specific meanings. For example, the name "Peter," the first name of one of your authors, originally meant a "rock." The name "Rita," the first name of your other author, meant a "pearl of great value." In the Middle Ages, many last names had meanings related to occupations. If someone was called "Baker," it was likely because that person made bread. If a person's last name was "Smith," this person was probably a blacksmith. The name "Mather," which is Peter's last name, means mower or reaper of hay. Although this may not sound too important, hay was used not only as feed for animals but also as bedding.

Robert Olen Butler's short story "Crickets," which is excerpted on the following pages, explores the significance of names in relation to the process of becoming part of a new culture. People new to this country might choose to "Americanize" their names to avoid difficulties in pronunciation or to better blend into the dominant culture. Thus "Katya" might become "Kathy," and "Jorge" might become "George."

In "Crickets," the Vietnamese father, Thieu, recognizes that his son, Bill, who was born in the United States, is now very different from him. Read the following profile of the author before beginning the short story.

Bio-sketch

Robert Olen Butler won the 1993 Pulitzer Prize for fiction for the collection of stories entitled *A Good Scent from a Strange Mountain.* The short story "Crickets," written from the perspective of an immigrant from Vietnam, describes the difficulties of adjusting to American society. Butler's extensive knowledge of the Vietnamese culture is the result of his Vietnam War experiences when he served as both a U.S. Army intelligence officer and an interpreter. Many of his novels are concerned with his Vietnam experience. Butler feels that fiction about Vietnam "has not dealt adequately with the Vietnamese people; it has not found their humanity." He says this is because most novels about the Vietnamese are written from the viewpoint of the American soldier facing an enemy in a time of war. Butler currently lives in Lake Charles, Louisiana, where he is a professor of English and creative writing at McNeese State University. Although he says he has probably written his last novel about Vietnam, his goal is to continue to publish one new book a year. His most recent work is the novel *Tabloid Dreams.*

Notes on Vocabulary

bowler—a low-crowned, hard felt hat.   *Bowler* is the common British name for what Americans call a "derby." Some say that the *bowler* was so named because of its resemblance to a bowling ball.

bayou—a small marshy stream or inlet.   The word *bayou* is the Louisiana French version of *bayuk,* used by the Choctaw Indians, the original inhabitants of the region.

Tuning In to Reading

Do you and your parents have different backgrounds? How has your special background made you different from your parents?

"Crickets"

by Robert Olen Butler

READING

Louisiana was named in 1682 by the French explorer, Sieur de LaSalle, after the King of France, Louis XIV. The French originally colonized the area, but sold the far larger Louisiana Territory to the United States for $15 million. This purchase by President Thomas Jefferson doubled the size of our country.

They call me Ted where I work and they've called me that for over a decade now and it still bothers me, though I'm not very happy about my real name being the same as the former President of the former Republic of Vietnam. Thieu is not an uncommon name in my homeland and my mother had nothing more in mind than a long-dead uncle when she gave it to me. But in Lake Charles, Louisiana, I am Ted. I guess the other Mr. Thieu has enough of my former country's former gold bullion tucked away so that in London, where he probably wears a bowler and carries a rolled umbrella, nobody's calling him anything but Mr. Thieu.

I hear myself sometimes and I sound pretty bitter, I guess. But I don't let that out at the refinery, where I'm the best chemical engineer they've got and they even admit it once in a while. They're good-hearted people, really. I've done enough fighting in my life. I was 18 when Saigon fell and I was only recently mustered into the Army, and when my unit dissolved and everybody ran, I stripped off my uniform and put on my civilian clothes again and I threw rocks at the North's tanks when they rolled through the streets. Very few of my people did likewise. I stayed in the mouths of alleys so I could run and then return and throw more rocks, but because what I did seemed so isolated and so pathetic a gesture, the gunners in the tanks didn't even take notice. But I didn't care about their scorn. At least my right arm had said no to them.

And then there were Thai pirates in the South China Sea and idiots running the refugee centers and more idiots running the agencies in the United States to find a place for me and my new bride, who braved with me the midnight escape by boat and the terrible sea and all the rest. We ended up here in the flat bayou land of Louisiana, where there are rice paddies and where the water and the land are in the most delicate balance with each other, very much like the Mekong Delta, where I grew up. These people who work around me are good people and maybe they call me Ted because they want to think of me as one of them, though sometimes it bothers me that these men are so much bigger than me. I am the size of a woman in this country and these American men are all massive and they speak so slowly, even to one another, even though English is their native language. I've heard New Yorkers on television, and I speak as fast as they do.

My son is beginning to speak like the others here in Louisiana. He is 10, the product of the first night my wife and I spent in Lake Charles, in a cheap motel with the sky outside red from refineries. He is proud to have been born in America, and when he leaves us in the morning to walk to the Catholic school, he says, "Have a good day, y'all." Sometimes I say good-bye to him in Vietnamese and he wrinkles his nose at me and says, "Aw Pop," like I'd just cracked a corny joke. He doesn't speak Vietnamese at all and my wife says not to worry about that. He's an American.

5 But I do worry about that, though I understand why I should be content. I even understood 10 years ago, so much so that I agreed with my wife and gave my son an American name. Bill. Bill and his father Ted. But this past summer I found my son hanging around the house bored in the middle of vacation and I was suddenly his father Thieu with a wonderful idea for him. It was an idea that had come to me in the first week of every February we'd been in Lake Charles, because that's when the crickets always begin to crow here. This place is rich in crickets, which always makes me think of my own childhood in Vietnam. But I never said anything to my son until last summer.

I came to him after watching him slouch around the yard one Sunday pulling the Spanish moss off the lowest branches of our big oak tree and then throwing rocks against the stop sign on our corner. "Do you want to do something fun?" I said to him.

"Sure, Pop," he said, though there was a certain suspicion in his voice, like he didn't trust me on the subject of fun. He threw all the rocks at once that were left in his hand and the stop sign shivered at their impact.

I said, "If you keep that up, they will arrest me for the destruction of city property and then they will deport us all."

My son laughed at this. I, of course, knew that he would know I was bluffing. I didn't want to be too hard on him for the boyish impulses that I myself had found to be so satisfying when I was young, especially since I was about to share something of my own childhood with him.

10   "So what've you got, Pop?" my son asked me.

"Fighting crickets," I said.

"What?"

Now, my son was like any of his fellow 10-year-olds, devoted to superheroes and the mighty clash of good and evil in all of its high-tech forms in the Saturday-morning cartoons. Just to make sure he was in the right frame of mind, I explained it to him with one word, "Cricketmen," and I thought this was a pretty good ploy. He cocked his head in interest at this and I took him to the side porch and sat him down and I explained.

I told him how, when I was a boy, my friends and I would prowl the undergrowth and capture crickets and keep them in matchboxes. We would feed them leaves and bits of watermelon and bean sprouts, and we'd train them to fight by keeping them in a constant state of agitation by blowing on them and gently flicking the ends of their antennas with a sliver of wood. So each of us would have a stable of fighting crickets, and there were two kinds.

15   At this point my son was squirming a little bit and his eyes were shifting away into the yard and I knew that my Cricketman trick had run its course. I fought back the urge to challenge his set of interests. Why should the stiff and foolish fights of his cartoon characters absorb him and the real clash—real life and death—that went on in the natural world bore him? But I realized that I hadn't cut to the chase yet, as they say on the TV. "They fight to the death," I said with as much gravity as I could put into my voice, like I was James Earl Jones.

The announcement won me a glance and a brief lift of his eyebrows. This gave me a little scrabble of panic, because I still hadn't told him about the two types of crickets and I suddenly knew that was a real important part for me. I tried not to despair at his understanding and I put my hands on his shoulders and turned him around to face me. "Listen," I said. "You need to understand this if you are to have fighting crickets." There are two types, and all of us had some of each. One type we called the charcoal crickets. These were very large and strong, but they were slow and they could become confused. The other type was small and brown and we called them fire crickets. They weren't as strong, but they were very smart and quick."

"So who would win?" my son said.

"Sometimes one and sometimes the other. The fights were very long and full of hard struggle. We'd have a little tunnel made of paper and we'd slip a sliver of wood under the cowling of our cricket's head to make him mad and we'd twirl him by his antenna, and then we'd each put our cricket into the tunnel at opposite ends. Inside, they'd approach each other and begin to fight and then we'd lift the paper tunnel and watch."

"Sounds neat," my son said, though his enthusiasm was at best moderate, and I knew I had to act quickly.

20   So we got a shoe box and we started looking for crickets. It's better at night, but I knew for sure his interest wouldn't last that long. Our house is up on blocks because of the high water table in town and we crawled along the edge, pulling back the bigger tufts of grass and turning over rocks. It was one of the rocks that gave us our first crickets, and my son saw them and cried in my ear, "There, there," but he waited for me to grab them. I cupped first one and then the other and dropped them into the shoe box and I felt a vague disappointment, not so much because it was clear that my boy did not want to touch the insects, but that they were both the big black ones, the charcoal crickets. We crawled on and we found another one in the grass and another sitting in the muddy shadow of the house behind the hose faucet, and then we caught two more under an azalea bush.

"Isn't that enough?" my son demanded. "How many do we need?"

I sat with my back against the house and put the shoe box in my lap and my boy sat beside me, his head stretching this way so he could look into the box. There was no more vagueness to my feeling. I was actually weak with disappointment because all six of these were charcoal crickets, big and inert and just looking around like they didn't even know anything was wrong.

"Oh, no," my son said with real force, and for a second I thought he had read my mind and shared my feeling, but I looked at him and he was pointing at the toes of his white sneakers. "My Reeboks are ruined!" he cried, and on the toe of each sneaker was a smudge of grass.

I glanced back into the box and the crickets had not moved, and I looked at my son and he was still staring at his sneakers. "Listen," I said, "this was a big mistake. You can go on and do something else."

25   He jumped up at once. "Do you think Mom can clean these?" he said.

"Sure," I said. "Sure."

He was gone at once and the side door slammed and I put the box on the grass. But I didn't go in. I got back on my hands and knees and I circled the entire house and then I turned over every stone in the yard and dug around all the trees. I found probably two dozen more crickets, but they were all the same. In Louisiana there are rice paddies and some of the bayous look like the Delta, but many of the birds are different, and why shouldn't the insects be different too? This is another country, after all. It was just funny about the fire crickets. All of us kids rooted for them, even if we were fighting with one of our own charcoal crickets. A fire cricket was a very precious and admirable thing.

The next morning my son stood before me as I finished my breakfast, and once he had my attention, he looked down at his feet, drawing my eyes down as well. "See?" he said. "Mom got them clean."

Then he was out the door, and I called after him, "See you later, Bill."

"Crickets" from A Good Scent from a Strange Mountain *by Robert Olen Butler, © 1992 by Robert Olen Butler. Reprinted by permission of Henry Holt and Company, Inc.*

IN YOUR OWN WORDS

1. What reasons does Thieu give for feeling somewhat bitter in his new homeland?

2. He has reservations about the name "Thieu" and also about the name "Ted." Why?

3. From the context of the second paragraph, how would you define an "isolated and . . . pathetic" gesture?

4. Why does Thieu feel compelled to share part of his culture with his son? What does he use as a "hook" to generate interest?

5. What is a James Earl Jones voice? What does the expression "cut to the chase" mean?

6. Why are the two types of crickets of such importance to Thieu? What do the two types of crickets represent in terms of human beings?

7. What actions on the part of the son disappoint the father?

8. What is the significance of the son's concern over his soiled Reeboks?

9. What is the father acknowledging when he excuses the son from searching for more crickets?

10. What does the father hope to gain by continuing the search alone?

11. How do we know that the father has come to terms with his son's allegiance to another culture?

Written Exercises

Choose one of the following activities to complete.

1. Go to a library (call number—CS 2367.H32) or a bookstore and do some research on the original meaning of your name. Write a short paragraph describing your findings.

2. Create a new name for yourself and explain, in paragraph format, why you have chosen it. For instance, you might choose the new name "Dawn" because that is your favorite part of the day.

3. If your name has special significance or was chosen for a particular reason, explain briefly how it was selected.

Chapter 1

How We Learn

Finding Out about Ourselves

Auditory, Visual, or Kinesthetic

What Is Your Learning Style?

In this chapter we are going to discover a little bit more about ourselves. Are we the kind of person who works best at night or during the day? Are we a visual learner or an auditory one? What kinds of things are most likely to cause stress in our lives? We will be trying to answer these and many other questions in the pages that follow.

Each of us is an individual with particular strengths and weaknesses. If we want to do better in school, we must learn how to use our strengths and minimize our weaknesses. Research is beginning to demonstrate that most of us have a learning style that will work best for us.

Your learning style is partially dependent on whether you are a visual, auditory, or kinesthetic learner. The test below will help you determine your learning style. Keep in mind that there are no right or wrong answers. Read each question and place a check mark on the appropriate line. If the question doesn't directly apply to you, think of a similar situation that might apply to you.

Adult Learning Styles Inventory

	Often	Sometimes	Seldom
1. You need to see a map or written directions to drive to someone's house.	_____	_____	_____
2. You remember material from a lecture without studying, or you have to tape the lecture and play the tape.	_____	_____	_____
3. You feel comfortable touching others, shaking hands, etc.	_____	_____	_____
4. You would rather learn a new recipe from a TV show than from a recipe book.	_____	_____	_____
5. When you watch sports on TV, you pay more attention to the play than to the explanation of the play by the announcers.	_____	_____	_____

	Often	Sometimes	Seldom
6. You enjoy sewing, cooking, gardening, or working with tools.	_____	_____	_____
7. You remember a news event best by reading about it in a newspaper or magazine.	_____	_____	_____
8. You are good at making and interpreting graphs and charts.	_____	_____	_____
9. In order to learn material, you write notes over and over again.	_____	_____	_____
10. Without writing them down, you remember oral directions for assignments well.	_____	_____	_____
11. You smoke, chew gum, or play with coins or keys in your pockets.	_____	_____	_____
12. In order to learn material, you read notes out loud to yourself.	_____	_____	_____
13. When taking a trip, you would rather drive than be responsible for giving directions or reading a map.	_____	_____	_____
14. When you encounter a new word while you are reading, you usually sound it out.	_____	_____	_____
15. When you are trying to learn something, you form pictures in your mind.	_____	_____	_____
16. When you are studying for a test, you can visualize your notes on the page.	_____	_____	_____
17. You frequently tap your pencil or your pen.	_____	_____	_____
18. When oral introductions are made at a party, you are likely to remember the names of people you have not met before.	_____	_____	_____

Score your test below. For each question, give yourself five points if you answered often, three points if you answered sometimes, and one point if you answered seldom. For example, if you answered "often" to question 1, you would place a 5 on the line next to that question. When you have finished, add up the points for each column.

Visual	Auditory	Kinesthetic
1._____	2._____	3._____
5._____	4._____	6._____
7._____	10._____	9._____
8._____	12._____	11._____
15._____	14._____	13._____
16._____	18._____	17._____

Totals   _____   _____   _____

Now look at the differences between the totals for each learning style. A small difference, say one less than four points, doesn't mean much, but larger differences do. The larger the difference, the more dominant your learning style. For example, if your total for visual learning far exceeds the other two totals, this would be a good indication that you are basically a visual learner.

What does it mean to be a **visual learner**? A visual learner is one who learns best by seeing. Visual learners like to use maps, diagrams, and charts; their goal is to be able to visualize the subject they are trying to learn. A visual learner would prefer a teacher who uses a blackboard or projector over one who primar-ily talks. Visual learners often have a superior ability to visualize pages of print. They learn material well by copying and recopying their notes. Most people are visual learners.

What does it mean to be an **auditory learner**? An auditory learner is one who learns best through hearing. Auditory learners have a superior ability to hear and remember sounds in their mind. Auditory learners like to listen, and they prefer teachers who lecture and encourage discussion. They learn material well by talk-ing to themselves and repeating words and phrases out loud. Many people are auditory learners.

What does it mean to be a **kinesthetic learner**? Kinesthetic learners, who are the smallest group, learn best by doing and performing. They have a superior abil-ity to remember their actions. Kinesthetic learners like to be in movement while learning; their special talent is in associating ideas and concepts with motion. When learning material, they may prefer to gesture or walk around.

Keep in mind, though, that even if one of your scores was way above the other two, all that the test results suggest is a tendency on your part. For example, if you have a high score for auditory learning, this just means that you tend to be an auditory learner, but you are still likely to have a significant ability to learn in visual and kinesthetic ways. Most of us will learn best by using some combina-tion of all three learning styles. The trick is to find the combination that works best for you.

Vocabulary: Words in Context

One technique for discovering the meaning of new words is the use of context clues. By paying attention to what an author is saying, we can often discover the meanings of words without having to look them up in the dictionary. As you will see, often our own background or experiences will also help us determine the meanings of unfamiliar words. Here are some common techniques for using con-text to determine the meaning of new words.

Definition:

Sometimes a writer simply provides us with a definition of a word somewhere within the sentence, especially if the word is one that we are unlikely to be familiar with.

> The FBI conducted *covert*, or secret, operations to find out information about the drug-smuggling ring.

Covert here is simply defined by the author as meaning "secret."

Synonym:

A synonym, which is another word with a similar meaning, may be used elsewhere in the sentence.

> Four types of objects *revolve* around the sun; however, the planets are the largest objects that circle our fiery star.

If you did not know the meaning of *revolve*, you could determine its meaning from the word "circle." To circle and to revolve mean approximately the same thing.

Antonym:

Sometimes you can determine the meaning of a word by finding an antonym, a word with an opposite meaning, somewhere in the sentence.

> Although scientists are certain that life has evolved over time, they are *dubious* about the exact dates of various events.

You can see that the writer is making a contrast, and that *dubious* has an opposite meaning from certain.

Examples:

Sometimes examples illustrate the meaning of a word.

> Examples of *nocturnal* animals are the owl and the raccoon.

You may know that owls and raccoons are active at night, which suggests to you the meaning of *nocturnal*.

Explanation:

Sometimes a writer simply gives the reader an explanation of what a word means.

> In your communications class, you will probably have to give an *impromptu* speech. For this type of speech, you will be given a topic and only a few minutes to prepare your talk.

The writer is telling you that an *impromptu* speech is one that is given with very little preparation.

Experience:

This way of discovering the meaning of a word draws on your personal experience.

> The football player jumped into the air, caught the ball, and then was knocked to the ground. When he tried to stand up, he experienced *vertigo*.

Perhaps you have experienced this or a similar situation, and you remember that you were dizzy when you got up. It would also help to know that the root word *vert* means "turn."

Knowledge of Subject: In this technique, you have just enough familiarity with the subject the writer is discussing to enable you to figure out the meaning of the unknown word.

> Many students are not *affluent* enough to attend college without working part-time or receiving financial aid.

You know that many students have limited financial resources, and so *affluent* here means "wealthy."

Combination: Can you use a number of these techniques at the same time to detect the meaning of a word? You bet!

> The man at the party was a real *extrovert*. He acted like a clown and had everyone laughing the whole evening.

Here you probably used explanation, experience, and familiarity with the subject to determine that an *extrovert* is a very outgoing person.

Now work with a partner on the following examples. Remember, no peeking at your dictionary. First, give your own definition for the italicized word, then on the second line give the technique you used to arrive at the definition. The first example is done for you.

1. Many boys in high school *aspire* to be professional athletes, but very few will make it to the big time of fame and fortune.
   Definition: <u> to hope for or desire   </u>
   Technique(s) used: <u> knowledge of subject, explanation, maybe experience </u>

2. Most students go into a *comatose* state when final exams are over.
   Definition: <u>   </u>
   Technique(s) used: <u>   </u>

3. Should football games be canceled because of *inclement* weather?
   Definition: <u>   </u>
   Technique(s) used: <u>   </u>

4. Should sexually *explicit* scenes be deleted from movies when they are shown on television?
   Definition: <u>   </u>
   Technique(s) used: <u>   </u>

5. If someone makes a *derogatory* remark about your mother, you may want to fight back.

   Definition: _____

   Technique(s) used: _____

6. We used to believe in the geocentric theory of the universe when we thought that the earth was at the center, but now we believe in the *heliocentric* theory.

   Definition: _____

   Technique(s) used: _____

Context Clue Practice No. 1

Directions: Use the second sentence to define the italicized word. Circle the clue or clue words in the second sentence.

1. "Yes, this computer is *obsolete*," said Matt. "But out of date or not, it's too expensive to replace."

2. "I can't accept any *remuneration* for taking care of your dog while you were in the hospital," said Carrie. "Nonsense dear," said Mrs. Watson, "you should get paid for doing a good deed."

3. It would be *presumptuous* to accuse him of the crime. Without solid evidence, it would simply be too bold.

4. Mountain climbing is full of *hazards*. However, the adventure is worth all of the risks.

5. He considered it an *indignity* for his parents to ignore his college graduation. He couldn't envision a worse insult.

6. Martha complained that she was getting tired of *goading* her son to do his homework. At his age, he should be able to finish it without her urging.

7. Some people *feign* injuries after their car is rear-ended. They don't stop pretending until they have received a cash settlement.

8. Todd, the pilot of our small airplane, seemed very *apprehensive* about taking off during the storm. His anxious behavior was upsetting the passengers.

9. I was certain he was *despondent* because he hadn't smiled all week. Perhaps he had good reason to be so depressed.

10. The teacher was *cognizant* of the difficulties involved in learning a new language. Her awareness was based on the fact that she too had once emigrated from her homeland.

11. Her *frivolous* behavior was a cause of great concern to her father. Spending $1,000 on a painting she didn't need clearly demonstrated a lack of sense.

Context Clue Practice No. 2

Directions: Using the context, determine the missing word. Briefly describe the clue or clues that you found.

1. If you believe that you control your own destiny, you have an internal locus of control; however, if you believe that your fate is determined by chance or outside forces, you have an _____ locus of control.

    Clue: _____

2. Successful students are naturally _____ because they have a hopeful attitude and believe that effort, good study habits, and self-discipline will make their grades go up. "They can because they think they can."

    Clue: _____

3. Students exhibit what is called self-serving bias. When they get an exam grade back, if they did well they tend to accept personal credit. They consider the exam to be a valid indication of their abilities. However, if they did very poorly, they are much more likely to _____ the teacher or the exam.

    Clue: _____

4. Interestingly enough, teachers do the same thing. They are likely to take credit for whatever success is associated with their students and blame the student for any _____. "Teachers, it seems, are likely to think, 'With my help, Maria graduated with honors. Despite all my help, Melinda flunked out.'"

    Clue: _____

5. College students need to be especially careful about those they associate with. Researchers have verified that students learn more from their friends and other students than they do from their _____ or from books. Out-of-class relationships are clearly the major influence in a student's life.

    Clue: _____

From Myers, David, Social Psychology, *5th edition, New York: McGraw Hill, 1997, pp. 47, 54, 57.*

Day versus Night People

Are You More of a Morning Lark or a Night Owl?

You probably already have some idea whether you are more alert in the morning, afternoon, or evening. Before we see how this might affect how you set up your class and study schedule, read the following article from *Reader's Digest*. The article describes our circadian, or daily, cycles, and how these cycles affect us. When you finish the article, you will have a chance to take a test to help you determine whether you are a morning or night person.

Notes on Vocabulary

circadian rhythm—A person's *circadian rhythm*, popularly known as one's "body clock," is a biological rhythm that governs our routine of working, eating, and sleeping through a 24-hour period. *Circadian* is derived from the Latin words *circa*, meaning "about," and *dies*, meaning "day."

"The Two Most Dangerous Hours of Your Day" *by Lowell Ponte*

READING

Your Interior Clock Has Far-reaching Effects on Your Health

You awaken after a good night's sleep and start to climb out of bed. Take care! You are beginning the most dangerous time of your day.

For the next two hours or so, you are two to three times more likely to suffer a heart attack or a stroke than you are in the late evening, the safest cardiovascular time of your day. According to a study headed by Merrill Mitler of Scripps Clinic and Research Foundation in La Jolla, California, 6 A.M. to 10 A.M. is the average peak time for many other major causes of death: ischemic heart disease, cancer, bronchitis, emphysema and asthma.

Until recently doctors were taught that the human body lives in homeostasis, changing little during the day. The science of chronobiology—the study of how time affects life—is sparking a medical revolution by revealing how much our bodies change through circadian (daily) rhythms.

"These natural biological rhythms are as vital as our heartbeat," says Lawrence E. Scheving of the University of Arkansas for Medical Sciences in Little Rock. "By learning their secrets, we are discovering new ways to prevent and cure illness. There isn't a function in your body that doesn't have its own rhythm. The absence of rhythm is death."

5   While you sleep, your blood pressure falls, your temperature drops more than a degree from its daily afternoon high, and some blood pools in your body's extremities. Come morning, the body has to "jump start" itself from its sleeping to waking stages with a surge of excitation chemicals called catecholamines. Heart rate increases and blood vessels constrict, raising blood pressure and reducing blood flow to heart muscle; this might cause ischemia, or angina, as well as sudden death from myocardial infarction. If hardened plaques of cholesterol coat arteries, fragments may break loose, causing the clots that lead to heart attacks.

Also, your blood swims with cell granules called platelets that are most likely to stick together during these morning hours. When a leap from bed and a surge of catecholamines combine to "get your blood moving," your blood is near its daily peak in thickness and tendency to clot. Packing kids off to school and rushing to get ready for work add emotional tension to the physical stress.

This circadian cardiovascular risk comes not from your bedside clock but from your interior biological clock. "Whatever hour you get up," says Dr. James Muller, chief of cardiology for New England Deaconess Hospital in Boston, "your peak risk of myocardial infarction will come within two to three hours after awakening."

The master timekeepers in our bodies help synchronize us with such outside cycles as day and night. Like orchestra conductors, they coordinate hundreds of functions inside us. Our body dances through the day to complex inner rhythms of rising and falling tides of hormones, immune cells, electrolytes and amino acids.

The long-held belief that some of us are "larks," or morning people, and others are "owls," or evening people, has now been confirmed. Measurements of circadian rhythms in morning people show heart rates peaking between 1 and 2 P.M., while evening people peak between 5 and 6:30 P.M. Larks produce more of the stimulating hormone adrenaline during the morning hours, followed by decreasing levels of performance through the day. Owls start the day more slowly, produce more nearly level amounts of adrenaline, and improve performance through the day and into early evening.

10   Most people enjoy a peak in short-term memory and mental quickness in the late-morning hours until shortly after noon. Then a measurable dip in energy and efficiency begins around 1 P.M. In some Mediterranean cultures, shops close during the afternoon for a period of siesta.

In the afternoon, exercise endurance, reaction time and manual dexterity are at their highest. Some research indicates that from then until early evening, athletes put in their best performances. From 6:30 P.M. until 8:30 P.M. is the sharpest time of day for long-term memory, an optimal time to study.

Our daily rhythms can bring a dark side to the early evening, however. These hours include a second daily peak in heart attacks, although smaller than the morning's. Around 7 P.M., alcohol takes longer to be cleared by your liver, and hence can be more intoxicating and performance-impairing than at other times of day—except 11 P.M., which brings a second peak of high ethanol susceptibility.

Students often cram during late-night and early-morning hours. Research, however, shows this is the time of the circadian cycle when long-term memory, comprehension and learning are at their worst.

Sensitivity to pain has generally increased throughout the day; it reaches its peak late at night. But by early morning the body may have almost doubled its night-time levels of beta endorphins, which help relieve pain. Researchers theorize that this is what increases the body's pain tolerance during the hours after awakening.

For most of us, sleep is a time of life's renewal. Within the first 90 minutes or
15 so of sleep, we reach our daily peak of growth hormone, which may help regenerate our bodies. And among pregnant women, the hours between midnight and 4 A.M. most commonly mark the start of labor. "Early morning labor and birth may be part of our genetic inheritance and may have had some survival value for the species," speculates chronobiologist Michael Smolensky of the University of Texas Health Science Center in Houston.

By understanding our body clocks, we can improve our health and continue to foster our survival. Without grasping, for instance, that our natural temperature rises one to two degrees from morning until evening, we could misjudge thermometer readings. A temperature of 99 degrees might signal perfect health at 5 P.M. but augur illness at 7 A.M.

The effects of drugs are also subject to our rhythms. For instance, many doctors are learning to give powerful cancer drugs with the patient's biological clocks in mind. A given chemotherapy drug may be highly toxic to the kidneys at one time of day, for example, and far less harmful at another. "For every 1 of more than 20 anti-cancer drugs, there is an optimal time of day," says Dr. William Hrushesky of the Stratton Veterans Administration Medical Center in Albany, New York.

Some prescription drugs can reduce morning heart-attack risk, as can aspirin. One major study found that taking an aspirin *every other day* reduced overall incidence of heart attack in men by almost 45 percent and morning risk by more than 59 percent. You should, of course, consult your doctor about the use of aspirin.

Aside from using medicine, there are ways to make your mornings less stressful and, perhaps, less risky. Set the alarm clock a bit earlier to give yourself time to stretch arms and legs slowly while still lying down, the way your dog or cat does. This gets the pooled blood in your extremities moving. Move slowly. Don't subject yourself to the thermal shock of a very hot or cold shower, which could boost blood pressure. Then eat breakfast. Dr. Renata Cifkova at Memorial University of Newfoundland at St. John's says, "Skipping breakfast apparently increases platelet activity and might contribute to heart attacks and stroke during morning hours."

20   To avoid the "Monday morning blues," don't change your schedule on weekends. Your body's clock naturally runs on a cycle of about 25 hours. During the

week, your body uses mechanical clocks, mealtimes, work schedules and other cues to reset itself to 24 hours each day. On weekends it is tempting to let the clock "free run" forward by staying up late Friday and Saturday, then sleeping late Saturday and Sunday. This action will leave you "jet-lagged," an unnecessary stress.

By turning the cycles of your biological clock in your favor, you may reduce your daily danger and increase your days of life.

From "The Two Most Dangerous Hours of Your Day" by Lowell Ponte. Reprinted with permission from the March 1992 Reader's Digest. *Copyright © 1992 by The Reader's Digest Assn., Inc.*

Vocabulary Checkup

Directions: In the previous section you were introduced to finding the meaning of new words by using context clues. In the following exercise, try to discover the meaning of each of the italicized words by looking closely at the way the word is used in the sentence or passage.

1. What is a synonym, or word that has a similar meaning, for *circadian*? ___
   _____

2. After reading paragraph 2, the word *cardiovascular* refers to what specific organ of the body? _____

3. After reading paragraph 3, what do you think *chronobiology* means?
   _____

4. According to the context of paragraph 3, what does *homeostasis* mean? ___
   _____

5. In paragraph 4, what does the word *rhythm* mean? _____

6. If your blood vessels *constrict*, are they getting larger or smaller?
   _____

7. In paragraph 6, what is the synonym for *platelets*? _____

8. In paragraph 7, what is the difference between *interior* and *exterior*?
   _____

9. In paragraph 8, what does *synchronize* mean? (Use the context clues given in the sentence following the word *synchronize*) _____

10. In paragraph 9, what is a synonym for a "human" lark or a "human" owl?
    _____

11. If something is *stimulating* to you, does it depress or energize you?
    _____

12. In paragraph 10, is a *peak* a high point or a low point? _____

13. What is a *siesta*? _____

14. In paragraph 11, define *endurance*, *dexterity*, and *optimal*. _____
    _____

15. If your teacher is *susceptible* to flattery and you're hoping to raise your grade, you will tell her . . .
    a. "Class was really enjoyable today!"
    b. "I was so bored I couldn't seem to stay awake."

16. In paragraph 15, what do you think the prefix *re* means, as in I need to *renew* my library book. _____

17. In paragraph 16, if we *misjudge,* are we judging badly or well? _____

18. In paragraph 16, what is the synonym for *augur?* _____

19. Use the context of paragraph 17 to define the word *toxic* _____

20. If you are *anti* something, are you for it or against it? _____

21. After reading paragraph 19, name some parts of your body that would be considered *extremities.* _____

22. How do you feel if you suffer from *jet lag*? _____

Comprehension Checkup

True–false—In the space provided, indicate whether each statement is true or false.

_____ 1. Cramming for exams late at night is unlikely to benefit most students.

_____ 2. Most people show a decline in energy around 1 P. M.

_____ 3. For most people, alcohol is more intoxicating in the morning.

_____ 4. If you need to have surgery, you should plan on having it in the early evening when you are least sensitive to pain.

_____ 5. Our body temperature increases as we go through the day.

_____ 6. If someone *speculates* about something, they are sure to know the answer.

_____ 7. If you're *sensitive* to pain, be sure to tell the dentist to avoid the use of all anesthetics.

Multiple choice—For each question, circle the letter for the best answer.

1. Your circadian rhythm is
   a. a daily cycle.
   b. a 1-hour cycle.
   c. a 1-month cycle.
   d. none of the above.

2. Which of the following statements is true based on paragraph 9?
   a. Owls are awake at night.
   b. Larks are more lively during the morning.
   c. Some people are morning people and some are evening people.
   d. All of the above.

3. When do you think you would be least likely to suffer a heart attack or stroke?
   a. just after you wake up
   b. early evening
   c. late evening
   d. two hours after you wake up

4. Which of the following statements is true based on the article?
   a. Orchestra conductors can help coordinate the functions of our body.
   b. Babies are most likely to be born in the early morning hours.

c. It's best to sleep in on Saturday and Sunday mornings to readjust to the 25-hour cycle.

d. None of the above.

5. The human body
   a. changes little during the day.
   b. lives in homeostasis.
   c. changes a lot through daily rhythms.
   d. has no rhythm.

Day versus Night People

The following test is intended to determine whether you are a morning person or a night person. Answer the questions and then add up your points to determine your score.

	Points Possible	Points Earned
1. I feel best if I get up around:		
5–6:30 A.M.	5	
6:30–7:30 A.M.	4	
7:30–9:30 A.M.	3	
9:30–11 A.M.	2	
11–noon	1	_____
2. If I had to describe how easy it is for me to get up in the morning, I would say:		
It is not easy at all!	1	
It is not very easy.	2	
It is fairly easy.	3	
It is very easy.	4	_____
3. The way I feel for the first half-hour after I wake up is:		
very tired	1	
fairly tired	2	
fairly refreshed	3	
very refreshed	4	_____
4. If I could choose the best time to take a difficult test, it would be:		
8–10 A.M.	4	
10 A.M.–1 P.M.	3	
1–5 P.M.	2	
7–9 P.M.	1	_____
5. If my job required that I work from 4 to 6 A.M. one day, I would choose to:		
not go to bed until after I worked	1	
take a nap before and sleep after	2	
sleep before work and nap after	3	
get all the sleep I need before work	4	_____
6. If someone asked me to jog with him/her at 7 A.M. one morning, I would perform:		
well	4	
reasonably well	3	

not very well	2
not well at all	1

7. If I have to wake up at a specific time each morning, I depend on my alarm:

not at all	4
slightly	3
quite a lot	2
desperately	1

8. I am usually tired and wanting to go to bed by:

8–9 P.M.	5
9–10:30 P.M.	4
10:30 P.M. to 12:30 A.M.	3
12:30–2 A.M.	2
2–3 A.M.	1

Total Number of Points Earned   _____

From Bradley, et. al., Thrills, Spills, and Study Skills, *Dubuque, Iowa: Kendall Hunt Publishing, 1992, pp. 65–66.*

An average score would be 17. The higher the score, the more of a morning or day person you are; the lower the score, the more of an evening person you are. In another section, we will show you how to use this information in making a study schedule. If at all possible, you should plan the activities that require the most concentration when you are the most alert. For example, if math is a difficult subject for you and you are a morning person, plan to take that class in the morning and do your homework while you are still fresh.

Left-Brain and Right-Brain Orientation

Which One Are You?

Over the past 20 years, psychologists have been studying how the two hemispheres of the brain operate. There is research that shows that the two sides of the brain think in quite different ways. In general, the left half is more analytical, logical, and likely to break down thoughts into parts. The right half is more likely to focus on the whole picture, to think in analogies, and to interpret things imaginatively. We use both halves of the brain together, but one side may be more dominant. Being right-brain oriented or left-brain oriented has little to do with whether you are right-handed or left-handed.

Take the following test to see which half of your brain is dominant.
Check the statements that apply to you.

_____ 1. When reading or watching TV, you prefer a true story to one that is fiction.

_____ 2. You like to read or write poetry.

_____ 3. You prefer to take tests that have no right or wrong answers rather than tests having objective and definite answers.

_____ 4. You find yourself solving a problem more by looking at the individual parts than by looking at the big picture.

_____ 5. You usually do several tasks at once rather than one task at a time.

Frank and Ernest

© 1994 Thaves. Reprinted with permission of Bob Thaves. Newspaper distribution by NEA, Inc.

_____   6. You would prefer a job with a set salary over one such as sales where your income might vary considerably.

_____   7. You usually follow new directions step by step rather than improvising or taking steps out of order.

_____   8. When planning a vacation you usually like to just go without doing much planning in advance.

_____   9. Your papers in your notebook are usually neat and orderly and not just thrown in every which way.

_____   10. When listening to someone else's problems, you usually become emotional instead of trying to come up with logical solutions.

To score your test, circle the number for each statement that you checked.

| Right-brain hemisphere | 2 | 3 | 5 | 8 | 10 |
| Left-brain hemisphere | 1 | 4 | 6 | 7 | 9 |

Now compare the results. Which hemisphere has the most circled numbers? The bigger the difference between the two scores, the greater your right-brain dominance or left-brain dominance. If you circled about the same number for both hemispheres, neither one of your hemispheres is extremely dominant.

What does all this mean? One hemispheric orientation is not better than the other, but the thinking processes are different. People who are more left-brain oriented tend to be more organized, be more analytical, and use more logic. So, it is not surprising that engineers, accountants, scientists, and auto mechanics are more likely to have a dominant left hemisphere.

Those with a dominant right hemisphere, on the other hand, tend to focus on the whole more than individual parts, be imaginative, jump to conclusions, and be emotional. People such as poets, artists, musicians, and inventors are more likely to have a dominant right hemisphere.

We will apply this information later on when we discuss study techniques. Students with a dominant left hemisphere will probably do better organizing material by outlining, while those with a dominant right hemisphere might find mapping easier. Those who are left-brain oriented will probably find study schedules easier to stick to than those who are right-brain oriented.

Left-brain oriented students will probably find it easier to do well in classes that require analysis and linear thinking than will students who are right-brain oriented. Examples of such classes are algebra, science, accounting, logic, computers, and engineering. Those of you who are more right-brain oriented might do better in classes such as art, social science, music, English, the humanities, and geometry.

Intuition becomes increasingly valuable in the new information society precisely because there is so much data.

John Naisbitt

Multiple Intelligences

What Are Your Strengths?

The Merriam Webster's Collegiate Dictionary defines intelligence as "the ability to learn or understand" and "the ability to cope with a new situation." We have discovered in the previous sections that we are all unique individuals who learn in different ways. Some psychologists believe that intelligence can also be expressed in a variety of ways. Many of you may remember taking the Stanford-Binet IQ test. After completing the test, you were assigned a score, and then evaluated based on that score. If your mental age, as measured by the test, and your age in years were the same, you received an IQ of 100. This meant that you were considered "average." The higher the score above 100, the more intelligent you were considered to be, while a score of 80 meant you were below average.

Critics argue that one problem with this test is that it is based on the principle that our intelligence is one-dimensional. Howard Gardner, a Harvard professor, has proposed the idea that there are seven different types of intelligence. His theory is based on biological research showing different parts of the brain to be the sites of different abilities. He says that "the concept of 'smart' and 'stupid' doesn't make sense. . . . You can be smart in one thing and stupid in something else." As you read a description of each different type of intelligence, try to determine your own strengths and weaknesses.

❝ The art of writing is the art of discovering what you believe. ❞

David Hare

❝ A word after a word after a word is power. ❞

Margaret Atwood

Verbal/linguistic intelligence—This intelligence relates to language skills. It includes the ability to express yourself verbally, to appreciate complex meanings, and to detect subtle differences in the meanings of words. It is considered to be a key intelligence for success in college.

Logical/mathematical intelligence—This intelligence deals with the ability to reason, solve abstract problems, and understand complex relationships. Intelligence in this area is also a good predictor of academic success.

Visual/spatial intelligence—This is the ability to think in three dimensions and to recreate one's experiences visually. A painter, sculptor, or an architect are all able to manipulate a form in space.

Musical/rhythmic intelligence—This is the ability to hear pitch, tone, and rhythm.

Bodily/kinesthetic intelligence—This intelligence places the emphasis on control of the body and the skillful handling of objects. The mind clearly coordinates the movements of the body. An athlete, pianist, or dancer might excel in this area.

Interpersonal intelligence—This is the ability to interact well with people. A person who excels in this area is especially skillful in detecting the moods and intentions of others. A politician might display this type of intelligence.

Intrapersonal intelligence—This is the ability to understand your own feelings and to use the insight gained to guide your actions.

Is there a relationship between these seven intelligences and the learning styles we have been studying? Probably, but our knowledge of how the brain functions is still in the early stages. One problem, of course, is that although we are all human beings, we are all distinctly different, making it difficult for scientists to generalize.

Another problem concerns the controversy over how much of our intelligence is fixed at birth and how much is determined by our environment. More than likely our intelligence is a combination of both of these factors, but the nature-versus-nurture debate is far from resolved. In the meantime, many educators and psychologists are not only attempting to define intelligence more broadly, but are also devising new methods to teach thinking skills once thought to be fixed for life.

Assignment

You are now going to read an essay by Isaac Asimov (1920–1992). This essay, written years before Gardner began his research in multiple intelligences, demonstrates how we can be "smart" in many different ways.

Bio-sketch

According to David N. Samuelson, in *Twentieth Century Science-Fiction Writers*, Asimov is "the world's most prolific science writer" who "has written some of the best-known science fiction ever written." In addition to writing science fiction, Asimov, a former professor of biochemistry, has written many essays explaining scientific principles to the general public. The essay excerpted below, "What Is Intelligence, Anyway?" is a sample of his autobiographical writings. In these essays, Asimov recounts many incidents from his own life, both painful and pleasurable. He never forgot his early origins and often invited the reader "to wonder, with him, at the rise to prominence of a bright Jewish boy brought to this country from Russia at the age of three and raised in a collection of Brooklyn candy stores." Throughout his lengthy career, he has received numerous honors and awards, including having his short story "Nightfall" chosen by the Science Fiction Writers of America as the best science fiction story of all time.

Notes on Vocabulary

private (in the Army)—the lowest rank in the army. Comes from the Latin *privare*, meaning "to separate or deprive." A *private* is separated from those of higher rank and is deprived of the privileges of higher rank.

oracle—any person of great knowledge or a wise statement or authoritative prediction. *Oracle* was originally the place where ancient Greeks and Romans consulted their gods and asked their advice. The *oracle* of Delphi was the most famous.

moron—fool. From the Greek word *moros*, meaning "foolish."

"What Is Intelligence, Anyway?" *by Isaac Asimov*

READING

What is intelligence, anyway? When I was in the Army, I received a kind of aptitude test that all soldiers took and, against a normal of 100, scored 160. No one at the base had ever seen a figure like that, and for two hours they made a big fuss over me. (It didn't mean anything. The next day I was still a buck private with KP—kitchen police—as my highest duty.)

All my life I've been registering scores like that, so that I have the complacent feeling that I'm highly intelligent, and I expect other people to think so, too. Actually, though, don't such scores simply mean that I am very good at answering the type of academic questions that are considered worthy of answers by the people who make up the intelligence tests—people with intellectual bents similar to mine?

For instance, I had an auto repairman once, who, on these intelligence tests, could not possibly have scored more than 80, by my estimate. I always took it for granted that I was far more intelligent than he was. Yet, when anything went wrong with my car I hastened to him with it, watched him anxiously as he explored its vitals, and listened to his pronouncements as though they were divine oracles—and he always fixed my car.

Well, then, suppose my auto repairman devised questions for an intelligence test. Or suppose a carpenter did, or a farmer, or, indeed, almost anyone but an academician. By every one of those tests, I'd prove myself a moron. And I'd *be* a moron, too. In a world where I could not use my academic training and my verbal talents but had to do something intricate or hard, working with my hands, I would do poorly. My intelligence, then, is not absolute but is a function of the society I live in and of the fact that a small subsection of that society has managed to foist itself on the rest as an arbiter of such matters.

5   Consider my auto repairman, again. He had a habit of telling me jokes whenever he saw me. One time he raised his head from under the automobile hood to say: "Doc, a deaf-and-mute guy went into a hardware store to ask for some nails. He put two fingers together on the counter and made hammering motions with the other hand. The clerk brought him a hammer. He shook his head and pointed to the two fingers he was hammering, the clerk brought him nails. He picked out the sizes he wanted, and left. Well, doc, the next guy who came in was a blind man. He wanted scissors. How do you suppose he asked for them?"

Indulgently, I lifted my right hand and made scissoring motions with my first two fingers. Whereupon my auto repairman laughed raucously and said, "Why you dumb jerk, he used his *voice* and asked for them." Then he said, smugly, "I've been trying that on all my customers today." "Did you catch many?" I asked. "Quite a few," he said, "but I knew for sure I'd catch *you*." "Why is that?" I asked. "Because you're so goddamned educated, doc, I *knew* you couldn't be very smart."

And I have an uneasy feeling he had something there.

From "What Is Intelligence, Anyway?" by Isaac Asimov. Published by permission of The Estate of Isaac Asimov c/o Ralph M. Vicinanza Ltd.

Directions: Write the letter of the correct answer on the blank without looking back at the story.

_____   1.   While serving in the Army, Asimov was (a) rewarded for receiving such a high score on the aptitude test; (b) belittled and made to feel inferior; (c) fussed over momentarily.

_____   2.   The people who write the tests are emphasizing the kinds of questions (a) they do poorly on; (b) they do well on; (c) they are indifferent to.

_____   3.   The auto repairman mentioned in the essay on a traditional aptitude test most probably would score (a) superior; (b) average; (c) below average.

_____   4.   When Asimov says that he listened to the auto repairman's pronouncements "as though they were divine oracles," he means he listened (a) closely; (b) with distrust; (c) angrily.

_____   5.   If a carpenter devised an aptitude test, Asimov would most probably score (a) superior; (b) average; (c) below average.

     6. When Asimov *indulgently* lifted his hand to make scissoring motions, he was indicating he (a) felt uncertain of the correct answer; (b) was confident he was correct; (c) knew he was wrong.

     7. When the auto repairman succeeded in fooling Asimov, he felt *smug*. In this context, the word "smug" most probably means (a) frustrated; (b) self-satisfied; (c) silly.

     8. Does the auto repairman have respect for Asimov's type of intelligence? (a) most probably; (b) not likely; (c) absolutely.

Vocabulary Practice

Directions: Choose one of the following words to complete each of the sentences below. Use each word only once. Be sure to pay close attention to the context clues provided.

mute	aptitude	fuss	raucous	complacent
foist	intricate	arbiter	hastened	indulgent

1. Tara's kids weren't turning out very well because she was far too _____ in disciplining them, letting them do whatever they felt like.

2. Sam's _____ test indicates that he would probably do well to consider law-enforcement as a possible career choice.

3. Eddie Murphy's trademark _____ laugh was most recently displayed in the movie *The Nutty Professor.*

4. The coffin cover of the ancient Egyptian King Tut features an _____ design of gold inlaid with enamel and semiprecious stones.

5. Realizing she had forgotten to turn off the oven, Tina _____ home before her turkey dinner was ruined.

6. Darryl was feeling smug and _____ over how well he did on the last test and so he quit working hard.

7. Whenever Cathy, the cartoon character by Cathy Guisewhite, goes home to visit her mother at the holidays, a real _____ is made over her.

8. The two sides can't agree on a deal, so Robyn has agreed to serve as an _____ in the dispute.

9. Mark gets really angry every time some of his co-workers try to _____ some of their work on him.

10. Tony pushes the _____ button whenever there is a loud, annoying commercial on TV.

Stress Inventory

How Much Stress Is There in Your Life?

Although there is no exact correlation between how well students do in college and the stress in their lives, students need to pay attention to personal stress. To be successful in college, you must be able to give full attention to your studies. This means that you must come to terms with all facets of your life, including whatever is causing you stress. If the stress in your life is controlling you, you need to do something about it. You may be able to solve the problem yourself, or you might want to consider seeking professional help. Most college campuses have a center to help students deal with too much stress and other emotional problems. When we have physical problems, most of us are willing to consult a doctor. On the other hand, many of us have difficulty seeking help for other personal problems. But if you need help and help is available, why not take advantage of it?

In 1967, Holmes and Rahe developed the following scale to determine how much stress there is in a person's life. The test is meant to be kept confidential and is for your use only. For each of the following "major life changes" that you have had in your life, write in its assigned value under the column for your score.

Major Life Changes	Value	Your Score
Death of a spouse	100	_____
Divorce	73	_____
Marital separation	65	_____
Jail term	63	_____
Death of a close family member	63	_____
Personal injury or illness	53	_____
Marriage	50	_____
Fired at work	47	_____
Marital reconciliation	45	_____
Retirement	45	_____
Change in health of family member	44	_____
Pregnancy	40	_____
Sexual difficulties	39	_____
Gain of a new family member	39	_____
Business readjustment	39	_____
Change in financial state	38	_____
Death of a close friend	37	_____
Change to a different line of work	36	_____
Change in arguments with spouse	35	_____
Foreclosure of mortgage or loan	30	_____
Change in responsibilities at work	29	_____
Son or daughter leaving home	29	_____
Trouble with in-laws	29	_____
Outstanding personal achievement	28	_____
Spouse begin or end work	26	_____
Begin or end school	26	_____
Change in living conditions	25	_____
Revision of personal habits	24	_____

Major Life Changes	Value	Your Score
Trouble with boss	23	_____
Change in work hours or conditions	20	_____
Change in residence	20	_____
Change in schools	20	_____
Change in recreation	19	_____
Change in church activities	19	_____
Change in social activities	18	_____
Change in sleeping habits	16	_____
Change in number of family get-togethers	15	_____
Change in eating habits	15	_____
Vacation	13	_____
Christmas	12	_____
Minor violations of the law	11	_____
Your Total Life Change Score		_____

Now add up your points. If you scored 150–200 points, you may be experiencing a "mild life crisis." A score between 200 and 300 may indicate a "moderate life crisis," and a score over 300 may indicate a "major life crisis." Studies have shown that the higher your score, the more likely you are to become ill.

From Holmes and Rahe, "Stress Inventory," 1967, found in Minkoff, Eli C., and Baker, Pamela G., Biology Today, *New York: McGraw-Hill, 1996, p. 362.*

Tuning In to Reading

The next article you will read describes a very unique teenager who has encountered many stresses in his young life. Faced with the prospect of losing his beloved grandmother, he makes a very unselfish decision to give one of his kidneys to her. What decision would you make if you were to find yourself facing the same circumstances?

Bio-sketch

The author, Rick Reilly, is an ABC golf commentator. His latest book is *Missing Links*, published in 1996. Reilly, who has been named National Sportswriter of the Year five times, is currently a senior writer for *Sports Illustrated*, which is where the story excerpted below appeared.

Notes on Vocabulary

scrimmage line—the imaginary line between opposing teams where the ball is put into play. In football, the ball is placed on the *scrimmage line* and the two teams face each other across it. The word *scrimmage* comes from *skirmish*, which is a brief fight or encounter between two groups.

fullback, halfback, quarterback—backfield positions on the offensive side in football. In the 1890s, when football was played quite a bit differently than it is today, the *quarterback* played a quarter of the way back directly behind the line of scrimmage; behind him on either side and halfway back played two *halfbacks*; and then behind them in the middle and all the way back played the *fullback*.

dicier—comes from *dicey* meaning "chancy." Derived from British slang, the word *dicey* was first made popular by RAF (Royal Air Force) pilots during World War II, who spoke of their missions, and the chances of their safe return, as *dicey*.

"An Easy Choice"   *by Rick Reilly*

READING

When Daniel Huffman quit football, he did exactly what his mom told him not to do and started messing around with needles, folks in tiny Rossville, Illinois, shook his hand. How else was he supposed to save his grandmother's life?

Still if there was one kid in town you hated to see quit the high school team, it was Daniel. "That kid *lived* for football," said his grandfather Daniel Allison. Young Daniel would count the days from the end of school to the start of summer two-a-day practices. He was the screamer on the team, the human pep rally. O.K., so maybe he wasn't going straight to Florida State, but at 6'2" and 275 pounds, Daniel was where a lot of enemy tailbacks ended up. "He would just engulf them like some huge amoeba," recalls his former coach, Dave McDonald. "And then he'd yell some more."

This is Daniel's senior year at Rossville High. He is an honor-roll student (A-plus average), a member of the school chorus, the class vice president, a writer of poetry, a part-time cleanup boy at a discount store and a onetime shot-putter on the track team, but none of those things have made him as proud as being a co-captain, starting defensive tackle and occasional offensive tackle on the football team. In a town such as Rossville (pop. 1,400), a hiccup of a place 118 miles south of Chicago, your senior year of football is precious, and Daniel had planned to make this season a doozy.

Though he played primarily on defense, he had the soul of an offensive lineman. He had no designs on stardom. Of the team's star running back, Zeb Stephenson, Daniel once said, "It will be my privilege to block for him."

5   Daniel is very big on making other folks' paths a little easier. When diabetes left his grandmother Shirlee Allison legally blind for a while, 14-year-old Daniel and his 13-year-old sister, Kristina, did the dishes and folded the laundry. Daniel became Shirlee's eyes, helping her walk, reading the mail to her. When Shirlee's husband had his quintuple bypass two years ago, Daniel got his grandmother through it. "Sometimes we raised them," Shirlee says of her grandchildren, "and sometimes they raised us."

Daniel is just as attentive to his friends. "He'll do anything for us," says Lisa Masengale, a high school classmate. "He writes me poetry when I'm down. He can always make me laugh."

Hard to figure where he got all the spare sunshine. Daniel's mother, Alice, left the family when he was four. His father, Barry, remarried, and an evil step-mother/ungrateful stepkids thing broke out. Daniel and Kristina were miserable, but Barry wasn't one to interfere. "He's kind of a partier," Daniel says. So the summer after Daniel finished seventh grade, he and Kristina moved to Florida to live with Alice. That didn't work out either, so after a year everyone agreed that the kids would be best off living with their grandparents, the Allisons.

"My grandparents kinda saved me," says Daniel. "There's a whole lot of drugs and stuff around here. I probably would've ended up all messed up." Kristina eventually moved back to Florida, which left Daniel and Shirlee as the oddest couple in town. Sure, they shared a love of books and a certain hardhead-edness, but he was a 17-year-old growing uncontrollably, and she was a 60-year-old disappearing before the town's eyes. After a time, her diabetes-ravaged kidneys were producing almost no urine. All that poison the kidneys were supposed to filter out was circulating through her.

As last spring grew warmer, Shirlee's trips to the hospital in nearby Danville for dialysis got more frequent, and her condition worsened. Her muscles were atrophying, her heart was enlarged, and her blood pressure was dangerously low. "We all figured there was no hope for her," says her neighbor Madge Douglas.

10　But then Daniel had this crazy idea. He was sitting at a Burger King with Shirlee after another brutal day of watching her on the dialysis machine ("the metal and plastic vampire," he called it in his diary). He had been thinking about how much he missed her. Where was Gran, the kidder? Gran, the one you couldn't get to shut up? Who was this 101-pound ghost? Who was this clothes hanger of a woman, all bone where he used to plant his good-night kiss? "Mrs. Allison," the doctor had told her, "many people can live on dialysis, but you aren't one of them."

Well, that made the situation sticky. She refused to take a kidney from a relative. She was on the waiting list for a cadaver kidney. That was good enough for her. "I'm not imposing on anybody," she said. Daniel was so scared that he couldn't watch her undergo treatment anymore. He started picking up medical handbooks about dialysis. He talked to Shirlee's doctors. He learned the dangers of becoming a kidney transplant donor. He knew that if he gave Shirlee one of his kidneys, he would have to give up contact sports forever—one hard hit from behind, and he could end up on life support. On the other hand, he learned that eight people die each day in the U.S. while waiting for an organ. The wait for a cadaver kidney can be two years. At the rate Shirlee was shrinking, that would be a year and a half too much.

And so, somewhere between the Whopper and the onion rings, Daniel made up his mind. "Gran," he said, "I can't take it anymore. I want you to take my kidney."

"No, no, no," she said. "You're too young. What if something happens?"

"Gran, I don't care what happens to me. I'm doin' this!"

15　"Absolutely not," she said. "Besides, when I think about you giving up football, it makes me sick to my stomach."

Daniel got good and mad. He yelled, "Gran, you always told me, 'Stand up for what you believe in.' Well, I'm standin' up! You're taking my kidney!"

You do not hear that every day at Burger King. Every head in the joint turned. "Well," Shirley whispered, sliding back in her chair, "we'll see if we match."

Getting around Daniel's mother was even dicier. Alice was foursquare against the donation. When Daniel decided to go ahead with the operation anyway, Alice took action. She wrote a letter to the University of Illinois Medical Center, where Daniel and his grandmother wanted the transplant to take place, and asked how the surgeons could take organs from minors. The center, which had not known Daniel's age, declined to allow the operation.

Daniel was dogged. If he waited until his 18th birthday—December 24—Shirlee might be too weak to survive the operation. "He was ready to go to court on this," says Jeff Miller, transplant coordinator for Dr. Frederick K. Merkel, who performs surgery at the Illinois Medical Center and Chicago's Rush Presbyterian Hospital and accepts living-relative transplant donors as young as 16. The operation was on, at Rush.

20　The night before the July 9 surgery, Daniel was scared for both Shirlee and himself. "Gran," he said, "I gotta ask you one thing: Is this worth risking your life for?"

"Oh, honey," she said, laying her withered hand on his huge one. "I have no life without this."

When she woke up in the intensive care unit, she already had her color back. "My stars!" she said to a nurse. "Now that I've got this 17-year-old kidney in me, I hope I don't feel like going out and tackling somebody!" Across the hall, though, Daniel was hurting. After a kidney transplant the donor gets months of tests—the constant blood work, the working knowledge of the hierarchy of hospital needles. Shirlee's scar is small and on her pelvis. Daniel's is 18 inches long and wraps from his navel nearly to his spine. It was Daniel who was in pain long after the surgery, not Shirlee. Who said it's more blessed to give than to receive?

But a lot of wonderful things also started happening. Daniel had quit the football team, but the football team refused to quit him. The players insisted that he wear his football jersey each Friday. He went to every practice when he wasn't working at the discount store. He rode on the senior players' float at homecoming and made the speech at the pep rally before the game. And on Friday nights you could hear his voice all over the field: "C'mon, everybody! *Clap!*" Funny, how somebody who wasn't even playing could be the toughest kid on the team.

Daniel is almost completely recovered. In fact, the doctors say his remaining kidney will soon be twice the size it used to be. They still haven't figured out how to measure his heart.

Daniel wants to be a writer, and he's applying for college scholarships like crazy. As for Shirlee, her weight is up to 128, she rarely uses her cane, and her vision has improved. She has even gone to some of Rossville's football games—something she couldn't do before the surgery. You should have seen her there, bursting with pride. "The boy loved his grandma more than football," she marveled, wiping a tear from the corner of her eye. "Whaddya think a that?"

Folks in town seem to think a lot of it. Folks out of town too. Governor Jim Edgar wrote Daniel to say how proud he was of him, and the story of Daniel's donation was on national as well as local TV programs.

The Rossville football team didn't do too well, finishing the season last Friday at 3–6. "We sure could have used Daniel to put a body on somebody," said lineman Chad Smith. With 24 seconds left in Rossville's final game, a 28-3 win over Palestine high, Rossville's Shaun York asked to leave the game and be replaced by Daniel—who with the coach's permission, had put on shoulder pads, a helmet and a borrowed pair of cleats. Daniel lined up 20 yards behind the line of scrimmage, and as his quarterback took the snap and downed the ball, Daniel raised his hands in a V for victory. "It was," he says, "the single best memory of my life."

Now Daniel hopes for a victory for his friend Lisa. When she was sick for two weeks last month, doctors discovered that she had a badly infected kidney. Now Lisa, too, is learning all about needles and even transplants. Luckily, she's got a 17-year-old Mayo Clinic encyclopedia to talk to on the phone, to keep her calm—and make her laugh. "He's getting me through it," she says.

Shirlee Allison knows how well Daniel can do that sort of thing. After she went home from the hospital, she ran a two-inch-by-one-inch ad in the Danville paper expressing her love for her grandson. She says, "Every morning I wake up, I get on my knees and thank two people: God and Daniel."

Reprinted courtesy of Sports Illustrated *November 4, 1996. Copyright © 1996, Time Inc. "An Easy Choice" by Rick Reilly. All rights reserved.*

IN YOUR OWN WORDS

1. Before his grandmother's illness, what stressful situations did Daniel experience?

2. How did he cope with these situations?

3. There are two points of view expressed in this article. Daniel's mother was clearly against the operation, and in fact tried to stop it. Despite misgivings just before surgery, Daniel was obviously in favor of it, as was his grandmother. What is your position? If you were faced with a similar set of circumstances, would you donate a kidney to a close relative? Would you be willing to accept the donation of a kidney from a close relative?

4. Try to analyze the article from the perspective of Daniel's mother and the first hospital that scheduled the surgery. What reasons do you think they gave for being against the surgery? Do you think these reasons have validity? Do you think Daniel, as a minor, should have been evaluated by a psychologist before his donation of his kidney? Since he was living with his grandmother at the time of the surgery, do you think she took unfair advantage of him?

5. Describe the point of view of Daniel's grandmother, Shirlee. Is her age, 60, a factor in this decision? Is her quality of life a factor?

6. Do you think the early stresses in Daniel's life contributed to his making the decision to save his grandmother's life? In Daniel's mind he made the right decision. Why does he feel that way?

7. How would you describe Daniel's personality? Given that personality, could he have decided in any other fashion? How do you think Daniel would have been personally affected if he had made the decision not to help his grandmother?

8. What do you think could be the repercussions of Daniel's unselfish act? Do you think there will be additional pressure placed on healthy children to donate organs to ailing relatives?

9. Several years ago, a mother faced with the inevitable death of her daughter deliberately conceived another child so that the second child could be a donor. As a result of the mother's action, both children are still alive and thriving. Would you approve of this type of situation? What is morally right or wrong about it?

Vocabulary Exercise

Directions: Below are some expressions used in the article. Try to determine the meaning of each italicized expression from its context and then write the definition.

1. He was the screamer on the team, the *human pep rally*. (paragraph 2)

   _____

2. Daniel had planned to make this season *a doozy*. (paragraph 3)

   _____

3. He had no *designs on stardom*. (paragraph 4) _____

4. Hard to figure where he got all the *spare sunshine*. (paragraph 7)

   _____

5. Who was this *clothes hanger of a woman*, all bone . . .(paragraph 10)

   _____

6. Alice was *foursquare against* the donation. (paragraph 18)_____

7. Daniel was *dogged.* (paragraph 19) _____

8. We sure could have used Daniel to *put a body on somebody . . .* (paragraph 27) _____

Written Assignment

Write a paragraph describing the stresses in your life and the way you handle them.

Study Schedules

How do you create a study schedule that makes you more efficient?

Where to Study

The last part of the puzzle we will work with, before writing up your study schedule, is looking at *where* you should study. It is important to separate your studying from the other phases of your life. There should be a time to study and a time to be with your children, spouse, or friends, and the two should be separate. You may want to study at your boyfriend's or girlfriend's apartment, but you may be studying something else other than your sociology.

Mary Kaye Perrin, at College of St. Theresa, asks students in her classes to complete the following Study Area Analysis handout. Completing this survey helps students recognize the best places to study. You will notice that you may be able to study in one place better than another depending on the time of day. Now take the following test, and later we will talk some more about how to choose a good place to study. This is not going to be turned in, but is only meant to help you.

List two or three places where you frequently study.

Place A _____

Place B _____

Place C _____

After reading each statement below, check the answer (T or F) that applies to each of these places. It's easiest to do all of the questions for Place A first, then all of the questions for Place B second, and then, if you have a third place, all of the questions for Place C.

		Place A	Place B	Place C
1.	Other people often interrupt me.	T F	T F	T F
2.	The environment reminds me of things not related to studying.	T F	T F	T F
3.	I can often hear the radio or TV.	T F	T F	T F
4.	I can often hear the phone ringing.	T F	T F	T F
5.	I take too many breaks.	T F	T F	T F
6.	I seem to be especially bothered by distractions.	T F	T F	T F
7.	My breaks tend to be too long.	T F	T F	T F

	Place A	Place B	Place C
8. I tend to start conversations.	T F	T F	T F
9. Temperature conditions are ideal.	T F	T F	T F
10. Chair, table, lighting arrangements are not conducive to studying.	T F	T F	T F

From Course Manual for Becoming a Master Student, *Seventh Edition by David B. Ellis. Copyright © 1994 by Houghton Mifflin Company. Used with permission*

What does this survey tell you about where you should study? Is that place best because of when you study there or because of the location? You will need to think about the answer to this question when you fill out the last part of your study schedule.

Before making your study schedule, read the following article written by Walter S. Minot and published in *The Christian Science Monitor* in 1988. Minot received his Ph.D. from the University of Nebraska and is presently a Professor of English and chair of the English Department at Gannon University. He is concerned that students are working too many hours a week while also trying to be full-time students. Although some colleges recommend that students work part-time on campus, the work hours should be kept to a minimum. We suggest that if you are a full-time student (12 hours per semester), you limit your work schedule to no more than 20 hours per week. If you play sports, you should not work at all during the season. If you work full-time (40 hours per week), you should take no more than 6 credit hours.

After reading Minot's article, decide which is more important—school or work, and begin to plan your life accordingly. You may want to apply for financial aid to reduce the number of hours you need to work. Remember, you can't do everything!

Notes on Vocabulary

scapegoat—a person, group, or thing made to take the blame for the crime or mistake of others   Under the law of Moses, the high priest of the ancient Jews would bring two goats to the altar on the Day of Atonement. The high priest then cast lots to see which goat would be sacrificed to the Lord and which would be the *scapegoat*. After the priest had confessed the sins of his people over the head of the *scapegoat*, it was taken to the wilderness and allowed to escape, carrying with it all the sins of the people. The other goat was then given in sacrifice.

tripe—slang for nonsense, or anything offensive; part of the stomach of cattle, goats, or deer when used for food.

"Students Who Push Burgers"

by Walter Minot

READING

A college freshman squirms anxiously on a chair in my office, his eyes avoiding mine, those of his English professor, as he explains that he hasn't finished his paper, which was due two days ago. "I just haven't had the time," he says.

"Are you carrying a heavy course load?"

"Fifteen hours," he says—a normal load.

"Are you working a lot?"

5 "No, sir, not much. About 30 hours a week."

"That's a lot. Do you have to work that much?"

"Yeah, I have to pay for my car."

"Do you really need a car?"

"Yeah, I need it to get to work."

10   This student isn't unusual. Indeed, he probably typifies today's college and high school students. Yet in all the lengthy analyses of what's wrong with American education, I have not heard employment by students being blamed.

I have heard drugs blamed and television—that universal scapegoat. I have heard elaborate theories about the decline of the family, of religion, and of authority, as well as other sociological theories. But nobody blames student employment. The world seems to have accepted the part-time job as a normal feature of adolescence. A parochial school in my town even had a day to honor students who held regular jobs, and parents often endorse this employment by claiming that it teaches kids the value of the dollar.

But such employment is a major cause of educational decline. To argue my case, I will rely on memories of my own high school days and contrast them with what I see today. Though I do have some statistical evidence, my argument depends on what anyone over 40 can test through memory and direct observation.

When I was in high school in the 1950s, students seldom held jobs. Some of us baby-sat, shoveled snow, mowed lawns, and delivered papers, and some of us got jobs in department stores around Christmas. But most of us had no regular source of income other than the generosity of our parents.

The only kids who worked regularly were poor. They worked to help their families. If I remember correctly, only about five people in my class of 170 held jobs. That was in a working-class town in New England. As for the rest of us, our parents believed that going to school and helping around the house were our work.

15   In contrast, in 1986 my daughter was one of the few students among juniors and seniors who didn't work. According to Bureau of Labor statistics, more than 40 percent of high school students were working in 1980, but sociologists Ellen Greenberger and Laurence Steinberg in "When Teenagers Work" came up with estimates of more than 70 percent working in 1986, though I suspect that the figure may be even higher now.

My daughter, however, did not work; her parents wouldn't let her. Interestingly, some of the students in her class implied that she had an unfair advantage over them in the classroom. They were probably right, for while she was home studying, they were pushing burgers, waiting on tables, or selling dresses 20 hours a week. Working students have little time for homework.

I attended a public high school, while she attended a Roman Catholic preparatory school whose students are mainly middle class. By the standards of my day, her classmates did not "have to" work. Yet many of them were working 20 to 30 hours a week. Why?

They worked so that they could spend $60 to $100 a week on designer jeans, rock concerts, stereo and video systems, and, of course, cars. They were living lives of luxury, buying items on which their parents refused to throw hard-earned money away. Though the parents would not buy such tripe for their kids, the parents somehow convinced themselves that the kids were learning the value of money. Yet, according to Ms. Greenberger and Mr. Steinberg, only about a quarter of these students saved money for college or other long-term goals.

How students spend their money is their business, not mine. But as a teacher, I have witnessed the effects of their employment. I know that students who work all evening aren't ready for studying when they get home from work. Moreover, because they work so hard and have ready cash, they feel that they deserve to have fun—instead of spending all their free time studying.

20   Thus, by the time they get to college, most students look upon studies as a spare-time activity. A survey at Pennsylvania State University showed that most freshmen believed they could maintain a B average by studying about 20 hours a

week. (I can remember when college guidebooks advised two to three hours of studying for every hour in class—30 to 45 hours a week.)

Clearly individual students will pay the price for lack of adequate time studying, but the problem goes beyond the individual. It extends to schools and colleges that are finding it difficult to demand quantity or quality of work from students.

Perhaps the reason American education has declined so markedly is because America has raised a generation of part-time students. And perhaps our economy will continue to decline as full-time students from Japan and Europe continue to outperform our part-time students.

From "Students Who Push Burgers" by Walter S. Minot as appeared in The Christian Science Monitor. *Copyright © 1988 Walter S. Minot. Reprinted by permission of author.*

**IN YOUR
OWN WORDS**

1. Although this article was written in 1988, the information presented is still relevant today. In fact, the actual percentage of working students has increased slightly. Minot's main idea is that student employment is a major cause of educational decline in this country. Do you agree or disagree with Minot's viewpoint? Why or why not?

2. Do you think parents today still support the notion that a student's "job" is going to school and getting good grades?

3. In grade school, most students are in class until 3 or 4 in the afternoon. Most high school students are dismissed much earlier than this. Why do you think older students are allowed to spend fewer hours in school? Do you think that high schools require fewer hours in class because they expect students to do more studying at home? Do you think they are allowing students to leave early because of extracurricular activities, such as jobs? Do you think high schools should require students to spend more time at school?

4. What do parents hope a student will learn from a work experience? What do you think students learn from a work experience? Do you think it would be better for students with free time to do volunteer work instead of working for a salary?

5. Is it likely that students are learning the value of money from their early work experiences? Why or why not?

6. Many teachers report that the number of students trying to do their homework in class has increased over the years. What key point does Minot make that supports these teachers' observations?

7. Many publishers over the years have lowered the readability levels of their textbooks. Today a social studies textbook meant for use by eighth graders might be written at a sixth or seventh grade readability level. Which of Minot's arguments would help explain why this has happened?

8. Many high school and college teachers comment that they no longer require the same amount of work from their students. For example, where once two research papers were required for English 101, now only one is required. What are some possible effects of these reduced standards?

9. Professor Minot concludes his article by contrasting American students to those in foreign countries. It is well known that students in the United States spend less time in school than do students in any other modern industrial country. According to Minot, what are the global implications of being a nation of part-time students?

When to Study

Now let's begin to put some of this information we have learned about ourselves to practical use. What we are going to be doing—making a study schedule—will probably make a lot of sense to a left-brain oriented person, but not as much sense to those of you who are extremely right-brain dominant. But that's even more reason for those of you with a dominant right hemisphere to make a study schedule—so that you can begin to get organized. Would you like to be prepared for a test two nights before the test is given? Would you like to have that paper written a day early? If so, follow along.

Following this discussion, you will find a practice form for a study schedule (see page 53). Another copy is located in the Appendix for your future use.

Step 1: First, fill in your class schedule. For example, if your math class is MWF from 9 to 10, write in Math in the three blocks for those days and time. You have no control over these items; you have to go to class.

Step 2: Now fill in your work schedule. We hope it is fairly regular, because if it is not, keeping a regular study schedule from week to week will be difficult. Write in "work" in the appropriate blocks.
If your schedule changes from week to week, try to approximate it.
If some weeks you work more than others, go by your busier weeks.

Step 3: Fill in time for school activities such as sports events, clubs, and student council.

Step 4: Fill in time for other regularly scheduled activities, such as church, meetings, and grocery shopping. If it's something you do almost every week, put it in. If you do something only about once a month, then leave it out.

Step 5: Fill in time commitments to your family, spouse, friends, and so forth. Remember that those people will also need your attention. This includes such things as putting your children to bed and time at your boyfriend's house. As we mentioned previously, begin to separate your academic life from your family and social life. Don't try to study and cook dinner simultaneously. Don't try to study at your girlfriend's or boyfriend's house. Plan time for studying and time for your personal life—but not at the same time. The two don't mix. You and your children will be happier. You and your significant other will be happier. You will be able to do higher quality schoolwork in a shorter period of time.

Step 6: Fill in other times when you are not likely to be studying. For example, Friday and Saturday nights, a time when you watch your favorite TV show, or times when you exercise. Remember exercise is also important for your health and well-being.

Step 7: At the bottom of the schedule sheet you are working on, make a list of the classes you are taking. After each of your classes, make an estimate of the total number of hours you think you will need to study in that class each week to achieve an A or B. This number may vary from class to class. For example, you may need only 4 hours per week for psychology, but 8 hours per week for math and 10 hours per week for biology. Remember that one of the differences between high school and college is that college requires more work outside the classroom. Generally speaking, you need to plan for about two hours outside of class for every hour in class. You need to include in your estimate time for studying the textbook, reviewing your

STUDY SCHEDULES

	Monday	Tuesday	Wednesday	Thursday	Friday	Saturday	Sunday
6:00–7:00							
7:00–8:00							
8:00–9:00							
9:00–10:00							
10:00–11:00							
11:00–12:00							
12:00–1:00							
1:00–2:00							
2:00–3:00							
3:00–4:00							
4:00–5:00							
5:00–6:00							
6:00–7:00							
7:00–8:00							
8:00–9:00							
9:00–10:00							
10:00–11:00							
11:00–12:00							
12:00–1:00							

notes, writing your papers, and studying for tests. If unsure, for example, whether to put six or seven hours down for your English class, put down the larger number.

Step 8: Now decide which class is the most difficult and will take the most concentration. Think back to the test you took on your circadian cycle. Also think about the test on study areas you just took. If math is your most difficult subject, then find a time when you can concentrate on it the most. Unless you are a real night owl, and wide awake at 11:00 P.M., don't try to study just before you go to bed. Also recall whether you are an auditory, visual, or kinesthetic learner and take this into account. For example, if you are a visual learner who is taking a class in psychology that involves mostly lectures, plan time the night before each lecture to read and study the textbook. That way you are emphasizing a strength rather than a weakness.

If you can plan a regular time every day for each subject, you will be better off because you will have put order into your life. Two-hour blocks of time work fairly well for many people, but you need to decide what your own attention span is. Don't try to study one subject for more than two hours because you will probably lose your concentration. If your attention span is a problem, try one-hour blocks at first.

Step 9: You now have a guide for your daily and weekly routine. Remember you have to go to class on a regular basis, so why not study on a regular basis? What should you be doing during your scheduled study time? You can read the chapter before going to class; review your notes from each day's class; review the previous chapter; begin to review and study for the test the following week; or you can work on that paper you have to write that is due next Friday.

This schedule does not have to be inflexible. It can be changed as your life changes. But if you have a regular study schedule that you use from week to week, you will finish your studying more quickly and do a better job at it. Don't be caught trying to cram for a test the night before or beginning to write your paper for English at 10:00 P.M. on Tuesday night when it is due at 10:00 A.M. on Wednesday morning. It won't work, or at least it won't work very well!

SQ3R

A Classic Way to Study

SQ3R is a system for reading and studying textbook material that was developed by Dr. Francis P. Robinson more than 50 years ago. Most "new" study techniques are variations of this old classic.

Step 1: Survey

You survey a reading selection by looking it over before actually beginning to closely read it. When you complete your survey, you should have a general understanding of what the selection is about. Following are some suggestions for surveying.

1. Read the title or subtitle, and any information given about the author.
2. Read the first paragraph or the introduction.
3. As you move through the material, notice the headings or subheadings.

4. Pick out any boldfaced or italicized words.

5. Read the first sentence of each paragraph.

6. Notice the charts, diagrams, pictures, or other graphic material.

7. Read the last paragraph, the conclusion, or the summary.

8. Read any questions at the end of the selection.

9. Think about what *you* already know about the topic.

Step 2: Question

After completing your survey, you should have some questions in mind about the material. If you can't think of any questions, try turning a subheading into a question. For a section with the title "SQ3R," you might ask, "What is SQ3R?" Or, "Why is it a classic technique of studying?" If the material you are reading doesn't have subheadings, try turning the first sentence of every paragraph into a question. It is much easier to keep yourself actively involved in the material if you are reading to answer specific *how, why,* or *what* questions. Your attention is less likely to wander if you actually write down the questions, and their answers, on a separate sheet of paper, or even in the textbook. You might want to try conducting an imaginary conversation with the author—talk to the author, ask the author for answers, keep a continuous conversation going.

Step 3: Read

Now carefully read the entire selection from the beginning to the end. Look for main ideas and the answers to your questions. You may also want to mark key points by underlining, highlighting, or jotting notes about important information in the margins. Remember, most textbook material will need to be read more than once. The first reading will give you only a limited understanding of the material. If the material is particularly long, divide it into sections, read a section at a time, and take a short break between sections if you need to.

Step 4: Recite

To do this step, you must put the information you have learned into your own words, and then say it either to yourself or out loud. While it might seem odd at first, talking out loud can be a very effective technique for remembering material because it involves hearing and saying at the same time. You might pretend someone has asked you a question about the material and then respond (out loud or to yourself) by giving the answer. Or you might pretend that you are the teacher giving a lecture on the material. Be sure you can recite the answers to *who, what, where, when, why,* and *how* questions. When you organize the material mentally and put it into your own words, you are demonstrating your understanding of the material.

Step 5: Review

In this last step, look over your questions, notes, and underlinings. Practice giving the answers to the questions you originally posed. By now you should be able to define special terms and give relevant examples. You might want to do your review with another person by explaining the material to that person, or by taking turns quizzing each other about the material. Review frequently so the material will stay with you.

Vocabulary: Homonyms and Other Confusing Words

U.S. Capitol (Gamma Liaison)

As you learned in the introduction, homonyms are words that sound the same but may have different spellings or meanings. There are other words that could be added to our list of homonyms below, but these are the ones students most commonly have trouble with. Mastering these words will help you make a good impression in written assignments, so we have included homonyms in Chapter 1. *Affect* and *effect* are discussed in a separate box because they are especially difficult.

accept	a verb meaning "to receive, take, or hold." Did you *accept* the money given to you by your rich uncle?
except	a preposition meaning "without." Everyone *except* you was invited to the party.
expect	a verb meaning "to look forward to an event." *Expect* is not technically a homonym, but students sometimes confuse it with *except*. I *expect* to get an A in English, but if I don't do well on the final I might end up with a B.
capitol	a noun meaning "the physical building where laws are made." From now on, you should use this word for the actual building. The *capitol* building in Washington, D.C., has two branches, the Senate and the House of Representatives.
capital	a noun or adjective meaning "most important or most serious," including the *capital* city, money, *capital* letters, *capital* punishment, and the top of a column of a building. What is the *capital* city of your state?

(capital) The highest capital city, before being taken over by China, was Lhasa, Tibet. Its elevation is 12,087 feet above sea level.

Think about This Sentence: Your state *capitol* building is located in the *capital* city of your state.

(know) "All men by nature desire to know."

Aristotle

know	a verb meaning "to understand." Did you *know* all the important information for the test?
no	adverb, sometimes an adjective, used to express something negative. Did you stay up all night studying for the test? *No*, you went to bed.
knew	a verb, past tense of the verb *know*. I *knew* the material for the test.
new	adjective meaning "present, modern"; an antonym of *old*. Did you spend your money on a *new* car?

(past) "This only is denied even to God: the power to undo the past."

Agathon

past	a noun meaning "former time." In the *past* you did not study as much as you should have.
	an adjective meaning "former." One of our *past* presidents was Thomas Jefferson.
	an adverb meaning "beyond something." Did you walk *past* the library on the way to the student union?
passed	the past tense of the verb *pass*. The quarterback *passed* the ball to the tight end who ran for a touchdown. The student *passed* the test with an A. My father *passed* away. Each of these sentences uses the word *passed* as a verb expressing action.

Think about This Sentence: Most of our *past* presidents have *passed* away.

principal	a noun meaning "head of a school, or other person who is the main person."
	a noun meaning "sum of money." When you buy a house, you will pay on *principal* and interest.
	an adjective meaning "main" or "chief." Was the *principal* cause of the Civil War the desire to abolish slavery or the need to keep our country unified?
principle	a noun meaning "fundamental moral beliefs." Cheating people out of their money should go against the *principles* your parents taught you.
	a noun meaning "fundamental theory," as in physics. A fundamental *principle* in physics is that the atoms or molecules in gases are more widely spaced than in solids or liquids.

Think about This Sentence: Your *principal* beliefs are the *principles* you live by.

quiet	an adjective meaning "silent." Are you a *quiet* person?
quite	an adverb meaning "very" or "extremely." The line of cars trying to get into the parking lot of the football stadium was *quite* long.
quit	a verb meaning "to discontinue" or "give up." This word is not really a homonym, but is often confused with *quiet* and *quite*. The student *quit* her job at McDonald's so that she could devote more time to her studies.
their	an adjective indicating possession; the possessive form of "they." *Their* car was stolen from the parking lot.
there	an adverb indicating direction, meaning "in that position." Notice how the word *here* appears in the word *there*. The computer lab is located over *there*.
	a pronoun used to begin a sentence or phrase. *There* are a few students absent from class today.
they're	a contraction for "they are." *They're* going to the party after the game.
to	a preposition indicating direction, and meaning "toward." Are you going *to* your house after you finish class?
	part of a verb indicating an infinitive statement. Unless you are independently wealthy, you will need *to* work for a living. You may want *to* study in the library.

Think about This Sentence: You are going *to* work because you need *to* work for a living. The first *to* is a preposition indicating direction; the second *to* is part of the verb "to work."

too	an adverb meaning "also" or "excessively." He, *too*, was allowed to leave class early. She drank *too* much at the party.
two	the number 2. The baseball team scored *two* runs in the fifth inning.

threw		the past tense of the verb *throw*. The shortstop *threw* out the runner at first base.
through		a preposition indicating direction. The drunk driver drove *through* the red light.
		a preposition meaning "finished." When the student was *through* with the test, he took it to the instructor at the front of the class.
		Finish the sentence: The boy *threw* the ball *through* the _____.
weather		a noun meaning "temperature, climate." The *weather* was so hot that you just had to stay inside with the air conditioner running.
whether		a conjunction similar to "if." Some people believe it really doesn't make much difference *whether* we have a Republican or Democratic president.
were		the past tense of the verb *are*. We *were* in the mountains when the fire broke out.
we're		a contraction for *we are*. *We're* going to go to the store.
wear		a verb meaning "to have on the body" or "to diminish." What are you going to *wear* to the party on Saturday? You are going to *wear* out the carpet walking back and forth so much.
where		an adverb, conjunction, or noun indicating location. *Where* did I leave my books?

(weather)   Don't talk on the phone or take a shower during a thunderstorm. The electrical current of lightning can travel through phone lines and water pipes.

Now for the difference between *affect* and *effect*. We won't insist on perfection in your use of these words, but you can get better. The key to working with these words is knowing the difference between a noun and a verb. Remember that a verb indicates *action* or *state of being*. A noun is a person, place, or thing; remember that things can be intangible (for example, feelings, causes, and hopes).

action	The team *won* the game last night.
state of being	The team *is* excellent because its players *are* quick and play good defense.
affect	a verb meaning "influence." This word will *almost always* be used as a verb. If one thing *affects* something else, it influences it. If you are using one of these words as a verb, you will use *affect* 95 percent of the time. Weather *affects* our personalities and how we feel. (The weather is influencing your personality.) In psychology, *affect* can be used as a noun meaning "emotional response." After her mother died, Maria became depressed and had a flat *affect*.
effect	Ninety-nine percent of the time this word will be a noun. *Effect* as a noun usually means "the result of an action." What will be the *effect* on you if Congress cuts back the financial aid program? Using *effect* as a verb is very tricky, but on the positive side you will probably need to use it this way very rarely. As a verb, *effect* means "to cause or bring about." Congress may *effect* a change in the income tax laws.

Now write your own sentences using *affect* and *effect*. (You may find it helpful to refer back to the sample sentences above.)

_____

_____

_____

Homonyms

ACROSS CLUES

2. _____ on their way to class.

4. We have all done things in the _____ that we later regretted.

7. All students need _____ study several times each week for each class.

9. Did you drive your car _____ the exit on the freeway?

10. _____ is a good program on TV tonight.

11. Will you _____ your friend's invitation to the party?

13. Will you go _____ your graduation ceremony?

14. The student was _____ upset when he was withdrawn from class.

15. Many students _____ college before they graduate.

16. Do you _____ who won the game last night?

17. One of the _____ ingredients in soda is sugar.

19. Why were you over _____ when you should have been over here?

20. _____ house was broken into several times last summer.

24. You must walk _____ the hallway to get to the classroom.

25. Did you _____ your job?

26. _____, I do not want any more ice cream.

27. Everyone _____ you received an A on the test.

28. _____ you at home last night studying?

29. The elderly person _____ away.

30. One _____ of life is to do unto others as you would want them to do unto you.

DOWN CLUES

1. We went to K-Mart to buy _____ clothes.

2. There are _____ wheels on a typical bike.

3. All of the student's grades were A's _____ for the B on the final.

5. Studying hard should positively _____ your grade.

6. The basketball player _____ the ball out-of-bounds, by accident.

8. What is the _____ city of your state?

12. Using drugs will have a negative _____ on a person.

13. _____ little sleep will probably make you drowsy and cranky.

14. Was the room _____ while students were taking the test, or was it too noisy?

16. The student _____ all the important information for the test.

17. Religious books lay down basic _____s of life.

18. Where is the _____ building located?

21. When will you be _____ with your work and able to go home?

22. _____ is the closest McDonald's?

23. The first letter of a sentence should be a _____ letter.

PART 2

Discovering Meaning through Structure

Written music is like a route map, or a set of instructions for a journey. It is a diagram which shows a musician how a piece of music should be played.

from Music Connections *by Caroline Grimshaw*

"[Musical] notation can be used as a point of reference, but the notation does not indicate music. It indicates a direction."

—Cecil Taylor
from Jazz Is *by Nat Hentoff*

A musician composing a piece of music has a purpose or direction in mind, which is to communicate a certain mood or feeling. This mood or feeling could be called the main idea of the piece. The composer will organize the piece around the main idea by finding instruments, notes, and chords that support the main idea and bring it to life. All of these elements will fit together in a smooth way to form the structure of the piece, which is what gives it meaning.

A writer works in a similar way. A writer constructing a paragraph has a purpose or direction in mind, which is to communicate a main idea. The writer organizes the paragraph around the main idea by stating the main idea and then presenting details that support it. How the supporting details relate to one another and to the main idea forms the structure of the paragraph. It is the structure of the paragraph that gives it meaning. What we will be discussing in Part 2 are the different ways that paragraphs can be organized or structured.

61

Chapter 2

Topics, Main Ideas, and Details

Description of Topics and Main Ideas

Most paragraphs are about a particular **topic** or **subject**. The topic is usually a single word or phrase, and is often the noun that is mentioned most frequently in a paragraph. We can identify the topic by asking ourselves, "What is this all about?" or "Whom is this all about?"

Paragraphs are supposed to be organized around a main idea with all sentences supporting this **main idea**, or key point, of the paragraph. The main idea can be identified by asking the question, "What key point does the author want me to know about the topic?"

The main idea may be directly stated in a paragraph—usually, but not always, in the first or last sentence—or it can be implied. When trying to find a main idea that is directly stated, it helps to remember that you are looking for a general statement, not a specific one. When main ideas are implied, you, the reader, are responsible for coming up with a general statement that unites the author's key details. This general statement should be no more than one sentence long.

Details are supporting sentences that reinforce the main idea. While the main idea is a general statement, supporting details provide specific information, such as facts, examples, or reasons, that explain or elaborate on the main idea.

As an illustration of the difference between main ideas and details, study the *Baby Blues* cartoon below. In it, Darryl provides Wanda with the main idea of the phone conversation, but is unable to provide her with any of the supporting details.

Those supporting sentences that directly reinforce the main idea are called **major** supporting details, and those sentences that serve only to reinforce the major supporting details are called **minor** supporting details. To gain understanding of how main ideas and major and minor supporting details work in a paragraph, read the following paragraph on posture as body language and study the outline.

Psychologist Albert Mehrabian has found that other postural keys to feelings are tension and relaxation. He says that we take relaxed postures in non-threatening situations and tighten up when threatened. Based on this observation, he says we can tell a good deal about how others feel simply by watching how tense or loose they seem to be. For example, he suggests that watching tenseness is a way of detecting status differences. The lower-status person is generally the more rigid, tense-appearing one, whereas the one with higher status is more relaxed. This is the kind of situation that often happens when an employee sits ramrod straight while the boss leans back in her chair. The same principle applies to social situations, where it's often possible to tell who's uncomfortable by looking at pictures. Often you'll see someone laughing and talking as if he were perfectly at home, but his posture almost shouts nervousness. Some people never relax, and their posture shows it.

From Adler, Ronald, and Towne, Neil, Looking Out/Looking In: An Introduction to Nonverbal Communication, *7th Edition, Fort Worth: Harcourt Brace, 1993, p. 219.*

MI (main idea), MSD (major supporting detail), msd (minor supporting detail)

I.   Tension and relaxation in a person's posture are keys to feelings (MI)
   A.   Person displays relaxed posture when not threatened (MSD)
   B.   Person displays tense posture when feeling threatened (MSD)
   C.   Tension or relaxation in posture may indicate status (MSD)
      1.   Tense-appearing person has low status (msd)
      2.   Relaxed-appearing person has high status (msd)
   D.   Posture indicates who's comfortable in a social setting (MSD)

In the following example, the general topic is sensitivity to nonverbal communication. The format is fairly typical of information presented in college textbooks. The main idea is given in the first sentence of the paragraph. The sentences following the main idea are all meant to serve as examples illustrating it. The last sentence concludes the paragraph and reinforces the main idea.

Affirmative action programs have brought diversity to the workplace, creating the need for greater sensitivity among managers and employees regarding people's cultural backgrounds. *For instance, white Americans define eye contact in the course of a conversation as showing respect. But many Latinos do not, and many Americans of Asian ancestry deem eye contact with a boss to be an exceedingly disrespectful behavior. Potential conflicts may arise when white bosses consider Hispanic or Asian employees furtive or rude for casting their eyes about the room.* Multicultural training programs seek to teach employers and employees to look beyond their culture-bound notions about what constitutes "proper" and "improper" behavior.

From Vander Zanden, James W., Sociology: The Core, *4th edition, New York: McGraw-Hill, 1996, p. 74.*

It is wise to remember that while all paragraphs have a topic, not all paragraphs have main ideas. Some background or descriptive paragraphs, which are meant to set the tone or mood of a piece of writing, may not have any main idea at all.

Distinguishing between General and Specific

In order to be able to recognize a main idea, you must be able to determine the difference between something that is general and something that is specific. Remember, a main idea is a general statement that is supported by specific details. In the first example below, a car is something that is general because there are more specific kinds of cars. A sedan would be one specific kind of car, and a convertible would be another. In the second example, a tree is the broad category. An ash tree is a specific kind of tree, as is an elm tree.

Car	**Tree**
sedan	ash
convertible	elm

Exercise #1 Practice in Writing General and Specific Terms

In the examples that follow, you need to give two specific terms for each general category.

Example:

Professional baseball teams
Los Angeles Dodgers
New York Yankees

1. Wild animals   2. Weekly magazines   3. College courses

   _____   _____   _____

   _____   _____   _____

4. Cosmetics   5. Universities   6. U.S. presidents

   _____   _____   _____

   _____   _____   _____

In the examples that follow, you need to give a general term.

1. _____   2. _____   3. _____
   Aleve   TWA   *101 Dalmatians*
   Bayer   Continental   *The Lion King*
   Excedrin   American   *Beauty and the Beast*

Exercise #2 Practice Writing Specific Sentences

Directions: A general or main idea sentence is given to you. Working in a group, try to come up with two sentences to support the main idea. Your sentences should provide specific details by giving reasons or examples.

Example: Many people do not use antibiotics properly.

   A. They stop taking the antibiotic when they start feeling better.

   B. They pass them around to their friends like candy.

1.   Children today don't treat their parents with much respect.

   A. They _____

   B. They _____

2. Young boys are more interested in active, aggressive play than little girls.

   A. Boys play _____

   B. Girls play _____

3. In the last ten years, a new kind of father has emerged.

   A. Fathers now _____

   B. Fathers now _____

4. For a student in the United States, school is just like a job.

   A. _____

   B. _____

5. Dying today has become more lonely and impersonal.

   A. _____

   B. _____

6. People are more isolated from their neighbors today than they were 50 years ago.

   A. _____

   B. _____

7. The traditional family (husband as breadwinner, wife as homemaker) has all but disappeared.

   A. _____

   B. _____

Exercise #3 Practice Writing General or Main Idea Sentences

Directions: Two specific detail sentences are given to you. Working in a group, try to write a main idea sentence that will cover both of the details.

1. _____

   A. Research shows a 15-minute nap can improve concentration.

   B. Truck drivers who pull over to the side of the road whenever they feel sleepy are less likely to have an accident on long haul trips.

2. _____

   A. Air bags have been responsible for the deaths of 31 young children.

   B. Air bags deploy with a 200-pound force sometimes injuring children and small adults in minor fender-bender accidents.

3. _____

   A. A local minister was caught telling a lie to a member of his church.

   B. Kids as young as two years of age routinely lie to avoid punishment.

4. _____

   A. Americans exercise very little and watch too much TV.

   B. Americans eat far too many foods classified by nutritionists as "junk."

5. _____

   A. Pet owners enjoy better health and have fewer visits to the doctor.

   B. Pet owners recover more quickly from surgery.

6. _____

    A. After a divorce, boys are more likely to be low achievers in school.

    B. After a divorce, many boys suffer from a poor self-image.

7. _____

    A. Toothpaste contains unappetizing ingredients like chalk, detergent, seaweed, and formaldehyde.

    B. Toothpaste can actually create cavities.

8. _____

    A. College athletes spend enormous amounts of time and energy on their sport.

    B. Although individual athletic departments generate large sums from team sports, the individual student-athlete receives no compensation.

Locating Topics and Main Ideas

Directions: Now locate the topic of each paragraph and the main idea sentence. The main idea can be identified by asking the question, "What key point does the author want me to know about the topic?"

Information on nonverbal cues is from Vander Zanden, James W., Sociology: the Core *4th Edition, New York: McGraw-Hill, 1996, pp. 74–75.*

1. Physical motions and gestures provide signals. The "preening behavior" that accompanies courtship is a good illustration. Women frequently stroke their hair, check their makeup, rearrange their clothes, or push the hair away from the face. Men may adjust their hair, tug at their tie, straighten their clothes, or pull up their socks. These are signals that say, "I'm interested in you. Notice me. I'm an attractive person."

    Topic: _____

    Main Idea: _____

2. Students who sit in the front rows of a classroom tend to be the most interested, those in the rear are more prone to mischievous activities, and students on the aisles are primarily concerned with quick departures. As you can see, the way we employ social and personal space also contains messages.

    Topic: _____

    Main Idea: _____

3. Through physical contact such as touch, we convey our feelings to one another. However, touch can also constitute an invasion of privacy, and it can become a symbol of power when people want to make power differences visible. For example, a high-status person might take the liberty of patting a low-status person on the back or shoulder, something that is deemed inappropriate for the subordinate.

    Topic: _____

    Main Idea: _____

4. It appears that some aspects of nonverbal communication, such as many gestures, are especially susceptible to cultural influence. For instance, the American "A-Okay" gesture made by joining the thumb and forefinger in a circle has quite different meanings, depending on the culture. An American tourist will find that what is taken to be a friendly sign in the United States has an insulting connotation in France and Belgium: "You're worth zero!" In southern Italy it means "You're a jerk," and in Greece and Turkey it conveys an insulting or vulgar sexual invitation.

Topic: _____

Main Idea: _____

Paragraph Diagrams

In previous exercises, we have seen that the main idea in a paragraph is frequently located at either the beginning or end of the paragraph. However, the main idea may also appear in other locations within a paragraph, such as in the middle, or at both the beginning and the end. Wherever the main idea is located, it must be supported by details. Most authors provide examples, illustrations, major points, reasons, or facts and statistics to develop their main idea. While a main idea can be either directly stated somewhere in the paragraph or implied, supporting details are always directly stated. The ability to recognize supporting details is of crucial importance in the reading process. Locating supporting details will tell you whether you have correctly identified the main idea.

For those of you who are visual learners, diagrams showing the development of a paragraph and the position of the main idea and supporting details might be helpful. The topic of each of the following paragraphs is the healing power of laughter.

All information was taken from 1996. Hafen, Karren, Frandsen, and Smith, Mind/Body Health, *Needham Heights, MA: Allyn and Bacon, Simon & Schuster, 1996, pp. 541, 542, 545, 547, and 551.*

Directions: After reading the explanation for each type of paragraph, write several key supporting details on the line provided.

1. *Laughter as medicine is probably as old as humankind.* One of the earliest written accounts recognizing the healing power of humor is found in the Bible, in which King Solomon remarked that a "merry heart doeth good like medicine" (Proverbs 17:22). Sixteenth-century physician Richard Mulcater prescribed laugh-ter for those afflicted with head colds and melancholy; a favorite "cure" was being tickled in the armpits. The famous seventeenth-century physician Thomas Sydenham said that "the arrival of a good clown exercises more beneficial influence upon the health of a town than twenty asses laden with drugs."

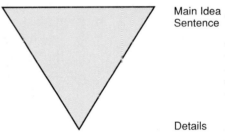

In paragraph 1, the main idea is stated in the first sentence. The supporting details are a series of examples illustrating the main idea. A diagram of this type of paragraph would be a triangle with the point aiming downward. The main idea is represented by the horizontal line at the top.

Supporting Details: _____

2. Some researchers have found that a humorous outlook on life can have far-reaching benefits such as enhancing self-esteem and promoting creativity. Others suggest that humor improves negotiating and decision-making skills. Still others have found that a healthy sense of humor helps maintain a balanced outlook, improves performance, and bestows a feeling of power. At the very least, humor helps to relieve stress and improves coping abilities. *As you can see, a sense of humor has tremendous psychological benefits.*

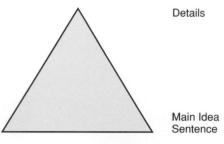

In paragraph 2, the author gives examples at the beginning and uses the main point to draw a conclusion. A diagram for this type of paragraph places the main idea at the bottom of the triangle.

Supporting Details: _____

3. Laughter requires no special training. It requires no special equipment. You don't have to do it at the gym or on the track or on a Nautilus machine. *Laughter is one of the best exercises around.* It improves your digestion, stimulates your central nervous system, improves and tones the cardiovascular system, thereby providing what some experts have called "a total inner body workout."

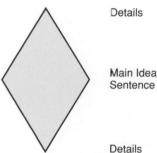

In paragraph 3, the author begins with reasons explaining why laughter is one of the best exercises, states the main idea, and then concludes with additional reasons. Because the main idea is in the middle, the diagram resembles a diamond.

Supporting Details: _____

4. *A sense of humor can give us a sense of power.* Anatoly Sharansky, the Russian human rights advocate, was confined for nine years in Soviet prisons. The Soviet police constantly threatened Sharansky with the *rastrel* (firing squad). Sharansky started to win the war against fear with humor. He started joking about the firing squad and talking about it on a daily basis. "You make jokes fifteen to twenty times," Sharansky remembers, "and the word becomes like any other word." *Humor can turn any situation around and give us a feeling of power over our circumstances.*

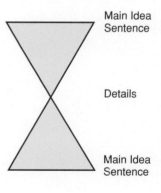

In paragraph 4, the author begins with the main idea, provides a detailed illustration of it, and concludes with a restatement of the main idea. A diagram of this type of paragraph would have an hour-glass shape.

Supporting Details: _____

5. In a study by University of Maryland psychologist Alice Isen, she split volunteers into two groups. One either watched a math film or did a monotonous exercise; the other group watched a clip of funny television "bloopers" or received candy.

In paragraph 5, the main idea is not stated in any specific sentence. Instead, all of the sentences are working together to create a word picture in your mind of an experiment in progress. Because no one sentence is clearly the main idea, a diagram of this paragraph might resemble a square or a rectangle.

For additional practice, identify the main idea in the paragraphs below. Then draw a diagram of the paragraph and list the supporting details.

6. Mark Twain once penned the sentiment that "against the assault of laughter nothing can stand." What the great American humorist and author believed more than a hundred years ago is being proven today by some of our most gifted scientists. A sense of humor, and the laughter that accompanies it, can actually banish pain and keep us well.

Diagram: _____

Main Idea: _____

Supporting Details: _____

7. Humor has been used across the span of cultures to make people feel better. A number of American Indian tribes—the Zunis, Crees, Pueblos, and Hopis among them—had ceremonial clowns whose sole purpose was to provide humor for their tribesmen. According to accounts, they were called in "to entertain and heal the sick with hilarity, frightening away the demons of ill health."

Diagram: _____

Main Idea: _____

Supporting Details: _____

8. A sense of humor can actually promote good health by strengthening the immune system. Researchers subjected volunteers to a set of "hassles," situations known to invoke stress. The researchers found that people with a low sense of humor reacted strongly to the hassles causing a significant drop in their ability to withstand disease. Those who rated high on the humor scale demonstrated a strengthened immune function, even when subjected to hassles and stressors. It appears that people who tend to have a humorous outlook have greater immunity against a variety of diseases as well as increased ability to fight off infection.

Diagram: _____

Main Idea: _____

Supporting Details: _____

Main Idea: Location of the Main Idea

Directions: The main idea sentence appears at different locations in the following paragraphs. Write the number of the main idea sentence on the line. Then draw a diagram of the paragraph and list the supporting details.

(1) American males may feel uncomfortable when Middle Eastern heads of state greet the U.S. president with a kiss on the cheek. (2) A German student, accustomed to speaking rarely to "Herr Professor," considers it strange that at American colleges most faculty office doors are open and students stop by freely. (3) An Iranian student on her first visit to an American McDonald's restaurant fumbles around in her paper bag looking for the eating utensils until she sees the other customers eating their French fries with, of all things, their hands. (4) Your best manners and my best manners may be exceedingly offensive to people of

different nationalities and may cause us to make a serious breach of etiquette. (5) Foreigners visiting Japan often struggle to master the rules of the social game—when to take their shoes off, how to pour the tea, when to give and open gifts, how to act toward someone higher or lower in the social hierarchy.

Main Idea Sentence: _____ Diagram: _____
Supporting Details: _____

(1) Cultures also vary in their norms for personal expressiveness and time. (2) To someone from a relatively formal northern European culture, a person whose roots are in an expressive Mediterranean culture may seem "warm, charming, inefficient, and time-wasting." (3) To the Mediterranean person, the northern European may seem "efficient, cold, and over concerned with time." (4) Latin American business executives who arrive late for a dinner engagement may be mystified by how obsessed their American counterparts are with punctuality.

Main Idea Sentence: _____ Diagram: _____
Supporting Details: _____

(1) Adults maintain more distance from each other than children. (2) Men keep more distance from one another than do women. (3) Cultures near the equator prefer less space and more touching and hugging. (4) Thus the British and Scandinavians prefer more distance than the French and Arabs; Americans prefer more space than Latin Americans. (5) As you can see, individuals and groups differ in their need for personal space.

Main Idea Sentence: _____ Diagram: _____
Supporting Details: _____

Information is from Myers, David G., Social Psychology, *5th Edition, New York: McGraw-Hill, 1996, p. 211.*

(1) Once in Mexico I raised my hand to a certain height to indicate how tall a child was. (2) My hosts began to laugh. (3) It turned out that Mexicans have a more complicated system of hand gestures to indicate height: one for people, a second for animals, and a third for plants. (4) What had amused them was that I had ignorantly used the plant gesture to indicate the child's height.

Main Idea Sentence: _____ Diagram: _____
Supporting Details: _____

(1) To get along in another culture, then, it is important to learn the gestures of that culture. (2) If you don't, you will not only fail to achieve the simplicity of communication that gestures allow but you will also miss much of what is happening, run the risk of appearing foolish, and possibly offend people. (3) In many cultures, for example, you would provoke deep offense if you were to offer food or a gift with your left hand, because the left hand is reserved for dirty tasks, such as wiping after going to the bathroom.

Main Idea Sentence: _____ Diagram: _____
Supporting Details: _____

Information is from Henslin, James, Sociology, *Needham Heights, MA: Allyn and Bacon, Simon & Schuster, 1993, pp. 38–39.*

Review Test 1

Each of the following groups contains a series of related statements: One of the statements gives a topic, another gives a main idea, and two give supporting details. Identify the role of each statement in the space provided using the following abbreviations:

T for Topic

MI for Main Idea

SD for Supporting Detail

Group 1

_____ a. An early human observing anger, for instance, could choose to flee or prepare to fight.

_____ b. For example, it might be more beneficial to know when someone is angry and likely to react in a violent way than to know when someone is happy.

_____ c. Darwin believed that the ability to recognize some emotions is more important for survival than the ability to recognize others.

_____ d. The benefits of recognizing emotion.

Group 2

_____ a. People are more sensitive to signs of anger than to those of happiness.

_____ b. Subjects asked to recognize and label facial expressions from a variety of pictures were more apt to correctly identify the angry expressions than the happy ones.

_____ c. Recognition of angry versus happy faces.

_____ d. One reason people are more sensitive to anger than happiness is that happiness is a non-threatening emotion.

Group 3

_____ a. The face of anger.

_____ b. Specifically, triangular eyes that point directly toward the nose and hard, downward lines in the forehead, cheeks, mouth, and chin indicate anger.

_____ c. Anger is universally recognized by fixed geometric patterns in the face.

_____ d. Some common examples of the geometric principle can be seen in the threatening ceremonial masks of the natives of Bali and other cultures and in the protective masks worn by National Hockey League goalies.

From Brehn, Sharon S. and Kassin, Saul M., Social Psychology, *New York: Houghton Mifflin, 1996, p. 87.*

Group 4

_____ a. Between 9 and 12 months of age, for example, Antonio pointed to things to show that he wanted an object, nodded his head to mean *yes*, and shook his head to mean *no*.

_____ b. Babies develop a rich repertoire of nonverbal gestures before saying their first words.

_____ c. At 13 months, he was using representational gestures such as holding up his arms to show that he wanted to be picked up.

_____ d. Symbolic gestures of babies.

From Papalia, Diane, and Olds, Sally Wendkos, Human Development, *6th Edition, New York: McGraw-Hill, 1995, p. 147.*

Group 5

_____ a. When we are exposed to both verbal and nonverbal messages, research indicates that we give the most credibility to the nonverbal signals especially when they contradict the speaker's words.

_____ b. A friend might say that she agrees with you, but a study of her nonverbal body language reveals that her body is stiff and her hands are clenched into fists.

_____ c. When asked how he feels about his daughter, a father replies that she means the world to him, but he speaks in a flat tone, doesn't look at his daughter, and keeps his legs tightly crossed.

_____ d. Verbal versus nonverbal impact.

From Bird, Gloria, and Melville, Keith, Families and Intimate Relationships, New York: McGraw-Hill, 1994, p. 297.

Group 6

_____ a. Demonstration of affection.

_____ b. For example, middle-class Brazilians teach their male and female children to kiss every adult relative they ever see.

_____ c. While females continue kissing throughout their lives, Brazilian men greet each other with a hearty handshake and a traditional male hug.

_____ d. Brazilians do not fear demonstrations of physical contact and affection.

From Kottak, Conrad Phillip, Anthropology, An Exploration of Human Diversity, *7th Edition, New York: McGraw-Hill, 1995, p. 39.*

Group 7

_____ a. First, Jane Goodall identified 25 distinct calls used by Gombe chimps.

_____ b. The natural communication systems of other primates, their call systems, are much more complex than used to be supposed.

_____ c.   Communication systems of other primates.

_____ d.   Each of the Gombe chimp calls had a distinct meaning and was used only in particular situations.

From Kottak, Conrad Phillip, Anthropology, An Exploration of Human Diversity, *7th Edition, New York: McGraw-Hill, 1995, p. 127.*

In this section you are going to learn how to paraphrase main ideas.

Exercise #1 Paraphrasing Quotations

When you paraphrase something, you are expressing the author's essential meaning in your own words. Some key words will remain the same.

> *Example:* "The man who most vividly realizes a difficulty is the man most likely to overcome it." (Joseph Farrell)
>
> *Paraphrase:* The man who clearly recognizes a problem is the one likely to solve it.

Directions: Working in a group, paraphrase the following quotations. When you finish, check to make sure the meaning of both statements is the same.

1.   Every man is the architect of his own fortune. (Anonymous)

2.   A life lived in fear is a life half-lived. (Spanish proverb)

3.   "The crisis of yesterday is the joke of tomorrow." (H. G. Wells)

4.   "I am a great believer in luck, and I find the harder I work, the more I have of it." (Thomas Jefferson)

5.   "Once you have been stung by a wasp, it is easier to tolerate a mosquito, and you can be downright friendly with a fly." (Ellen Marek)

6.   "Victory finds a hundred fathers, but defeat is an orphan." (Count Galeazzo Ciano)

7.   A man has to live with himself; so he should see to it that he is always in good company. (Anonymous)

8.   "Courage is resistance to fear, mastery of fear—not absence of fear." (Mark Twain)

Exercise #2 Paraphrasing Rhymes

Directions: Working with a partner, paraphrase each of these nursery rhymes using your *own* words. Leave the key names, such as Humpty Dumpty, the same.

> *Example:* There was an old woman who lived in a shoe,
> She had so many children she didn't know what to do;
> She gave them some broth without any bread;
> She whipped them all soundly and put them to bed.

An elderly woman, who was residing in a shoe, felt so overwhelmed by her large family that she fed all the children clear soup, spanked them, and sent them to bed.

1. Jack Sprat could eat no fat,
   His wife could eat no lean,
   And so betwixt them both, you see,
   They licked the platter clean.

2. Humpty Dumpty sat on a wall,
   Humpty Dumpty had a great fall.
   All the king's horses, and all the king's men,
   Couldn't put Humpty together again.

3. Tom, Tom, the piper's son,
   Stole a pig and away did run!
   The pig was eat, and Tom was beat,
   And Tom went howling down the street.

4. Three wise men of Gotham
   Went to sea in a bowl;
   If the bowl had been stronger
   My song had been longer.

5. Little Polly Flanders
   Sat among the cinders,
   Warming her pretty little toes;
   Her mother came and caught her,
   And whipped her little daughter
   For spoiling her nice new clothes.

6. Jack and Jill
   Went up the hill,
   To fetch a pail of water;
   Jack fell down,
   And broke his crown,
   And Jill came tumbling after.

Exercise #3 Paraphrasing a Poem

Directions: Read the entire poem carefully, noting the key words and main ideas. Then try to explain the meaning of the poem in your own words.

"Grandmother's Fable" from **Shallow Graves**   *by Tran Thi Nga*

Once upon a time there lived a farming family.
The mother died, leaving three sons
to live with their father.
When the father became ill
and thought he was going to die, he called his children to his bedside
and handed each of them
a large bunch of chopsticks tied together.

He said, "Whoever can break this,
I will reward."
Not one was able to.

The father then handed each of them
only one set.
This they broke easily.

The father said, "If you remain united,
no one can harm you,
but if you separate, then you will be hurt.
This is the advice I leave with you.
The heritage I have for you
is in the rice fields."

After the father's death,
the three brothers stayed together
even after they married.
They did not find any golden treasures
buried in the rice fields.
They plowed and planted
and the ground gave successful harvests.
They realized working together
and working hard were life's riches.

"Grandmother's Fable" from Shallow Graves *by Tran Thi Nga. Reprinted by permission of Leona P. Schecter Literary Agent.*

Implied Main Ideas

Not all main ideas are directly stated. Sometimes we have to look closely at the details the author has provided in order to determine the main idea. Read the following paragraph from *The Art of Public Speaking* by Stephen Lucas and try to identify the implied main idea.

It had been a long day at the office, and the going-home traffic was bumper to bumper. By the time Jason Whitehawk pulled his late-model car into the driveway at home, he was exhausted. As he trudged into the house, he routinely asked his wife, "How did things go with you at work today?"

"Oh, pretty well," she replied, "except for the terrorist attack in the morning and the outbreak of bubonic plague in the afternoon."

Jason nodded his head as he made his way toward the sofa. "That's nice," he said. "At least someone had a good day. Mine was awful."

From The Art of Public Speaking, *5th Edition, by Stephen Lucas. Reprinted by permission of The McGraw-Hill Companies.*

The topic of this paragraph is listening. The implied main idea is that sometimes without really listening, people give the appearance of being interested in what someone is saying.

In the next example, the topic could be parenting or child-rearing patterns. In order to formulate the main idea, we must mention the three categories of parents.

Authoritarian parents are rigid and punitive and value unquestioning obedience from their children. They have strict standards and discourage expressions of disagreement. Permissive parents give their children lax or inconsistent direction and, although warm, require little of them. Authoritative parents are firm, setting limits for their children. As the children get older, these parents try to reason with and explain things to them. They also set clear goals and encourage their children's independence.

From Feldman, Robert S., The Essentials of Understanding Psychology, *3rd Edition, New York: McGraw-Hill, 1997, p. 337.*

Train a child in a way he should go, and when he is old, he will never depart from it.

Proverbs 12:4

From the details presented, we can conclude that each parent's child-rearing style is likely to have a different effect. Our implied main idea should be stated something like this:

> *Main Idea:* Three different parenting styles, authoritarian, permissive, and authoritative, shape children in different ways.

Determining an implied main idea is simply reducing all of the key information contained in the paragraph to one sentence.

It is sometimes helpful to first identify the topic, and then ask *who, what, where, when, why,* and *how* about the topic.

Read the following paragraph and try to determine the main idea.

> *In general, young males tend to be more aggressive than girls. They play more boisterously; they roughhouse more and are more apt to try to dominate other children and challenge their parents. Boys argue and fight more often and are more apt to use force or threats of force to get their way, while girls try to diffuse conflicts by persuasion rather than confrontation. Girls are more likely to cooperate with their parents and they tend to set up rules to avoid clashes. Girls are more likely to be empathic, that is, to identify with other people's feelings.*

From Papalia, Diane, and Olds, Sally Wendkos, Human Development, *6th Edition, New York: McGraw-Hill, 1995, p. 246.*

> *Who:* boys and girls
>
> *What:* display different personality characteristics
>
> *Where:* in social settings
>
> *When:* during interactions with others
>
> *Why:* boys are more aggressive; girls are more cooperative and empathic
>
> *How:* boys dominate, fight, threaten; girls persuade, cooperate, set up rules

The topic of this paragraph appears to be personality differences between boys and girls. If we look at all the key details, our main idea will look something like this: Young boys are more likely to display an aggressive personality and young girls are more likely to display an empathic, cooperative personality.

The next paragraph provides an explanation for male behavior in interpersonal relationships.

> *The boys' play illuminates why men would be on the lookout for signs they are being put down or told what to do. The chief commodity that is bartered in the boys' hierarchical world is status, and the way to achieve and maintain status is to give orders and get others to follow them. A boy in a low-status position finds himself being pushed around. So boys monitor their relations for subtle shifts in status by keeping track of who's giving orders and who's taking them.*

From You Just Don't Understand, *by Deborah Tannen. Copyright © 1990 by Deborah Tannen, Ph.D. By permission of William Morrow & Company, Inc.*

> *Who:* boys/men
>
> *What:* try to achieve and keep status
>
> *Where:* in settings with others
>
> *When:* in relationships
>
> *Why:* to avoid being pushed around
>
> *How:* by monitoring who's giving and taking orders

When you put together these key details, you should arrive at a main idea that looks something like this: Boys and men are very concerned with status, with high status going to the person who gives orders and low status going to the person who must take orders.

Now look closely at these examples illustrating the differences between the way men and women communicate.

From Adler, Ronald, and Towne, Neil, Looking Out/Looking In: An Introduction to Nonverbal Communication, *7th Edition, Fort Worth: Harcourt Brace, 1993, pp. 191, 192, 195.*

> *In general, men value talks with friends for their freedom, playfulness, and camaraderie. When researchers asked them what they liked best about their all-male talk, the most frequent answer was its ease. A common theme was appreciation of the practical value of conversation: new ways to solve problems about everyday matters. Some men also mentioned enjoying the humor and rapid pace that characterized all-male conversations.*

The topic or title of the paragraph could be male-to-male conversation. The main idea is directly stated in the first sentence because freedom, playfulness, and camaraderie are illustrated by the remaining sentences. In the next paragraph the main idea is implied because no one sentence is broad enough to include all the key details. Try formulating the main idea by expanding the first sentence.

> *Women, on the other hand, seem to look for very different kinds of satisfaction when talking with their friends. The most common theme mentioned in surveys is a feeling of empathy or understanding—"To know you're not alone," as some put it, or "the feeling of sharing and being understood without a sexual connotation." Whereas men commonly describe same-sex conversations as something they* like, *females characterize their woman-to-woman talks as a kind of contact they* need.

Main Idea: Woman-to-woman conversations provide satisfaction by fulfilling a need for understanding and empathy.

In the next few paragraphs, the topic and part of the main idea are already provided for you.

> Nearly 50 percent of the women surveyed said they called friends at least once a week just to talk, whereas less than half as many men did so. In fact, 40 percent of the men surveyed reported that they never called another man just to chat.

Topic: Chatting

Main Idea: In contrast to men, women _____

_____

> Women ask more questions in mixed-sex conversations than do men— nearly three times as many, according to one study. Other research has revealed that in mixed-sex conversations, men interrupt women far more than the other way around.

Topic: Mixed-Sex Conversations

Main Idea: In mixed-sex conversations, women _____

_____

Exercise on Writing Implied Main Ideas

Excerpts from **You Just Don't Understand** *by Deborah Tannen*

Directions: Each of the following paragraphs is concerned with the topic of men's and women's conversational patterns. Write the implied main idea for each paragraph.

1.   [Alice] Deakins did what is called an eavesdropping study: While seated alone in a dining room where bank officers had lunch, she noted what people at adjacent tables were talking about. This was not a situation where the men were executives and the women their wives and secretaries. The men and women in Deakins's study were all bank officers, meeting as equals at work. Deakins found that when there were no women present, the men talked mostly about business and never about people, not even people at work. Their next most often discussed topic was food. Another common topic was sports and recreation. When women talked alone, their most frequent topic was people—not people at work so much as friends, children, and partners in personal relationships. The women discussed business next, and third, health, which included weight control.

Implied Main Idea: _____

_____

2.   When women and men got together, they tended to avoid the topics that each group liked best and settle on topics of interest to both. But in discussing those topics, they followed the style of the men alone. They talked about food the way men did, focusing on the food they were eating and about restaurants rather than diet and health. They talked about recreation the way men did, focusing on sports and vacations rather than exercising for diet or health, as the women did when they were alone. And they talked about housing in the way men did, focusing on location, property values, and commuting time, rather than the way women did, focusing on the interiors of houses (for example, layout and insulation) and what goes on among people inside houses (for example, finding cleaning help).

Implied Main Idea: _____

_____

<blockquote>
Of my two handicaps, being female put more obstacles in my path than being black.

Shirley Chisholm
</blockquote>

3.   Many women tell of having made a comment at a meeting or conference that is ignored. Later a man makes the same comment and it is picked up, approved or discussed, attributed to him rather than to her. Most women feel that this happens because people are less likely to pay attention to an idea that is raised by a woman, and the studies mentioned above indicate that there is truth to that. But the way ideas are raised may be a factor too.

Implied Main Idea: _____

_____

4.   [W]omen who attempt to adjust their styles by speaking louder, longer, and with more self-assertion will also better fit the model of masculinity. They may command more attention and be more respected, but they may also be disliked and disparaged as aggressive and unfeminine. Indeed, a woman need not be particularly aggressive to be criticized. A professor who invited a prominent woman researcher to speak to his students was shocked to hear some of his students— both female and male—comment later that they had found her arrogant. He had

seen nothing arrogant about her at all. She simply hadn't engaged in any of the womanly behavior they had come to expect, such as continually smiling, qualifying her statements, or cocking her head in a charming way.

Implied Main Idea: _____

_____

5.   *Ways of talking associated with masculinity are also associated with leadership and authority. But ways of talking that are considered feminine are not. Whatever a man does to enhance his authority also enhances his masculinity. But if a woman adapts her style to a position of authority that she has achieved or to which she aspires, she risks compromising her femininity in the eyes of others.*

Implied Main Idea: _____

_____

From Tannen, Deborah, You Just Don't Understand, *New York: Ballantine, 1990, pp. 236–237.*

The topic of many of the previous exercises has been communication, both verbal and nonverbal. Some of the exercises noted the differences between male and female styles of communication. After reading the article below by humorist Dave Barry, list the key communication differences.

Bio-sketch

Dave Barry, the Pulitzer Prize–winning columnist, is also the author of numerous best-selling books, including *Dave Barry's Complete Guide to Guys* from which this excerpt is taken. *The New York Times* calls Mr. Barry the funniest man in America. His life was featured in the hit TV show called *Dave's World*.

Tuning In to Reading

A popular advice book by John Gray is entitled *Men Are from Mars, Women Are from Venus*. Do you think that men and women are so different that they might as well be from different planets? Think about your own personal experiences with this issue before reading the following article.

"That was a fine report, Barbara. But since the sexes speak different languages, I probably didn't understand a word of it."

J.B. Handelsman. © 1995 from The New Yorker Collection. All rights reserved.

Excerpt from **"What Women Don't Understand about Guys"** *by Dave Barry*

READING

Contrary to what many women believe, it's easy to develop a long-term, intimate and mutually fulfilling relationship with a guy. Of course, the guy has to be a Labrador retriever. With human guys, it's extremely difficult. This is because guys don't really grasp what women mean by the word *relationship*.

Let's say a guy named Roger asks a woman named Elaine out to a movie. She accepts; they have a pretty good time. A few nights later he asks her out to dinner, and again they enjoy themselves. They continue to see each other regularly, and soon neither is seeing anybody else.

Then one evening when they're driving home, a thought occurs to Elaine. She says: "Do you realize that we've been seeing each other for exactly six months?"

Silence fills the car. To Elaine, it seems like a very loud silence. She thinks to herself: "Geez, I wonder if it bothers him that I said that. Maybe he feels confined by our relationship. Maybe he thinks I'm trying to push him into some kind of obligation."

5   And Roger is thinking: "Gosh. Six months."

And Elaine is thinking: "But hey, *I'm* not so sure I want this kind of relationship either. Are we heading toward marriage? Toward children? Toward a *lifetime* together? Am I ready for that level of commitment? Do I really even *know* this person?"

And Roger is thinking: "So that means it was . . . let's see . . . February when we started going out, which was right after I had the car at the dealer's, which means . . . lemme check the odometer . . . whoa! I am *way* overdue for an oil change here."

And Elaine is thinking: "He's upset. I can see it on his face. Maybe I'm reading this completely wrong. Maybe he wants *more* from our relationship—more intimacy, more commitment. Maybe he senses my reservations. Yes, that's it. He's afraid of being rejected."

And Roger is thinking: "I'm going to have them look at the transmission again. I don't care what those morons say—it's still not shifting right. And they better not try to blame it on cold weather this time. It's 87 degrees out, and this thing is shifting like a garbage truck, and I paid those incompetent, thieving cretins *600 dollars!*"

10   And Elaine is thinking: "He's angry, and I don't blame him. I'd be angry too. I feel so guilty, putting him through this, but I can't help the way I feel. I'm just not sure."

And Roger is thinking: "They'll probably say it's only a 90-day warranty. That's what they're gonna say!"

And Elaine is thinking. "Maybe I'm too idealistic, waiting for a knight to come riding up on his white horse, when I'm sitting next to a perfectly good person who's in pain because of my self-centered, schoolgirl fantasy."

And Roger is thinking: "Warranty? I'll give them a warranty!"

"Roger," Elaine says aloud.

15   "What?" says Roger.

"I'm such a fool," Elaine says, sobbing. "I mean, I know there's no knight and there's no horse."

"There's no horse?" says Roger.

"You think I'm a fool, don't you?" Elaine says.

"No!" Roger says, glad to know the correct answer.

20   "It's just that . . . I need some time," Elaine says.

There is a 15-second pause while Roger tries to come up with a safe response. "Yes," he finally says.

Elaine, deeply moved, touches his hand. "Oh, Roger, do you really feel that way?"

"What way?" says Roger.

"That way about time," Elaine says.

25 "Oh," says Roger. "Yes."

Elaine gazes deeply into his eyes, causing him to become very nervous about what she might say next, especially if it involves a horse. At last she says, "Thank you, Roger."

"Thank *you*," he responds.

Then he takes her home, and she lies on her bed, a conflicted soul weeping until dawn, whereas when Roger gets back to his place, he opens a bag of chips, turns on the TV and immediately becomes deeply involved in a rerun of a tennis match between two Czech players he never heard of. A tiny voice in his mind tells him that something major was going on back there in the car, but he figures it's better not to think about it.

The next day Elaine will call her closest friend, and they will talk for six straight hours. In painstaking detail they will analyze everything she said and everything he said. They will continue to discuss this subject for weeks, never reaching any definite conclusions but never getting bored with it either.

30 Meanwhile, Roger, playing racquetball with a friend of his and Elaine's, will pause just before serving and ask, "Norm, did Elaine ever own a horse?"

We're not talking about different wavelengths here. We're talking about different *planets* in completely different *solar systems*. Elaine cannot communicate meaningfully with Roger because the sum total of his thinking about relationships is *Huh?*

He has a guy brain, basically an analytical, problem-solving organ. It's not comfortable with nebulous concepts such as love, need and trust. If the guy brain has to form an opinion about another person, it prefers to base it on facts, such as his or her earned-run average.

Women have trouble accepting this. They are convinced that guys *must* spend a certain amount of time thinking about the relationship. How could a guy see another human being day after day, night after night, and *not* be thinking about the relationship? This is what women figure.

They are wrong. A guy in a relationship is like an ant standing on top of a truck tire. The ant is aware that something large is there, but he cannot even dimly comprehend what it is. And if the truck starts moving and the tire starts to roll, the ant will sense that something important is happening, but right up until he rolls around to the bottom and is squashed, the only thought in his tiny brain will be *Huh?*

35 Thus the No. 1 tip for women to remember is never assume the guy understands that you and he have a relationship. You have to plant the idea in his brain by constantly making subtle references to it, such as:

"Roger, would you mind passing me the sugar, inasmuch as we have a relationship?"

"Wake up, Roger! There's a prowler in the den and we have a relationship! You and I do, I mean."

"Good news, Roger! The doctor says we're going to have our fourth child—another indication that we have a relationship!"

"Roger, inasmuch as this plane is crashing and we have only a minute to live, I want you to know that we've had a wonderful 53 years of marriage together, which clearly constitutes a relationship."

40   Never let up, women. Pound away relentlessly at this concept, and eventually it will start to penetrate the guy's brain. Someday he might even start thinking about it on his own. He'll be talking with some other guys about women, and out of the blue he'll say, "Elaine and I, we have, ummm . . . we have, ahhh . . . we . . . we have this thing."

And he will sincerely mean it.

From Dave Barry's Complete Guide to Guys *by Dave Barry. Copyright © 1995 by Dave Barry. Reprinted by permission of Random House, Inc.*

Comprehension Checkup

1. From this article you could conclude that
   a. Men and women basically think alike about relationships.
   b. Men like to talk extensively about the status of their relationships.
   c. It is easy for women to develop long-term relationships with men.
   d. A woman must continually remind a man that they are having a relationship.

2. What is the meaning of the word *reservations* as used in the last sentence of paragraph 8?
   a. public lands set aside for special use.
   b. desires.
   c. arrangements to have something held for one's use.
   d. doubts.

3. The author suggests that
   a. Men are more right-brain oriented than women.
   b. Women are more right-brain oriented than men.
   c. Men like to deal with abstract concepts like "love."
   d. Men are more likely to be emotional than women.

4. Roger and Elaine's discussion about their "relationship" took place in
   a. February.
   b. April.
   c. August.
   d. December.

5. An idealistic person is likely to be
   a. practical.
   b. a dreamer.
   c. realistic.
   d. materialistic.

6. A definition for the word *conflicted* as used in paragraph 27 is
   a. competitive.
   b. state of emotional uncertainty.
   c. hostile.
   d. incompatible.

7. Something that is done in *painstaking detail*
   a. requires great care and attention.
   b. requires little care and attention.
   c. involves suffering.
   d. is done in a sloppy manner.

8. As used in paragraph 32, the word *nebulous* most nearly means
   a. vague.
   b. essential.
   c. life-threatening.
   d. distinct.

9. An antonym for the word *subtle* as used in paragraph 35 is
   a. elusive.
   b. cunning.
   c. obvious.
   d. delicate.

10. After Roger's date with Elaine, he
    a. feels confined because of the demands she has placed on him.
    b. feels angry and mistreated.
    c. turns on the TV and watches reruns.
    d. spends a great deal of his time thinking about what just occurred in the car.

11. After Elaine's date with Roger, she
    a. cries until the early morning hours.
    b. watches TV.
    c. calls Roger and apologizes to him for being a fool.
    d. goes off to find a knight on a white horse.

**IN YOUR
OWN WORDS**

1. Although Barry is humorously overstating his case, do you think his position has any validity? Are men and women really as different as he portrays them to be? Base your answers on your own personal experiences.

2. Why do you think Dave Barry wrote this article? What is his likely main idea?

3. List some of the differences between male and female styles of communication mentioned in this article.

More Practice with Main Ideas and Context Clues

This article from *U.S. News & World Report*, June 17, 1996, illustrates some problems in the way emergencies are reported to police, fire, and other municipal agencies. Many people are obviously confused about what constitutes a true emergency, and many others are careless about it, putting stress on an already overburdened system. Operators handling 911 calls can also be part of the problem because many have inadequate training and, as a result, can be rude, abrupt, or ineffective.

In February 1997, President Clinton proposed the use of 311 for non-emergency calls. Do you think the use of 311 is a good idea?

Excerpt of "This Is 911 . . . Please Hold"

READING

In a dismal subterranean pressure cooker four floors beneath Los Angeles's City Hall East, "police service representatives" bathed in muted blue neon hues clack on keyboards, their headsets plugged into the torrent of 911 calls that echo the panic and mayhem of Los Angeles. From a phone booth, a panicked caller is screaming that somebody has just been shooting at him. "OK, where's the man with the gun now, sir?" asks dispatcher Martin Ford matter-of-factly as the location of the phone booth pops up on his computer screen.

"OK, the guy that had the gun, was he black or white or Hispanic? Do you know what he's wearing? OK, what's the license plate again?" Almost before the caller hangs up, Ford has typed the relevant information into the computer and pushed a button to assign the call to an available police car. Next up: a woman who fears an intruder is still in her house.

Across the country in Baltimore's 911 center, another mostly windowless room with false ceilings and a few splashes of cafeteria-blue paint, dispatchers' consoles are spitting out rows of red numbers and new "jobs" to be assigned to the cops on the streets. A fight. A shoplifting suspect. Eighteen junkies in an alley with a drug dealer. A man bothering a woman. An elderly lady needs her pills. 3933 Kimble Road. 5706 Fenwick Avenue. 1403 Kingsway Road. 1700 East Northern Parkway. In Los Angeles, in Baltimore, in Chicago and Buffalo, in your town and mine, the numbers keep coming and the lights never stop blinking.

Police executives call it the "tyranny of 911"—the relentless drumbeat of calls that sends cops bouncing all over town like so many pinballs. The creation of 911 seemed like a good idea, and it regularly works in heroic fashion. But life-threatening situations do not always get the prompt attention they deserve because frivolous 911 calls send police off on unnecessary runs. And the sheer volume of calls sometimes overwhelms 911 operators and phone lines, meaning some desperate callers get a recording or are put on hold. During a Dallas storm last spring, hundreds of callers had to wait for more than 90 seconds. And in Los Angeles last year, 325,261 calls—13.5 percent of the total—were abandoned by callers before 911 operators could answer.

5   The vast majority of 911 calls are handled efficiently and courteously, but recent years have seen more than enough horror stories to cause concern. Perhaps the most infamous occurred in November 1994 in Philadelphia, where a fast-moving fight among rival groups of teens eventually led to the baseball-bat beating death of 16-year-old Eddie Polec.

More than 20 calls were made to report a roving teen rumble that chilly November night in Philadelphia. But by the time police arrived 45 minutes later, 16-year-old Eddie Polec lay dying, his head crushed, on the steps of St. Cecilia's Catholic Church, where he had been an altar boy. Since that cold 1994 night, the question keeps popping up: Was Philadelphia's 911 system an accessory to his murder?

People who called to report the fight say 911 operators were curt and hostile in response to their pleas for help. "Don't talk to me like that," barked one dispatcher to an angry and frightened caller. "I asked you a question. . . . "

Public and political outrage forced the city to audit its emergency system. Among the findings: Not enough patrol officers were available to handle 911 calls, and the system was being drained by requests for hospital transportation, abandoned-vehicle reports and other nonemergency calls. . . .

. . . The public has become so addicted to 911 that cops have time for little else, especially the sort of crime prevention and analysis that might actually be more effective in fighting crime. "We have created a monster," is the police chiefs' refrain. "So long as 911 persists in its present form, policing can not move forward," write Northeastern University criminal justice Prof. George Kelling and lawyer Catherine Coles in their forthcoming book, *Fixing Broken Windows: Restoring Order and Reducing Crime in Our Communities*.

10   Like so many other problems, 911 started out as a solution. In 1967, the Presidential Commission on Law Enforcement and Administration of Justice recommended that "a single number should be established" nationwide for reporting emergencies. AT&T soon announced its choice of 911, and the first 911 call was

made in Haleyville, Alabama, in February 1968. Today, some 85 percent of the population is covered by 911.

The number of 911 calls started growing in the 1970s and has mushroomed to an estimated 268,000 a day. About 80 to 85 percent of them summon the cops, though ambulances and fire departments use the system as well. Total calls to Columbus, Ohio's system jumped from 222,000 during July 1987—June 1988 to 310,000 in 1994–95. In New York City, the annual number of 911 calls is expected to grow to 12.5 million by 2005.

The sheer volume of calls isn't the only problem, however. An ever increasing percentage of 911 calls do not fit anyone's definition of an emergency. "It's so easy to use and easy to remember, people have begun calling 911 for anything," says AT&T's John Cohen, an ex-cop. In some places, 90 percent of the calls are for non-emergencies. In Columbus, callers want to know the kickoff time for Ohio State football games. In Los Angeles, says frustrated Police Chief Willie Williams, callers include "people who call 911 for the time of day. They call 911 for directions, as if we're Triple A. They'll call and ask what are the best seats at the Coliseum, at Dodger Stadium, how do I get to Disneyland, what happened at some meeting."

Cops admit they're partly to blame because they sold 911 so aggressively, failed to teach the public how to use it properly and went out of their way for so long to respond to all calls, emergency or not. "There was a failure on everybody's part to anticipate the downsides," says Joseph Brann, who runs the Justice Department's community-policing program.

For police chiefs, the [key] question is how to wean the public off frivolous 911 calls, weed out the nonemergencies, service the public in ways other than rapid response and give cops more time to work with neighborhoods in really fighting crime. In recent years many law enforcement executives have questioned the entire foundation on which 911 is built—the idea that police can stop crimes by responding rapidly to citizens' "emergency" calls. Landmark research in several cities has found that most of the calls in which officers are dispatched—50 to 90 percent in most places—are not about crime. Fewer than 5 percent of most cities' total dispatched calls, the researchers concluded, are made quickly enough for officers to intervene or make an arrest.

15   Research in Kansas City, Missouri; Jacksonville, Florida; Peoria, Illinois; Rochester, New York; and San Diego found that rapid police responses led to arrests in only 3 percent of serious reported crimes. "In many individual cases, 911 systems and police responses have had wonderful and heartwarming outcomes," write researchers Kelling and Coles. "Yet on an aggregate level, cases in which 911 technology makes a substantial difference in the outcome of criminal events are extraordinarily rare."

Nevertheless, in many cities, response time is still considered the key test of a police department's effectiveness. People want quick responses, and the press often focuses on the issue. Weaning the public away from rapid response is a tough sell. . . . The result is that 911 dominates the operations of most of America's police departments, "and you never have any of the discretionary time that community policing demands," says Baltimore Police Commissioner, Thomas Frazier. "The equation is simple," write Harvard's David Kennedy, Mark Moore and Malcolm Sparrow in their book, *Beyond 911: A New Era for Policing.* "The more officers a department reserves to answer 911 calls, the swifter and more sure the emergency response, but the fewer people and less time left for doing anything else, such as foot patrol, neighborhood organizing [or] crime prevention. . . . "

Everyone agrees public education is critical to solving the problem, but some argue education alone hasn't worked and must be accompanied by something else—like new, easy-to-remember phone numbers for nonemergency calls. Most police departments have nonemergency numbers, but they've rarely been memorable or marketed as aggressively because so much of the focus has been on 911.

Buffalo plans to inaugurate a new nonemergency number this summer and has hired a local advertising agency, the Schutte Group, to help launch the effort. The firm has copyrighted a sequence of rhyming slogans: "For a real emergency, call 911; we'll quickly send someone! Nonemergencies, it's 853-2222, and we'll tell you what to do." Officials feel a seven-digit number more clearly denotes a nonemergency. . . . Cops agree they've got to find some way to break the tyranny of 911. But no one watching the blinking lights thinks that will be easy. "Nine-one-one is almost like heroin," says communications Sgt. Louis Hopson of the Baltimore PD. "It's easier to get people on it than off."

From "This Is 911 . . . Please Hold." Copyright, June 17, 1996, U.S. News and World Report. *Reprinted by permission.*

Comprehension Checkup

1. What is the topic of this article? _____

2. What is the article's main idea? _____

   _____

3. List three details supporting the author's main idea.

   _____

   _____

   _____

Vocabulary in Context

Directions: Work with a partner to define the following words from context. Be sure to give the technique(s) used. It may be necessary to study the sentences before and after the sentence containing the word. Remember, no looking in the dictionary.

Paragraph 1: **subterranean**

Definition: _____

Technique(s) used: _____

Paragraph 1: **panicked**

Definition: _____

Technique(s) used: _____

Paragraph 4: **frivolous**

Definition: _____

Technique(s) used: _____

Paragraph 7: **hostile**

Definition: _____

Technique(s) used: _____

Paragraph 8: **audit**

Definition: _____

Technique(s) used: _____

Paragraph 11: **mushroomed**

Definition: _____

Technique(s) used: _____

Paragraph 14: **intervene**

Definition: _____

Technique(s) used: _____

Paragraph 15: **aggregate**

Definition: _____

Technique(s) used: _____

Paragraph 16: **discretionary**

Definition: _____

Technique(s) used: _____

Paragraph 18: **inaugurate**

Definition: _____

Technique(s) used: _____

IN YOUR OWN WORDS

1. Have you ever used 911? When? If you did, in retrospect, was the situation really an emergency? If it was not really an emergency, how could you have dealt with it more appropriately?

2. You arrive home and find that your house has been burglarized but the burglar is gone. Would you call 911 or a nonemergency number? Why?

3. Do you think a nonemergency number such as 311 is a good idea? Why or why not?

Chapter 2 Test: "This Is 911 . . . Please Hold"

Multiple Choice

1. Which of the following is true according to the article?
   a. Most 911 calls are handled efficiently and courteously.
   b. There are problems with the 911 emergency system.
   c. 911 operators are sometimes overburdened by the high volume of calls.
   d. All of the above.

2. From the article, you could conclude that
   a. A breakdown in 911 service was partially responsible for the death of Eddie Polec.
   b. Life-threatening situations always receive top priority by 911 operators.
   c. Police chiefs are satisfied with the current 911 system.
   d. There are more than enough police officers to handle 911 calls.

3. The first three paragraphs of this article were written to
   a. Give the main idea of the article.
   b. Relate an amusing story.
   c. Give examples of actual 911 calls.
   d. Show how inefficient the police department is.

4. According to the article
   a. The number of nonemergency calls has been about the same for the last few years.
   b. Police departments say the problem with the 911 system will not disappear until provision is made for more patrol cars.
   c. The Los Angeles police department is inefficiently run.
   d. Approximately 15 percent of the U.S. population is not covered by 911.

5. According to information presented in the article
   a. Very few 911 calls are made quickly enough to actually stop a crime in progress or make an arrest.
   b. In some areas of the country, 90 percent of the 911 calls are for nonemergencies.
   c. Policemen must share part of the blame for the failure of the 911 system.
   d. All of the above.

True or False

_____ 6. After a spring storm, hundreds of Dallas residents were put on hold by 911 operators for over 90 minutes.

_____ 7. In Los Angeles, callers asked 911 operators for directions to popular tourist attractions.

_____ 8. In many cities, rapid response to 911 calls is considered a gauge of a police department's effectiveness.

_____ 9. Suggestions have been made for both public education about the 911 system and the creation of a new nonemergency number.

_____ 10. In the Los Angeles area, the majority of calls are abandoned before reaching a 911 operator.

Determining an Author's Purpose

Most writers create a story, essay, article, or poem with at least one **general purpose** in mind. Because most writers do not directly state their general purpose, the reader must use indirect clues to determine it. We can identify the general purpose by asking the question, "Why did the author write this?" Usually, this purpose will fall into one of three broad categories: **to entertain, to inform or explain,** or **to persuade.**

An author whose purpose is **to entertain** will be trying to give the reader an enjoyable experience by telling a story or describing an event. A piece of writing meant to entertain will often make an appeal to the reader's imagination or sense of humor. Witty, unusual, dramatic, or exciting stories usually have entertainment as their purpose.

An author whose purpose is **to inform or explain** will be trying to provide readers with knowledge they did not possess before. Ordinarily, the material will be presented in an objective or neutral fashion. Authors who write textbooks presenting factual material often have this purpose in mind.

Finally, the author's purpose may be **to persuade.** Persuasion goes beyond merely being entertaining or providing information. This kind of writing tries to change our opinions by appealing to our emotions or intellect. If the author is presenting an emotional argument, we may be subjected to vivid descriptive passages designed to manipulate our feelings. If the author is presenting an appeal to our intelligence, a rational or logical argument may be presented. Political literature is a common example of writing meant to persuade.

Authors also take into account their **audience** (those they are writing for) when they select their general purpose. Writers of fiction usually want to entertain readers by creating interesting characters and stories. If an author writes an article for a wellness magazine, the general purpose will probably be to provide information about how to practice good health. If an author writes a letter to solicit campaign contributions for a political candidate, the general purpose will be persuasive because the author is trying to convince people to give money.

In addition to a general purpose, authors usually have a **specific purpose,** which gives more information about the article than the general purpose. Take the "wellness" example above. The general purpose is to "inform." The specific purpose might be "to inform people about foods that may prevent cancer."

Read the paragraph below and identify the writer's topic, main idea, and general and specific purposes.

When asked to advise youngsters about preparing for going to work, the experts are remarkably consistent. Rule 1, says labor consultant Malcolm Cohen, is become computer literate. And right alongside it, he says, is learn to communicate well through writing and speaking. Notes Audrey Freedman, an economist who specializes in labor issues: "Students should take the toughest courses they can to develop their logic and reasoning capacity." Essential too, she concurs, is expressing oneself "clearly and persuasively." Above all, in a job world where change is the only constant, the most valuable skill for the young—and their elders—is the ability to keep on learning.

From "Where the Jobs Are" by John Greenwald. Time, January 20, 1997. © Time Inc. *Reprinted by permission.*

Topic:	Preparing for work
Main Idea:	Young people need to develop good communication skills to prepare for going to work.
General Purpose:	To explain
Specific Purpose:	Explaining to the young that the most important step for preparing for work is developing good communication skills.

The following exercises will give you some practice in determining an author's general purpose.

Exercise 1

Directions: Label each sentence according to its general purpose: to inform (**I**), to entertain (**E**), or to persuade (**P**).

_____   1.   **CUBICLES**

Assuming your computer hasn't made you sterile, someday your descendants will look back and be amazed that people of our generation worked in things called "cubicles." They will view our lives much the way we now view the workers from the Industrial Revolution who (I've heard) worked twenty-three hours a day making steel products using nothing but their foreheads. Imagine our descendants' disbelief when they read stories about how we were forced to sit in big boxes all day, enduring a stream of annoying noises, odors, and interruptions. They might think it was the product of some cruel experiment.

From Adams, Scott, The Dilbert Principle, *New York: Harper Business, a Division of Harper Collins, 1996, p. 265.*

_____   2.   Most sharks are harmless—at least to humans. Actually we threaten the survival of sharks more than they threaten us. They reproduce slowly, and their numbers are already being depleted by over-fishing in many areas. This attitude toward sharks may be short-sighted, because they play an important role in marine communities. Some people catch shark only for the shark's fins or jaws. Others practice shark hunting for sport, leaving the meat to waste. A magnificent predator, the shark may soon be exterminated by human beings, the bloodiest predator of them all.

From Castro, Peter, and Huber, Michael E., "Sharks," Marine Biology, *Second Edition, Dubuque, IA: Wm. C. Brown, 1997, p. 47.*

_____   3.   Of the 10.6 million undergraduates enrolled in U.S. colleges, it's estimated that 45 percent are older than 25. *Modern Maturity* magazine reported that 1 in 10 college students is actually over 50. Furthermore, a much larger percentage of older students are women, the number of female students over 22 years of age having more than doubled in the past decade. In urban institutions, the average age of students is 28 years.

From Nickels, William, Understanding Business, *New York: McGraw-Hill, 1997, p. 11.*

Exercise 2

Read each of the following paragraphs in order to determine if the author's primary purpose is (1) to entertain, (2) to persuade, or (3) to inform or explain. Indicate the clues that enabled you to make your decision. In the space provided, write the directly stated or implied main idea.

1. In the past 10 years, the prison population has grown an average of 8 percent a year. There are 1.2 million inmates in state and federal institutions; by 2002, that figure is expected to swell by 4.3 percent. The adoption of mandatory sentencing guidelines and public concern about the spread of crime have led to longer sentences and reduced parole for inmates. To accommodate new arrivals, the number of prisons built between 1990 and 1995 increased a record 17 percent, and the boom has made corrections officer one of the fastest growing careers of the 90s. Forget the stereotypes: Today's position combines the duties of a police officer, social worker, counselor, security specialist, manager, and teacher. Look for opportunities in California, Florida, New York, and Texas, where nearly half of all inmates are concentrated.

From "When Less is More" by Amy Saltzman. Copyright, October 27, 1997, U.S. News and World Report. *Reprinted by permission.*

Purpose: _____ Clues: _____

Main Idea: _____

2. You know how when you buy your pants, there's a piece of paper in one of the pockets that says "inspected by #47." Who ARE these people anyway? Has anyone out there met one of these inspectors? What do they inspect? I mean seriously, if someone bends over and their pants rip, should we say, "Oh no! Who inspected that? Number 63? Whew. That was close. Mine were done by number 34." If there was a problem, what are you supposed to do? Call up the manufacturer and say, "Hello. I hate to be the one to break it to you, but you know number 63? She just isn't going to cut it anymore."

From The Cheeseburger Philosophy *by Tom Mather. Reprinted by permission.*

Purpose: _____ Clues: _____

Main Idea: _____

3. Child labor laws prohibit a 13-year-old from punching a cash register for forty hours a week, but that same child can labor for 40 hours or more inside a gym or an ice skating rink without drawing the slightest glance from the government. The U.S. government requires the licensing of plumbers. It demands that even the tiniest coffee shop adhere to a fastidious health code. It scrutinizes the advertising claims on packages of low-fat snack food. But it never asks a coach, who holds the lives of

his young pupils in his hands, to pass a minimum safety and skills test. Coaches in this country need no license to coach children, even in a high-injury sport like elite gymnastics.

From Ryan, Joan, Little Girls in Pretty Boxes, *New York: Warner Books, 1995, pp. 11–12.*

Purpose: _____   Clues: _____

Main Idea: _____

4. When people are unemployed, two major sources of stress are the loss of income (with its financial hardships) and the effect of this loss on their feelings about themselves. Workers who derive their identity from their work, men who define manhood as supporting a family, and people who define their worth in terms of their work's dollar value lose more than their paychecks when they lose their jobs. They lose a piece of themselves and their self-esteem.

From Papalia, Diane, and Olds, Sandy, Human Development, *6th Edition, New York: McGraw-Hill, 1995, p. 493.*

Purpose: _____   Clues: _____

Main Idea: _____

The articles presented in the next section all deal, directly or indirectly, with the world of work. Read each article noting the purpose and then answer the questions.

Author's Purpose: To Entertain

The following short story by William Saroyan has entertainment as its purpose.

Bio-sketch

William Saroyan (1908–1981) was an American writer of Armenian descent. Throughout his long and prolific career, he drew upon his heritage to provide him with inspiration for his short stories, novels, and plays. He is best known for the "Daring Young Man on the Flying Trapeze," "The Time of Your Life," which won the Pulitzer Prize, and "The Human Comedy." In many of his stories, Saroyan invents a family life much different from his own. At the age of 3, he lost his father and was placed in an orphanage by his mother. At the age of 8, he began selling newspapers and working at a variety of odd jobs. He learned to read at the age of 9, and shortly afterward began to write. Eventually, at the age of 15, he left school altogether. Over the years, he has said, it was his writing that kept him sane.

Notes on Vocabulary

humble—to lower in condition, rank, or position.   *Humble* is derived from the Latin word *humilis*, which in turn comes from *humus*, meaning "soil." The literal meaning of humble is "not far above the ground" or "low."

dungeon—a dark underground cell, vault, or prison.

Tuning In to Reading

Have your grandparents ever given you advice about how to conduct your life? Was it advice that you agreed or disagreed with?

"The Shepherd's Daughter"   *by William Saroyan*

READING

Ancient Persia was located in the Middle East where Iran is today.

It is the opinion of my grandmother, God bless her, that all men should labour, and at the table, a moment ago, she said to me: You must learn to do some good work, the making of some item useful to man, something out of clay, or out of wood, or metal, or cloth. It is not proper for a young man to be ignorant of an honourable craft. Is there anything you can make? Can you make a simple table, a chair, a plain dish, a rug, a coffee pot? Is there anything you can do?

And my grandmother looked at me with anger.

I know, she said, you are supposed to be a writer, and I suppose you are. You certainly smoke enough cigarettes to be anything, and the whole house is full of the smoke, but you must learn to make solid things, things that can be used, that can be seen and touched.

There was a king of the Persians, said my grandmother, and he had a son, and this son fell in love with a shepherd's daughter. He went to his father and he said, My Lord, I love a shepherd's daughter, and I would have her for my wife. And the king said, I am king and you are my son, and when I die you shall be king, how can it be that you would marry the daughter of a shepherd? And the son said, My Lord, I do not know but I know that I love this girl and would have her for my queen.

5   The king saw that his son's love for the girl was from God, and he said, I will send a message to her. And he called a messenger to him and he said, Go to the shepherd's daughter and say that my son loves her and would have her for his wife. And the messenger went to the girl and he said, The king's son loves you and would have you for his wife. And the girl said, What labour does he do? And the messenger said, Why he is the son of the king; he does no labour. And the girl said, He must learn to do some labour. And the messenger returned to the king and spoke the words of the shepherd's daughter.

The king said to his son, The shepherd's daughter wishes you to learn some craft. Would you still have her for your wife? And the son said, Yes, I will learn to weave straw rugs. And the boy was taught to weave rugs of straw, in patterns and in colours and with ornamental designs, and at the end of three days he was making very fine straw rugs, and the messenger returned to the shepherd's daughter, and he said, These rugs of straw are the work of the king's son.

And the girl went with the messenger to the king's palace, and she became the wife of the king's son.

One day, said my grandmother, the king's son was walking through the streets of Baghdad, and he came upon an eating place which was so clean and cool that he entered it and sat at the table.

This place, said my grandmother, was a place of thieves and murderers, and they took the king's son and placed him in a large dungeon where many great men of the city were being held, and the thieves and murderers were killing the fattest of the men and feeding them to the leanest of them, and making sport of it. The king's son was of the leanest of the men, and it was not known that he was the son of the king of the Persians, so his life was spared, and he said to the thieves and murderers, I am a weaver of straw rugs and these rugs have great value. And they brought him straw and asked him to weave and in three days he weaved three rugs, and he said, Carry these to the palace of the king of the Persians, and for each rug he will give you a hundred gold pieces of money. And the rugs were carried to the palace of the king, and when the king saw the rugs he saw that they were the work of his son and he took the rugs to the shepherd's daughter and he said, These rugs were brought to the palace and they are the work of my son who is lost. And the shepherd's daughter took each rug and looked at it closely and in the design of each rug she saw in the written language of the Persians a message from her husband, and she related this message to the king.

10 And the king, said my grandmother, sent many soldiers to the place of the thieves and murderers, and the soldiers rescued all the captives and killed all the thieves and murderers, and the king's son was returned safely to the palace of his father, and to the company of his wife, the little shepherd's daughter. And when the boy went into the palace and saw again his wife, he humbled himself before her and he embraced her feet, and he said, My love, it is because of you that I am alive, and the king was greatly pleased with the shepherd's daughter.

Now, said my grandmother, do you see why every man should learn an honourable craft?

I see very clearly, I said, and as soon as I earn enough money to buy a saw and a hammer and a piece of lumber I shall do my best to make a simple chair or a shelf for books.

"The Shepherd's Daughter," from The Daring Young Man on The Flying Trapeze *by William Saroyan. Reprinted by permission of the Trustees of Leland Stanford Junior University.*

Comprehension Checkup

True or False

Directions: Indicate whether each statement is true or false.

_____ 1. The grandmother has the most respect for someone who can create something useful.

_____ 2. The grandmother saved the life of the king's son.

_____ 3. Before the shepherd's daughter agreed to marry the king's son, she required that he learn a craft.

_____ 4. The grandmother approves of her grandson's chosen profession.

_____ 5. The king's son was grateful to the shepherd's daughter for helping to rescue him.

Multiple Choice

Directions: Select the best answer for each item.

6. At first the king of the Persians
   a. was pleased by his son's selection of a bride.
   b. was puzzled by his son's selection of a bride.
   c. ignored his son's selection of a bride.
   d. was angered by his son's selection of a bride.

7. The messenger was of the opinion that
   a. a king's son must do the bidding of a shepherd's daughter.
   b. a king's son is above doing tasks of manual labor.
   c. the shepherd's daughter should not be made queen.
   d. the king's son should not marry someone of a lowly station.

8. The grandson is going to please his grandmother
    a. by giving up his smoking habit.
    b. by learning to weave straw rugs.
    c. by abandoning his desire to be a writer.
    d. by earning enough money by writing to enable him to build something.

9. The king's son was initially spared by the thieves and murderers because
    a. he was lean.
    b. it was considered unwise to kill the son of a king.
    c. he was overweight.
    d. he was a well-known weaver.

10. After he was captured, the king's son was placed in a *dungeon.* The most likely meaning of the word *dungeon* is
    a. an earth-covered cellar for storing fruits.
    b. a dark underground cell or prison.
    c. a high rounded hill or ridge.
    d. a place for dumping rubbish.

IN YOUR OWN WORDS

1. What is the main idea of the story?

2. According to the grandmother, what kind of work is admirable? Would the grandmother think that the practice of law is honorable? What supporting details from the story helped you answer this question?

3. What character in the fable has the same opinion toward work as the grandmother?

4. What is the significance of the ending of the fable?

5. What is meant by the last sentence of the story? How will the grandson earn the money for the materials to build a chair or bookshelf?

Author's Purpose: To Inform or Explain

Read the following article, "From a Melted Candy Bar to Microwaves," by Ira Flatow, the host of National Public Radio's science show, *Talk of the Nation.* Flatow's purpose is to present information about the discovery of the microwave.

Bio-sketch

Ira Flatow demonstrates in his book *They All Laughed* "that truth is stranger than fiction . . ." Each of the stories, including this one about the invention of the microwave, is really a story about inquisitive people who won't take no for an answer. While doing research about inventors, Flatow discovered that most of them are hearty souls, unafraid of appearing ridiculous by asking silly questions. He calls this the "quack like a duck" discovery method. If something looks like a duck, walks like a duck, but doesn't quack like a duck, these bold inventors want to know why. In this particular excerpt, Perry Spencer, noticing the melted candy bar in a lab coat he'd been wearing all day long, should have assumed his own body temperature had been the culprit. Because that answer didn't make "quack noises," Spencer went on to invent the microwave oven.

Notes on Vocabulary

nuke—slang for cooking food in a microwave oven

cynical—disbelieving; sarcastic, sneering   In ancient Greece, a *Cynic* was a member of a school of philosophers who believed that being virtuous was the highest good. Because *cynics* had contempt for worldly needs and pleasures, they were extremely critical of the rest of society. Today the word refers to anyone who questions the motives or actions of other people.

maven—an expert, a really knowledgeable person   The word *maven* comes from Yiddish.

Tuning In to Reading

Survey this selection by reading the first two paragraphs and the last two paragraphs.

"From a Melted Candy Bar to Microwaves"

by Ira Flatow

READING

Little minds are interested in the extraordinary; great minds in the commonplace.

Elliot Hubbard

Next time you nuke a bag of Orville Redenbacher's, you'll be repeating an experiment that heralded the dawning of the age of microwave cooking.

Almost 50 years ago, 1946 to be exact, one of the great minds in the history of electronics accidentally invented microwave popcorn.

Shortly after World War II, Percy L. Spencer, electronic genius and war hero, was touring one of his laboratories at the Raytheon Company. Spencer stopped in front of a magnetron, the power tube that drives a radar set. Suddenly he noticed that a candy bar in his pocket had begun to melt.

Most of us would have written off the gooey mess to body heat. But not Spencer. Spencer never took anything for granted. During his 39 years with Raytheon, he patented 120 inventions. When England was battered by German bombs in the 1940 Battle of Britain, Spencer turned his creative mind toward developing a better version of the British invention radar. His improved magnetron allowed radar tube production to be increased from 17 per week to 2,600 per day. His achievements earned him the Distinguished Service Medal, the U.S. Navy's highest honor for civilians.

5   So when this inquisitive, self-educated, and highly decorated engineer who never finished grammar school came face to face with a good mystery, he didn't merely wipe the melted chocolate off his hands and shrug off the incident. He took the logical next step. He sent out for popcorn. Holding the bag of unpopped kernels next to the magnetron, Spencer watched as the kernels exploded.

The next morning Spencer brought in a tea kettle. He wanted to see what microwaves would do to raw eggs. After cutting a hole in the side of the kettle, Spencer placed an uncooked egg into the pot. Next he placed a magnetron beside the kettle and turned on the machine.

An unfortunate (cynical?) engineer poked his nose into the pot and was greeted by an explosion of yolk and white. The egg had been blown up by the steam pressure from within. Spencer had created the first documented microwave mess—an experiment to be inadvertently repeated by countless thousands of microwave cooks. He had also shown that microwaves had the ability to cook foods quickly.

Legend has it that this demonstration was reproduced before unsuspecting members of Raytheon's board of directors who had trouble visualizing exactly what microwaves could do to food. The ensuing egg shower convinced the board of directors to invest in the "high frequency dielectric heating apparatus" patented in 1953.

That demo and the fact that the military no longer needed 10,000 magnetron tubes per week for radar sets helped shape the future of microwaves. What better way to recover lost sales than to put in every American home a radar set disguised as a microwave oven?

10   But first the device needed a better name. Raytheon's marketing mavens felt few people would demand a high-frequency dielectric heating apparatus for their kitchens even if they could pronounce it. A contest followed to rename the apparatus. Seeing as how the oven owed its roots to radar, the winning entry suggested "Radar Range." The words were later merged to Radarange. But no words could hide the woeful inadequacies of this first-generation oven.

Weighing 750 pounds and standing five and a half feet [tall], the Radarange required water—and plumbing—to keep its hefty innards cool. Hardly the compact unit that fits under today's kitchen cabinets. The early 1953 design—with its three-thousand-dollar price tag—was strictly for restaurants, railroads (the Japanese railroad system bought 2,500), and ocean liners. These customers would be Raytheon's prime market for two decades.

The microwave oven was no pleasure to cook with, either. Culinary experts noticed that meat refused to brown. French fries stayed white and limp. Who could eat this ugly-looking food? Chefs were driven to distraction. As chronicled in the *Wall Street Journal*, "the Irish cook of Charles Adams, Raytheon's chairman, who turned his kitchen into a proving ground, called the oven 'black magic' and quit."

It would take decades before the consumer oven was perfected. The Tappan Company took an interest in the project and helped Raytheon engineers shrink the size of the magnetron. A smaller power unit meant the hideous plumbing could be done away with and air cooling fans could take over.

Then someone had the brilliant idea that perhaps the magnetron should not be pointed directly at the food but rather out of sight. That's it. Put the food in a box, put the microwave source at the back, and lead the microwaves into the box via a pipe. Now we could truly call it an oven.

15   And that's what happened. In 1955 Tappan introduced the first consumer microwave oven. Did you have one? Hardly anyone did. It was still too big and costly. Then came 1964 and a breakthrough. From Japan, the country that had a reputation for making "transistorized" (read: small) products out of everything, came an improved electron tube. Smaller and smaller than the old magnetron, it put Raytheon on track to placing a microwave oven under everyone's kitchen cabinet.

Needing a consumer-oriented vehicle to sell its new ovens, Raytheon bought up Amana Refrigeration, Inc., in 1965 and put out its first affordable ($495), compact, and practical microwave oven in 1967.

The specter of little microwaves leaking out of the oven scared a lot of people. Their worst fears were realized in 1968 when a test of microwave ovens at Walter Reed Hospital found microwaves did indeed leak out. Federal standards set in 1971 solved that problem.

Today more homes have microwave ovens than dishwashers. And we owe it all to an inquisitive man with a melted candy bar in his pocket and egg on his face.

From They All Laughed . . . *by Ira Flatow. Copyright © 1992 by Ira Flatow. Reprinted by permission of HarperCollins Publishers, Inc.*

Comprehension Checkup

True or False

Directions: Indicate whether each statement is true or false.

_____   1.   The magnetron caused the candy bar in Spencer's pocket to melt.

_____   2.   Spencer performed additional experiments with the magnetron using unpopped kernels and raw eggs.

_____   3.   The microwave oven was perfected quickly.

_____   4.   Spencer was chosen to select an appropriate name for his new invention.

_____   5.   Chefs were eager to work with the new oven.

_____   6.   Initially, microwaves leaked out of the ovens.

_____   7.   Homes are more likely to have a dishwasher than a microwave oven.

Multiple Choice

Directions: Select the best answer for each item.

8.   The original Radarange achieved little acceptance in which of the following situations
    a. restaurants.
    b. ocean liners.
    c. railroads.
    d. small kitchens.

9.   The original Radarange had all of the following qualities except for which?
    a. Cooked food to perfection.
    b. Had large size and weight.
    c. Required water for cooling.
    d. Was very expensive.

10.   All of the following led to our modern microwave oven except for which?
    a. Japan reduced the size of the electron tube.
    b. Air cooling fans were introduced.
    c. The microwave source was placed at the back.
    d. Microwave-safe dishes were invented.

IN YOUR OWN WORDS

1.   What does the author admire about Spencer?

2.   How was the timing of Spencer's discovery beneficial to the military?

3.   What were the drawbacks of the original microwave oven?

4.   Although Spencer lacked formal education, he was able to be a successful engineer. In the world today, how likely is it that a person without formal education could achieve success in a technical field?

5.   What does context tell us about the meaning of the word "inquisitive" in the last sentence? In the fifth paragraph?

Vocabulary Practice

Directions: Look through the given paragraph and find a word that matches the definition.

announced (1)   _____

pessimistic (7)   _____

unintentionally (7)   _____

resulting (8)   _____

experts (10)   _____

pitiful (10)   _____

kitchen (12)   _____

object of fear (17)   _____

Author's Purpose: To Persuade

In the following letter, Abraham Lincoln, our 16th president, is trying to persuade his stepbrother, John D. Johnston, to change his attitude toward work.

Bio-sketch

Lincoln was president of the United States during the bloody Civil War. Though largely self-taught while growing up, Lincoln managed to read the classics such as the Bible and Shakespeare, which helped him to develop his distinctive speaking and writing style. His two most famous speeches are *The Gettysburg Address* and his *Second Inaugural Address*, both noted for their brevity and the beauty and clarity of the language. Lincoln was assassinated by John Wilkes Booth while attending a play at Ford's Theater, plunging the nation into mourning. Today we remember him when we celebrate President's Day in February.

"Abraham Lincoln Denies a Loan"

READING

Dec. 24, 1848

Dear Johnston:
    Your request for eighty dollars, I do not think it best to comply with now. At the various times when I have helped you a little, you have said to me, "We can get along very well now," but in a very short time I find you in the same difficulty again. Now this can only happen by some defect in your conduct. What that defect is, I think I know. You are not *lazy*, and still you are an *idler*. I doubt whether since I saw you, you have done a good whole day's work, in any one day. You do not very much dislike to work, and still you do not work much, merely because it does not seem to you that you could get much for it.
    This habit of uselessly wasting time, is the whole difficulty; it is vastly important to you, and still more so to your children, that you should break this habit. It is more important to them, because they have longer to live, and can keep out of an idle habit before they are in it, easier than they can get out after they are in.
    You are now in need of some ready money; and what I propose is, that you shall go to work, "tooth and nail," for somebody who will give you money for it.
    Let father and your boys take charge of your things at home—prepare for a crop, and make the crop, and you go to work for the best money wages, or in dis-

charge of any debt you owe, that you can get. And to secure you a fair reward for your labor, I now promise you that for every dollar you will, between this and the first of May, get for your own labor either in money or in your own indebtedness, I will then give you one other dollar.

5 By this, if you hire yourself at ten dollars a month, from me you will get ten more, making twenty dollars a month for your work. In this, I do not mean you shall go off to St. Louis, or the lead mines, or the gold mines in California, but I mean for you to go at it for the best wages you can get close to home—in Coles County.

Now if you will do this, you will soon be out of debt, and what is better, you will have a habit that will keep you from getting in debt again. But if I should now clear you out, next year you will be just as deep in as ever. You say you would almost give your place in Heaven for $70 or $80. Then you value your place in Heaven very cheaply, for I am sure you can with the offer I make you get the seventy or eighty dollars for four or five months' work. You say if I furnish you the money you will deed me the land, and if you don't pay the money back, you will deliver possession—

Nonsense! If you can't now live *with* the land, how will you then live without it? You have always been kind to me, and I do not now mean to be unkind to you. On the contrary, if you will but follow my advice, you will find it worth more than eight times eighty dollars to you.

Affectionately

Your brother

A. Lincoln

From Bennett, William J., The Book of Virtues, *New York: Simon & Schuster, 1993, pp. 402–404.*

> *He that can work is born king of something.*
>
> **Thomas Carlyle**

Questions:

1. What distinction does Lincoln make between being a lazy person and being an idler?

2. Give a short description of Johnston's character based on Lincoln's comments about him.

3. What does this letter reveal to you about Lincoln's attitudes toward work?

4. What point is Lincoln making when he refers to Johnston's children?

5. Why does Lincoln want Johnston to stay close to home?

6. Why does Lincoln tell Johnston that he must value his place in Heaven very cheaply?

7. Do you think Lincoln's offer makes sense?

8. Is Lincoln's answer what Johnston expected? Why or why not? Do you think Johnston will accept Lincoln's offer?

9. The expression "tooth and nail" means
   a. elderly or old.
   b. with all one's strength or resources.
   c. a very small pointed stick for getting bits of food free from between the teeth.
   d. pleasing to the taste.

An Exercise on Determining the Author's Purpose

This last excerpt is about a welfare mother who graduated with honors from the University of California at Berkeley. In response to questions posed by Catherine Maclay, she shares her experiences. What do you think the general purpose of the article is? Be sure to notice the profile of Diana Spatz provided by the author in her introduction as well as the type of questions Maclay poses to Spatz.

Notes on Vocabulary

panic—sudden, unreasoning, hysterical fear   The word is derived from *Pan,* the Greek god of the fields and flocks who was usually depicted with a human torso and the legs, ears, and horns of a goat. *Pan* was considered to be something of a prankster who often darted out of the underbrush driving others into a "state of panic."

Excerpt from "A Conversation with Diana Spatz '95"   *by Catherine Maclay*

READING

While more than five thousand students earned undergraduate degrees at Berkeley last month, fewer than five hundred of them graduated with honors. One of those was also a single mother on welfare, and during her years at Cal, Diana Spatz '95 decided her classmates should know about it. "At first it was hard to tell people I was on welfare," she says. "It was like painting a bull's-eye on my forehead and passing out darts. But I felt I had a responsibility to tell them, to challenge their stereotypes of what a welfare mother is."

When Spatz crossed the stage at Zellerbach Auditorium on May 21 to accept her diploma, her nine-year-old daughter, Eden accompanied her. It was a big moment for both of them. . . . She and Eden have been on public assistance since Eden was born in 1986. . . .

When she first discovered she was pregnant with Eden, Spatz was 26, homeless, and living in her car in San Francisco. She had recently fled from her physically abusive boyfriend, only to find that the city's battered women's shelters were full. Going home to her parents in South Carolina was not an option; her father was an alcoholic who had beaten Spatz throughout her childhood and adolescence. So for three months a 1967 Chevrolet station wagon was home.

"It was a humbling experience," Spatz says. After nights in her car, she got up in the morning and went to work cleaning houses for $4.75 an hour. "I never told my clients I was homeless. They were usually out while I cleaned for them, so I could take a shower and do my laundry and warm up their leftovers in the microwave."

“ Fall seven times, stand up eight. ”   5

Japanese proverb

Spatz was unwilling to undergo the abortion everyone advised. Instead, with the birth approaching, she applied for public assistance, moved into an apartment shared by four other people, and waited.

Soon after Eden was born at Mt. Zion Hospital, Spatz began to think of ways to get off welfare. She entered San Francisco City College with a plan to take some accounting courses. She could work as a bookkeeper for $12 to $15 an hour. "I thought that would be my ticket to the good life," she says.

She took a set of standardized tests as part of the enrollment procedure and then reported to her counselor to arrange her schedule. "I'll never forget that day. I told her my plans to take a few courses and then look for work as a bookkeeper. She said, 'You kicked ass on these tests! Just tell me where you want to go and I'll get you a scholarship.' Do you want to go to Stanford? Or Berkeley?' I was stunned. It was the first time it occurred to me that I could have a future."

. . . [Today Spatz's] consuming passion in life is to improve the odds for other single mothers on welfare who want to complete a college education. In her quest, she has been involved with the National Organization for Women, debated senators on CNN about changes she believes are badly needed in the existing welfare system, and organized and taught classes for student parents, who are an increasing presence in today's diverse student body.

Spatz and her daughter share a two-bedroom apartment in University Housing's Albany Village. There is little furniture—a battered Formica table she found on the sidewalk, a washer her mother helped pay for, a dryer Diana bought for $20 at a garage sale (and which, to her amazement, still works). There is no carpet on the floor, just worn linoleum. The only place to sit in the living room is a tattered chaise longue draped with an Indian bedspread. A vintage computer occupies one corner of a large cluttered desk. The walls are covered with photographs of Eden.

10   At 35, Spatz describes herself as "getting old and getting fat," but she seems young, vital, and only slightly over fighting weight. She talks fast, laughs frequently, and appears unwearied by the challenges she has faced as a student, an activist, and a mother on welfare.

*   *   *   *

Q: How did other students react when you told them you were a welfare mother?

A: They always expressed shock. The first thing they said was, "You don't *look* like a welfare mother!" And I'd say, "Really? What is a welfare mother supposed to look like?" They'd say "You're different." And I would say, "No I'm not different. You just know me."

Q: How did you get into this situation?

A: I met Eden's father and fell in love. Mistake Number One! He had trouble getting and keeping a job. It took me a while to realize this was a permanent behavior pattern and not just a run of bad luck. And then he started drinking and doing drugs and getting abusive.

Q: So you left?

A: Not right away. People around you convince you it's your fault. And you think, Well, if it's my fault then I can solve it. If I can just find the right formula, he'll stop hitting me. Because, you know, he did love me. I never doubted that. . . .

Q: Does he see Eden much?

A: He's in jail. Alcohol and drugs got the better of him. But Eden visits him. His parents take her.

Q: What are some of the complications of being on welfare and going to school?

A: When I first got financial aid, I was kicked off welfare. I was told the financial aid made me ineligible. I got some legal advice and found out they were wrong—I was allowed to have additional funds beyond my welfare grant to pay for school expenses. So between classes I kept trying to call my caseworker, but the phone was invariably busy. This went on for days. I was panicking. My daughter was sick. I couldn't pay for the prescription she needed. I finally got hold of my worker and said, "You can't do this because of federal regulation such-and-such," and

I gave her the regulation numbers. She said, "I don't want to hear about your federal regulations" and hung up on me.

I was crying, and I was in a rage. I thought, This is why they have security guards in the social services department. People don't go there because they want a free ride. They go there because it's the end of the line. And then when you try to improve your situation you feel like they're trying to kick you down. I said, "If this is how it works, then it's going to change. I don't care how long it takes me." So I wrote a 13-page brief stating why my financial aid was necessary for school expenses, and I represented myself before a state appeals court, and I won my case.

Q: You seem to know how to stand up for yourself. Where did you learn that?

A: I always stood up to my father. I was the lightning rod in the family. I caught all the heat. It's a role I play to this day.

The first time I stood up to him I was about 11 years old. I'll never forget it. He hit me so hard I flew—I left the ground and hit the wall and slid down to the floor. I thought, Oh, my God!

Q: Did that happen a lot?

A: It got worse when I was in high school. I moved out as soon as I turned 18. Then I moved from South Carolina to California to get farther away. After I'd been here for a while I got really angry. I realized that wasn't how people treated each other. How could he do that to us?

I guess I have this crusader side to me that extends from my family background to the world at large. My own story is compelling enough, but when you connect it to all the other stories, you realize this isn't just about me, or my family. It's a lot bigger than that. And we need to make changes, not just for welfare mothers, but for families of all kinds. There's little accommodation in our society for parents, whether they're working or going to school.

Q: What changes would you like to see?

A: Welfare takes up 0.9 percent of the federal budget. Of that, 67 cents of every federal welfare dollar goes to the bureaucracy, and the bureaucracy spends most of its time and money trying to make sure that people *don't* get aid. To be eligible for childcare funding I have to fill out three separate forms a day; and each month all of my professors have to sign another form saying I've been attending classes regularly. Then all these forms have to be processed by the welfare office. I think we should dismantle the bureaucracy and just hand out cash grants to families in need.

Q: Does it make you feel good to speak out for your beliefs?

A: No. It's hard. But I feel compelled to make people better informed. For example, the savings-and-loan bailout cost more money than AFDC [Aid to Families of Dependent Children] has since its inception in 1935. But people don't know that. People don't know what the realities are. The biggest percentage of women on public assistance in California are divorced and separated mothers, and the numbers of white and African-American women on welfare are about equal.

Every time I do an interview or debate someone on television I get hate mail. One man wrote and said, "I see pregnant Mexican immigrant women in San Diego working at McDonald's. They don't go on welfare. If it's good enough for them, why isn't it good enough for you?" It made me feel terrible.

Q: Does this sort of criticism make you doubt yourself?

A: Always. My sense of self is constantly under siege. Criticism makes me think, Is this valid? Because sometimes you're wrong. And I always remember that my dad thought he was never wrong. So I have to stop and think, Is there something in this person's experience that allows them to know something I don't know?

* * * *

Q: Why do you think [your father] was so abusive?

A: In one of my English classes I read a story by James Joyce called "Counterparts." It was about an Irish Catholic family. The man is very low on the totem pole at work. He gets beaten up at the office every day, psychologically. And then he goes home and beats up his wife and kids. When I read that I cried. I thought, This is my dad! The only place he had any power was in his little home! And there's a legacy of violence in our family. He was abused by his father.

Q: What about you? Do you ever find yourself losing control with Eden?

A: Being a student and a single mother aren't always compatible. A friend described the feeling of being torn and panicky all the time, and that's how it is. I have to take care of my daughter, and I have a midterm tomorrow. How can I do both? Last spring I was on the speech team and taking 16 units. One afternoon I slapped Eden. Or I almost slapped her; I can't remember which. But that was it. Getting my work done on time wasn't worth subjecting my kid to the kind of treatment I'd grown up with. I went to my professors and told them I had to take incompletes.

* * * *

Q: What are you planning to do now that you're through with school?

A: The first thing I want to do is take some time off this summer to be with Eden. But I'm making plans for the future. I was asked to submit my résumé to David Ellwood, who's on the Clinton administration's Welfare Reform Task Force. And I'm writing a grant proposal for funding to be a community organizer for poor mothers who want to go to college.

Q: And how do you think your college degree will affect your future?

A: At this point in my life I don't know if anything will ever make me feel safe in the world. But I think a degree from Cal will make a big difference. It will get me a good job, I hope, and it will give me some credibility. I won't just be a former welfare mom. I'll be a former welfare mom who graduated from Cal—with honors! And I think people will listen to what I have to say and take me seriously because of that.

But most of all, it will help to provide a little place in the sun for Eden and me. That's what I want. A house with a back yard and a big, friendly dog—and that's what Eden wants more than anything on earth.

From "A Conversation with Diana Spats '95" by Catherine Maclay as appeared in California Monthly, *June 1995. Reprinted by permission of the author.*

**IN YOUR
OWN WORDS**

1. According to the article, what roadblocks did Spatz encounter in her quest to get an education and a better job?

2. Why do you think the author goes into such descriptive detail of Diana Spatz and her living accommodations? What stereotypes of welfare mothers is she trying to discredit? *Example:* Welfare mothers are lazy.

3. Spatz mentions that society does not offer much child care help for the children of parents who are working or going to school. Do you feel we should have more childcare programs? Why or why not?

4. Should there be a "safety net" for women who find themselves in a situation similar to Diana Spatz's—alone, pregnant, and with no real marketable skills? What kind of help does Spatz, and those like her, need most? To what extent does Spatz speak for all welfare mothers?

5. Were you surprised by the way Spatz was treated by the bureaucracy? What details about how the bureaucracy treated Spatz affected you the most? Is there a need for the bureaucracy to be more responsive to the people it is trying to help?

Written Assignment

Directions: Choose one of the following:

1. Both Diana Spatz's 1995 interview and Abraham Lincoln's letter to his stepbrother discuss ways to deal with the issue of welfare. Lincoln offers a concrete proposal of "matching funds" for those Johnston earns honestly. Spatz, on the other hand, suggests dismantling the current welfare structure and distributing cash grants to needy families instead. Write a paragraph comparing and contrasting these two viewpoints and add some concrete suggestions of your own on ways to solve the welfare dilemma. You might want to do some research on the welfare reform bill signed into law by President Clinton. How will that bill affect people like Diana Spatz?

2. What kind of work gives you the most satisfaction? What kind of work do you find least rewarding? Write a paragraph discussing your answers to these questions.

3. Write a paragraph describing your previous job history. Explain why you liked or disliked each previous job. What did each of your previous jobs teach you about what you like to pursue as a future career?

4. Write a paragraph describing the difference between a "good" boss and a "bad" boss.

5. What kind of work do you want to do? Interview some people already active in the career of your choice. How do these people feel about their work? Write a paragraph discussing your findings.

Chapter 3 Test: "A Conversation with Diana Spatz"

Multiple Choice

1. Diana Spatz's dream is to
   a. earn a college degree.
   b. have another child.
   c. be on the Welfare Reform Task Team.
   d. share a house with her daughter Eden.

2. The purpose of this article is to
   a. entertain and amuse.
   b. inform and persuade.
   c. entertain and persuade.
   d. explain and entertain.

3. Spatz believes which of the following?
   a. Our welfare system needs to be made more responsive to the individual's needs.
   b. The federal government is doing all it can.
   c. It's easy to be a student and a single mother.
   d. People take advantage of the welfare system because they want a free ride.

4. Paragraph 8 is organized as follows:
   a. details, main idea, details.
   b. main idea, details.
   c. details, main idea.
   d. no main idea sentence, just details.

5. In paragraph 9, the word "vintage" means
   a. a good time in history.
   b. representative of the best.
   c. dating from a period long past.
   d. the year of a particular wine.

True or False

_____ 6. Of the amount of money available for welfare, most of it goes to support the bureaucratic structure.

_____ 7. Spatz wanted to have an abortion, but couldn't afford one.

_____ 8. Spatz would like to help other single mothers obtain a college education.

_____ 9. Spatz's father, mother, and boyfriend were physically abusive.

_____ 10. Spatz's original goal was to become a college professor.

Review Test 2: Topics, Main Ideas, Details, and Author's Purpose

Directions: Read each passage. Then choose the best answer for each item.

If our business enterprises are to be as flexible and innovative at all levels as they need to be, our youngsters must be prepared to work with and through other people. While there will always be a need for a certain number of solo practitioners, the more usual requirement will be that combinations of individual skills are greater than their sums. Most of the important work will be done by groups, rather than by individual experts. . . . Young people must be taught how to work constructively together. Instead of emphasizing individual achievement and competition, the emphasis in the classroom should be on group performance. Students need to learn how to seek and accept criticism from their peers, to solicit help, and to give credit to others, where appropriate. They must also learn to negotiate—to articulate their own needs, to discern what others need and see things from others' perspectives, and to discover mutually beneficial outcomes.

From Reich, Robert, "Dick and Jane Meet the Next Economy" *in* The Resurgent Liberal, New York: Vintage Books, a Division of Random House, 1989, p. 102.

1. The main idea expressed in this passage is that
   a. Most of the work in the future will be done by individuals working alone.
   b. There are advantages and disadvantages to working collectively.
   c. Many students are capable of learning to work together productively.
   d. Young people need to be taught how to work together productively so that our business enterprises can successfully meet new challenges.

2. The author's primary purpose is to
   a. convince us of the necessity of emphasizing group activities in our educational systems.
   b. explain the dynamics of a business enterprise.
   c. entertain us with an interesting anecdote concerning the world of business.
   d. inform us of problems students are likely to face in the near future.

3. The examples of seeking and accepting criticism, soliciting help, and giving appropriate credit were used to illustrate
   a. skills students need to develop in order to work individually.
   b. skills students need to develop in order to work cooperatively.
   c. requirements of a top-notch school system.
   d. the complexity of a business organization.

4. The best title for the above paragraph would be
   a. "Group Dynamics in Action"
   b. "Cooperative Learning"
   c. "The Solo Practitioner"
   d. "Group Learning and Business"

According to a new U.S. News/Bozell Worldwide *poll conducted by KRC Research and Consulting, 49% of Americans say society puts too much emphasis on work and not enough on leisure. That's a big change from 11 years ago. In a study conducted by the Opinion Research Corp. in 1986, just 28 percent felt that way. "Job candidates are letting us know that they don't want their work to be their life and that they want a job with reasonable hours," says Eric Schwalm, vice president in charge of recruiting operations at Bain & Co., a Boston-based consulting firm. Marilyn Moats Kennedy, managing partner of Career Strategies in Wilmette, Illinois, says she sees more people in job interviews spelling out the number of hours they are willing to work. "I know of one young software engineer who told every employer he interviewed with that he would give them 40 spectacular hours a week and nothing more," she says. Nonetheless, he got two job offers. Benjamin Hunnicutt, a leisure studies professor at the University of Iowa says that, "We envision a reawakening of the American dream of progress as more time for family and leisure activities—not ever increasing wealth and consumption."*

From "20 Hot Job Tracks" by David Brindley, et al. Copyright, October 27, 1997, U.S. News & World Report. *Reprinted by permission.*

5. The topic of this paragraph could best be stated as
   a. work and leisure.
   b. less and more.
   c. young engineers.
   d. cutting hours.

6. All of the following were given as reasons for reducing the emphasis on work except
   a. Americans now view a shorter work week as progress.
   b. More emphasis should be placed on making money.
   c. More time should be spent in family-related activities.
   d. More time should be spent in leisure-related activities.

7. The most accurate expression of the main idea of this paragraph is
   a. Many people would like to spend fewer hours at work and more at family and leisure-type activities.
   b. There has been a change in the way many women feel about work.
   c. A person who refuses to work more than 40 hours a week can still get job offers.
   d. A shorter work week would give employees more reason to be productive.

8. The author's primary purpose in this paragraph is to
   a. persuade the reader to reduce the number of hours he or she spends on a job.
   b. persuade the reader to spend more time with family members.
   c. inform the reader of a new trend regarding work and leisure.
   d. entertain the reader with stories about the world of work.

   Want a job? Be prepared to answer a few true-or-false questions first:
   > *(1) People are basically kind-hearted.*
   > *(2) My sleep is fitful and disturbed.*
   > *(3) My sex life is satisfactory.*
   > *(4) I loved my father.*
   > *(5) Evil spirits possess me at times.*

   Some questions of job applicants are legal; others have been challenged in court. But all are being asked by employers on prehire tests to measure such traits as personality, honesty, and intelligence. Employers think the tests are good predictors of job success. Even candidates leery of the tests, they say, divulge information about themselves. Others, such as Lewis Maltby of the American Civil Liberties Union, say there are serious problems with the accuracy of these tests. Forcing job candidates to answer a barrage of questions is invasive and a bad hiring technique. Nevertheless, more than three million people each year are quizzed. No job is immune: Even rookies in the National Football League take such tests.

   From USA Today, *January 21, 1998, p. 2B.*

9. The best title for this paragraph would be
   a. "Invasive Tests"
   b. "Prehire Tests: Valuable or Invasive?"
   c. "Jobs"
   d. "A Good Predictor of On-The-Job-Success"

10. All of the following were given as reasons to dislike the tests except
    a. The tests can interfere with a right to privacy.
    b. There are problems with the accuracy of the tests.
    c. The tests are considered a bad technique for hiring someone.
    d. The tests are better predictors of job success than a standard interview.

Vocabulary: Word Structure and Unit 1

Introduction

The Greeks and Romans came up with a system for creating words by putting together smaller word parts. They used three types of word parts: prefixes, suffixes, and roots. *Pre* means "before," and so it makes sense that a prefix comes before the main part of a word. *Suf* means "after," and so a suffix comes at the end of a word. A root word is the main part of a word, and usually comes in the middle. Many English words are composed of at least one root, and many have one or more prefixes and suffixes.

Part of the Greek and Roman system was a set of prefixes that represented numbers. Split up into groups of two, three, or four, and appoint a secretary. On a separate sheet of paper (just one sheet for the whole group), make a list of numbers 1 through 10, followed by 100, 1,000, and 1,000,000. Your list will look something like this:

1

2

3

4

5

6

7

8

9

10

100

1,000

1,000,000

Now see how many of the prefixes for these numbers your group knows. Write your answers on the lines next to the numbers. For example, you can see below that a prefix for 1 is *uni*, as in "unicycle." What would be a prefix for 2? You can see below that the answer is *bi*, as in "bicycle." Notice also that *tri* means "3," *quad* means "4," and *oct* means "8."

Some numbers can have more than one prefix as the lines below indicate. Can you think of another prefix for 1, and two more for 2? Try to think of words that refer to number or quantity. For example, what is the word for a 10-year period of time? What is its prefix?

      1   uni, _____

      2   bi, _____, _____

      3   tri

      4   quad, _____

      5   _____, _____

      6   _____, _____

      7   _____, _____

8	oct
9	_____
10	_____
100	_____ , _____
1,000	_____ , _____
1,000,000	_____ , _____

As you can now see, there are many words in English derived from specific numbers.

One way that might help you remember many of these number prefixes is to think of the months of the year. For example, October has the prefix *oct*, meaning "eight." That might help you remember what *oct* means, except for one big problem—October is not the 8th month, but the 10th. How can this be? The answer is that our calendar evolved from the original Roman calendar, which began in March instead of January and had only 10 months. The months of Januarius and Februarius, named after Roman gods, were added later around 700 B.C. You can see that making March the first month makes October the eighth month.

Almost all cultures have attempted to organize the year through the use of calendars. The earliest calendars, based on the phases of the moon, resulted in a lunar year of 354 days. Our calendar is based on one revolution of the earth around the sun. A difficulty with making solar calendars such as ours is that the earth does not revolve around the sun in an exact number of days. In fact, one revolution of the earth around the sun takes 365 days, 5 hours, 48 minutes, and 45.5 seconds.

The Roman calendar had become so hopelessly confused that Julius Caesar, prior to his death, tinkered with it to make it catch up. It was so far off that one year he was forced to add 90 extra days. Citizens labeled that year "the year of confusion." At least they had a sense of humor! In addition to establishing the order of the months and the days of the week, Caesar added the concept of leap years. The result is that we have 365 days in most years, but we also have leap years (every fourth year), which have 366 days. Later, Caesar Augustus established the length of the months we still use today. Because the two Caesars made substantial changes to the calendar, the months of Quintilis and Sextilis (fifth and sixth months, *quint* meaning "five," and *sex* meaning "six") were renamed July and August in honor of them.

We currently use the Gregorian or Christian calendar named after Pope Gregory XIII. He added the idea that no century year, except if divisible by 400, should be a leap year. Thus 1600 was a leap year and we will have a leap year in the year 2000.

Vocabulary units 1 and 2 will draw on your knowledge of the numbering system. Make sure that you remember that the calendar began in March.

Vocabulary 1

Each of the following special vocabulary seven units, which are located in various chapters remaining in the book, will introduce you to important prefixes and root words, and give you vocabulary words using these word parts. Each unit will draw on what you learned in the previous units. You will find an exercise and a crossword puzzle at the end of each unit to reinforce your learning.

Now we are going to learn some number prefixes.

uni—one	tetra—four	oct—eight
mono—one	quint—five	nov—nine
bi—two	pent—five	dec—ten
duo—two	sex—six	lat—side
di—two	hex—six	ped—foot
tri—three	sept—seven	pod—foot
quad—four	hept—seven	

biped—One biped, the frigate bird, can fly 260 miles an hour.

biped	*Ped* means "foot" as in *pedal* and *pedestrian*, so a *biped* is an animal with two feet, such as a human.
tripod	Sometimes there are slight variations in the spellings of word parts. *Pod* also means "foot," so a *tripod* has three feet. An example would be a stand for a camera.
quadruped	An animal with four feet, such as a dog or cat.
hexapod	An organism with six feet, such as an insect. Why aren't spiders *hexapods*? Because they have eight feet.
unicorn	That mythical animal with one horn.
unison	An instance of sounding the same note at the same time.
monopoly	A company that has no competition is called a *monopoly*. The electric and gas companies in your area are probably *monopolies* because they are the only companies allowed to give you service.
monolog(ue)	Log means "to speak," so a *monolog* is one person speaking without anyone responding. Jay Leno and David Letterman give *monologs* at the beginning of their shows. Why is the "ue" in parentheses? Many words such as *monologue*, *dialogue*, and *catalogue* are in the process of losing their last two letters. As time passes, there is a tendency to drop unneeded letters from words. A dictionary 50 years from now will probably not list any of these words with the "ue" at the end.
lateral	toward the side, sideways. The quarterback threw a *lateral* pass.
unilateral	one-sided. The mother made a *unilateral* decision and told her child to go to bed. This was not a decision that was made by discussing it with the child.
bilateral	two-sided. We signed a *bilateral* agreement with Russia.
bicuspids	your teeth with two points.
dual	two of a kind, such as *dual* mufflers.
duel	a formal combat with weapons fought between two people in the presence of witnesses.
duet	a musical composition written for two musicians to perform simultaneously.
duo	two musical performers; a pair.
trio	three people in a group.
quartet	four people in a group. A jazz *quartet* has four musicians.

hexapod—There are over five million species of insects in the world and the total insect population of the world is at least 1,000,000,000,000,000,000.

Trivia Question #1

How many opening monologs did Johnny Carson deliver during his 30 years as host of *The Tonight Show*? You will find the answer at the end of this unit.

Trivia Question #2

Who were the two people who fought in the most famous duel in American history? Answer at the end of this vocabulary unit.

biplane—The first plane flight by Orville Wright lasted 12 seconds, went to a height of 8–12 feet, and traveled 120 feet. The name of their plane flown at Kitty Hawk, North Carolina, was Bird of Prey.

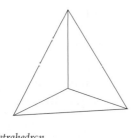

tetrahedron

Pentagon: Gamma Liaison

Pentagon—The Pentagon has 17.5 miles of corridors, 7,754 windows, and 23,000 people working there.

hexagon—All snow crystals are hexagonal.

Trivia Question #3

What number did the ancient Mayan civilization base their numbering system on? Answer at end of this vocabulary unit.

triathlon—The oldest participant in the Hawaii triathlon was 73-year-old Walt Stack who participated in 1981. His time of 26 hours and 20 minutes was also the longest time for any participant in this event.

quintuplets	five children of the same mother born at one time.
sextuplets	six children of the same mother born at one time.
septuplets	seven children of the same mother born at one time. Bobbi and Kenny McCaughey of Carlisle, Iowa, had *septuplets* in 1997.
monoxide	one oxygen atom, as in carbon *monoxide* (CO).
dioxide	two oxygen atoms, as in carbon *dioxide* (CO_2).
biplane	a plane with two sets of wings, one over the other, such as the one the Wright brothers flew.
triplane	a plane with three sets of wings, one over the other. The Germans, and specifically the "Red Baron," flew *triplanes* for a short period during World War I, but they were not practical for combat.
tetrahedron	a four-sided, three-dimensional object.
pentagon	a five sided figure. The military has its headquarters in this five-sided building located in Virginia just across the Potomac River from Washington, D.C.
Pentateuch	The first five books of the Old Testament (Genesis, Exodus, Leviticus, Numbers, and Deuteronomy) are called the *Pentateuch*. The Jews considered these books central to their faith and called them the Torah (law).
hexagon	a six-sided figure.
octagon	an eight-sided figure.
octave	eight notes of the musical scale.
octane	You know it has to do with gas, but *octane* acquired its name because it has eight carbon atoms in its chemical formula (C_8H_{18}).
decade	a 10-year period.
decimal	Our numbering system is called a *decimal* system because it is based on units of 10.
September	originally the seventh month.
October	originally the eighth month.
November	originally the ninth month.
December	originally the tenth month.
biathlon	two events, usually sporting.
triathlon	an endurance race combining three consecutive events usually swimming, bicycling, and running. The Hawaiian *Triathlon* requires participants to swim 2 miles, ride a bike 100 miles, and last, but not least, run 26 miles—all of which is done in one day.
heptathlon	an athletic contest for women that requires participants to take part in seven different events (100-meter hurdles, shot-put, high jump, 200-meter dash, long jump, javelin throw, and 800-meter run). Jackie Joyner-Kersee won the gold medal in the *heptathlon* at the Olympics in 1992.

Copyright © 1999 by The McGraw-Hill Companies, Inc.

Answer to Trivia Question #1

Johnny Carson gave 4,531 *monologs* in his 30 years on *The Tonight Show*.

Answer to Trivia Question #2

One of the participants was Alexander Hamilton whose picture you will find on a $10 bill. He's the one who lost the *duel*. The other participant was Aaron Burr.

Answer to Trivia Question #3

The Mayans based their numbering system on units of 20.

decathlon	an athletic contest in which each contestant takes part in 10 different athletic events: 100-meter dash, 400-meter dash, long jump, 16-pound shot-put, high jump, 110-meter hurdles, discus throw, pole vault, javelin throw, and 1500-meter run. The winner is usually proclaimed "the world's greatest athlete." Dan O'Brien won the gold medal in the *decathlon* in 1996.
sexagenarian	a person in his or her sixties.
septuagenarian	a person in his or her seventies.
octogenarian	a person in his or her eighties.
nonagenarian	a person in his or her nineties.

Draw a line between the number prefixes in the first column and their corresponding numbers in the second column. Do as many as you can without looking back for the answers.

hex	3
quint	10
sept	4
di	6
nov	1
mono	5
tetra	2
dec	8
tri	9
oct	7

Now that you have studied Vocabulary Unit 1, practice your new knowledge by trying the crossword puzzle on the next page.

Vocabulary 1

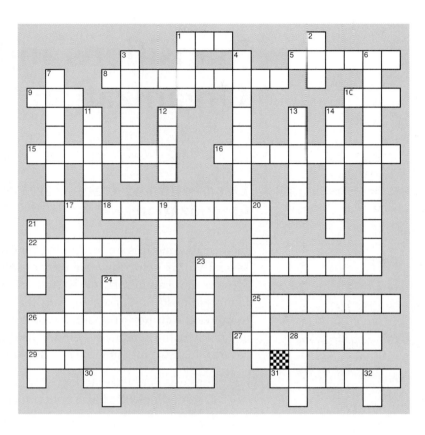

ACROSS CLUES

1. The abbreviation for what was once the tenth month.
5. A chemical found in gas.
8. The Torah, or the first five books of the Old Testament.
9. A word part meaning "side."
10. A word part meaning "one."
15. What the Red Baron flew in World War I.
16. One of five children born at one time.
18. Teeth with two points.
22. All the voices or instruments together.
23. A contest involving seven track events.
25. A business that has no competition.
26. Carbon _____ is one thing that comes out of a car exhaust pipe.
27. The building in Washington, D.C. where the military has its headquarters.
29. The abbreviation for what was once the ninth month.
30. What Jay Leno delivers at the start of the show.
31. We exhale carbon _____.

DOWN CLUES

1. Two of a kind.
2. The abbreviation for what was once the eighth month.
3. A numbering system that is based on units of ten.
4. An animal with four legs.
6. A person in his or her nineties is a _____.
7. Passing the ball to the side is a _____.
11. An animal with two legs.
12. What Aaron Burr and Alexander Hamilton fought.
13. The eight notes of the musical scale.
14. What the Wright Brothers flew.
17. The mythical animal with one horn.
19. A decision made without consulting the other party is _____.
20. What was originally the seventh month.
21. A musical piece written for two musicians to perform at the same time.
23. A word part meaning "seven."
24. A scientific name for insects.
26. A word part meaning "one."
28. Three in a group.
32. A word part meaning "two."

Chapter 4

Transitions and Patterns of Organization

Description of Transition Words and Patterns of Organization

In your reading it is important to pay close attention to **transition** words. These special words help show the relationships between ideas within sentences and ideas within paragraphs. Good drivers learn to closely watch the road ahead, utilizing signposts or markers to make their trips easier and safer. Good readers learn to utilize the author's transition words, which signal what is ahead.

Look at the sentences below. The addition of a transition word signaling a reversal makes a big difference in our ability to understand Tom's situation.

1. Tom was very eager to leave for college. The thought of leaving familiar surroundings filled him with dread.

2. Tom was eager to leave for college. **Nevertheless**, the thought of leaving familiar surroundings filled him with dread.

The first example doesn't really make a lot of sense. If Tom is so eager to leave, why is he filled with dread? The addition of the transition word makes the situation clear in the second example. Although Tom wants to leave for college, he is understandably reluctant to give up his safe and comfortable surroundings.

Now look at these two sentences.

1. Carmen loves tea. It keeps her awake at night unless she drinks decaffeinated.

2. Carmen loves tea; **however**, it keeps her awake at night unless she drinks decaffeinated.

Again, the first example doesn't make much sense, but the addition of the transition word in the second example clarifies the situation. Carmen likes tea, but must be careful to drink only decaffeinated or else she is likely to experience a sleepless night.

In the following sentences, provide an appropriate transition word. If you need help, use the chart on the next page. Be sure your completed sentence makes sense.

1. (contrast) _____ he was failing all of his classes, he still had a positive attitude about school.

2. (cause) _____ he worked so many hours at his job, he had no time left for a social life.

3. We can (classification or division) _____ parents into two categories: those who are willing to use physical punishment on their children and those who are not.

Transition Words

Words that can be used to show **classification or division (categories):**

break down	combine	lump
categorize	divide	split
class and subclass	group	type
classify	kind	

Words that can be used to show **cause-and-effect** relationships:

as a consequence	due to	resulting
as a result	for	since
because	for this reason	so
begin	hence	then
bring about	lead to	therefore
consequently	reaction	thus

Words that can be used to show **comparison:**

all	both	like
and	in comparison	likewise
as	just as	similarly

Words that can be used to show **contrast:**

although	in contrast	on the other hand
but	in opposition	rather than
despite	instead	though
even so	nevertheless	unlike
however	on the contrary	yet

Words that can be used to show **steps in a process:**

after	finally	process
afterwards	first, second, third	step
at this point	next	then
at this stage	now	

Words that can be used to show **examples:**

for example	specifically	to illustrate
for instance	such as	
in particular	to demonstrate	

Words that can be used to **define:**

is defined as	is called	refers to
is described by	means	term or concept

Words that can be used to show **chronological order:**

after	first, second, third	next
at last	finally	seasons
before	following	soon
currently	in a year, month, day	then
during	in the meantime	until

4.   Aggression is (definition) _____ any physical or verbal behavior that is directly intended to hurt someone.

5.   (example) _____ a slap, a punch, and even a direct insult are all considered forms of aggression.

6.   Suppose your boss insults you (steps in a process) _____ you go home and yell at your wife, _____ she yells at your son, _____ he kicks baby sister, _____ she pulls the dog's tail, and _____ the dog bites the mail carrier.

7.   In the winter months of (months of the year in order) _____, _____, and _____, assaults are at an all-time low. In the hotter seasons of _____, _____, and _____, violent crimes are more likely to occur.

Writers organize their supporting sentences and ideas in ways called **patterns of organization**. The most common kinds of patterns of organization are (1) classification and division, (2) cause and effect, (3) comparison and contrast, (4) steps in a process, (5) examples, (6) definition, and (7) chronological order. A writer's chosen pattern of organization will affect the sort of transition words he or she uses. In the sections that follow, we will discuss patterns of organization and the relationships between patterns of organization and transition words.

Classification Pattern

Classification is the process of organizing information into categories. A category is created by noticing and defining group characteristics. The categories we create make it easier to analyze, discuss, and draw conclusions.

Have you ever scanned the classified ads section of the newspaper? If you have, you are already familiar with classification and division. Ads are not arranged randomly in the newspaper; otherwise we would never be able to quickly locate the information we need. Instead, ads are grouped into categories, with each category further subdivided as much as needed.

For instance, if you wanted to buy your son a dog for his birthday, you would first locate the section entitled **Livestock/Pets/Produce**. Under this heading, you would locate the section on **Dogs**. In some newspapers, the category **Dogs** may be

LIVESTOCK/PETS/PRODUCE

Birds & Fish 4045

Cats 4060

Dogs. 4070

Farmers Market 4085

Farm/Ranch Machinery 4105

Livestock 4140

Livestock Services & Supplies 4145

Pets. 4155

Poultry & Rabbits 4172

so large that it is further subdivided into **Beagles, Boxers, Poodles,** and other breeds of dogs.

The details in many paragraphs are also organized by using classification. Look at the three short paragraphs below describing unhealthy expressions of anger. The author uses two specific categories to make it easier for us to understand the information being presented.

> *According to University of Arizona psychologist Roger J. Daldrup, there are* **two classic ways** *of expressing anger in an unhealthy way: misdirecting it, and suppressing it completely.*
>
> *Misdirected anger, Daldrup says, "is the classic kicking the cat because you're angry at your spouse maneuver. Though people who misdirect their anger seem to be expressing it, they are just burying the real problem and creating more problems along the way."*
>
> *The other classic response, complete suppression of anger, doesn't work either, because, says Daldrup, it creates what he calls "the keyboard effect." When a person starts repressing one emotion, he begins repressing them all, something he likens to pressing down the soft pedal on the piano: "That practice softens all the notes on the piano, just as dulling one emotion will dull them all."*

From Mind/Body Health, *by Brent Hafen, Keith Karren, Kathryn Frandesen, and N. Lee Smith. Copyright © 1996 by Allyn and Bacon. Reprinted by permission.*

The following words are clues to classification and division pattern:

Classification	Division
classify	divide
group	split
lump	break down
combine	
categorize	
class and subclass	

In recent years, many Americans have become fascinated with investigating their ancestral background. They use the information they gather to assemble family trees or genealogy charts showing the names, birth dates, marriages, and deaths of ancestors. In addition to being fun, studying the details of a family's medical past can provide early warning of health problems that might lie ahead for current family members. Many ailments are known to have genetic links, including cancer, diabetes, and alcoholism.

To practice classification, try making a genealogy chart or family tree. Talk with family members to try to gather information about your ancestors. Then record the information on a genealogical chart.

Your family tree shows your pedigree. The word *pedigree* came to English in the fifteenth century from the French phrase *pied de grue* meaning "foot of a crane." The lines showing descent (in the earliest genealogies) strongly resembled the footprint of a crane. In time, the symbol came to represent the study of genealogy itself.

Written Assignment

In the process of doing your research, you may discover some interesting stories about your family. Some of these stories are likely true, but others may be part family myth. Write three of these stories in paragraph format and share them with the class.

Four Generation Genealogical Chart

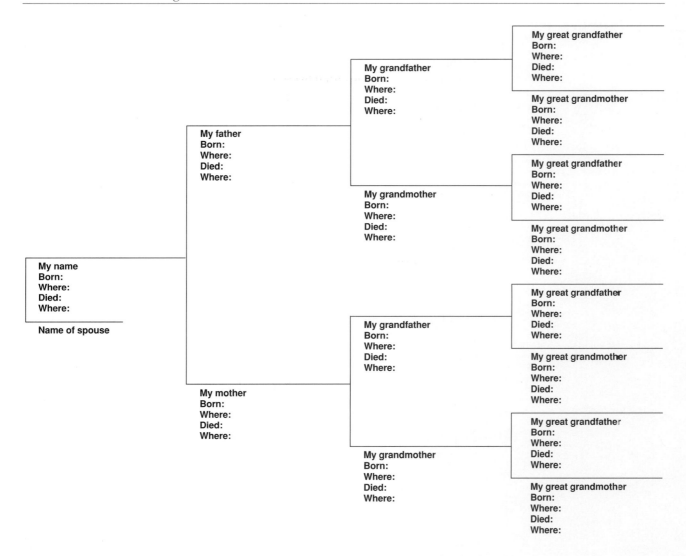

Practice Exercise: Classification and Division

Directions: Fill in the blank with an appropriate transition word or phrase from the list below. Some of the transition words will fit in more than one of the sentences, but try to use a different transition word in each of the sentences. Make sure the sentence makes sense with the transition word you choose.

      break down   classify   combine   divide   group

1. We can _____ cohabitating relationships into five types.

2. The first _____ is called *temporary casual* and involves two people sharing living space simply because it is convenient and less expensive. Neither party is romantically involved.

3. If we _____ together all those who have cohabited at some point in their lives, we discover that the figure is about 50 percent.

4. We can _____ this category into those who expect to eventually marry their partners and those who do not.

5. We can further _____ those couples into those who intend to have children and those who do not.

Cause-and-Effect Pattern

In a cause-and-effect relationship, one thing causes another thing to happen. The second event is the effect or result of the first event.

Try reading the following anecdote to locate cause-and-effect relationships. You will need someone to read the narrator's part, the farmer's part, and the field hand's part.

Adapted from Contemporary's Building Basic Skills in Reading Book 1, *Chicago: Contemporary Books, Inc., 1988, pp. 93–94.*

Narrator:	It happened in the days before mail service and telephones. A wealthy farmer took a long trip. When he arrived home, he asked the first field hand he saw what had happened while he was away. This is how their conversation went:
Field hand:	Well, the dog died.
Farmer:	The dog died! How?
Field hand:	The horses ran over him when they became frightened and ran out of the barn.
Farmer:	What scared the horses? Why did they run?
Field hand:	They were running from the flames when the barn caught on fire.
Farmer:	My God! How did the barn catch on fire?
Field hand:	Well, sir, flames jumped from the house and caught the barn on fire.
Farmer:	From the house! Did the house burn down, too?
Field hand:	Yep. The house is gone, too.
Farmer:	How on earth did the house burn down?
Field hand:	You see, one of the candles around your wife's casket fell over and caught the house on fire.

Now complete the cause-and-effect sentences.

1. Because the candles on the wife's casket fell over, the _____.

2. Because flames jumped from the house, the _____.

3. Because the horses were scared, they _____.

The following transition words are clues to the cause-and-effect pattern:

Cause	Effect
because	as a result
for	consequently
for this reason	reaction
since	then
begin	lead to
	bring about
	hence
	therefore
	so
	resulting

You will encounter many cause and effect relationships in the textbooks you read for your various classes. The following paragraphs from a health textbook illustrate a cause-and-effect relationship

*Anger has as many different **causes** as there are situations and people. The most common **cause** is physical or psychological restraint—being held back from something we intensely want or want to do. Others include being forced to do something against our will, being taken advantage of, being frustrated, being insulted, being ridiculed, or having plans defeated. Sometimes other emotions (such as distress, sorrow, or fear) can **lead to** anger.*

*The most recent research shows that the **effects** of anger are diverse and widespread. Consider the wide range of physiological **reactions** that go with it: changes in muscle tension, scowling, grinding of teeth, glaring, clenching of fists, flushing, goose bumps, chills and shudders, prickly sensations, numbness, choking, twitching, sweating, losing control, or feeling hot or cold. One of the major physiological **effects** of anger is on the release of chemicals and hormones, principally adrenaline and noradrenaline. When the release of adrenaline and noradrenaline is chronic or prolonged, **resulting** in chronic or prolonged anger, some of the most serious **effects** are high blood pressure, headache, heart attack, stroke, and kidney problems. If there's enough anger, almost any part of the body can be harmed. The **effects** can be as serious as cancer and heart disease or as minor (but annoying) as the common cold or skin disorders.*

From Mind/Body Health, *by Brent Hafen, Keith Karren, Kathryn Frandesen, and N. Lee Smith. Copyright © 1996 by Allyn and Bacon.*

Practice Exercise: Cause and Effect

Directions: Fill in the blank with an appropriate transition word or phrase from the list below. Some of the transition words will fit in more than one of the sentences, but try to use a different transition word in each of the sentences. Make sure the sentence makes sense with the transition you choose.

as a result   because   bring about   therefore   reaction

1. _____ working moms with children under the age of five want a familiar face to care for their children, many are turning to grandparents and other relatives for help with child care.

2. Teens who begin drinking before they are old enough to drive have a higher chance of becoming alcoholics at some time in their lives. _____ many organizations want to begin early intervention programs with those teens who begin drinking early.

3. Last year, U.S. residents spent $207 billion on meals prepared by restaurants, with 51 percent of that total for takeout and delivery; _____ on-line food order companies are beginning to see the potential for big business.

4. In _____ to criticism by the Food and Drug Administration, R. J. Reynolds Tobacco Co. discontinued the use of Joe Camel, the cartoon character, in its smoking ads.

5. In order to _____ positive changes in race relations, more and more open forums discussing problems are being held around the country.

Compare/Contrast Pattern

A comparison shows the similarities between two or more things, while a contrast shows the differences. Sometimes a writer both compares (tells the similarities) and contrasts (tells the differences) at the same time. The following information from the Internet on Presidents Lincoln and Kennedy illustrates comparison.

Lincoln and Kennedy
There are many curious parallels in the deaths of President Abraham Lincoln and John Fitzgerald Kennedy. Among these are:

1. *President Lincoln was elected in 1860. Exactly 100 years later, in 1960, Kennedy was elected president.*
2. *Both were assassinated on a Friday in the presence of their wives.*
3. *Both presidents were deeply involved in civil rights for blacks.*
4. *Both President Lincoln and President Kennedy were succeeded by vice-presidents named Johnson who were southern Democrats and former senators.*
5. *Both men were killed by a bullet that entered the head from behind.*
6. *Lincoln was killed in Ford's Theater. Kennedy met his death while riding in a Lincoln convertible made by the Ford Motor Company.*
7. *Both assassins were killed before they could be brought to trial.*

On the other hand, there are significant dissimilarities between the two. To name just a few: Lincoln, largely self-educated, was born poor and was raised by his father and a stepmother. *In contrast,* Kennedy was born to a wealthy family and attended elite private schools. Lincoln was president when the country was at war with itself during the Civil War. *In contrast,* Kennedy served during the Cold War when the country was unified against an enemy outside the United States.

The following transition words are clues to this pattern:

Comparison	Contrast	
all	on the other hand	nevertheless
and	though	in contrast
as	unlike	on the contrary
both	yet	in opposition
like	although	instead
similarly	but	
in comparison	despite	
likewise	even so	
just as	however	

In the two paragraphs that follow, the author explores the differences between cultures in regard to the subject of anger.

*Besides individual **differences** in the way we feel and express anger, there are also some important cultural **differences**. In a number of Latin and Arab cultures the free expression of anger is heartily endorsed; two who are angry at each other may fight because they figure that a strong third party (such as a neighbor or family member) will intervene before things go too far. The Utku Eskimos fall at the **opposite** end of the spectrum: They ostracize anyone who loses his temper, regardless of the reason. Between these two extremes are all kinds of middle ground. The Japanese don't display anger as their traditional Western counterparts do; **instead** of lashing out verbally, the Japanese assume a neutral* *expression and a polite demeanor when angry. The Mbuti hunter-gatherers of northeast Zaire take it a step further; when angry, they laugh. Some individual disputes have become "full-scale tribal laugh fests."*

*There are also profoundly **different** "rules" from one culture to another for the way anger is choreographed. Members of Anglo societies follow a fairly predictable course of action: hints, indirect efforts, involvement of a third party, direct confrontation, escalating anger, lawsuits, and, when all else fails, violence. The steps are quite **different, however,** in Iran, Latin America, and some American Indian cultures: There you might observe silent brooding (for five years or even five hundred years) while the tribe decides what to do; an act of violent revenge; then more resolute measures, such as discussion, direct negotiation, or the involvement of a third party.*

From Mind/Body Health, *by Brent Hafen, Keith Karren, Kathryn Frandesen, and N. Lee Smith. Copyright © 1996 by Allyn and Bacon.*

Practice Exercise: Compare and Contrast

Directions: Fill in the blank with an appropriate transition word or phrase from the list below. Some of the transition words will fit in more than one of the sentences, but try to use a different transition word in each of the sentences. Make sure the sentence makes sense with the transition you choose.

   although   both   however   just as   on the other hand

1.   In order to live a healthy lifestyle, people are increasingly being told to _____ eat right and exercise.

2.   Joan's adviser gave her some good reasons for going to graduate school, but, _____ , he also gave her some good reasons for directly starting her career.

3.   There are two ways to go to get to the mall, and one way is _____ good as the other.

4.   _____ linemen on a professional football team need to be large, they also need to be fast.

5.   Judging by all the dark clouds in the sky, it looked like it was going to rain. _____ , around noontime the sun came out.

Written Assignment

For practice, write a short paragraph comparing and contrasting two ordinary household objects such as a pencil and a pen, or a fork and a spoon. Or, you might want to try comparing and contrasting a typewriter and a computer. Include some of the "compare and contrast" words found on the previous page.

Steps in a Process Pattern

In the steps in a process pattern, something is explained or described in a step-by-step manner. The sequences are clearly identified by specific transition words. A lot of scientific writing uses this particular pattern. In addition, anytime we try to show how to make or do something, we are probably using this pattern of organization. Just for fun, try following these directions explaining how to draw cartoon characters. (You will need a separate piece of paper for your sketches.)

Step 1. *Draw a basic shape lightly and loosely in pencil.*   **Step 2.** *Lightly sketch in the features.*

Step 3. *Go back over the drawing darkening some of your lines.*   **Step 4.** *Erase pencil lines and add details to make your drawing personal.*

From *Cartooning* by Lloyd Littlepage. Reprinted by permission.

It's easy to draw a cartoon. Just take it step by step. First, start by drawing a shape in pencil, and then lightly sketch in the features. Remember to exaggerate!

The following transition words are clues to the steps in a process pattern:

first, second, third	then
next	finally
at this point	at this stage
after	afterwards
now	process, step

In the two paragraphs that follow, the author gives a step-by-step account of the physical changes that accompany anger.

Medical research shows that no matter how many times you work out at the gym or how careful you are to eat correctly, you're putting yourself at risk if you *don't manage your anger effectively. The body reacts to anger with immediate physical changes. **First,** blood rushes to the face, the heartbeat speeds up, and the body undergoes a physical reaction much like that of stress. **Next,** respiration speeds up, blood pressure rises, the digestive **process** slows down, and the muscles tense up, all in readiness for action. Our blood "boils," our muscles tense up, our stomach feels like it's tied up in knots, and our cheeks feel like they're burning up. **At this point,** the more angry we become, the stronger and more powerful we feel—and the more pressed to "strike out." Back when people needed the fight-or-flight response to defend themselves against aggressors, they needed anger. It was important to survival. The surge of energy helped early people defend themselves. Anger enabled them to fight with vigor and great strength.*

*Our culture evolved much more rapidly than our bodies. We are **now** a society and a civilization who are expected to deal calmly and rationally with each other. We don't need to fight saber-toothed tigers; our battles are waged in boardrooms and bedrooms. **At this stage,** we no longer need the fight-or-flight response, but our bodies still respond that way. We call it stress. We no longer need the physical stimulus of anger either, but we still get angry. Instead of being a benefit, most regard the **process** of anger as a liability.*

From Mind/Body Health, *by Brent Hafen, Keith Karren, Kathryn Frandesen, and N. Lee Smith. Copyright © 1996 by Allyn and Bacon. Reprinted by permission.*

Practice Exercise: Steps in a Process

Directions: Fill in the blank with an appropriate transition word or phrase from the list below. Some of the transition words will fit in more than one of the sentences, but try to use a different transition word in each of the sentences. Make sure the sentence makes sense with the transition you choose.

> stages   at this point   first   final   process   second

1. The _____ of sleeping is complicated, with people progressing through four distinct, 90-minute stages during a night's rest.

2. Each of these four sleep _____ is associated with a unique pattern of brain waves.

3. In the _____ stage, as people begin to go to sleep, images sometimes appear as if a person were viewing still photos.

4. It is _____, in stage 1, that rapid eye movement, or REM, sleep occurs. REM sleep is usually accompanied by dreams, which, whether people remember them or not, are experienced by *everyone* during some part of the night.

5. As sleep becomes deeper, people enter the _____ stage, which is characterized by a slower, more regular wave pattern.

6. By the time sleepers arrive at the _____ stage, they are least responsive to outside stimulation. Stage 4 sleep is most likely to occur during the early part of the morning.

From Feldman, Robert S., adapted from The Essentials of Understanding Psychology, 3rd Edition, *New York: McGraw-Hill 1997, p. 120–121.*

Examples Pattern

A paragraph of examples usually gives a general statement of the main idea and then presents one or more concrete examples to provide support for this idea. Many writers place the most important or convincing example either first, as an attention-getter, or last, as a dramatic climax. While the terms *example* and *illustration* are used interchangeably, an illustration is usually longer, and there may be only one in the paragraph.

In this poem, Richard Armour gives a series of short examples about the different ways people relate to money.

Money

Workers earn it,
Spendthrifts burn it,
Bankers lend it,
Women spend it,
Forgers fake it,
Taxes take it,
Dying leave it,
Heirs receive it,
Thrifty save it,
Misers crave it,
Robbers seize it,
Rich increase it,
Gamblers lose it,
I could use it.

From "Money" by Richard Armour. Reprinted by permission of Kathleen Armour on behalf of her husband.

Watch for these transitional words in paragraphs of illustration or examples:

for example	for instance	to illustrate	such as
in particular	specifically	to demonstrate	

The main ideas in the following paragraphs on aggression are underlined. Aggression is defined as hostile assault intended to inflict harm.

*We need look no further than our daily paper or the nightly news to be bombarded with **examples** of aggression, both on a societal level (war, invasion, assassination) and on an individual level (crime, child abuse, and the many petty cruelties that humans are capable of inflicting on one another).*

Sometimes aggressive behavior is a reaction to frustration. Suppose you've been working on a paper due in class early the next morning, and your word processor printer runs out of ink just before you can print out the paper. You rush to the store to buy more ink, only to find the salesclerk locking the door for the day. Even though the clerk can see you gesturing and literally begging him to open the door, he refuses, shrugging his shoulders and pointing to a sign that indicates when the store will open the next day. At that moment, the feelings you experience toward the salesclerk probably place you on the verge of real aggression, and you are undoubtedly seething inside. Frustration produces anger, leading to a readiness to act aggressively.

From Feldman, Robert S., adapted from The Essentials of Understanding Psychology, 3rd Edition, *New York: McGraw-Hill, 1997, p. 496.*

Americans today are much more likely to take out their frustrations on other drivers. *You can't drive if you're blind, or blind drunk, but an alarming number of Americans find themselves, at least occasionally, driving in a blind rage. "It's a major social issue," says Dr. Ricardo Martinez, administrator of the National Highway Traffic Safety Administration. "A 3,000-pound car in the hands of a rude, hostile person is a lethal weapon." A report on "road rage" by the American Automobile Association concluded that "motorists . . . are increasingly being shot, stabbed, beaten and run over for inane reasons." The report cites the most common **examples** of road rage as aggressive tailgating, followed by headlight flashing, obscene gestures, blocking other vehicles, and verbal abuse. **In particular,** drivers have been assaulted with weapons ranging from partially eaten burritos to canes (a favorite with the elderly and disabled) to golf clubs—and other vehicles, including buses, bulldozers, forklifts and military tanks.*

From Adler, Jerry, "Road Rage: We're Driven to Destruction," Newsweek, June 2, 1997, p. 70.

Practice Exercise: Example

Directions: Fill in the blank with an appropriate transition word or phrase from the list below. Some of the transition words will fit in more than one of the sentences, but try to use a different transition word in each of the sentences. Make sure the sentence makes sense with the transition you choose.

for example   for instance   in particular   specifically   such as

1. Today's college classrooms include many different kinds of students, _____ Donna who entered college after working for eight years after high school.

2. One avenue of self-discovery in college is the exploration of new career choices. _____, James was originally interested in a career in teaching, but has since decided to pursue a career in business.

3. _____, James has decided to become a marketing major.

4. In the 70s, high school girls were less likely to go to college. Today, girls _____ are more likely than boys to go to college.

5. However, even today many women avoid taking academic risks. _____, they stay away from taking mathematics and science classes.

Definition Pattern

A paragraph of definition will define, clarify, or explain a key term. Definitions can be developed by providing dictionary meanings or personal meanings. They can also be developed by means of examples or by comparing and contrasting the key word to other words.

In *The Adventures of Tom Sawyer,* Mark Twain defines work as "whatever a body is obliged to do while play consists of whatever a body is not obliged to do."

The following words are clues to a paragraph of a definitive pattern:

means   is called   is defined as
refers to   is described by   term or concept

In the paragraphs below, the author of *Mind/Body Health* attempts to clarify the meaning of anger by providing concrete illustrations, describing its distinguishing characteristics, and comparing and contrasting it to other similar words.

Everyone experiences it. Just watch two toddlers fighting over a favorite set of blocks, a teenager challenging an unreasonable curfew, an executive whose car gets rear-ended on the way to an important business presentation.

*Anger is an emotion. It's temporary. It combines physiological arousal with emotional arousal. It can range in severity all the way from intense rage to "cool" anger that doesn't really involve arousal at all (and might more accurately be **described** as an* attitude, *such as resentment). People express anger in all sorts of ways such as hurling verbal insults, using profanity, slamming doors, or smashing a fist into the nearest available object.*

*The words we use **to describe** our anger strongly hint at the turmoil that is going on inside our bodies when we're angry. Some of the most common ones were pointed out by social psychologist and anger expert Carol Tavris:*

> *You make* my blood boil.
> *His pent-up anger* welled up *inside him.*
> *He was* bursting with anger.
> *I* blew my stack.
> *She* flipped her lid.
> *He* hit the ceiling.

*The **terms** anger and* hostility *are often used interchangeably **to describe** a set of negative emotions, but they are not the same. Anger has been **defined** as a temporary emotion that may or may not be accompanied by outward expression (physical or verbal). Hostility, on the other hand, is not a temporary emotion, but rather an attitude. It is anger that is expressed in aggressive behavior motivated by animosity and hatefulness.*

*"Anger is generally considered to be a simpler concept than hostility or aggression," explain researchers Margaret A. Chesney and Ray H. Rosenman. The **concept** of anger usually refers to an emotional state that consists of feelings that vary in intensity, from mild irritation or annoyance to fury and rage.*

From Mind/Body Health, *by Brent Hafen, Keith Karren, Kathryn Frandesen, and N. Lee Smith. Copyright © 1996 by Allyn and Bacon.*

Practice Exercise: Definition

Directions: Fill in the blank with an appropriate transition word or phrase from the list below. Some of the transition words will fit in more than one of the sentences, but try to use a different transition word in each of the sentences. Make sure the sentence makes sense with the transition you choose.

is called   is defined as   means   refers to   term

1. Middle age _____ the years between 40 and 65.

2. A person _____ middle-aged if he or she has grown children or elderly parents.

3. In middle age, many people now need glasses for *presbyopia,* which _____ the farsightedness associated with aging.

4. The pressures created by a society that believes in looking young, acting young, and being young—added to the real physical losses that people may

suffer as they get older—may contribute to what _____ the midlife crisis.

5. The _____ *empty nest* refers to the period when the last child leaves home.

From Papalia, Diane, and Olds, Sandy, Human Development, *6th edition, New York: McGraw-Hill, 1995, pp. 250–251.*

Chronological Order Pattern

The word *chronological* comes from the Greek root *chron*, which means "time." This pattern of organization involves arranging events in time in the order that they actually happened. For this reason, historical essays and articles that are date-oriented are usually organized by this method. Paragraphs written with this pattern are usually very easy to recognize.

This short poem illustrates the key elements of the chronological pattern because the events are ordered by time.

> **Solomon Grundy**
> Solomon Grundy
> Born on a Monday,
> Christened on Tuesday,
> Married on Wednesday,
> Took ill on Thursday,
> Worse on Friday,
> Died on Saturday,
> Buried on Sunday,
> This is the end
> Of Solomon Grundy.
>
> —Anonymous

The following are some key transition words for chronology:

before	after
during	following
in the years	a year later
any month (May, etc.)	any year (1996, etc.)
then	finally
always	at last
currently	frequently
first, second (etc.)	in the meantime
until	when
soon	next
any time (12:00, etc.)	any season (winter, etc.)

The following paragraphs from *Anger, The Misunderstood Emotion* are in the chronology pattern.

> *Popular opinion has it that time heals all wounds, that human beings are naturally resilient. But some people do not heal from the wounds of divorce. In* **1971,** *Judith Wallerstein, then working with Joan Kelly, began a study of 131 children and adolescents from sixty families, and their divorcing parents, in Marin County, California. The researchers reinterviewed all family members* **eighteen**

months later, again *five years after* divorce, *and again* **ten and fifteen years after** *divorce. The parents were upper-middle-class, mostly white, and had been married anywhere from four to twenty-three years. The children were all developmentally normal, doing well in school, and in good psychological health—* **until** *the divorce hit them.*

Wallerstein found that even **after ten years,** *half of the women and one-third of the men in her study were still intensely angry at their former spouses, and that the consequences of this anger and conflict for their children were often disastrous.*

Tavris, Carol, Anger, The Misunderstood Emotion, *New York: A Touchstone Book published by Simon & Schuster, 1989, p. 300.*

Practice Exercise: Chronological Order

Directions: Fill in the blank with an appropriate transition word or phrase from the list below. Some of the transition words will fit in more than one of the sentences, but try to use a different transition word in each of the sentences. Make sure the sentence makes sense with the transition you choose.

following   frequently   1853   1890   then   until

1. In _____ , Vincent Van Gogh was born to a Dutch Protestant minister in the town of Groot-Zundert, in Holland.

2. His early life was spent as a lay preacher to the miners of the region and so not _____ the age of 27 did he begin to take a serious interest in art.

3. _____ , he went to live with his brother Theo, an art dealer in France, where he met the painter Paul Gauguin.

4. The two artists _____ quarreled, and after one very intense argument, Van Gogh cut off a portion of his ear.

5. _____ that bizarre incident, Van Gogh committed himself to an asylum where much of the work we now admire, including "Starry Night," was created.

6. Unfortunately, his despair deepened, and so in July of _____ he shot himself to death.

From Gilbert, Rita, from Living with Art, *4th edition, New York: McGraw-Hill, 1995, p. 13.*

Exercise #1 on Patterns of Organization

Directions: Identify the dominant pattern of organization for each paragraph. You may look at the preceding pages of transition words if necessary.

1. Quick French Onion Soup (serves 4–6)
   In medium fry pan, first saute onion in butter until golden and tender, about 15 minutes. Next, stir in flour. Then add remaining ingredients. Simmer uncovered at least 20 minutes, stirring occasionally. Serve piping hot. For a final touch, if desired, top with melba toast and shredded Gruyere cheese.

Clues: _____

2. In ancient Rome, whenever a man wished to be elected to a public office, he canvassed for votes wearing a white robe or toga. The purpose of this was to enable the populace to easily recognize him. The Latin word for white is *candidus*, so the potential official came to be known as a *candidatus*, meaning "a person clothed in white." From this derivation comes our English word *candidate*.

Clues: _____

3. If you were a child growing up in the 50s and you used the f-word, there would probably have been at least a discussion, and more than likely, a bar of soap would have been put to good use. In contrast, today this word is uttered routinely just about everywhere. Kids hear the word riding the bus to school, in class, in the lyrics of many songs, and on regular network TV. In the 50s, profanity was a shocking rarity. But, in the 90s, profanity has become part of our language. Some psychologists even say using curse words is healthy because it allows us to express our deepest emotions. Young people of today are so used to hearing the f-word that many linguists predict it will end up meaning as little as the standard curse word of the 50s, "hell."

Clues: _____

4. One hundred years ago, no one "exercised" because their daily life was strenuous enough. As a direct result of the many labor-saving devices we have today, the typical American's weight is rising. Most Americans don't participate in athletics, and many hire others to do their routine home-maintenance chores. Thus, they get almost no vigorous exercise. The most exercise many get is changing the channel on the remote control. The sad consequence of becoming a sedentary, TV-watching nation is that one in three adults are currently overweight.

Clues: _____

5. The Ripley's Museum in Orlando, Florida, is apparently the place to go for those seeking to start a family. In late 1994, two ebony fertility statues were placed in the office lobby. Three employees immediately became pregnant after rubbing the belly of the statue. In another instance, three wives of office personnel all became pregnant despite the fact one was using birth-control pills. In another example, eight women who visited the office became pregnant, including a woman who accidentally bumped into the statue while delivering a package. One Texas woman with five daughters recently came to make the pilgrimage in the hope of having a son. She's convinced the "reproductive magic" will work for her.

Clues: _____

6. Is the cartoon character of Krusty the Clown, in the popular *Simpsons* TV show, based on David Letterman? Krusty and Letterman, in addition to their ever-present cigarette/cigar, have many things in common. Both are compulsive, irascible, perfectionistic, and generally difficult to be around, especially for their staff. Also, neither one is supposed to like kids. If you

look closely the next time you see Krusty, you will even notice a strong physical resemblance to Letterman.

Clues: _____

Exercise #2 on Patterns of Organization

Directions: Choose the correct pattern of organization by noting the transitional words.

1. After the Thanksgiving holiday is over, many people have gained an average of six pounds. They tend to feel both fat and remorseful. Here are some suggestions from experts in exercise and nutrition in how to lose excess pounds. Dietitian Keith Thomas Ayoob suggests treating the television as an activity box. Whenever the TV is on, do things such as stretching exercises or marching in place. Anything is better than just sitting there. Mary Lee Chin, dietitian, suggests donating fattening holiday gifts such as boxes of candy to charity. She also suggests packaging small bags of dried fruit to keep in the car for snacks. Mackie Shilstone, sports performance director, suggests participating in a half-hour of moderate physical activity every day. Other suggestions include drinking lots of water, pushing your plate away when you're full, and eating special treats early in the morning rather than late at night. Hopefully these examples from nutritionists will help people lead a healthier lifestyle that might lead to eventual weight loss.

(From USA Today, *January 13, 1996, "Life" Section, p. 1.)*

Clues: _____

2. As the car became more important in American lives, it radically altered the homes we live in. First, the garage was moved from the back of a plot of land to the front. Next, the garage was integrated into the actual design of the home. Later, primarily in the suburbs, the garage provided an entry from the kitchen and took over the function of the front porch. Finally, the car was included as part of the family and even took on petlike characteristics.

(From Marsh, Peter, and Collett, Peter, "Driving Passion," Psychology Today, *June 1987, p. 18.)*

Clues: _____

3. Psychologists define thoughts as daydreams if they are about something apart from the person's immediate situation, if they are spontaneous, and if they happen in ways that are perceived as being contrary to reality. Most daydreams are pleasant, wishful creations of the imagination.

(From Klinger, Eric, "The Powers of Daydreams," Psychology Today, *October 1987, p. 37.)*

Clues: _____

4. Questionnaires have found some key gender differences in regard to sexual fantasy. Men usually daydream about real events they have experienced in their past or in the present. Women, on the contrary, have daydreams about imaginary situations.

(From Klinger, Eric, "The Powers of Daydreams," Psychology Today, October 1987, p. 39.)

Clues: _____

5. Psychologists Karen Dion, Ellen Berscheid, and Elaine Hatfield found in 1972 that when people are good-looking, we assume many other good things about them. Most researchers have uncovered a self-fulfilling prophecy. Because attractive people are treated as if they have more to offer, they live up to our positive expectations. As a result, good-looking people turn out to have higher self-esteem and to be happier, less neurotic, and more resistant to peer pressure than those who are less attractive. Because of our affirmation, those blessed with good looks also have more influence on others, get higher salaries, receive more lenient decisions in court, are thought by their students to be superior teachers, and are more valued as friends, colleagues, and lovers. "The way we treat attractive versus unattractive people shapes the way they think about themselves," says University of Hawaii psychologist Hatfield, "and as a consequence, the kind of people they become."

(From Kohn, Alfie, "You Know What They Say . . .," Psychology Today, April 1988, p. 39.)

Clues: _____

6. Psychologist Liz Zelinski of the University of Southern California tested people's ability to read and understand brief passages. In a study comparing the elderly to young people, she discovered that people in their 70s and 80s showed no significant decline in comprehension. Similarly, Zelinski found that older men and women read her tests just as fast as younger people do. In most areas, the elderly learn to substitute experience for speed. Psychologist Neil Charness discovered that in bridge, if given enough time, the bids and the moves that the elderly chose were every bit as good as those of younger players. This is good news for the over-65 population.

(From Meer, Jeff, "The Reason of Age," Psychology Today, June 1986, p. 63.)

Clues: _____

Exercise #3 on Patterns of Organization

The paragraphs below have been taken from the college textbook *Public Speaking for College and Career* by Hamilton Gregory.

Directions: Choose the correct pattern of organization by noting the transitional words.

1. In the late 80s, Aldrich "Rick" Ames, the infamous CIA agent who sold out to the Russkies, starts arriving at work in clothes more appropriate for a banker than a bureaucrat, and *nobody cares*. Then he flies to Switzerland to stash a million bucks, and *nobody notices*. Next, he plunks down cash for a new Jaguar, new teeth, and a new house, and *nobody raises a fuss*. So what finally trips him up? His directory of computer files. In 1993, Ames and his CIA boss attend a conference in Turkey. Ames brings along a notebook personal computer packed with computer games . . . and megabytes of purloined government secrets. His boss asks to play one of the games, and when he looks to see what's on the hard disk, just happens to notice a file for Rick's Russian contact along with tons of classified info. Ames is nabbed. (153)

Clues: _____

2. Our daily lives are enriched by other countries and by the diversity of American society. Consider this example of a typical American citizen. Each morning she wakes up in a bed (an invention from the Near East). She puts on clothes made in Taiwan, Mexico, and Jamaica, shoes from Spain and a wristwatch from Switzerland, jewelry from Kenya and perfume from France. She eats breakfast at a table made in Sweden, using plates from Korea and a tablecloth from India. Her breakfast includes a banana from Honduras and coffee from Colombia. While driving to work in a car made in Japan, she listens to music performed by a band from Cuba. For lunch at a restaurant, she can choose from a wide variety of ethnic cuisines—Thai, Italian, Chinese, Mexican, Korean, Vietnamese, Egyptian, and more. Throughout the day, she is likely to use or benefit from products invented by immigrants to the United States and their descendants. Her health, for example, is protected by an oral polio vaccine, developed by Albert B. Sabin, a Polish immigrant. (14)

Clues: _____

3. Medical researchers have found that the average human needs about eight hours of sleep each night in order to function well on the job, on the highway, in school, and in the home. But the majority of Americans try to get by on less than eight hours; in fact, 80 percent get six hours of sleep or less each night. Perhaps the most insidious consequence of skimping on sleep is the irritability that increasingly pervades society. Weariness corrodes civility and erases humor, traits that ease the myriad daily frustrations, from standing in supermarket lines to refereeing the kids' squabbles. Because people go without sufficient sleep, tempers flare faster and hotter at the slightest offense. (32)

Clues: _____

4. Which of the following kinds of speakers have you ever encountered?

    Robots are lifeless speakers who have no energy and no desire to reach the audience. They prepare dull, uninteresting speeches which they deliver without a trace of enthusiasm.

    Fountains of Knowledge, who are enthusiastic and knowledgeable about their subject, expect the audience to absorb their ideas as easily as a sponge soaking up water. So they pour out a huge amount of information.

Jerks are thoughtless speakers who wrongly assume that listeners share their prejudices or their twisted notions of what is funny.

Performers at first seem to be perfect speakers: they have good eye contact, strong voices, confident posture. But they talk *at* their listeners rather than *with* them. They perform rather than communicate, and they are oblivious to their listeners' needs and interests.

What all four of these types have in common is a low sensitivity to their audience—a failure to understand and reach the people sitting in front of them. (64–65)

Clues: _____

5. Albert Einstein could present his incredibly complex theories to his scientific peers in language that was appropriately sophisticated for their level of understanding; yet he could also adjust his speech for the benefit of the 99.9 percent of the population who couldn't begin to comprehend his theories. He once made part of his theory of relativity understandable to the average person by using this analogy: "Time is relative. If you sit on a park bench with your girl friend for an hour, it seems like a minute. But if you sit on a hot stove for a minute, it seems like an hour." By emphasizing the differences between the two events, Einstein demonstrated that time seems to speed up or slow down in relation to other events. (78)

Clues: _____

Additional Transition Words

While lists of transition words are helpful, the groupings of the words given in this section are not perfect, and many of these words may be placed in more than one category. The only way to truly determine the function of a transition word is by studying the context of the sentence and the paragraph.

Summary and Conclusion	Spatial Order
finally	above
in brief	below
in short	beyond
overall	on top
hence	underneath
so	near
therefore	next to
thus	front
to conclude	center
to sum up	left
in summary	right
in conclusion	

Reversal	**Addition**
unlike	again
nevertheless	also
instead	and
yet	another
still	further
granted that	furthermore
	in addition
Emphasis	moreover
as indicated	as well as
as noted	besides
here again	too
once again	
to repeat	**Concession**
it's important to remember	despite
truly	although
certainly	in spite of
without a doubt	even though
unquestionably	
to emphasize	

More Practice with Transitions

Directions: To gain additional practice with transitions, read the following excerpt and then answer the questions that follow. You may need to refer to both of the transition word charts.

"Police Power in Japan"

READING

It is midnight in Tokyo. Downtown streets are filled with pedestrians, strollers abound in the park, bicycles sit unchained on the street, many front doors are unlocked, and children under eight years of age are even seen riding alone on the subway. As much of a culture shock as this may be to a visitor from the United States, an additional surprise comes the next morning when virtually no crimes are reported.

Tokyo has the lowest rates of murder, rape, robbery, and theft of any major city in the world. A **comparison** of crime rates in the United States **and** Japan per 100,000 inhabitants shows that the United States has about 6 times **as** many burglaries, more than 9 times as many murders, 19 times as many reported rapes, about 45 times as many cases of arson, and close to 90 times as many aggravated assaults. **Yet** Japan has fewer police officers per capita: 1 for every 557 residents, compared with 1 for every 357 residents in the United States.

Why is there so little crime in Japan? The country's low rate of unemployment and comparatively egalitarian distribution of wealth contribute to social cohesiveness and harmony. **Moreover**, the cultural values of the Japanese help to promote law-abiding behavior and cooperation with police officers. As part of their early socialization, children are encouraged to respect authority figures and place great value on self-discipline. In schools, young people are taught to accept codes of responsible behavior associated with citizenship. Throughout Japan, there is persistent community disapproval of wrongdoing and socially deviant behavior is not excused. Indeed, Japanese culture ostracizes offenders and demands that they confess and show remorse.

Gun control is also a factor in the comparatively low rates of serious crime in Japan. Apart from those held by the police, there are only 49 legal handguns in Japan, all held at shooting ranges for highly skilled marksmen. While shotguns and hunting rifles are allowed, there are strict restrictions on their ownership and use. A person caught with a loaded gun faces a 15-year prison term, **so** many street criminals do not carry guns. **Consequently,** in 1994, only 38 people in Japan were murdered by a person using a firearm.

5   Still another factor contributing to low crime rates is the absolute trust that the Japanese have in the police. Outside observers believe that people's faith in the police results in good part from their extraordinary 99.83 percent conviction rate. **But** an examination of police–community interactions offers quite a different explanation for the power of the police and the low rate of crime. Once or twice a year, the police knock on every door in Japan to speak with residents or business owners about conditions in the building and neighborhood. Japanese people do not regard this as harassment, but rather as an example of the police taking a personal interest in their welfare.

Small police boxes, known as *kobans,* are located in all urban neighborhoods and are staffed by two officers at all times. These 1,250 *kobans* report to Tokyo's 99 police stations, which in turn report to nine district headquarters. The *koban* officials are the first line of police response to a crime or crisis, **yet** they more often function as information brokers, providing information about locations and addresses in Tokyo's confusing maze of houses and businesses. When a person seeks police assistance, he or she typically goes to a *koban.* Consequently, the Japanese tend to look favorably on the *koban* system, rather than fearing its social functions.

In recent years the power of Japan's police has come under fire. International human rights groups criticize the police for such practices as conducting investigations without allowing suspects access to a lawyer and jailing suspects for up to 23 days without filing criminal charges. Yet there are no broad public demands for curtailing the power of the police. Indeed, even in death penalty cases, the Japanese seem to completely trust the police. When convicted criminals are executed, the police make no announcement and the media offer no coverage. These executions come to light only at the end of each year when the police release crime data.

From Sociology: A Brief Introduction, *by Robert T. Schaefer and Robert P. Lamm, 1989. Reprinted by permission of The McGraw-Hill Companies.*

Questions:

1. What is the function of paragraph 1? _____

2. In paragraph 4, describe the cause-and-effect relationship.

Cause: _____

Effect: _____

Vocabulary

Using context from the essay, define the following words. Then consult your dictionary to see how accurate your definition is.

3. strollers *abound* in the park (Paragraph 1)

Definition: _____

4. social *cohesiveness* and harmony (Paragraph 3)

Definition: _____

5. Japanese culture *ostracizes* offenders (Paragraph 3)

Definition: _____

6. confess and show *remorse* (Paragraph 3)

Definition: _____

7. Tokyo's confusing *maze* of houses and businesses (Paragraph 6)

Definition: _____

8. public demands for *curtailing* the power of the police (Paragraph 7)

Definition: _____

**IN YOUR
OWN WORDS**

1. Violent crimes are far more common in the United States than in Japan. What factors mentioned in the essay help explain why the United States has such a high rate of violent crime?

2. Do you think the easy availability of guns contributes to the higher rates of violent crime in the United States? Are you in favor of more gun control? Why or why not?

3. Do you think putting more police officers on the streets would help solve the U.S. crime problem? Or will it turn the United States into a "police state"? Why or why not?

4. Although the United States already has the highest percentage of its population in prison of any country in the world, many say we need to get tougher on crime. What is your opinion?

Chapter 4 Test: "Police Power in Japan"

Multiple Choice

1. The main idea expressed in this selection is that
    a. Japanese respect for police is a major factor in keeping the crime rate low.
    b. The average Japanese citizen believes the police have too much power.
    c. Media coverage of executions helps keep the crime rate low.
    d. International human rights groups are highly critical of the power of the Japanese police.

2. The transition words in paragraph 2 indicate the following pattern of organization.
    a. cause and effect.
    b. compare and contrast.
    c. definition.
    d. steps in a process.

3. The transition word *moreover* in paragraph 3 indicates
   a. contrast.
   b. addition.
   c. reversal.
   d. conclusion.

4. The best definition of the word *egalitarian* as used in paragraph 3 is
   a. equal.
   b. unequal.
   c. coordinated.
   d. synonymous.

5. In paragraph 5, what does the transition word *but* signal?
   a. addition
   b. conclusion
   c. comparison
   d. contrast

6. In paragraph 6, the transition word *yet* indicates
   a. spatial order.
   b. reversal.
   c. addition.
   d. steps in a process.

True or False

_____   7. The U.S. has a lower rate of aggravated assaults than does Japan.

_____   8. Only 38 people were murdered in Japan by a person using a gun.

_____   9. In Japan, it is possible to be in jail for over three weeks without having a criminal charge filed.

_____   10. Violent crimes are less common in Japan than in the United States.

Writing Summaries

In your reading and English classes, you will be called upon to write summaries. **Summarizing** simply means restating the main ideas in your own words. Because many supporting details are omitted, a summary is much shorter than the original on which it is based. When you write summaries, you need to present the main ideas in order of importance in an objective fashion. Keep in mind that you are reporting the author's viewpoints and not your own. When writing a summary, you never write something like "I feel," "I think," or "it seems to me." Instead, you always write only the author's opinions. A summary is always a recapturing of what the author feels, thinks, or believes.

It takes a great deal of practice to learn how to write a good summary. However, since we have now learned how to identify directly stated main ideas and how to write implied ones, we are ready to begin learning how to write a summary of a short article. In Chapter 1, you read an article by Walter S. Minot entitled "Students Who Push Burgers." This is a relatively easy article to summarize because the author presents his main ideas in a logical sequence. Try to locate the directly stated main ideas. Because not all of the main ideas are stated directly, you are also going to have to come up with several implied main ideas.

In order to identify the key supporting details, try to answer as many of the question words (who, what, where, when, why, and how) about the topic as possible.

Directions for Assignment

1. Provide answers to who, what, where, when, why, and how. (Not all of these question words will apply to every article.)

2. List five to six main ideas from the article. Paraphrase each main idea. The overall main idea of the article is: *Student employment is a major cause of the decline in American education.*

3. Write at least a half-page summary of the article. Be sure to include the information from numbers 1 and 2 in your summary.

Who: _____

_____

What: _____

_____

Where: _____

_____

When: _____

_____

Why: _____

_____

How: _____

_____

1st Main Idea: _____

_____

2nd Main Idea: _____

_____

3rd Main Idea: _____

_____

4th Main Idea: _____

_____

5th Main Idea: _____

_____

When you have finished recording all of this information, you are ready to begin writing a summary. Your completed summary should contain no trivia (useless information), and should not be redundant (give the same information more than once). Remember to present the information in an organized way by using transition words. After writing your summary, compare your version with the student sample given below.

Your summary: _____

_____

_____

_____

_____

_____

Student Sample:

Who: high school and college students

What: are spending too little time studying and too much time working

Where: in the United States in contrast with other industrialized countries

When: the author compares attitudes in the 50s with attitudes in the late 80s

Why: students work to buy luxury items parents won't pay for

How: because of increased acceptance on the part of parents and teachers

Overall Main Idea:

Student employment is a major cause of the decline in American education.

Other Main Ideas:

1. Today student employment is widely accepted as normal for teens, but in the past going to school was a student's "job."

2. Working students have little time for homework. (Directly stated.)

3. Students work to buy luxury items and then feel they need to go out and have fun.

4. Thus, by the time they get to college, most students look upon studies as a spare-time activity. (Directly stated.)

5. The problem doesn't just affect the individual student, but our country as a whole, because the full-time students from other countries outperform the part-time students from the United States.

Student Summary

Walter S. Minot in his article "Students Who Push Burgers" feels that U.S. education has declined because students hold part-time jobs. Minot compares the educational system of the 1950s with that of the 1980s. In the past, kids only worked to help their families out financially. In contrast, he says, today's students work to buy luxury items, fooling their parents into thinking that they are learning the value of a dollar. Because these students work so hard at their jobs, they feel they deserve to have a good time after work, and they don't have enough time or energy to do their homework. As a result, schools are finding it difficult to get quality work from their students and have had to reduce their standards. Minot feels this problem doesn't just affect individual students or schools, but our country as a whole. According to Minot, one reason our economy has slowed is because the part-time students of the United States are being outperformed by the full-time students of other countries.

Review Test 3: Main Idea, Details, Purpose, Transitions, and
Patterns of Organization

Directions: Each of the following paragraphs related to aggressive behavior was adapted from commonly used psychology textbooks. Read each passage. Then choose the best answer for each item.

> *Psychologists define* aggression *as behavior intended to hurt. Throughout the world, hunting, fighting, and warring are primarily men's activities. In surveys, men admit to more aggression than women do. In laboratory experiments, men exhibit more physical aggression by administering what they believe are hurtful shocks. In Canada, the male-to-female arrest rate is 11 to 1 for murder and 8 to 1 for assault. In the United States, it is 10 to 1 for murder and 5 to 1 for assault.*

Across the world murder rates vary. Yet in all regions, men are roughly 20 times more likely to murder men than women are to murder women. However, in less violent forms of aggression—say, slapping a family member or verbally attacking someone—women are no less aggressive than men.

From Myers, David, Social Psychology, *5th Edition, New York: McGraw-Hill, 1996, p. 200.*

1. In the first sentence of this paragraph, the author uses a(n)
    a. cause-and-effect relationship.
    b. definition.
    c. example.
    d. contrast.

2. The body of the paragraph is organized to
    a. make a contrast.
    b. show steps in a process.
    c. show events in chronological order.
    d. give a definition.

3. The last sentence of the paragraph is written to
    a. define what was described above it.
    b. show a cause-and-effect relationship.
    c. show steps in a process.
    d. show a contrast with the body of the paragraph.

It is 9 o'clock on a warm evening. Tired and thirsty, after two hours of studying, you borrow some change from a friend and head for the nearest soft-drink machine. As the machine devours the change, you can almost taste the cold, refreshing cola. But when you push the button, nothing happens. Yet you push it again. Then you hit the buttons. You slam them. And finally you shake and whack the machine. A few minutes later, you stomp back to your studies, empty-handed, and short-changed. Should your roommate beware? Are you now more likely to say or do something harmful?

From Myers, p. 441.

4. The author has written this paragraph using the following method:
    a. definition
    b. comparison
    c. classification
    d. chronological order

5. The example of the student and the vending machine was used to illustrate
    a. the difficulties of a student's life.
    b. the relationship between frustration and aggression.
    c. the problems with vending machines.
    d. the wide variety of things that can go wrong in a day.

*One of the first psychological theories of aggression, the popular frustration–aggression theory, says that a person who has suffered frustration is more likely to do or say something harmful. "Frustration always leads to some form of aggression," said John Dollard and his colleagues. **Frustration** is anything (such as the malfunctioning vending machine) that blocks our attaining a goal. Frustration grows when our desire to achieve a goal is very strong, when we expected satisfaction, and when the blocking is complete.*

From Myers, pp. 441–442.

6. The main purpose of this paragraph is to
   a. entertain.
   b. inform or explain.
   c. persuade.
   d. criticize.

7. Which of the following best describes the organizational pattern of this paragraph?
   a. definition and explanation
   b. examples and classification
   c. comparison and contrast
   d. classification and division

Our aggressive energy doesn't necessarily explode directly against the cause. We learn to inhibit direct retaliation, especially when others might disapprove of us or punish us; instead we displace our hostilities to safer targets. Displacement occurs in the old anecdote about a man who, because he is humiliated by his boss, scolds his wife, who yells at their son, who kicks the dog, which bites the mail carrier.

From Myers, p. 442.

8. The author in the last sentence of this paragraph uses which of the following:
   a. comparison
   b. classification
   c. cause and effect
   d. definition

What kind of stimuli act as aggressive cues? They can range from the most obvious, such as the presence of weapons, to the subtlest, such as the mere mention of the name of an individual who has behaved violently in the past. For example, in one experiment, angered subjects were more aggressive when in the presence of a rifle and revolver than in a similar situation in which no guns were present. It appears, then, that frustration does lead to aggression, at least when aggressive cues are present.

From Feldman, Robert S., The Essentials of Understanding Psychology, 3rd Edition, New York: McGraw-Hill 1997, p. 496.

9. Which of the following does the author <u>not</u> use in this paragraph?
   a. an example
   b. a contrast
   c. a definition
   d. a cause and effect statement

10. The main idea expressed in this passage is that
    a. frustration can more easily lead to aggression when aggressive cues are present.
    b. aggressive cues can be subtle or obvious.
    c. people behave more aggressively when in the presence of weapons.
    d. psychologists don't know what kind of stimuli act as aggressive cues.

PART 3 | Interpreting What We Read

In jazz, each player must be a clever musician, an originator as well as an interpreter.

from Carl Engel, head of the music division of the Library of Congress

Just as musicians interpret a piece of music, so readers interpret written material. The author of a written piece will try to use words in the way that best communicates the intended meaning. In seeking to understand an author's meaning, a reader must interpret the words the author has written down, and the only way the reader can do this is through the filter of his or her own skills, experiences, and personality. While no two readers end up with precisely the same understanding of what the author has meant, some interpretations will be better than others in discovering the author's intended meaning. Being a good interpreter requires a knowledge of inference, figurative language, and tone, and the purpose of Part 3 is to increase your understanding of these topics.

Chapter 5

Inference

Introduction and Exercises

We make inferences, or intelligent guesses, every day of our lives. If a teacher sees a student looking at his watch and tapping his foot, the teacher will likely assume the student is anxious to leave class. If a person comes home from work and slams the door, most of us will deduce that the person is angry or upset about something. If Maria's dog doesn't move all day, she's likely to assume her pet is sick and needs to go to the vet.

We negotiate through life by means of "cues." We are constantly "reading" situations and adjusting our actions. If we see a car weaving down the road late at night, most of us will become concerned that the driver may be intoxicated and so we try to stay out of the way.

Look at the picture below and see if you can make some logical inferences.

1. _____
2. _____
3. _____
4. _____

We can infer that the scene is probably a child's birthday party at a fast-food restaurant, even though no birthday cake is present. We note the tables and chairs, the decor, the age of the children, the paper hats, and especially the balloons,

146

which usually indicate a celebration of some sort. Our inference could still be wrong, but we took the available evidence and put it together in a plausible way. We do the exact same thing in our reading.

In prose or poetry, we must be alert for cues to determine the writer's true meaning. The following paragraph describes an incident that occurred between Elliott Roosevelt, son of President Franklin Roosevelt, and Elliott's mother, Eleanor, in the White House.

> *Elliott Roosevelt used to tell this story about his mother, Eleanor. At a state dinner where she was seated next to him, she leaned over and whispered into his ear. When a friend later asked Elliott, then in his forties, what she had said, he answered, "She told me to eat my peas."*

From Papalia, Diane, and Olds, Sandy, Human Development, *6th edition, New York: McGraw-Hill, 1995, p. 516.*

The key to understanding this anecdote is Elliott Roosevelt's age. It is normal behavior for a mother to tell a 4-year-old to clean his plate, but not a 40-year-old, and definitely not at a formal state dinner in the White House. We can infer that Eleanor Roosevelt had difficulty treating Elliott like an adult.

Now read the poem "Indian Names," by Lydia Sigourney, and record the inferences you can make.

> Ye say they all have pass'd away
>> That noble race and brave;
> That their light canoes have vanish'd
>> From off the crested wave;
> That mid the forests where they roam'd,
>> There rings no hunter's shout;
> But their name is on your waters,
>> Ye may not wash it out . . .

From Sigourney, Lydia Huntley, 1st stanza from "Indian Names," found in Donald Hall, editor, The Oxford Book of Children's Verse in America, *New York: Oxford University Press, 1985, p. 24.*

1. _____
2. _____
3. _____
4. _____

We can infer that the speaker is not a Native American, or is writing as though she is not one, because she uses the pronoun "their." It also appears as if a conversation is occurring between two or more people because the speaker says "ye say." Because of the speaker's use of the word "but," signaling a contrast, it seems likely that an opposing viewpoint is being expressed. The speaker is challenging the ideas of either another person or society in general. You can also infer from the tone of the poem, and the use of the word "noble," that the speaker's point of view toward Native Americans is respectful. At the end, the speaker reminds us that even though particular Native American tribes may have vanished, their influence is present in the names of many places (for example, Lake Huron).

You have probably heard the expression "to read between the lines." This means figuring out an idea that is not directly stated in what you are reading.

No matter how old a mother is, she watches her middle-age children for signs of improvement.

Florida Scott-Maxwell

When you "draw inferences," you make educated guesses using the clues provided by the writer, your own experience, and logic.

In order to understand the next passage, you must determine the meaning of the word *hora*, which can only be accomplished by reading the last two sentences of the paragraph. After reading the passage, circle the letter of the most logical answer to the questions.

A corporate president recently made a visit to a nearby reservation as part of his firm's public relations program. "We realize that we have not hired any Native Americans in the five years our company has been located in this area," he told those assembled, "but we are looking into the matter very carefully." "Hora, hora," said some of the audience. "We would like to eventually hire 5 percent of our total workforce from this reservation," he said. "Hora, hora," shouted more of the audience. Encouraged by their enthusiasm, the president closed his short speech by telling them that he hoped his firm would be able to take some hiring action within the next couple of years. "Hora, hora, hora," cried the total group. With a feeling of satisfaction the president left the hall and was taken on a tour of the reservation. Stepping in a field to admire some of the horses grazing there, the president asked if he could walk up closer to the animals. "Certainly," said his driver, "but be careful not to step in the hora."

From Langan, James, Ten Steps to Improving Reading Skills, *Marlton, NJ: Townsend Press, 1992, pp. 267–268.*

1. To get the main point of the passage, the reader must infer
   a. the location of the reservation.
   b. what kind of company the president headed.
   c. the meaning of the word *hora*.

2. From the president's speech, we can infer that
   a. his firm had great interest in hiring Native Americans.
   b. his firm had little interest in hiring Native Americans.

3. From the passage, we can infer that
   a. the audience believed the president's speech.
   b. the audience did not believe the president's speech.

4. From the passage we can infer that the president
   a. thought the Native Americans deserved to be hired.
   b. thought his company should not hire the Native Americans.
   c. misinterpreted the Native Americans' reaction to his speech.

5. From the passage, we can infer that the main reason the president spoke to the Native Americans about jobs was that
   a. they needed the jobs.
   b. he thought promising jobs to Native Americans would make his company look good.
   c. he thought hiring Native Americans would be good for his company.

If we understand the meaning of the word *hora*, we realize that the Native Americans recognized early on that the corporate president was engaging in "empty promises" and had no intention of hiring very many of them. We noted the fact that the firm had been in the area for five years and had not yet hired a single Native American. Moreover, the president was not promising to remedy the situation immediately, but was promising 5 percent employment within "the next couple of years," again indicating no real commitment on his firm's part.

You can see how experience can play a role in our ability to understand inferences. Those of us who know more about how businesses sometimes handle problems with community relations may more easily see the cues indicating the president's lack of sincerity. In this case, the joke was on the corporate president, whose feeling of satisfaction with his speech was completely unjustified.

In your reading, you are more likely to encounter the need to draw inferences in imaginative literature. Nonfiction is likely to rely on direct statements calling for no interpretation on your part. In the first sentence below, the happiness described is not open to debate. In the second sentence, we must infer Marilyn's happiness based on our experience, which tells us that a smile usually indicates happiness.

Example:

1. Marilyn was happy.

2. Marilyn's face was wreathed with a smile.

In the exercises that follow, you will be given an opportunity to practice making inferences.

Exercise #1 Drawing Inferences

After reading the dialogue in the cartoon, try to answer the following questions. Write down the clues that helped you. If there are not enough clues in the cartoon to enable you to answer the question, write "can't tell."

DOONESBURY   **BY GARRY TRUDEAU**

Doonesbury © 1995 G. B. Trudeau. Reprinted with permission of UNIVERSAL PRESS SYNDICATE. All rights reserved

                                                                              Clues

1. What class is the student writing a paper for?   _____

2. What is the student using for reference material?   _____

3. Is the student working in the library?   _____

4. Is the student guilty of plagiarism?   _____

5. Is the student showing his paper to a teacher?   _____

6. Does the adult believe the paper is the student's
   own work?   _____

Try to analyze this cartoon just as we did on the other page. Remember to read between the lines to discover the attitudes and values that are expressed indirectly.

Shoe

© Tribune Media Services, Inc. All Rights Reserved. Reprinted with permission.

1. What kind of booth is the smoker expecting to get?_____
2. Why did the maitre'd send him to a phone booth? _____
3. Does the cartoon reflect a positive or a negative view of smoking?_____
4. Could proponents of smoking find something in this cartoon to support their viewpoint? _____

Exercise #2 Inferences/Proverbs

A proverb is a traditional saying that offers advice or presents a moral. In order to understand proverbs, you must be able to read between the lines. Proverbs cannot be read in the literal sense. For example, the proverb "Don't put all your eggs in one basket" is not really concerned with collecting eggs. What it implies is that it is not a good idea to rely on just one thing.

Directions: What can you logically infer about the meaning of these proverbs? Working with a partner, see how well you can explain them.

1. The leopard does not change his spots.
2. The early bird catches the worm.
3. The squeaky wheel gets the grease.
4. Every cloud has a silver lining.
5. Don't cross the bridge till you come to it.
6. A bad workman blames his tools.
7. You can lead a horse to water, but you can't make him drink.

Can you identify these well-known proverbs? They have been rewritten with synonyms for key words. Use your dictionary if necessary.

1. Birds of similar plumage assemble.
2. Sanitation is next to piousness.
3. An examined kettle does not bubble.
4. It is not possible to instruct ancient canines in fresh wiles.
5. Where there is fume, there is blaze.
6. Inspect before you bound.
7. Persons who dwell in crystal domiciles should not fling pebbles.

Exercise #3 Drawing Inferences from Popular Literature

Read each of the following excerpts from popular literature and use inferential reasoning to answer the questions that follow.

I suppose it was inevitable that my brother and I would get into one big fight which also would be the last one. When it came, given our theories about street fighting, it was like the Battle Hymn, terrible and swift. There are parts of it I did not see. I did not see our mother walk between us to try to stop us. She was short and wore glasses and, even with them on, did not have good vision. She had never seen a fight before or had any notion of how bad you can get hurt by becoming mixed up in one. Evidently, she just walked between her sons. The first I saw of her was the gray top of her head, the hair tied in a big knot with a big comb in it; but what was most noticeable was that her head was so close to Paul I couldn't get a good punch at him. Then I didn't see her anymore.

From Maclean, Norman, A River Runs Through It, *New York: Pocket Books, 1992, p. 9.*

1. What happened to the boys' mother? _____

All he would have to do would be to slip the translation out of his desk, copy it, put it away, and he would pass the examination. All of his worries would be over. His father would be happy that he passed the examination. He wouldn't have to go to summer school. He and Charlie could go out to Colorado together to work on that dude ranch. He would be through with Latin forever. The Latin grade would never pull his average down again. Everything would be all right. Everything would be fine. All he would have to do would be to copy that one paragraph. Everyone cheated. Maybe not at V.P.S. But in other schools they bragged about it. . . . Everyone cheated in one way or another. Why should that one passage ruin everything? Who cared what problems the Romans had!

From Bryan, C.D.B., "So Much Unfairness of Things," in Ten Top Stories, *edited by David A. Sohn, New York: Bantam, 1964, p. 55, from* New Yorker Magazine, *1962.*

1. What subject is the student having difficulty with? _____
2. How is he rationalizing his decision? _____

"C'mon, mama's boy," Bull whispered. "Bring little mama's boy up to Daddy Bull." Right hand, left hand, right hand, left hand, the ball drummed against the cement as Ben waited for his father to move out against him and Bull held back, fearing the drive to the basket. At the foul line, Ben left his feet for the jump shot, eyed the basket at the top of his leap, let it go softly, the wrist snapping, the fingers pointing at the rim and the ball spinning away from him as Bull lunged forward and drove his shoulder into Ben's stomach, knocking him to the ground. Though he did not see the ball go in, he heard the shouts of his mother and sisters; he saw Matthew leaping up and down on the porch. He felt his father rise off him slowly, coming up beaten by a son for the first time in his life. Screaming with joy, Ben jumped up and was immediately flooded by his family, who hugged, slapped, pummeled, and kissed him.

From Conroy, Pat, The Great Santini, *New York: Bantam, 1994, p. 121.*

1. What kind of relationship does Ben have with his father? _____

2. Is the family rooting for the father or the son? _____

3. What can we infer about Bull's character from this excerpt? _____

_____

> *In the few days between arrival at Harvard Law School and the first classes, there are rumors. And stories. About being singled out, made to show your stuff.*
>
> *Mostly they're about people who made some terrible mistake. Couldn't answer a question right.*
>
> *One concerns a boy who did a particularly bad job. His professor called him down to the front of the class, up to the podium, gave the student a dime and said, loudly:*
>
> *"Go call your mother, and tell her you'll never be a lawyer."*
>
> *Sometimes the story ends here, but the way I heard it, the crushed student bowed his head and limped slowly back through the one hundred and fifty students in the class. When he got to the door, his anger exploded. He screamed:*
>
> *"You're a son of a bitch, Kingsfield."*
>
> *"That's the first intelligent thing you've said," Kingsfield replied. "Come back. Perhaps I've been too hasty."*

From Osborn, John Jay, Jr., The Paper Chase, *New York: Avon Books, 1973, p. 15.*

1. What does this anecdote demonstrate about Harvard Law School?

_____

2. In what way did the student redeem himself? _____

3. Why does the professor feel he might have made a mistake?

_____

Exercise #4 Personal Ads/Inferences

In the United States, personal ads have become increasingly popular as a way of meeting people. These ads appear in many newspapers and magazines throughout the country.

The ads below are all from men seeking women.

WANT TO MEET a terrific, communicative, bright, very educated man in time for the holidays? If you are under 50, educated, bright, urban, and slender, Santa may have a wonderful gift for you.   23238

WANTED: CLASSY, FINANCIALLY independent, easygoing F to enjoy life and to dabble in business, 35-55. SM, 50s, financially secure, 5'11/187, fit and healthy. No close relatives or dependents.   23219

NEW ON THE market, won't last long, DM, 39, 6'/180, brown/blue, fun-loving, down-to-earth; seeks slender F, under 40, who likes Harley's.   23216

007's WOMAN, Yes, I have the savoir faire of James. You have the beauty of his women. Let's make life an adventure. I'm 46, great black hair, athletic build, love life. Get everything you desire in one great package. A dream come true.   8902

PERFECT MATCH, If you were born on any of the following dates: 5-28-41, 2-16-49, 2-17-49, 6-3-52, 6-4-52, 1-24-54, 1-25-54, 1-26-54, 2-1-66, 2-2-66. A kindred soul searches for you—let's talk.   9656

The following ads are from women seeking men.

DEAR SANTA, This year, instead of a turkey, please bring me a dashing reindeer. Any color coat OK. Please make him 40s to 50s and nonsmoking and well-employed. But not too well-fed or with a red nose. Thanks, Santa.   9778

GO BULLS & A SF, The Bulls are down by 3 but I'm up by 5'5. My number is 36 and I enjoy traveling around. My uniform is attractive and I'm in shape for the season. My special draft pick is a professional SM; a team player whose number is 33-39. Extra points given if you're attractive, fun-loving and enjoy bicycling and tennis. Take a time out and call. Shot clock's a ticking.   8765

ATTRACTIVE & ADVENTUROUS SF, 40 is seeking physically fit, attractive man with a professional degree. Nonsmokers ONLY. Please send phone number and a recent photo.   5347

What can you logically infer from these ads? Include the specific details that help you make your inferences.

1. Which ads are from people who are likely to be health conscious? _____

2. Which ads demonstrate that the individual has a sense of humor?_____

3. Although it is generally considered to be unwise to meet people through personal ads, which ad conveys a special sense of danger? _____

4. In which ad does the individual appear to be familiar with astrology? _____

5. Which ads convey a sense of self-importance, or a touch of the egotistical?_____

6. What physical characteristics are emphasized in the ads? _____

Exercise #5 Drawing Inferences from the Social Sciences

A good reader makes educated guesses based upon observable details. We use our intuition and experiences to create a likely interpretation of what is happening in a story, while being careful that our interpretation is logical and realistic.

Read the following excerpt. In order to answer the questions at the end of the passage, you must read between the lines.

Even from the dim glow of the faded red-and-white exit sign, its light barely reaching the upper bunk, I could see that the sheet was filthy. Resigned to another night of fitful sleep, I reluctantly crawled into bed—tucking my clothes firmly around my body, like a protective cocoon.

The next morning, I joined the long line of disheveled men leaning against the chain-link fence. Their faces were as downcast as their clothes were dirty. Not a glimmer of hope among them.

No one spoke as the line slowly inched forward. When my turn came, I was handed a Styrofoam cup of coffee, some utensils, and a bowl of semi-liquid that I couldn't identify. It didn't look like any food I had seen before. Nor did it taste like anything I had ever eaten.

My stomach fought the foul taste, every spoonful a battle. But I was determined. "I will experience what they experience," I kept telling myself. My stomach reluctantly gave in and accepted its morning nourishment.

The room was eerily silent. Hundreds of men were eating, but each was sunk deeply into his own private hell, his head aswim with disappointment, remorse, bitterness.

As I stared at the Styrofoam cup holding my solitary post-breakfast pleasure, I noticed what looked like teeth marks. I shrugged off the thought, . . . concluding, "That must be some sort of crease from handling."

I joined the silent ranks of men turning in their bowls and cups. When I saw the man behind the counter swishing out Styrofoam cups in a washtub of water, I began to feel sick at my stomach. I knew then that the jagged marks on my cup really had come from a previous mouth.

How much longer did this research have to last? I felt a deep longing to return to my family—in a world of clean sheets and healthy food.

From Henslin, James, Sociology, *Needham Heights, MA: Allyn and Bacon, Simon & Schuster, 1993.*

Directions: Answer the questions and then write the clue on which your inference is based.

1. What is the likely sex of the writer? _____

2. Where is the writer? What is the writer's location? _____
   _____

3. What is the writer's purpose? _____

4. What is the likely occupation or profession of the writer? _____

5. How do we know the writer is accustomed to a better life? _____
   _____

6. Use one word to describe the demeanor of the men in line. _____

Bio-sketch

Fannie Flagg is the author of the national bestseller *Fried Green Tomatoes at the Whistle Stop Cafe,* which was made into a movie. She has been an actress, screenwriter, director, and a comedian.

Directions: Read the passages from *Daisy Fay . . .* and then do the exercise that follows. In order to understand this excerpt, you must pay close attention to the clues the author provides.

Excerpt from **Daisy Fay and the Miracle Man**   *by Fannie Flagg*

READING

September 6
Daddy and I are excited because the Big Speckled Rodeo Trout Contest is next week and he and I are going to enter and we are going to win. I know that for a fact.

Daddy already bought the winning fish off Harvey Underwood a month ago and put it in the freezer. He told Momma it was a fish, he was going to stuff later on this year. It weighs twelve pounds and two ounces. I don't see how anybody could catch a fish bigger than that. The all-time record holder weighed thirteen pounds and that was six years ago. Our chances are excellent!

The person who catches the biggest speckled trout during three days of fishing wins first prize and first prize is an Evinrude outboard motor, valued at

$146.90 and second prize is a Ply-Flex fishing rod valued at $36. Now all we need is a boat to go with it!

September 15

Tomorrow is the last day of the Speckled Trout rodeo and everything is going just as Daddy and I planned. We went down to the Speckled Trout Rodeo Headquarters the first day and registered early in the morning and headed on up to our spot on the river. Daddy made a big show of how he didn't expect to win, but thought it would be fun for his little girl since he had been so busy all summer and hadn't had a chance to spend any time with her. He made me paddle up and down the river for a while every day so people could see us fishing.

5 Then every day we went and napped and didn't even fish at all. I took my Red Ryder BB gun and shot at snakes. I ate candy and Daddy drank his beer and told me war stories. At five o'clock we would go back to the Speckled Trout Rodeo Headquarters at the live bait shop. Daddy would say, "Well no luck today. Those fish just aren't biting," and act real disappointed to throw them off the track. . . .

We are going to take the winning speckled trout out of the freezer tonight before we go to bed so it will be good and thawed for tomorrow.

September 18

The trout was still frozen stiff as a board when we took it out of the freezer. So Daddy put it in a pan of boiling water and locked it in the trunk of the car. When we got up to the Speckled Trout Rodeo Headquarters, Daddy carried on some more how he had not caught one fish and how he hoped he caught something today. What kind of fisherman would his little girl think he was? We rowed up and down the river long enough for everyone to see us, just as we always did. Then we went back up to our spot and waited for that trout to thaw out. . . . About two o'clock in the afternoon the trout finally thawed, but putting it in the hot water had turned his eyes all cloudy. It didn't look like a fresh fish to me. Daddy didn't think so either and started cussing. Then he got an idea.

He said, "Don't move from this spot. If anybody comes up here, tell them I have gone to the bathroom." I sat there and waited and I tell you nothing smells worse than a dead trout.

About an hour later he came sneaking through the bushes and nearly scared me half to death. He had me drag the fish up to the bushes where he'd brought his whole taxidermy kit, right down to the artificial eyes, and some airplane glue. It took us forever, but we found some trout eyes. They were a little too big and the wrong color, but he said he didn't think the judges would notice. He cut the real eyes out of that trout and glued those plastic eyes in their place. We sat there and blew on them so they'd dry and at about four o'clock that fish started to look pretty good. The glue had dried funny, but Daddy said it made it appear like the trout had died terrified. I told you my Daddy likes to see the bright side of things.

10 We were just getting ready to go when some old country man came by in a boat and saw us and yelled out, "I heard Emmet Weaverly caught a thirteen-pounder this morning." Our trout was only twelve pounds and two ounces. I thought Daddy was going to be sick. But he's a quick thinker. He grabbed my box of BBs and stuffed every one of them down that trout's throat. By the time we got to the headquarters, everyone had weighed in but us.

So far the winner was Emmet Weaverly's fish that weighed twelve pounds and eight ounces, not thirteen like that man had said.

When Daddy got in the room, do you know what he did? He handed me that trout and said, "Hey, folks, look what my little girl just caught."

I couldn't believe it. I said, "Oh, no, Daddy. You're the one who really caught it."

He said, "No, honey, you caught it. Run up there and have it weighed."

15   If looks could kill, he'd be deader than that fish with the plastic eyes. I knew what he was doing. He was acting like he really caught it, but he was letting his little girl get all the glory. I tried to hand it back to him, but by then everybody thought the idea was so cute they pushed me up to where the scales were. I put the fish down on the scales very carefully. I didn't want those plastic eyes making a noise if they hit anything.

Our trout weighed twelve pounds and nine ounces. I did some fast figuring in my head; that was seven ounces of BBs. Everybody started applauding and saying "Bill Harper's little girl won." I looked around and there was Daddy, smiling, getting patted on the back, taking all the credit. . . .

I never took my eyes off the trout. Just as a judge was about to pick it up, I grabbed it in the nick of time. The official Speckled Trout Rodeo photographer started posing me for the picture for the paper. They said for me to hold it up by the tail and smile real big. It was hard to smile because if one of those plastic eyes fell out on the floor and they found out that fish had been dead for a month, I would go to jail. . . . The more I thought about it, the worse it got. My heart started pounding and my lips began to tremble. I couldn't smile if my life depended on it. They made me stand there longer and said, "We're not going to let you go until you give us a big smile. So smile big, honey." My hands started to shake and that trout was shaking like crazy, too. I just knew those eyes were going to fall out. One had slipped a little anyway, but I needn't have worried about the eyes because at that moment the BBs started coming out of that trout's mouth one by one all over the floor. I was in a cold sweat, but you never saw anybody smile as big as I did.

I knew they had to get that picture fast! Mrs. Dot said, "Oh look she caught a female fish, it's just full of caviar!" I sure was glad she didn't know the difference between BBs and caviar. Thank goodness Daddy came over and grabbed the fish out of my hand and turned it right side up and said, "I'm taking this trout home and stuffing it to make it into a trophy to donate to the Speckled Trout Rodeo as a gift." Everybody thought that was a fine idea, especially me. He said he had to get it home right away before the trout went bad.

Momma was waiting up for us. Daddy said, "Look what Daisy caught," and didn't even give her time to look at it good before he threw it back in the freezer. He told Momma not to open the freezer until at least twenty-four hours because it would ruin the trout if she did. She believed him. . . .

20   Daddy won't have a hard time stuffing the fish. He's already got the eyes in. . . . [Now] my daddy has an outboard motor in the shack out by the side of the malt shop. He doesn't have a boat yet, so I don't know what good it is doing him. Momma and I want him to sell it. We need the money for the payment on the malt shop, but Daddy says as soon as he starts stuffing his animals, he will have enough money to pay the note and buy a boat besides.

From Coming Attractions *by Fannie Flagg. Reprinted by permission of the author.*

IN YOUR OWN WORDS

1.   What could you infer about Bill Harper's character? List the details from the story that support your conclusions.

2.   Would Daisy Fay's mother have approved of the scheme to win the fishing contest? What evidence do you have for your answer?

3.   Bill Harper would probably be considered an **optimist.** What details in the story show that he always looks on the bright side of things.

4. What evidence shows that Bill Harper is resourceful?

5. How do we know that Daisy Fay was not comfortable with the scheme?

Review Test #4 Too Much of a Good Thing

An exercise in inference: "Too Much of a Good Thing" by Geoffrey Cowley.

This article on antibiotics demonstrates that the need to draw inferences is not restricted to literature and the social sciences. Read each paragraph below and circle the letter of the sentence that can be directly inferred from the passage.

The desire to take medicine is perhaps the greatest feature which distinguishes man from other animals.

William Osler

Like any internist, Dr. Robert Moellering of Boston's Deaconess Hospital has felt the pressure to hand out antibiotics on demand. When he served as director of student health services at Emerson College, he saw a steady stream of students with colds and flus, and many knew just which drug they wanted. Instead of dashing off prescriptions, Moellering would dutifully explain that their ailments were caused by viruses, and that no antibiotic—however new or expensive—can kill a virus. His campaign didn't get very far. As he now recalls, the kids would return days later waving bottles of pills in his face. "They'd tell me, 'My doctor said I almost had pneumonia.'"

1. We can infer that
   a. students were willing to follow the advice of Dr. Moellering.
   b. students were able to obtain antibiotics from their own personal physicians.
   c. Dr. Moellering acceded to the demands of the college students.

If the golden age of antibiotics is ending, the reasons should be no mystery. Bacteria gradually adapt to any antibiotic, and when one is misused, its power to heal is squandered. "If I give my patient too much hypertensive medicine, I might hurt that patient but there's no way I'm going to hurt the next patient," says Dr. Frank Rhame, director of infection control at the University of Minnesota Hospital and Clinic. "If I use an antibiotic too much, I'm making it less useful for everyone." Unfortunately, doctors have been slow to act on that insight. Confronted with a miserable patient, they tend to write a prescription. Antibiotic sales are soaring as a result (sales have already doubled since the mid-1980s), and so are drug-resistant infections.

2. We can infer that
   a. overuse of antibiotics by one person has repercussions for many others.
   b. overuse of heart medication by one person causes problems for others.
   c. doctors are unlikely to prescribe antibiotics to those with a viral infection.

The misuse of antibiotics isn't a new problem. Since the 1970s, various studies have concluded that 50 to 60 percent of all outpatient prescriptions are inappropriate. Other studies have found that 7 in 10 Americans receive antibiotics when they seek treatment for common colds. "Essentially," says Dr. Lee Green, a family practitioner at the University of Michigan, "we have a tradition of prescribing antibiotics to anybody who looks sick."

3. We can infer that
   a. doctors are unlikely to prescribe antibiotics to relieve the symptoms of the common cold.
   b. the problem of misusing antibiotics is a relatively new phenomenon.
   c. a large percentage of prescriptions for antibiotics are unnecessary.

There's plenty of blame to go around. As Moellering has learned in Boston, Americans like quick fixes, and when a doctor doesn't offer one, they look for a doctor who will. Patients aren't the only culprits. When insurance companies fail to cover bacterial tests, they encourage sloppy prescribing. Drug companies, for their part, promote the use of their products by advertising them widely and supplying doctors with free samples. Experts in health policy agree that the latest patented medications, which can cost 10 times as much as older generics, should be reserved for uniquely stubborn infections. "The more widely you use these newer antibiotics," says Dr. David Kessler, commissioner of the U.S. Food and Drug Administration, "the greater the chances that [bacteria] will develop resistance." But when a manufacturer touts a new product as a high-octane alternative that every patient deserves, doctors can feel duty-bound to prescribe it. "It's another form of defensive medicine," says Dr. Thomas O'Brien of Harvard.

4. We can infer that
   a. doctors are unlikely to feel pressure to prescribe the newest "wonder drugs."
   b. promotion on the part of drug companies increases the likelihood of abuse of antibiotics.
   c. overusing the new "high-octane" antibiotics increases their effectiveness.

Even when doctors dispense antibiotics properly, there is no guarantee they'll be used that way. Studies suggest that a third of all patients fail to use the drugs as prescribed. Many stop taking their medication after just a few days, when it has killed the most susceptible invaders but left hardened survivors to flourish. Besides being harder to treat, those resistant germs can then spread through the community. Besides quitting treatments early, some patients save unused drugs to take later, or pass them around like vitamins. "I've heard of people on trips who take a fellow traveler's antibiotic, thinking it will protect them from illness," says Dr. Stuart Levy of Tufts University. "It just causes widespread resistance."

5. We can infer that
   a. patients closely follow the directions on their antibiotic prescriptions.
   b. doctors are entirely to blame for the current antibiotic dilemma.
   c. a few days of antibiotic treatment kills off only the least-resistant bacteria.

Drug-resistant microbes don't threaten us all equally. A healthy immune system easily repels most bacterial invaders, regardless of their susceptibility to drugs. But when resistant bugs take hold among the weak, the sick or the elderly, they're hellishly hard to control. "I believe resistant infections are present in every hospital and nursing home," says Dr. Thomas Beam of the Buffalo, N.Y., VA Medical Center. "The only question is whether the institution is releasing that information." In the past 18 months alone, Beam has seen 51 patients stricken with drug-resistant staphylococcus aureus, *a microbe that infects surgical wounds and can cause pneumonia and systemic blood infections. Twelve of those infections have been lethal.*

6. We can infer that
   a. it is unlikely that a patient can contract a bacterial infection in a hospital.
   b. the elderly are more susceptible to resistant bacterial infections.
   c. hospitals and nursing homes are likely to inform the patients of any outbreak of drug-resistant infections.

Penicillin and tetracycline lost their power over staph back in the 1950s and 60s. Another antibiotic, methicillin, provided a backup for a while, but methicillin-resistant staph is now common in hospitals and nursing homes worldwide. "If it's not in your hospital already," says Dr. David Shlaes of Cleveland's Case Western Reserve University, "the only way to keep it out is to screen patients and keep [carriers] in some kind of holding center until you treat them." Last month officials at the VA nursing home in Sioux Falls, SD, quarantined half of the facility's 42 residents to control an outbreak of drug-resistant staph. Two of them are still in isolation.

7. We can infer that
   a. staph infections are uncommon in hospitals and nursing homes.
   b. antibiotics never lose their effectiveness against bacteria.
   c. a return to isolating patients is sometimes the only way to control infection.

Like staph infections, bugs known as enterococci flourish among weak and elderly hospital patients. Shlaes recalls that when a resistant strain of enterococci took hold in a Pittsburgh liver-transplant unit, 50 people were infected over the course of two years. The only survivors were patients whose infected tissues could be removed surgically (a trick from the pre-antibiotic era), or whose infections were confined to the urinary tract, where drugs can be used in high concentrations.

8. We can infer that
   a. prior to the availability of antibiotics, doctors used to excise the infected body part.
   b. it is unwise to administer high concentrations of antibiotics in the treatment of urinary tract infections to save the life of a patient.
   c. *staphylococcus* is the only bacteria likely to be a problem for the elderly.

Though they're concentrated in hospitals and nursing homes, the superbugs aren't confined to such settings. Out in the community, many bacterial diseases are becoming even harder to treat. Some 20 percent of the nation's gonorrhea is now resistant to one or more antibiotics. A similar proportion of TB now resists the drug isoniazid. As any doctor who has spent a winter throwing one drug after another at a toddler's ear infection can tell you, resistance is common in other bugs as well. But because the government doesn't track drug resistance, clinicians rarely know when to expect it.

9. We can infer that
   a. clinicians are not kept well-informed of outbreaks of resistant infections.
   b. you are not as likely to encounter a resistant form of bacteria in the community at large.
   c. gonorrhea and TB are no longer serious health threats.

To give doctors a better sense of what germs are circulating in their communities, the Centers for Disease Control and Prevention now encourage local health officials to conduct regular surveys for drug resistance. Meanwhile, the World Health Organization is funding a global computer database that doctors can use to report drug-resistant outbreaks. Surveillance alone won't stop the erosion of the wonder drugs. "The classic response has been to develop new and more powerful antibiotics," says Moellering. With luck and perseverance, scientists

❦ One of the first duties of the physician is to educate the masses not to take medicine. ❦

William Osler

will discover unimagined new weapons. But the immediate challenge is to get doctors, and patients, to stop abusing the weapons we still have.

From "Too Much of a Good Thing" by Geoffrey Cowley, Newsweek, March 28, 1994. Copyright © 1994 Newsweek, Inc. All rights reserved. Reprinted by permission.

10. We can infer that
   a. keeping a closer watch on drug-resistant outbreaks is likely to alleviate the problem.
   b. new and powerful antibiotics are readily available.
   c. something must be done to educate both doctors and the populace at large to the danger of using antibiotics inappropriately.

This last section on inference skills combines an excerpt from an art history textbook giving a chronological account of *Guernica*, Picasso's masterpiece, and an excerpt from a history textbook describing the discovery of the concentration camps. Both selections have the effects of war as a theme.

Practice your ability to read inferences by learning about one of the greatest achievements of twentieth-century art.

Notes on Vocabulary

fury—comes from Latin *furia* meaning violent passion, rage, or madness. In classical mythology, the three Furies were winged female monsters with snakes for hair. Their goal was to pursue and punish those who had committed evil deeds.

procrastinate—to put off doing something unpleasant or burdensome until a future time. The word *procrastinate* can be broken down into parts, *pro* meaning "toward" and *cras* meaning "tomorrow." So when you *procrastinate*, you are pushing something toward tomorrow.

Excerpt from **Guernica**

READING

❝All art is a revolt against man's fate.❞

Andre Malraux

[*G*uernica] was created by an artist whose sympathies lay with those not in power, an artist who took up his brush with a sense of fury at the "ins" who caused devastation. From his fury came one of the great masterpieces of twentieth-century art. The artist was Picasso, and the painting is called *Guernica*.

It is necessary to know the story behind *Guernica* to understand its power. In 1937 Europe was moving toward war, and a trial run, so to speak, occurred in Spain, where the forces of General Francisco Franco waged civil war against the established government. Franco willingly accepted aid from Hitler, and in exchange he allowed the Nazis to test their developing air power. On April 28, 1937, the Germans bombed the town of Guernica, the old Basque capital in northern Spain. There was no real military reason for the raid; it was simply an experiment to see whether aerial bombing could wipe out a whole city. Being totally defenseless, Guernica was devastated and its civilian population massacred.

At the time Picasso, himself a Spaniard, was working in Paris and had been commissioned by his government to paint a mural for the Spanish Pavilion of the Paris World's Fair of 1937. For some time he had procrastinated about fulfilling the commission; then, within days after news of the bombing reached Paris, he started *Guernica* and completed it in little over a month. Despite the speedy execution, however, this was no unreasoning outburst of anger. Picasso controlled his rage, perhaps knowing that it could have better effect in a carefully planned canvas, and he made many preliminary drawings. The finished mural had a shocking effect on those who saw it; it remains today a chillingly dramatic protest against the brutality of war.

Picasso always intended *Guernica* as a gift to the people of Spain, his homeland, but at the time of its creation in 1937, he did not trust the Spanish government. So, he shipped the picture off to the Museum of Modern Art in New York, where it was to be held "on extended loan" until such time as a "democratic" government was established in Spain.

5 In New York, *Guernica* was simply hung on a wall—a large wall to be sure. Its impact was staggering when the viewer came around a corner and, suddenly, there it was. If the museum guards decided you were all right, and if you held your breath carefully, you could get quite close to the canvas. Or you could stand far back to take in the whole work at a gulp. So the situation remained for 40 years. Only one unpleasant event marred the open relationship between artwork and viewers. In 1974 an Iranian artist splashed the *Guernica* with red paint as a political protest, but no permanent damage was done.

By 1981, eight years after Picasso's death, there was general agreement that Spain's government had become sufficiently "democratic" to satisfy the artist's conditions. Under tight security *Guernica* was sent to Madrid, where it was installed in an annex of the Prado museum. The Prado was taking no chances with its newly acquired masterpiece. *Guernica* was quickly sealed up in what some observers called a "cage"—an immense riot-resistant enclosure under an armor-plated ceiling, with bulletproof glass set some 14 feet in front of the canvas' surface. Obviously, one could no longer move in close to study details. Museum visitors complained that glare on the glass prevented any overall view of the painting. Some grumbled that the protective box dominated the picture, making even a 25-foot-wide painting seem puny. *Guernica* was safe, all right, but at what cost to its expression?

The controversy escalated in 1992, when *Guernica* was moved yet again, this time to the Reina Sofía museum a mile or so from the Prado. This new journey had all the drama of a spy movie. A special steel box, climate-controlled and weighing 3,500 pounds, was built to carry the painting. The transport company practiced its run down the road for weeks in advance, using stand-in paintings. Finally, on the fateful day, an armored truck carried *Guernica* through heavily guarded streets to its new home. The trip took half an hour and cost $200,000. Arriving intact at the Reina Sofía, *Guernica* was once again secured behind bulletproof glass.

One cannot help wondering what Picasso would have thought about all this hullabaloo. His eldest daughter has accused the Spanish art ministry of "murdering" the *Guernica*. Perhaps "jailing" it would be a better term. The issue is one of balance. If *Guernica* should be damaged or destroyed, there is no way ever to replace it. But what is the point of keeping this masterpiece so *very* safe that no one can properly see it?

From Living With Art *by Rita Gilbert, 1995. Reprinted by permission of The McGraw-Hill Companies.*

IN YOUR OWN WORDS

1. How does Rita Gilbert feel about the way the Spanish government has chosen to exhibit Picasso's *Guernica*? What clues enable you to make this inference?

2. How do you think Picasso might feel about the safekeeping of his masterpiece?

3. Why do you think Picasso chose to paint *Guernica* in black, white, and shades of gray?

Picasso: © Copyright ARS, N.Y. Giraudon/Art Resource, N.Y.

4. What might the gaping mouths and distorted figures in his painting signify?

5. Picasso was fascinated by the ancient sport of bullfighting. What do you think the bull in *Guernica* might represent?

6. In an otherwise bleak picture, what is the significance of the flower and the light?

Read this account of the liberation of the Nazi concentration camps and then answer the questions that follow.

Notes on Vocabulary

holocaust—slaughter and destruction on a very wide scale, especially by fire When used with a capital H, it refers to the Nazi slaughter of Jews in World War II. Originally, a *holocaust* was a sacrificial burnt offering to pagan gods in pre-Christian times. It is derived from the Greek words *holos*, meaning "whole," and *kaustos*, meaning "burnt."

"Inside the Vicious Heart"

READING

5.1 million to 6 million Jews were murdered during the Holocaust.

The liberation of the Nazi death camps near the end of World War II was not a priority objective; nor was it a planned operation. Convinced that military victory was the surest way to end Nazi oppression, Allied strategists organized their campaigns without specific reference to the camps; they staged no daring commando raids to rescue the survivors of Nazi genocide. It was by chance that Allied forces first stumbled upon the camps, and the GIs who threw open the gates to that living hell were totally unprepared for what they found.

Not until November 1944 did the U.S. Army discover its first camp, Natzwiller-Struthof, abandoned by the Germans months before. Viewing Natzwiller from a distance, Milton Bracker of the *New York Times* noted its deceptive similarity to an American Civilian Conservation Corps camp: "The sturdy green barracks buildings looked exactly like those that housed forestry trainees in the U.S. during the early New Deal."

As he toured the grounds, however, he faced a starker reality and slowly came to think the unthinkable. In the crematorium, he reported, "I cranked the elevator tray a few times and slid the furnace tray a few times, and even at that moment, I did not believe what I was doing was real."

"There were no prisoners," he wrote, "no screams, no burly guards, no taint of death in the air as on a battlefield." Bracker had to stretch his imagination to its limits to comprehend the camp's silent testimony to Nazi barbarism. U.S. military personnel who toured Natzwiller shared this sense of the surreal. In their report to headquarters, they carefully qualified every observation. They described "what appeared to be a disinfection unit," a room "allegedly used as a lethal gas chamber," "a cellar room with a special type elevator," and "an incinerator room with equipment obviously intended for the burning of human bodies." They saw before them the evidence of German atrocities, but the truth was so horrible, they could not quite bring themselves to draw the obvious conclusions.

5   *Inside the Vicious Heart*, Robert Abzug's study of the liberation of the concentration camps, refers to this phenomenon as "double vision." Faced with a revelation so terrible, witnesses could not fully comprehend the evidence of mass murder without meaning or logic. But as the Allied armies advanced into Germany, the shocking evidence mounted. On April 4, 1945, the Fourth Armored Division of the Third Army unexpectedly discovered Ohrdruf, a relatively small concentration camp. Ohrdruf's liberation had a tremendous impact on American forces. It was the first camp discovered intact, with its grisly array of the dead and dying. Inside the compound, corpses were piled in heaps in the barracks. An infantryman recalled, "I guess the most vivid recollection of the whole camp is the pyre that was located on the edge of the camp. It was a big pit, where they stacked bodies—stacked bodies and wood and burned them."

On April 12, Generals Eisenhower, Bradley, and Patton toured Ohrdruf. The generals, professional soldiers familiar with the devastation of battle, had never seen its like. Years later, Bradley recalled, "The smell of death overwhelmed us even before we passed through the stockade. More than 3,200 naked, emaciated bodies had been flung into shallow graves. Others lay in the street where they had fallen."

Eisenhower ordered every available armed forces unit in the area to visit Ohrdruf. "We are told that the American soldier does not know what he is fighting for," said Eisenhower. "Now at least he will know what he is fighting against." He urged government officials and journalists to visit the camps and tell the world. In an official message Eisenhower summed it up:

> We are constantly finding German camps in which they have placed political prisoners where unspeakable conditions exist. From my own personal observation, I can state unequivocally that all written statements up to now do not paint the full horrors.

On April 11, the Timberwolf Division of the Third Army uncovered Nordhausen. They found 3,000 dead and only 700 survivors. The scene sickened battle-hardened veterans.

10   *The odors, well there is no way to describe the odors. . . . Many of the boys I am talking about now—these were tough soldiers, there were combat men who had been all the way through the invasion—were ill and vomiting, throwing up, just at the sight of this. . . .*

For some, the liberation of Nordhausen changed the meaning of the war.

> I must also say that my fellow GIs, most thought that any stories they had read in the paper . . . were either not true or at least exaggerated. And it did not sink in, what this was all about, until we got into Nordhausen.

If the experience at Nordhausen gave many GIs a new sense of mission in battle, it also forced them to distance themselves from the realities of the camps. Only by closing off their emotions could they go about the grim task of sorting out the living from the dead and tending to the survivors. Margaret Bourke-White, whose *Life* magazine photographs brought the horrors of the death camps to millions on the home front, recalled working "with a veil over my mind."

People often ask me how it is possible to photograph such atrocities. In photographing the murder camps, the protective veil was so tightly drawn that I hardly knew what I had taken until I saw prints of my own photographs.

15   By the end of 1945, most of the liberators had come home and returned to civilian life. Once home, their experiences produced no common moral responses. No particular pattern emerged in their occupational, political, and religious behavior, beyond a fear of the rise of post-war totalitarianism shared by most Americans. Few spoke publicly about their role in the liberation of the camps; most found that after a short period of grim fascination, their friends and families preferred to forget. Some had nightmares, but most were not tormented by memories. For the liberators the ordeal was over. For the survivors of the hell of the camps, liberation was but the first step in the tortuous process of rebuilding broken bodies and shattered lives.

From America Past and Present *by Divine et al. Copyright © 1991 by HarperCollins Publishers Inc. Reprinted by permission of Addison Wesley Educational Publishers Inc.*

Vocabulary Practice

Directions: Each question below has a sentence from the selection and another sentence. A particular word is italicized in both sentences. Use the context clues from the two sentences to choose the definition of the word that makes sense.

1. "Viewing Natzwiller from a distance, Milton Bracker of *The New York Times* noted its *deceptive* similarity to an American Civilian Conservation Corps camp. . . . " (paragraph 2)

   The clear sky in the morning was *deceptive* because by noon a bad storm had blown in.

   deceptive means
   a. truthful.
   b. misleading.
   c. dangerous.
   d. ornamental.

2. "The liberation of the Nazi death camps near the end of World War II was not a *priority* objective. . . . " (paragraph 1)

   The student had to decide whether her *priority* concern was going to be studying or watching TV.

   priority means
   a. insignificant.
   b. believable.
   c. more important.
   d. historical.

3. " 'There were no prisoners,' he wrote, 'no screams, no *burly* guards. . . .' " (paragraph 4)

In the football game, the *burly* linebacker was making a lot of tackles.

burly means

a. weak

b. relaxed

c. big and strong

d. handsome

4. "U.S. military personnel who toured Natzwiller shared this sense of the *surreal*." (paragraph 4)

The *surreal* painting, "The Persistence of Memory," by Salvador Dali, which shows one watch hanging limply from a tree, others covered by flies and ants, and the final watch melted over a form representing the artist, illustrates the decay of time.

surreal means

a. romantic

b. realistic

c. funny

d. bizarre

5. "It was the first camp discovered intact, with its *grisly* array of the dead and dying." (paragraph 5)

The movie *Silence of the Lambs* portrays a *grisly* killer.

grisly means

a. pleasing

b. frightful

c. unusual

d. well-known

6. " 'I can state *unequivocally* that all written statements up to now do not paint the full horrors.' " (paragraph 8)

He stated *unequivocally* that he was innocent of his wife's murder.

unequivocally means

a. proudly

b. humorously

c. with certainty

d. doubtfully

7. "a room 'allegedly used as a *lethal* gas chamber' " (paragraph 4)

If you are a boxer like Mike Tyson, your fists can be considered *lethal* weapons.

lethal means

a. useful

b. simple

c. mild

d. deadly

8. " 'The *sturdy* green barracks buildings . . .' " (paragraph 2)

The old woman, despite her recent hospitalization, was still very *sturdy* on her feet.

sturdy means

a. practical

b. weak

c. strong or stable

d. attractive

IN YOUR OWN WORDS

Directions: Use supporting details from the essay to answer the following questions.

1. Why did the soldiers who discovered the camps have difficulty believing what they were seeing? In their reports, why did they qualify their observations about the camps?

2. What did Eisenhower mean when he said that if the Americans did not know what they were fighting for, they at least now knew what they were fighting against?

3. Do you think the concentration camps were deliberately designed to look innocuous? Why might they have been designed that way?

4. How did the photographer Margaret Bourke-White close off her emotions?

5. Did the battle-hardened soldiers have difficulty viewing the dead at Nordhausen? What was their reaction?

6. Are you surprised that the soldiers who liberated the death camps were not affected more by their experiences?

7. Lee Miller, a former model for *Vogue*, became a war correspondent in 1944. While on assignment, she photographed Dachau, the German concentration camp. She sent her photographs to British *Vogue* and followed with a telegram that said: I IMPLORE YOU TO BELIEVE THIS IS TRUE. Why would she find it necessary to have a cable like this accompany her photographs? How do comments like this help explain America's initial reluctance to believe in the existence of the camps?

Chapter 5 Test: "Inside the Vicious Heart"

Multiple Choice

1. You could infer from the article that
   a. throughout the war, the United States was fully aware of the existence of concentration camps.
   b. U.S. soldiers had little idea what they would discover in the concentration camps.
   c. inmates were still alive in the Natzwiller-Struthof concentration camps.
   d. U.S. soldiers who entered the concentration camps could be characterized as being "fresh" troops.

2. The primary organizational pattern used in this article is
   a. classification and division.
   b. definition.
   c. chronological order.
   d. steps in a process.

3. The author's primary purpose in writing this article was to
   a. explain what happened when U.S. soldiers entered the concentration camps.
   b. persuade people to become more interested in the Holocaust.
   c. give a summary of one person's account of what he saw when he entered the camps.
   d. provide an explanation of Hitler's Jewish "relocation" policy.

4. The best definition of the word *atrocities* as used in the article is
   a. good deeds.
   b. graves.
   c. dead bodies.
   d. acts of cruelty.

5. The purpose of the first paragraph is to
   a. give an example.
   b. discuss the strategy of the Allies.
   c. give a general introduction.
   d. discuss Nazi oppression.

True or False

_____ 6. The Allies discovered more than 3,000 dead bodies in the Ohrdruf concentration camp.

_____ 7. Eisenhower wanted as many soldiers as possible to view the camps.

_____ 8. The liberation of the camps was a planned operation for the military.

_____ 9. Allied forces staged a daring raid to rescue prisoners at Natzwiller-Struthof.

_____ 10. The discovery of Ohrdruf had a tremendous effect on American forces because it was the first concentration camp discovered intact.

Vocabulary: Unit 2

In this unit, we will continue working with word parts involving number and amount.

centi—100   milli—1,000

century	100 years. In the year 2001, we will enter the twenty-first *century*.
centennial	a 100-year anniversary. *Ann* and *enn* mean "year." Since *centi* means "100," and *enn* means "year," we are simply putting word parts together to make a word meaning 100 years. In 1876, we celebrated the first *centennial* of our independence from England.
bicentennial	a 200-year anniversary.
tricentennial	a 300-year anniversary.
cent	A penny is called a *cent* because it is 1/100 of a dollar.
centipede	*Centi* means "100" and *ped* means "foot," so a *centipede* would be an animal with 100 feet. Actually, *centipedes* don't have 100 feet; they just look like they do.
centigrade	divided into 100 parts. On the centigrade, or Celsius, scale, water freezes at 0 degrees and boils at 100 degrees. While most other nations use the *centigrade* scale, the United States uses the Fahrenheit scale. On this scale, water freezes at 32 degrees and boils at 212 degrees.

What does the word *quadricentennial* mean? When will your state celebrate its quadricentennial? _____

centipede—The largest centipede in the world, Himantarum gabrielis, has 171 to 177 pairs of legs and is found in southern Europe.

Trivia Question 1

On the *centigrade* scale, at what temperature does beer freeze? Answer found at the end of the lesson.

Trivia Question 2

What famous centenarian died in 1996?

polyglot—Ziad Fazah of Brazil is a true polyglot. He can speak and write in 58 languages.

centimeter	a unit of length in the metric system; 1/100 of a meter, or approximately two-fifths of an inch.
centenarian	a 100-year-old person. There are more women who are *centenarians* than there are men.
millennium	a period of 1,000 years.
millipede	an animal that looks like it has 1,000 feet. The technical difference between a *centipede* and a *millipede* is that a *millipede* has two pairs of legs on each segment, while a *centipede* has only one pair of legs on each segment.
millimeter	1/1000 of a meter. Metric wrenches used for working on bikes and cars made in Europe are measured in millimeters.
million	The word *million* probably came about by multiplying $1{,}000 \times 1{,}000$. Maybe this will help you remember that *milli* means 1,000.

multi—many   graph—write
poly—many   gam—marriage

multiply	a system of repeating addition many times ($3 \times 3 = 3 + 3 + 3$).
multimedia	a combination of many media. A *multimedia* computer presentation might appeal to more than one of our senses simultaneously with film, music, and special lighting all in one performance.
multilateral	many-sided. Remember that *lat* means "side." A treaty signed by more than two nations would be a *multilateral* treaty.
polygon	a many-sided figure. A decagon is a *polygon* that has 10 sides and 10 angles. The simplest *polygon* is the triangle.
polygraph	You probably know that *polygraph* machines are used on someone suspected of lying. *Graph* means "write." The machine works by recording (writing) the many bodily changes (blood pressure, respiration, pulse rate) thought to occur when a person lies in answering questions.
polygamy	being married to more than one person at the same time.
polyglot	speaking or writing several languages.

semi—half   demi—half   hemi—half

semester	half an academic year.
semicircle	half a circle.
semiprofessional	not fully professional. The baseball player was not good enough to play professionally, so he played in a *semiprofessional* league, or what is commonly called a semi-pro league.

semicentennial	half of 100 years, or 50 years; a 50th anniversary. Here you are just putting together *semi* meaning "half," *cent* meaning "100," and *enn* meaning "year."
semilunar	shaped like a half-moon; crescent-shaped.
hemisphere	half of a sphere or a globe. We live in the Western *Hemisphere*. The word *hemisphere* is also used when referring to the left half or right half of our brain.
demitasse	a small (half) cup. This cup is used for drinking very strong black coffee similar to espresso. A *demitasse* is usually served following dinner.

equi—equal

Don't get *equi* confused with *equus*, which means "horse." *Equestrian* competition involves horse-riding.

equal	evenly proportioned.
equator	the imaginary line around the middle of the earth that splits it into two equal parts.
equidistant	equally distant.
equinox	*equi* meaning "equal" and *nox* meaning "night." The *equinox* happens twice a year, once in March and then again in September, when day and night are of exactly *equal* length.
equilibrium	The state of being evenly balanced. Your *equilibrium*, or balance, is controlled by your inner ear.
equilateral	a figure having *equal* sides. A square is an *equilateral*.

equator—The earth is not a perfect sphere because it is slightly flattened at the poles. The greatest circumference of the earth is at the equator and is 24,901,458 miles.

omni—all

omnivorous	eating all sorts of food, especially both animal and vegetable food. Human beings are *omnivorous*.
omnipotent	all-powerful. Many religions consider God to be *omnipotent*.
omniscient	all-knowing. The professor thought he was *omniscient* in his subject area.
omnipresent	present in all places at the same time. Cartoons are *omnipresent* on TV on Saturday mornings.

ambi, amphi—both; around

These two word parts have the same meaning, one coming from Latin and the other from Greek.

ambidextrous	able to use both hands equally well.
ambiguous	vague; having two or more meanings. Because the teacher's directions were *ambiguous*, many students failed to complete the assignment correctly.

ambivalent	*Ambi* means "both" and *valens* means "worth," so *ambivalent* means "an inability to decide between two conflicting feelings or thoughts." My parents are *ambivalent* about my getting a job. On the one hand, they would like me to earn money; on the other, they think my grades will suffer.
amphibian	an organism that is able to live or operate on land and in the water. A salamander is an *amphibian*.
amphitheater	a type of theater or stadium that has seats going all around the stage or arena. The Greeks and Romans built outdoor *amphitheaters,* many of which are still in use today. You may have an *amphitheater* in your hometown for summer concerts.

Find some other words using the following prefixes. Write out the meaning of your word, using a dictionary as needed. Do not just copy the dictionary definition; instead try to put the definition into your own words.

Prefix	Your word	Meaning
ambi	_____	_____
omni	_____	_____
cent	_____	_____
multi	_____	_____
poly	_____	_____
equi	_____	_____

Answer to Trivia Question 1

The freezing point of beer on the centigrade scale is approximately −10 degrees. Beer freezes at a lower temperature than water because it contains alcohol. The exact freezing point of beer will depend upon the percentage of alcohol in the drink.

Now use each of your words in a sentence. Be sure to use the word correctly according to its part of speech (noun, verb, adjective, etc.).

1. _____
   _____
2. _____
   _____
3. _____
   _____
4. _____
   _____
5. _____
   _____
6. _____
   _____

Answer to Trivia Question 2

George Burns, a famous comedian and actor, died in 1996.

Vocabulary 2

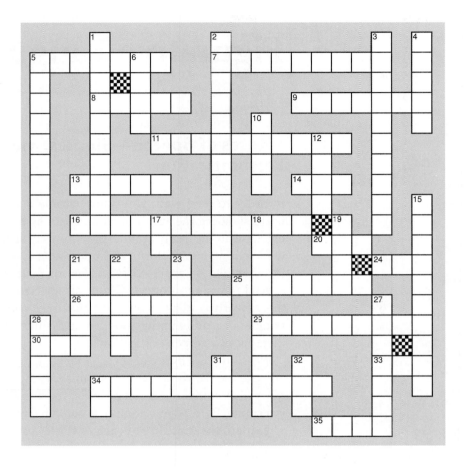

ACROSS CLUES

5. This event happens in September and March.
7. This "critter" has two pairs of legs on each of its segments.
8. A root word meaning "moon."
9. The imaginary line dividing the northern and southern hemispheres.
11. 1/100 of a meter.
13. Word part meaning 1,000.
14. Word part meaning two.
16. Being able to use both hands equally well.
20. The abbreviation for what was once the ninth month.
24. Abbreviation for what was once the eighth month.
25. 1,000 × 1,000.
26. A person who can speak many languages.

29. A "critter" that appears to have 100 legs.
30. Word part for one.
33. Word part for three.
34. 200-year anniversary.
35. Word part for many.

DOWN CLUES

1. 1,000 years.
2. In ancient Greece, you might have gone to an _____ to watch a play.
3. Water freezes at 0 degrees on this scale.
4. A word part meaning "four."
5. A square is an _____ figure.
6. Word part meaning "all."
10. A word part meaning "both."
12. A word part meaning "equal."
15. Movies are _____ experiences because they combine images and sound.

17. A word part meaning "two."
18. All-knowing.
19. A word part meaning "one."
21. A word part meaning "both."
22. A word part for "many."
23. A figure with many sides.
27. In the year 2001, we will enter the twenty-first _____.
28. A word part meaning "five."
31. An abbreviation for what was once the 10th month.
32. A word part meaning "marriage."
34. A word part meaning "two."

Figurative Language

Figures of Speech—Similes, Metaphors, and Personification

In order to read well, you must become a **critical** reader. This means not only understanding the author's literal meaning but also the author's implied or inferential meaning. Many authors use figures of speech or figurative language to make their writing more colorful and interesting. These figures of speech are expressions in which words are used regardless of their true meanings in order to create a special meaning or effect. Often this specialized language enables the author to more clearly convey meaning by making a comparison to something that is more familiar or readily understood. Some frequently used figures of speech are similes, metaphors, and personification.

A **simile** is a figure of speech that compares two dissimilar things. Similes usually use the words *like*, *as*, or *as if* to show the comparison. "Sam is as energetic as Mary" is a comparison, not a simile. "Sam is as energetic as the Energizer bunny" is a simile. Both poems and prose contain similes.

Explain the meaning of each of these similes:

She is as confused as a rat in a maze.

His muscles are like iron bands.

The fullback charged as if he were a locomotive.

_____

_____

_____

A **metaphor** connects two unlike things directly without using *like*, *as*, or *as if*. One thing is spoken of as though it were something else. In "Dreams," the poet Langston Hughes uses a metaphor to show the hopelessness of a life without any dreams.

> Hold fast to dreams
> For if dreams die
> **Life is a broken-winged bird**
> **That cannot fly.**
>
> Hold fast to dreams
> For when dreams go
> **Life is a barren field**
> **Frozen with snow.**

From Collected Poems *by Langston Hughes. Copyright © 1994 by the Estate of Langston Hughes. Reprinted by permission of Alfred A. Knopf Inc.*

An **extended metaphor** sustains the comparison for several lines or for the entire poem or story.

In the following excerpt from *How Good Do We Have to Be?*, Rabbi Harold S. Kushner uses an extended metaphor to express his feelings about life. What comparison is he making?

> *Life is not a spelling bee, where no matter how many words you have gotten right, if you make one mistake you are disqualified. Life is more like a baseball season, where even the best team loses one-third of its games and even the worst team has its days of brilliance. Our goal is not to go all year without ever losing a game. Our goal is to win more than we lose, and if we can do that consistently enough, then when the end comes, we will have won it all.*

From Rabbi Harold S. Kushner, How Good Do We Have to Be? *Boston: Little, Brown, and Company, 1996, pp. 180–181.*

Create your own metaphor for life. Include a short explanation of why you have chosen this metaphor. *Example:* Life is like a tidal wave; it doesn't stop for anybody or anything.

_____

_____

_____

_____

_____

Personification is a type of figurative language that gives human attributes to a nonhuman subject. When Longfellow said, "Time has laid his hand upon my heart, gently," he was personifying the concept of time and his feelings about growing old. In the poem "The Eagle" by Alfred, Lord Tennyson, the first line of each stanza makes use of personification.

> **He clasps the crag with crooked hands;**
> Close to the sun in lonely lands,
> Ringed with the azure world he stands.
>
> **The wrinkled sea beneath him crawls;**
> He watches from his mountain walls,
> And like a thunderbolt he falls.

What figure of speech is the last line of the poem? _____.

What does it mean to fall like a thunderbolt? _____

_____

Choose five inanimate objects. Then write a sentence giving each object a human attribute.

Example: My computer sighed, wheezed, and then expired.

_____

_____

_____

_____

_____

Exercise #1 Literal or Figurative Comparisons

Directions: Label the comparison **L** for literal or **F** for figurative.
Reminder: Not all comparisons are figures of speech.
A figure of speech makes a comparison between unlike things.
A literal comparison compares things that are from the same category.

Example: Lucille is as thin as a bookmark. (F) Different categories
Lucille is as thin as her grandmother. (L) Same categories

_____ 1.   Evergreen trees bent **like old people leaning out of the wind.**

_____ 2.   The baby's breathing was choked and rough, like something pulled through tightly packed gravel.

_____ 3.   She was as strong-willed as her father.

_____ 4.   The animal was as white as cream cheese.

_____ 5.   He was eating as well and sleeping as well as the other students.

_____ 6.   I am a willow swaying gently in the wind.

_____ 7.   The waves beside them danced.

_____ 8.   He complained all day as if no one had anything better to do than listen to him.

_____ 9.   Like her brother before her, she chose to live at home while attending college.

_____ 10. A gray mist rose on the sea's face.

List the numbers of the sentences above that contain a personification.
Sentence #'s _____ and _____.
What is the number of the sentence containing a metaphor?
Sentence # _____
Change the words in boldface in sentence number one to make an original simile.
Reminder: You need something that bends or is bent.

New simile: _____

Exercise #2 Creating Original Comparisons

Comparisons are considered to be **trite** when they are overused or worn. Read the following overused comparisons and try to think of a way to create a fresh or original comparison.

Definition of **trite**: worn, overused, hackneyed; a platitude

1. thin as a rail_____

2. red as a beet_____

3. flat as a pancake _____

4. nutty as a fruitcake_____

5. light as a feather _____

Directions: Rewrite this paragraph by substituting original comparisons of your own for the italicized trite expressions.

It was late at night and I was working alone at the office. *Quick as a flash,* a robber dashed in and pulled a gun on me demanding I oper. the office safe. I managed to stay *cool as a cucumber* despite his gun at my temple and his *viselike grip* around my chest. Unfortunately, while escorting me over to the wall safe, he knocked my glasses off my face and stepped on them with a resounding thud. There I was *blind as a bat* unable to see the numbers well enough to open the lock. I began to *sweat like a pig,* realizing I would soon be *dead as a doornail,* when without any warning the police came to my rescue. To conclude my story, I am now *as happy as a lark.*

A special type of comparison is called an **analogy**. A writer uses an analogy to make something understandable or clear by comparing it to something that is different from it but that does have something in common with it. Sometimes an attempt to create a fresh and original comparison can go too far. These analogies recently posted on the Internet were labeled "the worst ever written in high-school essays." Try conveying the same information in a meaningful comparison of your own.

1. Her hair glistened in the rain like nose hair after a sneeze.

   _____

2. He was as tall as a six-foot-three-inch tree.

   _____

3. The politician was gone but unnoticed, like the period after the Dr. on a Dr. Pepper can.

   _____

4. His thoughts tumbled in his head, making and breaking alliances like underpants in a dryer without Cling Free.

   _____

5. The little boat gently drifted across the pond exactly the way a bowling ball wouldn't.

   _____

Exercise #3 Analyzing Figurative Comparisons

Directions: Each of the following sentences contains a figurative comparison. In the space provided, write down the real subject, what it is compared to, and the meaning of the sentence.

Example: Oliver Wendell Holmes once attended a meeting in which he was the shortest man present. "Doctor Holmes," quipped a friend, "I should think you'd feel rather small among us big fellows." "I do," retorted Holmes, "I feel like a dime among a lot of pennies."

Subject: Dr. Holmes
Compared to: dime among pennies
Meaning: Dr. Holmes did not let his short stature bother him. Just as a dime, though smaller than a penny, is worth more, Holmes is "worth more" than his friends.

1. Whenever I try to speak to him, his mind wanders everywhere, like a cow following green grass.

    Subject: _____

    Compared to:_____

    Meaning: _____

2. Her face looked like it had just come out of a dryer and needed to be pressed.

    Subject: _____

    Compared to:_____

    Meaning: _____

3. He bobbed through life's turbulences like driftwood on a sea.

    Subject: _____

    Compared to:_____

    Meaning: _____

Exercise #4 Figurative Comparisons in Fiction

Directions: The figurative expressions (set in boldface) in the excerpts below were chosen by the authors to create a fresh effect or demonstrate a new insight. Determine whether the expression is a metaphor, simile, or a personification, and then decide what image or insight the author is trying to convey.

For speech is so much more than words and sentences. It seemed to me that regional speech is in the process of disappearing, not gone but going. Forty years of radio and twenty years of television must have this impact. Communications must destroy localness, by a slow, inevitable process. I can remember a time when I could almost pinpoint a man's place of origin by his speech. That is growing more difficult now and will in some foreseeable future become impossible. **It is a rare house or building that is not rigged with spiky combers of the air.** *Radio and television speech becomes standardized, perhaps better English than we have ever used.* **Just as our bread, mixed and baked, packaged and sold without benefit of accident or human frailty, is uniformly good and uniformly tasteless, so will our speech become one speech.**

From Steinbeck, John, Travels with Charlie, *New York: Bantam Pathfinder Edition, 1972, p. 106.*

1. What is Steinbeck referring to when he uses the expression **spiky combers of the air**?

2. Do you think Steinbeck is in favor of a uniform manner of speaking?

Until I was thirteen and left Arkansas for good, the Store was my favorite place to be. Alone and empty in the mornings, **it looked like an unopened present from a stranger. Opening the front doors was pulling the ribbon off the unexpected gift.** *The light would come in softly (we faced north), easing itself over the shelves of mackerel, salmon, tobacco, thread. It fell flat on the big vat of lard and by noontime during the summer the grease had softened to a thick soup.* **Whenever I walked into the Store in the afternoon, I sensed that it was tired. I alone could hear the slow pulse of its job half done.** *But just before bedtime, after numerous people had walked in and out, had argued over their bills, or joked about their neighbors, or just dropped in "to give Sister Henderson a 'Hi y'all,' " the promise of magic mornings returned to the Store and spread itself over the family in washed life waves.*

From Angelou, Maya, I Know Why the Caged Bird Sings, New York: Bantam, 1970, p. 13.

1. What does Maya Angelou mean when she refers to the Store as **an unopened present**? Is this a simile or a metaphor?

2. To what does Angelou compare the opening of the front doors? Does this comparison involve a simile or a metaphor?

3. What figurative device does the following phrase use: **I sensed that it [the store] was tired?**

Exercise #5 Figurative Comparisons in Non-Fiction

It is important to realize that not all figures of speech come from fiction. Many writers of nonfiction also use figurative language in their writing. To convey information to readers who are not well-versed in scientific procedures, a science writer will often construct an appropriate metaphor. Keeping in mind that the word *metaphor* literally means "to transfer or bring across," Ted Anton and Rick McCourt, editors of *The New Science Journalists*, state that "almost every piece of really good science writing will connect its subject to an unexpected object or larger meaning."

Each of these figures of speech is taken from a scientific article. Determine what the figurative language suggests in each example and then answer the true/false questions that follow each description.

A description of a common roundworm . . .

Through a microscope, they look like tiny crystal serpents, curving and slithering across the dish with an almost opiated languor, doubling back on themselves as though discovering their tails for the first time, or bumping up against a neighbor clumsily and then slowly recoiling.

From Angier, Natalie, "The Very Pulse of the Machine," The Beauty of the Beastly, Boston: A Peter Davison Book, Houghton Mifflin, 1995, p. 53.

_____ 1. The roundworm moves quickly in a purposeful fashion.

_____ 2. The roundworm appears well-coordinated.

A description of proteins . . .

The concentration of proteins in the cell is as thick as honey, and young proteins must be sequestered from the ambient ooze. During the early stages of folding, the polypeptide may form characteristic corkscrew shapes, or linked loops that resemble a Christmas bow, or slender fingerlike projections.

From Angier, Natalie, "Chaperoning Proteins," The Beauty of the Beastly, *Boston: A Peter Davison Book, Houghton Mifflin, 1995, p. 70.*

_____　1.　The ooze might jeopardize the development of the young proteins.

_____　2.　Proteins are highly concentrated in cells.

A description of a bat cave . . .

The air screams, rustling movements feather against the skin, squeaks and screeches bounce off the stone walls, and a sweet acrid stench rolls across the room. My mouth chews the darkness like a thick paste. . . . The rock walls feel like cloth to the touch. . . . The feces and urine continue to shower down, the mites tickle the surface of my body, the atmosphere tastes like a bad meal and always the air drifting like a thick fog promises the whisper of rabies.

From Bowden, Charles, "Bats," in Ted Anton and Rick McCourt, editors, The New Science Journalists, *New York: Ballantine Books, 1995, pp. 284–285.*

_____　1.　Bat caves are quiet, pleasant-smelling environments.

_____　2.　Visibility is good inside the cave.

_____　3.　Visitors emerging from a bat cave are likely to be covered in excrement.

A description of the brain . . .

Brain *is easy to define: It is the wet, oatmeal-colored organ, weighing about three pounds, that resides inside the skull. . . . Mind is not the all-knowing monarch of the brain, but a little circle of firelight in a dark, Australia-sized continent where the unconscious brain processes carry on.*

From, "The Interpreter," in Ted Anton and Rick McCourt, editors, The New Science Journalists, *New York: Ballantine Books, 1995, p. 31.*

_____　1.　The conscious mind forms a much smaller part of the operations of the brain than the unconscious.

_____　2.　The mind is not really "running the show."

A description of chromosomes . . .

Human chromosomes, shaped like cinch-waisted sausages and sequestered in nearly every cell of the body, are famed as the place where human genes reside.

From Angier, Natalie, "A Clue to Longevity," The Beauty of the Beastly, *Boston: A Peter Davison Book, Houghton Mifflin, 1995, p. 31.*

_____　1.　The chromosomes contain human genetic material.

_____　2.　Chromosomes reside in only a few dominant areas of the human body.

_____　3.　The chromosome is smallest at the top and at the bottom.

Exercise #6　Practice with the Extended Metaphor

In an extended metaphor, the figurative comparison is developed throughout the entire article. This lengthy comparison helps the reader to visualize the event much more clearly. As you read the following article, note the extended metaphor and then answer the questions that follow.

Notes on Vocabulary

quarry—an animal that is being hunted down, prey; anything being hunted or pursued.   The word *quarry* originated from the Latin *corium,* meaning "hide."

query—to question, to ask about.

stalk—to pursue game or an enemy.

Tuning In to Reading

As you are reading this article, think about your own experience buying a new or used car.

Car Buying Turns Men into Big Game Hunters   *by Karen Peterson*

READING

The total number of cars sold worldwide during 1994 was 36,289,127.

Men hunt a new car for up to three months before buying; they sneak up on their quarry, peer into dealership windows after-hours and bring their prey home like a trophy, a new study indicates.

"Men hunt for cars the way an experienced tracker hunts for wild game," says Mike Lafavore, of *Men's Health* magazine. "They spend a lot of time planning their attack, arming themselves with the necessary weapons and stalking their prey when hopefully it can't see them."

Nearly half (48%) of men spend between three weeks and three months thinking about buying a new car before they buy it, says a survey of 2,153 men done for the magazine by J. D. Power and Associates. The average span is fourteen weeks.

Thirty-two percent deliberately stalk cars at closed dealerships, checking them out when no other hunters are around. "They want to sneak up, kick the tires on the lot, peer into car windows when they are alone," he says.

5   And dealers, don't approach the hunter on Sunday, his "stealth day" for tracking. Only 4% buy then; the most popular day is Saturday, 21%. "Men who encounter salespeople on Sundays are like hunters who walk into a flock of wild game without their weapons."

Almost 30% of hunters were irritated with dealers whenever they bought. Reasons: Dealers withheld a better price, 34%; were dishonest, 27%; too pushy, 22%; charged extra fees, 21%; used jargon, 10%; didn't provide test drive, 5%; smoked, 5%; criticized other dealers, 4%.

The men's magazine did not query women. But if men are hunters of cars, women are the gatherers of truly useful information: "Women tend to be much more practical than men," says Lafavore, whose father was a car salesman. "His car is a trophy; hers is transportation."

From "Car Buying Turns Men Into Big Game Hunters" by Karen S. Peterson, USA Today, September 20, 1995. Copyright © 1995 USA TODAY. Reprinted with permission.

Cathy © 1995 Cathy Guisewite. Reprinted with permission of UNIVERSAL PRESS SYNDICATE. All rights reserved.

IN YOUR OWN WORDS

1. Peterson uses an extended metaphor to describe the car buying habits of men. Specifically, she compares a man hunting for a new car to a big game hunter tracking wild game. List the similarities between the two activities.

2. Would a salesman have much success approaching a man looking at cars on a Sunday? Why?

3. In the last paragraph, the writer compares the attitudes of men and women toward the acquisition of a car. In the author's view, what do men want from a new car? What do women want from a new car?

4. How does the cartoon by Cathy illustrate the difference between male and female attitudes toward the acquisition of a new car?

5. In the last panel of the cartoon, Cathy is using figurative language to describe her feelings. What does she mean when she says, "They splattered self-doubt particles all over my nice new windshield"?

The Use of Symbols

A symbol is a person, object, or event that stands for more than its literal meaning. It is representative of something else. A good symbol captures in a simple form a more complicated reality. For example, a white dove symbolizes peace, a flag symbolizes a country's values and aspirations, a budding flower may symbolize birth and new beginnings, and a logo on a shirt may signify wealth and status. Writers use symbols to create a particular mood or to reinforce a specific theme.

In his poem "The Road Not Taken," Robert Frost uses an extended metaphor to compare life to a journey along a road. The fork in the road is a more specific symbol that represents a major decision in life—a decision that must be made and that likely cannot be taken back. To preserve its symbolic value, the poem does not discuss the particulars of a decision or choice. In this way, the choice made in the poem can stand for any important choice made in life.

The Road Not Taken   *by Robert Frost*

Two roads diverged in a yellow wood,
And sorry I could not travel both
And be one traveler, long I stood
And looked down one as far as I could
To where it bent in the undergrowth;

Then took the other, as just as fair,
And having perhaps the better claim,
Because it was grassy and wanted wear;
Though as for that the passing there
Had worn them really about the same,

And both that morning equally lay
In leaves no step had trodden black.
Oh, I kept the first for another day!
Yet knowing how way leads on to way,
I doubted if I should ever come back.

I shall be telling this with a sigh
Somewhere ages and ages hence:
Two roads diverged in a wood, and I—
I took the road less traveled by,
And that has made all the difference.

Exercise #1 Identifying Symbols

Directions: Identify what each of these common symbols represents.

1. wedding ring _____
2. white wedding dress _____
3. rabbit's foot _____
4. the American flag _____
5. a Lexus or Infiniti _____
6. Springtime _____
7. a skull and crossbones _____
8. a gavel _____

Nowadays, nearly everyone is involved in our Society's sick sad scramble to acquire "things." For the most part, these "things" are acquired to impress other people, and they actually carry this message rather clearly, as though they were printed signs. In fact, here is what we almost see when we look at these . . .

MAD Magazine is a trademark of E.C. Publications, Inc. © 1998 All rights reserved. Used with permission.

Directions: After reading the descriptions on this status symbol, write a sentence clarifying what the possession represents to the owner:

_____

Exercise #2 "Thunderbolts"

In this excerpt from *The Winner Within,* Pat Riley uses an extended metaphor to explain how individuals should learn to cope with adversity.

Bio-sketch

Pat Riley is generally considered to be one of America's greatest coaches and is known for using psychological techniques to inspire his players to work as a team. In his recent book, *The Winner Within*, he shares his ideas for developing success, not just in basketball, but in all walks of life. Riley, a former player and broadcaster, coached the 1980s Los Angeles Lakers to four championship titles in nine years. From 1991 to 1995, he was coach of the New York Knicks and inspired them to playoff greatness. Riley is currently the coach and general manager of the Miami Heat. Overall, Riley has the best regular-season winning percentage of any coach in NBA history. In his book, he shares his techniques to create a winning attitude and demonstrates how adversity can open the door to new opportunities.

Notes on Vocabulary

adversity—a state of wretchedness or misfortune; trouble.

divestiture—a stripping or taking away of possessions. To *divest* originally meant to strip of clothing or equipment. Later to *divest* came to mean to remove ranks or privileges.

Tuning In to Reading

Survey the following article by reading the introductory quotations, the first paragraph and the last paragraph. Have you ever been faced with something that seemed like a bad setback for you, but then after you worked and struggled with it, something good came out of the whole experience?

"Thunderbolts" an excerpt from **The Winner Within**   *by Pat Riley*

READING

"Sweet are the uses of adversity." William Shakespeare

"Now you're lookin' at a man that's gettin' kinda mad; I've had lots of luck, but it's all been bad. No matter how I struggle and strive I'll never get out of this world alive." Hank Williams

"Success in life comes not from holding a good hand, but in playing a poor hand well." Denis Waitley and Rem L. Witt

August 30, 1992, Florida City: A young couple walked through rubble where their house used to stand, the same house where the young man had been a boy, where his father had lived for fifteen years. Looking around, they saw ripped-up hunks of aluminum siding from destroyed trailer houses, pink tufts of fiberglass insulation scattered, cracked two-by-fours and wet, shiny-looking spots in the grass which turned out to be shards of broken glass.

Two framed photographs were the only family possessions they could find. The man looked across all the adjacent home sites, each one as demolished as his own.

"It doesn't look like a town," he said. "The trees are all naked or gone. It's a whole other world."

Because of a natural phenomenon called Hurricane Andrew, the husband and wife who searched their home's wreckage for belongings were among more than a quarter of a million people who were left homeless overnight across a two-hundred-mile-wide swatch of South Florida. Their houses, as well as the shops and businesses where they used to work, were equally swept away.

5   "People want to know what's going to happen to them," the mayor of Florida City said. "But there is no quick fix." A woman with three children told a reporter, "It hurts to think about the future."

Still, human beings are a lot more resilient than they realize. With the phone lines down, storm survivors communicated by painting messages on the sides of buildings. A spray-can telegram on the side of one house told friends, GRANDMA NEWTON IS OK.

Hurricane Andrew (August 24, 1992) was the costliest hurricane in United States history. The total losses amounted to approximately $20.6 billion. Hurricane Andrew killed 76 people and left approximately 258,000 homeless.

Andrew was a disaster greater than most of us will ever experience. The scars it left will be slow to heal. But the people of Florida will build again. They will be back. That's what a Thunderbolt experience should teach you to do: take on adversity and come back, better than before.

A Thunderbolt is something beyond your control, a phenomenon that one day strikes you, your team, your business, your city, even your nation. It rocks you, it blows you into a crater. You have no choice except to take the hit. But you do have a lot of choice about what to do next. That much is in your power. In the coming years, expect the sky to blaze with Thunderbolts. They're part of the game of constant change.

Our whole planet seems to be a collection of flash points. Only about sixty of the world's one hundred and ninety current states existed at the beginning of the century. Most of the globe's new nations emerged in just the past five decades. In Africa, in Eastern Europe, everywhere—governments and borderlines are changing at accelerating speed. More often than not, those changes are introduced through coups, strife, and bloodletting.

10   The *Winner Within* must know how to field the strife-filled change of Thunderbolts—and that includes winners of every sort, because Thunderbolts can strike businesses as easily as they do governments, communities, or individuals. In fact, business columns and magazines are chock full of Thunderbolt reports every day.

• A two-year-old child dies and as many as 300 people are stricken when a fast-food chain is hit with an outbreak of bacterial poisoning.

• Terrorists sabotage the World Trade Center, exposing thousands of people to great danger, causing multimillion-dollar damage and disrupting countless businesses.

• Two people die and another becomes seriously ill when, despite three layers of tampering protection, someone puts cyanide in a brand of cold capsules.

Some Thunderbolts are sheer shots out of the blue. Others spring out of partly cloudy skies, where vigilant attention to the weather reports could have provided advance warning. That means monitoring trends, public policy issues, and regulatory agencies.

15   • In January 1984, AT&T implements the divestiture of its regional subsidiaries decreed by the U.S. Department of Justice—thus shrinking the size of Ma Bell and affecting the destiny of more than a million employees.

****

All of these are Thunderbolt situations, and Thunderbolts are a prime factor in upsetting the competitive applecart. Whether it is a powerful competitor drastically lowering its pricing or a quality inspector dramatically increasing standards, a Thunderbolt spells immediate adversity for someone. But that adversity also carries a positive charge: it strips away all the nonessentials and forces you back to your basic strengths. Adversity shoves you down to your core values and beliefs, to the things that matter most. Back on bedrock, you find the reasons and the strength to carry on and carry through.

Sometimes when adversity strikes, we rail against fate. We brutally and unfairly punish ourselves or we lash out at the people around us. We blame others. We stop and wait for someone else to show us the way, to open the door. Or we play the victim: "That's the way it goes. There's nothing I could do. It was meant to be."

That's what happened to the Lakers in 1983. We were the defending champions, with yet another chance at becoming the first team to win back-to-back NBA championships since 1969. Then disaster struck.

Our last regular season game was a completely meaningless contest against the Phoenix Suns. We were down to the last few minutes, already plotting playoff strategy. James Worthy, a brilliant 22-year-old rookie who played the game with the same kind of sweet intensity that Marvin Gaye brought to soul music, swooped into the lane to rebound a missed shot. He collided in midair with the Suns' power forward and fell to the floor. At the instant he hit the wood, he heard a bone in his lower leg snap.

20   I was aghast. James was the top draft pick in the entire league and had been named to the NBA All-Rookie Team. He was scoring for us in double figures. "Why did this have to happen now?" I thought bitterly.

Still we had more than enough to win. We advanced to the finals with eight victories against just three losses. But in the very last game prior to the finals, lightning struck again. Bob McAdoo, one of the chief reasons we had won the previous year's title, tore a hamstring muscle and was lost to us. Then, in game one of the finals, our first string shooting guard, Norm Nixon suffered a shoulder separation.

Taken together, Worthy, McAdoo and Nixon had generated 40 percent of the points our team had scored all year. Losing all three destroyed our attitude. We all silently decided that if anyone had the right to lose, it was us. This simply wasn't our year—what else could we do?

Never mind that we still had three of the finest players in the league—Magic Johnson, Kareem Abdul-Jabbar and Jamaal Wilkes—all in perfect health. Never mind that our bench was strong, and that we were actually ahead in the third quarter in every single game of the finals. Instead of focusing on our remaining strengths and letting them blossom even more, we mentally gave in. We drank in all the solace that our injuries had elicited from fans and media. We assumed that we were off the hook, that the consequences of losing somehow wouldn't fall on our shoulders. With that attitude, it's easy to understand how we lost four straight to the Philadelphia 76ers, one of the few sweeps in NBA finals history.

Rocked by adversity, people often get so much empathy and caring poured on them that their own misfortune actually starts to feel good . . . sort of special: "What a tough break," everybody tells them. "You don't deserve it." What soothing consolation this is!

25   But sympathy is like junk food. It has no real nourishment. The emptiness comes back very quickly. And nothing gets accomplished in the meantime. There is never, really, any release from the consequences of adversity until you decide to do something about them.

Forget about sympathy. Strengthen your state of mind instead. Even if the odds have shifted against you, go after your goal with the same effort, the same belief and the same faith.

Somewhere in the 1983 finals we made the classic resignation to adversity. We decided: "It's OK. We're not supposed to win." And that decision made us let down even more. When we went into the locker room after the last loss, we all had our heads down for a moment. Then we looked at each other and said, "Hey, it was a good season anyway." This is the subconscious autosuggestion of blameless defeat.

It took us an entire year to realize what we were doing wrong. If you're going to be a championship team, you have to think championship thoughts. "It's OK to lose" will never be one of them. If you hear yourself or your teammates starting sentences with "If only" or "I could've" or "We should've," you've heard thoughts that are going in the wrong direction. After our "Thunderbolts" season, the Lakers of the 1980s developed a standard saying for whenever they heard a teammate make an excuse: "Shoulda, coulda and woulda won't get it done." And they were right.

Reprinted by permission of The Putnam Publishing Group from The Winner Within *by Pat Riley. Copyright © 1993 by Pat Riley.*

Questions on "Thunderbolts"

Directions: Answer the questions below in complete sentences. At the end of the section, choose either to create your own metaphor to explain how to handle adversity or write a paragraph explaining how you successfully coped with some difficulty in your life.

1. Explain Riley's definition of a "Thunderbolt." How does the word serve as a symbol? _____

    _____

2. In paragraph 8, what does Riley mean when he says "it rocks you, it blows you into a crater"? _____

3. Why is Riley expecting the sky "to blaze with Thunderbolts" in the future?

    _____

    _____

4. What does Riley mean when he says we should pay attention to "weather reports"? Does he mean this literally or figuratively? _____

    _____

5. What is a "competitive applecart"? _____

    _____

6. Give an example of a "positive charge" when you are "back on bedrock."

    _____

    _____

7. What does Riley mean when he says the Lakers should have focused on their remaining strengths and "let them blossom even more"? _____

    _____

8. What does it mean to "drink in solace"? _____

    _____

9. In what way is sympathy like "junk food"? Think of another simile for sympathy. _____

10. What is Riley's purpose? What is his main idea? _____

_____

11. Define the following words from their context and then give the technique(s) you used to discover the meanings of the words. You may want to refer to the different "context clues" techniques discussed in the vocabulary section at the beginning of Chapter 1.

resilient (paragraph 6) Definition:_____

Technique(s) used: _____

aghast (paragraph 20) Definition: _____

Technique(s) used: _____

Bio-sketch

Pete Hamill (1935–   ), a correspondent during the Vietnam War, has been an active journalist, publishing a nationally acclaimed syndicated newspaper column. He is also a novelist whose most recent work is *The Drinking Life*, published in 1995. "The Yellow Ribbon," originally published in his *New York Post* column, has since become the inspiration for a TV movie and a song by Tony Orlando entitled "Tie a Yellow Ribbon 'round the Old Oak Tree." Today, many people use yellow ribbons to welcome home soldiers or to serve as a reminder for those still missing in action.

Notes on Vocabulary

solitude—the state of being solitary or alone.   It comes from the Latin word *solus*, meaning "sole" or "alone." It is often used to describe the state of being cut off from human contact. The loneliness of such a situation is sometimes stressed.

"The Yellow Ribbon"   *by Pete Hamill*

READING

Florida—This area of our country was named by Ponce de Leon after the pascua florida, *or Spanish Festival of Flowers, an annual celebration held during the Easter season. This famous Spanish explorer arrived in Florida in April 1513, and thus named the territory after this festival.*

5

They were going to Ft. Lauderdale, the girl remembered later. There were six of them, three boys and three girls, and they picked up the bus at the old terminal on 34th Street, carrying sandwiches and wine in paper bags, dreaming of golden beaches and the tides of the sea as the gray cold spring of New York vanished behind them. Vingo was on board from the beginning.

As the bus passed through Jersey and into Philly, they began to notice that Vingo never moved. He sat in front of the young people, his dusty face masking his age, dressed in a plain brown ill-fitting suit. His fingers were stained from cigarettes and he chewed the inside of his lip a lot, frozen into some personal cocoon of silence.

Somewhere outside of Washington deep into the night, the bus pulled into a Howard Johnson's, and everybody got off except Vingo. He sat rooted in his seat, and the young people began to wonder about him, trying to imagine his life: Perhaps he was a sea captain, maybe he had run away from his wife, he could be an old soldier going home. When they went back to the bus, the girl sat beside him and introduced herself.

"We're going to Florida," the girl said brightly. "You going that far?"

"I don't know." Vingo said.

I've never been there," she said. "I hear it's beautiful."

"It is," he said quietly, as if remembering something he had tried to forget.

"You live there?"

"I did some time there in the Navy. Jacksonville."

Chianti—Did you 10
know that this red
wine is called "Chianti"
because it was originally
produced in the Chianti
Mountains of Italy?

"Want some wine?" she said. He smiled and took the bottle of Chianti and took a swig. He thanked her and retreated again into his silence. After a while, she went back to the others, as Vingo nodded in sleep.

In the morning they awoke outside another Howard Johnson's, and this time Vingo went in. The girl insisted that he join them. He seemed very shy and ordered black coffee and smoked nervously, as the young people chattered about sleeping on the beaches. When they went back on the bus, the girl sat with Vingo again, and after a while, slowly and painfully and with great hesitation, he began to tell his story. He had been in jail in New York for the last four years, and now he was going home.

"Four years!" the girl said. "What did you do?"

"It doesn't matter," he said with quiet bluntness. "I did it and I went to jail. If you can't do the time, don't do the crime. That's what they say and they're right."

"Are you married?"

15 "I don't know."

"You don't know?" she said.

"Well, when I was in the can I wrote to my wife," he said. "I told her, I said, Martha, I understand if you can't stay married to me. I told her that. I said I was gonna be away a long time, and that if she couldn't stand it, if the kids kept askin' questions, if it hurt her too much, well, she could just forget me. Get a new guy— she's a wonderful woman, really something—and forget about me. I told her she didn't have to write me or nothing. And she didn't. Not for three-and-half years."

"And you're going home now, not knowing?"

"Yeah," he said shyly. "Well, last week, when I was sure the parole was coming through I wrote her. I told her that if she had a new guy, I understood. But if she didn't, if she would take me back she should let me know. We used to live in this town, Brunswick, just before Jacksonville, and there's a great big oak tree just as you come into town, a very famous tree, huge. I told her if she would take me back, she should put a yellow handkerchief on the tree, and I would get off and come home. If she didn't want me, forget it, no handkerchief, and I'd keep going on through."

20 "Wow," the girl said. "Wow."

She told the others, and soon all of them were in it, caught up in the approach of Brunswick, looking at the pictures Vingo showed them of his wife and three children, the woman handsome in a plain way, the children still unformed in a cracked, much-handled snapshot. Now they were 20 miles from Brunswick and the young people took over window seats on the right side, waiting for the approach of the great oak tree. Vingo stopped looking, tightening his face into the ex-con's mask, as if fortifying himself against still another disappointment. Then it was 10 miles, and then 5 and the bus acquired a dark hushed mood, full of silence, of absence, of lost years, of the woman's plain face, of the sudden letter on the breakfast table, of the wonder of children, of the iron bars of solitude.

Then suddenly all of the young people were up out of their seats, screaming and shouting and crying, doing small dances, shaking clenched fists in triumph and exaltation. All except Vingo.

Vingo sat there stunned, looking at the oak tree. It was covered with yellow handkerchiefs, 20 of them, 30 of them, maybe hundreds, a tree that stood like a banner of welcome blowing and billowing in the wind, turned into a gorgeous yellow blur by the passing bus. As the young people shouted, the old con slowly rose from his seat, holding himself tightly, and made his way to the front of the bus to go home.

"The Yellow Ribbon" by Pete Hamill. Copyright © 1972 by Pete Hamill. Reprinted by permission of International Creative Management, Inc.

Review Test 5 "The Yellow Ribbon"

1. The main idea expressed in this article is that
   a. a prison sentence can easily ruin a marriage.
   b. young people on vacation can meet interesting people.
   c. love is better the second time around.
   d. after serving his time in prison, Vingo returned to Brunswick and discovered that his wife wanted him back after all.

2. The author's primary purpose in writing this article is to
   a. inform the reader about unjust prison sentences.
   b. explain to the reader how prison disrupts family life.
   c. entertain the reader with a heartwarming story.
   d. persuade the reader to show compassion to those returning from prison.

3. The pattern of organization used in this article is
   a. division and classification.
   b. comparison and contrast.
   c. chronological order.
   d. cause and effect.

4. You can conclude that Pete Hamill obtained the information needed to write this article by
   a. interviewing Vingo.
   b. interviewing a girl who was on the bus with Vingo.
   c. interviewing Vingo's family and friends.
   d. interviewing the boys who were riding on the bus.

5. We can infer that the young people aboard the bus are going to Florida
   a. to visit relatives.
   b. to celebrate Spring Break.
   c. to interview for jobs.
   d. to take a vacation.

6. We can infer that Vingo's wife was
   a. willing to forgive Vingo.
   b. angry for having to raise their children alone.
   c. a compassionate and caring woman.
   d. both *a* and *c*.

7. We can infer that the young people began their trip in
   a. Washington, D.C.
   b. New York.
   c. Florida.
   d. Pennsylvania.

8. In paragraph 3, the word *rooted* in "He sat *rooted* in his seat. . . . " means
   a. to become established or anchored.
   b. to search about.
   c. to work hard.
   d. to dig.

9. In paragraph 21, the word *fortifying* in "as if *fortifying* himself against still another disappointment" means
   a. strengthening.
   b. weakening.
   c. praising.
   d. condemning.

True or False

_____ 1. Vingo was in prison for four years before receiving a parole.

_____ 2. There were eight young people and two chaperones making the trip.

_____ 3. Vingo had never been to Jacksonville before.

_____ 4. Vingo looked at the pictures of his wife and children a lot.

_____ 5. Vingo felt that you shouldn't commit crimes if you aren't willing to do the time.

IN YOUR OWN WORDS

1. In the last paragraph, Hamill says that the tree covered with yellow handkerchiefs "stood like a banner of welcome." In Vingo's case, what does the tree symbolically represent?

2. What does a yellow ribbon symbolize to returning soldiers? Why do families with soldiers who are POWs or MIAs wear or display yellow ribbons?

3. Make a profile sketch of Vingo by listing his key character traits. Some traits are directly stated in the text, and others must be inferred from the evidence presented. Be able to justify each of your descriptions by citing specific passages.

4. What does it mean to be "frozen into some personal cocoon of silence"?

5. What does Vingo's face look like when he tightens it "into the ex-con's mask"?

6. What inference can you make about why Vingo's wife did not keep in regular contact with him while he was in prison? What kind of woman do you think she is?

Written Assignment

All of us make assumptions about other people just by looking at them. We also judge people by their friends. You can often tell a lot about a person from the people he or she associates with. What do your friends "say" about you? That is, what can someone tell *about you* from knowing or observing your friends? Write a paragraph about yourself from this perspective.

Literary Allusions

A literary allusion is a reference to something that is supposed to be common cultural knowledge. Allusions are a technique writers use to quickly express a complex thought or evoke a certain image or reaction. In this sense, they are much like symbols. To fully understand a literary work, you need to be able to recognize and understand the allusions used by the author. Often, research must be done to discover the meaning of an allusion.

Study the following example from the opening stanza of "Travel" by Robert Louis Stevenson.

> I should like to rise and go
> Where the golden apples grow;—
> Where below another sky
> Parrot islands anchored lie,
> And, watched by cockatoos and goats,
> Lonely Crusoes building boats;—

The word *Crusoe* refers to the main character of Daniel Defoe's eighteenth century novel, *Robinson Crusoe*. In the novel, Crusoe is shipwrecked and washed ashore on an uninhabited island. Crusoe has come to symbolize a person who can overcome hardships and survive in isolation. The second literary allusion, Parrot islands, refers to the Canary Islands located in the Atlantic Ocean directly off the northwest coast of Africa. The Canaries, because of their beauty and relative isolation, symbolize serenity. Thus, in the beginning of this poem, the poet is expressing a longing to journey to a remote area.

Assignment

Directions: Form into groups of four. Each group will then be assigned either Quiz A or Quiz B. You are allowed to help each other. (This activity may be done in the library where resource materials to check answers are readily available, or it may be done in class as a contest to see which group can correctly complete the most answers in a given amount of time.)

Cultural Literacy Quiz A

Mythology and Folklore

1. A weak or sore point in a person's character. A_____ H_____

2. A magician who acted as King Arthur's primary adviser. M_____

Proverbs

3. Physical beauty is superficial. B_____ is _____ _____ d_____.

4. If we want to achieve our goal, we must get an early start. The _____ b_____ gets the w_____.

Idioms

5. A disgrace to the family. B_____ sh_____

6. If something can go wrong, it will. M_____ L_____

Literature

7. Author of *Diary of a Young Girl.* A_____ F_____

8. "I'll huff and I'll puff, and I'll blow your house down." T_____ _____ P_____

9. A novel by J. D. Salinger recounting the adventures of the young Holden Caulfield. *The Catcher in the R_____*

Art

10. The creator of the paintings on the ceiling of the Sistine Chapel. M_____

11. The statue features the words—"Give me your tired, your poor, your huddled masses. . . . " S_____ of L_____

History

12. A king of England who beheaded two wives. H_____ the _____

13. A Roman emperor alleged to have fiddled while Rome burned. N_____

14. The inventor of the lightning rod, bifocal glasses, and a stove. B_____
    F_____

15. A seamstress who made flags in Philadelphia during the Revolutionary
    War. B_____ R_____

16. A battle between Custer and Native Americans.
    L_____ B_____

17. The championship game of the NFL held in January.
    S_____ B_____

Bible

18. The principle of justice that requires punishment equal in kind to the
    offense. An _____ for an _____

19. "Do unto others as you would have them do unto you." The G_____
    R_____

Science

20. Large, white, puffy clouds—some carry rain. C_____

21. The shuttle that exploded in space. C_____

Cultural Literacy Quiz B

Mythology and Folklore

1. A very handsome man. A_____

2. Small men who resemble elves capable of revealing the whereabouts of a
   pot of gold at the end of the rainbow. L_____

Proverbs

3. Apples keep us healthy. An _____ a day k_____ the
   d_____ a_____.

4. Don't assume that you'll get the things you want until you have them.
   D_____ c_____ y_____ ch_____ b_____
   they h_____.

Idioms

5. Smooth, flattering talk (Irish derivation). B_____

6. To blow an event out of proportion. Don't m_____ a m_____
   out of a m_____ h_____.

Literature

7. Ali Baba and the _____ Thieves.

8. "All animals are equal, but some animals are more equal than others."
   A_____ F_____

9. "Elementary, my dear Watson." Sh_____ H_____

Art

10. A painting by Leonardo Da Vinci of a woman with a mysterious smile.
    M_____ L_____

11. The Spanish painter of "Guernica." P_____

History

12. The queen of Egypt famed for her beauty; lover of Marc Antony.
   C_____

13. A female French military leader who claimed God spoke to her in voices.
   J_____ of A_____

14. An English nurse of the nineteenth century, and a symbol for all nursing.
   F_____ N_____

15. The commander of the Confederate troops. R_____ E. L_____

16. His most famous speech is "I Have a Dream." M_____ L_____
   K_____, Jr.

17. The oldest and most famous of the "bowl games." R_____ B_____

Bible

18. The reason people of the Earth are scattered speaking different languages.
   The T_____ of B_____

19. The first children of Adam and Eve. C_____ and A_____

Science

20. Lacy or wispy clouds that form at high altitudes. C_____

21. A very "unlucky" space mission. A_____ _____

Imagery

In addition to the figures of speech mentioned earlier, writers use **imagery** to create word pictures. This means that they describe a person, object, or setting by relying on sensory images. The words or phrases that they use may emphasize any one, or all, of our five senses—sight, sound, taste, touch, and smell. The reader must not only be able to recognize these images, but also understand the author's intent in presenting a particular image to us. In "The Runner," the poet Walt Whitman uses imagery to convey the sensation of running. The descriptive words in the poem primarily appeal to our **visual sense**.

> On a flat road runs the well-train'd runner;
> He is lean and sinewy, with muscular legs;
> He is thinly clothed—he leans forward as he runs,
> With lightly closed fists, and arms partially rais'd.

The next poem, in addition to creating a visual picture of the horses, also creates an image of physical sensation, particularly in the fourth and fifth lines.

> With flowing tail, and flying mane
> Wide nostrils never stretched by pain,
> Mouths bloodless to the bit or rein,
> And feet that iron never shod,
> And flanks unscarred by spur or rod,
> A thousand horses, the wild, the free
> Like waves that follow o'er the sea.

Neptune: Erich Lessing from Art Resource

Study the painting (above) by Walter Crane entitled "Neptune." In what way does the painting express the sensory images conveyed by the poem?

Exercise #1 *L is for Lawless*

In the excerpt below, Kinsey Millhone, private investigator, finds herself trying to escape from a hotel fire started by the murderer she is trying to apprehend. Notice how the use of sensory images involves the reader in Kinsey's distress. These images were chosen by the author to heighten the sense of excitement and danger.

Bio-sketch

Sue Grafton, Edgar award nominee, helped usher in the era of the modern, female, hard-boiled private eye. Grafton, a former screen writer, is the daughter of C. W. Grafton, a lawyer and part-time mystery writer. As a direct consequence of "life with father," Grafton claims she was raised on a steady diet of detective fiction. Grafton's mysteries, which are titled after letters of the alphabet (*A Is for Alibi, B Is for Burglar,* etc.), are considered to be "humorous" in the sense that they exhibit the wit of her female sleuth, Kinsey Millhone. According to the author, Kinsey is partially based on Grafton herself, but is younger and feistier. Grafton's first mystery, *A Is for Alibi,* was selected by the Mystery Writers of America as one of the top 100 mystery novels of all time.

Notes on Vocabulary

abyss—a bottomless pit.   Comes from the Greek word *abyssos* with *a* meaning "without" and *byssos* meaning "bottom."

tawny—tan   The word is derived from the Latin verb *tannare*, meaning "to tan hides," and is associated with the brownish-yellow of tanned leather.

Excerpt from **L is for Lawless**   *by Sue Grafton*

READING

Blindly, I measured the width of the catwalk, sensing the cavernous abyss on my left where my hand plunged suddenly into nothingness.

The entire area was pitch black, but I could hear an ominous crackling noise. A blistering wind blew, sending a shower of sparks in my direction. I could smell hot, dry wood, undercut by the acrid odor of petroleum-based products changing chemical states. I inched my way forward. Ahead, I could now discern a soft reddish glow defining the wall where the corridor curved left. A long finger of smoke curled around the corner toward me. If the fire caught me on the catwalk, it would probably sweep right past, but the rising cloud of toxic fumes would snuff me out as effectively as the flames.

While the water from the sprinkler system hissed steadily, it seemed to have no effect on the fire that I could see. The play of tawny light on the walls began to expand and dance, pushing fine ash and black smoke ahead of it, gobbling up all the available oxygen. The metal catwalk was slippery, the chain railing swinging wildly as I propelled myself onward. The public address system came to life again. The same announcement was repeated, a garbled blend of consonants. I reached the top of the ladder. I was afraid to turn my back on the encroaching fire, but I had no choice. With my right foot, I felt for the first rung, gauging the distance as I moved down from rung to rung. I began descending with care, my hands sliding on the wet metal side rail. Hanging lengths of chain turned gold in the light, sparks flying up, winking out like intermittent fireflies on a hot summer night. By now, the fire was providing sufficient illumination to see the air turn gray as smoke accumulated.

I reached the bottom of the ladder and moved to my left. The fire was heating the air to an uncomfortable degree. I could hear a snapping sound, glass shattering, the merry rustle of destruction as the flames roared toward me. Despite the liberal use of concrete, the hotel had sufficient combustible material to feed the swiftly spreading blaze. I heard the dull boom of thunder as something behind me gave way and collapsed. This entire portion of the hotel had apparently been engulfed. I spotted a door on my left. I tried the knob, which was cool to the touch. I turned it and pushed through, spilling abruptly into a second-floor hall.

5   Here the air was much cooler. The rain birds in the ceiling showered the deserted corridor with irregular sprays. I was getting used to the dark, which now seemed less dense, a chalky gloom instead of the impenetrable black of the inner corridor. The carpet was saturated, slapping wetly beneath my feet as I stumbled down the darkened hallway. Afraid to trust my eyes, I held my arms out stiffly, waving my hands in front of me like a game of blindman's bluff. The fire alarm continued its monotonous clanging, a secondary horn bleating gutturally. In a submarine movie, we'd be diving by now. I felt my way across another door frame. Again, the knob seemed cool to the touch, suggesting that, for the time being, the fire wasn't raging on the other side. I turned the knob, pushing the door open in front of me. I found myself on the fire stairs, which I knew intimately by now. I went down through the blackness, reassured by the familiarity of the stairwell. The air was cold and smelled clean.

From "L" is for Lawless by Sue Grafton, © 1995 by Sue Grafton. Reprinted by permission of Henry Holt and Company, Inc.

Vocabulary Check

Directions: Look through the paragraphs indicated and find a word that correctly matches the definition given.

anything too deep for measurement (1) _____

threatening (2) _____

sharp or bitter to the taste or smell (2) _____

poisonous (2) _____

stopping and starting again at intervals; periodic (3) _____

distorted or confused (3) _____

generous (4) _____

flammable (4) _____

thoroughly soaked (5) _____

going on and on in the same tone (5) _____

closely, familiarly (5) _____

Optional Assignment

1. Make a chart with each one of the senses as a category. On your chart, place each relevant detail from the excerpt under the appropriate category.

2. Identify all similes, metaphors, and personification, and explain their meaning.

3. Write a metaphor or simile about fire. Choose a characteristic about fire that you wish to describe or emphasize. Next, select something else that possesses the same characteristic as fire. Finally, put it all together by comparing the two subjects.

Example:

Subject:	Fire
Characteristic:	Shine
Second Subject:	Gold
Simile:	Fire is like gold, shining ever bright

Exercise #2 "Blizzard under Blue Sky"

The short story "Blizzard under Blue Sky" comes from a collection of short stories entitled *Cowboys Are My Weakness*, written by Pam Houston. The collection was named a *New York Times* Notable Book in 1992. In this particular story, Ms. Houston describes the curative powers of nature. Her character, at a crossroads in life, is suffering from depression. Rather than resort to pills, she seeks to heal herself by being self-reliant in the great outdoors. Houston uses many sensory details to describe her character's experience camping out in Utah in winter with her two dogs as her only companions.

As you read Houston's short story, be sure to notice the descriptive elements used to convey the key character's loneliness, as well as those used to describe the beauty of her surroundings.

Notes on Vocabulary

rampant—spreading unchecked; widespread.

inversion-cloaked—obscured by a temperature inversion   Salt Lake City sits in a valley surrounded by high mountains. In the winter, an inversion layer, or a layer of warmer air over cooler air, often forms over this region. The combination of the mountains around the valley and the inversion layer over the top traps the pollution in, leading to high levels of smog.

translucent—shining through   Something that is translucent allows some light through, but not as much as clear glass. Stained glass windows and skylights are translucent because they allow light through, but you cannot see through them.

"Blizzard Under Blue Sky"   *by Pam Houston*

READING

The doctor said I was clinically depressed. It was February, the month in which depression runs rampant in the inversion-cloaked Salt Lake Valley and the city dwellers escape to Park City, where the snow is fresh and the sun is shining and everybody is happy, except me. In truth, my life was on the verge of more spectacular and satisfying discoveries than I had ever imagined, but of course I couldn't see that far ahead. What I saw was work that wasn't getting done, bills that weren't getting paid, and a man I'd given my heart to weekending in the desert with his ex.

The doctor said, "I can give you drugs."

I said, "No way."

She said, "The machine that drives you is broken. You need something to help you get it fixed."

5   I said, "Winter camping."

She said, "Whatever floats your boat."

One of the things I love the most about the natural world is the way it gives you what's good for you even if you don't know it at the time. I had never been winter camping before, at least not in the high country, and the weekend I chose to try and fix my machine was the same weekend the air mass they called the Alaska Clipper showed up. It was thirty-two degrees below zero in town on the night I spent in my snow cave. I don't know how cold it was out on Beaver Creek. I had listened to the weather forecast, and to the advice of my housemate, Alex, who was an experienced winter camper.

"I don't know what you think you're going to prove by freezing to death," Alex said, "but if you've got to go, take my bivvy sack; it's warmer than anything you have."

"Thanks," I said.

10   "If you mix Kool-Aid with your water it won't freeze up," he said, "and don't forget lighting paste for your stove."

"Okay," I said.

"I hope it turns out to be worth it," he said "because you are going to freeze your butt."

When everything in your life is uncertain, there's nothing quite like the clarity and precision of fresh snow and blue sky. That was the first thought I had on Saturday morning as I stepped away from the warmth of my truck and let my skis slap the snow in front of me. There was no wind and no clouds that morning, just still air and cold sunshine. The hair in my nostrils froze almost immediately. When I took a deep breath, my lungs only filled up halfway.

I opened the tailgate to excited whines and whimpers. I never go skiing without Jackson and Hailey: my two best friends, my yin and yang of dogs. Some of you might know Jackson. He's the oversized sheepdog-and-something-else with the great big nose and the bark that will shatter glass. He gets out and about more than I do. People I've never seen before come by my house daily and call him by name. He's all grace, and he's tireless; he won't go skiing with me unless I let him lead. Hailey is not so graceful, and her body seems in constant indecision when she runs. When we ski, she stays behind me, and on the downhills she tries to sneak rides on my skis.

15   The dogs ran circles in the chest-high snow while I inventoried my backpack one more time to make sure I had everything I needed. My sleeping bag, my Thermarest, my stove, Alex's bivvy sack, matches, lighting paste, flashlight, knife. I brought three pairs of long underwear—tops and bottoms—so I could change once before I went to bed, and once again in the morning, so I wouldn't get chilled by my own sweat. I brought paper and pen, and Kool-Aid to mix with my water. I brought Mountain House chicken stew, and some freeze-dried green peas, some peanut butter and honey, lots of dried apricots, coffee and Carnation Instant Breakfast for morning.

Jackson stood very still while I adjusted his backpack. He carries the dog food and enough water for all of us. He takes himself very seriously when he's got his pack on. He won't step off the trail for any reason, not even to chase rabbits, and he gets nervous and angry if I do. That morning he was impatient with me. "Miles to go, Mom," he said over his shoulder. I snapped my boots into my skis and we were off.

There are not too many good things you can say about temperatures that dip past twenty below zero, except this: They turn the landscape into a crystal palace and they turn your vision into Superman's. In the cold thin morning air the trees and mountains, even the twigs and shadows, seemed to leap out of the background like a 3-D movie, only it was better than 3-D because I could feel the sharpness of the air.

I have a friend in Moab who swears that Utah is the center of the fourth dimension, and although I know he has in mind something much different and more complicated than subzero weather, it was there, on that ice-edged morning, that I felt on the verge of seeing something more than depth perception in the brutal clarity of the morning sun.

As I kicked along the first couple of miles, I noticed the sun crawling higher in the sky and yet the day wasn't really warming, and I wondered if I should have brought another vest, another layer to put between me and the cold night ahead.

20   It was utterly quiet out there, and what minimal noise we made intruded on the morning like a brass band: the squeaking of my bindings, the slosh of the water in Jackson's pack, the whoosh of nylon, the jangle of dog tags. It was the bass line and percussion to some primal song, and I kept wanting to sing it, but I didn't know the words.

Jackson and I crested the top of a hill and stopped to wait for Hailey. The trail stretched out as far as we could see into the meadow below us and beyond, a double track and pole plants carving through softer trails of rabbit and deer.

"Nice place," I said to Jackson, and his tail thumped the snow underneath him without sound.

We stopped for lunch near something that looked like it could be a lake in its other life, or maybe just a womb-shaped meadow. I made peanut butter and honey sandwiches for all of us, and we opened the apricots.

"It's fabulous here," I told the dogs. "But so far it's not working."

25   There had never been anything wrong with my life that a few good days in the wilderness wouldn't cure, but there I sat in the middle of all those crystal-coated trees, all that diamond-studded sunshine, and I didn't feel any better. Apparently clinical depression was not like having a bad day, it wasn't even like having a lot of bad days, it was more like a house of mirrors, it was like being in a room full of one-way glass.

"Come on, Mom," Jackson said. "Ski harder, go faster, climb higher."

Hailey turned her belly to the sun and groaned.

"He's right," I told her. "It's all we can do."

After lunch the sun had moved behind our backs, throwing a whole different light on the path ahead of us. The snow we moved through stopped being simply white and became translucent, hinting at other colors, reflections of blues and purples and grays. I thought of Moby Dick, you know, the whiteness of the whale, where white is really the absence of all color, and whiteness equals truth, and Ahab's search is finally futile, as he finds nothing but his own reflection.

30   "Put your mind where your skis are," Jackson said, and we made considerably better time after that.

The sun was getting quite low in the sky when I asked Jackson if he thought we should stop to build the snow cave, and he said he'd look for the next bank. About one hundred yards down the trail we found it, a gentle slope with eastern exposure that didn't look like it would cave in under any circumstances. Jackson started to dig first.

Let me make one thing clear. I knew only slightly more about building snow caves than Jackson, having never built one, and all my knowledge coming from disaster tales of winter camping fatalities. I knew several things *not* to do when building a snow cave, but I was having a hard time knowing what exactly to do. But Jackson helped, and Hailey supervised, and before too long we had a little cave built, just big enough for three. We ate dinner quite pleased with our accomplishments and set the bivvy sack up inside the cave just as the sun slipped away and dusk came over Beaver Creek.

The temperature, which hadn't exactly soared during the day, dropped twenty degrees in as many minutes, and suddenly it didn't seem like such a great idea to change my long underwear. The original plan was to sleep with the dogs inside the bivvy sack but outside the sleeping bag, which was okay with Jackson, the super-metabolizer, but not so with Hailey, the couch potato. She whined and wriggled and managed to stuff her entire fat body down inside my mummy bag, and Jackson stretched out full-length on top.

One of the unfortunate things about winter camping is that it has to happen when the days are so short. Fourteen hours is a long time to lie in a snow cave under the most perfect of circumstances. And when it's thirty-two below, or forty, fourteen hours seems like weeks.

35   I wish I could tell you I dropped right off to sleep. In truth, fear crept into my spine with the cold and I never closed my eyes. Cuddled there, amid my dogs and water bottles, I spent half of the night chastising myself for thinking I was Wonder Woman, not only risking my own life but the lives of my dogs, and the other half trying to keep the numbness in my feet from crawling up to my knees. When I did doze off, which was actually more like blacking out than dozing off, I'd come back

to my senses wondering if I had frozen to death, but the alternating pain and numbness that started in my extremities and worked its way into my bones convinced me I must still be alive.

It was a clear night, and every now and again I would poke my head out of its nest of down and nylon to watch the progress of the moon across the sky. There is no doubt that it was the longest and most uncomfortable night of my life.

But then the sky began to get gray, and then it began to get pink, and before too long the sun was on my bivvy sack, not warm, exactly, but holding the promise of warmth later in the day. And I ate apricots and drank Kool-Aid flavored coffee and celebrated the rebirth of my fingers and toes, and the survival of many more important parts of my body. I sang "Rocky Mountain High" and "If I Had a Hammer," and yodeled and whistled, and even danced the two-step with Jackson and let him lick my face. And when Hailey finally emerged from the sleeping bag a full hour after I did, we shared a peanut butter and honey sandwich and she said nothing ever tasted so good.

We broke camp and packed up and kicked in the snow cave with something resembling glee.

I was five miles down the trail before I realized what had happened. Not once in that fourteen-hour night did I think about deadlines, or bills, or the man in the desert. For the first time in many months I was happy to see a day beginning. The morning sunshine was like a present from the gods. What really happened, of course, is that I remembered about joy.

40   I know that one night out at thirty-two below doesn't sound like much to those of you who have climbed Everest or run the Iditarod or kayaked to Antarctica, and I won't try to convince you that my life was like the movies where depression goes away in one weekend, and all of life's problems vanish with a moment's clear sight. The simple truth of the matter is this: On Sunday I had a glimpse outside of the house of mirrors, on Saturday I couldn't have seen my way out of a paper bag. And while I was skiing back toward the truck that morning, a wind came up behind us and swirled the snow around our bodies like a blizzard under blue sky. And I was struck by the simple perfection of the snowflakes, and startled by the hopefulness of sun on frozen trees.

"A Blizzard Under Blue Sky," from Cowboys Are My Weakness *by Pam Houston. Copyright © 1992 by Pam Houston. Reprinted by permission of W.W. Norton & Company, Inc.*

Comprehension Checkup

Completion:

1. At the outset of the story, the narrator is feeling _____.

2. List three things that have gone wrong in the narrator's life.
   _____, _____, and _____.

3. In the first paragraph, what sentence demonstrates to the reader that the narrator feels self-pity? _____

   _____

4. What analogy does the doctor use to describe the narrator's condition?

   _____

5. What does this analogy mean? _____

   _____

Multiple Choice

6. "I noticed the sun crawling higher in the sky" is an example of a
   a. simile.
   b. metaphor.
   c. personification.
   d. symbolism.

7. The organizational pattern of paragraph 15 is
   a. main idea sentence followed by details.
   b. details followed by the main idea in the last sentence.
   c. details, main idea sentence in the middle, followed by more details.
   d. just details with no stated main idea.

8. "What minimal noise we made intruded on the morning like a brass band."
   This sentence makes use of
   a. simile.
   b. symbol.
   c. literary allusion.
   d. metaphor.

9. The imagery of this sentence refers to
   a. the beauty of the surrounding area.
   b. the silence of the woods before their arrival.
   c. the bitter cold of the woods.
   d. the life-and-death situation they were facing.

10. The narrator's purpose in writing this selection was to
    a. recommend that we all go to the mountains to fix our "machines."
    b. show how her life has changed since her weekend experience in the mountains.
    c. give the reader a visual and sensory understanding about her weekend experience.
    d. explain how to survive in cold weather.

**IN YOUR
OWN WORDS**

1. Compare and contrast Jackson's and Hailey's personalities. What does the narrator mean when she refers to Jackson and Hailey as "my two best friends, my yin and yang of dogs." Use specific details from the story to support your answers.

2. Referring to specific details from the story, describe what the landscape looks like at 20 degrees below.

3. Explain the meaning of the title "Blizzard under Blue Sky."

Written Assignment

1. Have you ever felt as depressed as the narrator's description? What did you do to restore the "joy" in your life?

2. Have you ever been on a winter or summer camping trip? If you have, describe the preparations you made for the trip and what you saw and how you felt while actually camping.

3. Do you have pets? What kind of relationship do you have with them? Do you think your animals are capable of thinking and feeling?

Chapter 6 Test: "Blizzard Under Blue Sky"

Multiple Choice

1. The squeaking of bindings, slosh of water, whoosh of nylon, and jangle of dog tags are all images that appeal to our sense of
   a. smell.
   b. taste.
   c. touch.
   d. hearing.

2. The narrator refers to clinical depression by saying it is "like a house of mirrors, it was like being in a room full of one-way glass." These similes suggest that the narrator
   a. feels hopeless.
   b. is unmoved by the beauty of her surroundings.
   c. feels there is no way to escape.
   d. All of the above.

3. When the narrator refers to Superman, Moby Dick, Captain Ahab, and Wonder Woman, she is using a
   a. simile.
   b. metaphor.
   c. literary allusion.
   d. personification.

4. What is the narrator saying in this sentence? "The morning sunshine was like a present from the gods."
   a. She has rediscovered her joy in being alive.
   b. She is glad it is morning and she has survived the night.
   c. Her personal problems no longer seem as important.
   d. All of the above.

5. A likely title for this selection would be
   a. "A Tale of Two Dogs."
   b. "Utah in the Winter."
   c. "A Weekend to Remember."
   d. "How to Keep Warm in Sub-Zero Temperatures."

True or False

_____ 6. The narrator took along Kool-Aid to keep her water from freezing.

_____ 7. The narrator's two dogs have similar personalities.

_____ 8. The narrator believes her pets act and think like human beings.

_____ 9. The narrator used drugs to cure her depression.

_____ 10. Hailey likes to be "in charge."

Tone

Inferring Tone

The word **tone** refers specifically to the emotional quality of an article. Just as a speaker's voice can convey a wide range of feelings, so can a writer's **voice.** Because tone reveals an author's attitude toward a subject, understanding it is crucial to interpreting what an author has written. Tone is expressed by the words and details an author selects and can often be described by a single adjective.

Here is a list of words that are sometimes used to describe tone.

1. excited	24. sentimental
2. loving	25. compassionate
3. surprised	26. self-pitying
4. tragic	27. alarmed
5. cruel	28. critical
6. angry	29. depressed
7. bitter	30. solemn
8. formal	31. informal
9. serious	32. objective
10. cheerful	33. amused
11. humorous	34. remorseful
12. arrogant	35. ironic
13. cynical	36. vindictive
14. optimistic	37. pessimistic
15. whining	38. befuddled
16. witty	39. sarcastic
17. peevish	40. admiring
18. charming	41. playful
19. outraged	42. irreverent
20. amazed	43. disgusted
21. scolding	44. appreciative
22. sorrowful	45. nostalgic
23. dictatorial	46. perplexed

Exercise #1 on Tone

The following conversations took place at a local restaurant at lunchtime. Choose an appropriate tone for each conversation from those highlighted below. Use key words and punctuation as clues in identifying the correct tone. Be able to justify your choice.

amazed	appreciative	cheerful	dictatorial
disgusted	outraged	nostalgic	perplexed
scolding	sorrowful		

1. "Don't you dare talk to me like that! I'm your mother and you owe me a little respect. Sit up straight, stop slouching, and please chew with your mouth closed. Don't you have any manners?"

2. "Wow! This is really a nice restaurant. From the outside it certainly doesn't look like much."

3. Mike looks up at the servers singing Happy Birthday and says, "What is this? What's going on? It's not my birthday."

4. "Mommy, I hate this macaroni," Susie said with a sob. "I don't want to be here anymore," she cried. "Please take me home."

5. "I'd like to speak to your manager. You've completely ignored me while you've flirted with the young men at the next table. I want you to know I've never been treated like this before. You're going to be sorry your behavior was so rude when you're out of a job."

6. "Gene, clean up the spill at table 6 and then take four glasses of water to table 7."

7. "We hope you had a pleasant time and will come back soon. Please tell all your friends about us. We've only been open for two weeks and are grateful for all new customers."

8. "Hello everybody! How are you all today? I'm Susan, your server! The tuna looks terrific today! Can I get you an appetizer to start off?"

9. "This food is awful! My lettuce is soggy and it's turning brown. There's a hair in my tomato soup and my sandwich is burnt!"

10. "Oh, honey. Look at that picture on the wall. Remember when we were in Italy? We were so young then and we had such a wonderful time. I wish we could go back to those carefree days."

Exercise #2 Detecting tone

Humor is generally defined as anything that is comical, amusing, or witty. The goal of a writer of humor is to entertain and amuse us, and this may be accomplished in a variety of ways. Some humorists relate absurd events using a serious tone (like Jerry Seinfeld telling a joke while keeping a straight face). Others use a tone of exaggeration to get their laughs (like the slapstick of Jim Carrey). It is important to realize that humor can take many forms.

Bio-sketch

Art Buchwald is one of the foremost humorists in the United States today. His job, as he sees it, is to expose us to our failings as human beings and as members of society. Buchwald has written numerous books, is a regular contributor to a syndicated newspaper column, and is also the recipient of the Pulitzer Prize. In this particular article, he writes about a generational problem concerning morals that many parents are currently facing with their college-age offspring.

Directions: As you and your group members read the article, try to determine the tone of each speaker. Use the list of tone words provided at the beginning of this chapter. Be prepared to justify your choice! You each might want to take a part and play it.

"Daughter's Friend Is A Boy"   *by Art Buchwald*

READING

In the good old days when your daughter said she was bringing home a friend for the weekend, it meant she was bringing home a girlfriend—and when your son said he was bringing home a friend for the weekend, it was a boy. This is not the case anymore, and it is causing houseguest problems throughout the country.

I was over at Ripley's house the other evening, when his daughter, Joan, arrived home for the weekend with her "friend," a tall strapping fellow named Mickey.

1. Mrs. Ripley: "Oh, my goodness! Oh, my goodness! Well, Mickey, I guess you want to put your things away."

2. Joan: "Put them in my room."

3. Mrs. Ripley: "Oh, I think it would be a lot nicer if we put Mickey in the attic."

4. Joan's mouth fell open. "Why can't he sleep in my room?"

5. Mr. Ripley: "I know he'd rather sleep in the attic."

6. Mickey: "That's really nice of you, but Joan's room will be fine."

7. Mr. Ripley: "Well, it isn't going to be fine with me. We need to talk to Joan alone. There's a beer in the refrigerator. Make yourself at home."

8. Joan: "How could you humiliate me in front of my friend?"

9. Mr. Ripley: "My dear girl, perhaps you don't realize, but there's a certain propriety about people sharing rooms when they're not married."

10. Joan: "What propriety could there possibly be?"

11. Mrs. Ripley: "Calm down sweetheart. I know you think we're old-fashioned and out-of-date, but your father and I get very nervous when we know two unmarried people of the opposite sex are in the same room under our roof."

12. Joan: "This is ridiculous. Mickey and I aren't strangers. Where do you think we live in Cambridge?"

13. Mr. Ripley: "I don't want to know where you live in Cambridge. You're not in Cambridge this weekend! You're in our house."

14. Joan: "Well, I guess I was mistaken. I thought it was my house, too."

15. Mrs. Ripley: "Sweetie, please listen to reason. It is your house—but it's not Mickey's house. After all it would

seem to me you would enjoy one weekend sleeping alone in your own room."

_____ 16. Joan: "If I'd known it was going to be such a big deal, I wouldn't have come home. All the way down in the car Mickey was counting on sleeping in my room. He wouldn't have come if he had known he had to sleep in the attic."

_____ 17. Mr. Ripley: "He'll sleep in your room over my dead body."

I decided to intercede. "I have a suggestion. Since Mickey was counting on sleeping in Joan's room, why don't you let him sleep there and have Joan sleep in the attic?"

All three looked at me.

Then Mr. Ripley said, "Wait a minute. Suppose Joan decides to come down from the attic in the middle of the night?"

"It's simple," I said. "Make Mickey promise to lock his door."

From "Daughter's Friend Is A Boy" by Art Buchwald. Reprinted with permission of the author.

Question: What is humorous about Buchwald's solution to the problem? What is the solution meant to illustrate?

Review Test 6: Figurative Language, Inference, and Tone

Directions: Read the following excerpt from Annie Dillard; then answer the questions at the end.

Bio-sketch

Annie Dillard was born in 1945 in Pittsburgh, Pennsylvania, and received her B. A. and M. A. degrees from Hollins College in Roanoke, Virginia. She has received numerous awards for her writings, which include essays, poetry, memoirs, literary criticism, and even a western novel. The following selection is taken from *Pilgrim at Tinker Creek,* for which she received the 1975 Pulitzer Prize for non-fiction writing. This book was the result of Dillard's stay on Tinker Creek in Virginia's Roanoke Valley, where she observed the natural world while exploring the subjects of theology, philosophy, and science. Many have compared this work to Thoreau's *Walden.* The section of Dillard's book that you will be reading is based on her childhood memories.

"The Fixed" *by Annie Dillard*

READING

Once, when I was 10 or 11 years old, my friend Judy brought in a Polyphemus moth cocoon. It was January; there were doily snowflakes taped to the schoolroom panes. The teacher kept the cocoon in her desk all morning and brought it out when we were getting restless before recess. In a book we found what the adult moth would look like; it would be beautiful. With a wingspread of up to six inches, the Polyphemus is one of the few huge American silk moths, much larger than, say, a giant or tiger swallowtail butterfly. The moth's enormous wings are velveted in a rich, warm brown, and edged in bands of blue and pink delicate as a watercolor wash. A startling "eyespot," immense, and deep blue melding to an almost translucent yellow, luxuriates in the center of each hind wing. The effect is one of masculine splendor foreign to the butterflies, a fragility unfurled to strength. The Polyphemus moth in the picture looked like a mighty wraith, a beating essence of the hardwood forest, alien-skinned and brown, with spread, blind eyes. This was the giant moth packed in the faded cocoon. We closed the book and turned to the cocoon. It was an oak leaf sewn into a plump oval bundle; Judy had found it in a pile of frozen leaves.

We passed the cocoon around; it was heavy. As we held it in our hands, the creature within warmed and squirmed. We were delighted, and wrapped it tighter in our fists. The pupa began to jerk violently, in heart-stopping knocks. Who's there? I can still feel those thumps, urgent through a muffling of spun silk and leaf, urgent through the swaddling of many years, against the curve of my palm. We kept passing it around. When it came to me again it was hot as a bun; it jumped half out of my hand. The teacher intervened. She put it, heaving and banging, in the ubiquitous Mason jar.

It was coming. There was no stopping it now. January or not. One end of the cocoon dampened and gradually frayed in a furious battle. The whole cocoon twisted and slapped around in the bottom of the jar. The teacher fades, the classmates fade, I fade: I don't remember anything but that thing's struggle to be a moth or die trying. It emerged at last, a sodden crumple. It was a male; his long antennae were thickly plumed, as wide as his fat abdomen. His body was very thick, over an inch long, and deeply furred. A gray, furlike plush covered his head; a long, tan furlike hair hung from his wide thorax over his brown-furred, segmented abdomen. His multijointed legs, pale and powerful, were shaggy as a bear's. He stood still, but he breathed.

He couldn't spread his wings. There was no room. The chemical that coated his wings like varnish, stiffening them permanently, dried, and hardened his wings as they were. He was a monster in a Mason jar. Those huge wings stuck on his back in a torture of random pleats and folds, wrinkled as a dirty tissue, rigid as leather. They made a single nightmare clump still wracked with useless, frantic convulsions.

5   The next thing I remember, it was recess. The school was in Shadyside, a busy residential part of Pittsburgh. Everyone was playing dodgeball in the fenced playground or racing around the concrete schoolyard by the swings. Next to the playground a long delivery drive sloped downhill to the sidewalk and street. Someone—it must have been the teacher—had let the moth out. I was standing in the driveway, alone, stock-still, but shivering. Someone had given the Polyphemus moth his freedom, and he was walking away.

He heaved himself down the asphalt driveway by infinite degrees, unwavering. His hideous crumpled wings lay glued and rucked on his back, perfectly still now, like a collapsed tent. The bell rang twice; I had to go. The moth was receding down the driveway, dragging on. I went; I ran inside. The Polyphemus moth is still crawling down the driveway, crawling down the driveway hunched, crawling down the driveway on six furred feet, forever.

From Pilgrim At Tinker Creek *by Annie Dillard. Copyright © 1974 by Annie Dillard. Reprinted by permission of HarperCollins Publishers, Inc.*

The greatest joy in nature is the absence of man.

Bliss Carman

Questions

1. Describe the young Annie Dillard's mood (a) at first and (b) by the end of the essay.

   a. _____

   b. _____

2. At what point in the essay does Dillard's reaction to what is happening in the classroom change?

    _____

3. How can we tell that the other children were not as concerned as Dillard about the moth's fate?

    _____

4. To what does Dillard compare the moth in the fourth paragraph of the essay?

    _____

5. What do you suppose caused the moth to start working its way out of the cocoon?

    _____

6. When was the moth supposed to be born?

    _____

7. Why do you think Dillard felt guilty about what happened?

    _____

8. Does this essay have any symbolic value for humankind's relationship to the environment?

    _____

9. By use of context in paragraph 2, give a definition of the word "intervened."

    _____

10. List the similes and metaphors Dillard uses to describe the body parts of the moth. What part of the moth's body is described most vividly? What overall image is created by Dillard's figures of speech?

    _____

    _____

Vocabulary

Find the word in paragraph 1 that means

1. _____ partially transparent; clear
2. _____ brightness; brilliance; glory
3. _____ delicateness; the state of being easily damaged
4. _____ open or spread out
5. _____ a ghost; a spectral vision seen before death
6. _____ foreign; strange

Find the word in paragraph 2 that means

1. _____ calling for haste; insistent
2. _____ present everywhere

Find the word in paragraph 3 that means

1. _____ the body segment between the head and abdomen

Find the word in paragraph 4 that means

1. _____ a physical torment; a wrenching upheaval

Find the word in paragraph 6 that means

1. _____ endless; very great

2. _____ showing no doubt or indecision

3. _____ wrinkled or puckered

Irony

When there is a contrast between what people say and what they actually mean, they are using **verbal irony**. Since the meaning is usually expressed indirectly, you must use inference to understand this *reversed* meaning, or you will misinterpret the author.

Another form of irony is **situational**. In this form, there is a contrast between what is expected to occur and what actually does happen. Many stories or poems that end with an unexpected twist are based on this type of irony.

Study the verbal irony in Stephen Crane's poem, "War Is Kind." Crane is best known as the author of *The Red Badge of Courage*, a novel about a young man whose romantic notion of heroism is shattered in the trenches of the Civil War.

"War Is Kind"   *by Stephen Crane*

Do not weep, maiden, for war is kind.
Because your lover threw wild hands toward the sky
And the affrighted steed ran on alone,
Do not weep
War is kind.
    Hoarse, booming drums of the regiment,
    Little souls who thirst for fight,
    These men were born to drill and die.
    The unexplained glory flies above them,
    Great is the battle-god, great, and his kingdom—
    A field where a thousand corpses lie.
Do not weep, babe for war is kind.
Because your father tumbled in the yellow trenches,
Raged at his breast, gulped and died,
Do not weep.
War is kind.
    Swift blazing flag of the regiment,
    Eagle with crest of red and gold,
    These men were born to drill and die.
    Point for them the virtue of slaughter,
    Make plain to them the excellence of killing
    And a field where a thousand corpses lie.
Mother, whose heart hung humble as a button
On the bright splendid shroud of your son,
Do not weep.
War is kind.

// In peace sons bury their fathers; in war fathers bury their sons. //

Herodotus

**IN YOUR
OWN WORDS**

1. What images of war does Crane convey?

2. Why does Crane mention the mother, the babe, and the maiden?

3. Why does he repeat the refrain, "a field where a thousand corpses lie"?

4. Explain the simile in the last stanza. How can a heart hang "humble as a button"?

Cartoons: Understanding Irony

By permission of Leigh Rubin and Creators Syndicate.

1. Underline the word in the cartoon that most expresses irony.

2. What can you infer has happened in the cartoon?

_____

3. What key point is being made in the cartoon? What situation is being criticized?

_____

4. Describe the tone or attitude you think is really being expressed in the cartoon.

_____

The cartoon above concerns the environment. The sign proclaims the new headquarters of a forest conservation group. This cartoon is ironic because instead of preserving timberland, ground has been cleared to erect another building. The foundation has destroyed what it was supposed to be protecting. This action has defeated the group's fundamental goal. This is the exact **opposite** of what we would reasonably expect. In the cartoon, the meaning is expressed indirectly, so you must use inference to decipher the reversed meaning.

Exercise #1 Irony

Directions: Read the fable and answer the questions that follow.

> *Once, a long time ago, Death came riding into the city of Baghdad looking for Ali Haj, a proud and wealthy merchant. Death was in no hurry to meet Ali Haj, for he had many other old friends whom he wished to honor by a visit. On hearing that Death was in the town and had already called on some of his friends, Ali Haj, who had not gained his riches by stupidity, spoke to his old, blind servant:*
>
> *"There is a great prince come to town, whom I am eager to see, for I wish to give him a rare jewel to win his friendship. Unfortunately, I cannot hope he would visit the poor home of a humble merchant like myself. Therefore I shall go to seek him. But if he should by chance come here while I am away, welcome him with the choicest of food and drink, and beg him only to wait for me a little while. But see you keep him here."*
>
> *Then Ali Haj gathered his favorite treasures, his wives and children, and fled on his swiftest horses to Damascus.*
>
> *When Death knocked at his door the next day, the blind servant appeared. "I seek your master, Ali Haj," Death said.*
>
> *"He has gone out to seek a great prince to give him a precious jewel," answered the servant. "But if you, my lord, are that prince, then my master begs you to consider this house your own and to stay only a little while till he returns."*
>
> *"There are many who call me Prince," said Death, "but few so joyful to greet me as Ali Haj. But that is what I expected of him." Then he stared at the ancient man, who was indeed rich in white hairs and wrinkles. "Since you are sure to see him soon, kindly remind him that he need not have gone out today to seek me, for I wished only to ask him to meet me tomorrow in Damascus."*

**IN YOUR
OWN WORDS**

1. What is the moral of this fable? What is the fable saying about Death?

2. What is ironic about Ali Haj's departure? Why does he ask the servant to keep Death well-entertained in Baghdad?

3. Is Ali Haj going to succeed in avoiding Death? Explain your answer.

4. Whom does Ali Haj succeed in fooling?

5. What does Death mean when he tells the old servant that he is sure to see his master, Ali Haj, soon?

6. Why was Death in no hurry to see Ali Haj? Why is this ironic? What does Death mean when he says he expected this type of welcome from Ali Haj?

Exercise #2 Irony

Bio-sketch

Gregorio Lopez y Fuentes was a highly acclaimed author who received Mexico's National Prize for Literature in 1935. As the son of a small farmer, he understood the difficulties the farmer faced in trying to make a living off the land. This story was translated from Spanish by Donald A. Yates.

"A Letter to God"   *by Gregorio Lopez y Fuentes*

READING

The house—the only one in the entire valley—sat on the crest of a low hill. From this height one could see the river and, next to the corral, the field of ripe corn dotted with the kidney-bean flowers that always promised a good harvest.

The only thing the earth needed was a rainfall, or at least a shower. Throughout the morning Lencho—who knew his fields intimately—had done nothing else but scan the sky toward the northeast.

"Now we're really going to get some water, woman."

The woman, who was preparing supper, replied:

5   "Yes, God willing."

The oldest boys were working in the field, while the smaller ones were playing near the house, until the woman called to them all:

"Come for dinner . . . "

It was during the meal that, just as Lencho had predicted, big drops of rain began to fall. In the northeast, huge mountains of clouds could be seen approaching. The air was fresh and sweet.

The man went out to look for something in the corral for no other reason than to allow himself the pleasure of feeling the rain on his body, and when he returned he exclaimed:

10 "Those aren't raindrops falling from the sky, they're new coins. The big drops are ten-centavo pieces and the little ones are fives. . . . "

With a satisfied expression he regarded the field of ripe corn with its kidney-bean flowers, draped in a curtain of rain. But suddenly a strong wind began to blow and together with the rain very large hailstones began to fall. These truly did resemble new silver coins. The boys, exposing themselves to the rain, ran out to collect the frozen pearls.

'It's really getting bad now," exclaimed the man, mortified. "I hope it passes quickly."

It did not pass quickly. For an hour the hail rained on the house, the garden, the hillside, the cornfield, on the whole valley. The field was white, as if covered with salt. Not a leaf remained on the trees. The corn was totally destroyed. The flowers were gone from the kidney-bean plants. Lencho's soul was filled with sadness. When the storm had passed, he stood in the middle of the field and said to his sons:

"A plague of locusts would have left more than this. . . . The hail has left nothing: this year we will have no corn or beans. . . . "

15 That night was a sorrowful one:

"All our work, for nothing!"

"There's no one who can help us!"

"We'll all go hungry this year. . . . "

But in the hearts of all who lived in that solitary house in the middle of the valley, there was a single hope: help from God.

20 "Don't be so upset, even though this seems like a total loss. Remember, no one dies of hunger!"

"That's what they say: no one dies of hunger. . . . "

All through the night, Lencho thought only of his one hope: the help of God, whose eyes, as he had been instructed, see everything, even what is deep in one's conscience.

Lencho was an ox of a man, working like an animal in the fields, but still he knew how to write. The following Sunday, at daybreak, after having convinced himself that there is a protecting spirit, he began to write a letter which he himself would carry to town and place in the mail.

It was nothing less than a letter to God.

25   "God," he wrote, "if you don't help me, my family and I will go hungry this year. I need a hundred pesos in order to resow the field and to live until the crop comes, because the hailstorm . . . "

He wrote "To God" on the envelope, put the letter inside and, still troubled, went to town. At the post office he placed a stamp on the letter and dropped it into the mailbox.

One of the employees, who was a postman and also helped at the post office, went to his boss laughing heartily and showed him the letter to God. Never in his career as a postman had he known that address. The postmaster—a fat amiable fellow—also broke out laughing, but almost immediately he turned serious and, tapping the letter on his desk, commented:

"What faith! I wish I had the faith of the man who wrote this letter. To believe the way he believes. To hope with the confidence that he knows how to hope with. Starting up a correspondence with God!"

So in order not to disillusion that prodigy of faith, revealed by a letter that could not be delivered, the postmaster came up with an idea: answer the letter. But when he opened it, it was evident that to answer it he needed something more than good will, ink and paper. But he stuck to his resolution: he asked for money from his employee, he himself gave part of his salary, and several friends of his were obliged to give something "for an act of charity."

30   It was impossible for him to gather together the hundred pesos, so he was able to send the farmer only a little more than half. He put the bills in an envelope addressed to Lencho and with them a letter containing only a single word as a signature: GOD.

The following Sunday Lencho came a bit earlier than usual to ask if there was a letter for him. It was the postman himself who handed the letter to him, while the postmaster, experiencing the contentment of a man who has performed a good deed, looked on from the doorway of his office.

Lencho showed not the slightest surprise on seeing the bills—such was his confidence—but he became angry when he counted the money. . . . God could not have made a mistake, nor could he have denied Lencho what he had requested!

Immediately, Lencho went up to the window to ask for paper and ink. On the public writing table, he started in to write, with much wrinkling of his brow, caused by the effort he had to make to express his ideas. When he finished, he went to the window to buy a stamp which he licked and then affixed to the envelope with a blow of his fist.

The moment that the letter fell into the mailbox the postmaster went to open it. It said:

35   "God: of the money that I asked for, only seventy pesos reached me. Send me the rest, since I need it very much. But don't send it to me through the mail, because the post-office employees are a bunch of crooks. Lencho."

From "A Letter to God" by Gregorio Lopez y Fuentes, translated by Donald Yates. Reprinted by permission.

Questions

1. Record your first impressions about Lencho, his wife, the postman, and the postmaster. Give a brief description of each.

   _____

   _____

2. Study the following list of key details and explain what could reasonably be inferred from each.
   a. Lencho knows his fields "intimately."

   _____

   b. Lencho's only hope is "the help of God."

   _____

   c. The postman goes to his boss "laughing heartily."

   _____

   d. Never had the postman "known that address."

   _____

   e. The postmaster answers the letter "in order not to disillusion that prodigy of faith."

   _____

   f. The postmaster experiences "the contentment of a man who has performed a good deed."

   _____

   g. Lencho affixes the stamp "with a blow of his fist."

   _____

3. Why did Lencho react the way he did? Would you react as Lencho does? Explain why or why not.

   _____

4. Identify and explain a simile and a metaphor in the story.

   _____

5. In what way is the story ironic? Explain your answer.

   _____

Written Assignment

Have you ever tried to help someone, and it turned out that the person resented your efforts? If so, how did you feel about that person? Describe your experience in a short paragraph.

Satire

Satire is a kind of writing that uses ridicule to create awareness of flaws and to bring about change. Almost anything can be satirized, including people, institutions, and ideas. Because it relies on exaggeration and distortion, satire often has a humorous effect.

Caricature is a form of satire in which certain characteristics, such as physical features, are exaggerated. Look at the caricature of President Clinton. Which of his features are distorted?

CLAY JONES
Courtesy Mississippi Business Journal

IN MY SECOND TERM, AL AND I WILL BUILD A BRIDGE INTO THE 21st CENTURY...

Reprinted by permission of Clay Jones.

In **hyperbole**, language is used to exaggerate a situation. In Mark Twain's classic novel *The Adventures of Huckleberry Finn*, the author gives the reader the following warning at the start of the book:

> *NOTICE: Persons attempting to find a motive in this narrative will be prosecuted; persons attempting to find a moral in it will be banished; persons attempting to find a plot in it will be shot.—By Order Of The Author*

The satirist may also use **understatement**, which is saying less about something than is appropriate. As an example of understatement, consider the following incident. In 1897, Samuel Clemens (Mark Twain) was staying in London at the same time as his cousin, Dr. James Ross Clemens. Dr. Clemens became ill and died, but the press mistakenly reported that it was Mark Twain who had died. To untangle the mix-up, Twain sent a cable from London to the Associated Press that read, "The reports of my death are greatly exaggerated."

In May, 1997, the long-running, popular television show, *The Simpsons*, received the prestigious George Foster Peabody Award for excellence in television. *The Simpsons* was cited for satire and social commentary. If you are not a frequent viewer of the show, try watching an episode or two. What kinds of things does Matt Groening, creator of *The Simpsons*, satirize? Using "Grandpa" as an example, how does Groening feel about how the elderly are treated in this country?

A satirist is a man who discovers unpleasant things about himself and then applies it to other people.

Peter McArthur

The Calvin and Hobbes cartoon below uses satire to demonstrate how power-ful the popular media is in influencing behavior. Even Calvin, who is portrayed as being very sophisticated about the media, is not immune. Is the cartoonist making a valid point about the media? Do you think, in addition to Calvin, other young children are easily influenced by messages they receive from television? Why or why not?

Calvin and Hobbes © Watterson. Reprinted with permission of UNIVERSAL PRESS SYNDICATE. All rights reserved.

When reading satire, pay close attention to the goals of the satirist, the devices he uses to accomplish his goals, and his tone. While a satire can have any tone, the most common is irony.

Exercise #1 Satire

Directions: Read this short satire and then answer the questions that follow.

"The Animal School"
by George H. Reavis

READING

THE ANIMAL SCHOOL:
The Administration of the School Curriculum
with References to Individual Differences
Dr. George H. Reavis
Assistant Superintendent, Cincinnati Public Schools, 1939–1948

Once upon a time, the animals decided they must do something heroic to meet the problems of "a new world." So they organized a school.

They adopted an activity curriculum consisting of running, climbing, swim-ming, and flying. To make it easier to administer the curriculum *all* the animals took *all* the subjects.

The duck was excellent in swimming, in fact better than his instructor; but he made only passing grades in flying and was very poor in running. Since he was slow in running, he had to stay after school and also drop swimming in order to practice running. This was kept up until his web feet were badly worn and he was only average in swimming. *But average was acceptable in school so nobody worried about that except the duck.*

The rabbit started at the top of the class in running, but had a nervous breakdown because of so much make-up work in swimming.

5   The squirrel was excellent in climbing until he developed frustration in the flying class where his teacher made him start from the ground up instead of from the treetop down. He also developed a "charlie horse" from overexertion and then got a C in climbing and a D in running.

The eagle was a problem child and was disciplined severely. In the climbing class he beat all the others to the top of the tree, but insisted on using his own way to get there.

At the end of the year, an abnormal eel that could swim exceedingly well, and also run, climb, and fly a little, had the highest average and was valedictorian.

The prairie dogs stayed out of school and fought the tax levy because the administration would not add digging and burrowing to the curriculum. They apprenticed their children to a badger and later joined the groundhogs and gophers to start a successful private school.

From "The Animal School" by Dr. George H. Reavis.

IN YOUR OWN WORDS

Question: Does this fable have a moral?

1. What makes this story satirical?

2. In regard to the school system, what changes would Dr. Reavis like to see implemented?

3. What criticism is the author making about the way schools are run?

4. Why was the eel chosen as the valedictorian?

5. What is the significance of this choice?

6. Is the prairie dogs' course of action similar to any contemporary trends in education?

Exercise #2 Satire

1. Study Matt Groening's satirical cartoon on the following page. What is he saying about the current school situation?

2. What attitude about learning does the cartoon express?

3. Do you see yourself in this cartoon? Has your school experience been similar? Explain.

4. What attitude about adults does the cartoon express?

LIFE IN HELL   ©1984 BY MATT GROENING

Panel 1: SO WHAT DID YOU LEARN IN SCHOOL TODAY?

Panel 2: PICTURE THIS: ROW AFTER ROW OF KIDS CHEATED OF ENLIGHTENMENT, NUMBED INTO SUBMISSION BY TEDIUM AND BLANDNESS.

Panel 3: DAY AFTER DAY OF OBEDIENCE TRAINING BY DRONING ADULTS WHO RESPOND TO INCONVENIENT QUESTIONS WITH SWIFT PUNISHMENT.

Panel 4: IT IS EASIER TO SQUELCH A KID FOR SHOWING BOREDOM THAN IT IS TO BE INTERESTING.

Panel 5: KIDS ARE CONDESCENDED TO, MISUNDERSTOOD, OR JUST PLAIN IGNORED. OUR FEARS ARE BELITTLED, OUR HOPES DISMISSED.

Panel 6: WE GET UNNECESSARY RESTRAINTS PLACED ON OUR NARROW LITTLE LIVES, EXAGGERATING OUR PHYSICAL LIMITATIONS AND TAKING ADVANTAGE OF OUR NATURAL IGNORANCE OF PRACTICAL AFFAIRS.

Panel 7: BUT THEY WON'T GET ME. I WILL NOT BE DORMANT, I WILL NOT BE DOCILE. I WILL NOT GIVE IN, I WILL NOT BE BURIED ALIVE.

Panel 8: IT'S HARD TO BELIEVE ADULTS DON'T REMEMBER WHAT IT WAS LIKE TO BE A KID.

Panel 9: SO WHAT DID YOU HAVE FOR LUNCH TODAY?

From *The Big Book of Hell* © 1990 by Matt Groening. All Rights Reserved. Reprinted by permission of Pantheon Books, a division of Random House, Inc., NY.

Exercise #3 Satire

In this excerpt from the book *Lighten Up, George*, Art Buchwald, well-known humorist, uses satire to convey his feelings about "direct" dialing.

"When You Hear the Beep"   *by Art Buchwald*

READING

Not since Alexander Graham Bell invented the whatchamacallit has the phone system gone through so many gyrations. The big breakthrough recently is that companies are installing direct dialing so that you are never able to speak to a live operator. Every employee has his or her own line and it's up to the caller to figure out how to get through.

The other day I needed to talk to Dumphries at my favorite utility company. This is how it went:

The recorded voice said, "You have reached the Darkness Unlimited Telephone Company. If you know the extension of the party you wish to speak to, you may key it in at any time. If you do not have that number, dial 233-5570 or 554-6784. If you wish to talk to the service department, ring 312-6789, or if you have questions regarding a bill, dial 908-7654, or 345-7890. If you prefer to speak to the advertising department or public relations, then ring 800-234-5670. If you get a busy signal, drop the 800 and add area code 999 instead. Any questions regarding the environment will be answered by calling our branch office in Toronto. You can obtain this number by requesting information through our Atlanta substation at 900-345-789-000."

I wasn't having much luck finding Dumphries, so I telephoned his wife at home. She gave me his direct line at work, 897-6550.

5   My problem was far from solved. When I dialed his extension I got the recorded voice of Dumphries: "This is Harcourt Dumphries. I am sorry I am not at my desk right now. If you wish to leave a message, you may do so at the sound of the beep, and I will get back to you, If you don't hear from me within three days, call my secretary at 456-7800. If she's not there, you can leave a message with the receptionist at 403-4557. You'll know you have reached the correct number because she always plays 'The Ride of the Valkyries' on her line when she asks you to wait."

Dumphries did not get back to me, so I called him again. He told me that he had received my call on his answering service but he could not return it because the tape jammed up.

"What gives with the direct dialing?" I asked.

"The company installed it for ten thousand employees because it enabled Darkness to lay off two telephone operators and save twelve hundred dollars a year."

"But it's so impersonal," I protested. "A caller feels at a terrible loss trying to get through to the person he wants to contact."

10   "That's because you don't pay enough attention when you phone us. We give you the choice of every telephone number in the system. Next month we're going to put out a company phone book which you can buy for nine ninety-five. Direct dialing is the wave of the future. The more live people a company eliminates from its telephone system payroll, the more efficient that company will become."

"No doubt, but I'm old-fashioned and I feel a lot less helpless when I hear a human voice at the other end of the line. Why couldn't customers have a choice, the same as in restaurants? Instead of Smoking or Nonsmoking, we could choose Human Voice or Recorded Voice. It would be wonderful for your clients."

Dumphries said, "We are not going to placate customers who are against computer technology. Direct dialing has been a breakthrough comparable to man landing on the moon. Just because the public is confused doesn't mean that the system is unworkable. The money saved is channeled into research to find better ways of dialing people *without* having to go through the switchboard.

"We try very hard to make our recorded voices sound human. We auditioned two hundred applicants before we found a woman who could give us the perfect, 'All our lines are busy. Please do not hang up.' "

Reprinted by permission of G.P. Putnam's Sons, a division of Penguin Putnam Inc. from Lighten Up, George *by Art Buchwald. Copyright © 1991 by Art Buchwald.*

**IN YOUR
OWN WORDS**

1. Why was the fictitious phone company given the name *Darkness Unlimited*?

2. What is the phone company's reason for installing direct dialing? Why does Buchwald include this detail?

3. What reasons does Buchwald give for returning to the sound of a human voice?

4. What is Dumphries' response to Buchwald's arguments?

5. What is ironic about the last paragraph?

6. What is Buchwald pointing out about the status of technology in this country? Is he for or against these "improvements"?

Written Assignment

1. Write a paragraph about a so-called time-saving device that at times makes your life more difficult.

2. How do you feel about answering machines, cellular phones, and pagers?

Frank and Ernest

© 1996 Thaves. / Reprinted with permission. Newspaper distribution by NEA, Inc.

Chapter 7 Test: "When You Hear the Beep"

Multiple Choice

1. The author's primary purpose in writing this article was to
   a. persuade.
   b. entertain.
   c. explain.
   d. define.

2. The tone of this article could be described as
   a. sentimental.
   b. admiring.
   c. humorous.
   d. cheerful.

3. The structure used in paragraph 5 is
   a. main idea followed by details.
   b. no stated main idea, just details.
   c. details with the main idea sentence at the end.
   d. the main idea sentence at the beginning and at the end.

4. The word *placate* in the first sentence of paragraph 12 means
    a. anger.
    b. appease.
    c. tolerate.
    d. convince.

5. The organizational pattern used in paragraph 8 is
    a. definition.
    b. steps in a process.
    c. cause and effect.
    d. classification and division.

True or False

_____   6. The general organizational pattern of the article is chronological.

_____   7. You can infer from the article that Buchwald believes computer technology will make the future brighter and happier.

_____   8. Dumphries believes that his company can save money by installing a direct dialing system.

_____   9. Dumphries has never had any difficulty with answering machines.

_____ 10. Alexander Graham Bell invented the telephone.

Vocabulary: Unit 3

In vocabulary 2, you learned that *enn* and *ann* mean year. In this lesson, we will study some more words using these word parts. We will also introduce you to word parts related to the five senses, size, and writing.

	ann—year **enn—year**
anniversary	the yearly return of a date or event, as in a wedding *anniversary*.
annual	*Annual* usually means "yearly," but it is also a term used to describe a plant living only one year or season. A sunflower is an example of an *annual* because it completes its life cycle, produces seeds, and dies after growing only one season. *Annual* flowers will not bloom again.
biannual	happening twice a year. The equinox is a *biannual* event.
biennial	happening every two years; also a plant that lasts for two years. Congressional elections take place *biennially*.
perennial	continuing for a long time; year after year; also a plant which has roots that remain alive during the winter and which blooms year after year, such as the Iris. The San Francisco 49ers are *perennially* a good football team.

audience—The largest television audience for any show or event was the 134.4 million people who listened to and watched the 1994 Super Bowl. Dallas beat Buffalo 30–13.

| | anno Domini (A.D.) | *Anno* means "year," and *Domini* means "Lord," so A.D. does not mean "after death," but "Year of Our Lord." The Civil War began in 1860 A.D. |

audio—hear
ology—the study of; the science of
spec(t)—to see

| | audience | a group of people gathered to hear (and see) a speaker, play, or concert; also a formal interview with someone in a high position.   The local parish priest was granted an *audience* with the Pope. |

spectators—The largest number of spectators at a one day sporting event is the approximately 2.5 million people who line the streets of New York every year to watch the New York Marathon.

	audiology	the science of hearing.
	auditorium	a room where an audience usually gathers to listen.
	audition	a hearing to judge the skills of a musician or actor for a job When you *audition* for a part in a play, the director will be interested in hearing how you read your lines. There were no microphones in ancient Greece, so actors who were in plays had to be able to say their lines loud enough so that the people in the back row of the amphitheaters could hear them.

spectrum—One beautiful spectrum, the rainbow, can be seen only in the morning or late afternoon when the sun is 40 degrees or less above the horizon.

	auditory	having to do with the sense of hearing; also your listening skills. In the first part of this textbook, you discovered whether or not you were an *auditory* learner.
	spectator	a person who sees or watches something without being an active participant. You might be a *spectator* at a football game.
	speculate	to mentally see something in a serious way. Are you *speculating* about what you are going to do tonight?
	spectrum	A *spectrum* is a range of color, as in a rainbow or in light shining through a prism. The word also sometimes refers to a range of ideas. In the college classroom, there was a wide *spectrum* of opinion on the subject of abortion.

vis—see   in—not; into, within

visible—The farthest object visible to the naked eye is the Great Galaxy of Andromeda. It was first observed by a German, Simon Marius (1570–1624). This galaxy is 2,310,000 light-years from the earth. A light-year is how far light will travel in a year and is equivalent to 5,878,499,814,000 miles.

	visible	capable of being seen. The mountains were *visible* from a great distance.
	invisible	not capable of being seen. Here *in* means "not." The Latin prefix *in* appears in many English words. At times it means "not," and at other times it means "into." When you come to a word using *in*, you may need to use context clues or your dictionary to determine the correct meaning.
	vista	a view or outlook seen from some distance.

visionary	looking into the future. He had a *visionary* scheme to create human colonies on Mars. *Visionary* also means a prophet or seer. In the Old Testament, prophets were *visionaries* because they looked into the future.
audio-visual	involving both hearing and seeing. VCRs are examples of *audio-visual* equipment.

phono—sound

phonograph	a device for reproducing sound recorded in a turning record. The word literally means "sound written down." We used to listen to records on a *phonograph*. What's the modern-day equivalent of the *phonograph*?
phonics	the study of speech sounds and their written symbols (letters). Your teacher might have taught you *phonics* when you were learning to read.

Frank and Ernest

© 1995 Thaves. / Reprinted with permission. Newspaper distribution by NEA, Inc.

macro—large
micro—small, or one-millionth part; enlarging, amplifying
bio—life
scope—an instrument for seeing

microwave	a small electromagnetic wave; also an oven that cooks with *microwaves*. The literal meaning is "small wave."
micrometer	one millionth of a meter.
microphone	an instrument for amplifying sound. In this word *micro* means "amplifying what is small or weak."
microscope	an instrument for making very small objects look larger. In this word *micro* means "enlarging what is small."
microeconomics	an economic analysis of small-scale parts of the economy, such as the growth of a single industry or demand for a single product.
macroeconomics	the part of economic theory that deals with the larger picture, such as national income, total employment, and total consumption.

microphone—The smallest microphone is 0.06 by 0.03 inches.

microbiology	the branch of biology that deals with small life organisms.

magna—large	**mega—large; one million**	**tele—distance**

magnify	to make larger.
megaphone	a device for magnifying the voice; literally means "large sound." Police may use *megaphones* to be heard over the noise of the crowd.
megabyte	one million pieces of information; a unit of capacity on your computer equal to 1,048,576 bytes (bits).
telescope	an optical device for seeing distant objects; use of a *telescope* makes these distant objects appear to be closer.
telephone	a device for transmitting speech or computerized information over distances; "sound from a distance."
telephoto	a camera lens that magnifies a distant object so that it appears to be close. A photographer working for a tabloid magazine was able to get a picture of Madonna's baby girl by using a camera equipped with a *telephoto* lens.
telepathy	mind reading; knowledge communicated from one person to another without using any of the five senses; "feeling from a distance."
teleconference	a conference of persons in different locations by means of the telephone or TV.
television	"seeing from a distance."

scribe, script—write	**biblio—book**	**pre—before**	**post—after**

scribble	to write carelessly, quickly.
inscription	something engraved; a short, signed message. (Here *in* means "into.") Because Thomas Jefferson wanted to be remembered for the things he had left to the people, and not for the high offices he had held, the *inscription* on his tomb reads: "Here was buried Thomas Jefferson, author of the Declaration of American Independence, of the Statute of Virginia for religious freedom, and father of the University of Virginia."
prescription	something advised or ordered; a written direction for the preparation and use of medicine; "written before." Following her attack of the flu, her doctor's *prescription* was lots of fluids and complete bed rest.
postscript	a note written after the signature in a letter (P.S.).
scribe	a writer, author, or secretary. Before the invention of printing, the *scribes* were professional penmen who copied manuscripts and documents.

telescope—The largest telescope in the world is located on Mauna Loa, Hawaii. Its mirror is 394 inches wide.

telephone—The first telephone book was published in 1878 in New Haven, Connecticut. It listed only 50 names.

television— All television is educational television. The question is: what is it teaching?

Nicholas Johnson

Scripture   any sacred writing or book; a Bible passage.

Bible—The Bible is the   *Bible*   the sacred book of Christianity; the Old Testament
best-selling book in the   and New Testament.
world. The American
Bible Society has pub-   *bibliography*   Since *graph* means "write," a *bibliography* literally
lished almost a billion   means "books written down." A *bibliography* is a list
copies since 1816. The   of sources of information on a particular subject.
whole Bible has been   When you write a research paper for one of your
translated into at least   classes, you will include a *bibliography* at the end of
337 languages.   your paper listing the books and articles you used
                                                    for your research.

Write sentences for the following words. Add whatever endings are necessary.

audiologist_____

_____

perennial _____

_____

speculate _____

_____

scribe _____

_____

biennial _____

_____

visionary _____

_____

telepathy _____

_____

scribble_____

_____

Vocabulary 3

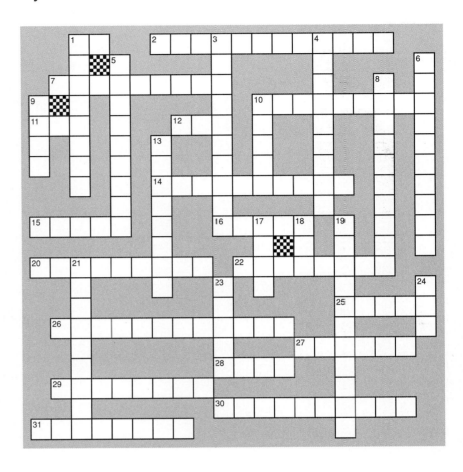

ACROSS CLUES

1. Word part for "two."
2. Written before.
7. Instrument to see from a distance.
10. Roses are _____ flowers. They bloom year after year.
11. Word part for "year."
12. Word part for "side."
14. "Year of Our Lord" (no space between words).
15. The sacred book of Christianity.
16. Word part for "to see."
20. A person who looks into the future.
22. The _____ for the Opening Ceremony of the 1998 Olympics was the largest in history.
25. View seen from a distance.
26. A list of books or references at the end of a paper.
27. A writer.
28. Word part meaning "half."
29. Your listening skills.
30. P.S.
31. A range of light or ideas.

DOWN CLUES

1. Every other year.
3. A group that watches an event.
4. Sound from a distance.
5. Police might use one of these.
6. Seeing from a distance.
8. An instrument for amplifying sound.
9. Word part meaning 1,000,000.
10. Word part meaning "sound."
13. The equinox is a _____ event.
17. Word part meaning "the same amount or size."
18. Word part meaning "three."
19. Happening once a year, such as a wedding _____.
21. Sacred writing.
23. Word part meaning "write."
24. Word part meaning "marriage."

PART 4 Recognizing Modes of Writing

*Music is a collection of sounds that are arranged into patterns. These
sounds, or notes, may be produced by human voices, instruments, or
even nature itself. When sound, or noise, is organized or manipulated
by a person into some kind of pattern it may become music.*

from Music Connections *by Caroline Grimshaw*

*Even jazz—that glorification of the senses . . . is organized [and]
obeys the principles of form and structure.*

from The Forms of Music *by Andre Hodeir*

It may surprise you that jazz, which often seems so lively and
creative, has structure. Writing too has structure. On a general
level, writing is structured into what we will call modes of writing. These modes of writing are narrative, descriptive, expository,
and persuasive. And then within these general structures there
are more specific structures, which we will call modes of organizing. Understanding the ways in which writing may be structured
will make you a better, more efficient reader. The purpose of Part
4 is to develop your understanding of modes of writing and
modes of organization.

Four Primary Methods

An Introduction to Modes of Writing (Rhetorical Modes)

In longer reading selections, the main idea is often referred to as the **thesis.** The thesis, just like the main idea in paragraphs, expresses the most important point the writer is trying to make. You may also hear the thesis referred to as the *controlling idea* because its primary purpose is to hold the essay or story together.

In the process of creating written work, most writers select a **mode of writing** (sometimes called a rhetorical mode) that helps them achieve their purpose. There are four primary modes of writing: *narrative, descriptive, expository*, and *persuasive.*

Material written in a **narrative mode** tells a story, either true or fictional. With material written in a **descriptive mode,** the emphasis is on providing details that describe a person, place, or object. An author who is trying to explain something will likely use an **expository mode.** Much of the material that you read in your textbooks follows an expository mode. Material written in a **persuasive mode** is meant to convince you of something.

Once a writer has selected a mode of writing, he needs to select one or more **modes of organization.** The modes of organization are (1) cause and effect, (2) compare and contrast, (3) definition, (4) examples or illustrations, (5) steps in a process, (6) classification and division (categories), and (7) chronology. (These categories should seem familiar to you because they previously appeared in this book as *patterns of organization* for paragraphs.) Thus, a writer who wishes to write in a persuasive mode might choose as modes of organization *compare and contrast, definition,* and *examples.* Or, an author who wishes to write in a descriptive mode might select *examples* and *chronology* as modes of organization. Sometimes an author may organize the entire article using only one mode of organization.

Writers select the modes of writing and organization that will best enable them to communicate with their audience. Being able to recognize the different modes of writing and organization will help you become a better reader.

The reading selections that follow illustrate modes of writing and organization. Though these articles come from a variety of sources, they all, either directly or indirectly, concern the topic of relationships.

Narrative

Bio-sketch

Langston Hughes (1902–1967) is one of the best-known African-American writers of the twentieth century and the first to live solely from his writings and lectures. Shortly after his birth in Joplin, Missouri, his parents were divorced. As a result, Hughes spent much of his early childhood living in poverty with his maternal grandmother. In the following short story, the character of Mrs. Jones is most probably based on his grandmother. Hughes, a graduate of Lincoln University, was a prolific writer of poems, short stories, and plays. He also wrote two books. Throughout his literary career, he was sharply criticized by other African-American writers who believed that he portrayed an unattractive view of African-American life.

As you read this narrative, notice how the action of the story is told in sequence, with a clear beginning, middle, and end. Try to discover the larger message about relationships that Hughes is illustrating.

Notes on Vocabulary

thank-you-ma'm—a small bump in the road sometimes put there to force drivers to go slowly. In earlier times, if a young couple were out riding, the male was entitled to a kiss every time he hit one of the bumps. He acknowledged that kiss with a polite *"Thank you, ma'm."*

pocketbook—the original *pocketbook* was a man's purse that resembled an open book with a clasp at the top and conveniently fit into the owner's pocket.

Tuning In to Reading

What would you do if someone attempted to steal your purse or wallet? After reading the first paragraph of this story, what do you think is going to happen next?

"Thank You Ma'm"

by Langston Hughes

READING

She was a large woman with a large purse that had everything in it but a hammer and nails. It had a long strap, and she carried it slung across her shoulder. It was about eleven o'clock at night, dark, and she was walking alone, when a boy ran up behind her and tried to snatch her purse. The strap broke with the sudden single tug the boy gave it from behind. But the boy's weight and the weight of the purse combined caused him to lose his balance. Instead of taking off full blast as he had hoped, the boy fell on his back on the sidewalk and his legs flew up. The large woman simply turned around and kicked him right square in his blue-jeaned sitter. Then she reached down, picked the boy up by his shirt front, and shook him until his teeth rattled.

After that the woman said, "Pick up my pocketbook, boy, and give it here."

She still held him tightly. But she bent down enough to permit him to stoop and pick up her purse. Then she said, "Now ain't you ashamed of yourself?"

Firmly gripped by his shirt front, the boy said, "Yes'm."

5 The woman said, "What did you want to do it for?"

The boy said, "I didn't aim to."

She said, "You a lie!"

By that time two or three people passed, stopped, turned to look, and some stood watching.

"If I turn you loose, will you run?" asked the woman.

10 "Yes'm," said the boy.

"Then I won't turn you loose," said the woman. She did not release him.

"Lady, I'm sorry," whispered the boy.

"Um-hum! Your face is dirty. I got a great mind to wash your face for you. Ain't you got nobody home to tell you to wash your face?"

"No'm," said the boy.

15   "Then it will get washed this evening," said the large woman, starting up the street, dragging the frightened boy behind her.

He looked as if he were fourteen or fifteen, frail and willow-wild, in tennis shoes and blue jeans.

The woman said, "You ought to be my son. I would teach you right from wrong. Least I can do right now is to wash your face. Are you hungry?"

"No'm," said the being-dragged boy. "I just want you to turn me loose."

"Was I bothering *you* when I turned that corner?" asked the woman.

20   "No'm."

"But you put yourself in contact with *me*," said the woman. "If you think that that contact is not going to last awhile, you got another thought coming. When I get through with you, sir, you are going to remember Mrs. Luella Bates Washington Jones."

Sweat popped out on the boy's face and he began to struggle. Mrs. Jones stopped, jerked him around in front of her, put a half nelson about his neck, and continued to drag him up the street. When she got to her door, she dragged the boy inside, down a hall, and into a large kitchenette-furnished room at the rear of the house. She switched on the light and left the door open. The boy could hear other roomers laughing and talking in the large house. Some of their doors were open, too, so he knew he and the woman were not alone. The woman still had him by the neck in the middle of her room.

She said, "What is your name?"

"Roger," answered the boy.

25   "Then, Roger you go to that sink and wash your face," said the woman, whereupon she turned him loose—at last. Roger looked at the door—looked at the woman—looked at the door—*and went to the sink.*

"Let the water run until it gets warm," she said. "Here's a clean towel."

"You gonna take me to jail?" asked the boy, bending over the sink.

"Not with that face, I would not take you nowhere," said the woman. "Here I am trying to get home to cook me a bite to eat, and you snatch my pocketbook! Maybe you ain't been to your supper either, late as it be. Have you?"

"There's nobody home at my house," said the boy.

30   "Then we'll eat," said the woman. "I believe you're hungry—or been hungry—to try to snatch my pocketbook!"

"I want a pair of blue suede shoes," said the boy.

Suede was first used in gloves in Sweden and France in the 1880s.

"Well, you didn't have to snatch *my* pocketbook to get some suede shoes," said Mrs. Luella Bates Washington Jones. "You could of asked me."

"M'am?"

The water dripping from his face, the boy looked at her. There was a long pause. A very long pause. After he had dried his face, and not knowing what else to do, dried it again, the boy turned around, wondering what next. The door was open. He could make a dash for it down the hall. He could run, run, run, *run!*

35   The woman was sitting on the daybed. After a while she said, "I were young once and I wanted things I could not get."

There was another long pause. The boy's mouth opened. Then he frowned, not knowing he frowned.

The woman said, "Um-hum! You thought I was going to say *but,* didn't you? You thought I was going to say, *but I didn't snatch people's pocketbooks.* Well, I wasn't going to say that." Pause. Silence. "I have done things, too, which I would not tell

An ice box was what people used before electricity. It literally held a block of ice to keep food cold.

you, son—neither tell God, if He didn't already know. Everybody's got something in common. So you set down while I fix us something to eat. You might run that comb through your hair so you will look presentable."

In another corner of the room behind a screen was a gas plate and an icebox. Mrs. Jones got up and went behind the screen. The woman did not watch the boy to see if he was going to run now, nor did she watch her purse, which she left behind her on the daybed. But the boy took care to sit on the far side of the room, away from the purse, where he thought she could easily see him out of the corner of her eye if she wanted to. He did not trust the woman *not* to trust him. And he did not want to be mistrusted now.

"Do you need somebody to go to the store," asked the boy, "maybe to get some milk or something?"

40   "Don't believe I do," said the woman, "unless you just want sweet milk yourself. I was going to make cocoa out of this canned milk I got here."

"That will be fine," said the boy.

She heated some lima beans and ham she had in the icebox, made the cocoa, and set the table. The woman did not ask the boy anything about where he lived, or his folks, or anything else that would embarrass him. Instead, as they ate, she told him about her job in a hotel beauty shop that stayed open late, what the work was like, and how all kinds of women came in and out, blonds, red-heads, and Spanish. Then she cut him a half of her ten-cent cake.

"Eat some more, son," she said.

When they were finished eating, she got up and said, "Now here. Take this ten dollars and buy yourself some blue suede shoes. And next time, do not make the mistake of latching onto *my* pocketbook *nor nobody else's*—because shoes got by devilish ways will burn your feet. I got to get my rest now. But from here on in, son, I hope you will behave yourself."

45   She led him down the hall to the front door and opened it. "Good night! Behave yourself, boy!" she said, looking out into the street as he went down the steps.

The boy wanted to say something else other than, "Thank you, Ma'm," to Mrs. Luella Bates Washington Jones, but he couldn't do so as he turned at the barren stoop and looked back at the large woman in the door. He barely managed to say, "Thank you," before she shut the door. And he never saw her again.

"Thank You Ma'm" from Short Stories *by Langston Hughes. Copyright © 1996 by Ramona Bass and Arnold Rampersad. Reprinted by permission of Hill and Wang, a division of Farrar, Straus, & Giroux, Inc.*

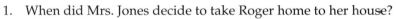

IN YOUR OWN WORDS

1. When did Mrs. Jones decide to take Roger home to her house?
2. Why didn't Mrs. Jones call the police? Do you think Roger had tried to steal anything before?
3. Why didn't Roger run when he finally was given the opportunity?
4. When they were finally at her home, why did Mrs. Jones give Roger the chance to steal her purse?
5. Why does Mrs. Jones want Roger to make himself "presentable"? How are her suggestions interpreted by Roger?
6. At the end of their meal together, why did Mrs. Jones give Roger the money to buy his blue suede shoes?
7. What lesson do you think Mrs. Jones was trying to teach Roger?
8. Look at the *Notes on Vocabulary* for an unusual meaning of the phrase "thank you ma'm." What do you think Hughes means to imply by the title of this story? Do you think he made use of this special meaning?

9. Do you think a similar incident could happen today? Or, are people too frightened to get involved in another person's life?

Directions: Number the sentences in correct time order sequence according to the story.

_____ Roger tells Mrs. Jones that he wants some blue suede shoes.

_____ Roger thanks Mrs. Jones.

_____ Roger combs his hair.

_____ Roger offers to go to the store for Mrs. Jones.

_____ Mrs. Jones kicks Roger and shakes him roughly.

_____ Mrs. Jones serves Roger dinner and tells him about her job.

_____ Mrs. Jones drags Roger behind her.

_____ Roger washes his face.

_____ Mrs. Jones gives Roger ten dollars to buy some blue suede shoes.

_____ Roger tries to steal Mrs. Jones's purse.

Written Assignment

1. Describe the character of Mrs. Jones. Use as many descriptive details as possible.

2. Trace the character development of Roger. How does his behavior change as the result of Mrs. Jones's actions?

3. Discuss how you helped someone or someone helped you. Give details about what happened and how you felt.

Descriptive

Four years after her death, a son reflects on his mother's struggle with Alzheimer's.

Bio-sketch

John Daniel is a poet and essayist living in Oregon. He is the author of two books of poetry, *Common Ground* (1988) and *All Things Touched by Wind* (1994). His mother died in 1992.

While reading this essay, notice how the key details serve to describe both the author's mother and the author's experience giving her a shower. Because of the emphasis on sensory images, the reader is able to visualize the scene being depicted.

Notes on Vocabulary

Alzheimer's—a progressive, irreversible disease characterized by deterioration or loss of function of brain cells causing severe mental dementia   Former President Ronald Reagan is an acknowledged sufferer of Alzheimer's, which has been called "the disease of the century." The disease is named after Alois Alzheimer, the German physician who first described the condition.

Tuning In to Reading

Have you ever helped someone who was very ill for an extended period of time? Do you recall what the experience was like?

"A Son's Memoir"

by John Daniel

READING

❝ The only gift is a portion of thyself. ❞

Ralph Waldo Emerson

My mother was tough as lobster shell, solid as New England granite, lively as the wind. . . .

In 1988, when she was 80, my mother agreed to leave her home on the Maine coast and live with my wife and me in Portland, Oregon. She was frail, slowed to a stooped-back shuffle. Her memory was failing. She was frequently disoriented and confused. She lived her last four years with us, and it was to understand those years, their burdens and their blessings, that I wrote *Looking After*. The story that follows is composed of an excerpt from the book.

I never looked forward to helping my mother with her shower. She wasn't the least self-conscious about baring her body in my presence, but something in me shrank from it. To be with her in her nakedness seemed too intimate for a grown son. And some other part of me, the child who wants always to be cared for and never burdened with responsibility, felt put upon and put out. Why was I having to do this? It seemed an indignity, and it touched an open wound. I had no child to bathe, to make faces at, to splash and laugh with. Most likely I never would. What I had was a frail and failing old woman who couldn't take a shower on her own.

Talking her into it was the first challenge. "Oh, I don't need a shower," she would say. "I just had one yesterday, didn't I?"

5   "You haven't had one for a week."

"But I don't *do* anything. Why do I need a shower?"

It wasn't only bad memory and lapsing judgment that made her resist, of course. It was also that the shower was strenuous for her, and she didn't want to acknowledge, or couldn't, that she needed help with anything so simple. In her own mind, the mind I believe she inhabited most of the time, she was perfectly capable of taking a shower by herself if she wanted to. In this mind, she was still the woman she had been five years ago, a woman who came and went and drove a car, a woman who lived on her own on the coast of Maine and was only temporarily exiled in a distant place. This woman was honestly perplexed when we bought her a cane and asked her, over and over again, to use it. What need had Zilla Daniel for a cane? Somewhere inside her she was not only an able-bodied woman but still a Sea Scout, climbing the rigging in a bright clear wind.

But in her present mind she knew, whenever she leaned far forward in a chair and tried to stiff-arm herself to her feet, whenever she steadied herself with a hand on the wall as she shuffled to the bathroom, just how incapable she had become. She knew, and she hated it. How could she not have hated it? And if she had to bear it, she didn't want me or my wife, Marilyn, or anyone else to have to help her bear it. She wanted to carry herself on her own stooped shoulders. I can still hear her making her way to the toilet with her left hand pulling her nightgown tight behind her, disgustedly whispering "No, no" to her bladder that could not hold back what it should have held back. As if she were castigating an unbroken puppy, but without the tolerance she would have granted an innocent thing. Standing for any length of time was hard for my mother, and so the shower was a kind of siege. She would grip the soap tray with both hands as I got the water temperature right—"Aaant!" she would holler, "too cold!"—and soaped a washcloth to scrub her sway-spined back. Even the soap met resistance.

. . . "It's just one more thing that has to come off."

10   "Well, it does come off," I answered, peeling open a bar of Dial. "It rinses off."

"My dear, it leaves a residue. Plain water is enough."

"Mother, for God's sake. . . . You need soap to get clean."

"Yes, Father," she said with a scowl.

Eventually we worked out a mulish compromise. We used Ivory, which we both agreed was the most natural. I washed her back and buttocks with a soaped washcloth, she held the cloth for a few seconds in the shower spray before washing her front . . . Then I helped her down to the bath stool, where she rested a while and washed her lower legs and feet. The skin of her shins was dry and papery, perpetually blotched with dark purple—not impact bruises but bruises of age.

15   As I lathered shampoo into her wet white curls, her head would bow from the pressure of my fingers. I'd ask her to hold it up and she would for a second or two, then it would slowly sink again. It must have taken a major effort just to hold herself as upright as she did in her last years. All the while she was slowly bending, slowly folding, curling toward the fetal comfort of the grave.

She squeezed her eyes shut as I rinsed her hair in the shower stream. She scrunched up her face, stuck her lips out, and sputtered through the soapy runoff. It was in that recurring moment of her life with us, her hair flattened to her head, darkened a little with that soaking spray, that I could almost see my mother as a girl—swimming the cold swells off Hancock Park, splashing and laughing, shouting something toward shore, laying into the water with strong, even strokes that would take her where she wanted to go.

She would let me stop rinsing only when she could rub a bit of her hair between finger and thumb and make it squeak. Then I would steady her out of the shower stall, her two hands in mine. It felt at moments like a kind of dance, a dance that maybe I knew how to do and needed to do. Who was that, doing the dance? Who was it who allowed himself those moments of pleasure helping his mother from the shower? When I look back at that scene in the bathroom, I see a boy in my place. A solemn boy with a bit of a smile, a boy attending his mother out of love and duty blended as one. The boy was there, and he was there now and then at other times in those years my mother was with us. He was there when I'd let him be there.

I helped my mother down into a straight-backed chair and left her in the bathroom with towels, clean underwear, and a little space heater to keep her warm. She took her time, as with everything. Often it was half an hour or longer before she emerged in her dressing gown, her hair beginning to fluff, her face smiling. No matter how hard she might have resisted the idea, a bath or shower always seemed to renew her. Soap, or no soap, the old woman came forth cleaner of spirit.

"She was pure as the driven snow," she usually quoted, gaily, then a pause: "But she drifted."

20   I guess I came out of the bathroom cleaner of spirit myself. Soap or no soap, whatever the tenor of our conversation, I appreciate now what a privilege it was to help my mother with her shower. I wish I'd seen it more clearly at the time. We don't get to choose our privileges, and the ones that come to us aren't always the ones we would choose, and each of them is as much burden as joy. But they do come, and it's important to know them for what they are.

One morning as my mother came out of her shower she paused at the bottom of the stairs. I was reading the paper in the living room.

"Do you feel them sprouting?" She said, smiling in her white gown.

"Do I feel what sprouting?"

"Your wings," she said. She stood there, barefooted and bright, smiling right at me and through me, smiling as though she weren't feeble of body and failing of mind but filled with an uncanny power that saw things I could only glimpse.

25 "Mother, I don't have wings," I said.

But she was still smiling as she headed up the stairs, gripping the banister hand over hand, hauling herself up 15 carpeted steps to her room and her bed made of seaweathered posts and boards, where she would read for a while, gaze out her window at sky and treetops, then drift into sleep.

From Looking After: A Son's Memoir, *by John Daniel © 1996. Published by Counterpoint. Reprinted by permission.*

**IN YOUR
OWN WORDS**

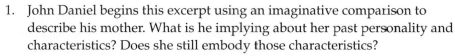

1. John Daniel begins this excerpt using an imaginative comparison to describe his mother. What is he implying about her past personality and characteristics? Does she still embody those characteristics?

2. Why does Daniel feel resentful about having to help his mother with her shower?

3. Why does his mother initially resist taking a shower? What is the larger issue in their battle over the soap? What is the implication of his mother saying "Yes, Father" to him?

4. When does Daniel catch a glimpse of his mother as she might have been as a young girl? From his descriptions of her throughout the excerpt, what do you think she was like when she was young?

5. What is the son implying when he describes attending to his mother as a kind of "dance"?

6. What image does the author use to describe his mother's encroaching death?

7. How do both mother and son feel at the conclusion of the shower?

8. What is the mother implying by her comment about "wings sprouting"?

9. What is the main idea of this selection?

10. What was the author's purpose in writing it?

Practice Using Context Clues

Directions: A sentence from the essay is quoted first and then an additional sentence is provided using the same word. After reading both sentences, use the clues to determine the meaning of the word and write your guess on the line provided. Then consult your dictionary to check how closely you came to the correct definition.

1. "It was also that the shower was *strenuous* for her, and she didn't want to acknowledge, or couldn't, that she needed help with anything so simple."

   After engaging in a *strenuous* workout at the Y, he would come home and take a long nap.

   strenuous: _____ Your Guess
   _____ Dictionary Meaning

2. "As if she were *castigating* an unbroken puppy, but without the tolerance she would have granted an innocent thing."

   After the teacher finished *castigating* the student for his sloppy classwork, she made him stay after class for an hour.

   castigating: _____ Your Guess
   _____ Dictionary Meaning

3. "The skin of her shins was dry and papery, *perpetually* blotched with dark purple—not impact bruises but bruises of age."

   He was *perpetually* late to class even though he got up early enough each morning.

   perpetually: _____ Your Guess
   _____ Dictionary Meaning

4. "A *solemn* boy with a bit of a smile, a boy attending his mother out of love and duty blended as one."

   When she was naturalized as a new citizen of the United States, she *solemnly* swore her allegiance to her new country.

   solemn: _____ Your Guess
   _____ Dictionary Meaning

5. "Soap or no soap, whatever the *tenor* of our conversation, I appreciate now what a privilege it was to help my mother with her shower."

   If you persist in using that *tenor* with me, I'll have to ask you to leave my house.

   tenor: _____ Your Guess
   _____ Dictionary Meaning

6. "In this mind, she was still the woman she had been five years ago, a woman who came and went and drove a car, a woman who lived on her own on the coast of Maine and was only temporarily *exiled* in a distant place."

   When Juan Peron lost political power in Argentina, he was forced to live in *exile* in Spain.

   exile: _____ Your Guess
   _____ Dictionary Meaning

Expository

Bio-Sketch

Traditional IQ tests have been accepted since the early 1900s as a way to measure intelligence. Lately, however, many experts have been calling their use into question. These experts point out that traditional tests are actually capable of measuring only a fraction of the skills and talents included in intelligence. They also suggest that these tests fail to predict who will later be successful in life. In 1995, Daniel Goleman, former editor of *Psychology Today,* published the bestseller, *Emotional Intelligence: Why It Can Matter More Than IQ.* His basic thesis is that the ability to control emotional impulses is crucial to determining success in all endeavors. In the excerpt that follows, Goleman provides an explanation for how the ability to control one's impulses at the age of four can have far-reaching consequences.

Notes on Vocabulary

inhibition—a mental or psychological process that holds back an action, emotion, or thought.

limbic system—primitive part of the brain, located near the brain stem, thought to control emotions and behavior.

Tuning In to Reading

Read the first paragraph of the essay. What choice do you think you would have made at that age? Have there been times in your life when you wanted the immediate short-term reward? Even when you knew that waiting would guarantee a bigger "payoff"? Do you think you can teach people to control their impulses?

"Impulse Control: The Marshmallow Test" *by Daniel Goleman*

READING

Just imagine you're four years old, and someone makes the following proposal: If you'll wait until after he runs an errand, you can have two marshmallows for a treat. If you can't wait until then, you can have only one—but you can have it right now. It is a challenge sure to try the soul of any four-year-old, a microcosm of the eternal battle between impulse and restraint, id and ego, desire and self-control, gratification and delay. Which of these choices a child makes is a telling test; it offers a quick reading not just of character, but of the trajectory that child will probably take through life.

There is perhaps no psychological skill more fundamental than resisting impulse. It is the root of all emotional self-control, since all emotions, by their very nature, lead to one or another impulse to act. The root meaning of the word *emotion*, remember, is "to move." The capacity to resist that impulse to act, to squelch the incipient movement, most likely translates at the level of brain function into inhibition of limbic signals to the motor cortex, though such an interpretation must remain speculative for now.

At any rate, a remarkable study in which the marshmallow challenge was posed to four-year-olds shows just how fundamental is the ability to restrain the emotions and so delay impulse. Begun by psychologist Walter Mischel during the 1960s at a preschool on the Stanford University campus and involving mainly children of Stanford faculty, graduate students, and other employees, the study tracked down the four-year-olds as they were graduating from high school.

Some four-year-olds were able to wait what must surely have seemed an endless 15 to 20 minutes for the experimenter to return. To sustain themselves in their struggle they covered their eyes so they wouldn't have to stare at temptation, or rested their heads in their arms, talked to themselves, sang, played games with their hands and feet, even tried to go to sleep. These plucky preschoolers got the two-marshmallow reward. But others, more impulsive, grabbed the one marshmallow, almost always within seconds of the experimenter's leaving the room on his "errand."

5   The diagnostic power of how this moment of impulse was handled became clear some 12 to 14 years later, when these same children were tracked down as adolescents. The emotional and social difference between the grab-the-marshmallow preschoolers and their gratification-delaying peers was dramatic. Those who had resisted temptation at four were now, as adolescents, more socially

competent: personally effective, self-assertive, and better able to cope with the frustrations of life. They were less likely to go to pieces, freeze, or regress under stress, or become rattled and disorganized when pressured; they embraced challenges and pursued them instead of giving up even in the face of difficulties; they were self-reliant and confident, trustworthy and dependable; and they took initiative and plunged into projects. And more than a decade later, they were still able to delay gratification in pursuit of their goals.

The third or so who grabbed for the marshmallow, however, tended to have fewer of these qualities, and shared instead a relatively more troubled psychological portrait. In adolescence they were more likely to be seen as shying away from social contacts; to be stubborn and indecisive; to be easily upset by frustrations; to think of themselves as "bad" or unworthy; to regress or become immobilized by stress; to be mistrustful and resentful about not "getting enough"; to be prone to jealousy and envy; to overreact to irritations with a sharp temper, so provoking arguments and fights. And, after all those years, they were still unable to put off gratification.

What shows up in a small way early in life blossoms into a wide range of social and emotional competencies as life goes on. The capacity to impose a delay on impulse is at the root of a plethora of efforts, from staying on a diet to pursuing a medical degree. Some children, even at four, had mastered the basics: They were able to read the social situation as one where delay was beneficial, to pry their attention from focusing on the temptation at hand, and to distract themselves while maintaining the necessary perseverance toward their goal—the two marshmallows.

Even more surprising, when the tested children were evaluated again as they were finishing high school, those who had waited patiently at four were far superior *as students* to those who had acted on whim. According to their parents' evaluations, they were more academically competent: better able to put their ideas into words, to use and respond to reason, to concentrate, to make plans and follow through on them, and more eager to learn. Most astonishingly, they had dramatically higher scores on their SAT tests. The third of children who at four grabbed for the marshmallow most eagerly had an average verbal score of 524 and quantitative (or "math") score of 528; the third who had waited longest had average scores of 610 and 652, respectively—a 210-point difference in total score.

At age four, how children do on this test of delay of gratification is twice as powerful a predictor of what their SAT scores will be as is IQ at age four; IQ becomes a stronger predictor of SAT only after children learn to read. This suggests that the ability to delay gratification contributes powerfully to intellectual potential quite apart from IQ itself. (Poor impulse control in childhood is also a powerful predictor of later delinquency, again more so than IQ.) . . . [W]hile some argue that IQ cannot be changed and so represents an unbendable limitation on a child's life potential, there is ample evidence that emotional skills such as impulse control and accurately reading a social situation *can* be learned.

10   What Walter Mischel, who did the study, describes with the rather infelicitous phrase "goal-directed self-imposed delay of gratification" is perhaps the essence of emotional self-regulation: the ability to deny impulse in the service of a goal, whether it be building a business, solving an algebraic equation, or pursuing the Stanley Cup. His finding underscores the role of emotional intelligence as a meta-ability, determining how well or how poorly people are able to use their other mental capacities.

From Emotional Intelligence, *by Daniel Goleman. Copyright © 1995 by Daniel Goleman. Used by permission of Bantam Books, a division of Doubleday Dell Publishing Group, Inc.*

Questions:

1. *Microcosm* as used in paragraph 1 means which of the following?
   a. something regarded as a world in miniature
   b. a small inexpensive computer
   c. a small organism causing disease
   d. so small as to be invisible except through a microscope

2. *Trajectory* as used in paragraph 1 means which of the following?
   a. the curve that a body (as a planet or comet) makes in space
   b. a path, progression, or line of development
   c. to throw over

3. Here are some word pairs from paragraph 1: impulse/restraint, id/ego, desire/self-control, gratification/delay. These word pairs are all
   a. homonyms.
   b. antonyms.
   c. synonyms.

4. In paragraph 2, *to squelch the incipient movement* means
   a. to stop that which is just beginning to appear.
   b. to lead from movement to movement.
   c. to stop something from reappearing.

5. *Speculative* as used in paragraph 2 means which of the following?
   a. taking part in a risky venture on the chance of making huge profits
   b. buying or selling certain stocks
   c. leading to no definite result

6. Write the main idea of paragraph 2 below.

   _____

   _____

7. What words in paragraph 4 demonstrate that it was not easy for the four-year-olds to resist temptation? List a few of them below.

   _____

   _____

8. Write the main idea of paragraph 5 below.

   _____

   _____

9. The story discusses children who gave in to temptation and grabbed the marshmallows. What consequences did this have for them when they were adolescents?

   _____

   _____

10. In paragraph 7, a *plethora of efforts* means
    a. a fullness.
    b. an abundance.
    c. a delighted feeling.

11. What is the overall main idea of this excerpt?

    _____

    _____

Persuasion/Argumentation

Bio-Sketch

Dr. Mary Pipher is a clinical psychologist, part-time instructor at the University of Nebraska, nationwide lecturer, and best-selling author. Her book *Reviving Ophelia*, published in 1994, explored the stresses placed on teenage girls by modern society. In her most recent book, *The Shelter of Each Other*, published in 1996, Pipher turns her attention to the stresses placed on the family as a whole. In Pipher's view, the family is so burdened with problems that it can no longer protect family members from the "enemy within," which she defines as inappropriate stimulation from a variety of sources, with TV being at the top of her list.

In the following excerpt, written in a persuasive mode, Pipher compares and contrasts the community of the past with the new MTV community.

Tuning In to Reading

How has TV affected you positively? Negatively? How much TV do you watch in a day?

"TV"   *by Mary Pipher*

READING

The average family in 1994–1995 watched TV 7 hours and 20 minutes per day.

In a college class I asked, "What would it be like to grow up in a world without media?" A student from the Tonga Islands answered, "I never saw television or heard rock and roll until I came to the United States in high school." She paused and looked around the room. "I had a happy childhood. I felt safe all the time. I didn't know I was poor. Or that parents hurt their children or that children hated their parents. I thought I was pretty."

Television has probably been the most powerful medium in shaping the new community. The electronic community gives us our mutual friends, our significant events and our daily chats. The "produced" relationships of television families become our models for intimacy. We know media stars better than we know our neighbors. Most of us can discuss their lives better than we can discuss those of our relatives. We confuse personas and persons. That is, we think a man who plays a doctor on TV actually knows something about medicine. We think a chatty talk show host is truly good-natured. This confusion is especially common with young children, who are developmentally incapable of distinguishing between reality and fantasy. But even adults get mixed up about this.

Most real life is rather quiet and routine. Most pleasures are small pleasures—a hot shower, a sunset, a bowl of good soup or a good book. Television suggests that life is high drama, love and sex. TV families are radically different from real families. Things happen much faster to them. On television things that are not visually interesting, such as thinking, reading and talking, are ignored. Activities such as housework, fund raising and teaching children to read are vastly underreported. Instead of ennobling our ordinary experiences, television suggests that they are not of sufficient interest to document.

These generalizations even fit the way TV portrays the animal kingdom. Specials on animals feature sex, births and killing. Dangerous and cuddly-looking animals are favored. But in reality, most animals are neither dangerous nor cute. Sharks and panda bears are not the main species on the planet. Most animals, like most people, spend most of their time in rather simple ways. They forage and sleep.

5   TV isolates people in their leisure time. People spend more time watching music videos but less time making music with each other. People in small towns now watch international cable networks instead of driving to their neighbor's

Television has proved that people will look at anything rather than each other.

Ann Landers

house for cards. Women watch soaps instead of attending church circles or book clubs. When company comes, the kids are sent to the TV room with videos. Television is on during meals and kids study to television or radio.

Parents are not the main influences in the lives of their children. Some of the first voices children hear are from the television; the first street they know is Sesame Street. A child playing Nintendo is learning different lessons than a child playing along a creek or playing dominoes with a grandfather. Many children have been conditioned via the media into having highly dysfunctional attention spans.

Adults too have diminished concentration. Neil Postman in *Amusing Ourselves to Death* writes of the 1858 Lincoln/Douglas debates. The average citizen sat for up to seven hours in the heat and listened to these two men discuss issues. People grasped the legal and constitutional issues, moral nuances and political implications. In addition, they could listen to and appreciate intricate and complex sentences. Today the press and the public decry President Clinton's speeches if they last more than an hour. To an audience socialized to information via sound bite, an hour seems like a long time.

The time devoted to violence on TV in no way reflects its importance in real life. In real life, most of us exercise, work, visit our friends, read, cook and eat and shop. Few of us spend any significant amount of our time solving murders or fleeing psychotic killers. On television there are many more detectives and murderers than exist in the real world. A rule of thumb about violence is "If it bleeds, it leads." Violence captures viewer attention. Our movies have become increasingly violent, and as James Wolcott wrote in *The New Yorker*, "Violence is the real sex now."

Some might argue that there is nothing new under the sun. Of course, in a narrow sense, they are correct. There have always been murderers and rapists, and stories about violence have been themes of literature and song. But things are different now. Children, including toddlers, are exposed to hundreds of examples of violence every day. The frequency and intensity of these images is unprecedented in the history of humanity. We have ample documentation that this exposure desensitizes children, makes it more likely they will be violent and increases their fear levels about potential violence.

10   Another difference is in the attitudes about violence. *Romeo and Juliet*, for example, was a tragedy. The deaths in the play were presented as a cause of enormous suffering to friends and families and as a terrible waste. When Juliet and Romeo died, something momentous happened in the universe. The very gods were upset. Often today, death is a minor event, of no more consequence than, say the kicking of a flat tire. It's even presented as a joke.

It is one thing to read Shakespeare, which at least requires that the person can read. It's another to, day after day, see blood splattered across a screen by "action heroes." It is one thing to show, as Shakespeare did, that violence can be the tragic consequence of misunderstandings, and another to show violence as a thrill, as a solution to human problems or merely as something that happens when people are slightly frustrated or men need to prove they are men.

Of course, one could argue that parents can keep televisions out of their homes. This is extremely hard for the average parent to do. Even if they succeed, their children go from these "protected environments" to play with children who have watched lots of TV and who behave accordingly.

I don't often go to violent movies, but I do have a stake in them. I don't like living in a world where thousands of teenage boys, some of whom own guns, have been reared on them. Walking city streets, I may be accosted by a youth who has spent most of his life watching violent media. Unfortunately, needy children are the ones most affected. Children with the least available parents watch the most TV. Violent television is like secondhand smoke; it affects all of us.

Heavy viewers develop the "mean world syndrome." This leads to a vicious-cycle phenomenon. Because children are afraid and the streets are not safe, they come home right after school and stay indoors. They watch more TV, which makes them more afraid and thus more likely to stay indoors. With everyone indoors the streets are less safe. Families watch more TV and are more fearful and so on.

15   Television and electronic media have created a new community with entirely different rules and structures than the kinds of communities that have existed for millions of years. Families gather around the glow of the TV as the Lakota once gathered around the glow of a fire on the Great Plains or as the Vikings once huddled around fires in the caves of Scandinavia. They gather as New England families gathered in the 1800s around a fireplace that kept them warm and safe. But our TVs do not keep us warm, safe and together. Rapidly our technology is creating a new kind of human being, one who is plugged into machines instead of relationships, one who lives in a virtual reality rather than a family.

Reprinted by permission of The Putnam Publishing Group from The Shelter of Each Other, *by Mary Pipher, Ph.D. Copyright © 1996 by Mary Pipher, Ph.D.*

Answer the Following Questions:

1. Write the main idea implied in paragraph 1.

     _____

     _____

2. Write the main idea that is directly stated in paragraph 2. Explain what Pipher means when she says we have trouble distinguishing between "personas and persons." Are children the only ones who have trouble with this?

     _____

     _____

3. Summarize the key points that Pipher makes in paragraph 3. How does what you see on the evening local or national news reinforce Pipher's argument?

     _____

     _____

4. In paragraph 4, Pipher says that TV distorts our impression of animals. How does TV do this?

     _____

5. What does Pipher say in paragraph 5 about what is happening to our sense of belonging to a community? Is the Internet likely to create strong community ties or weaken them?

     _____

     _____

6. Do you agree with Pipher's assertion that parents are not the primary influences in their children's lives? Why do you agree? Why don't you agree? How does the media contribute to children's short attention spans?

     _____

     _____

7. Paragraphs 8–13 are devoted to a discussion of violence on TV. Why does television portray so much violence? What are some of the effects of violent TV programs on the young?

   _____

   _____

8. Pipher compares and contrasts the modern media's attitude to violence and death to that portrayed in *Romeo and Juliet*. What is the difference she perceives?

   _____

   _____

9. Many people would suggest that parents are responsible for their own children and so should just restrict the amount of time their kids spend watching TV. What is Pipher's response to these critics?

   _____

   _____

10. Explain what Pipher means in paragraph 13 when she says: "Violent television is like secondhand smoke; it affects all of us."

    _____

    _____

11. Explain the cause-and-effect relationships in paragraph 14.

    Cause: _____

    Effect: _____

    Cause: _____

    Effect: _____

12. Paragraph 15 compares and contrasts two communities. List the similarities and differences between the two.

    _____

    _____

Written Assignment

1. Summarize the information presented in a local news show. Identify the subject of each story (murder, robbery, fire, accident, etc.), and the approximate amount of time given to coverage of the story.

2. Watch a TV drama, detective show, soap opera, or movie, and keep track of how many specific acts of violence the show portrays.

Chapter 8 Test: "TV"

Multiple Choice

1. The organizational pattern used in paragraph 2 is
   a. main idea, details.
   b. details, main idea, details.
   c. details, main idea.
   d. no directly stated main idea.

2. The transition word *but* in paragraph 4 indicates
   a. comparison.
   b. contrast.
   c. cause and effect.
   d. definition.

3. From this selection you could conclude that
   a. no one should watch TV.
   b. people should limit the amount of television they and their families watch.
   c. people should spend more time on the Internet.
   d. the government should regulate the content of TV programs.

4. A likely title for this selection would be
   a. "TV—The Cause of Violence"
   b. "TV versus Shakespeare"
   c. "TV in the Tonga Islands"
   d. "TV and Its Effects on Relationships"

5. If the author was reading this selection orally, her tone of voice would probably be
   a. admiring.
   b. optimistic.
   c. critical.
   d. amused.

6. "Violent television is like secondhand smoke. . . . " (paragraph 13) would best be described as an example of a
   a. definition.
   b. metaphor.
   c. simile.
   d. personification.

True or False

_____   7. Pipher suggests that children whose parents are most available watch the least TV.

_____   8. Watching television is likely to significantly increase a person's ability to concentrate.

_____   9. According to Pipher, things happen much more quickly in real life.

_____ 10. Pipher sees a cause-and-effect relationship between a child's exposure to a great deal of televised violence and violent behavior.

Vocabulary: Unit 4

supersonic—Chuck Yaeger made the first supersonic flight October 14, 1947, over Edwards Air Force Base in California.

All of the word parts in this unit are related to either direction or position.

super—above or over
sub—under, below, beneath

supersonic   *Super* means "above," and *sonus* means "sound," so *supersonic* means moving at a speed greater than that of sound.

supervisor	a person who oversees or directs work or workers. The original meaning of the word was to see from above.
superscript	a figure, letter, or symbol written above the line. In math, 10 squared would be written 10^2, with the "2" being *superscript*.
subscript	a figure, letter, or symbol written below the line. The chemical formula for water, H_2O, has a *subscript*.
subscribe	to agree to pay for a service or periodical. Originally, when you *subscribed* to a magazine, you signed your name at the bottom of the contract on the dotted line.
subliminal	*Limen* means "threshold." If something is *subliminal*, it is below the threshold of consciousness. The sale of audiocassette tapes with *subliminal* self-help messages is a big business in the United States. While you are sleeping, you could listen to a weight-loss tape with a *subliminal* message saying "eat less."

retro—backward, back, behind

<table>
<tr><td>

Trivia Question #1

Which space vehicle does not use retrorockets to reduce speed? The answer will be found at the end of this lesson.

</td><td>

retroactive	having an effect on things that are past; going back in time. If you received *retroactive* pay, you would be paid for work that was done in the past.
retrorocket	a small rocket that produces a backward thrust in order to reduce speed.
retrogress	to move backward toward an earlier or worse condition; to decline. After learning new study techniques, the student *retrogressed* to her old methods of studying and just read the chapter the night before the quiz.
retrospect	to see back in time; hindsight. In *retrospect*, the cook should have added more garlic to her soup.

</td></tr>
</table>

ante(i)—before, in front of, prior to
ad—toward

Sometimes spellings of word parts change over the years. In the word part *anti*, sometimes the "e" changes to "i." This causes confusion with the word part *anti* meaning "opposite of." What do you think was the original meaning of the word *antifreeze*? Sometimes you have to use the context of a sentence to determine the meaning of a word part. When in doubt, consult a dictionary.

anticipate	to look forward to something before it happens. She was *anticipating* a pleasant two-week vacation in Hawaii.
ante	In poker, each player must *ante* up before receiving cards.
anteroom	a small room before a larger or more important room. *Anterooms* can be lobbies, vestibules, or waiting rooms.
antecedent	coming before in time, order, or logic. In English grammar, the *antecedent* of a pronoun is the noun to which the pronoun refers. In the sentence, "The team will win the game if it plays well," the *antecedent* of the pronoun "it" is the word "team."

advertise—The largest and tallest freestanding advertising sign is at the Hilton Hotel and Casino in Las Vegas. Originally, it had a total area of 82,328 square feet. Part of it fell down during a storm in July 1994, but it is still the largest and tallest sign.

circulate—In one year, the human heart circulates 770,000 to 1.6 million gallons of blood. This is enough to fill 200 tank cars, each with a capacity of 8,000 gallons.

circumference—The circumference of a quarter has 119 groves; a dime has one less.

circumnavigate— The fastest trip circumnavigating the globe in a catamaran was completed by Peter Blake from New Zealand and Robin Knox-Johnson from Great Britain. The trip took 74 days, 22 hours, and 17 minutes and was completed April 1, 1994.

antebellum	*Bellum* means "war," so *antebellum* means "before the war." The word is often used in relation to the American Civil War. The *antebellum* days of the South were approximately 1820–1860.
advance	"*Ance*" originally came from *ante*, and so the word *advance* literally translates to "toward before." The hurricane rapidly *advanced* on the helpless town.
adolescent	a person moving toward adulthood or maturity.
advent	*Ven* means "come." *Advent* means "to come toward." To Christians, the season of *Advent* includes the four Sundays before Christmas.
advertise	*Vert* means "to turn," so *advertise* means "to turn toward." *Advertising* praises a service or product so that people will want to turn toward it, or buy it.

circ—ring; around   cycle—circle; wheel

circle	a *circle* is a plane figure, but the word also means to surround or move around.
circulate	to move in a circle and return to the same point; to move around freely. Blood *circulates* through the body.
circumference	the measure of the distance around a circle.
circumnavigate	to sail or fly around, as in *circumnavigating* the earth. Magellan's crew was the first to *circumnavigate* the earth. Magellan himself was killed on the voyage.
circumscribe	to draw a line around. The student *circumscribed* the correct answer on the quiz by drawing a circle around it.
circumspect	to look all around or to consider all circumstances before deciding.
circadian	relating to a person's daily biological cycle.
circa	*Circa* means "around" or "approximately," in reference to a period of time or the date of an event, especially when the exact dates are not known. Jazz began in the United States circa 1920.
bicycle	to ride or travel on a two-wheeled vehicle.
cyclorama	No, not a track for bicycles. A *cyclorama* is a series of large pictures put on the wall of a circular room so that a spectator standing in the middle can see all around (360 degrees). If you have been to Disneyland, you might have seen a movie in the *cyclorama*.
cyclical	moving or occurring in a circular pattern. Fashions in clothing tend to be *cyclical*. Men's ties gradually become wider, and then gradually become narrower, and then start the cycle over.

Trivia Question #2

Who was the first American to circumnavigate the earth in a space vehicle? Hint: He served as a U.S. Senator from Ohio. The answer will be found at the end of the lesson.

bicycle—The longest true tandem bicycle with just two wheels measures 72.96 feet. In 1988, it was ridden 807 feet by four riders. Needless to say, turning corners presented problems.

Pan-American—The Pan-Am Highway is the longest driveable road in the world. It is 15,000 miles long. It goes from northwest Alaska, down through Santiago, Chile, east through Argentina, and ends in Brasilia, Brazil.

Answer to Trivia Question #1

the space shuttle

Answer to Trivia Question #2

John Glenn

pan—all; every; around   peri—around; about

Panavision	see all around. The movie was in *Panavision* Movies in *Panavision* are not really all around you, but are simply on a large screen.
Panasonic	sound all around. Do you think you really get sound all around you from a *Panasonic* transistor radio?
panorama	a wide view. A synonym for *panorama* is *vista*. From the top of the mountain, the sunset produced a beautiful *panorama*.
panacea	a cure-all; or the act of going around the problem. Owners of sports teams often resort to firing the coach as a *panacea* for the team's failure to win enough games. Some people view building more prisons as a *panacea* to our crime problem.
Pan-American	common to North, South, and Central America together. The diplomats negotiated a *Pan-American* treaty to deal with poaching of endangered species.
perimeter	the outer boundary or measurement around a figure or area. The soldiers guarding the camp walked along its *perimeter*.
peripheral	lying at the outside. Because he has so much money already, it is of only *peripheral* importance to him whether he gets a job. You might have your driver's license revoked if you have poor *peripheral* vision.
periscope	an optical instrument used on submarines that goes up to the surface and allows a person to "look around."

Fill in the blank with one of the following words. Not all of the words will be used.

circa	subscripts	retroactive	retrospect	advertise
advent	superscripts	circadian	anteroom	retrogress

1. Congress passed a law in September that will lower your taxes. This law was made _____ to last January.

2. The chemical formula for octane, C_8H_{18}, has _____ in it.

3. After the team lost, the coach felt that in _____ he should have left his star player in the game in the fourth quarter.

4. If students pay attention to their _____ cycle, their study times might prove to be more effective.

5. Does the auditorium of your college have an _____ before you go into the main area where the stage and seats are located.

6. Spring training indicates the _____ of the baseball season.

Vocabulary 4

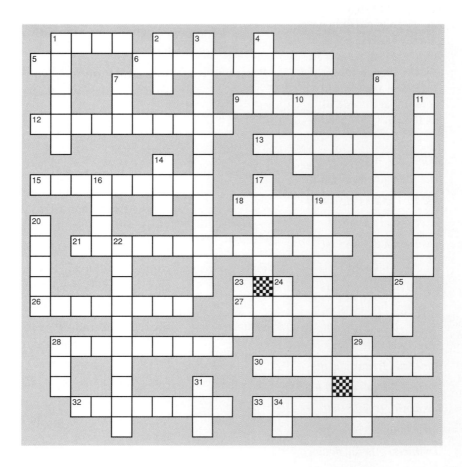

ACROSS CLUES

1. What you might do at the beginning of a poker game before receiving your cards.
5. A word part meaning "toward."
6. _____ vision is to the side.
9. You might see a beautiful _____ (synonym for vista) from the top of a mountain.
12. The _____ days of the South were those preceding the Civil War.
13. A cure-all.
15. To sign your name at the bottom of a contract.
18. A person who oversees.
21. John Glenn was able to _____ the earth.
26. A lobby or vestibule.

27. Your daily biological rhythm is your _____ cycle.
28. The formula for carbon dioxide has a _____ in it.
30. An outer boundary is called a _____.
32. Occurring in cycles.
33. The literal meaning is "to turn toward."

DOWN CLUES

1. The period of time before Christmas.
2. The abbreviation for what was once the 10th month.
3. The distance around a circle.
4. A word part meaning "large."
7. A word part meaning "under."
8. The movie was in _____.
10. A word part meaning "all."

11. Large pictures all around you in a circular room.
14. A word part meaning "see."
16. A word part meaning "half."
17. A word part meaning "hear."
19. Back pay is _____.
20. The antique was _____ 1900.
22. In hindsight or _____.
23. The abbreviation for what was once the eighth month.
24. A word part meaning "three."
25. A word part meaning "one."
28. A word part meaning "six."
29. A word part meaning "100."
31. A word part meaning "around."
34. A word part meaning "two."

Chapter 9

Modes of Organization

Cause and Effect

Bio-sketch

John Collier was born in London in 1901 and died in California in 1980. Throughout his lengthy career, he was a successful novelist, playwright, and screenwriter, but is primarily remembered today for his sinister short stories. Many of these stories, though focused on evil, were written with great wit and irony. Each word in a Collier short story was carefully chosen to heighten a particular effect. Most critics consider Collier's particular strength his use of dialogue.

This short story, a descriptive narrative, demonstrates a cause and effect relationship. Alan, the young man, wishes to change his beloved Diana forever by making her more responsive to him. He pursues his dream without ever realizing the unintended, or ironic, effects.

Notes on Vocabulary

sinister—ominous, threatening harm or evil   The original Latin meaning was simply "left" or "on the left." The origins of this word have to do with an ancient prejudice favoring what is to the right over what is to the left. So, the more important guests at a banquet would be seated to the right of the host or hostess.

Tuning In to Reading

Try to determine the personality of the old man after reading the first three paragraphs of the short story. Do you think Allan is being "suckered" into doing something against his will?

"The Chaser"   *by John Collier*

READING

Alan Austen, as nervous as a kitten, went up certain dark and creaky stairs in the neighborhood of Pell Street, and peered about for a long time on the dim landing before he found the name he wanted written obscurely on one of the doors.

He pushed open this door, as he had been told to do, and found himself in a tiny room, which contained no furniture but a plain kitchen table, a rocking-chair, and an ordinary chair. On one of the dirty buff-coloured walls were a couple of shelves, containing in all perhaps a dozen bottles and jars.

An old man sat in the rocking-chair, reading a newspaper. Alan, without a word, handed him the card he had been given. "Sit down, Mr. Austen," said the old man very politely. "I am glad to make your acquaintance."

250

"Is it true," asked Alan, "that you have a certain mixture that has—er—quite extraordinary effects?"

5   "My dear sir," replied the old man, "my stock in trade is not very large—I don't deal in laxatives and teething mixtures—but such as it is, it is varied. I think nothing I sell has effects which could be precisely described as ordinary."

"Well, the fact is . . ." began Alan.

"Here, for example," interrupted the old man, reaching for a bottle from the shelf. "Here is a liquid as colourless as water, almost tasteless, quite imperceptible in coffee, wine, or any other beverage. It is also quite imperceptible to any known method of autopsy."

"Do you mean it is a poison?" cried Alan, very much horrified.

"Call it a glove-cleaner if you like," said the old man indifferently. "Maybe it will clean gloves. I have never tried. One might call it a life-cleaner. Lives need cleaning sometimes."

10   "I want nothing of that sort," said Alan.

"Probably it is just as well," said the old man. "Do you know the price of this? For one teaspoonful, which is sufficient, I ask five thousand dollars. Never less. Not a penny less."

"I hope all your mixtures are not as expensive," said Alan apprehensively.

"Oh dear, no," said the old man. "It would be no good charging that sort of price for a love potion, for example." Young people who need a love potion very seldom have five thousand dollars. Otherwise they would not need a love potion."

"I am glad to hear that," said Alan.

15   "I look at it like this," said the old man. "Please a customer with one article, and he will come back when he needs another. Even if it *is* more costly. He will save up for it, if necessary."

"So," said Alan, "you really do sell love potions?"

"If I did not sell love potions," said the old man, reaching for another bottle, "I should not have mentioned the other matter to you. It is only when one is in a position to oblige that one can afford to be so confidential."

"And these potions," said Alan. "They are not just—just—er—"

"Oh, no," said the old man. "Their effects are permanent, and extend far beyond the mere casual impulse. But they include it. Oh, yes, they include it. Bountifully, insistently. Everlastingly."

20   "Dear me!" said Alan, attempting a lock of scientific detachment. "How very interesting!"

"But consider the spiritual side," said the old man.

"I do, indeed," said Alan.

"For indifference," said the old man, "they substitute devotion. For scorn, adoration. Give one tiny measure of this to the young lady—its flavour is imperceptible in orange juice, soup, or cocktails—and however gay and giddy she is, she will change altogether. She will want nothing but solitude and you."

"I can hardly believe it," said Alan. "She is so fond of parties."

25   "She will not like them anymore," said the old man. "She will be afraid of the pretty girls you may meet."

"She will actually be jealous?" cried Alan in a rapture. "Of me?"

"Yes, she will want to be everything to you."

"She *is*, already. Only she doesn't care about it."

"She will, when she has taken this. She will care intensely. You will be her sole interest in life."

30   "Wonderful!" cried Alan.

"She will want to know all you do," said the old man. "All that has happened to you during the day. Every word of it. She will want to know what you are thinking about, why you smile suddenly, why you are looking sad."

"That *is* love!" cried Alan.

"Yes," said the old man. "How carefully she will look after you! She will never allow you to be tired, to sit in a draught, to neglect your food. If you are an hour late, she will be terrified. She will think you are killed, or that some siren has caught you."

"I can hardly imagine Diana like that!" cried Alan, overwhelmed with joy.

35   "You will not have to use your imagination," said the old man. "And, by the way, since there are always sirens, if by any chance you *should*, later on, slip a little, you need not worry. She will forgive you, in the end. She will be terribly hurt, of course, but she will forgive you—in the end."

"That will not happen," said Alan fervently.

"Of course not," said the old man. "But if it did, you need not worry. She would never divorce you. Oh, no! And, of course, she will never give you the least, the very least grounds for—uneasiness."

"And how much," said Alan, "is this wonderful mixture?"

"It is not as dear," said the old man, "as the glove-cleaner, or life-cleaner, as I sometimes call it. No. That is five thousand dollars, never a penny less. One has to be older than you are, to indulge in that sort of thing. One has to save up for it."

40   "But the love potion?" said Alan.

"Oh, that," said the old man, opening the drawer in the kitchen table, and taking out a tiny, rather dirty-looking phial. "That is just a dollar."

"I can't tell you how grateful I am," said Alan, watching him fill it.

"I like to oblige," said the old man. "Then customers come back, later in life, when they are better off, and want more expensive things. Here you are. You will find it very effective."

"Thank you again," said Alan. "Good-bye."

"*Au Revoir*," said the old man. [Good-bye. Until we meet again.]

From "The Chaser" by John Collier, renewed 1968. Permission granted by Harold Matson Co., Inc. as agent for the estate of John Collier.

True or False Checkup

Directions: Answer the following questions without referring back to the story.

_____   1.   Someone referred Alan to the old man.

_____   2.   The old man sells many items that could be considered ordinary.

_____   3.   The old man's shop is in an affluent area.

_____   4.   The mixture referred to as a "glove-cleaner" is actually poison.

_____   5.   In contrast to the "glove-cleaner," the love potion is inexpensive.

_____   6.   The old man makes his money on customers returning for more-expensive items.

_____   7.   The love potion will cause Diana to be incapable of anything but permanent devotion to Alan.

_____   8.   The old man says that if Alan becomes tempted by another woman, Diana will never forgive him.

_____ 9.   The old man indicates that he likes to please his customers.

_____ 10. The old man implies that at some point in Alan's life he will grow tired of Diana.

IN YOUR OWN WORDS

1. In the very first sentence of this story, what descriptive words give the setting a sinister aspect?

2. What word or words are used to describe Alan?

3. What effects does Alan think the potion will have? Why does Alan want to purchase it?

4. How will the potion actually affect Diana?

5. A chaser is a drink that takes away the taste of another drink. What will be Diana's chaser?

6. Does the old man think that Alan will return later in life? Refer to specific details in the story to support your answer. At the end of the story what does the old man mean by "more expensive things"?

7. What does the old man mean when he says: "Young people who need a love potion very seldom have five thousand dollars. Otherwise they would not need a love potion"? What viewpoint about love is he expressing?

8. What point is Collier making about love? How can something that we want very badly end up causing us grief?

9. Why is one bottle referred to by words such as a "glove-cleaner," or a "life-cleaner"?

10. What is ironic about this particular story? What does Alan expect to happen? What is really going to happen?

Optional: The dialogue in this story reads very much like a play. Have two people in your class act out the part of Alan and the old man.

Understanding the Vocabulary in the Story

Directions: Choose one of the words in the following list to complete each of the sentences below. Use each word only once.

creaky	obscure	imperceptible	scorn
solitude	indulge	peered	autopsy
confidential	detachment	sole	

1. Although I try to stay away from rich foods, every once in a while I _____ myself by having a hot fudge sundae with nuts, whipped cream, and a cherry.

2. A tiny baby was the _____ survivor of American Airlines flight 209.

3. Sue wanted to surprise her husband on his birthday with a special present, and so she looked everywhere for an _____ hood ornament for his 1965 Corvette.

4. Unable to see a thing without his glasses, the old man _____ closely at the bus schedule in his hand.

5. Although Raymond tried to be a fair and open-minded person, he felt only revulsion and _____ for the man who had cut off the young girl's arms.

6. The _____ revealed that the young child had died of a fractured skull.

7. Investigative reporters who work for *The National Enquirer* claim that they frequently search people's garbage in order to obtain private, _____ information.

8. Although she had her heart set on a sleek, modern home with up-to-date conveniences, her husband was resolved to own the Victorian mansion with the _____ stairs.

9. There was so much chaos at the rock concert, that Tom found himself longing for the peace and _____ of his home.

10. Because our dog Bandit didn't like to swallow pills, they had to be hidden in the middle of a hot dog where they became _____ to his taste and sight.

11. The judge tried not to be biased in favor of one side or the other, and so maintained a level of professional _____ .

Categories

The following expository essay makes good use of categories. When you read the essay, notice how the author organizes information into categories, defines the categories, and uses the categories to analyze and draw conclusions.

Russell Belk, Ph.D., is a professor of business administration at the Graduate School of Business, University of Utah.

JFK Library

Tuning In to Reading

Have you ever been burglarized? If so, how did the experience make you feel?

"My Possessions Myself"   *by Russell W. Belk*

READING

Burglary victims often say that they feel they have been personally polluted, even raped. Since they never had any personal contact with the burglar, what has been violated is the sense of self that exists in their jewelry, clothing, photographs and other personal possessions.

The feeling of violation goes even deeper since the burglar has also wounded the family's sense of identity by penetrating its protective skin, the family home. Clearly, the sense of self is not only individual. Heirlooms, for example, can represent and extend a family's sense of identity, while public buildings, monuments and parks help us develop regional and national identities. Although we Americans think of ourselves as highly individualistic, aggregate identity is important to us, as the willingness to preserve and restore symbols such as the Statue of Liberty shows.

What we possess is, in a very real way, part of ourselves. Our thoughts and our bodies are normally the most central part of our self-concept. But next in importance are what we do—our occupations and skills—and what we have—our unique set of possessions. The fact that jewelry, weapons and domestic utensils are found in prehistoric burial sites is evidence that we have long considered possessions as part of the person, even after death.

We find the same identification of people with possessions in examples as diverse as the reverence religions pay to relics of saints and prophets, the intensity of autograph hounds, the emphasis auctioneers place on the previous ownership of objects up for bid and the difficulty secondhand stores have in selling used underwear and other garments worn close to the body. In each case a sense of the prior owners is thought to remain in the things that touched their lives.

5   We generally include four types of possessions in our personal sense of self: body and body parts, objects, places and time periods, persons and pets. Body parts are normally so well integrated into our identities that we think of them as "me" rather than mere "mine." But several studies have shown that body parts vary widely in their importance to us.

Recently, doctoral student Mark Austin and I gave 248 adults a group of cards, each of which listed a single item in one of the four categories: body parts such as kidneys, hearts and knees; objects such as a favorite dessert or the contents (other than money) of your wallet; places and times such as a favorite city or time of life; and particular people or pets.

We asked people to put the 96 cards in two piles, things they considered self and non self. They then sorted each of these into two piles representing a little or a lot of self or non self. We then gave each pile a "self" score (1,2,3,4) and calculated average scores for each card. This gave us a rating of how central each item was to the sense of identity.

Eyes, hair, heart, legs, hands, fingers, genitals and skin were the most important body parts, while throat, liver, kidneys, chin, knees and nose were least essential to the sense of self. In general, women saw their bodies—particularly external parts such as eyes, hair, legs and skin—as more central to their identities than men did to theirs. In interviews, we found that many willing donors, men and women, believed that having part of themselves live on in someone else's body promised a kind of immortality.

Objects were somewhat less central than body parts to the sense of self. Not surprisingly, the most important material possessions were dwellings, automobiles and favorite clothes—each a kind of second skin that embellishes the self we present to others. Automobiles were particularly important to the identities of men.

10   For both houses and cars, the more recently they had been acquired and the better their condition, the more important they were to someone's sense of self; and the more important they were, the better care they got—dusting, painting, and remodeling in the case of houses; washing, waxing, and oil changing for the cars. The similarities stopped when it came to the possession's age. Here older houses and newer cars were considered more important parts of the self. It may be that houses are looked on as heirlooms, for which age is a virtue, while new cars run and look better.

Other objects important to a sense of self included favorite rooms, artwork, jewelry and clothing—all meaningful attachments to the body and the home. We found that academics were especially likely to cite books as favorite possessions, perhaps because they represent the knowledge on which their work is based. For other people, sporting goods represent what they can or could do, while the contents of wallets or purses were important because they indicated central characteristics such as age, sex, and organizational memberships, as well as personal power to spend (credit cards) and travel (driver's license).

For some, collections were a significant part of their extended selves—possessions that had been acquired through considerable personal effort. For others, heirlooms were vital parts of family self, providing a sense of the past and of continuity with prior generations.

The third category of possessions important to the extended self is the less tangible one of time and place. To most of the people in our study, and others we interviewed, childhood was an especially important time of life. They tended to cherish memories, accurate or otherwise, of this period. We found that older people were most likely to name nearby cities, states, and countries as important to their sense of self, while younger ones generally named places farther away.

Our interviews showed that people can be as acquisitive of places they visit as they are of objects they collect. We even found a sedentary form of place acquisition. An Amish man whose religion forbids him to drive a motorized vehicle collected the hometowns of people who visited his community. While speaking to us, he reeled off a list of their states and countries much as other people mention the places they have visited personally.

15   There were few surprises in the final major category of possessions—people and pets—that individuals used to define themselves. The most important were generally parents, spouses, siblings, children and favorite friend of the same sex. Prominent political figures and favorite stars of movies and television were usually at the opposite end of the "selfness" continuum, unrelated to the sense of identity.

The common idea that some people consider their pets part of the family (and therefore of themselves) was supported by a series of interviews with people who owned dogs, cats, ferrets, birds and various other animals. While not all owners identified strongly with their pets, some felt closer to them than to their immediate families.

Is the fact that we are what we possess desirable or undesirable? There is no simple answer, but certain advantages and disadvantages seem evident. Among the advantages is that possessions provide a sense of the past. Many studies have shown that the loss of possessions that follows natural disasters or that occurs when elderly people are put in institutions is often traumatic. What people feel in these circumstances is, quite literally, a loss of self. Possessions also help children develop self-esteem, and learning to share possessions may be important in the growth of both individual and aggregate senses of self.

Incorporating possessions deeply into the sense of self can also have undesirable consequences. Too much attachment to pets can reflect an unhealthy drive to dominate and possess power and result in less devotion to family and friends. Investing too much of the self in collections and other possessions may displace love from people to things. Regarding other people as parts of our self can lead to jealousy and excessive possessiveness. Or by identifying too strongly with a spouse or child, we may end up living vicariously, instead of developing our own potential. As Erich Fromm asked in his book *To Have or To Be*, "If I am what I have and if what I have is lost, who then am I?"

From "My Possessions Myself" by Russell W. Belk, Psychology Today, *Vol. 22 No. 718, 1988. pp. 50–53. Reprinted by permission of the author.*

Questions:

1. List the four categories of possessions and give an example for each.

   a. _____   _____

   b. _____   _____

   c. _____   _____

   d. _____   _____

2. Write the main idea of the essay. In which paragraph did you find the main idea?

   _____

   _____

3. Archaeologists have recovered finely worked jade artifacts and marble vessels from a series of burial caves in Honduras. What directly stated main idea from the essay does this information reinforce?

   _____

   _____

4. When the possessions of Jacqueline Kennedy Onassis were sold at an auction at Sotheby's, people paid far more for her things than their actual appraised value. Write the directly stated main idea from the essay that helps explain why this occurred.

   _____

   _____

5. In Italy recently, an American family devastated by their son's untimely death donated his heart, lungs, liver, and corneas to others. What main idea from the essay supports their action?

   _____

   _____

6. Susan has a cup and saucer collection that once belonged to her maternal grandmother. What are these objects likely to represent to her?

    _____

    _____

7. What is the author's purpose in writing this article?

    _____

    _____

8. An elderly woman, estranged from her family, risked her life to retrieve her dog from her burning apartment. What is positive about her attachment to her dog? What is negative?

    _____

    _____

    _____

9. A mother distraught over a diagnosis of cancer fatally wounded both her two children and herself. This incident reinforces what main idea from the essay?

    _____

    _____

10. In paragraph 4, the organizational pattern could be described as
    a. comparison and contrast.
    b. cause and effect.
    c. chronological order.
    d. examples.

11. For paragraph 7, the author uses an organizational pattern that indicates
    a. the definition of something.
    b. division and steps in a process.
    c. a cause-and-effect relationship.
    d. examples of something.

12. "We found that academics were especially likely to cite books as favorite possessions, perhaps because they represent the knowledge on which their work is based." This sentence in paragraph 11 is an example of
    a. definition.
    b. classification.
    c. cause and effect.
    d. steps in a process.

13. The author's primary purpose in the final two paragraphs of the article is to
    a. discuss the advantages and disadvantages of strong identification with possessions.
    b. discuss the loss of self that the elderly experience when they give up their possessions.
    c. discuss the problems of living through others.
    d. discuss how possessions help build self-esteem in young children.

14. The author's overall tone in the article could be described as
     a. critical.
     b. matter-of-fact.
     c. concerned.
     d. sympathetic.

Working with Vocabulary

Directions: Try to determine each of the italicized words by means of context clues. Then consult your dictionary to find the precise definition.

1. "Burglary victims often say that they feel they have been personally *polluted*, even raped."

     Polluted:_____ Your Definition

     _____ Dictionary Definition

2. "Although we Americans think of ourselves as highly individualistic, *aggregate* identity is important to us, as the willingness to preserve and restore symbols such as the Statue of Liberty shows."

     Aggregate: _____ Your Definition

     _____ Dictionary Definition

3. "Body parts are so well *integrated* into our identities that we think of them as 'me' rather than merely 'mine.' "

     Integrated: _____ Your Definition

     _____ Dictionary Definition

4. "In general, women saw their bodies—particularly *external* parts such as eyes, hair, legs and skin—as more central to their identities than men did to theirs."

     External:_____ Your Definition

     _____ Dictionary Definition

5. "In interviews, we found that many willing donors, men and women, believed that having part of themselves live on in someone else's body promised a kind of *immortality*."

     Immortality: _____ Your Definition

     _____ Dictionary Definition

6. "We found that *academics* were especially likely to cite books as favorite possessions, perhaps because they represent the knowledge on which their work is based."

     Academics: _____ Your Definition

     _____ Dictionary Definition

7. "Many studies have shown that the loss of possessions that follows natural disasters or that occurs when elderly people are put in institutions is often *traumatic*."

     Traumatic: _____ Your Definition

     _____ Dictionary Definition

Written Assignment:

After reading the article, *My Possessions Myself*, describe which possessions you would save from a fire at your own home if you could safely retrieve anything (assuming all your family members and pets were safely removed). Tell why you would save these particular items and why they are so important to you.

Chronological Order and Summaries of Longer Articles

You summarize a reading selection by stating the main ideas and key supporting details in your own words. A summary condenses the original material, and good summaries are about one-fourth the length of the original. If a summary is written well, you do not have to go back and read the selection again.

Your ability to summarize will help you in college because summarizing information is a good way to learn it. Summarizing may also help you at work. For instance, a nurse might summarize a patient's condition, a sports writer might summarize the action in a basketball game, and a police officer might summarize the events leading up to an accident.

In Chapter 4, we did a summary of a fairly short article. You are now going to be working with a longer article about a nineteenth-century woman who took on a role usually reserved for a man. The information in the article is presented chronologically making it easier to summarize.

Use the survey and question steps of SQ3R before actually beginning to read the article. Study the bibliographic heading at the top. Who wrote the article? What is the title? What journal is it from? When was it written? All of this information will suggest what the article is about, how it is organized, and what the author's viewpoint is. In your survey, read the first two paragraphs, the last two paragraphs, and the first sentence of the other paragraphs. After completing your survey of the entire article, write the main idea below.

Main Idea: _____

"Charley's Secret," *American History*, June 1997   *by Shannon Moon Leonetti*

READING

On December 28, 1879, Charley Parkhurst lost his battle against crippling rheumatism and cancer. The well-known stagecoach driver had been seriously ill for weeks when he mentioned to his friend Charles Harmon, that he had something to tell him, but "there was no hurry." The tough old driver had less time than he knew, however, and died without speaking to Harmon.

The local undertaker, beckoned to prepare Charley's body for burial, was not prepared for what he discovered. When he started to change Charley out of his bed clothes, he was shocked to find that the tobacco-chewing man who had handled a black snake whip and a gun as well as anyone, was, in fact, a woman.

At first the undertaker did not know what to do. After gathering his wits, he called out for Frank Woodward, Charley's closest friend for more than 20 years. Frank had kept a daily vigil during Charley's illness and was by his side at the end. But when informed of the startling discovery, Woodward forgot his grief and started to "wax profane."

The truth was almost impossible to comprehend. It confounded those closest to Charley and shocked the people who had respected their friend's prowess as a reinsman, skills that had earned Parkhurst a spot in an elite group nicknamed the

"Kings of the Road." A lifetime spent within a small circle of friends had not prevented Charley Parkhurst from keeping her secret from everyone.

5   While the written history of nineteenth century America is dominated by the exploits of men, the bizarre story of Charley Parkhurst is not unique. A number of women disguised themselves as men in order to fight in the Civil War. Whatever had motivated Charley Parkhurst, and whether or not her "secret" was one she kept willingly, the truth remains that opportunities for women of her day to lead the kind of lives they wanted were very limited.

Facts about Charley's life are difficult to come by, and harder to prove. Much of what has been written about her is based on hearsay and legend. Still, enough is known about her 67 years to categorize her life as another example of how, in the history of the American West, the truth is often more interesting than fiction.

Born around 1812, in Lebanon, New Hampshire, Parkhurst spent her youth in an orphanage. There is no record of who left her there, or of whether her birth name was Charlotte, as many have assumed. Orphanages of this era were not happy places in which to grow up. Rules were adopted for the convenience of the staff, and with so many children under one roof, child-care institutions could not supply the warmth, affection, and attention of a normal household. Boys and girls often were dressed alike in easy-to-care-for overalls, with their hair cut in identical bobs. This sort of generic environment must have encouraged Charley's sense of independence, and shaped her outlook on life.

By the time she was a teenager, Charley had had enough of the harsh, restricted life of the orphanage and decided to run away. She went to work in a livery stable in Worcester, Massachusetts, cleaning stalls, keeping the tack in good repair, washing the coaches, and currying and feeding the horses. The new stable "boy" turned out to be a natural with the horses, and his employer, Ebenezar Balch began teaching him to drive the coaches, beginning with a one-horse buggy. It was not long before he could handle as many as six horses at a time.

Charley moved with Balch to Providence, Rhode Island, where he earned a reputation as both a smooth and careful driver and the perfect coachman for parties and dances. Long after he moved west, Charley was remembered back east as a quiet man who "struck a handsome figure when he showed up driving six grays exactly matched." He grew restless with driving livery, however, and reportedly left Rhode Island for Georgia with another driver in the mid-1840s. His exact whereabouts for this period are unclear, but presumably, he continued to ply the trade at which he had become so skilled, until he returned to Rhode Island in 1849.

10   A pair of young businessmen and expert reinsmen from that state named Jim Birch and Frank Stevens went west to take advantage of the money-making opportunities that followed the recent gold rush in California. In 1851, when Birch desperately needed good reinsmen for the rapidly growing stage and mail lines he had established, he induced Charley to come and work for him. Two years later, Birch and Stevens, in an effort to head off growing competition, formed the California Stage Company, with Charley as one of their top drivers.

By 1856, stagecoaching had grown enormously in the West, particularly in California, where Sacramento had become the largest stagecoach center in the world. The California Stage Company, the largest stagecoach firm in the country, dominated the business within the state, with 28 daily lines that covered nearly two thousand miles of roads. The company owned two hundred Concord stagecoaches and wagons, and employed three hundred drivers, agents, hostlers, and others. Drivers, such as the famed Frank Monk who both terrified and impressed *New York Tribune* editor Horace Greeley during an 1859 excursion, earned inflated reputations because of their speed and skill on mountain roads. A good driver, given a change of teams and a Concord coach, could cover nearly one hundred miles in 24 hours.

Like Monk, Charley earned a reputation of heroic proportions while driving local routes for the California Stage Company. Passengers considered it an honor to be asked by the veteran reinsman to ride up on the box with him. Parkhurst worked hard to maintain his record as one of the fastest and safest stagecoach drivers in California. His incessant tobacco chewing did nothing to diminish his high, booming voice or his loud whistle; valuable tools when it came time to shout over the clamor of the coach or signal his approach on a particularly narrow road.

One day, not long after Charley arrived in California, a road agent surprised and robbed his stage. From then on he carried a weapon beside him. The next time he faced a similar threat, Parkhurst, better prepared, reportedly fired a shot as he kept the stage rolling. The partner of a notorious stage robber called "Sugarfoot" was wounded in the fray; he died later, after making a deathbed confession. "Old Charley," as the nearly middle-aged reinsman was called by younger drivers, never again had serious trouble with highwaymen.

Over time, Charley drove stages on almost every route in northern California. Once, on a run from San Francisco to San Jose, he was said to have lost his left eye while shoeing a horse who "ungratefully kicked him in the face." From then on, Charley wore a patch over the damaged eye socket, enhancing the aura of mystery that surrounded this "unsociable feller."

15   Having only one good eye did not prevent Charley from becoming famous for feats of skill and bravery. While driving at a fast clip, he could, some claimed, run over a half dollar that was lying in the road, with the front and rear wheels of his stage. Some found his proficiency with a whip "downright spooky"; Parkhurst could, the stories went, "cut the end off an envelope held at arm's length at 15 paces, or cut the cigar from a man's mouth at the same distance without hurting anyone."

Sometime around the 1860s, Charley was carrying a load of liquor to the Pleasant Valley ranch owned by Andrew Jackson Clark. Charley was said to have arrived so drunk that Clark and his 14-year-old son put him to bed. The young Clark came running and told his mother that Charley ain't no man, he's a woman." For some unknown reason, Mr. Clark chose this occasion to teach his young son a lesson in not telling stories about others, and the Clarks kept Charley's secret until after his death. Charley was never seen drunk again.

Around that same time, Parkhurst's rheumatism convinced him it was time to give up driving. He wanted to leave the roads before an accident or a runaway marred his clean record. In 1864, he settled on a small tract of land on the road from San Jose to Santa Cruz, built a two-room house and stable, and planted wheat, turnips, and an apple orchard. The worn-out driver noted: "I'm no better now than when I commenced. Pay's small and work's heavy. I'm getting old. Rheumatism in my bones."

Parkhurst continued working, however. His place became a stage stop where he changed horses and refreshed travelers. Then, joining in a venture with his good friend Frank Woodward, Charley started raising cattle. When times were slow, the pair hired themselves out as lumberjacks. Before long, however, his rheumatism forced Charley to slow down further. Heavy physical work was becoming too tough, and his limbs were starting to shrivel. Nearly sixty, he had to give up his long habit of sleeping out in the woods wrapped only in a blanket. And, he grew increasingly reticent and private.

Never one to talk about himself, Charley shined when the subject turned to politics. He firmly believed that it was both the right and the obligation of every citizen to pay attention to the political situation and to vote. In November 1868, Charley Parkhurst cast his first recorded vote; having lived for so long as a man, it may never have occurred to him that he did not have that right. The voting entry recorded in the Great Register of Santa Cruz County, California, lists one "Charley Darkey Parkhurst, age 55, occupation farmer, native New Hampshire, resident Soquel."

20   The country was changing rapidly as the 1870s approached, yet women still had almost no property or inheritance rights, and the doors were just beginning to open in the job market. Only because she sacrificed her identity as a woman was Charley able to exercise one special privilege, the right to vote, almost 52 years before anyone else of her gender.

Sometime around 1872, Parkhurst sold off all of his cattle and property, and moved into a small vacant house on land owned by Charles Harmon. A few years later, in 1879, Charley complained of a sore throat, but refused to see a doctor. Even when the sore throat became a swelling on the side of his tongue, Charley—the person who took the best care possible of his horses—still did not seek medical attention. Nearly a year went by before he could be coerced into seeing Mr. Plumm, Soquel's "Cancer man." By then it was too late.

As Christmas approached, Charley's health was rapidly deteriorating. Frank Woodward starting visiting him every day. The two tired old-timers mostly sat in front of the fire, sometimes breaking the silence to reminisce or to share fresh gossip.

Finally, death came, and word of Charley's secret spread. Shock and anger overwhelmed "his" closest friends, and much time passed before their sense of loss settled in. Woodward is said to have sworn aloud at the corpse as he accompanied it to the carpenter's shop to be fitted for a coffin. Old Charley had no money, but an acquaintance donated a plot in the Odd Fellow's cemetery in Watsonville, California. In 1880, Charles Harmon donated a small headstone.

Another donation provided a plaque that was hung on the Soquel, California, fire station. The inscription noted that "On this site on November 3, 1868 was cast the first vote by a woman in California. A Ballot by Charlotte 'Charley' Parkhurst who disguised herself as a man."

"Charley's Secret" by Shannon Moon Leonetti. This article is reprinted from the May/June 1997 issue of American History Illustrated *magazine with the permission of Cowles Enthusiast Media, Inc. (History Group), A PRIMEDIA Publication, Copyright American History Illustrated magazine.*

Do you still agree with your original main idea? _____
If not, rewrite your main idea below.

Main Idea: _____

_____

Answer the following questions about the topic. Your answers will provide you with important details about the story.

Who? _____

What? _____

Where? _____

When? _____

Why? _____

How? _____

In your own words, write four main points from the article along with two supporting details for each main point.

Point 1: _____

Detail 1: _____

Detail 2: _____

Point 2: _____

Detail 1: _____

Detail 2: _____

Point 3: _____

Detail 1: _____

Detail 2: _____

Point 4: _____

Detail 1: _____

Detail 2: _____

If you have difficulty with any of the steps, check the following examples.

Now you are ready to write your summary. The introductory paragraph will present the main idea of the selection. Each of the next paragraphs will focus on one of the main points. Include just enough details to support each main point. Use transitional words to smoothly connect everything together.

Main idea of the article: *Charley Parkhurst, disguising herself as a man, became a well-known and respected stagecoach driver living a life of independence unknown to women at the time.*

Who?	*Charley Parkhurst (Charlotte?)*
What?	*became a well-known stagecoach driver*
Where?	*the West, mainly California*
When?	*middle nineteenth century before women had the vote*
Why?	*lived a life of great independence*
How?	*disguised herself as a man*

Point 1:	*Charley's early years in an orphanage encouraged her independence and shaped her outlook on life.*
Details:	Born 1812 and abandoned at harsh orphanage where all dressed alike; ran away to work in livery stable where learned to drive coaches
Point 2:	*Charley became a well-respected reinsman for the largest stagecoach company in the world.*
Details:	Worked for California Stage Co; was part of the "Kings of the Road"; known as a fast, safe driver and a hero

Point 3:	*Charley, disguised as a man, exercised the right to vote long before other women.*
Details:	In 1868, at 55, voted as a man, 52 years before other females allowed; first owned a stagecoach rest stop and then in 1872 moved to a house
Point 4:	*When Charley became ill with cancer and died, friends were shocked and angry about the deception.*
Details:	Even after sore throat was diagnosed as cancer, failed to tell secret; fell to undertaker to announce that Charley was a woman

The following summary was written by a student:

> This article is about a woman named Charley Parkhurst who, disguising herself as a man, became a well-known and respected stagecoach driver, living a life of independence unknown to women at the time.
>
> Charley's early years in an orphanage probably shaped her outlook on life. She was born around 1812 and as a small child was abandoned at [the] orphanage. Her name is assumed to have been Charlotte. Orphanages at the time were harsh places. Both male and female children were dressed alike and given the same haircuts. Being in this type of environment could have encouraged Charley to "act like a man." In her teens, she ran away and became a worker in a livery stable. She was trained to drive coaches and one horse buggies, and finally six horse buggies.
>
> As a top reinsman, Charley was persuaded to go to California to work for the largest stagecoach company in the world, the California Stage Company. There she was a well-respected driver earning a place in a group nicknamed, "Kings of the Road." Many passengers considered it a great honor to be invited by Charley to ride up on the box next to him. In addition to being considered one of the fastest and safest drivers, Charley also earned the reputation of a hero.
>
> At a time when women were not allowed to own property or vote, Charley managed to do both. In 1868, at the age of 55, Charley voted as a man, having lived that life for so long that no one thought to ask questions. This was 52 years before other females were given the right to vote. When Charley gave up driving, he owned a small place that became a stagecoach rest stop. In 1872, he sold off all his property and moved into a vacant house owned by a friend.
>
> Charley, suffering from rheumatism and other symptoms of old age, complained of a sore throat, but refused to see a doctor. Eventually the sore throat was diagnosed as cancer. At no time during his illness did Charley confide his secret to any close friends. At his death, it was the undertaker who made the announcement that old Charley was in fact a woman. When the truth of Charley's deception was discovered, his friends were both shocked and angry. Tobacco-chewing Charley, who had handled a whip and a gun with the best of them, had become a legend in the Old West.

Now you are going to write a summary of a previous selection in this chapter. Select either "Impulse Control: The Marshmallow Test" or "The Chaser." Because you have already read your chosen selection, you can skip the survey questions.

What is the main idea of your selection?

_____

_____

Answer the following questions about the topic:

Who?   _____

What?   _____

Where? _____

When?   _____

Why?   _____

How?   _____

In your own words, list three or four main points from the article along with two supporting details for each main point.

Point 1: _____

Details: _____

_____

Point 2: _____

Details: _____

_____

Point 3: _____

Details: _____

_____

Point 4: _____

Details: _____

_____

Using this information, write your summary on a separate sheet of paper.

Chapter 9 Test: "Charley's Secret"

Multiple Choice

1. The author's purpose in writing this article was to
    a. encourage women to enter predominantly male occupations.
    b. inform us of the life of one lady who assumed the role of a man.
    c. explain the life of 19th century stage-coach drivers.
    d. entertain the reader with an amusing story.

2. You can infer from this article that Charley
    a. had many friends who knew she was a woman.
    b. would have been allowed to vote if her true sex had been known.
    c. probably could not have become a stage-coach driver if she had not pretended to be a man.
    d. was a transsexual.

3. The most likely modes of writing and organization for this article are
   a. descriptive and chronological.
   b. expository and cause and effect.
   c. narrative and definition.
   d. persuasive and examples.

4. The word *incessant* in paragraph 12 means
   a. disliked by others.
   b. off-and-on.
   c. constant or continual.
   d. frequent.

5. The last sentence of paragraph 20 indicates
   a. comparison/contrast.
   b. cause/effect.
   c. definition/example.
   d. classification/division.

True or False

_____ 6. Charley stopped driving stage coaches because of cancer.

_____ 7. Charley died in poverty.

_____ 8. Charley led other women to fight for the right to vote.

_____ 9. The undertaker was the first person to discover that Charley was a woman.

_____ 10. Charley had a difficult childhood.

Review Test 7: Modes of Writing

The following paragraphs are taken from college textbooks. The general purpose of each author is to present information about the topic or explain a specific idea.
   Directions: Read each paragraph. Then choose the best answer for each item.

(1) Psychologist John Reisman divides enduring friendships into three types: "associative," "receptive," and "reciprocal." An *associative friendship* endures because of circumstances that bring the partners together. Associative friendships include relationships with colleagues at work, at church, at school and members of the same club, athletic team, fraternity, or sorority. The sense of commitment that each partner feels toward the other is due to the situation (belonging to the same club). A *receptive friendship* is based on a difference in status or control. One member is the giver and the other is the taker. Leaders and followers create receptive friendships, as do instructors and students, mentors and trainees, masters and apprentices, or any sets of people whose relationship is based on a relational difference of complementary roles in which one person is the giver and the other is the receiver. A very close relationship is most likely to be a *reciprocal friendship* rather than an associative or receptive one. Partners in a reciprocal friendship feel a commitment specifically to their interpersonal relationship. Moreover, reciprocal friends tend to consider themselves as equals in the relationship. They will switch back and forth between giving and receiving roles and will typically not maintain one role throughout the relationship.

From Interpersonal Communication, *2nd edition, by Aubrey Fisher and Katherine L. Adams, 1994. Reprinted by permission of The McGraw-Hill Companies.*

1. The organizational patterns used in this paragraph are
   a. persuasion, and cause and effect.
   b. expository, and classification and division.
   c. narrative and comparison/contrast.
   d. description and chronological order.

2. Your relationship with a supervisor at work would be an example of which type of friendship?
   a. associative
   b. receptive
   c. reciprocal

3. You work as a teacher's aide at a local high school and have become friends with a fellow teacher's aide. The two of you often take lunch and recess breaks together. This is an example of a(n) _____ friendship.
   a. associative
   b. receptive
   c. reciprocal

    (2) The Beatles—the singer-guitarists Paul McCartney, John Lennon, and George Harrison, and the drummer Ringo Starr—have been the most influential performing group in the history of rock. Their music, hairstyle, dress, and lifestyle were imitated all over the world, resulting in a phenomenon known as Beatlemania. All four Beatles were born during the early 1940s in Liverpool, England, and dropped out of school in their teens to devote themselves to rock. Lennon and McCartney, the main songwriters of the group, began working together in 1956 and were joined by Harrison about two years later. In 1962 Ringo Starr became their new drummer. The group gained experience by performing in Hamburg, Germany; and in Liverpool, a port to which sailors brought the latest American rock, rhythm-and-blues, and country-and-western records. In 1961, the Beatles made their first record, and by 1963 they were England's top rock group. In 1964, they triumphed in the United States, breaking attendance records everywhere and dominating the record market. Audiences often became hysterical, and the police had to protect the Beatles from their fans. Beatle dolls, wigs, sweatshirts, and jackets flooded the market. Along with a steady flow of successful records, the Beatles made several hit movies: *A Hard Day's Night*, *Help!*, and *Yellow Submarine*.

From Music: An Appreciation, *2nd Edition by Roger Kamien, 1994. Reprinted by permission of The McGraw-Hill Companies.*

1. For this paragraph, the author uses an organizational pattern that
   a. gives examples to support a point.
   b. describes a series of events in chronological order.
   c. compares and contrasts key details.
   d. defines key terms.

2. You can infer from this paragraph that the Beatles
   a. took college classes in music theory.
   b. had little effect on rock music.
   c. were well-known musicians before joining the group.
   d. changed the course of rock music.

3. Ringo Starr
   a. was the Beatles' first drummer.
   b. was born in the late 1940s.
   c. joined the group after the Beatles released their first hit.
   d. was one of the group's main songwriters.

PART 5 | Reading Critically

The jazz of any period needs critical comment and evaluation, but criticism must be based on something more than personal preference or personal opinion. Discussion and debate over the relative merits of different kinds of jazz can be healthy and rewarding provided they are based not merely on opinion but on significant analysis and interpretation.

from Understanding Jazz *by Leroy Ostransky*

When we hear a musical piece played, most of us have an opinion whether or not we like it. Few of us, though, have the knowledge necessary to be able to evaluate the piece on its technical merits. Only someone with enough expertise about music would be able to do that. Often there is a need to be able to critically evaluate reading selections, especially those that are meant to explain or persuade. The purpose of Part 5 is to teach you some techniques for performing such an evaluation. What we will be discussing are (1) the difference between fact and opinion, (2) what it means for a writer to have a bias and how to identify a writer's bias, and (3) how to look at the evidence presented in a reading selection to determine whether it supports the writer's conclusions.

Chapter 10

Fact and Opinion

Learning to Read Critically

Listening: To Tell Fact from Opinion

*by Shirley Haley-James
and John Warren Stewig*

READING

You spend a good part of your day listening to other people—teachers, friends, parents, radio and TV announcers. Sometimes they tell you facts; other times they offer their opinions. Can you tell the difference? If you cannot, you will have a hard time knowing what to believe.

Fact   A fact is a statement that can be proved. You can prove it yourself, or you can use a reliable authority. Here are some examples of facts and how they can be proved.

Statements of Fact	Sources of Proof
Abraham Lincoln was assassinated.	History book
Mr. Guthrie teaches math.	Experience
Jeff won the election.	Number of votes
Your kitchen table is 52 inches long.	Measurement

Laws and observations are also forms of fact. A law may be based on science (the law of gravity) or an established government authority (the speed limit). You can prove an observation, such as "Some stars are brighter than others," by pointing it out yourself or by testing it scientifically.

So many men, so many opinions.

Terence

Opinion   An opinion cannot be proved. It is based only on someone's thoughts, feelings, or judgment.

Opinions: Abraham Lincoln was a great man.

Mr. Guthrie works his students too hard.

Jeff is the better candidate.

You should have a larger table.

Some people may think that these statements are true; others may disagree. Listen for words like *good, nice, bad, wonderful,* and *should.* They can help you identify opinions.

Some opinions, however, are sounder than others. While they cannot be proved, they can be backed up with facts. Someone who tells you that Jeff is the better candidate can support this opinion by giving facts about Jeff's experience

270

and past actions. Historians who believe Lincoln was great can support their opinion with facts about his achievements.

A hypothesis is a form of opinion. It is a reasonable guess made to explain an observation. Each hypothesis must be tested to make sure it is a good guess.

Hypotheses: Objects move only when they are pushed or pulled.

                  The car stopped because it ran out of gas.

                  Green food makes me sneeze.

You can test the last hypothesis by seeing if you really do sneeze whenever you eat something green. If you also sneeze when you eat something yellow, you may have to change your hypothesis.

A theory is also an opinion, but it is not a guess. A theory is an accepted explanation of a set of observations. A theory often includes several hypotheses that belong together and have been tested successfully. If a theory is good, it can be used to explain other things.

Theories: Heat results from the movement of tiny particles.

             All the forces of nature are interrelated.

Here are some examples of some other kinds of opinions.

Speculative Statement:	Allison Packer is going to win the seat in the state legislature.
Value Judgment:	She is the best candidate.
Exaggeration:	Allison Packer will get billions of votes.
Belief:	She will change the government as she has promised.

When you listen to someone—in a lecture, a commercial, an election campaign, or even just conversation—be aware of the difference between a fact and an opinion. Do not be persuaded by an opinion unless the speaker supports it with facts.

From Houghton Mifflin English, Level 8 by Haley-James, et al. Copyright © 1988 by Houghton Mifflin Company. Reprinted by permission of Houghton Mifflin Company. All rights reserved.

Note: It is important to realize that "facts" can change over time for a variety of reasons. At one time in the past, it was considered to be a "fact" that the earth was at the center of the universe. Of course, we now know that this is not true. Until recently, the following statement was considered to be a fact:

Star Wars is the top domestic money-earner of all time.

This is no longer a "fact" because in 1997 the release of the movie *Titanic* surpassed *Star Wars* in box office receipts.

Even facts that we take for granted today may not stand the test of time. Should estrogen-replacement therapy for women be widely prescribed? Is caffeine bad for your health? Is the consumption of one alcoholic drink a day beneficial to your cardiovascular system? Until scientists discover new information, the answer to these questions seems to be yes.

Some statements of fact are false because our information is erroneous. Comedians like to joke that if you ask most women over the age of 40 their age, you're going to get a false answer. Other "facts" that are based on numbers and statistics may be false because numbers and statistics can be easily manipulated. In evaluating factual information, it is best to keep in mind what Mark Twain used to say, "There are lies, damn lies, and statistics."

Clues to Identifying an Opinion

Opinions are beliefs or judgments that cannot be proved by any objective means. Any statement that deals with probabilities or future events is considered to be an opinion because it cannot be proved. Opinions rely on abstract words that are not quantifiable such as value-judgment words. Below are some examples of typical opinion words.

Words and Phrases That Signal an Opinion

I believe	Perhaps	This suggests
Apparently	In my view	Presumably
It seems likely	Many experts agree	In my opinion
One interpretation is	One possibility is	

In addition, any word that indicates a value judgment on someone's part signals an opinion. Many people disagree about what is the best or the worst, and so forth. Because of our different values, the use of these words makes any statement that contains them impossible to prove.

Value Judgment Words

necessary	interesting	successful
beautiful/attractive, etc.	worst	effective
best	highest	most
greatest	bad	nice

Most of what we read and hear is a combination of fact and opinion. Because of this, it is important to be able to distinguish between the two. Remember, not all opinions are of equal validity. Poorly supported opinions are of little value, while opinions from an expert, or someone knowledgeable in the field, are considered to be more reliable.

Exercise #1 Writing Personal Facts and Opinions

Directions: Using complete sentences, write six facts about yourself. Then, think about some opinions you have and write six of them down.

Facts about You

1. _____
2. _____
3. _____
4. _____
5. _____
6. _____

Opinions You Have

1. _____
2. _____
3. _____
4. _____
5. _____
6. _____

Exercise #2 Working with Facts and Opinions

Directions: Place an **F** in the blank for those statements that are mostly fact and an **O** in the blank for those statements that are mostly opinion. Circle the abstract or value-judgment words in the statements of opinion.

_____ 1. The community college is a better place to attend school for the first two years than a university or a four-year school.

_____ 2. *U.S. News and World Report* found that 100 percent of the students at Harvard University were in the top quarter of their high school graduating class.

_____ 3. Martin Gilbert's *In Search of Churchill* is a convincing portrait of one of the dominant men of the World War II era.

_____ 4. According to Sharon Thompson's 1986 research study, teenagers' rates of drug use, eating disorders, depression, and suicide are rising.

_____ 5. Patricia Cornwell's book, *From Potter's Field,* is number one after its second week on the *New York Times* fiction bestseller list.

_____ 6. At $13.95 a copy, the book is a real bargain.

_____ 7. In a 1996 study, The American Medical Association reported that drinking is heaviest among singles and the newly divorced.

_____ 8. In 1995, there were only 84 surviving liberal arts colleges for women—down from 298 in 1960.

_____ 9. According to data reported in *Retirement Places Rated,* Las Vegas, with a grade of 84.5, is America's #1 retirement destiny.

_____ 10. Researchers from the University of Arizona recently tested 500 used kitchen dishcloths and found that two-thirds contain bacteria that can make people sick.

_____ 11. Toothpaste containing peroxide and baking soda is far better at producing clean and attractive teeth.

_____ 12. Researchers at Ohio State University found that women experience anxiety and depression about 30 percent more often than men.

_____ 13. Women have greater burdens and limitations placed on them in both the workplace and the family.

Exercise #3 Recognizing Facts and Opinions

Directions: Read the following sentences and put an **O** in the blank if the statement is an opinion or an **F** if the statement is a fact. Circle the opinion words that indicate probabilities or future events.

_____ 1. The *Victoria's Secret* catalog offers 45 items in satin.

_____ 2. You will learn more from reading books than you will from watching television.

_____ 3. In the next century, we will be unable to function as a society without computers.

_____ 4. A recent Ohio State study showed that playing the violin or cello burns 40 percent more calories than watching TV.

_____ 5. In 1923, F. Scott Fitzgerald called a collection of his short stories "Tales of the Jazz Age."

_____ 6. The National Highway Department, in its 1995 study, concluded that elderly drivers (those over the age of 70) are responsible for the majority of driving fatalities in the United States.

_____ 7. The United States is certain to do better in the 2000 Olympics because 56 percent of the 1996 Olympic team will be returning to competition.

_____ 8. The United Nations Human Development Program reports that the divorce rate in the United States is now the highest of any major industrialized nation.

_____ 9. An Education Department survey showed that 70 percent of 5,500 secondary school principals approve of requiring school uniforms.

_____ 10. Schools that maintain a dress code will tend to have fewer instances of assault, robbery, and vandalism, while at the same time will tend to report improved academic performance.

Exercise #4 Rewriting Opinion Statements

Directions: Working in a group, determine whether the given statement is a fact or an opinion, and write your answer on the line provided. Then on a separate piece of paper rewrite all statements of opinion as statements of fact. Be sure to eliminate all abstract and value-judgment words. Your fact sentence should use concrete words and be verifiable.

Example:

Opinion: My current house is **too small** for my family.

Fact: I have a one-bedroom house and 10 people in my family.

                                                 or

Fact: I have a 900-square foot-home and 10 people in my family.

_____ 1. My husband and I took a three-mile hike on Sunday.

_____ 2. My spring break was much too short.

_____ 3. My Honda Accord gets excellent gas mileage.

_____ 4. The yearly salary for the principal of John F. Kennedy School is $65,000.

_____ 5. He is a reckless and irresponsible driver.

_____ 6. The Macintosh Performa computer was very reasonably priced.

_____ 7. The temperature in the oven is 375 degrees.

_____ 8. My English teacher graded my last essay unfairly.

_____ 9. Of all my college classes, my computer class has been the most helpful.

_____ 10. Tiger Woods is the best golfer in Professional Golf Association (PGA) history.

Exercise #5 Movie Reviews Fact and Opinion

Directions: Study these Quick Flick reviews from a movie guide. If the review is entirely factual, mark **F.** If the review is entirely opinion, mark **O.** Mark the reviews containing both facts and opinions with **FO.**

_____ 1. **Boys on the Side.** A surprisingly fresh, funny, and sad story about three women who have nothing in common but their friendship. Bring Kleenex!

_____ 2. **Billy Madison.** Starring *Saturday Night Live's* Adam Sandler. A kid has to go back to first grade in order to earn his inheritance.

_____ 3. **Quiz Show.** Starring Ralph Fiennes. The story of the Senate investigation into the quiz shows of the 1950s. Features Charles Van Doren.

_____ 4. **Roommates.** Peter Falk turns in a superb performance as a cantankerous old man. This wonderful comic drama will be particularly meaningful for people with parents or grandparents who came to America as immigrants and worked harder than we can now imagine to make new lives here for their families.

_____ 5. **Nobody's Fool.** Paul Newman nominated for best actor and a cast that includes Bruce Willis, Melanie Griffith, and the late Jessica Tandy.

_____ 6. **The Quick and the Dead.** Sharon Stone of *Basic Instinct* fame starring as the sexiest gunslinger in the West. Also starring a miscast Gene Hackman. Director Sam Raimi tries to make this shoot-em-up a serious Western and a Western spoof at the same time, but he fails at both.

_____ 7. **Forrest Gump.** A wonderful comic drama with Tom Hanks as the low-I.Q. Gump and his journeys through life. Winner of Academy Awards for Best Picture, Best Actor, and Best Director. Also a Golden Globe winner.

_____ 8. **Outbreak.** Story concerns a virus that threatens the human race. Features Dustin Hoffman and Rene Russo as Drs. Sam Daniels and Roberta Keough, two infectious-disease specialists tracking a deadly virus that comes out of Africa and spreads to a small California town. *Outbreak* is rated R for profanity. There is no nudity or sex. So frightening you'll need to hang onto your seat. Be sure to cover your mouth when you cough!

Exercise #6 Separating Fact from Opinion

Many writers try to convince readers of the wisdom of their arguments by combining both facts and opinions, often within the same sentence. The following sentences contain both fact and opinion. The facts have been italicized.

1. *With half of all American marriages failing,* it appears that "till death do us part" simply means until the going gets rough.

2. *A USA Today poll showed that 65 percent of Americans were unable to identify* The Bill of Rights, thus demonstrating the widespread ignorance of the population at large.

Directions: After reading each sentence, underline only the facts.

1. Even though African-Americans make up 12 percent of the U.S. population and 25 percent of the moviegoing audience, they are virtually invisible at the annual Academy Awards celebration.

2. Immediately after divorce, the income of households with kids declines by 21 percent, thereby creating an unfortunate new class of people in poverty—divorced women with children.

3. Male adults who enjoy light or moderate drinking should keep right on enjoying imbibing since research done by Serge Renaud of the National Institute of Health on 36,000 middle-age men demonstrated that those who drank two to four glasses of wine a day had a 30–40 percent reduction in mortality from all causes.

4. In the state of Illinois, the delicate balance between a boss's right to know what's going on in the office and an employee's right to privacy has been upset by a 1995 state law that permits bosses to eavesdrop on employees' work telephones.

5. California, the state where 1.6 million lawsuits were filed in 1993, perhaps should have a new motto emblazoned on all license plates—Home of Litigators.

6. In 1981, the product NutraSweet was introduced to the public as a boon to the overweight, yet the Centers for Disease Control recently reported that U.S. obesity rates have actually increased since that time.

7. Despite the fact that many physicians, scientists, and consumer advocates regard homeopathic medicines as ineffective at best and dangerous at worst, the National Center for Homeopathy reports that Americans are spending more than $165 million annually on homeopathic preparations.

Fact and Opinion Exercise

Excerpt from "Truth Is More Than Skin Deep—The Lie Detector"

READING

Directions: Read the following excerpt and answer the questions that follow.

As credibility and trust have declined in American society, the popularity of lie detectors has increased. Once limited to law enforcement applications, lie detectors (also called polygraphs) came to be routinely used by corporations, banks, and even fast-food chains to question job applicants about their honesty in past jobs. In 1983, President Reagan ordered polygraph tests of certain federal employees in an effort to plug leaks to the press of classified or embarrassing information.

But by December of 1988, the employee Protection Act prohibited the use of polygraphs for random examinations or as part of a preemployment screening process. The growing use of the polygraph prompted a controversial question: What does a lie detector measure? Is it only the act of telling a lie that produces the telltale patterns of inked lines on graph paper? Or can other factors, such as emotional reactions to the content of the questions or the testing situation itself, cause truthful people to appear to be liars?

Lie detectors do not register lies; they rely on the fact that emotions and inner conflict are typically accompanied by physiological changes. When a person lies, there are changes in blood pressure, in breathing, and in the resistance of the skin to electrical current, known as *galvanic skin response.* There is no single pattern of responses unique to lying, however; the pattern varies from person to person.

In a typical lie detector examination, failing the test can have serious consequences. Subjects are thus generally quite nervous as a blood pressure cuff is strapped to one arm, sensors designed to measure breathing are attached to the chest and stomach, and electrodes are placed on the fingertips to measure galvanic skin response. Because the blood pressure cuff soon becomes uncomfortable, the examination must be short—three to four minutes long.

The form and mix of the questions is a key to the examination. A typical set of questions includes just a few that are critical: "Did you take money from the cash register on the evening of July 21?" The rest are control questions, designed to be answered dishonestly even if the subject is telling the truth about the relevant questions. For example, to a control question such as "Have you ever taken anything in your life?" even most truthful people will choose to lie, given the circumstances, since just about everyone has stolen something sometime. Polygraph examiners assume that an otherwise truthful person will react more strongly to the control questions, while an untruthful subject will react more strongly to the relevant ones.

Lie detectors are far from error-free. Figures vary widely, but according to one estimate, examinations in the field correctly identify about 75 percent of those lying. Unfortunately, about 49 percent of those telling the truth are also identified as lying. One major source of error is the fact that galvanic skin response changes in reaction to all kinds of emotions, not just those connected with deception. When someone is asked if he or she committed a murder, the lie detector is likely to jump. Of course, this may reflect guilt, but it may also reflect anxiety, fear, or loathing—all possible reactions to being questioned about a murder. If a suspect were questioned about marital problems, relationships with parents, or even attitudes toward work, the polygraph might make a similar jump in emotional response regardless of whether the person told the truth when answering.

It is also easy to fool the polygraph machine, given the proper knowledge. Some tactics do not work, however. Conscious efforts not to sweat or not to alter one's respiratory patterns will not succeed. Nor will efforts to increase one's response to control items, such as by clenching one's teeth. But taking tranquilizers does seem to reduce the physiological response to lying. So does not paying attention to the questions. In one experiment, subjects counted backward by sevens during their examination to distract themselves from the questions, and they were able to escape detection more often as a result.

Personal and social factors can also affect the physiological signs monitored by the machine. The galvanic skin response of some people changes spontaneously at a high rate, thus increasing the chances that their truthful answers will appear to

//The lie is a condition of life.//

Friedrich Nietzsche

5

be lies. Finally, the degree to which examiner and subject are matched in terms of sex, age, race, or ethnicity may also have an effect. In one study, the lie detector was least successful when examiner and subjects shared the same ethnicity, possibly because the subjects felt most at ease in this situation.

It is possible to increase the accuracy of polygraphs by testing only for "guilty knowledge"—that is, knowledge about details of the crime that only the guilty person could know. For example, if a list of banks is read, a guilty subject should react more strongly to the name of the bank that he or she actually robbed. However, in many of the 500,000 to 1 million testings taken each year in the United States, the most sophisticated methods are not used in formulating questions or interpreting results, partly because the vast majority of the 4,000 to 8,000 examiners have had little or no training in physiology or psychology.

From Understanding Psychology, *3E by Charles G. Morris, © 1996. Reprinted by permission of Prentice-Hall, Inc., Upper Saddle River, NJ.*

IN YOUR OWN WORDS

1. Do you think employers should be able to use lie detector tests to screen job applicants? Why or why not?

2. If a prospective employer asked you to take a lie detector test, would you agree to do it?

3. Do you think lie detector tests should be used to determine the guilt or innocence of criminal defendants? Why or why not?

Understanding the Vocabulary in the Essay

Directions: Choose one of the words in the following list to complete each of the sentences below. Use each word only once.

credibility	prohibited	randomly
controversial	physiologically	resistance
relevant	deception	loathe
tactics	alter	spontaneous
ethnicity	sophisticated	formulating

1. At the University of Texas Law School, an applicant's _____ will no longer be a factor in admissions decisions.

2. Girls attending high school proms frequently wear black strapless gowns and other types of _____ clothing.

3. The issue of cloning has become increasingly _____ with many scientists supporting continued research and other groups opposing the idea on moral or religious grounds.

4. Even though Jennifer was naturally a pretty girl, she spent a lot of time at the cosmetic counter searching for new ways to _____ her appearance.

5. After telling so many lies to his mother and father, the young child has completely lost his _____.

6. Many of Martha Graham's dances were completely _____ and unrehearsed.

7. Minors are _____ from smoking cigarettes or drinking alcohol.

8. Since so many students wanted to see the Final Four of the NCAA Championship Tournament, the tickets were distributed _____ by lottery.

9. When deciding what college to attend, a _____ consideration for the prospective student to consider is cost.

10. It is not only important to keep yourself healthy psychologically, but also _____.

11. Some people have a natural _____ or immunity to chicken pox; no matter how many times they are directly exposed they do not catch it.

12. After years of being mistreated by Bill, Marsha came not only to dislike him, but to actively _____ him.

13. During the war in Southeast Asia, the Vietcong employed guerrilla warfare _____, using small bands of fighters to harass U.S. troops.

14. Because John spent so much time _____ his ideas and too little time writing his paper, he missed the deadline.

15. Many Jewish leaders accuse Swiss banks of _____ for failing to be truthful about funds the Nazis had confiscated from victims of the Holocaust.

Chapter 10 Test: "Truth Is More Than Skin Deep—
The Lie Detector"

Multiple Choice

1. Based on the article, the author would probably believe that
   a. polygraph machines should never be used in any court cases.
   b. polygraph tests need to be used with caution and be administered by qualified professionals.
   c. lie detectors are so accurate that they can definitely determine whether a person is guilty or innocent.
   d. both the government and business should increase their use of the polygraph machine.

2. The mode of writing used in this article is
   a. narrative.
   b. descriptive.
   c. expository.
   d. persuasive.

3. The tone of this article is
   a. objective.
   b. optimistic.
   c. outraged.
   d. bitter.

4. "By December of 1988, the Employee Protection Act prohibited the use of polygraphs for random examinations. . . ." This sentence makes a statement of
   a. fact.
   b. opinion.

5. The main idea expressed in paragraph 6 is that
   a. polygraphs mistakenly say that 49 percent of those telling the truth are lying.
   b. the polygraph machines identify about 75 percent of those who are lying.
   c. lie detectors are far from error-free.
   d. emotional reactions can cause the polygraph machine to say that the subject is lying when the subject is telling the truth.

True or False

_____ 6. The article is supported by more fact than opinion.

_____ 7. Lie detector tests may be more successful when the examiner and the subject have similar ethnic backgrounds.

_____ 8. There are ways to fool polygraph machines.

_____ 9. A subject's emotional reactions can affect the results of polygraph testing.

_____ 10. Subjects of polygraph exams can easily change their respiratory responses.

Vocabulary: Unit 5

Copyright © 1999 by The McGraw-Hill Companies, Inc.

Trivia Question #1

Who invented the automobile? The answer is at the end of this lesson.

automobile—The largest car is 100 feet long and has 26 wheels. Inside this limousine is a swimming pool with diving board and a king-sized bed.

autograph—The highest price paid for a single autographed letter was $748,000. In 1991, Profiles in History of Beverly Hills paid this amount for a letter written by Abraham Lincoln in which he defended the Emancipation Proclamation.

This unit begins with the word part *auto*, found in many English words. It then looks at word parts having opposing meanings, such as "over" and "under," and "same" and "different." The last section covers some words that are commonly confused.

auto—self or same

automobile	*Auto* means "self," so an *automobile* is a self-moving vehicle.
autograph	*Graph* means "write," and *auto* means "self," so an autograph is a person's own signature. The literal meaning is self-written.
automaton	acting unthinkingly or automatically, like a robot. After the policeman had informed the Millers of their daughter's murder, the couple acted like *automatons* in making arrangements for her funeral.
autonomous	*Auto* means "self" and *nomos* means "law," so the literal meaning of *autonomous* is "self law." The word refers to self-government or being independent. The United States is an *autonomous* country. Individual states in the United States are not totally *autonomous* because they are part of the United States. Are individual citizens in the United States *autonomous*?

co, com, con—with, together
contra—against; opposite

cooperate	to act or work together with another or others

committee	a group of people chosen to work together on a particular matter.
consensus	Comes from *con* meaning "with" and *sentire* meaning "to think or feel." It means a thinking together or a general agreement.
compare	*Par* means "make equal," so if you *compare* two things, you are technically showing their similarities. But people, including college instructors, often use this word when they really mean to show similarities and differences. If one of your instructors asks you to do a *comparison*, find out whether the instructor wants you to show similarities only, or really wants you to show similarities and differences.
contrast	*Contra* means "against," so *contrast* means "to point out differences," or how one thing goes against another.
contradict	Comes from *contra* meaning "against" and *dict* meaning "say," as in *diction* and *predict*. The literal meaning of *contradict* is "say against." To *contradict* means to deny the statement of another person.
contraband	*Ban* originally means to officially forbid, so *contraband* means "to forbid against." Today it refers to something that is illegal to import or export. Cocaine would be considered *contraband*.

extra—over; more than; beyond
ultra—over; more; beyond
infra—under, below, beneath

extramarital	relating to a sexual relationship with someone other than one's spouse.
extraterrestrial	*Terra* means "earth," so an *extraterrestrial* is a being from outside the earth's limits. The title character from the movie *E.T.* was an *extraterrestrial*. Scientists are actively searching for signs of *extraterrestrial* intelligence.
extrasensory	Some people believe that they have a power of perception beyond the normal senses. They credit this *extrasensory* perception, or ESP, for their ability to predict the future, read someone else's thoughts, or visualize an unknown event. For example, have you ever felt that something tragic has happened to a close friend and it turned out you were right? That might be E.S.P. Scientists, though, are very skeptical about the validity of E.S.P.
ultraviolet	*Ultraviolet* light is above violet on the color spectrum. It is invisible because its wavelengths are too short. The ozone layer blocks most, but not all, of the harmful *ultraviolet* radiation, which is what causes sunburns.
ultramicroscope	an instrument that allows a person to see things too small to be seen by an ordinary microscope.

infrared	*Infrared* light is below red on the color spectrum. It is invisible because its wavelengths are too long for the human eye. The Army uses *infrared* light to see at night. TV remote controls use *infrared* light.
infrastructure	the basic structure or underlying foundation of something. The *infrastructure* of a house is its foundation and framing. The *infrastructure* of a community is its roads, schools, power plants, transportation, and communication systems.

trans—across

transportation	*Port,* as in portable, port-a-potties, and import, means "to carry." So, *transportation* is the act of carrying something from one place to another.
transmission	*Mis,* as in missile and missionary, means "to send," so *transmission* means "the act of sending across." The *transmission* of a car sends energy from the engine across the drive shaft to the wheels. You can also *transmit* a message to another person by writing a letter, or using e-mail or voice mail.
transsexual	a person who undergoes surgery and hormone treatments to change his or her sex. So, it could be said that a *transsexual* goes across sexual boundaries.
transvestite	A *transvestite* dresses in the clothing of the opposite sex. So, a *transvestite* dresses across sexual boundaries. If you can't remember the difference between this word and the one above, keep in mind that a vest is a piece of clothing. It comes from *vestire,* which means "to dress."

homo—same; equal; like
hetero—different

homosexual	having sexual desire for the same sex.
heterosexual	having sexual desire for the opposite sex.
homogeneous	the same in structure or quality; having similar parts. Your class is fairly *homogeneous* in terms of age if you are all of a comparable age.
heterogeneous	dissimilar, composed of unlike parts. Your class may be *heterogeneous* because you come from different backgrounds, cultures, and countries.
homogenization	The *homogenization* process of milk mixes the fat particles of the cream evenly throughout so that the cream doesn't separate. In milk taken straight from the cow, the lighter cream rises to the top. This is different from the process of pasteurization, named after inventor Louis Pasteur, which uses heat to kill bacteria.

Trivia Question #2

On what liquid did Pasteur conduct his initial experiments? Answer found at the end of this lesson.

Here are some words that are often confused with one another. Though some may appear to use the word parts mentioned in this unit, they really do not.

compliment	something said in praise; to make a nice remark about someone.
complement	that which completes or makes whole or perfect; to balance. The team plays well because the players *complement* each other; they fit together well. Steve needs to get his date a corsage that will *complement* the color of her dress.
supplement	Comes from *sub* meaning "under" and *plere* meaning "to fill," and means something added to make up for a lack. Physicians often prescribe vitamin *supplements* to pregnant women.
council	a group of people called together for discussion or advice.
counsel	a mutual exchange of ideas; to give or take advice.
consul	a government official appointed to live in a foreign country and look after his or her country's citizens who are in the foreign country. If you were in a foreign country and having passport problems, you might go to the U.S. *consulate* for help. If you are from another country, you may wish to visit your country's *consulate*.
continuous	going on without any interruption; unbroken. Think of "ous" to help you remember the meaning of this word, as in "one uninterrupted sequence." The cars backed up in a *continuous* line on the freeway.
continual	repeated often; over and over again but with interruptions. The weather forecaster predicted continual showers over the Labor Day weekend.

Make up your own sentences using each of the following words:

complement _____

_____

homogeneous _____

_____

autonomous _____

_____

infrastructure _____

_____

continuous_____

_____

extrasensory _____

_____

automaton _____

_____

Answer to Trivia Question #1

Pasteur conducted his original experiments on beer. Most of our beer is pasteurized. Non-pasteurized beer, such as keg beer, needs to be kept at a cold temperature so that bacteria don't form.

Answer to Trivia Question #2

Henry Ford did not invent the automobile; rather, his contribution was to mass-produce them. The two persons commonly given much credit for the invention of the automobile are the German engineers Gottlieb Daimler and Karl Benz.

Vocabulary 5

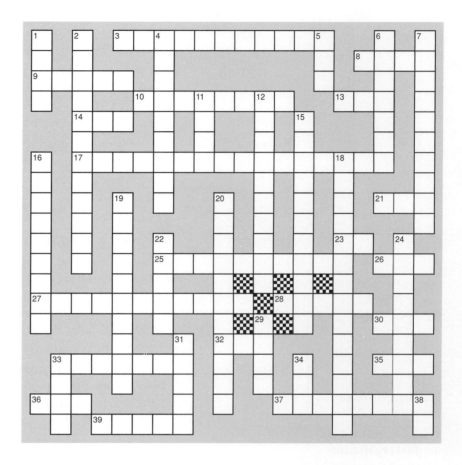

ACROSS CLUES

3. A person who has had a sex change operation.
8. A word part meaning "same."
9. A word part meaning "across."
10. To point out differences.
13. A word part meaning "around."
14. A word part meaning "below."
17. E.T.
21. An abbreviation for what was once the 10th month.
23. A word part meaning "toward."
25. Your state is not _____ because it is part of the United States.
26. A word part meaning "two."
27. _____ milk has been heated to kill bacteria.
28. A word part meaning "back."
30. An abbreviation for what was once the eighth month.
32. A word part meaning "year."
33. A group called together for discussion.
35. A word part meaning "see."
36. A word part meaning "three."
37. _____ light has wavelengths longer than ordinary light.
39. A word part meaning "over, more, beyond."

DOWN CLUES

1. A word part meaning "self."
2. A person who wears the clothing of the opposite sex.
4. Self-written.
5. A word part meaning "side."
6. To give advice.
7. To deny the statement of someone.
11. A word part meaning "distance."
12. A person who directs work or workers.
15. Light that causes sunburn.
16. The chemical formula for water has a _____ in it.
18. The foundation and frame of a building.
19. That which completes; to balance.
20. In a _____ group, the members are alike.
22. A word part meaning "large."
24. To sign your name at the bottom of a document.
29. A word part meaning "before."
31. A word part meaning "more or over."
33. A word part meaning "around."
34. A word part meaning "with."
38. A word part meaning "two."

Chapter 11

Bias

Eyewitness Testimony

In the previous chapter, we learned how important it is to be able to distinguish between fact and opinion. In order to be a critical reader, we also need to be aware of our biases and the biases of others. **A bias is defined as a strong leaning in either a positive or a negative direction.**

Authors have biases, and it is the critical reader's job to discover what they are. A careful reader will study the author's line of reasoning, notice whether opinions have been supported by facts and reasons, and then decide if the author's bias has prevented the making of a good argument.

In the drawing depicted below, the suspect in the investigation is in the center. Each of the individuals (and the Martian life form?) briefly describe his appearance. Notice how the descriptions they give the interviewer reflect their personal biases. Can you list some of these biases? Now read the essay on the following page while noting the effect bias can have on legal judgments.

THE INVESTIGATION

Reprinted by permission of John Jonik.

Notes on Vocabulary

Clarence Darrow—a lawyer known for his legal writing and for his defense of unpopular causes in the late nineteenth and early twentieth century. Darrow was the defense attorney in the famous Scopes trial of 1925. John Scopes, a high school biology teacher, was arrested for teaching the theory of evolution to his students. Although Scopes was eventually found guilty and had to pay a $100 fine, Darrow was considered to be the winner in the trial.

Cicero—a famous orator and statesman who lived in Rome from 106 B.C. to 43 B.C. He is known as one of ancient Rome's finest writers of prose. Many of his essays on philosophy are based on the works of Aristotle and Plato.

Tuning In to Reading

Have you ever served on a jury? Did you enjoy the experience? Can you think of any instances when a jury verdict was not popular with the public? Was the defendant found guilty or not guilty? Can you explain the difference between popular perception and the verdict?

"The Defendant's Characteristics"

READING

According to the famed trial attorney Clarence Darrow, jurors seldom convict a person they like or acquit one they dislike. He argued that the main job of the trial attorney is to make the jury like the defendant. Was he right? And is it true, as Darrow also said, that "facts regarding the crime are relatively unimportant"?

Darrow overstated the case. One study of more than 3,500 criminal cases and some 4000 civil cases found that 4 times in 5 the judge agreed with the jury's decision. Although both may have been wrong, the evidence usually is clear enough that jurors can set aside their biases, focus on the facts, and agree on a verdict. Darrow was too cynical; facts do matter.

Nevertheless, when jurors are asked to make social judgments—would *this* defendant commit *this* offense? intentionally?—facts are not all that matter. Communicators are more persuasive if they seem credible and attractive. Jurors cannot help forming impressions of the defendant. Can they put these impressions aside and decide the case based on the facts alone? To judge from the more lenient treatments often received by high-status defendants it seems that some cultural bias lingers. But actual cases vary in so many ways—in the type of crime, in the status, age, sex, and race of the defendant—that it's hard to isolate the factors that influence jurors. So experimenters have controlled such factors by giving mock jurors the same basic facts of a case while varying, say, the defendant's attractiveness or similarity to the jurors.

There is a physical attractiveness stereotype: Beautiful people seem like good people. Michael Efran wondered whether this stereotype would bias students' judgments of someone accused of cheating. He asked some of his University of Toronto students whether attractiveness should affect presumption of guilt. Their answer: "No, it shouldn't." But did it? Yes. When Efran gave other students a description of the case with a photograph of either an attractive or an unattractive defendant, they judged the most attractive as least guilty and recommended that person for the least punishment.

5　To see if these findings extend to the real world, Chris Downs and Phillip Lyons asked police escorts to rate the physical attractiveness of 1,742 defendants appearing before 40 Texas judges in misdemeanor cases. Whether the misdemeanor was serious (such as forgery), moderate (such as harassment), or minor (such as public intoxication), the judges set greater bails and fines for less-attractive defendants. What explains this dramatic effect? Are unattractive people also lower in status? Are they indeed more likely to flee or to commit crime, as the judges perhaps suppose? Or are judges simply ignoring the Roman statesman Cicero's advice: "The final good and the supreme duty of the wise man is to resist appearance."

If Clarence Darrow was even partly right in his declaration that liking or disliking a defendant colors judgments, then other factors that influence liking should also matter. Among such influences is the principle that likeness (similarity) leads to liking. When people pretend they are jurors, they are indeed more sympathetic to a defendant who shares their attitudes, religion, race, or (in cases of sexual assault) gender. For example, when Cookie Stephan and Walter Stephan had English-speaking people judge someone accused of assault, they were more likely to think the person not guilty if the defendant's testimony was in English, rather than translated from Spanish or Thai.

It seems we are more sympathetic toward a defendant with whom we can identify. If we think *we* wouldn't have committed that criminal act, we may assume that someone like us is also unlikely to have done it.

Ideally, jurors would leave their biases outside the courtroom and begin a trial with open minds. So implies the Sixth Amendment to the U.S. Constitution: "The accused shall enjoy the right to a speedy and public trial by impartial jury." In its concern for objectivity, the judicial system is similar to science: Both scientists and jurors are supposed to sift and weigh the evidence. Both the courts and science have rules about what evidence is relevant. Both keep careful records and assume that others given the same evidence would decide similarly.

When the evidence is clear and jurors focus on it, their biases are indeed minimal. The quality of the evidence matters more than the prejudices of the jurors.

From Social Psychology *5E by David G. Myers, 1996. Reprinted by permission of The McGraw-Hill Companies.*

Answer the following questions:

1. According to the context clues in paragraph 2, what does the word *cynical* mean?

    "Darrow was too *cynical;* facts do matter."

    Cynical means_____.

2. Paragraph 2 contains the following statement: "Darrow overstated the case." This is a statement of
    a. fact.
    b. opinion.

3. In the third paragraph, what does the transition word *nevertheless* signal?

    Nevertheless signals _____.

4. As used in paragraph 3, the word *credible* means
    a. easily deceived.
    b. believable.
    c. childish.
    d. doubtful.

5. In paragraph 4, the example of Efran's University of Toronto students was used to illustrate that
    a. attractive people receive more-lenient sentences in court.

    b. the way we treat attractive and unattractive people shapes the way they think about themselves.

    c. attractive people are thought to be less likely to have committed a crime.

6. In paragraph 5, the author helps the reader understand the different types of misdemeanors by providing
   a. definitions.
   b. examples.
   c. cause-and-effect relationships.
   d. chronological order.

7. Based on Cicero's statement, the reader can conclude that he would advise jurors to
   a. carefully consider the appearance of the defendant during jury deliberations.
   b. disregard the appearance of the defendant during jury deliberations.

8. According to the context clues in paragraph 6, what does the word *colors* mean?

   "If Clarence Darrow was even partly right in his declaration that liking or disliking a defendant *colors* judgments . . ."

   Colors means_____.

9. What two things are being compared in paragraph 8?

   _____and_____.

10. According to the context clues in paragraph 8, what does the word *objectivity* mean?

    "In its concern for *objectivity* . . ."

    Objectivity means_____.

11. Paragraph 8 contains the following statement: "Ideally, jurors would leave their biases outside the courtroom and begin a trial with open minds." This is a statement of
    a. fact.
    b. opinion.

12. The mode of writing used in this selection is
    a. narrative.
    b. descriptive.
    c. expository.
    d. persuasive.

13. The main idea expressed in this selection is that
    a. jurors can be influenced by the physical appearance and actions of a defendant.
    b. jurors are unlikely to pay attention to the physical characteristics of a defendant.
    c. in Texas, judges were affected by the attractiveness of the defendants.
    d. jurors are unlikely to be sympathetic to those who are like them.

Exercise #1 Practice Spotting Biased Words

When you look up a word in your dictionary, you are determining its **denotation,** or dictionary meaning. However, words also have **connotations,** or meanings beyond simple dictionary definitions. These words carry an extra emotional "charge." We can think of these words as being positive, negative, or neutral.

For example, even though the words *thin, slender,* and *skinny* all have similar dictionary definitions, they have different connotative meanings. Most of us think *slender* has a positive connotation and *skinny* a negative one. *Thin* has a more neutral meaning. In using words that have connotative meanings, we reveal our personal biases.

Authors can do exactly the same thing as speakers by choosing one particular word over another. If an author begins a novel by referring to the title character as someone who is *thrifty*, what picture of that person comes to your mind? How about if the author referred to the title character as *cheap* or *stingy*?

Directions: Read the following parent–teacher conference and circle the words with the most positive connotation.

> *I am very proud of Tommy and his* diligent/plodding *effort to improve his arithmetic grade. He does seem to have a(n)* self-confident/arrogant *approach toward the work at this grade level. However, he is not placing enough emphasis on producing quality homework. It is done in a(n)* sloppy/untidy *way. In general, he is a very* able/gifted *child. He does, however, need to improve his social and emotional conduct. His contributions to the class are made in a(n)* enthusiastic/hyperactive *way, and he is sometimes* rude/insensitive *in his comments to others. He does seem* eager/willing *to participate in most activities in the classroom, but he needs to learn to do so in a less* assertive/aggressive *manner. On the playground and in his relations with his peers, he is often* shy/reserved, *but he is beginning to be asked to enter into new activities. I enjoy having Tommy in my room and I hope we can make the rest of the year a pleasant one.*

Euphemisms

When someone substitutes an inoffensive word or phrase for one that is likely to be offensive to someone, they are using a **euphemism.** Most of the time euphemisms are used to be polite or to avoid controversy. The *Farside* cartoon by Gary Larson shows a "swamp thing" who would rather be referred to as a "wetlands-challenged mutant" because it has a more positive connotation.

THE FARSIDE by Gary Larson

"Well, actually, Doreen, I rather resent being called a 'swamp thing.' ... I prefer the term 'wetlands-challenged mutant.'"

Euphemisms can also be used to purposely mislead and obscure the truth. In the working world, layoffs have become commonplace, but because the word "layoff" has a negative connotation, many new euphemisms have been created to appease both the person being fired and the general community. In his book *The New Doublespeak*, William Lutz discusses this new "downsizing lingo." In general, Lutz says that the "doublespeak" for firing thousands of employees falls into three categories, which are described below.

Excerpt from "How Do I Fire Thee? Let Me Count the Ways."   *by William Lutz*

READING

" His words were softer than oil, yet they were drawn swords."

Psalms 55:21

Some companies want to make it sound as if laying off workers is a positive experience for the workers and not a negative one, as in "constructive dismissal," which means losing your job is good for you, kind of like that bad-tasting medicine you had to take as a kid. However, I am willing to bet that the experience is more constructive for the company than for the people who have just lost their jobs.

Then there are the companies that don't really fire workers; they just make some other changes that only incidentally happen to result in the layoff of thousands of workers. There might be a "product cessation," which means the factory is closed and everyone working there is left without a job, or the "elimination of positions," which means that since the jobs have been eliminated there's no need for all those workers to hang around.

Finally, there is the new strategic plan that will make the company even better, ready to face the challenges of the future, engage in global competition, and, oh, by the way, lay off 13,000 workers. Such is the result of Procter & Gamble's plan for "Strengthening Global Effectiveness." Meanwhile, General Motors of Canada was working on its "lean concept of Synchronous Organizational Structures." Officials at GM conceded that this "concept" would result in layoffs. How many workers would lose their jobs, they wouldn't say.

However, I think the winner for the best doublespeak for firing comes from the computer industry, where you're not fired; you're "uninstalled." Call a vice president at this company and the voice mail message will tell you that "you have reached the number of an uninstalled vice president." I'm sure we all hope he gets installed someplace else real soon.

From The New Doublespeak *by William Lutz. Copyright © 1996 by William Lutz. Reprinted by permission of HarperCollins Publishers, Inc.*

Here are some additional examples from *The New Doublespeak* as reprinted in *Newsweek*, August 12, 1996.

Hit the Road, Jack

As companies try to put a positive spin on the ugly practice of layoffs, they've invented a new lexicon. Some downsizing lingo:

Company	Euphemism
AT&T	Force management program
Bank of America	Release of resources
Bell Labs	Involuntary separation from payroll
Clifford of Vermont	Career-change opportunity

Digital Equipment Corp.	Involuntary severance
G.M.	Career-transition program
Harris Bank of Chicago	Rightsizing the bank
National Semiconductor	Reshaping
Newsweek	Reduction in force (RIF)
Pacific Bell	Elimination of employment security policy
Procter & Gamble	Strengthening global effectiveness
Stanford University	Repositioning
Stouffer Foods Corp.	Schedule adjustments
Tandem Computers	Reducing duplication or focused reduction
Wal-Mart	Normal payroll adjustment

From Lutz, William, "Hit the Road Jack," Newsweek, *August 12, 1996, from the* New Doublespeak, *New York: Harper Collins, 1996.*

Note: Lutz suggests that people fight doublespeak by becoming "first-rate crap detectors." One way to accomplish this is to start collecting and trading examples of doublespeak. Try to bring in examples to your class on a topic like the economy, unemployment, or foreign aid.

Exercise #2 Practice Detecting Bias in Magazines and Newspapers

Directions: On the line to the left of each passage, write the letter for the group of words that suggest the writer's bias.

> 1. *They are required to put in long hours of hard work for next to nothing, often in hostile conditions, always under the intense scrutiny of their bosses. They are imported from faraway places, then isolated from the rest of the population and ultimately exploited for their sweat. Migrant farm workers? No, we're talking here about major college-football players. The ideal notion that a lad should just be grateful for the education he receives in exchange for a few hours of practice and the glory of Saturday afternoon is as dead as the dropkick.*

From "Tote That Ball, Lift That Revenue" by Steve Wulf, Time, *October 21, 1996. © 1996 Time Inc. Reprinted by permission.*

_____ a. required, migrant, major, nothing

b. lad, football players, sweat, practice

c. hostile, exploited, imported, isolated

> 2. *Perhaps we'll thank Roberto Alomar someday. The second baseman's despicable act of contempt, a spit in the face of umpire John Hirshbeck, somehow landed on the window of the baseball establishment, washing off just enough film to reveal who was minding the store. We looked inside and nobody was there. . . . Fans deserve far better baseball leadership. For now, we're just being spit upon.*

From "The Spit Hits the Fan" by Steve Wulf, Time, *October 14, 1996. © 1996 Time Inc. Reprinted by permission.*

_____ a. despicable, contempt, spit upon

b. baseball establishment, film, minding the store

c. deserve, leadership, umpire

3.   *Who ever would have thought that good old PB&J could be a health hazard?
Sad but true: the peanut-butter-and-jelly sandwich is under assault, along with
its cousin the fluffer nutter, the peanut-butter cracker, the Reese's Piece, the
peanut M&M and all the other delectable forms the humble peanut comes in.
At the Breck School in Minneapolis, PB&J sandwiches must now be eaten at
separate tables. The Bradstreet Early Childhood Center in North Andover,
Massachusetts, is one of many kindergartens to have created peanut-free classrooms this fall, and the Trinity School in New York City has expelled all forms of
the peanut from the premises. Why the frenzy over goobers? Because 1 percent
of American children are now estimated to have a peanut allergy.*

From "Goodbye to the Goober" by John Sedgwick, Newsweek, October 14, 1996.
Copyright © 1996 Newsweek, Inc. All rights reserved. Reprinted by permission.

_____   a.   hazard, sad, expelled, frenzy, assault

           b.   goobers, separate, peanut-free, premises

           c.   cracker, estimated, allergy, health

4.   *Thick swordfish steaks, orange roughy fillets. Great mounds of red-fleshed
tuna. Judging from the seafood sections of local supermarkets, there would seem
to be plenty of fish left in the oceans. But this appearance of abundance is an
illusion, says Sylvia Earle, former chief scientist for the National Oceanic and
Atmospheric Administration. Already, Earle fears, an international armada of
fishing vessels is on the verge of exhausting a storehouse of protein so vast that
it once appeared to be infinite. "It's a horrible thing to contemplate," shudders
Earle. "What makes it even worse is that we know better. Yet here we go, making
the same mistake over and over again." It is overfishing that constitutes the
most urgent threat and demands the most immediate action.*

From "The Fish Crisis" by J. Madeleine Nash, Time, August 11, 1997. © 1997 Time Inc.
Reprinted by permission.

_____   a.   swordfish, appearance, international, vessels

           b.   illusion, urgent, horrible, shudders

           c.   action, protein, scientist, storehouse

5.   *There was blood, sweat, and a puddle of tears on kitchen tables across
America this morning, the detritus of a long afternoon, stretching into evening,
of yesterday's homework. Sure, some students probably whipped out their perfectly organized assignment pad, did each task cheerfully and finished with time
to spare for reading, television, or play. We just don't know any. Something that
infuriates parents, sabotages family time, and crowds out so much else in a
child's life might be tolerable if it also helped kids learn and if it imbued them
with good study habits and a lifelong love of learning. Unfortunately, "for
elementary-school students the effect of homework on achievement is trivial,
if it exists at all," concludes psychologist Harris Cooper of the University of
Missouri, whose analysis of more than 100 studies has stood up for 10 years.*

From "Death of the Stick" by Daniel McGinn, Newsweek, October 14, 1996. Copyright
© 1996 Newsweek, Inc. All rights reserved. Reprinted by permission.

_____   a.   infuriates, sabotages, crowds out, trivial

           b.   puddle, learning, imbued, exists

           c.   analysis, sweat, task, family

6. You slip into your leather seat. You don't tussle for the armrest with some sweaty stranger in the middle, because there is no middle; everyone sits two by two with loads of legroom in coach—the only class there is. On breakfast flights, the chilled champagne is free. At lunch and dinner, you can choose a quality merlot or Chardonnay poured from bottles with actual corks. Next comes the hot food on real china. Yes, food—not pretzels or a deli bag, but lobster or salmon, served by certifiably cordial airline employees. You can cover your shirt with a linen napkin. And, in a burst of true genius, the glass you're drinking from is made of . . . glass! This isn't a frequent flier's fantasy; it's a real utopia on a shockingly civilized airline called Midwest Express.

From "Concerns Grow That Doctor-Assisted Suicide Would Leave the Powerless Vulnerable" by Gina Kolata, The New York Times, *October 20, 1996. Copyright © 1996 by The New York Times. Reprinted by permission.*

_____ a. poured, shirt, legroom, frequent flier

b. cordial, quality, utopia, civilized

c. glass, pretzels, tussle, loads

Exercise #3 Detecting Bias: Group Activity "Who Gets In?"

The college can admit only five more students. As a member of the board, it is your responsibility to rank the 10 students listed below according to who most deserves to be accepted. Descriptions of their precollege situation and performance are given.

In your group, keep in mind the following factors as you select the **five** you consider the most deserving:

1. The person's potential, abilities, or capabilities.
2. The person's motivation to perform.
3. The probability of successful completion of a college education.

Your group must be in complete agreement about your choices. After selecting your five, write a brief sentence or two explaining the rationale for your choices. When everyone has completed the assignment, the group leader should write the selections on the chalkboard. Be prepared to defend your selections to the rest of the class.

Angela

Very intelligent; senior class valedictorian; has won awards in the National Science Fair for exhibits; has definite plans to major in chemistry; high school counselor says she has difficulty relating to others; she was involved in several disputes with high school classmates over chemistry experiments.

Albert

An all-state center in high school; plans to play college basketball and would help the team; scored poorly on the college admittance test although his high school grades were average; plans to become a physical therapist.

Jill

Ranked in the middle of her graduating class; did well in high school math; has good study habits; high school counselor says she has interfering, confrontational parents.

Carolyn

A divorced mother with two children; 24 years old, trying to return to college to continue her education after dropping out six years ago; works and raises her family; no financial support from her former husband; will need financial aid; wishes to become an elementary schoolteacher.

Dominique

An applicant from Venezuela; has already earned a degree in her own country; did very well academically; she wants to enroll to experience our lifestyle and perfect her English; not interested in any specific subject; plans to return home.

Thomas

High school counselor says he is outgoing and well-liked among his peers; poor grades; studied little in high school and has poor study skills; test results reveal a very high I.Q.

Howard

Ranked in the top 5% of his graduating class; high school counselor says he is a loner who lacks social skills; had no extracurricular activities in high school; has a great deal of academic potential; wants to be a doctor like his father.

Gina

Had attendance problems in high school; grades were mediocre; worked in excess of 40 hours a week; I.Q. in gifted range; will need financial aid.

Evelyn

She is 58 years old; worked in a day care center for the past 15 years; prior to that she was a housewife and mother; wants to earn a degree in child psychology; high test scores.

Karl

Average grades; works 28 hours a week to pay for his education; is aiming for a degree in engineering; high potential in math; a very hard worker

"Who Gets In," adapted from a supplement to Ellis, David, Becoming a Master Student—*originally titled "Who Stays? A Values-Clarification exercise."*

Exercise #4 Detecting Bias: Group Practice with Sex-Based Words

A. Each word or phrase below is usually associated with only one sex. Using your knowledge of cultural history, determine why these phrases are associated with one sex but not with the other.

Feminine Based	Masculine Based
1. mother nature	1. old man winter
2. black widow spider	2. daddy longlegs spider
3. lazy Susan serving tray	3. LA-Z-BOY lounging chair
4. The Clarissa (clipper ship)	4. man-of-war (battleship)
5. the statue of justice	5. a father of modern science
6. a ladybug	
7. a bombshell	

Write a general statement about your findings.

_____

B. The (animal) words listed below are nearly always used with one sex or
    the other. Mark **M** for the terms you would most likely use with males and
    F for terms you would most likely use with females. See if you can come
    to any conclusions as to how the lists differ and what they show about
    cultural expectations for males and females.

_____ 1.	a beast	_____ 1.	to be mousy
_____ 2.	a bird	_____ 2.	a rat
_____ 3.	to be bullheaded	_____ 3.	a loan shark
_____ 4.	a social butterfly	_____ 4.	a shrew
_____ 5.	to be catty	_____ 5.	a tiger
_____ 6.	a chick	_____ 6.	a tigress
_____ 7.	a jackass	_____ 7.	a vixen
_____ 8.	to be kittenish	_____ 8.	a vulture
_____ 9.	a hog	_____ 9.	a wolf
_____ 10.	a lamb	_____ 10.	doe eyes
_____ 11.	a fox		

Conclusion: _____

_____

_____

C. Change the following "man words" to "gender-inclusive" alternatives.
    Example: congressman—congressional representative

    1. mankind _____

    2. man-made _____

    3. the best man for the job _____

    4. man-hours _____

    5. foreman _____

    6. businessman _____

    7. salesman _____

    8. mailman _____

    9. insurance man _____

    10. fireman _____

    11. cameraman _____

    12. freshman _____

    13. manpower _____

    14. man-sized job _____

    15. sportsmanship _____

D. Change the following "female words" to "gender-inclusive" alternatives.

1. cleaning lady _____

2. gal Friday _____

3. housewife _____

4. ladylike _____

5. maid _____

6. coed _____

E. Change the following titles, used to distinguish female workers from males, to neutral terms for both men and women.

1. lady doctor _____

2. stewardess _____

3. policewoman _____

4. career girl _____

F. What is the problem with using language that is sexist or biased?

_____

_____

_____

Adapted from material by Alleen Pace Nilssen, Changing Words in a Changing World, *Newton, MA, WEEA Publishing Center.*

Exercise #5 Bias and Publications

Directions: Study the list of publications and the given topic. Would you expect the publication to be biased or objective (neutral) on this particular topic? Write an **O** for objective or a **B** for biased on the line.

Publication	Topic	
1. an editorial in *The Los Angeles Times*	marijuana	_____
2. *The New England Journal of Medicine*	marijuana	_____
3. *The Catholic Star Church Newsletter*	marijuana	_____
4. *The American Medical Association Encyclopedia*	marijuana	_____
5. *The Partnership for a Drug-Free America Newsletter*	marijuana	_____
6. *The Scourge of Drugs* by Wendell Collins	marijuana	_____
7. *Sociology* by James N. Henslin	marijuana	_____
8. *Understanding Psychology* by Charles G. Morris	marijuana	_____

Directions: Study the list of individuals and the given topic. Write **B** for biased and **O** for objective.

Individual	Topic	
1. Catholic priest	birth control	_____
2. Planned Parenthood counselor	birth control	_____
3. General practitioner	birth control	_____
4. Local psychologist	birth control	_____
5. School nurse	birth control	_____
6. School counselor	birth control	_____
7. National Organization of Women	birth control	_____

All of us have strong opinions on a variety of subjects. Our particular backgrounds and experiences have helped determine our points of view. Authors, also, have a point of view that may be directly expressed in their work or simply implied. As you read "A Hanging" by George Orwell, keep in mind that he is presenting a classic argument against capital punishment. Try to determine how you feel about this issue.

Notes on Vocabulary

Burma—a republic in Southeast Asia on the Bay of Bengal.   *Burma* was colonized by the British in 1824. In 1948, *Burma* overthrew its colonial government and became an independent nation. The official name for *Burma* today is Union of Myanmar.

pariah—Today, the word *pariah* means any person (or animal) who is a social outcast. However, originally *Pariahs* were members of one of the lowest castes in India, who served as slaves to the higher castes. The word is derived from a Tamil word meaning "drummer." Members of the *Pariah* caste frequently beat the drum (parai) at various festivals. At the time of Orwell's essay, the *Pariah* served as household servants to the British, and the term *pariah* was used to designate anyone of low caste.

warder—a person who guards something.   A *warder* is the British term for a prison guard or officer.

rupee—the basic monetary unit of India, Pakistan, Nepal, and Burma (Myanmar).

Bio-sketch

George Orwell (1903-1950) is best known as the author of the novels *1984* and *Animal Farm. 1984* is Orwell's version of the future and was meant to serve as a warning to mankind. It was completed just before his death at the age of 46. *Animal Farm*, a clever satire of dictatorships, was published in 1945 just after the end of World War II. During his lifetime, Orwell published ten books and two collections of essays. The essay "A Hanging," originally published in 1931, is considered to be a classic. It is the only surviving example of his early years as a writer, and the only work originally published under his real name of Eric Blair.

Blair was born in Bengal, a province of British India, to a father who was a minor official in the Indian customs office. From 1917 to 1921, he attended Eton, a preparatory school in England, and then instead of going on to a university, he served with the British Imperial Police in Burma, the setting of "A Hanging." It is obvious from the details carefully described in the essay that the incident of the hanging made a deep impression on him.

"A Hanging" takes place at Insein, where the second largest prison in Burma was located. At the time of the essay, the prison held approximately 2,000 inmates. It was while serving as a police officer that Orwell's lifelong hatred of imperialism began. His experiences in Burma allowed him to see "the dirty work of Empire at close quarters." What was especially painful to him was the power of life and death that the British officials held over their subjects. He agonized when he saw human beings being treated as though they were "things." Blair felt that in order to hang a man for a crime, one had to see him as less than human. Otherwise, one would be forced to admit the "unspeakable wrongness" of taking his life.

Upon his return from Burma, Orwell struggled with his need to be a writer, and his need to rid himself of the guilt he felt over his Burma experiences. At first he lived in Paris, writing stories that he later destroyed. Later, when money ran out, he washed dishes and performed other odd jobs. Finally, he returned to London where he held a series of teaching positions.

When "A Hanging" was published in the *Adelphi*, it received such good critical reviews that Orwell's career as a writer was launched. In the essay, the now-mature Blair is reflecting back on an event that took place five years before. The story is deceptively simple. A condemned man, a Hindu, is taken out of his cell and escorted across the jail yard where the gallows are located. During his walk, two things of importance occur. First, he is greeted by a large, friendly dog, and second, he steps aside to avoid a puddle in his path. Years later, Blair, now using the pen name of George Orwell, wrote: "I watched a man hanged once; it seemed to me worse than a thousand murders. I never went into a jail without feeling that my place was on the other side of the bars." As you read the essay, keep in mind that Orwell is presenting a classic argument against capital punishment.

"A Hanging"   *by George Orwell*

READING

It was in Burma, a sodden morning of the rains. A sickly light, like yellow tinfoil, was slanting over the high walls into the jail yard. We were waiting outside the condemned cells, a row of sheds fronted with double bars, like small animal cages. Each cell measured about ten feet by ten and was quite bare within except for a plank bed and a pot for drinking water. In some of them brown silent men were squatting at the inner bars, with their blankets draped round them. These were the condemned men, due to be hanged within the next week or two.

One prisoner had been brought out of his cell. He was a Hindu, a puny wisp of a man, with a shaven head and vague liquid eyes. He had a thick, sprouting moustache, absurdly too big for his body, rather like the moustache of a comic man in films. Six tall Indian warders were guarding him and getting him ready for the gallows. Two of them stood by with rifles and fixed bayonets, while the others handcuffed him, passed a chain through his handcuffs and fixed it to their belts, and lashed his arms tightly to his sides. They crowded very close about him, with their hands always on him in a careful, caressing grip, as though all the while feeling him to make sure he was there. It was like men handling a fish which is still alive and may jump back into the water. But he stood quite unresisting, yielding his arms limply to the ropes, as though he hardly noticed what was happening.

Eight o'clock struck and a bugle call, desolately thin in the wet air, floated from the distant barracks. The superintendent of the jail, who was standing apart from the rest of us, moodily prodding the gravel with his stick, raised his head at the sound. He was an army doctor, with a gray toothbrush moustache and a gruff voice. "For God's sake hurry up, Francis," he said irritably. "The man ought to have been dead by this time. Aren't you ready yet?"

Francis, the head jailer, a fat Dravidian in a white drill suit and gold spectacles, waved his black hand. "Yes sir, yes sir," he bubbled. "All iss satisfactorily prepared. The hangman iss waiting. We shall proceed."

5   "Well, quick march, then. The prisoners can't get their breakfast till this job's over."

We set out for the gallows. Two warders marched on either side of the prisoner, with their rifles at the slope; two others marched close against him, gripping him by arm and shoulder, as though at once pushing him and supporting him. The rest of us, magistrates and the like, followed behind. Suddenly, when we had gone 10 yards, the procession stopped short without any order or warning. A dreadful thing had happened—a dog, come goodness knows whence, had appeared in the yard. It came bounding among us with a loud volley of barks and leapt round us wagging its whole body, wild with glee at finding so many human beings together. It was a large woolly dog, half Airedale, half pariah. For a moment it pranced round us, and then, before anyone could stop it, made a dash for the prisoner and, jumping up, tried to lick his face. Everyone stood aghast, too taken aback even to grab at the dog.

"Who let the bloody brute in here?" said the superintendent angrily. "Catch it, someone!"

A warder, detached from the escort, charged clumsily after the dog, but it danced and gamboled just out of his reach, taking everything as part of the game. A young Eurasian jailer picked up a handful of gravel and tried to stone the dog away, but it dodged the stones and came after us again. Its yaps echoed from the jail walls. The prisoner, in the grasp of the two warders, look on incuriously, as though this was another formality of the hanging. It was several minutes before someone managed to catch the dog. Then we put my handkerchief through its collar and moved off once more, with the dog still straining and whimpering.

It was about 40 yards to the gallows. I watched the bare brown back of the prisoner marching in front of me. He walked clumsily with his bound arms, but quite steadily, with that bobbing gait of the Indian who never straightens his knees. At each step his muscles slid neatly into place, the lock of hair on his scalp danced up and down, his feet printed themselves on the wet gravel. And once, in spite of the men who gripped him by each shoulder, he stepped lightly aside to avoid a puddle on the path.

10   It is curious, but till that moment I had never realized what it means to destroy a healthy, conscious man. When I saw the prisoner step aside to avoid the puddle I saw the mystery, the unspeakable wrongness, of cutting a life short when it is in full tide. This man was not dying, he was alive just as we were alive. All the organs of his body were working—bowels digesting food, skin renewing itself, nails growing, tissues forming—all toiling away in solemn foolery. His nails would still be growing when he stood on the drop, when he was falling through the air with a tenth of a second to live. His eyes saw the yellow gravel and the gray walls, and his brain still remembered, foresaw, reasoned—reasoned even about puddles. He and we were a party of men walking together, seeing, hearing, feeling, understanding the same world; and in two minutes, with a sudden snap, one of us would be gone—one mind less, one world less.

The gallows stood in a small yard, separate from the main grounds of the prison, and overgrown with tall prickly weeds. It was a brick erection like three sides of a shed, with planking on top, and above the two beams and a crossbar with the rope dangling. The hangman, a gray-haired convict in the white uniform of the prison, was waiting beside his machine. He greeted us with a servile crouch as we entered. At a word from Francis the two warders, gripping the prisoner more closely than ever, half led half pushed him to the gallows and helped him clumsily up the ladder. Then the hangman climbed up and fixed the rope around the prisoner's neck.

We stood waiting, five yards away. The warders had formed in a rough circle round the gallows. And then, when the noose was fixed, the prisoner began crying out to his god. It was a high, reiterated cry of "Ram! Ram! Ram! Ram!" not urgent and fearful like a prayer or a cry for help, but steady, rhythmical, almost like the tolling of a bell. The dog answered the sound with a whine. The hangman, still standing on the gallows, produced a small cotton bag like a flour bag and drew it down and over the prisoner's face. But the sound, muffled by the cloth, still persisted, over and over again: "Ram! Ram! Ram! Ram!"

The hangman climbed down and stood ready, holding the lever. Minutes seemed to pass. The steady, muffled crying from the prisoner went on and on, "Ram! Ram! Ram!" never faltering for an instant. The superintendent, his head on his chest, was slowly poking the ground with his stick; perhaps he was counting the cries, allowing the prisoner a fixed number—fifty, perhaps, or a hundred. Everyone had changed color. The Indians had gone gray like bad coffee, and one or two of the bayonets were wavering. We looked at the lashed, hooded man on the drop, and listened to his cries—each cry another second of life; the same thought was in all our minds; oh, kill him quickly, get it over, stop that abominable noise!

Suddenly the superintendent made up his mind. Throwing up his head he made a swift motion with his stick. "Chalo!" he shouted almost fiercely.

15   There was a clanking noise, and then dead silence. The prisoner had vanished, and the rope was twisting on itself. I let go of the dog, and it galloped immediately to the back of the gallows; but when it got there it stopped short, barked, and then retreated into a corner of the yard, where it stood among the weeds, looking timorously out at us. We went round the gallows to inspect the prisoner's body. He was dangling with his toes pointed straight downward, very slowly revolving, as dead as a stone.

The superintendent reached out with his stick and poked the bare brown body; it oscillated slightly. "*He's* all right," said the superintendent. He backed out from under the gallows, and blew out deep breath. The moody look had gone out of his face quite suddenly. He glanced at his wristwatch. "Eight minutes past eight. Well, that's all for this morning, thank God."

The warders unfixed bayonets and marched away. The dog, sobered and conscious of having misbehaved itself, slipped after them. We walked out of the gallows yard, past the condemned cells with their waiting prisoners, into the big central yard of the prison. The convicts, under the command of warders armed with lathis, were already receiving their breakfast. They squatted in long rows, each man holding a tin pannikin, while two warders with buckets marched round ladling out rice; it seemed quite a homely, jolly scene, after the hanging. An enormous relief had come upon us now that the job was done. One felt an impulse to sing, to break into a run, to snigger. All at once everyone began chattering gaily.

The Eurasian boy walking beside me nodded toward the way we had come, with a knowing smile: "Do you know sir, our friend [he meant the dead man] when he heard his appeal had been dismissed, he pissed on the floor of his cell. From fright. Kindly take one of my cigarettes, sir. Do you not admire my new silver case, sir? From the boxwalah, two rupees, eight annas. Classy European style."

Several people laughed—at what, nobody seemed certain.

20   Francis was walking by the superintendent, talking garrulously. "Well, sir, all hass passed off with the utmost satisfactoriness. It was all finished—flick! like that. It iss not always so—oah no! I have known cases where the doctor wass obliged to go beneath the gallows and pull the prisoner's legs to ensure decease. Most disagreeable!"

"Wriggling about, eh? That's bad," said the superintendent.

"Ach, sir, it iss worse when they become refractory! One man, I recall, clung to the bars of hiss cage when we went to take him out. You will scarcely credit, sir, that it took six warders to dislodge him, three pulling at each leg. We reasoned with him. 'My dear fellow,' we said, 'think of all the pain and trouble you are causing to us!' But no, he would not listen! Ach, he wass very troublesome!"

I found that I was laughing quite loudly. Everyone was laughing. Even the superintendent grinned in a tolerant way. "You'd better all come and have a drink," he said quite genially. "I've got a bottle of whiskey in the car. We could do with it."

We went through the big double gates of the prison into the road. "Pulling at his legs!" exclaimed a Burmese magistrate suddenly, and burst into a loud chuckling. We all began laughing again. At that moment Francis' anecdote seemed extraordinarily funny. We all had a drink together, native and European alike, quite amicably. The dead man was a hundred yards away.

"A Hanging" from Shooting An Elephant And Other Essays *by George Orwell, copyright 1950 by the Estate of Sonia B. Orwell, reprinted by permission of Harcourt Brace & Company. Copyright © George Orwell 1931. Reprinted by permission of Mark Hamilton as the Literary Executor of the Estate of the Late Sonia Brownell Orwell and Martin Secker & Warburg Ltd.*

Vocabulary

Directions: Use your dictionary to find the correct definition according to the context.

1. _____ a *sodden* morning of the rains (1)
2. _____ a *puny* wisp of a man (2)
3. _____ a bugle call, *desolately* thin in the wet air (3)
4. _____ Everyone stood *aghast* (6)
5. _____ it danced and *gamboled* (8)
6. _____ All *toiling* away (10)
7. _____ It was a high, *reiterated* cry (12)
8. _____ never *faltering* for an instant (13)
9. _____ looking *timorously* out at us (15)
10. _____ it *oscillated* slightly (16)
11. _____ Francis was . . . talking *garrulously* (20)
12. _____ when they become *refractory* (22)
13. _____ he said quite *genially* (23)
14. _____ Francis' *anecdote* seemed extraordinarily funny (24)
15. _____ native and European alike, quite *amicably* (24)

IN YOUR OWN WORDS

1. What was the author's purpose in writing the essay?

   _____

2. What is the overall main idea of the essay?

   _____

3. Orwell is noted for his use of figurative language. List a few examples from the first paragraph.

   _____

4. As a writer, Orwell was often preoccupied with detail. At the beginning of the essay, he is concerned with using concrete details to set the scene for the reader. Give an example of this type of detail. What is the tone of paragraph 1?

   _____

5. Give some descriptive details about the prisoner's appearance at the start of the essay.

   _____

6. Considering Orwell's emphasis on details, why doesn't he tell us more about the prisoner, such as his name, and the reason he was being hanged?

   _____

7. What is ironic about the dog's reaction to the prisoner? How does the dog's behavior serve as a contrast to the behavior of the human beings in the story?

   _____

   _____

8. Analyze the simile Orwell uses to describe the way the guards handle the prisoner.

   "It was like men handling a fish which is still alive and may jump back into the water."

   Subject: _____

   Compared to:_____

   Meaning: _____

9. In paragraph 10, the author discovers that he is opposed to capital punishment. What are his reasons for opposing it? What trivial incident on the part of the prisoner brought him to this realization?

   _____

   _____

10. After the author realizes he is opposed to capital punishment, how does the way he describes the prisoner change? What words does he use to describe our common bond with the prisoner?

    _____

    _____

11. Identify the similes in paragraphs 13 and 15.

    _____

    _____

12. What is ironic about the superintendent's statement in paragraph 16?

    _____

13. What is ironic about the description of the scene in paragraph 17?

    _____

14. After the hanging, what clues does the author give us indicating that those who participated in the execution were uncomfortable with their role?

    _____

    _____

15. What is the irony in paragraph 22?

    _____

Chapter 11 Test: "A Hanging"

Multiple Choice

1. The first paragraph of the narrative serves to
   a. express Orwell's feelings about capital punishment.
   b. introduce the reader to the person being executed.
   c. introduce the reader to the setting of the story.
   d. describe the hanging process in detail.

2. From the story, you could infer that Orwell
   a. would support the continued use of capital punishment.
   b. viewed the death penalty process as ironic.
   c. saw no problems in executing a man.
   d. had been opposed to the death penalty before he went to Burma.

3. Orwell serves as the narrator of the story. Which role does the narrator play?
   a. the person responsible for hanging the prisoner
   b. a fellow prisoner due to be executed later
   c. the superintendent of the prison
   d. an observer to the hanging process

4. The organizational pattern used in paragraph 17 is
   a. cause and effect.
   b. compare and contrast.
   c. chronological order.
   d. definition and example.

True or False

_____ 5. The prisoner was accused of committing murder in a fit of rage.

_____ 6. A British official was responsible for serving as the hangman.

_____ 7. On the way to the gallows they were interrupted by a large, friendly dog.

_____ 8. After the hanging, everyone felt a great deal of grief and began to wail and cry.

_____ 9. The men, both British and local, later drank together quite amicably.

_____ 10. It was possible to see the prisoner's face when he was executed.

Review Test 8 Identifying the Author's Bias

Directions: Identify the author's bias and then briefly state it in your own words.

1.   *As it happens, some of the most disturbing images of environmental destruction can be found exactly halfway between the North and South poles—precisely at the equator in Brazil—where billowing clouds of smoke regularly blacken the sky above the immense but now threatened Amazon rain forest. Acre by acre, the rain forest is being burned to create fast pasture for fast-food beef; as I learned when I went there in 1989, the fires are set earlier and earlier in the dry season now, with more than one Tennessee's worth of rain forest being slashed and burned each year. According to our guide, the biologist Tom Lovejoy, there are more different species of birds in each square mile of the Amazon than exist in all of North America—which means we are silencing thousands of songs we have never even heard.*

Gore, Al, Earth in the Balance, *New York: a Plume Book by Penguin, 1993, p. 23.*

Bias: _____

_____

2.   *I can think of some pretty good reasons why vouchers for private schools are a bad idea. First of all, and probably most important, these schemes deprive public schools of the support they deserve. Parents who choose to send their kids to private school still have a responsibility to support public education, not the other way around. Pat Robertson, one of the biggest endorsers of voucher schemes, has said: "They say vouchers would spell the end of public schools in America. To which we say, so what?" What in the world is he thinking? Look, 42 million of our kids go to public school each day. Their future is America's future. No matter what we choose for our own kids, we all have a stake in the success of public education.*

    There's something else I want you to understand. Just because vouchers are public money doesn't mean that the participating private schools will be accountable to the public. Wondering about the curriculum at the David Koresh Academy? How about the expulsion policy at the Louis Farrakhan School? Well, stop wondering. It ain't any of your business now, and it will never get to be your business, even if they used your tax dollars to send somebody to these schools.

Carville, James, We're Right, They're Wrong, *New York: Random House, 1996, p. 102.*

Bias: _____

_____

3.   *Girls today are much more oppressed. They are coming of age in a more dangerous, sexualized and media-saturated culture. They face incredible pressures to be beautiful and sophisticated, which in junior high means using chemicals and being sexual. As they navigate a more dangerous world, girls are less protected.*

    As I looked at the culture that girls enter as they come of age, I was struck by what a girl-poisoning culture it was. The more I looked around, the more I listened to today's music, watched television and movies and looked at sexist advertising, the more convinced I became that we are on the wrong path with our daughters. America today limits girls' development, truncates their whole-ness, and leaves many of them traumatized.

Pipher, Mary, Reviving Orphelia, *New York: Ballanatine Books, 1994, p. 12.*

Bias: _____

_____

4.   *The information age has brought us many wonders, but it has also made possible an unprecedented level of record keeping and high-tech snooping into the lives of others. While we dazzle ourselves in virtual worlds and strange new digital communities that stretch around the globe, it's easy to forget that the same technology that connects us can keep track of us as never before.*

Employers have more freedom to infringe on the privacy of employees than do the police, who still need court approval to tap most telephone or data lines, notes Andre Bacard, author of the Computer Privacy Handbook. *Supervisors, he says, "can tap an employee's phones, monitor her e-mail, watch her on closed-circuit TV, and search her computer files, without giving her notice."*

From "The Invasion of Privacy" by Reed Karaim. Originally appeared in Civilization, *Oct/Nov 1996. Reprinted by permission.*

Bias: _____

_____

5.   *Consider for a moment a neighborhood in which most working-age women are not in paid jobs. This may conjure up a picture of tidy homes, children at play and gossip. Now think of a neighborhood in which most men are jobless. The picture is more sinister. Areas of male idleness are considered, and often are, places of deterioration, disorder and danger. Nonworking women are mothers; nonworking men, a blight.*

Men tend to commit most crimes. In America, they commit 81% of all crime and 87% of violent crime. Adolescent boys are the most volatile and violent of all. Those under 24 are responsible for half of America's violent crime; those under 18 commit a quarter.

Now ask yourself what restrains such behavior? The short answer is: a two-parent home. Without belaboring the complexity of family policies, two-parent families are demonstrably better at raising trouble-free children than one-parent ones. Fatherless boys commit more crimes than those with father at home. . . . Having a man in the house (preferably the biological father) is, it seems, more important than any other single factor.

From "Men tomorrow's second sex," The Economist, September 28, 1996. Copyright © 1996 The Economist Newspaper Group, Inc. Reprinted with permission. Further reproduction prohibited.

Bias: _____

_____

6.   *Stress is only a burden when you respond to it with the feeling you have lost control. Most of the time, this happens when there is a mismatch between your expectations and your environment. In other words, what you hope will happen doesn't, and you begin to think it never will. In the face of this mismatch, you may withdraw and resign yourself to losing control, or you may struggle to make things happen in order to regain control. Either way, if the event is not resolved as you want it to be, you will usually feel stressed. But there are alternatives.*

*You can regain your sense of balance and control by changing your environ-
ment (the conditions under which you work and live), and by changing your
expectations (which are often overreactions to your environment and events in
it). Usually a combination works best. But it is crucial to realize that you can
never make everything in the environment go your way. If you focus only on the
environment, you cannot succeed in controlling stress. Your own reactions—
and overreactions—are the key.*

Eliot, Robert S., Is It Worth Dying For, *New York: Bantam Books, 1989, p. 21.*

Bias: _____

_____

7.   *The author's message was headlined APOLOGY and inserted in 250 fresh-
off-the-press children's books given to guests at a Congressional Black Caucus
Foundation luncheon in Washington. "I apologize to you all for the atrocities
which I and others committed against our race through gang violence," wrote
Stanley (Tookie) Williams, who in 1971, co-founded the nation's largest and
arguably most violent street gang, the Crips. "I pray that one day my apology
will be accepted."*

*The founder's atonement, of course, is overdue. By current law-enforcement
tallies, Crips colors fly in 42 states, and the gang is linked annually to thousands of murders, robberies and drug deals. But if Williams, 42, has much to
regret, he has also done more than apologize. Writing with stubby pencils from
San Quentin's death row in California, the convicted murderer recently published the first half of a 17-book series titled* Tookie Speaks Out against Gang
Violence. *"You can learn from my mistakes," Williams advises readers in
simple, effective prose. "It's the best set of books I've ever read on this subject,"
says Franklin Tucker, director of Washington's National Center to Rehabilitate
Violent Youth. "And it's coming from the choir."*

From *"Lessons Learned on Death Row" by James Willwerth,* Time, *October 21, 1996.*
© *1996 Time Inc. Reprinted by permission.*

Bias: _____

_____

Chapter 12

Propaganda Techniques

What Are They and How Are They Used?

We have now discussed the difference between fact and opinion, and we have also discussed bias. Now we are going to look at the related topic of propaganda.

The word "propaganda" was first used by Pope Urban VIII who created a "congregation for propagating the faith." Thus, **propaganda** originally meant spreading the Christian faith with missionary activity throughout the world. Today **propaganda** simply means the spreading of ideas to further a cause. Political parties often use propaganda to persuade people to vote for their candidates or support their programs. Advertising such as you see in the media is a form of propaganda that is designed to persuade consumers that certain products or brands are superior.

Because modern propaganda often makes use of distortion and deception, the word "propaganda" now has a negative sound to it. Not all propaganda is destructive, though. Cigarette companies made use of propaganda to persuade people to smoke, and more specifically to persuade people to smoke particular brands of cigarettes. Many people would characterize this use of propaganda as destructive because smoking is damaging to health. But in recent years propaganda has been used in anti-smoking campaigns to inform people of the dangers of smoking and to try to persuade them to stop smoking. These anti-smoking campaigns use propaganda for a positive, beneficial purpose.

Propaganda works by using certain techniques to manipulate reason and emotion. Because propaganda is manipulative, it is important for you to be familiar with these techniques so that you will know when propaganda is being directed at you. Once you are aware that propaganda techniques are being used, your knowledge of these techniques will also help you evaluate the accuracy and fairness of the message. Does the message really make sense? Is the cause being promoted by the propaganda something that you want to support? Our special focus is on the use of propaganda techniques in written material. You want to know when a writer is using propaganda techniques so that you can more accurately and fairly evaluate what is being said.

The Institute for Propaganda Analysis was formed in 1937 to study propaganda and educate the American public about it. The institute identified seven propaganda techniques. Other techniques have since been added to the list. We will discuss the main propaganda techniques in this chapter, and give you some practice in identifying them.

1. *Name-calling*—This technique consists of attaching a negative label to a person or a thing. During the presidential campaign of 1992, when President Bush dismissively called Bill Clinton "a bozo," he was engaging in name-calling. When politicians engage in this type of behavior, they are

usually trying to avoid supporting their own position with facts. Rather than explain what they believe in, they prefer to try to tear their opponent down. Many of us engage in the same type of technique when someone disagrees with us. We might call someone we disagree with "radical," "reactionary," "foolish," or "stupid."

2. *Glittering generalities*—This technique uses important-sounding "glad words" that have little or no real meaning. These words are used in general statements that cannot be proved or disproved. Words like "good," "honest," "fair," and "best" are examples of "glad" words. When an automobile manufacturer says in an advertisement that its cars are the "best," what does the manufacturer really mean? Does that particular car have the "best" safety record? The "best" warranty? Get the "best" mileage?

3. *Transfer*—In this technique, an attempt is made to transfer the prestige of a positive symbol to a person or an idea. At both the Republican and Democratic national conventions, the backdrop is always the American flag. Politicians want us to think that they are patriotic and will do what is right for the country.

4. *False analogy*—In this technique, two things that may or may not really be similar are portrayed as being similar. The store brand can of peas may look like the name brand, but is it exactly the same? We have to ask ourselves several questions in order to determine the answer. For instance, are the peas of the same quality? Are there as many peas in the can? In most false analogies, there is simply not enough evidence available to support the comparison.

5. *Testimonial*—This technique is easy to understand. Often "big name" athletes, as well as movie and TV stars, are paid huge amounts of money to endorse a product. For example, Michael Jordan promotes athletic shoes, Elizabeth Taylor promotes perfume, and Rosie O'Donnell and Penny Marshall promote discount stores. Whenever you see someone famous endorsing a product, ask yourself how much that person knows about the product, and what he or she stands to gain by promoting it. In the area of politics, national political leaders often give ringing endorsements of members of their party running for office at the local level. They hope to use their prestige to influence the voting.

Propaganda Exercise #1

The following statements make use of propaganda techniques 1–5. For each statement, identify the techniques used.

1. Vote for Jack Hazelhurst. Governor Brown is voting for him.

   _____

2. E-Z LIVING recliners are the best that money can buy.

   _____

3. My opponent has been *stingy* in spending the public's money, and he voted against all the bills for building a rapid transit system.

   _____

4. Yang Chow Chinese dinners are just as good and appetizing as what is served in expensive Hong Kong restaurants. _____

5. Before giving his speech, Senator Jones had the band play "The Star Spangled Banner." _____

6. Basketball star Michael James says, "You should buy QuickLift tennis shoes. They'll help you lift off for a great day." _____

7. The National Vehicle Insurance Association has backed the bill going through Congress allowing state governments to build new freeways with federal tax dollars. _____

8. ShopRight laundry soap has as much cleaning power as the more expensive CleanEase detergent. _____

9. Congressional candidate Fred Goodheart says that people should vote for him because he is fair, honest, and kind. _____

10. In a recent interview Governor Herman said that those who oppose his reform measures are "misguided, arrogant fools."

_____

More Propaganda Techniques

Keep in mind that there is often overlap among these propaganda techniques, and propagandists commonly use more than one of these techniques at the same time. Also, we all are propagandists at times, such as when we are trying to persuade someone to do or believe something. Understanding propaganda techniques helps us to be more effective, and to think more clearly and logically.

6. *Plain folks*—This technique uses a folksy approach to convince us to support someone or something. At election time, politicians appear at local diners, coffee shops, or malls to prove they are just like us. A man running for president will be photographed making his own breakfast or taking out the garbage. In order to sell products such as headache remedies, cereal, or toilet bowl cleaners, advertisers will depict people with ordinary looks doing ordinary activities.

❝A half truth is a whole lie.❞

Jewish Proverb

7. *Card stacking*—This term comes from stacking a deck of cards in your favor. Propagandists effectively use "card stacking" to slant the message. Key words or unfavorable statistics may be omitted in an ad or commercial, leading to a series of half-truths. Keep in mind that an advertiser is under no obligation "to give the truth, the whole truth, and nothing but the truth." If you go to a car dealership to purchase a new car, the salesman is not likely to inform you that the model you are interested in has a problem with paint discoloration. The telemarketer trying to solicit funds to feed hungry children in Asia is unlikely to reveal how much of your donation goes to pay his salary and other administrative costs.

8. *Bandwagon*—The "bandwagon" approach encourages you to think that because everyone else is doing something, you should do it too, or you'll be left out. The technique embodies a "keeping up with the Joneses" philosophy. This technique got its name from the days when politicians would hire a band to play while they were seated on a horse-drawn wagon. As the wagon rolled through town, crowds of people would gather and follow, eager to be a part of the action. Those who didn't immediately join in felt they might be missing something. Teenagers today often feel the same way. If they don't wear certain clothes, say and do certain things, then

they fear they won't be accepted by their peers. Commercials or ads, such as those for beer, exploit this fear. During World War II, Hitler, a master propagandist, would frequently gather the German citizens in large arenas. As he spoke, a type of "herd mentality" would occur. Since people wanted to be accepted and not labeled as "different," they tended to follow blindly like a bunch of cattle.

9. *Either/or fallacy*—This technique is also called "black-and-white thinking" because only two choices are given. You are either for something or against it; there is no middle ground or shades of gray. People who exhibit this type of thinking have a "bumper sticker" mentality. They say things like "American—love it or leave it," or "Put up or shut up." According to this line of reasoning, either you are in favor of gun control or against it, in favor of abortion or opposed to it. When we attempt to polarize issues, we negate all attempts to find a common ground.

Propaganda Exercise #2

In this exercise, work with propaganda techniques 6–9.

1. Hurry down to our car dealership before we sell our last sale car. _____
   _____

2. If you don't buy our SureShine kitchen polish, your floor will look dull and dirty. _____

3. Governor Swellguy put on a hardhat and took a tour of the new mining operation at National Mining Company. _____

4. McDougal's has sold 50 billion hamburgers. _____

5. You are either part of the solution or part of the problem._____

6. All the guys down at Barney's Bar drink Blitz beer. _____

7. Brightwhite toothpaste makes your smile bright again. It gets rid of ugly discoloration caused by coffee and tea. It makes that special person in your life eager to get close. _____

8. Almost everyone in the office has given $5.00 to buy a present for Jim, who is retiring. Would you like to give a donation? _____

9. Mayor Walker is for the little guy. You don't see him driving an expensive car or sending his daughter to a private school. _____

Last Major Propaganda Technique

10. *Faulty cause and effect*—This last propaganda technique suggests that because B follows A, A must *cause* B. When we hear people say, "I know it's going to rain today because I just washed my car," they are guilty of faulty cause and effect. During the 1996 election, President Clinton took credit for the improved economy, reduced dependence on welfare, and the increase in employment. His opponent, Robert Dole, objected, saying Clinton could not prove that he was the "cause" of the economic upturn. According to Dole, the economy was beginning to improve *before* Clinton was elected as president. Remember, just because two events or two sets of data are related does not necessarily mean that one caused the other to happen. It is important for us to evaluate the data carefully and not jump to the wrong conclusion.

Review Test 9: Propaganda Techniques

Directions: For each passage, identify the propaganda technique being used.

_____ 1. Get behind the wheel of the most popular car on the road today!

_____ 2. You need a toothpaste that does it *All*. *All* toothpaste fights cavities, plaque, bad breath, and gingivitis. Plus it brightens your smile. Face the day the *All*-prepared way!

_____ 3. Either this community votes to fund mass transit or all of us will be personally affected by gridlock on our streets.

_____ 4. Sports star: "I've tried every brand of pain-relief medication on the market, and, believe me, nothing out there works better than *Pain-away*."

_____ 5. A politician running for election: "When I was very young, my father died, leaving my mother with debt and no way to support our family. Unlike my opponent, I know what it's like to struggle to put food on the table and pay the bills. Give me your vote on election day."

_____ 6. Broncos fan watching the Super Bowl on TV: "I better go away. Every time I come in to watch the game, the Packers score a touchdown."

_____ 7. "My opponent for the school board has the morals of an alley cat. Maybe his wife can tolerate his 'affairs' but the rest of us should not allow him to become a role model to our children."

_____ 8. A lot of us want only the best—the best house, in the best neighborhood, with the best car in our garage. Don't you think it's about time to be thinking about the best phone service? Call 1-800-BEST for a free consultation.

_____ 9. "Your sister has always gotten good grades and worked part-time to pay for her expenses. Don't you think you should be able to follow her example?"

_____ 10. "This is Chuck Jones standing in front of 'Old Faithful' in Yellowstone National Park. Remember to use *Old Faithful* laxative if you have problems with irregularity."

Many of you will take courses in introductory psychology or sociology. An ongoing controversy in these two fields has to do with the relationship between viewing violence on television and behaving in an aggressive manner. Study the chart below from *Social Psychology.* The vertical scale measures the seriousness of a criminal act by age 30. The horizontal scale measures frequency of TV viewing at age 8 for males and females. The graph seems to indicate that television watching does cause violence. Do you agree with this finding? Can you think of other possible explanations for these rates of violence? If you can, list them below.

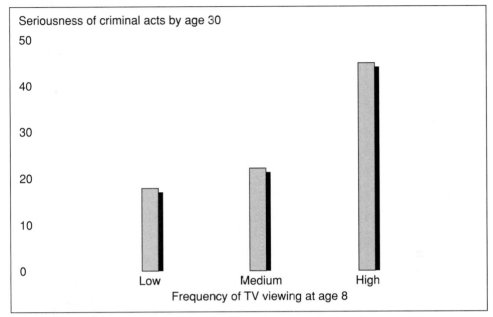

Children's television viewing and later criminal activity. Violence viewing at age 8 was a predictor of a serious criminal offense by age 30. (Data from Eron & Huesmann, 1984.)

1. _____

2. _____

3. _____

The excerpt below is found in *The Essentials of Understanding Psychology* by Robert S. Feldman. The author of this textbook sees a correlation between violence in the media and a child's aggressive behavior, but hesitates to state that there is a direct cause-and-effect relationship between the two. Does Feldman address any of the causes of criminal behavior that you mentioned above? He also discusses one approach to reducing aggression in frequent television viewers. While reading the article, be thinking of other ways to decrease aggression among children who frequently watch TV.

"Violence on Television and Film: Does the Media's Message Matter?"

READING

Beavis and Butt-head, MTV cartoon characters, discuss how much fun it is to set fires. On one occasion, one of them lights a fire in the other's hair by using aerosol spray cans and matches. Later five-year-old Austin Messner, who had watched the cartoon, sets his bed on fire with a cigarette lighter. Although he and his mother escape the subsequent blaze, his young sister dies.

Does observation of violence and antisocial acts in the media lead viewers to behave in similar ways? Because research on modeling shows that people frequently learn and imitate the aggression they observe, this question is among the most important ones being addressed by social psychologists.

Certainly, the amount of violence in the mass media is enormous. The average American child between the ages of 5 and 15, is exposed to no fewer than 13,000 violent deaths on television; the number of fights and aggressive sequences that children view is still higher. Saturday mornings, once filled with relatively peaceful fare, now include cartoon programs, for example, that sport titles such as *Power Rangers* and *Robo Cop,* which include long sequences of aggressive action.

Most research does in fact suggest that a significant association exists between watching such violent television programs and displaying aggressive behavior. For example, one experiment showed that subjects who watched a lot of television as third-graders became more aggressive adults than those who didn't watch as much. Of course, these results cannot prove that viewing television caused the adult aggression. Some additional factors such as particular personality characteristics of viewers may have led both to high levels of viewing aggressive shows and to high aggression.

5   Still, most experts agree that watching media violence can lead to a greater readiness to act aggressively . . . and to an insensitivity to the suffering of victims of violence. Several factors help explain why the observation of media violence may provoke aggression. For one thing, viewing violence seems to lower inhibitions against the performance of aggression—watching television portrayals of violence makes aggression seem a legitimate response to particular situations.

Furthermore, viewing violence may distort our understanding of the meaning of others' behavior. We may, for example, be predisposed to view even nonaggressive acts by others after watching media aggression, and subsequently may act upon these new interpretations by responding aggressively. Finally, a continued diet of aggression may leave us desensitized to violence, and what previously would have repelled us now produces little emotional response. Our sense of the pain and suffering brought about by aggression may be diminished, and we may find it easier to act aggressively ourselves.

Given the probable links between violence and exposure to media aggression, psychologists are working on ways to reduce aggression in frequent viewers. One approach has been to explicitly teach children that television violence is not representative of the real world, that the viewing of violence is objectionable, and that they should refrain from imitating behavior on television. The lessons appear to be effective. As a group, children who are given lessons act less aggressively than those who have not received lessons . . . During the sessions, the students learned that the aggressive behavior on television does not approximate what happens in the real world. They were taught about camera effects used to produce the illusion of aggression. Moreover, they learned that people generally used alternatives in seeking solutions to their problems. Finally, they were directly taught the undesirability of watching television violence and ways to avoid imitating aggression.

From The Essentials of Understanding Psychology, 2E *by Robert S. Feldman, 1994. Reprinted by permission of The McGraw-Hill Companies.*

The following excerpt is taken from the daily newspaper *The Oregonian.* Read the excerpt and then answer the questions that follow.

SALEM—Bush Elementary School officials tightened security and invited counselors to help children cope after a "gang" of second-grade boys allegedly tried to murder a second-grade girl on the playground. The Monday incident stunned parents and school officials when they discovered that the boys had plotted and carried out a plan to suffocate the girl because she broke up with the gang's alleged leader.

Salem police said that the boy "had a change of heart and let her go." One boy told police he got the idea for the attack from television. Many parents expressed concern about a generation growing up watching violent television programs.

Bill Pfohl, president of the National Association of School Psychologists, said statistics on elementary school violence are limited because it is a relatively new phenomenon. Pfohl blames television and movie images, growing child abuse, broken families, and drug and alcohol abuse. He said that these children, poorly nurtured at home, haven't learned to cope with anger and are bringing it to school.

Article from Oregonian, *combination of articles, December 20, 1996.*

Questions:

Assuming that there is a cause-and-effect relationship between television watching and violent behavior, can you think of ways to help solve this problem? Is there anything the media could do? What about parents?

Arguments for and against Proposition 200 (California)

Now let's try to identify propaganda techniques used to persuade voters to support a specific proposition. Many states give citizens the right to vote on issues. In the November 1996 election in Arizona, residents voted on Proposition 200, which (1) would change the sentencing of persons convicted of illegal drug use to put more emphasis on treatment and (2) would allow for the use of otherwise illegal substances for medicinal purposes with a doctor's recommendation. This proposition, similar to one previously passed in California, was approved by the voters.

Six other states are considering similar propositions. In addition, *The New England Journal of Medicine* has called for extending this policy across the nation. Federal drug enforcement agencies are strongly opposed to these new initiatives. Sheryl Massaro, an official with the National Institute on Drug Abuse, says "seeming to legalize marijuana for anything would give young people the wrong impression," which "doesn't even seem to enter the minds of a lot of people who are promoting it for medicinal use."

Below are "pro" and "con" statements for this proposition that appeared on the 1996 Arizona ballot. Where do these statements make use of propaganda techniques? What techniques are used?

Argument "For" Proposition 200

When John Kennedy was elected President, he asked Stewart Udall, Congressman from Tucson, to be his Secretary of the Interior. Stewart brought a small cadre of Arizonans to work for him in Washington. I was lucky enough to be in the group—as Special Assistant to the Solicitor.

Young people serving in the Kennedy Administration met twice a month in an informal group called the New Frontier Club. I remember at one meeting having an extensive discussion about our drug laws. There was general consensus that the criminalization of narcotic drug use was not working—just as

Both George Washington and Thomas Jefferson grew marijuana on their plantations.

prohibition didn't work. We were concerned that the Government was spending a lot of money and the situation was only getting worse. I thought that the laws would be reformed soon since their failure was so obvious. That was 34 years ago!

Today, the failed drug war continues. At the state level, drug control spending is over $16 billion with 80% going to the criminal justice system and 20% to education and treatment. We need to reverse these priorities so that we spend at least the same amount on treatment and education to what we spend on enforcement and prisons.

The Drug Medicalization, Prevention, and Control Act seeks to equalize the spending on treatment and education. Rather than wasting money on prison for minor drug users, the Act invests in treatment for users and prevention for our youth.

There is strong evidence that this approach will be more effective. A Rand Corporation study in 1994 found that treatment is much more effective than enforcement and prisons in reducing cocaine use. It is time to adopt rational, cost-effective measures that deal with drugs in ways that benefit rather than harm society.

> Marvin S. Cohen
> Former Chairman, Civil Aeronautics Board
> Treasurer, Arizonans for Drug Policy Reform
> Phoenix
> *Arizonans for Drug Policy Reform: John Norton, Chairman*

Argument "Against" Proposition 200

This proposition sounds deceptively appealing, but it gives less freedom with the one hand than it takes away with the other.

Proposition 200 contains some libertarian-sounding provisions that would restore a measure of freedom that has been denied by current drug laws—such as allowing the medical use of controlled substances to alleviate pain and suffering, and treatment instead of incarceration for nonviolent drug users. Cost reductions in our prisons sounds good, too.

But, on balance, this proposition is anti-freedom—and certainly anti-responsibility.

Proposition 200 creates another tax-hungry government entity (a Parents Commission) and creates compulsory business for the lucrative (and highly ineffectual) "drug abuse treatment" industry. Convicted drug users must undergo treatment as a requirement of Proposition 200 (whether they need it or not). If they can't pay for their own treatment, we, the taxpayers, pick up the tab.

It's high time government stopped treating responsible adults as children.

If you care about the suffering of patients who are denied the medical benefits of controlled drugs . . .

If you care about the lives wasted in prison for the mere possession of recreational substances . . .

If you want real, meaningful drug reform . . .

. . . then stop prosecuting people for using drugs. Control the sale of drugs just as we now control the sale of alcohol and tobacco.

Suddenly there will be room in our jails for truly violent offenders.

Suddenly there will be far fewer violent crimes, when drugs are no longer worth fighting over, stealing for, or pushing on our children.

Vote "NO" on 200.

Kent B. Van Cleave
Libertarian Candidate for
State Representative
District 25
Phoenix

Scott Grainger
Libertarian Candidate for
State Representative
District 21
Mesa

Robert Anderson
Libertarian Candidate for
U.S. Congress
District 6
Phoenix

John Williams
Libertarian Candidate for
State Senate
District 25
Phoenix

Rickie Duncan
Libertarian Candidate for
State Senate
District 20
Phoenix

Ted Louis Glenn
Libertarian Candidate for
Pima County Supervisor
District 4
Tucson

Ernest Hancock
Libertarian Candidate for
State Representative
District 18
Phoenix

John Wilde
Libertarian Candidate for
State Representative
District 20
Phoenix

Maricopa County
Libertarian Party
Steering Committee
Mesa

On the following page is a chart for you to fill in. First, take the argument in favor of Proposition 200 and see how many propaganda techniques you can identify. When you find a propaganda technique being used, record it in the appropriate box. One box has already been filled in for you. Then look at the argument against Proposition 200, and see how many propaganda techniques you can identify. Record these too.

Should marijuana be used as medicine, as its advocates say? Or is it a dangerous drug that should remain illegal?

Those opposed to the legalization of marijuana say that if it is made available, even for medicinal purposes, addiction to drugs will increase. Marijuana is regarded as the "gateway" drug because most individuals who go on to more dangerous drugs began by experimenting with marijuana. Others who object to marijuana's use for medical treatment note that smoking marijuana is even harder on the lungs than smoking tobacco. It may also subject the user to cognitive and motor impairments. Even limited legalization is seen as undermining efforts to convince children to avoid drugs. Former drug czar William Bennett says that "legalization will give us the worst of both worlds: millions of *new* drug users *and* a thriving criminal black market." Many of those opposed to the recent propositions to legalize marijuana for medicinal purposes view such efforts as a "backdoor" attempt to legalize all drugs.

Those in favor of legalization of marijuana feel that it causes less harm than either alcohol or tobacco. They cite research showing that it is much less addictive than either of those two drugs and is not likely to cause death from an overdose. Further, smoking marijuana may be an effective alternative to more commonly prescribed drugs for advanced AIDS and terminal cancer. The active ingredient THC found in marijuana may reduce extreme nausea and vomiting commonly found in chemotherapy treatment for cancer patients. One of the effects of AIDS is reduced appetite and loss of muscle mass. Marijuana treatment may improve the appetite through a process referred to as "the munchies." Many of those in favor of legalization of marijuana feel that doctors should be free to administer marijuana in a "caring and compassionate" manner.

As you are reading the following pro and con arguments, try to determine your position on the issue.

Marcus Conant, a doctor at the University of California, San Francisco, has treated more than 5,000 HIV-positive patients in his private practice.

PROPOSITION 200

Propaganda Techniques	Arguments "For"	Arguments "Against"
Name-calling	government bureaucrats and political appointees are seen as bad people, thus name-calling	
Glittering generalities or "glad" words		
Transfer		
False analogy		
Testimonial		
Plain folks		
Card stacking		
Bandwagon		
Faulty cause and effect		
Either/or fallacy		

"This Is Smart Medicine"

by Marcus Conant

READING

Anyone who has ever smoked marijuana will tell you he gets hungry afterward. That kind of anecdotal evidence led doctors and patients to experiment with marijuana as a treatment for extreme nausea, or wasting syndrome. I have seen hundreds of AIDS and cancer patients who are losing weight derive almost immediate relief from smoking marijuana, even after other weight-gain treatments—such as hormone treatments or feeding tubes—have failed. But it's not just individuals who have recognized the medicinal benefits of marijuana. No less an authority than the FDA has approved the use of Marinol, a drug that contains the active ingredient in marijuana.

The problem with Marinol is that it doesn't always work as well as smoking marijuana. Either you take too little, or 45 minutes later you fall asleep. Even though insurance will pay for Marinol—which costs about $200 a month—some patients spend their own money, and risk breaking the law, for the more effective marijuana. That's fairly good evidence that smoking the drug is superior to taking it orally. How would we keep patients from giving their prescribed marijuana to friends? The same way we keep people from abusing other prescription drugs: by making patients understand the dangers of giving medication to other people. A physician who prescribes marijuana without the proper diagnoses should be held up to peer review and punished. There are drugs available at the local pharmacy—Valium, Xanax, Percodan—that are far more mood-altering than marijuana. They aren't widely abused. It's not important that a few zealots advocate the wholesale legalization of marijuana. The federal government can't craft policy based on what a few irrational people say. This is a democracy, and what the people of California voted for was to make marijuana available for medicinal use for seriously ill people.

For skeptics, a study devised at San Francisco General Hospital would test the benefits of smoking marijuana once and for all. It, too, was endorsed by the FDA—but the federal government won't provide the marijuana for the study. Washington recently offered to fund a $1 million review of literature on medical marijuana, but it refuses to allow a clinical trial, which is what's really needed.

When citizens even speak up in favor of legalizing marijuana for medicinal use, as happened this fall in California and Arizona, the government tries to stop them. General Barry McCaffrey and the Justice Department have threatened to revoke the prescription-drug licenses of doctors who prescribe marijuana. This is a truly dangerous step. The government has no place in the examination room. Our society has long felt that certain relationships require privileged communication, such as those between a priest and a parishioner or a lawyer and a client. If a patient wants to discuss marijuana, I don't want to have the responsibility of reporting him, and I have to feel comfortable that the patient will not report me. This is a First Amendment issue of freedom of speech between doctor and patient.

5   Perhaps the most persuasive argument for medicinal marijuana I've encountered came two years ago, when the California Assembly was debating a medical-marijuana bill. One GOP assemblyman said he had had a great deal of trouble with the issue. But when a relative was dying a few years before, the family had used marijuana to help her nausea. That story helped the bill pass. Wouldn't it be awful if people changed their minds only after someone close to them had died?

From "This Is Smart Medicine" by Marcus Conant, Newsweek, *February 3, 1997. Copyright © 1997, Newsweek, Inc. All rights reserved. Reprinted by permission.*

Barry R. McCaffrey, a retired Army general, is the director of the Office of National Drug Control Policy.

"We're on a Perilous Path"   *by Barry R. McCaffrey*

READING

Why is it dangerous for Americans to use marijuana as a medicine? The answer is: it may not be. It may surprise you to hear the national drug-policy director say this, but I don't think we should automatically reject the possibility that marijuana may have some medicinal benefits. In fact, a synthetic version of THC, the main active ingredient in marijuana, is already approved by the FDA and available with a doctor's prescription. Called Marinol, it's used to ease nausea in cancer patients and help people with AIDS keep up their appetites.

Does that mean the new California law (Proposition 215) legalizing marijuana as medicine is a good idea? Absolutely not. The truth is, despite the insistence of legalization activists, there is no proof that smoked marijuana is the most effective available treatment for anything. Don't take my word for it. The National Institutes of Health recently examined all of the existing clinical evidence about smoked marijuana. Its conclusion: "There is no scientifically sound evidence that smoked marijuana is medically superior to currently available therapies." This isn't an argument between advocates for legalizing marijuana and the federal government. It's an argument between the legalizers and the American Medical Association, and the American Cancer Society, and the American Ophthalmological Society—all of which oppose the California marijuana initiative.

It seems to me entirely sensible that before we go rushing to embrace the medicinal use of marijuana—or LSD, heroin or any other illicit drug—we ought to find out if it is safe and effective. Every other drug on the market was required to undergo exhaustive testing by the FDA before it was made available to the public. As far as I'm concerned, the door is wide open to marijuana or any other substance—but first it has to pass scientific scrutiny and be subject to peer-group review. (It surprises many people to learn that methamphetamines and even cocaine have been approved for specific medical purposes.)

We have made $1 million available to the Institute of Medicine at the National Academy of Sciences to ask physicians and scientists for all that is known about smoked pot, and what questions need to be asked about it. And I have asked Dr. Harold Varmus, the Nobel laureate and head of the National Institutes of Health, to examine the potential benefits of marijuana. If researchers find there are compounds in marijuana that may have medicinal benefits (cannabis is made up of more than 400 different substances), we must immediately make them available to the American medical community. If they can demonstrate that they are safe and effective, then let's approve them.

5   Until then, though, it is inconceivable to allow anyone of any age to have uncontrolled use of marijuana for any alleged illness—without a doctor's examination or even prescription. But that is precisely what the California law lets people do. Can you think of any other untested, homemade, mind-altering medicine that you self-dose, and that uses a burning carcinogen as a delivery vehicle?

I think it's clear that a lot of people arguing for the California proposition and others like it are pushing the legalization of drugs, plain and simple. It sends a very mixed and confusing message to the young. We've got 68 million kids age 18 and below. They're using drugs in enormously increasing numbers. Drug use among eighth graders alone has more than tripled in the last five years. Pretending pot is just another choice makes their decision to stay off drugs that much harder.

From "We're on a Perilous Path" by Barry R. McCaffrey, Newsweek. *February 3, 1997. Copyright © 1997, Newsweek, Inc. All rights reserved. Reprinted by permission.*

**IN YOUR
OWN WORDS**

1. Does Dr. Conant believe there would be a problem with patients who obtain marijuana for medicinal purposes giving or selling it to others? What are his reasons?

2. According to Dr. Conant, what has the federal government threatened to do to doctors who prescribe marijuana?

3. Does General McCaffrey seem to be saying that Marinol is as effective as smoked marijuana in treating medical problems? Does Dr. Conant agree?

4. Why does Dr. Conant want to portray the federal government as being opposed to the medical use of marijuana? Why does General McCaffrey want to portray the federal government as being neutral?

5. Does Dr. Conant believe that the federal government wishes to conduct scientific studies to test the effectiveness of marijuana for medical treatment? Does General McCaffrey agree?

6. Is General McCaffrey saying that the California proposition will make marijuana available without a doctor's prescription? Does Dr. Conant agree? What could we do to determine who is right?

7. According to General McCaffrey, what effect will the California proposition have on drug use by children? Does Dr. Conant address this issue? What do you think Dr. Conant would say about this?

8. General McCaffrey feels that anything that diminishes society's rejection of marijuana should trouble us. In an interview for the *New York Times Magazine* (July 20, 1997), he expresses concern for the "terrible message" that California Proposition 215 is sending. He says that "kids are hearing that marijuana is a medicine, that it can cure these various illnesses," and as a result they are thinking, "How can anything that's medicine be that bad?" How would Dr. Conant respond to General McCaffrey's concerns?

9. Many people recognize the therapeutic value of THC, but are troubled by the "delivery system." They do not think it is wise for people, even those who are seriously ill, to inhale smoke that contains over 400 compounds, many of which are known to be carcinogenic. How do you feel about this issue?

10. Both opponents and proponents of Proposition 215 feel that over time the country's acceptance of medical marijuana will change the face of the drug war. Do you think that allowing the medical use of marijuana will make it more difficult for society to condemn the use of other problem drugs, such as cocaine and heroin?

11. What propaganda techniques were used in the articles?

Multiple Choice

1. Which of the following best expresses the main idea of the selection?
   a. Legalizing use of marijuana would be a mistake because it would inevitably lead to the use of hard drugs.
   b. General McCaffrey is opposed to the use of marijuana under any conditions.
   c. Marinol is just as effective as smoked marijuana.
   d. Before we legalize the use of marijuana for medical purposes, we should first make sure that it is safe and effective.

2. McCaffrey's purpose in writing this article is to
   a. explain.
   b. persuade.
   c. entertain.
   d. define.

3. In paragraph 2, McCaffrey states that various medical organizations are opposed to legalizing marijuana. This is an example of which propaganda technique?
   a. plain folks
   b. either/or fallacy
   c. testimonial
   d. false analogy

4. In the last paragraph, McCaffrey
   a. presents a faulty cause-and-effect situation.
   b. shows his bias against the legalization of marijuana.
   c. uses card stacking.
   d. all of the above

5. Comparing marijuana to Marinol is an example of
   a. name-calling.
   b. testimonial.
   c. false analogy.
   d. bandwagon.

True or False

_____ 6. The title of McCaffrey's article demonstrates his bias.

_____ 7. Cocaine has been approved for specific medical purposes.

_____ 8. You can infer from the article that all scientists are opposed to the use of marijuana for medical purposes.

_____ 9. The Institute of Medicine has $1 million available to discover what is known about smoked marijuana.

_____ 10. McCaffrey is worried about a confusing message being sent to the young.

Vocabulary: Unit 6

This vocabulary unit will continue with word parts having opposite or nearly opposite meanings. Some of these, such as *hyper* and *hypo,* and *inter* and *intra,* are commonly confused. The middle section discusses word parts having to do with phobias. The last section discusses a word part meaning "false."

syn—same; together	**pro—for**
anti—opposite, against	**nym—name**

synonym—There are 2,660 synonyms for being intoxicated, more than for any other condition or object	synonym	same name. *Synonyms* are words that have the same or similar meanings. For example, *vista* and *panorama* are *synonyms*.
	antonym	different name. *Antonyms* are words having opposite meanings. *Homogeneous* and *heterogeneous* are words with opposite meanings.
symphony—Beethoven was totally deaf when he wrote his Ninth Symphony.	symphony	*Sym* means "together" and *phono* means "sound," so, a *symphony* orchestra produces music by blending sounds together.
	antiphony	opposition of sounds. An *antiphony* is a musical piece that has half of a choral group singing in front of the audience and half in back. Such singing was popular in the Middle Ages.
	analyze	to separate into its parts. *Ana* means "up" and *lyze* means "to loosen," so the literal meaning of the word is "to loosen something up." When you *analyze* why you did not do very well on your psychology test, you try to take apart what happened to see what went wrong.
	synthesize	*Syn* means "together," and so *synthesize* means to form a whole by bringing together the separate parts. What does a *synthesizer* do in music? It combines different sounds to produce a new sound.
	antithesis	*Anti* means "opposite," so an *antithesis* is something that is in opposition. The *antithesis* of segregation is integration.
	pro-abortion	*Pro* means "in favor of," so a person who is *pro-abortion*, or *pro-choice*, is supportive of *abortion* rights.
	anti-abortion	If you are *anti-abortion*, you are opposed to legalized *abortion*.
	antidote	*Dote* comes from the root word meaning "to give," so an *antidote* is something given to counteract something else. If your child drinks a toxic liquid that is acidic, the container may give instructions recommending bicarbonate of soda as an *antidote*. (Remember that you should still call a doctor.)
syndicated—Ann Landers is the most widely syndicated columnist. Her column appears in over 1,200 newspapers and is read by an estimated 90 million readers.	syndicated	*Syn* means "same" and *dic* means "to say," so *syndicated* means "saying the same thing." If something is *syndicated*, it appears in many newspapers, magazines, or radio or TV stations. Abigail Van Buren, or *Dear Abby*, writes a *syndicated* advice column that appears in newspapers around the country.

hypo—under, below   hyper—above, over, excessive

hyperactive	A *hyperactive* child is excessively active. If you were *hyperactive* as a child, there's a good chance you still are.
hypoactive	meaning "under active." Depressed people are often *hypoactive*.
hyperthermia	the state of being overheated or too hot; very high temperature. Long-distance runners in hot weather need to be careful to drink enough water to avoid *hyperthermia*.
hypothermia	the state of being too cold or of having a below-normal body temperature. A person lost in a snowstorm might die of *hypothermia*.
hypodermic	Many of you know that *derm* means "skin," so a *hypodermic* needle is one that goes under the skin.
hyperbole	A *hyperbole* is an exaggeration, such as "strong as an ox." In the cartoon below, Calvin says that his bad day makes him feel as though he has been run over by a train. This is an example of *hyperbole*. *Hyperbole* is discussed in the section on satire.

hypothermia—A person may die of hypothermia when the body temperature is 95 degrees or less.

Calvin and Hobbes

mania—craving
phobia—irrational fear of something

phobias—Twenty-five percent of women and 12 percent of men have at least one type of phobia. Some of the most common phobias are related to injections, the dentist, and heights.

claustrophobia	irrational fear of small, tightly enclosed places.
acrophobia	fear of high places. Acrobats obviously do not have this *phobia*.
monophobia	fear of being alone.
homophobia	fear of homosexuals or homosexuality.
pyromania	a compulsion to start fires.
monomania	an excessive interest in just one thing. A *monomaniac* has a mental disorder characterized by preoccupation with one subject.

intra—within or inside   inter—between or among

Copyright © 1999 by The McGraw-Hill Companies, Inc.

intercollegiate	between or among colleges or universities. Your college's *intercollegiate* baseball team plays other colleges.
intramurals	Literally, this word means "within the walls." So, an *intramural* sports program would be one that takes place within the walls of your college. In *intramural* athletics, student teams play against each other.
interstate	between or among states. The *interstate* highway system connects 48 states.
intrastate	within a state. Your telephone bill may have a list of your *intrastate* calls.
international	between or among nations.
intravenous	within or directly into a vein, such as an *intravenous* injection or I.V. bottle.

para—alongside, beside, side; partial; similar

parallel	*Parallel* lines run side by side. *Parallel* ideas are similar thoughts.
paraphrase	literally, a similar phrase. When you *paraphrase* something, you put it into your own words.
paraprofessional	alongside a professional. This word refers to a person who is not a member of a given profession but who assists those who are. *Paramedics* and *paralegals* are *paraprofessionals*.
paramedic	a person with limited medical duties such as a nurse's aide; a person trained to rescue others.
paralegal	persons trained to aid lawyers but not licensed to practice law.
paranoid	*Para* means "beside" and *noid* refers to the mind. *Paranoia* is characterized by extreme suspiciousness or delusions of persecution.
paraplegic	A *paraplegic* has a paralysis of the lower half of the body, or is partially paralyzed.
quadriplegic	total paralysis of the body from the neck down; having all four limbs paralyzed.

pseudo—false

pseudoscience	a false science; a system of theories that presumes without warrant to have a scientific basis. Astrology, which studies the placement of the moon, sun, and stars to predict the future, is considered by many to be a *pseudoscience*. Astronomy is the real scientific study of the universe.

Trivia Question:

Why was our inter-state highway system originally built? Answer at the end of this lesson.

pseudonym—The deceased Russian author, Konstantine Arsenievich Mikhailov, holds the record for the author with the most pseudonyms. He used 325 different pen names, most of which were abbreviations of his real name.

pseudonym	a false name; a fictitious name, such as a pen name used by a writer to preserve anonymity. The book *Primary Colors*, describing an insider's look at the American political system, was written by Joe Klein using the *pseudonym* of Anonymous. Who is the most famous American author to write under a *pseudonym*? Hint: His two most well-known books are *The Adventures of Tom Sawyer* and *The Adventures of Huckleberry Finn*.
alias	also a false name, but usually used by criminals to disguise their identity.
misnomer	to attach the wrong name to a person or a thing. What do you call that cuddly, tree-dwelling little animal from Australia? If you called this animal a Koala bear, you have just used a *misnomer*, because Koalas aren't bears at all. They are marsupials and carry their young in pouches like a kangaroo.

Make a word using each of the following word parts. Then, in your own words, define or explain the meaning of your word. Do not create any nonsense words.

Word part	Your word	Meaning
hyper	_____	_____
hypo	_____	_____
syn or sym	_____	_____
anti	_____	_____
phobia	_____	_____
mania	_____	_____
inter	_____	_____
intra	_____	_____

Vocabulary 6

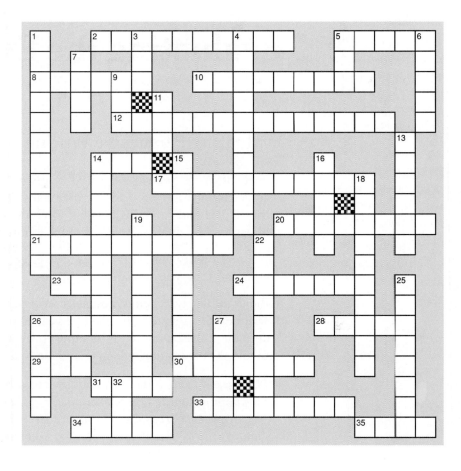

ACROSS CLUES

2. Underactive.
5. A word part meaning "above."
8. A word part meaning "false."
10. An opposition of sounds.
12. The fear of enclosed spaces.
14. A word part meaning "six."
17. Team sports on campus.
20. A person with delusions of persecution.
21. Within a state.
23. A word part meaning "two."
24. To separate into parts.
26. A word part meaning "different."
28. Used by a criminal to disguise identity.
29. A word part meaning "all around."
30. A _____ of vista might be a panorama.
31. A word part meaning "same."
33. Lines running side by side.
34. A word part meaning "within" or "inside."
35. A word part meaning "alongside."

DOWN CLUES

1. Overheated.
3. A word part meaning "in favor of."
4. Between or among states.
5. A word part meaning "same."
6. A word part meaning "back."
7. A word part meaning "around" or "about."
9. An abbreviation for what was once the 10th month.
11. A word part meaning "marriage."
13. A word part meaning "irrational fear."
14. An exaggeration.
15. I.V.
16. A word part meaning "large."
18. To bring elements together.
19. Mark Twain is the _____ of Samuel Clemens.
22. An excessive interest in one thing.
25. The wrong name for an object.
26. A word part meaning "above" or "over."
27. A word part meaning "craving."
32. An abbreviation for what was once the eighth month.

Evaluating the Evidence

Evaluating Persuasive Writing

Instead of using neutral, objective language, authors sometimes use language designed to arouse the reader emotionally. This is often a sign of bias on the author's part and serves as a signal to you that the author is trying to influence you. Authors might use any or all of the following persuasive techniques:

1. **Emotionally loaded language designed to appeal directly to your feelings rather than your reasoning abilities**

In the example given below, notice Dr. William Nolen's use of loaded words in his description of a severely disabled 90-year-old woman who develops pneumonia. A decision must be made on whether to treat the pneumonia with penicillin or withhold the medication, which would likely cause death within three or four days.

> *On the one hand, you cannot bear to see your **once vivacious** mother living the **painful, limited** life to which the stroke has **condemned** her. On the other hand, you hate to be the one to decide to let nature take its course. Until you are actually faced with such a decision, you probably won't be able to predict which course you would take.*
>
> *I'll tell you what choice I would make. I'd say, "Don't give her any penicillin. Keep her as comfortable as possible and let's see what happens. Maybe she'll have the resistance to fight off the pneumonia on her own and if she doesn't, she'll die a **peaceful** death. I don't want to be responsible for **condemning** my mother to a **living hell.**"*

From Nolen, William, "Deciding to Let Your Parents Die," permission from Blassingame, McCauley, and Wood, in Deanne Milan, Improving Reading Skills, *2nd edition, New York: McGraw-Hill, 1992, p. 345.*

2. **Tear-jerking stories or references to people and causes that you empathize with**

After the jurors found Timothy McVeigh guilty of murder and conspiracy in the bombing of the Alfred P. Murrah Federal Building in Oklahoma City, they had to determine whether he should be executed. During the first day of the penalty phase of the trial, prosecutors called upon both rescuers and relatives of the victims to tell their stories.

> *Diane Leonard, the wife of Secret Service agent Don Leonard, described how she and her sister-in-law searched for her husband's name on the list of wounded survivors. "I started on one side, she on the other and we met in the middle," Leonard said, her voice breaking. "Still no Don." She didn't give up hope until the day she was notified his body had been found. "I knew it would take a miracle," she said. "But I believe in miracles. I thought if there was any opportunity*

to defend himself, he would have." Leonard, who had protected five presidents, left behind three adult sons. One night, shortly after the bombing, one of the sons "came to me at 3 A.M. He was crying very hard. He said, 'I want my dad. I want him to meet my wife.' " At her son's wedding, a rose was left where Don Leonard would have sat. "I feel my heart looks like that building did," Leonard said. "It has a huge hole."

From USA Today, *Life Section.*

3. Figurative analogies

A widely known death-row case concerns journalist Mumia Abu-Jamal. In 1981, Philadelphia police officer Daniel Faulkner was killed after he stopped a Volkswagen traveling in the wrong direction on a one-way street. Evidence implicated Abu-Jamal, the brother of the driver of the Volkswagen. He was convicted and sentenced to die. Since that time, he has managed to raise doubts about some of the evidence used to convict him. A stay of execution was granted in August 1995. An appeal is currently pending before the Pennsylvania Supreme Court.

In his book *Live from Death Row,* Abu-Jamal used a metaphor when he said:

Unlike other prisoners, death row inmates are not 'doing time.' Freedom does not shine at the end of the tunnel. Rather, the end of the tunnel brings extinction.

4. Manipulation of tone

The author uses irony in the following description of an execution.

It didn't quite go as planned in Florida recently. The humming of the electricity was joined by a more ominous crackling sound like cellophane crinkling. Then great waves of gray smoke poured out and flames leaped from the prisoner's head. The smell of cooked human flesh and burning hair became pronounced. Despite the evidence to the contrary, proponents of capital punishment hasten to insist that the execution was not "cruel and unusual."

From Abu-Jamal, Live from Death Row, *New York: Avon Trade Books, 1996 p.*

5. Propaganda techniques such as bandwagon, plain folks, name-calling, testimonial

Animal rights activists are frequently at odds with medical researchers. The activists may refer to those conducting research as "cruel" or "sadistic." Researchers, on the other hand, may call the activists names like "fanatic" or "kook."

Those in support of animal research may use a testimonial such as this one from Dr. Michael E. DeBakey, chairman of surgery, and director of the DeBakey Heart Center at Baylor College of Medicine in Houston, Texas.

Even with today's technology, I could not have developed on a computer the roller pump that made open-heart surgery possible or the artificial artery that restored to health previously doomed patients with aneurysms. Nor could we have attempted the first successful coronary artery bypass or implanted the first temporary mechanical heart with which we saved a patient's life two decades ago.

From Rottenberg, Annette T., *found in* Elements of Argument, *New York: Bedford Books of St. Martin's Press, 1991, p. 383, originally an editorial "Holding Human Health Hostage," in* Journal of Investigative Surgery, *Vol. 1, 1988.*

When an author uses a testimonial, ask yourself the following questions:

A.   Is the writer an authority in that particular field?

B.   Is this the writer's specific area of competence?

C.   Is the writer biased?

D.   Is the writer likely to gain some advantage from the testimonial?

6.   Psychological appeals

This technique is used frequently by the media to create ads that appeal directly to our desire for power, prestige, sex, or popularity.

For example, People for the Ethical Treatment of Animals (PETA) used "sex appeal" when it had five well-known models pose naked, "wearing only their skins," to protest the buying of fur coats.

7.   Moral appeals

Authors may seek to appeal to your sense of morality or fair play.

C. S. Lewis was a professor of English literature at Oxford and Cambridge Universities. He is known for his writings on Christianity and morality. His tales for children include the popular *The Lion, the Witch, and the Wardrobe* series. Lewis, in arguing against experimental surgery on animals, said:

> *If we cut up beasts simply because they cannot prevent us and because we are backing our own side in the struggle for existence, it is only logical to cut up imbeciles, criminals, enemies, or capitalists for the same reason.*

From Rottenberg, Annette T., found in Elements of Argument, *New York: Bedford Books of St. Martin's Press, 1991 p. 378, originally in C.S. Lewis, "Vivisection," pamphlet by Anti-Vivisection Society, 1947.*

On this same issue, PETA has publicized an ad showing a bulbous-headed alien looking for humans for scientific experiments. The caption in this ad says:

Powerful, big-brained aliens from outer space with government grants to spend seek human beings for experimentation. Although our diseases do not occur naturally in your species, we plan to infect humans to test experimental drugs. Subjects can expect to convulse, vomit, go blind, develop painful rashes, bleed internally, lose bladder and bowel control, and die. Survivors may be recycled into other tests. Among the most desirable specimens are the homeless, orphans, and other strays who have little or no protection. Your participation may help our superior species or at least satisfy our curiosity.

PETA ad: Courtesy of People for the Ethical Treatment of Animals

PETA officials say they began the campaign because laboratories that use animals for research often justify their action by assigning a superior status to human beings. PETA spokesman Joey Penello said, "We are trying to address the issue of vivisection (surgery on living animals) in a new way. How would we feel if they did to us what we've been doing to animals for years?"

From Rottenberg, p. 378

8. Appeal to authority

Authors may call attention to their integrity, intelligence, and knowledge to convince you to trust their judgment and believe them.

Judge Alex Kozinski wrote an article for *The New Yorker* magazine supporting the death penalty. Near the beginning of the article, he established his authority on this topic by saying:

> *As a judge on the United States Court of Appeals for the Ninth circuit, I hear cases from nine states and two territories spread over the Western United States and Oceania.*

In addition to the above techniques, be sure to note the author's

A. Affiliations: Look for information in the introduction that tells you what types of people or organizations the author associates with.

B. Assumptions: Be sure to note the author's principal beliefs. What ideas does the author hold that enable him to present this particular argument?

C. Organization: Authors are more likely to be trying to persuade you of something when they withhold the purpose or the main idea until the end.

In summary, authors who are trying to persuade do not usually write material that is entirely objective and meant solely to inform. Instead, such authors tend to use factual material to bolster their opinions on a particular subject. By recognizing persuasive techniques and understanding the author's motives, you can avoid being manipulated and become better able to evaluate the issue on its own merits.

Drawing Conclusions: Inductive and Deductive Reasoning

In the final step of analyzing a selection, the reader must evaluate the soundness of the author's reasoning.

All of us draw conclusions based on what we think is reasonable and acceptable. Often these conclusions are based on **inductive** or **deductive** reasoning.

Inductive Reasoning

The word parts for "inductive" are *in* meaning "into" and *duc* meaning "to lead." In inductive reasoning, specific examples, evidence, or propositions lead to a more general conclusion. We reason inductively all the time.

An example of inductive reasoning is the following:

> It's time for me to plan my vacation. The last time Steve flew on Snoozy Airlines, they lost his luggage. My friend Greg says Skyloft is never on time. Tony says RightAir is always too crowded. Ryan and Bonnie have flown many miles on SureFlight and have never had any problems. Therefore, I think I'll fly on SureFlight too.

As this example implies, a conclusion reached by inductive reasoning is only as valid as the specific information on which it is based. Maybe if I had talked to more people, I would have heard some critical comments about SureFlight or some flattering comments about Snoozy or SkyLoft.

So, you can see that inductive reasoning leads to a conclusion that is only probably correct. A conclusion becomes more likely to be correct when the specific information on which it is based improves.

Deductive Reasoning

Deductive reasoning goes in the opposite direction from inductive reasoning. *De* means "away from," and deductive reasoning moves away from the general to the specific. A conclusion reached through deductive reasoning is seen as following logically from more general propositions or statements. Just as we often reason inductively, we also often reason deductively.

A syllogism is a common kind of deductive reasoning. The following is an example of a syllogism.

> All men are mortal.
> Harrison Ford is a man.
> Harrison Ford is mortal.

Here is another example of a syllogism.

> "All of the action movies starring Harrison Ford have been really enjoyable. He's starring in the movie *Air Force One*. This movie is going to be really enjoyable, too."

You can see that whether a conclusion drawn by deductive reasoning is valid depends on whether the general statements on which it is based are correct. If all Harrison Ford action movies have not been really enjoyable—maybe some were boring—then it does not follow that his movie *Air Force One* has to be enjoyable. Or, maybe all Harrison Ford action movies have been enjoyable, but he is not really starring in *Air Force One*, and instead is just playing a supporting role. Again, the conclusion would not follow.

Does the cartoon below make use of a syllogism? Is the conclusion a valid one?

Reprinted with permission of King Features Syndicate.

The Scientific Process

Inductive and deductive reasoning are both involved in the "scientific process." Scientists do research, which involves collecting data and analyzing it, and then they seek to draw a general conclusion or *hypothesis* from their research. This process of formulating hypotheses from research involves inductive reasoning. Scientists then use deductive reasoning to test their hypotheses. A hypothesis tells a scientist what should happen when the scientist collects further data or performs a further test. If the new data or test is consistent with the hypothesis, the hypothesis is confirmed; if not, the hypothesis needs to be modified or rejected. Scientists often have to revise their hypotheses to keep up with new research.

For example, assume that a friend of yours offers to set you up on a blind date. You have some reservations about blind dates, so you decide to do a little informal scientific research on the subject. You collect data on blind dates by talking to a number of people who have been on blind dates. All of these people tell you that they had a terrible experience. So, using inductive reasoning, you formulate a hypothesis based on your research. This hypothesis might say: Anyone who goes on a blind date will have a miserable time.

Then, reasoning deductively from your hypothesis, you would conclude that should you accept your friend's offer of a blind date, you will have a miserable time. But you're either courageous or desperate, and you decide to go on the blind date anyway. If it turns out that you have a miserable time, your hypothesis is confirmed. But if it turns out that you have a good time, your hypothesis has been contradicted and needs some further work. You might then formulate a new hypothesis that would say: If you go on a blind date, chances are high that you will have a miserable time, but you might get lucky and have a good time.

In the pages that follow, you, as a critical reader, will need to evaluate the author's reasoning to see how valid or persuasive it is.

This article on DNA demonstrates how scientists evaluate evidence in order to come to a reasonable conclusion. Read the article carefully, noting the inductive and deductive reasoning, and then answer the questions that follow.

"DNA Fingerprinting"   *by Ruth Bernstein and Stephen Bernstein*

READING

DNA, or deoxyribonu-cleic acid, is a protein which is a building block of life. It disappears rapidly from carcasses and thus is rarely found in fossils. However, in 1993 in Lebanon, DNA was found in a 120–135-million-year-old weevil.

John and Susan Gladstone had a young child and a bad marriage. They decided to divorce, but both of them wanted to keep their three-year-old daughter, Katie. Susan shocked her husband when she claimed the child was not his. Katie's biological father, she said, was the man next door. Susan planned to move in with him and take Katie with her.

John couldn't believe he wasn't Katie's father but arranged a paternity test to make sure. Samples of blood were taken from all three Gladstones as well as from the man next door, and DNA fingerprints were made of the DNA molecules in the white blood cells. A DNA fingerprint would identify with greater accuracy than any other test the biological father of Katie.

DNA fingerprinting was developed in 1985 by a British geneticist, Alec Jeffreys, at the University of Leicester. He coined the term *DNA fingerprinting* and was the first to use techniques of genetic engineering in paternity and murder cases.

Jeffreys observed that human DNA contains particular sequences of bases that are repeated many times. The repetitive sequences, which appear within genes (as introns) and between genes, do not code for proteins. The number of times the sequences are repeated varies from one person to the next. Thus, when the same DNA molecule in different people is cut with the same restriction enzyme (which cuts the DNA at the same base sequences), the lengths of the fragments vary: someone with a longer fragment has more repetitive sequences than someone with a shorter fragment. Moreover, the number of repetitive sequences, and so the fragment length, is inherited. A child inherits fragment lengths from both parents. The array of fragments should contain some like the mother's array and others like the father's array.

5   DNA molecules taken from white blood cells of the Gladstones and the man next door were fragmented by restriction enzymes and the fragments lined up according to length by gel electrophoresis. The fragments were then labeled with DNA probes (built to match the repetitive sequences) so that they could be seen and photographed. The array of fragments for each person appears as a pattern of bands, similar to the bar codes used in supermarkets.

A DNA fingerprint is remarkably precise. Virtually everyone, except an identical twin, has a unique banding pattern. And all that is needed to identify a person is a tiny sample of blood, semen, skin, or hair.

Try to help unravel the mystery of Katie's parentage. Remember that Katie's fingerprint is a mixture of her mother's fragments and her father's. A child inherits half the fragment lengths from each parent.

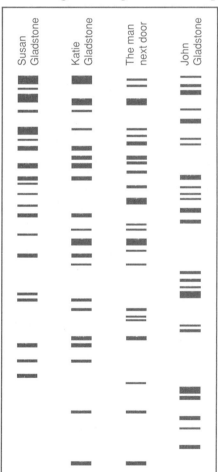

Katie's Father

The fingerprints of Susan, Katie, and John Gladstone, as well as the man next door, are shown in the figure. Each column of bars is a DNA fingerprint. Each bar in a column represents a fragment of DNA. The vertical arrangement of bars represents the DNA fragments sorted according to length. The four fragments shown are from a mother (Susan), a child (Katie), and two men (the man next door and John) who claim to be Katie's father.

The bars reveal that the man next door is Katie's real father. Katie's fingerprint is a mixture of her mother's fragments and fragments in the fingerprint of the man next door. Note that Katie has bands found in the fingerprint of the man next door but not found in either her mother's fingerprint and John's fingerprint. John had helped raise Katie, but the man next door gave her his genes. The court ruled that Katie should live with her biological mother and father.

From Biology *by Ruth Bernstein and Stephen Bernstein, 1996. Reprinted by permission of The McGraw-Hill Companies.*

IN YOUR OWN WORDS

1. When Jeffreys was collecting data and drawing conclusions about its usefulness for "fingerprinting," was he thinking primarily inductively or deductively? (Hint: Keep in mind that inductive reasoning goes from the specific to the general, and deductive reasoning goes from the general to the specific.)

2. If Jeffreys' hypothesis is correct, matching bands should exist between Katie and her mother, and Katie and her natural father. Is this conclusion—that these matching bands should be present—reached by inductive or deductive reasoning?

3. Why must a criminal be careful not to leave a single cell at the scene of the crime?

4. Can you see any potential problems with DNA evidence?

What follows is an odd tale of the use of nonhuman DNA in a murder trial. A Canadian man was convicted of murdering his former wife after hairs in a blood-stained jacket were genetically matched to his parents' cat.

The body of the ex-wife was found in a shallow grave two months after she had been reported missing. At the same site, a bloody leather jacket in a plastic sack was also discovered. Tests revealed that the bloodstains on the jacket belonged to the woman. Inside the lining of the jacket, cat hairs were discovered.

The man had been living with his parents and Snowball, a white short-haired cat. The police sent a blood sample from Snowball and the hair from the jacket to Stephen O'Brien of the National Cancer Institute in Maryland. O'Brien has studied cat genetics for over 20 years. According to O'Brien, Snowball's DNA matched genetic material from the root of one of the hairs.

In order to determine that the match was not the result of chance, a local veterinarian drew blood randomly from 19 cats. O'Brien studied the DNA in those samples and data from a survey of nine cats from the United States. His research concluded that the likelihood that the jacket hair DNA would match Snowball's DNA just by chance was about 1 in 45 million. As a result, the ex-husband was convicted of second-degree murder.

Non-human DNA evidence has been used to successfully prosecute other murderers before. Another famous case occurred in Arizona in 1993, when a man was convicted after DNA from seed pods in his pickup truck was matched to a Palo Verde tree at the site where the victim's body was discovered.

5. What the investigators did in the case of the Canadian man was collect evidence that he had killed his former wife. Was this reasoning process primarily inductive or deductive?

6. Would you feel comfortable convicting someone of murder on the basis of a scientific analysis of nonhuman DNA? Why or why not?

7. When DNA is used to solve crimes, what assumptions about DNA are being made?

A new study reported in *Nature* magazine suggests that DNA can be found on everyday objects, such as pens, keys, telephones, and glasses that were only casually touched by our hands. We apparently leave DNA in many places that can be traced back to us. Researchers have also determined that people can pick up other people's DNA, particularly on their hands. If a person can pick up your DNA from a handshake or something you touched, that at least raises the possibility that a person could "plant" or accidentally leave your DNA at a crime scene, thus implicating you in a crime you didn't commit.

8. Based on the information that has been presented here, do you think DNA evidence should be admissible in a court of law to convict people of crimes? Give your reasons.

In the last few years, a number of prisoners have been set free because of further DNA testing. Sometimes, prosecutors remained convinced of the guilt of these prisoners despite the new testing. As a result, some prosecutors have begun to change their view of DNA testing. Instead of viewing it as something that absolutely shows guilt or innocence, they may now view it as just another important piece of evidence. As these prosecutors are beginning to realize, while DNA testing can theoretically provide positive proof of guilt or innocence, the validity of the results can be compromised by problems in handling the evidence and interpreting the testing.

9. If, as some prosecutors say, DNA testing has been used to wrongly gain freedom for some prisoners, is it fair or right for prosecutors during a trial to tell jurors that DNA testing conclusively proves the defendants' guilt?

10. Do you think that DNA testing is more or less persuasive than simple fingerprinting?

11. Is DNA playing an important role in any criminal investigation that has recently been in the news?

Each of the next two sections deals with a separate topic: death and dying, and animal experimentation. There are two essays for each of these topics. Carefully evaluate the evidence in each essay you read so that you can answer the questions that follow it.

Tuning In to Reading

In the United States today, deciding how to treat the terminally ill or those in chronic pain is harder than ever because of the existence of life-prolonging medical technology. As a result, the whole concept of a "good death" has been called into question. One of the top fears of many Americans is dying in a hospital hooked up to machines. The author of this article, a physician, describes the dilemma of caring for a patient who has no realistic chance of recovery.

Paired Selections Related to Death and Dying

"Dreaming of Disconnecting a Respirator"   *by Elissa Ely*

READING

Late one night in the intensive care unit, one eye on the cardiac monitor and one on the Sunday paper, I read this story:

An infant lies in a hospital, hooked to life by a respirator. He exists in a "persistent vegetative state" after swallowing a balloon that blocked the oxygen to his brain. This "vegetative state," I've always thought, is a metaphor inaccurately

*The art of living well
and the art of dying well
are one.*

Epicures

borrowed from nature, since it implies that with only the proper watering and fertilizer, a comatose patient will bloom again.

One day his father comes to visit. He disconnects the respirator and, with a gun in hand, cradles his son until the infant dies. The father is arrested and charged with murder.

In the ICU where I read this, many patients are bound to respirators. I look to my left and see them lined up, like potted plants. Some will eventually be "weaned" back to their own lung power. Others will never draw an independent breath again.

5   In Bed No. 2, there is a woman who has been on the respirator for almost two months. When she was admitted with a simple pneumonia, there were no clues she would come apart so terribly. On her third day, she had a sudden and enigmatic seizure. She rolled rapidly downhill. Her pneumonia is now gone, but her lungs refuse independence: she can't come off the machine.

I know little about this patient except that she is elderly and European. (It is the peculiar loss of hospital life that patients often exist here with a medical history, but not a personal one.) I sometimes try to picture her as she might have been: busy in a chintz kitchen smelling of pastries. She might have hummed, rolling dough. Now there is a portable radio by the bed, playing Top Ten, while the respirator hisses and clicks 12 times a minute.

The family no longer visits. They have already signed the autopsy request, which is clipped to the front of her thick chart. Yet in their pain, they cannot take the final step and allow us to discontinue her respirator. Instead, they have retired her here, where they hope she is well cared for, and where she exists in a state of perpetual mechanical life.

I have dreamed of disconnecting my patient's respirator. Every day I make her death impossible and her life unbearable. Each decision—the blood draws, the rectal temperatures, the oxygen concentration—is one for or against life. No action in the ICU is neutral. Yet many of these decisions are made with an eye toward legal neutrality—and this has little to do with medical truth. The medical truth is that this patient exists without being alive. The legal neutrality is that existence is all that is required.

Late at night, reading in the ICU, the story of that father—so dangerous and impassioned—puts me to shame. I would never disconnect my patient from her respirator; it is unthinkable. But this is not because I am a doctor. It is because I feel differently toward her than the father toward his son.

10   I do not love her enough.

From "Dreaming of Disconnecting a Respirator" by Elissa Ely as appeared in The Boston Globe, *July 1, 1989. Reprinted by permission of the author.*

Evaluating the Evidence

1. Is the author's primary purpose to inform or to persuade? What evidence do you have to support your conclusion?

    _____

    _____

    _____

2. What is the author's background? Does the author have the qualifications to write seriously about this topic?

    _____

    _____

    _____

3. Is the content of the article primarily factual or expressing opinion?

   _____

   _____

   A. List some facts from the article:

      _____

      _____

      _____

   B. List some opinions from the article:

      _____

      _____

      _____

4. If the author has a strong bias, write it below. Can you give examples
   of emotionally loaded language, or material that has been included to
   create an emotional response on your part?

   _____

   _____

   _____

   _____

5. What is your opinion on the topic of euthanasia (mercy killing,
   assisted suicide)? Do you think that your opinion is biased? If so,
   does your bias interfere with your ability to fairly evaluate what
   the author is saying?

   _____

   _____

   _____

   _____

6. Does the author use any specific propaganda devices? List them below.
   How did you react to these techniques?

   _____

   _____

   _____

   _____

7. How would you describe the author's tone? What does the tone tell you
   about the author's bias?

   _____

   _____

   _____

The article below explores some fundamental questions about death and dying in the United States today.

"The Good Death: Embracing a Right to Die Well" *by Sheryl Gay Stolberg*

READING

The cold bare facts of Barbara Logan Brown's death are these: On July 17, 1996, Mrs. Logan Brown, a 38-year-old mother of two from Rochester, New York, died of AIDS, another statistic in an epidemic that has killed more than 362,000 Americans. Cancer had seeped into her brain; thrush had clogged her throat, making swallowing impossible. An intravenous diet of morphine had rendered her comatose.

Those are the cold bare facts. But there are other facts—achingly poignant, indeed, beautiful, some might argue—about Barbara Logan Brown's death. They are recounted here by Roberta Halter, herself a mother of four who cared for her dying friend and is today the guardian of Mrs. Logan Brown's son and daughter.

"The last time Barbara was able to go outside, she sat on the front porch. The girls and I went upstairs and took poster paint and painted a big huge smiley face above her bed. The next day, everyone put hand prints all over the wall. The children called it 'The Hands of Love,' and they started to paint messages on the wall. After the paint had dried, we let visitors come. By the end of the day, there were messages everywhere. It was kind of a tribute to her while she was still living. And it was wonderful."

It was, in Mrs. Halter's view, a good death.

5 A good death. It is a provocative phrase.

A Mystery Profaned

Death was much talked about last week, as the Supreme Court finally weighed in [on] one of the most divisive moral, legal and medical questions of the day: whether the Constitution gives Americans a fundamental right to a physician's help in dying. The justices said it does not, leaving the battle over whether to permit or prohibit assisted suicide to rage on among lawyers and legislators, doctors and ethicists across the country.

While the court ruled on the constitutional issue, what remains unsettled—indeed, unsettling—is the idea at the heart of the assisted-suicide question: that for most Americans, modern medicine has made dying worse.

America is often called a "death-denying" society; each year the United States spends millions on efforts to conquer death, or at least to postpone it. The self-help shelves of bookshelves overflow with such pearls as *Stop Aging Now!* and *Stay Young the Melatonin Way.*

If Americans don't deny death, they often trivialize it, said Joan Halifax, a Zen Buddhist priest who founded the Project on Being With Dying in Santa Fe, New Mexico. "By the time a kid gets into high school, he has seen 20,000 homicides on television," she said. "Death as a mystery to be embraced, entered into and respected has been profaned in our culture."

10 Courtesy of the assisted-suicide debate, the concept of a good death has now emerged, though many experts reject the phrase as simplistic. Dr. Ira Byock, president of the Academy of Hospice and Palliative Medicine, prefers "dying well." Dr. Timothy Keay, an end-of-life care expert at the University of Maryland, says "the least worst death."

There is no blueprint, however, for a good death. Death can't be neatly packaged with a red bow. It is messy, irrational, most often filled with sorrow and pain. More than two million Americans die each year; there are as many ways to die as to live. And so unanswerable questions arise: Not only what constitutes a good death and how can it be achieved, but who, ultimately, it is for—the person dying, or those going on living?

"I'm a little cynical about this whole notion of good death," said Dr. David Hilfiker, the founder of Joseph's House in Washington, which cares for homeless men dying of AIDS. "Death is really hard for most people. Why should people who are dying have to have a beautiful death? That's putting the burden on them to have some kind of experience that makes us feel good."

Indeed, said Dr. Sherwin B. Nuland, the author of "How We Die," the patient's needs often get lowest priority. "A good death," he said, "is in the eye of the beholder."

In centuries past, a good death was celebrated in art and literature as *ars moriendi,* the art of dying. Death marked salvation of the soul, neither an ending nor a beginning but, like birth, part of the cycle of life. "True philosophers," Plato wrote, "are always occupied in the practice of dying."

15   Buddhism is filled with stories of Zen masters who write poems in the moments before death, embracing it as the only time in life when absolute freedom may be realized. In the Middle Ages, Christian monks greeted one another with the salutation *Momento mori,* remember that you must die.

Today, it seems, most Americans would rather forget. Asked their idea of a good death, they say, "quick." Keeling over in the garden, trowel in hand, is one ideal, going to bed and not waking up another.

That is a reaction against medical technology; if Americans want anything from death, they want to remain in control, to avoid making their exits tethered to a machine. It is fear of a painful, lonely and protracted high-tech death that has fueled the movement to make assisted suicide legal.

"The classic idea of the good death is the sudden death," Dr. Nuland said, "but if you think seriously about it, that isn't what you want. What you really want is a tranquil, suffering-free last few weeks where you have the opportunity for those near you to express what your life has meant to them."

A century ago such opportunities could be elusive. Infectious disease caused most deaths; cholera struck, and there was a burial two days later. Dr. Joanne Lynn, director of George Washington University's Center to Improve Care of the Dying, said: "When people went to bed and said 'If I should die before I wake,' they meant it."

20   Today the leading causes of death are heart disease, cancer, and stroke. For older people, disproportionately affected by these ailments, dying can drag on for months or years. Most women, Dr. Lynn said, have eight years of disability before they die; most men, five or six. It might seem, then, that people have time to plan for their deaths, but many don't take advantage. A study to be published in this week's *Annals of Internal Medicine* found that most seriously ill adults in the hospital do not talk to their doctors about being kept alive on life-support machines. They prefer not to discuss it.

Americans have been reticent to talk about death; only recently have doctors and families felt obliged to tell a terminally ill person that he was, in fact, dying. Often the truth simply went unremarked, like an elephant in the dining room.

In 1969, Elisabeth Kubler-Ross shattered the silence with *On Death and Dying.* In it, she described the progression of a patient's coping mechanisms in five stages of dying: denial, anger, bargaining, depression and finally acceptance.

❝Death—the last voyage, the longest, the best.❞

Thomas Wolfe

Dr. Byock, the author of *Dying Well,* offers what he calls the "developmental model" of dying. When he began caring for the terminally ill 20 years ago, he noticed that when he asked patients how they were feeling, often the reply was something like this: "Despite it all, doctor, I am well."

The juxtaposition of wellness and dying seemed a paradox, but he has concluded that the two can exist side by side. "In dying," he said, "there are opportunities to grow even through times of severe difficulty, which we would label suffering."

25 In his view, dying well includes love and reconciliation, a settling of worldly affairs and a life's summing up, as stories are recounted and passed to new generations. By these standards, Barbara Logan Brown most certainly had a good death. "Barbara," Mrs. Halter said, "had an opportunity to put her life here on earth in order."

In the End, Liberation

Conventional wisdom holds that people die as they have lived; a crotchety old man in life will be a crotchety old man in death. Not so, say experts in end-of-life care: death can be both transforming and liberating.

Dr. Halifax, the Buddhist priest, tells of a woman whose daughter was a hospice nurse. Throughout her life, the mother had adhered to strict codes of politeness and propriety. A few days before her death, she began screaming in rage and pain.

As a nurse, her daughter knew that narcotics could subdue her mother's pain. But she chose to do nothing; the screaming, she believed, was her mother's way of finally expressing herself. "The screaming went on for four days and four nights," Dr. Halifax said. "And about an hour before she died, she lit up, and became extremely peaceful, and relaxed completely. And then she died."

Was it a good death? Dr. Halifax paused.

30 "A good death," she finally allowed, "sounds a little polite. It's like death with manners. I don't want to adorn death. Death is death."

From "The Good Death: Embracing a Right to Die Well" by Sheryl Gay Stolberg. The New York Times, Sunday, June 29, 1997. Copyright © 1997 by The New York Times. Reprinted by permission.

Vocabulary

Directions: For each italicized word from the article, use your dictionary to find the best definition according to the context.

1. other facts—achingly *poignant* (paragraph 2) _____
2. they often *trivialize* it (paragraph 9) _____
3. has been *profaned* in our culture (paragraph 9) _____
4. exits *tethered* to a machine (paragraph 17) _____
5. lonely and *protracted* high-tech death (paragraph 17) _____
6. a *tranquil*, suffering-free last few weeks (paragraph 18) _____
7. such opportunities could be *elusive* (paragraph 19) _____
8. *reticent* to talk about death (paragraph 21) _____
9. *juxtaposition* of wellness and dying (paragraph 24) _____
10. *crotchety* old man (paragraph 26) _____
11. *adhered* to strict codes (paragraph 27) _____

12. politeness and *propriety* (paragraph 27)   _____

13. *subdue* her mother's pain (paragraph 28)   _____

14. to *adorn* death (paragraph 30)   _____

Content and Structure

Directions: Choose the best answer for each of the following questions. Refer back to the article.

1. The mode of rhetoric in this selection is primarily (a) narration; (b) description; (c) exposition; (d) persuasion. Answer: _____.

2. The pattern of organization in paragraph 3 is primarily (a) compare and contrast; (b) example; (c) chronological order; (d) cause and effect. Answer: _____.

3. In paragraphs 14–16, two types of death are contrasted. Describe the two types below.

    a. _____

    b. _____

4. Explain the cause-and-effect relationship in paragraph 17.

    Cause:_____

    Effect: _____

5. In paragraphs 18–20, Stolberg implies several contrasts. State two specific things being contrasted.

    a. _____

    b. _____

6. In paragraph 21, Stolberg uses a figure of speech to describe Americans' reluctance to speak of death. Explain the meaning of this figure of speech.

    _____

7. According to Dr. Byock, what does "dying well" include?

    a. _____

    b. _____

8. Explain the meaning of "death with manners" described in the last paragraph.

    _____

    _____

9. Write the overall main idea of the selection below.

    _____

    _____

10. The author's purpose is to (a) inform; (b) entertain; (c) persuade. Answer: _____.

11. To support her ideas, the author primarily relies on (a) statistics from research studies; (b) expert opinion from health-related fields; (c) her own observations and opinions. Answer: _____.

12. The author's tone throughout the article is (a) loving; (b) angry; (c) serious; (d) humorous. Answer: _____.

IN YOUR OWN WORDS

1. Do you think dying today is more dehumanizing than in the past? Why or why not?

2. Compare and contrast the dying experience described at the beginning of the selection with that described at the end. From the perspective of the patient, which one would you call a "good death"? From the perspective of the family?

3. Do you have a living will? Why are so many Americans reluctant to make provisions for death?

4. The Greek word parts *eu* meaning "good," and *thantos* meaning "death," appear in the word *euthanasia*, so the literal meaning of this term is "good death." Euthanasia is also thought of as "mercy killing." Euthanasia may be either active or passive: In the first case, death is deliberately inflicted, sometimes by a relative; in the second case, life-support systems are withdrawn and the patient dies naturally. Controversy surrounding the morality of euthanasia has increased in recent years because of advances in medical technology that make it possible for human beings, both newborn and old, to be kept alive almost indefinitely, even when severely impaired. Where do you stand on euthanasia? Do you think life is sacred, so that euthanasia is always wrong? Do you think that the patient's ability or inability to continue to enjoy life should influence the decision? Who should make the decision? The patient? The family? The doctor? The courts?

5. Dr. Jack Kevorkian, the so-called Dr. Death, insists that those in chronic pain with no chance of recovery have a right to a physician-assisted suicide with the administration of mercy-killing drugs. The Supreme Court has decided that no such general right can be found in the Constitution. Do you think that laws should be passed authorizing physician-assisted suicide? Or do you think that laws should be passed banning it?

6. The June 1997 issue of *The Journal of the American Medical Association* reported that "a new analysis of doctor-assisted suicide in the Netherlands suggests that caregivers there have increasingly taken the next, troubling step: ending patients' lives without their permission." The Netherlands has long been considered a model by advocates of assisted suicide in the United States. This new information seems to confirm the fears of U.S. opponents of assisted suicide, which remains illegal in most states. Do you think that the acceptance of euthanasia would lead to a more relaxed attitude toward the taking of life in general, and toward taking the lives of those in need of constant attention in particular? What effect would this have on patients' ability to trust their doctors?

Paired Selections Related to Animal Experimentation

Excerpt from **"Animal Experimentation Raises Ethical Questions"**

READING

Uses and Abuses of Animals

Human societies have kept animals at least since the origin of agriculture. There are few societies of any kind that do not have some tradition of keeping animals as pets, as workmates, or as food. Most societies that practice agriculture use animals for all three purposes. Love of animals and use of animals can go hand in hand.

By far the largest number of animals used by any society are raised for use as food for humans. Animal products are used for clothing. Animals are also used, even in many industrial societies, for recreational hunting, fishing, and trapping. An estimated 7 percent of the United States population has a hunting or fishing license. Many people keep pets or "companion" animals. Pets can offer benefits beyond companionship. For example, studies have shown that heart attack victims who are pet owners live longer and suffer fewer repeat attacks than heart attack victims who do not own pets. Work animals include animals that are used for riding, for pulling and carrying loads, for police work, and for helping handicapped people in various ways, such as seeing eye dogs for the blind and also a small but growing number of monkeys and other animals trained to assist patients confined to wheelchairs. Finally, animals are often used in research, although the number of animals used annually in research is only a tiny fraction of numbers used each day as food and for other purposes.

Justifications for the Use of Animals   A variety of reasons have been given to justify the use of animals by humans, including (1) saving human lives (e.g., serving as stand-ins for humans in dangerous situations), (2) improving human health (e.g., testing medical and surgical procedures), (3) providing food for people, (4) providing nonmedical information, (5) serving our recreational needs (hunting other than for food, entertainment uses such as circus acts), and (6) serving as status symbols (e.g., wearing furs). A large number of people will accept reasons 1 to 4 as adequate to justify the use of animals, or their more extensive use, while fewer people will accept reasons 5 and 6.

Animals as Test Subjects   Nearly all new drugs, cosmetics, food additives, and new forms of therapy and surgery are tested first on animals before they are tested on humans. The use of animals in research is considered critical to continued progress in human health. Over 40 Nobel Prizes have been awarded in medicine or physiology for research using experimental animals. Organ transplants, open-heart surgery, and various other surgical techniques were first performed and perfected on animals before they were performed on humans. All major vaccines, including those for smallpox, polio, mumps, measles, rubella, and diphtheria, were tested on animals before they were used on human patients. Despite the vociferous opposition of the animal rights movement, the general concept of using animals in research has received widespread support in most industrial societies.

5   In most cases, animals are used in research as stand-ins for humans. If we were to abolish the use of animals for these purposes, we would be using many more procedures on humans without benefit of prior animal testing. In effect, the first few dozen or few hundred human patients would be serving as human guinea pigs—the experimental subjects on which the new technique is tested. Most

people favor the use of animals as substitutes for humans in those cases where the use of animals can lessen the suffering of human beings. This is especially true in those cases (the majority) in which the animal testing is limited to the initial development of a drug but the human benefit continues for many generations or longer.

Regulation of Animal Use   Very few people would object to the use of animals if human lives were saved as a consequence. Most people would also agree that we should alleviate unnecessary suffering among animals, whether the animals are pets, work animals, or research animals. It is in the best interest of science for scientists to conduct their tests on healthy, well-treated animals, and the U.S. Guide for the Care and Use of Laboratory Animals reflects this concern. The United States Department of Agriculture keeps statistics on the use of experimental animals in research. According to these statistics, 62 percent of the animals used in research experienced no pain, and another 32 percent were given anesthesia, painkillers, or both, to alleviate pain. Only in 6 percent of cases were animals made to suffer pain without benefit of anesthesia. Federal law in the United States requires the use of anesthesia and/or painkillers in animal research whenever possible. Exceptions are allowed only when the experimental design would be compromised by the use of anesthesia and when no other alternative method is available for conducting the test. Each such exception must be approved by the same institutional animal care and use committee that supervises animal research in general. All research using live animals must, by law, be scrutinized and approved by such committees, and the committees are required to minimize both the number of animals used and the amount of pain that those animals experience. Although it is assumed that researchers will design their experiments with these criteria in mind, the review process ensures that the researcher(s) are not the ones making the final decision on whether their experiments conform to ethical guidelines.

The Animal Rights Movement

Like many other movements, the animal rights movement is a heterogeneous mixture of believers, partial believers, zealots, and sympathizers. Bernard Rollin, a philosopher on the faculty at the College of Veterinary Medicine at Colorado State University, focused on the animal rights issue in a 1992 book:

> *The main problem, which continues to concern me the most . . . , is polarization*
> *and irrationality on the animal ethics issues by both sides. . . . The American*
> *Medical Association's recent paper on animal rights labels all animal advocates*
> *as "terrorists," and scientific and medical researchers continue to equate animal*
> *rights supporters with lab trashers, Luddites, misanthropes, and opponents of*
> *science and civilization. Animal rights activists continue to label all scientists as*
> *sadists and psychopaths. Thus an unhealthy pas de deux is created that blocks*
> *rather than accelerates the discovery of rational solutions to animal ethics issues.*

Those concerned with animal rights vary from traditional humane societies like the Society for the Prevention of Cruelty to Animals (SPCA) and various national, state, and local humane societies, through groups like People for the Ethical Treatment of Animals (PETA, founded in 1980), to groups like the Animal Liberation Front (ALF, founded in 1972). From the start, the ALF concentrated on such tactics as breaking into animal research labs, wrecking their facilities and equipment (often beyond repair), and "liberating" the animals. Because these activities are illegal, leading members of the ALF are sought by law enforcement authorities, and most of them are now in hiding. This is the organization most often labeled as "terrorist."

10   Some animal rights activists use a utilitarian ethic to support their position; others write as deontologists. An example of an deontological position would be that animals have inviolable rights, or that it is always wrong to do harm to them, regardless of the circumstances or consequences. A utilitarian animal rights position might insist on a comparison of costs and benefits (or good and bad consequences) but with equal value placed on the lives (or the pain) of humans and animals.

Current Debates

Fur Clothing   The wearing of furs has long been one of the major targets of animal rights activists, and the elimination of fur clothing has consistently been one of their strongest aims. In most cases, fur clothing is made from very small animals like mink or chinchilla, so it takes many dozens of animals to produce a jacket and many more to produce a coat. These animals are either trapped in the wild or are ranch-raised.

What would a cost-benefit analysis of fur clothing reveal? In addition to the death and suffering of the fur-bearing animals themselves, the death and suffering of animals inadvertently caught in the traps must be calculated on the cost side. On the benefit side, there is the utility for humans of having warm clothing. A number of people (fur trappers, shippers, processors, salespeople) are economically dependent on the fur industry, but many of these people could use their skills equally well in other jobs.

None of these costs and benefits are easily measured in a way that permits comparison in the same units. Pain and suffering are particularly difficult to measure or quantify. As in many other cases, after listing all the costs and all the benefits, we then leave it up to each of us as individuals to decide whether or not the benefits outweigh the costs. If we approach this question instead from a rights perspective, we must balance the rights of animals to go on living and to be free from pain against the rights of people to wear whatever they please.

Among the alternatives to animal-derived clothing are synthetic fabrics such as polyester, which are made from, and therefore use up, nonrenewable petroleum products. Other forms of warm clothing may not require using a nonrenewable resource. For example, wool can be obtained as a renewable resource from sheep; the shearing causes them no apparent harm, and they simply regrow a new coat of wool. Other fibers for fabrics can be made from plants such as cotton. Leather is generally obtained from animals that are killed for other purposes (such as food). Most of these are much less expensive than fur and raise none of the ethical issues mentioned here.

15   Testing of Pharmaceuticals   Of all the types of experiments to which animals are subjected, none are as often justified in the eyes of the public as the testing of medicines intended for human use. In fact, a pharmaceutical company would be considered remiss if it marketed a new drug without first testing it on animals. In many countries, including the United States, animal testing is required by law before a new drug can be brought to market. If a drug causes adverse effects in even a small fraction of humans who use it, then the failure of the drug company to identify such adverse effects in animal testing could be used against them in a very expensive lawsuit.

New drugs are tested every year, and most of the tests use experimental animals. In fact, a good deal of the expense involved in bringing a new drug to market is the cost of animal testing. In addition to the lives of the animals, the costs of the experimental testing of new drugs include the salaries of the experimenters and animal handlers. On the other side of the cost-benefit equation are the human lives saved or symptoms relieved. If the drug is successful, its benefits may continue far into the future.

Those people who value human life above the lives of animals are only being consistent when they insist that drugs or new procedures be tested on animals before they are used on humans. Some animal rights advocates, such as Ingrid Newkirk of PETA, have adopted the viewpoint that a human life is no more valuable than an animal life, or, in her words, "a rat is a pig is a dog is a boy." A direct logical consequence of this viewpoint is that the pain and suffering of animals in any experiment can no more be justified than an equivalent amount of pain and suffering for a human subject. On this issue, as on many others, the cost-benefit equation can come out differently according to the relative values placed on the lives of humans and the lives of nonhuman animals.

Improving the Treatment of Animals

Attempts to improve the status of animals in research include attempts to prevent animal abuse and neglect and to minimize pain and suffering. Most current legislation deals with the prevention of abuse and neglect by setting minimum standards for housing and care. For example, the U.S. Animal Welfare Act sets standards for the housing of various species (including minimum cage sizes and similar details); the provision of adequate food, water, and sanitation; and such other matters as ventilation, protection from temperature extremes, veterinary care, and the use of anesthetics, painkillers, and tranquilizers whenever it is appropriate.

Animal rights groups have advocated what are known as the three Rs: reduction, refinement, and replacement. *Reduction* would mean using methods that require fewer animals; such measures would also in most cases reduce costs. *Refinement* would mean using methods that get more information from a given amount of experimentation. Among other refinement measures, researchers should always make sure they are not repeating earlier work. *Replacement* would mean using tissue culture and other in vitro methods in preference to whole animals, or avoiding the use of animals entirely whenever this can be done without compromising experimental goals.

From Biology Today, *7E by Eli C. Minkoff and Pamela J. Baker, 1996. Reprinted by permission of The McGraw-Hill Companies.*

**IN YOUR
OWN WORDS**

1. In paragraph 3, the author lists reasons for the use of animals. Which ones do you agree with?

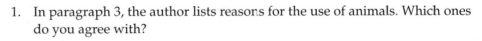

© 1994 Thaves. Reprinted with permission of Bob Thaves. Newspaper distribution by NEA, Inc.

2. Look at the cartoon above. Can this cartoon be seen as making an argument in favor of animal testing? In what way?

3. Summarize the information on animals as research subjects in paragraph 4. Define the term *vociferous* according to the context of the sentence in which it appears. Does the use of that particular word indicate a bias on the author's part? If so, what is the bias?

4. Summarize the author's arguments in paragraph 5. Are any propaganda or persuasive techniques used? If so, what are they?

5. What persuasive or propaganda techniques are used in paragraph 6? Can you see any problems with the safeguards currently in place for the treatment of animals?

6. In paragraph 8, Bernard Rollin discusses the polarization of those favoring and opposing the use of animals in research. What propaganda technique does each group use in referring to the other?

7. Explain the differences, as described in paragraph 10, between the utilitarian and deontological animal rights' positions.

8. After reading the information on the fur industry, do you favor or oppose raising animals for fur clothing? List your arguments.

9. Do you agree or disagree with Ingrid Newkirk of PETA (see paragraph 17) on the issue of drug testing? Explain your reasoning.

10. Do you think improving the treatment of experimental animals is a valid goal? What, if any, additional safeguards for their treatment should be put in place? Do you think an outside agency would be better able to monitor the care of the animals?

Read the following article by Deborah Blum for a more personal perspective on the debate on animal rights.

Bio-sketch

Deborah Blum wrote the Pulitzer Prize–winning series "The Monkey Wars" while working as a reporter for the *Sacramento Bee.* The excerpt that follows is the lead article in that series, which was first published in 1991 and has since been republished as a book. Blum received her education at the University of Wisconsin, where she was trained specifically as a science writer. Although she writes in a novelistic style, her essays are the product of a great deal of research on her part. Originally rebuffed by both sides, Blum ultimately gained the confidence of both the scientists engaged in animal research and the animal rights activists. Because she was perceived as fair, she was given unlimited access to the notes of long-time animal activist Shirley McGreal. Dr. Allen Merritt, over his department chair's objections, also allowed Blum full access to his lab. Blum herself likened her reporting on primate research as something similar to a "religious quest." At the outset, the questions that drove her were "Who are we?" and "How do we treat our fellow species?"

"The Monkey Wars"   *by Deborah Blum*

READING

On the days when he's scheduled to kill, Allen Merritt summons up his ghosts.

They come to him from the shadows of a 20-year-old memory. Eleven human babies, from his first year out of medical school. All born prematurely. All lost within one week when their lungs failed.

"We were virtually helpless," said Merritt, now head of the neonatal intensive care unit at the University of California–Davis Medical Center.

"There's nothing worse than being a new physician and standing there watching babies die. It's a strong motivator to make things different."

5   On this cool morning, he needs that memory. The experiment he's doing is deceptively simple: a test of a new chemical to help premature babies breathe. But it's no clinical arrangement of glass tubes. He's trying the drug on two tiny rhesus monkeys, each weighing barely one-third of a pound. At the end of the experiment, he plans to cut their lungs apart, to see how it worked.

Even his ghosts don't make that easy. Nestled in a towel on a surgical table, eyes shut, hands curled, the monkeys look unnervingly human. "The link between people and monkeys is very close," Merritt said. "Much closer than people would like to think. There's a real sense of sadness, that we can only get the information we need if we kill them."

Once, there was no such need to justify. Once, American researchers could go through 200,000 monkeys a year, without question. Now, the numbers are less—perhaps 20,000 monkeys will die every year, out of an estimated 40,000 used in experiments. But the pressures are greater.

These days, it seems that if researchers plan one little study—slicing the toes off squirrel monkeys, siphoning blood from rhesus macaques, hiding baby monkeys from their mothers—they face not just questions, but picket signs, lawsuits and death threats phoned in at night.

The middle ground in the war over research with monkeys and apes has become so narrow as to be nearly invisible. And even that is eroding.

10   Intelligent, agile, fast, but not fast enough, these non-human primates are rapidly being driven from the planet, lost to heavy trapping and vanishing rain forests. Of 63 primate species in Asia—where most research monkeys come from—only one is not listed as vulnerable.

Primate researchers believe they are making the hard choice, using non-human primates for medical research because they must, because no other animal so closely mirrors the human body and brain. During the 1950s, American scientists did kill hundreds of thousands of monkeys for polio research, using the animals' organs to grow virus, dissecting their brains to track the spread of the infection. But out of those experiments came a polio vaccine. Using monkeys, scientists have created vaccines for measles, learned to fight leprosy, developed anti-rejection drugs that make organ transplants possible.

Outside the well-guarded laboratory wall, that choice can seem less obvious. Animal rights advocates draw a dark description of research. They point out that AIDS researchers have used endangered chimpanzees, without, so far, managing to help people dying of the disease. Further, conservationists fear that the research is introducing dangerous infection into the country's chimpanzee breeding program, badly needed to help counter the loss of wild animals.

"They're guzzling up money and animals, and for what?" asked Shirley McGreal, head of the nonprofit International Primate Protection League. "Why not use those resources in helping sick people, why infect healthy animals?"

Her argument is that of animal advocates across the country—that scientists are sacrificing our genetic next-of-kin for their own curiosity, dubious medical gains and countless tax dollars.

15   No one is sure exactly how much money scientists spend experimenting on monkeys, although the National Institutes of Health alone allocates almost $40 million annually to its primate research programs, including one in Davis. Overall,

more than half of NIH's research grants—approaching $5 billion—involve at least some animal research.

Rats and mice are the most abundant; some 15 million are used in experiments every year. But primates are the most expensive; monkeys cost a basic $1,000, chimpanzees start at $50,000.

For people such as McGreal, these are animals in a very wrong place. McGreal's long-term goal for monkeys is simple: out of the laboratory, back into what remains of the rain forests.

"I used to think that we could persuade these people to understand what we do," said Frederick King, director of the Yerkes Regional Primate Research Center in Atlanta. "But it's impossible. And that's why I no longer describe this as a battle. I describe it as a war."

The rift is so sharp that it is beginning to reshape science itself.

20   "Science has organized," marveled Alex Pacheco, founder of the country's most powerful animal rights group, People for Ethical Treatment of Animals. "Researchers are out-lobbying us and outspending us. They've become so aggressive that it puts new pressure on us. We're going to have to fight tougher too."

In the past year, researchers have made it clear just how much they dislike the role of victim. If Pacheco wants to call scientists "sadistic bastards"—which he does frequently—then Fred King is more than ready to counter with his description of PETA: "Fanatic, fringe, one of the most despicable organizations in the country."

But beyond name-calling, the research community is realizing its political power. Its lobbyists are pushing for laws that would heavily penalize protesters who interfere with research projects. And this year, to the fury of animal rights groups, primate researchers were able to win a special exemption from the public records laws, shielding their plans for captive monkey care.

For researchers, the attention focused on them is an almost dizzying turnabout. Not so long ago, they could have hung their monkey care plans as banners across streets and no one would have read them.

"When I first started 20 years ago, monkeys were $25 each," said Roy Henrickson, chief of lab animal care at the University of California, Berkeley. "You'd use one once and you'd throw it away. I'd talk to lab vets who were under pressure about dogs and I'd say, I'm sure glad I'm in nonhuman primates. Nobody cares about them."

25   He can date the change precisely, back to 1981, the year Pacheco went undercover in the laboratory of Edward Taub. Taub was a specialist in nerve damage, working in Silver Springs, Maryland. To explore the effects of ruined nerves, he took 17 rhesus monkeys and sliced apart nerves close to the spinal column, crippling their limbs. Then he studied the way they coped with the damage.

Pacheco left the laboratory with an enduring mistrust of scientists and an armload of inflammatory photographs: monkeys wrenched into vices, packed into filthy cages. Monkeys who, with no feeling in their hands, had gnawed their fingers to the bone. Some of the wounds were oozing with infection, darkening with gangrene.

Many believe those battered monkeys were the fuse, lighting the current, combative cycle of animal rights. In the fury over the Silver Springs monkeys, Pacheco was able to build People for Ethical Treatment of Animals into a national force, and across the country, the movement gained power. Today, membership in animal advocacy groups tops 12 million; the 30 largest organizations report a combined annual income approaching $70 million.

And primate researchers have suddenly found themselves under scrutiny of the most hostile kind.

There are experiments, such as Allen Merritt's work to salvage premature infants, that the critics will sometimes reluctantly accept. The compound that Merritt is testing on young monkeys is a kind of lubricant for the lungs, a slippery ooze that coats the tissues within, allowing them to flex as air comes in and out.

30   Without the ooze—called surfactant—the tissues don't stretch. They rip. The problem for premature babies is that the body doesn't develop surfactant until late in fetal development, some 35 weeks into a pregnancy. Although artificial surfactants are now available, Merritt doesn't believe they're good enough. Two-thirds of the tiniest premature babies, weighing less than a pound at birth, still die as their lungs shred. He's trying to improve the medicine.

"There could be a scientific defense for doing that, even though it's extremely cruel," said Elliott Katz, head of In Defense of Animals, a national animal rights group, headquartered in San Rafael.

But Katz finds most of the work indefensible. He can rapidly cite examples of a different sort: a U.S. Air Force experiment, which involved draining 40 percent of the blood from rhesus macaques and then spinning them on a centrifuge, to simulate injured astronauts; a New York University study of addiction in which monkeys were strapped into metal boxes and forced to inhale concentrated cocaine fumes.

Last year, animal advocates rallied against a proposed study at the Seattle center, a plan to take 13 baby rhesus macaques from their mothers and try to drive them crazy through isolation, keeping them caged away from their mothers and without company. The scientists acknowledged that they might drive the monkeys to self-mutilation; rhesus macaques do badly in isolation, rocking, pulling out their hair, sometimes tearing their skin open.

This year, protesters have been holding candlelight vigils outside the home of a researcher at a Maryland military facility, the Uniformed Services University of the Health Sciences. That project involves cutting the toes from kittens and young squirrel monkeys and then, after they've wobbled into adjustment, killing them to look at their brains.

35   In both cases, there are scientific explanations. The Washington scientists wanted to analyze the chemistry of a troubled brain, saying that it could benefit people with mental illness. The Maryland researchers are brain-mapping, drafting a careful picture of how the mind reorganizes itself to cope with crippling injury.

But these are not—and may never be—explanations acceptable to those crusading for animal rights. "This is just an example of someone doing something horrible to animals because he can get paid for it," said Laurie Raymond, of Seattle's Progressive Animal Welfare Society, which campaigned against the baby monkey experiment and takes credit for the fact that it failed to get federal funding.

Researchers are tired of telling the public about their work, documenting it in public records—and having that very openness used against them. The Washington protesters learned about the baby monkey experiment through a meeting of the university's animal care committee—which is public. The Maryland work came to light through a listing of military funded research—which is public.

When the U.S. Department of Agriculture, which inspects research facilities annually, complained about the housekeeping at the Tulane Regional Primate Research Center in Louisiana, the director wrote the agency a furious letter. Didn't administrators realize that the report was public—and made scientists look bad?

"The point I am making is that USDA, without intending to do so, is playing into the hands of the animal rights/anti-vivisectionists whose stated goal is to abolish animal research," wrote center head Peter Gerone, arguing that the complaints could have been handled privately. "If you are trying to placate the animal rights activists by nit-picking inspections . . . you will only serve to do us irreparable harm."

40   When Arnold Arluke, a sociologist at Boston's Northeastern University, spent six years studying lab workers and drafted a report saying that some actually felt guilty about killing animals, he found himself suddenly under pressure. "I was told putting that information out would be like giving ammunition to the enemy," he said.

He titled his first talk "Guilt Among Animal Researchers." The manager of the laboratory where he spoke changed "guilt" to stress. When he published that in a journal, the editors thought that stress was too controversial. They changed the title to "Uneasiness Among Lab Workers." When he gave another talk at a pharmaceutical company, he was told uneasiness was too strong. They changed the title to "How to Deal with Your Feelings." Arluke figures his next talk will be untitled.

"People in animal research don't even want to tell others what they do," he said. "One woman I talked to was standing in line at a grocery store, and when she told the person next to her what she did, the woman started yelling at her: 'You should be ashamed of yourself.' "

And when new lab animal care rules were published this year, it was clear that researchers were no longer willing to freely hand over every record of operation.

The new regulations resulted from congressional changes in 1985 to the Animal Welfare Act. They included a special provision for the care of laboratory primates; legislators wanted scientists to recognize that these were sociable, intelligent animals.

45   The provision—perhaps the most controversial in the entire act—was called "psychological well-being of primates." When the USDA began drafting rules, in response to the new law, it received a record 35,000 letters of comment. And 14,000 consisted of a written shouting match over how to make primates happy. It took six years before the agency could come up with rules that the research community could accept.

Originally, the USDA proposed firm standards: Laboratories would have to give monkeys bigger cages, let them share space, provide them with puzzles and toys from a list.

Researchers argued that it was unreasonable. Every monkey species was different, the rigid standards might satisfy one animal and make another miserable. Now, each institution is asked to do what it thinks best for its monkeys; USDA inspectors will be free to study, criticize and ask for changes in those plans.

But animal rights groups will not. Research lobbyists persuaded the USDA to bypass the federal Freedom of Information Act; the president of the American Society of Primatologists told the agency that making the plans public would be like giving a road map to terrorists. Under the new rules, the plans will be kept at the individual institutions rather than filed with the federal government, as has been standard practice. That makes them institutional property—exempted from any requests for federal records.

Tom Wolfle, director of the Institute for Laboratory Animal Resources in Washington, D.C., the federal government's chief advisory division on animal issues, said the research community simply needed some clear space. "The idea was to prevent unreasonable criticism by uninformed people," he said.

50   Advocacy groups have sued the government over the new rules, saying they unlawfully shut the public out of research that it pays for. "In the end, they just handed everything back to the researchers and said, here, it's all yours," said Christine Stevens, an executive with the nonprofit Animal Welfare Institute.

    Stevens, daughter of a Michigan physiology researcher, finds this the ultimate contradiction, as well as "foolish and short-sighted." She thinks that science, of all professions, should be one of open ideas.

    On this point, she has some unlikely allies. Frederick King, of Yerkes, no friend to the animal rights movement, is also unhappy with the research community's tendency to withdraw. "I don't know about the law," he said. "But our plans for taking care of our primates will be open.

    "We are using taxpayers' money. In my judgment, we have an obligation to tell the public what we're about. And the fact that we haven't done that, I think, is one of the greatest mistakes over the last half-century, hell, the last century, that scientists have made."

    Against that conflict, Allen Merritt's decision to make public an experiment in which he kills monkeys was not an easy one. His wife worried that anti-research fanatics would stalk their home. His supervisors worried that animal lovers would be alienated; one administrator even called the Davis primate center, suggesting that Merritt's work should not be publicly linked to the medical school's pediatrics department.

55   But Merritt, like King, believes that his profession will only lose if it remains hidden from the public. "People need to understand what we're doing. If I were to take a new drug first to a nursery, and unforeseen complications occurred, and a baby died—who would accept that?"

    So, on a breezy morning, he opens the way to the final test of lung-lubricating surfactants that he will do this year, a 24-hour countdown for two baby monkeys. Those hours are critical to whether these drugs work. If human premature babies last from their first morning to the next one, their survival odds soar.

    The tiny monkeys—one male, one female—taken by C-section, are hurried into an intensive care unit, dried and warmed with a blow drier, put onto folded towels, hooked up to ventilators, heart monitors, intravenous drip lines. During the experiment, they will never be conscious, never open their eyes.

    "OK, let's treat," Merritt says. His technician gently lifts the tube from the ventilator, which carries oxygen into the monkey's lungs. A white mist of surfactant fills the tube, spraying into the lungs. And then, through the night, the medical team watches and waits.

    The next morning, they decide to kill the female early. An intravenous line going into her leg is starting to cause bleeding problems. The monkey is twitching a little in her unconsciousness, as if in pain. Merritt sees no point in dragging her through the experiment's official end.

60   But the male keeps breathing. As the sun brightens to midday, the scientists inject a lethal dose of anesthesia. Still, the monkey's chest keeps moving, up and down, up and down with the push of the ventilator. But, behind him, the heart monitor shows only a straight green line.

    For a few seconds, before they shut the machines down and begin the lung dissection, Allen Merritt stands quietly by the small dead monkey, marshaling the ghosts of the babies he couldn't save, a long time ago.

From "The Monkey Wars" by Deborah Blum. Copyright, The Sacramento Bee, 1998. *Reprinted by permission.*

Note: As a postscript, after the publication of this article, Dr. Allen Merritt received threatening phone calls and for his children's protection was forced to send them away from home for a short time. Though he has no real regrets about participating in the interviews, he has not spoken to Blum since the article's publication.

1. Look at paragraph 8. Explain why the phrase "one little study" is used ironically.

   _____

   _____

2. Responding to objections from the research community, Arnold Arluke had to continually change the title of his speech "Guilt Among Animal Researchers." What does this demonstrate about the attitudes of the research community as a whole?

   _____

   _____

Vocabulary

Directions: In the space before each word in column I, write the letter of its correct meaning (according to the context of the essay) in column II.

	Column I		Column II
_____	1. agile	A.	to stop from being angry; appease
_____	2. alienated	B.	fatal or deadly
_____	3. despicable	C.	relating to newborn children
_____	4. dissecting	D.	with a feeling of weakness or nervousness
_____	5. dubious	E.	nimble
_____	6. fanatic	F.	cutting apart for purpose of study
_____	7. inflammatory	G.	questionable
_____	8. lethal	H.	taking pleasure from inflicting pain
_____	9. neonatal	I.	zealous beyond reason (a person)
_____	10. placate	J.	contemptible
_____	11. sadistic	K.	likely to rouse anger, violence
_____	12. unnervingly	L.	estranged; withdrawn from

**IN YOUR
OWN WORDS**

1. How do the beliefs of the animal rights activists and the animal researchers conflict?

2. Summarize the arguments made by Shirley McGreal. Summarize Fred King's attack on animal rights activists. Which side's arguments do you believe are more persuasive? Why?

3. Which issues do you think Dr. Merritt argues most persuasively? Summarize his reasons for publicizing an experiment in which he kills monkeys.

4. Are you convinced by the arguments of the animal rights activists that there is too much animal experimentation today?

5. Do you think Deborah Blum is truly neutral? Where do you think she would draw the line killing animals?

6. Some people believe that it is acceptable to experiment on animals such as rats and rabbits, but that it is unacceptable to experiment on animals such as dogs, cats, or monkeys. How do you feel about this issue? Explain your reasoning.

7. Do you think that it is morally acceptable to experiment on humans who possess extremely low intelligence?

8. Would it be morally acceptable to experiment on persons incarcerated for particularly heinous crimes such as murder?

Chapter 13 Test: "The Monkey Wars"

Multiple Choice

1. Allen Merritt was motivated to pursue his experiments with the baby rhesus monkeys because of
    a. pressure from the animal rights activists.
    b. the deaths of premature human infants.
    c. the amount of money involved in animal experimentation.

2. A likely title for this selection would be
    a. "Animal Research—The Controversy Continues"
    b. "Allen Merritt's Animal Research"
    c. "The Increased Cost of Animal Research"
    d. "Animal Research—Too Much Red Tape"

3. Animal rights activist Shirley McGreal feels it would make more sense to
    a. spend more money on experiments with monkeys.
    b. spend money to help sick people get better rather than infect healthy animals with disease.
    c. send the chimpanzees to zoos around the country.

4. Researchers won a major victory against animal rights activists because their plans for the care of their primates
    a. will be open to inspection by animal activists.
    b. will be kept hidden from public view at the individual research institutions.
    c. will apply the same standards to each monkey species.

5. From this selection, you could infer that the term "animal advocates" refers to people who
    a. want more animal research.
    b. believe that animal research should be both humane and limited.
    c. do not take a position in relation to animal experimentation.

True or False

_____ 6. In the 1990s fewer animals are used in animal experiments and fewer animals lose their lives.

_____   7.   In the past, animal researchers faced considerably more protest than they do today.

_____   8.   The USDA has enacted strict standards to improve the mental health of primates.

_____   9.   The condition of the animals at the Silver Springs Lab helped spur a national movement to improve the treatment of animals.

_____   10. Research on animals is relatively inexpensive and is paid for by private donations.

PART 6 # Becoming Ready for Content-Area Classes

In a logically organized piece of music, one thought grows from another, and all the parts are interrelated.

from Music, An Appreciation *by Roger Kamien*

Look for connections. No matter what you're doing, everything is related. That's why we can relate practicing an instrument to building a house, learning a language, improving in a sport, cooking, getting along with people, and many other things. When you look for connections in life, you and your ideas don't have to be lonely. The more you discover similarities in things that seem different, the greater the world you can participate in.

from Marsalis on Music *by Winton Marsalis*

In Part 6 of this text we will connect what you have been learning in previous chapters to the kind of reading you will be called upon to do for your classes. We will begin with a chapter on skimming and scanning that will show you how to connect the skills you use every day to more challenging reading material. Our final chapter on jazz will introduce you to various study and test-taking skills that you can use when you are reading your own college textbooks.

Scanning and Skimming

Scanning Exercises

Scanning is the process of quickly searching reading material in order to locate specific bits of information. When you scan, you don't start at the beginning and read through to the end. Instead, what you do is jump around in the text trying to find the information you need. You probably already scan when you search for a phone number in a telephone book, go through the TV guide looking for a program to watch, or look up an unknown word in the dictionary. The purpose of this unit is to improve your scanning skills.

This section has three exercises. We will first practice doing the type of scanning you are probably already familiar with. Then we will practice scanning some more-difficult reading material.

Exercise 1

The first exercise involves scanning a page from a telephone book. The purpose of the exercise is to increase your scanning speed. Complete the exercise as quickly as you can by moving your eyes rapidly across the page to find the answers to the following questions:

1. What is A. G. Corssen's telephone number?_____

2. How many people on this page have the name of Corrigan? _____

3. Where does Rex Corsbie live? _____

4. Where does Brian Corte live? _____

5. What is Mark Corrie's phone number? _____

Exercise 2

This second exercise involves scanning a television guide (see page 360). Again, work as quickly as you can to find the answers to the following questions:

1. How many movies are being shown between 9:30 A.M. and 12:30 P.M.?

   _____

2. What time is "Mouse and the Monster"? _____

3. The website for "Computer Connection" is run by _____

4. What auto race is being shown? _____

5. What channel carries the program "Great Chefs of Hawaii"? _____

Corrgan - Cortez

CORRGAN Joseph & Judith
11011 N 92 St Sctsdl 314-1426
CORRICE B R 1242 S 80 St Mesa 373-9262
CORRICELLI W & S Phoenix 849-5202
CORRICK Marvin 46630 N 13 Av Nw Rvr 465-0258
CORRIDAN Lisa & Michael
6980 E Sahuaro Dr Sctsdl 905-3835
Timothy R 2000 W Calle Del Norte Chndlr 786-1663
CORRIDINO Nicholas 2719 E Glenrosa Av 955-7617
Nick 2256 E Ross Av 569-1604
CORRIE A 10420 N 11 St 870-7592
Darin 16819 N 42 Av 843-9257
David 8232 E Minnezona Av Sctsdl 945-0243
Joanna E 1421 S Rita Ln Tempe 894-9248
John R 12027 S Half Moon Dr Ahwtke 893-2907
M 14005 N 54 Av Glndl 938-3863
M L & Joan 8203 W Sweetwater Av Peoria 412-7906
Mark 25407 S Pinewood Dr Sn Lks 895-0282
Michael 501 E Vaughn Av Glbrt 926-2090
Mike 606 S 79 Pl Mesa 380-0967
CORRIERE Charles 2034 N 21 Pl 267-9585
E 8607 E Coronado Rd Sctsdl 945-4791
Vickie 903 N Lesueur Mesa 835-7266
CORRIERO Donald G
14416 N Calle Del Oro Fntn Hls 837-3852
Frank 977-1230
CORRIGAN Betsy 4700 E Main Mesa 641-3560
Betty 6444 N 67 Av Glndl 934-1358
Brendan 1415 N Country Club Dr Mesa 964-4625
C E Phoenix 956-0857
Chris 1711 S Extension Rd Mesa 898-9188
Dan 7508 N 21 St 861-3390
Daniel J 2623 S Patterson Mesa 820-0178
Mesa American L L 2623 S Patterson St Mesa 756-2607
Debbie & Patrick 9152 E Wier Av Mesa 986-1999
Dennis 7601 W John Cabot Rd Glndl 938-9870
Don & Jean 301 S Signal Butte Rd Mesa 986-4459
Earl J & Lavon M
10545 E Cinnabar Av Sctsdl 614-1645
Ed 5501 E Dallas St Mesa 985-2744
Edward 10120 Candlewood Dr Sn Cy 933-2213
Fritz 36402 N Peaceful Pl Crfree 488-2586
Fritz W & Glenda
6214 E Evening Glow Dr Sctsdl 595-0360
Fritz W & Glenda
10160 E Old Trail Rd Sctsdl 595-1157
Gerry 1103 W Marconi Av 866-7425
J 4530 E Hearn Rd 485-1026
Jack 854-1795
James F 13131 E Ocotillo Rd Chndlr 802-4885
John 4010 W Angela Dr 938-3876
John 15236 N 6 Cir 863-6281
John J 12734 Paintbrush Dr Sn Cy W 584-5934
Karen D 2916 E Amber Ridge Wy 759-2767
M 4530 E Hearn Rd 485-1026
M 5625 W Crocus Dr Glndl 843-9308
M C 5333 E Thomas Rd 952-1226
Martin 704 W Mission Dr Chndlr 899-5252
Michael 7115 E Bell Cir Mesa 396-3363
Michael F 13010 S 42 Pl 893-3593
Michael & Janice 18250 N Cave Creek Rd 493-3330
Michele 4010 W Angela Dr 938-3876
Mike 1324 E Bayview Dr Tempe 345-9381
Mike G 3338 N 67 St Sctsdl 675-0341
R 482-0933
Rebecca 2045 S McClintock Dr Tempe 731-9187
Rhea 837-2082
Robert 17407 N 56 Wy 971-0848
Steve 6599 E Thomas Rd Sctsdl 423-5294
Thomas 3811 E University Dr Mesa 832-5587
Toni & Keith 658 S Windsor Mesa 655-1031
Victoria 8724 E Heatherbrae Dr Sctsdl 946-4660
CORRIN Pat 7633 E Rancho Vista Dr Sctsdl 970-3408
CORRINGTON Carol 3125 W Claremont St 841-6034
Christi 815 N 52 St 231-0151
David L & Jennifer 4517 W Kristal Wy 516-1265
Janet 18328 E Riggs Rd Chndlr Hts 988-1493
Jim & Kristen 28638 N 46 Pl 502-8448
M J 12814 N 26 Pl 992-4520
Maurice (Mike) 3322 N 17 Av 264-0432
Moira 8936 W Peck Dr Glndl 872-2793
Paul D 2647 E Kenwood St Mesa 827-8904
S L 12814 N 26 Pl 992-4520
CORRINS Ron 4700 E Main Mesa 396-8302
CORRION Edward 14823 S 20 Pl 759-2309
CORRIS Brian 6052 E Thunderbird Rd 922-5763
Brian 6052 E Thunderbird Rd 991-1101
John W 3311 E Dry Creek Rd 706-1681
CORRISTON William 910 N Stapley Dr Mesa 898-0132
CORRITORE Bob 8221 E Garfield St Sctsdl 994-1234
Fax Line 8221 E Garfield St Sctsdl 994-1693
John
Mobile Service Dial 1 & Then 377-1234
John 6601 E Fanfol Dr Prds Vly 948-1423
John 6601 E Fanfol Dr Prds Vly 948-8865
Paul J 7558 E Bogart Av Mesa 985-0921
Sam J 1825 W Emelita Av Mesa 844-8694
CORRIVEAU Jason & Jennifer
1519 N Warner Dr Apch Jctn 288-9943
Mike 303 W 16 Av Apch Jctn 983-3561
Norman 5832 E Boston St Mesa 807-8780
Roland W 3255 S Dorsey Ln Tempe 491-4394
CORRON A R 2607 N 36 St 231-0836
Evelyn 3104 E Broadway Rd Mesa 924-0108
CORROO Matthew J 1602 E Culver St 257-1546
William 10943 E Gary Rd Sctsdl 451-8953
CORROW Matt 3645 N Marshall Wy Sctsdl 423-0369
Richard 3645 N Marshall Wy Sctsdl 423-0606
CORRUGEDO Rosario 1724 W Glenrosa Av 265-4735
CORRY B 79 W Buena Vista Dr Tempe 345-2417
Beverly C MD
Children's Health Center Of St Joseph's
124 W Thomas Rd 406-6947
2nd Floor
David R 14222 S 44 St 961-5181
F Sctsdl 391-3373
Loretta 22701 N Black Canyon Hwy 582-0406
Tracey & Robert 4124 W Alameda Rd 780-4957

CORRY Tyler Sctsdl 314-7374
W 1780 W Ivanhoe St Chndlr 963-3618
William A 23415 N 39 Ln 582-0890
William J 22701 N Black Canyon Hwy 582-0406
CORS Alvin 938 S Rochester Mesa 832-8068
M E 14010 N Wendover Dr Fntn Hls 837-2024
CORSAIR D J 7310 E Palm Ln Sctsdl 994-1158
CORSARO Joseph R 4861 E Hobart St Mesa 981-7978
R 837 E Grandview St Mesa 964-9647
CORSAUT Chuck & Jo
1797 W 28 Av Apch Jctn 671-4261
CORSBERG Herbert R
13840 N Desert Harbor Dr Peoria 933-7589
S 15757 N 90 Pl Sctsdl 614-1617
CORSBIE Rex 1101 S Ellsworth Rd Mesa 380-0520
CORSCADDEN Robert A
7728 W Maui Ln Peoria 412-1130
CORSE Donald J 6308 S Sundown Dr Chndlr 895-5053
Phil 9708 E Via Linda St Sctsdl 661-6957
Taylor & Michelle 756-0957
CORSENTINO Joseph 7529 E Ed Rice Av Mesa 807-4958
CORSETTE B 3113 E Highland Av 957-0516
CORSETTI B 874-9176
Benita 6520 W Becker Ln Glndl 487-8234
Daniel & Maryellen
8639 S Maple Av Tempe 820-9055
Tanja 13775 N 103 Wy Sctsdl 314-7491
CORSI C 4925 E Desert Cove Av 905-0332
D R 1631 E Villa Maria Dr 482-3907
J 610 E Gilbert Dr Tempe 921-0992
L B 10133 Pinehurst Dr Sn Cy 974-5973
N 523 S Hilton Rd Apch Jctn 982-6627
Nicholas J 9684 E Sutton Dr Sctsdl 614-8492
CORSICA Carol J 6445 S Maple Av Tempe 839-8505
CORSINI Gerardo 4348 E Coolbrook Av 404-4615
CORSINO S F 8207 E Berridge Ln Sctsdl 948-6110
CORSO D 5420 E Via Del Cielo Prds Vly 991-8264
David 322 E Beatrice St Tempe 945-5027
Frank D 11018 E Santan Blvd Sn Lks 895-8502
George P 22852 N 91 Wy Sctsdl 585-7713
Henry 7785 E Via Del Futuro Sctsdl 991-7894
James P 2015 Old West Hwy Apch Jctn 671-3668
Leroy 13622 W Bolero Dr Sn Cy W 546-1060
Les & Elsie 702 S Meridian Dr Mesa 984-4681
Nanette 12218 N 104 St Sctsdl 451-3010
Nanette ins 7202 E Ho Rd Crfree 488-2766
Phil 5420 E Via Del Cielo Prds Vly 998-0340
Robert 10336 Cumberland Dr Sn Cy 974-1720
S F Dr 946-9109
Susan Dr 945-2402
Victoria 510 W Pebble Beach Dr Tempe 966-9953
Wayne 2055 E Hampton Av Mesa 813-4243
CORSON A J 2002 W Sunnyside Dr 943-2220
A W 7844 S 9 St 268-1138
Alan 650 W Elena Av Mesa 834-4920
Alvin W 10937 E Pueblo Av Apch Jctn 986-7710
Barbara 2842 E Cholla St 788-8387
Crystal 2921 W Potter Dr 581-1801
Crystal Nicolet & Eric 9420 N 48 Dr Glndl 934-4342
F Todd 1819 S Heritage Mesa 839-1381
Francis 4129 E Ridge Rd 437-2612
George 14534 W Moccasin Tr Srprse 546-1810
Glen 9420 N 48 Dr Glndl 931-8059
H T Sctsdl 991-4734
Harry E 17200 W Bell Rd Srprse 214-1537
Helen Sctsdl 905-1540
Jack 1349 N Entrada St Chndlr 899-0851
Jack 7710 E Gainey Ranch Rd Sctsdl 951-3321
Janice 3501 N 64 St Sctsdl 994-8237
Kimball J 35808 N 15 Av 581-3769
Kimball J atty 40 N Central Av 253-1740
Len & Beth 6730 E McDowell Rd Sctsdl 423-9747
Len & Beth 13611 N Woodside Dr Fntn Hls 837-9322
R 1734 E Tara Dr Chndlr 963-7794
Randall 585-5727
Roy R 3823 E Glenrosa Av 955-0798
S G 13213 Cedar Dr Sn Cy 977-8934
Stephen F 4950 N Miller Rd Sctsdl 423-8332
W 995-9382
CORSSEN A G 6210 E Laurel Ln Sctsdl 991-4948
CORSTANGE Bruce R 3040 E Shea Blvd 482-8306
CORTABITARTE Rick 5963 W Gary Dr Chndlr 940-0153
CORTAZZO Fred 8215 E Cambridge Av Sctsdl 990-2099
L 5225 E Hearn Rd 996-4742
CORTE Brian 1131 N 71 St Sctsdl 994-1640
Curt & Arlene 818 N Ahoy Dr Glbrt 507-5675
Guenter 2524 S El Paradiso Dr Mesa 838-3963
Jerome 16453 N 29 Dr 504-6521
Jose Daniel 3802 N 27 St 912-0749
Joseph A 10901 E Palomino Rd Sctsdl 860-1731
Leonard phD 31 E Vernon Av 229-1233
Rosalie 3302 E Campbell Av 381-1071
CORTELL George 13015 N 37 Pl 493-0995
John P 12425 Fieldstone Dr Sn Cy W 546-1725
CORTELLESSA Anne 115 W Diana Av 331-4363
CORTEN James & Edith 4328 E Capri Av Mesa 654-0453
CORTER Carol 7127 W Reade Av Glndl 846-4975
CORTES Alfred B 3619 W Ocotillo Rd 841-8164
Bryon 3800 W Chandler Blvd Chndlr 821-9276
Cirilo F 2502 N 32 St 955-6564
Daniel 8650 S 17 Wy 268-1259
Dawn 1050 S Longmore Mesa 610-8670
Elduvina 2222 E Burgess Ln 268-4910
Esperanza 4252 E Minton St 437-0312
Gabriel A 4707 E McDowell Rd 220-9548
Hector M 4822 W Altadena Av 439-0299
Helen 9018 W Sheridan St 907-0513
Jorge 6231 W McDowell Rd 245-3310
Jose 264 E 9 Dr Mesa 464-7671
Juan 2055 E Broadway Rd Mesa 965-6476
Juan C 872-3988
Juan M 2139 E Howe Av Tempe 303-9621
Karen 1966 E Vinedo Ln Tempe 839-8534
Luis A 4335 W Royal Palm Rd Glndl 939-1697
Manuel 17030 N 15 St 482-6506
Matthew 3543 W Lamar Rd 973-1735
Mayra 625 W 1 St Tempe 350-9573
O 863 N Cherry Mesa 833-8294
Ozzie & Addie 8933 W Echo Ln Peoria 872-8137

- **PREFER NOT TO BE CONTACTED BY TELEMARKETING OR DIRECT MAIL ORGANIZATIONS**

C

CORTES Raul 2108 S Rural Rd Tempe 303-0061
Richard D 1540 E Mission Ln 997-4172
CORTESE B 736-0691
Bruno 930 N 86 Wy Sctsdl 990-7318
Charles & Debbie
4301 E Saint Catherine Av 437-1960
David 3831 E Camelback Rd 468-3112
Doug Phoenix 277-5828
Duilio A 12503 W Rampart Dr Sn Cy W 546-8330
Felix 2039 E Glenhaven Dr 460-2735
G M 999 E Baseline Rd Tempe 413-1429
Jim & Donna 5732 E Monte Cristo Av 493-0306
Marcia marriage & family counselor
2211 E Highland Av 468-9338
Phil 7909 E Wilshire Dr Sctsdl 946-9110
Rodolfo 5860 W Coolidge St 846-6654
CORTESE-CALDWELL Linda
1320 N McQueen Rd Chndlr 857-3355
CORTESI Susan MD
2248 N Alma School Rd Chndlr 899-1500
CORTEZ A E 326 W Earll Dr 241-9178
Abigel 4545 N 15 St 265-4097
Alfredo N 5008 E Thomas Rd 808-0662
Amado Salas 3337 E Taylor St 273-6616
Anthony 15425 N 25 St 485-9263
Armando 17031 N 11 Av 863-3283
Arnold & Wendy 3021 E Menlo St Mesa 854-7856
B 6302 W Rose Ln Glndl 939-1146
Brian J 5927 W Harmont Dr Glndl 435-9138
C P 610 W La Donna Dr Tempe 839-0659
Carlos 1821 E Covina St Mesa 964-7462
Charles 13602 N 44 St 996-6452
Dan 8204 S 40 St 437-3747
David 625 N Alma School Rd Chndlr 899-5633
Devin & Kate 4731 N 105 Dr 877-1418
E L 8319 E San Miguel Av Sctsdl 994-4322
Eduardo R 4141 W McDowell Rd 455-9154
Edward 3428 E El Moro Av Mesa 830-6626
Edward 9361 W Fillmore St Tllsn 907-0089
Edward M 1603 W Garfield St 256-9136
Eldio S 644 W Main St Mesa 969-9485
Elvin O 4305 W Claremont St Glndl 435-5639
Eric 6112 N 67 Av Glndl 934-2220
Estrella Z 1748 E Yale St 340-0710
Evelyn 11600 N 75 Av Peoria 487-8362
Frank 938 E Jones Av 243-4190
Frank 4707 E McDowell Rd 275-3719
Gil & Lolly Glbrt 892-7481
Gilbert 706-5893
Gilbert 5756 W Avalon Dr 247-0935
Greg 5738 W Pierson St 247-1040
Guadalupe 3316 W Polk St 269-3464
Hubertino 5701 W Roma Av 247-6422
Imelda 5954 W Geronimo Ct Chndlr 940-3605
Ismael 6041 W Medlock Dr Glndl 435-5510
Jaime 1555 W 7 Dr Mesa 461-1894
Jaime A 1029 S Vineyard Mesa 649-0841
Jesse 6231 N 67 Av Glndl 934-0656
Jesus Manuel 6711 N 35 Av 589-5065
Joaquin 1105 N 8 St Avndl 932-5732
Joe 924 S Oakwood Dr Tempe 834-9201
John Anthony 1833 E Oak St 253-7509
Johnny 2917 W Palm Ln 269-9639
Johnny 10100 N 89 Av Peoria 486-1262
Jose Luis 14633 N 31 Av 789-6242
Juan 4741 S 36 Av 276-9102
Juan 7832 W Julie Dr Glndl 572-0408
K 8030 W Elm St 846-1577
Leticia 614 W Apache St 238-9692
Lucas 1538 W McDowell Rd 257-4218
Luis & Rhonda M
1054 N Golden Key St Glbrt 892-0318
Luz 918 S Fontana Mesa 396-8584
Magdaleno 946 E Illini St 276-1349
Manuel 1722 W Peoria Av 870-8491
Maria 108 N 15 St 253-9680
Maria 516 W Euclid Av 276-2283
Maria 4620 W McDowell Rd 233-8756
Maria 10002 N 7 St 997-8172
Maria Del Socorro A
12717 W Tasha Dr Srprse 583-3409
Maria Lourdes 7113 N 53 Av Glndl 939-4074
Maria Pano 2336 W Pinchot Av 495-1316
Maria Pano 2822 E Adams St 275-2733
Marta 743 W Ray Rd Chndlr 786-3538
Miguel 11350 W Tennessee Av Yngtwn 876-9848
Mike 5308 W Edgemont Av 269-1156
N P chf mstr sgt ret 5809 N 45 Dr Glndl 931-7076
Nestor 4326 N 35 Av 246-7936
Obtabia D 1463 E Fillmore St 257-8172
Pam L 1862 S Loma Del Sur Cir Mesa 831-6508
Pedro 2525 W Campbell Av 249-9532
Pedro 4211 W Roosevelt St 352-8438
R 2726 E Villa Theresa Dr 971-7021
R C 2054 W Gila Ln Chndlr 899-7518
R M 8604 W Mariposa Dr 846-7108
Raul M 10305 N 15 Av 944-3004
Ray L Sr 6013 W Gardenia Av Glndl 939-4951
Ricardo 2319 E McArthur Dr Tempe 731-3041
Rick 2343 W Village Dr 866-3940
Rolando 2942 E Indian School Rd 553-8655
Ronald 8602 E Cambridge Av Sctsdl 990-7674
Ruben 1234 E Georgia Av 279-9269
Rufina 2836 E Garfield St 681-3824
S 132 W Riverside St 305-9958
S 2226 W Heatherbrae Dr 265-3365
S 4731 N 105 Dr 877-3511
S H 242-0292
Sandy 17625 N 7 St 404-3743
Steve 17625 N 7 St 992-3517

From U.S. West Direct Metro Phoenix 1997/98 White Pages. *Reprinted by permission*

Saturday

9:30AM
11AM

9:30 (2)(11) U.S. Open Golf (CC) 6:00
Third-round play at the Congressional Country Club in Bethesda, Md. See the Close-up on p. 59. (Live) 6480207/33175/30/33151725

(5)(13) Ninja Turtles (CC) 24443/69153
(7) Americana Outdoors 19511
(8) Baking with Julia (CC) 17153
(9) Eerie, Indiana (CC)—Comedy 38269
(10) Infomercial
(13) DuckTales (CC)—Cartoon 94849
(21) Colby's Clubhouse (E)—Religion 92269
(33) Oscar's Orchestra—Cartoon 85917
(61) Spider-Man (CC)—Cartoon 614917
(A&E) Zorro's Fighting Legion 95911
(DIS) Arts and Minds 360559
(CNB) Infomercials 2:00
(CNN) Travel Guide 155733
A tour of Denver. Valerie Voss hosts.
(DIS) Animal Adventures (CC) 362917
(DSC) Great Chefs of Hawaii—Cooking 519917
(ES2) Motoworld 5114199
(FAM) Boogies Diner—Teenagers 780443
(FSA) Outdoor Trails—Fishing 717443
(HBO) Long Shots: The Life and Times of the...
(ABA) (CC) 1:00 498761
(MTV) Grind 788085
(SCI) Making of 'Batman & Robin' 2187269
(TLC) Renovation Guide—Bob Villa 702511
(TNN) Bassmasters—Fishing 717443

10 AM (5)(13) Cooking with Beth and Bill 82269—Children 36375/88375
(7) Gold Hour 1:00 46240
(8) Jacques Pepin's Kitchen 29085
(9) Life with Louie (CC) (E)—Cartoon 81849
(10)(WGN) Xena: Warrior Princess (CC)—Adventure 1:00 64248/877424
(13) New Adventures of Winnie the Pooh (CC) (E) 1:00 14820
(20) Kids' Club (CC) 97627
(33) TeleDla 73443
(45) Eagle Riders—Cartoon 68153
(61) Goosebumps (CC)—Thriller 419559
(A&E) Auto Racing 2:00 92849
The Jasper Engines 200. (Live)
(BRV) [M] Our Miss Brooks 1:25 6150581
(CNN) On the Menu—Cuisine 960375
(COM) Make Me Laugh—Game 80337
(DIS) [M] We're Back: A Dinosaur's Story (CC)—Cartoon 1:15 2855379
(DSC) Home Matters 1:00 462606
(ESN) Coming Attractions 404627
(ES2) The Jasper Engines 200. (Live)
(FAM) Family Challenge—Game 1:00 217172
(FSA) Ride Guide Mountain Bike Show 96559
(FX) Vegas—Crime Drama 1:00 3829443

For details of movies on premium channels, see page 199.

(FAM) [M]★★★ Rhubarb—Comedy (BW) 1:35 1967646 Ray Milland, Jan Sterling.
(MTV) Jams 1:00 215714
(NIK) Rugrats (CC)—Cartoon 312191
(SCI) Sci-Fi Buzz—Magazine 8266356
(TLC) Home Pro—Home Improvement 507153
(TNN) My Classic Car—Automobiles 512085
(TNT) [M]★★ Zone Troopers—Science Fiction 2:00 720917
(1986) In WWII Italy, extraterrestrials help GIs battle Nazis. Tim Thomerson, Art La Fleur.
(USA) WWF Livewire—Wrestling 1:00 660240

10:30 (8) Martha Stewart Living (CC) 71849
(13) Storybreak (OC) 8433752375
(8) Pierre Franey's Cooking in Europe 27725
(9) X-Men (CC)—Cartoon 14191
(21) Faithville—Children 87849
(45) Flash Gordon (CC)—Cartoon 47269
(61) Eerie, Indiana (CC)—Comedy 9677511
(BET) Benson—Comedy 329337
(CNN) Parenting Today—Magazine 408337
A Father's Day-themed program. Pat Etheridge hosts.
(COM) Make Me Laugh—Game 70559
(DSC) Behind the Scenes 992207
(ESN) Futbol Mundial—Soccer 47207
(HBO) [M] Revenge of the Nerds III: The Next Generation (CC)—Comedy 1:30 168733
Robert Carradine, Ted McGinley.
(NIK) Angry Beavers—Cartoon 860153
(SCI) Trailer Park (CC) 5556375
(TLC) Renovation Guide—Home Improvement 1207743
(TNN) Hot Rod TV—Magazine 720527
(TNT) [M]★★ The Bad News Bears—Comedy 1:45 98197882
(1976) Walter Matthau coaches an inept sandlot-baseball team. Tatum O'Neal, Vic Morrow.

10:50 (THC) [M]★ Teenage Mutant Ninja Turtles III (CC)—Fantasy 1:40 27524191 Elias Koteas.

10:55 (MAX) [M]★★★ Eye of the Wolf (CC)—Drama 1:40 23299795 Jeff Fahey.

11 AM (5) To Be Announced 1:00
(7) WCW Wrestling 1:00 66004
(8) Home Cooking with Amy Coleman 44733
(9) Infomercial
(10) American Gladiators (CC) 1:00 84424
(13) Bill Nye the Science Guy (CC) (E) 11443
(15) Mi Gente My People 1:00 18004
(21) Carol Lawrence 44375
(33) Super sábado—Variedades 2:00 336202
(45) Dragon Ball Z—Cartoon 15801
(A&E) Life with Louie (CC) 442627
(BET) 20th Century 1:00 309838
(CNN) Caribbean Rhythms—Music 1:00 417066
(DIS) Your Health 990733
A series on men continues with a report on baldness and a segment on prostate health.
(COM) Saturday Night (CC) 1:00 25898
(DSC) Lynette Jennings (CC) 1:00 404022
(ESN) 'Batman & Robin' Premiere 1:00 149288
(ES2) Karate 1:00 7491849

11AM
12:30PM

Saturday

(FAM) Bowling (CC) 1:30 29608
The final round of the Wichita Open. Jess Stayrook defeated Butch Stoper in the final game last year. (Live)
(21) Up on Melody Mountain 61801
(45) [M]★★ The Duellists (CC)—Drama 2:00 88917
(British; 1978) Striking swashbuckler, with Keith Carradine and Harvey Keitel as rival cavalry officers of the Napoleonic Wars.
(61) Dragon Flyz—Cartoon 98191
(A&E) Investigative Reports 1:00 594608
(BET) Infomercials 98191
(CNN) Computer Connection (CC) 422917
A Web site run by Georgia Tech University's French campus. Brian Nelson hosts.
(COM) Daily Show 54511
(DSC) Popular Mechanics 1:00 592240
(ESN) Talk Soup Weekend 1:00 689608
(ES2) Road to Indy—Auto Racing 246559
(FNC) Rev It Up—Motor Sports 2562882
(FSA) Crier Report 1:00
(FX) Bowling 1:30 23904
ABC World Team Challenge competition in Kansas City. Taped June 8, 1997.
(FX) Trapper John, M.D. 1:00 4825424
(HBO) [M]★★ Armed and Dangerous (CC)—Comedy 1:30 115240 John Candy.
(LTF) Men's Room—Discussion 103761
(MTV) News 3:00 5070207
(NIK) House of Style—Fashion 303789
(NIK) Rocko's Modern Life (CC) 884733
(SHD) My Life as a Dog (CC) 424375
(TLC) Renovation Guide—Bob Villa 425135
(TNN) Auto Racing 2:00 53849
The Winston, NASCAR's all-star event at the Charlotte Motor Speedway in Concord, N.C. Taped May 17, 1997.
(TNT) [M] Broken Trust (CC)—Drama 2:00 525559
(Made for Cable; 1995) A respected judge (Tom Selleck) gets entangled in a sting operation to trap some colleagues, but his involvement could alter the outcome of a murder trial.
(USA) [M] Hush Little Baby (CC)—Thriller 2:00 965207
(Made for Cable; 1993) A psychopath (Diane Ladd) is reunited with the daughter she gave up for adoption years earlier. Wendel Meldrum.
(WGN) Andy Griffith—Comedy (BW) 631559

12:30 (3) Emergency Call (CC) 82443
(7) Infomercial
(9)(10) In the Zone (CC) 32085/30627
(21) God's News—Religion 96085
(61) Dinosaurs (CC)—Comedy 616733
(CNN) Moneyweek (CC) 166849
(COM) Daily Show 89795
(ESN) Pool 1:00 387207
The Ultimate 9-Ball Challenge in Orlando. Taped Jan. 9, 1997.

(FAM) [M]★★★ The Scalphunters—Western 2:00 599714
(1968) A fur trapper (Burt Lancaster) and a runaway slave team up against cutthroats.
(FNC) Movietone News 1:00
(FSA) Pennant Chase—Baseball 91269
(FX) Hart to Hart 1:00 3849207
(LTF) The Dish—Magazine 604559
(MTV) Singled Out—Game 699627
(NIK) Hey Arnold! (CC)—Cartoon 352559
(SCI) [M] Deep Red (CC)—Science Fiction 2:00 5762882
(1994) A detective (Michael Biehn) must guard an alien protein that ensures immortality.
(TLC) Furniture to Go—Restoration 554801
(TNN) Motor Trend TV 569733
(USA) Pacific Blue (CC) 1:00 680004
(WGN) Hercules: The Legendary Journeys (CC)—Adventure 1:00 897288

11:15 (DIS) [M]★★★ Muppet Treasure Island (CC)—Comedy 1:40 31287191 Tim Curry.

11:30 (2)(11)(12) U.S. Open Golf Continues
(9) Infomercial
(3) Travels in Europe 45462
(9) Mouse and the Monster 74998
(13) Nick News (E)—Children 14172
(21) Date with Dale—Dale Evans 45004
(45) WMAC Masters—Martial Arts 16530
(45) X-Men (CC)—Cartoon 443356
(AMC) [M]★★★ Sayonara (CC)—Drama 2:35 9132795
(1957) Love and prejudice in postwar Japan. Marlon Brando, Miiko Taka, Red Buttons. [Shown in letter-box format.]
(BRV) [M]★★ A Day In October—Drama 1:40 718849
(Danish-U.S.; 1992) Jews shelter a Resistance fighter (D.B. Sweeney) in Nazi-held Copenhagen. Kelly Wolf, Tovah Feldshuh.
(CNB) Infomercials 2:30
(CNN) Your Money 991462
(FSA) Fantasy Baseball Weekly 92998
(LTF) The Wire—Magazine 605288
(MTV) Darla—Cartoon 690356
(NYK) Aaahh!!! Real Monsters (CC) 353288
(TLC) Home Savvy 555530
(TNT) Truck Competition 560462

11:45 (MAX) [M]★★★ Eye of the Wolf (CC)—Drama 1:40 23299795 Jeff Fahey.

AFTERNOON

Noon (3) Pets on Parade 55801
(5)(13) Sports Show (CC) 2:00 1651/68511
Top men and women compete in the U.S.A. Outdoor Track and Field Championships in Bloomington, Ind. Tim Ryan, Craig Masback.
(7) Real Estate Classifieds 93085
(8) This Old House (CC)—Children 91627
(9) Gladiators 2000—Children 32153
(10) Extremists—Adventurers 32135

TV Guide, Phoenix Edition, June 14–20, 1997, pp. 60–61.

Exercise 3

The following exercises make use of an excerpt from *Biology Today* by Eli C. Minkoff and Pamela J. Baker (McGraw-Hill). The excerpt appears below the exercises. Work as quickly as you can to find the answers to the following questions.

A. Scan the excerpt below on pesticides to answer the following questions:

   1. What chemical did the ancient Romans use on their grapes? _____

   2. Twentieth-century pesticides are derived from what substance?

       _____

   3. Approximately how many insect species are DDT-resistant? _____

   4. What do the initials IPM stand for? _____

   5. The term _____means that all available tools are used in a mix of strategies.

   6. What is the name of a crop that has long been of commercial importance in the South?_____

   7. The _____bug is a natural enemy of the boll weevil.

   8. _____ (state) and _____ (country) have successfully controlled cotton pests.

   9. _____ are chemicals normally used in animal communication.

   10. _____ is used by female pink boll worms to attract mates.

B. Now carefully read the article and answer the following questions:

True or False

   _____ 1. It is not necessary to know a pest's natural enemies in order to use IPM.

   _____ 2. Chemical pesticides are used in many countries because they increase crop yield.

   _____ 3. DDT is now banned in most industrialized countries.

   _____ 4. In order to control pests, it is better to plant crops in pure stands.

   _____ 5. Sometimes corn and wheat are interplanted with cotton to control the spread of pests.

Multiple Choice

   6. Chemical pesticides
      a. are a modern invention.
      b. began with DDT.
      c. have been used for many centuries.

   7. What pesticide was commonly used in the nineteenth century?
      a. sulfur
      b. arsenic
      c. DDT

   8. The term *management* in IPM means
      a. budget controls.
      b. decreasing the use of DDT.
      c. keeping pest populations under control.

9. Spraying cotton with chemical pesticides
   a. initially reduced the level of pests.
   b. caused an eventual increase in pest populations.
   c. Both *a* and *b*.

10. Most DDT pesticides are derived from
    a. plastic.
    b. petroleum.
    c. corn and wheat.

11. Which of the following would be the best title for this article?
    a. "The Use and Misuse of DDT"
    b. "Advantages of Integrated Pest Management over Chemicals"
    c. "Control of Pests by Spraying Pheromones"

12. In the context of paragraph 3, the word *derivatives* means
    a. things mixed with.
    b. things abandoned by.
    c. things obtained from.

13. The mode of writing used in this article is primarily
    a. descriptive.
    b. narrative.
    c. expository.

14. The author of this article is likely to support
    a. the use of pheromones and predator species.
    b. the manufacturing and selling of DDT.
    c. None of the above.

15. In relation to paragraph 6, paragraph 7 was written to
    a. give a definition of predator species.
    b. discuss the successful use of chemical pesticides.
    c. explain the problems chemical pesticides cause.

"Pesticides" *by Eli C. Minkoff and Pamela J. Baker*

READING

Pesticides   Chemical pesticides were used in ancient times. (The Romans dusted sulfur, which we now know acts as a fungicide, on their grapes.) Enormous increases in the use of chemical pesticides occurred during the late nineteenth and twentieth centuries. Arsenic and copper compounds were widely used in the nineteenth century, but an increasing number of twentieth-century pesticides have been derived from petroleum. During the first several decades of their use, chemical pesticides greatly reduced the level of crop damage due to pests, and they continue to be used in many countries because they increase crop yields.

For much of the twentieth century, economic pressure encouraged the use of chemical pesticides, both for crop treatment and for postharvest treatment with fungicides. The postharvest treatments have given many farm products longer shelf lives, allowing transportation across longer distances. As a result, people in the industrialized world have come to expect perfect, blemish-free produce in every store and at most any time of the year, even for crops that do not grow at all in their local area.

Consequences of Pesticide Use   There are many problems associated with the use of chemical pesticides such as DDT. The pesticides themselves are generally expensive; most of them are petroleum derivatives, and a great deal of energy is used in their extraction and further synthesis. Attempts to control pests with chemical pesticides have in several cases brought about increased levels of pest-related devastation several decades later. Pesticides like DDT are toxic to a wide variety of harmful and beneficial species alike. They may kill so many of the target species' natural enemies that the population size of the target species subsequently increases (after a time delay) above its earlier levels. Another problem with frequent pesticide use is that the target species develop pesticide-resistant mutations so that the pests no longer respond to the spraying. Over 400 insect species, for example, are now DDT-resistant. Widespread use of the same pesticide year after year favors the evolution of pesticide-resistant mutant strains. Once they originate, these resistant strains of pest species spread rapidly because of selection by the pesticide itself.

DDT is now banned in most of the industrialized countries, though it is still used in some parts of the Third World. Unfortunately, the banning of DDT use in many countries has resulted in the development and use of other chemicals that are even more toxic to nontarget species, including humans.

5 **Integrated Pest Management (IPM)** (IPM) is a newer approach to crop pest management, one that uses a combination of techniques. The term *management* is meant to convey the intent to keep pest populations under control, so that they stay below the levels at which they cause economic harm. Total pest eradication is in most cases viewed as a goal that can only be achieved at an unacceptably high cost (including the cost to the environment or to society as a whole) or which cannot be achieved at any cost. The term *integrated* means that all available tools are used in a mix of strategies that includes chemical controls (such as pesticides), biological controls (such as the maintaining of a population of the pest's natural enemies), cultural control (such as public education), and regulatory control (such as public policy legislation). Integrated pest management requires the monitoring of pest populations to assess the possible damage that they may do and to allow the application of no more pesticide than is necessary to control pest populations below acceptable limits. Because integrated pest management relies more on biological controls than previous techniques, it requires a good working knowledge of the ecology of the pest species, especially a knowledge of its natural enemies and the other factors that control its numbers.

Introduction of Predator Species Planting crops in smaller, separated patches instead of pure stands [a field planted with a single crop] is one way in which the spread of pest species can be controlled without the use of chemical pesticides. Planting seasons may be modified so as to interrupt the life cycles of the pests. The most important techniques in integrated pest management, however, are those that take advantage of the natural enemies that keep the pest species in check. Rather than focusing on killing the pest directly, an effort is made to identify a predator that specifically targets the crop pest. If such a species can be identified, then any measure that encourages the growth, development, and proliferation of the predators will keep the pests in check.

For example, cotton has long been a crop of commercial importance in the southern United States, India, Egypt, and elsewhere. Traditional pests included the boll weevil and the pink boll worm. Spraying with chemical pesticides initially reduced the levels of these pests, but, by the 1960s, pesticide resistance had developed in both species. Despite increased spraying, pest populations continued to increase. Worse yet, the chemical sprays destroyed many of the pests' natural enemies, such as the spined soldier bug, and the destruction of the natural predators allowed other pest species, such as the tobacco bud worm (previously unimportant as a pest of cotton), to become significant pests—in some cases more devastating than the traditional ones.

In both Texas and Peru, integrated pest management techniques have been successfully used to control cotton pests. Soldier bugs and other natural predators are collected, reared, and released on the cotton fields, while chemical spraying has been greatly reduced and is used only selectively, though not eliminated entirely. The planting season is timed so as to disrupt the life cycle of the boll worm moth; when the moths emerge, they can find no cotton plants on which to lay their eggs. Stalks and other unused parts of the plants are shredded and plowed under soon after each harvest, denying to the pests places to hide until the next growing season. In some places, corn and wheat are interplanted with the cotton in order to encourage the growth of natural predators and to reduce the ability of the cotton pests to spread from one field to the next.

Use of Pheromones   Also part of integrated pest management is the spraying of *pheromones*, chemicals normally used in animal communication. The insect pheromone *glossyplure* is used by female pink boll worms to attract their mates. Spraying this pheromone on cotton fields confuses the male insects and interferes with their ability to locate the females, resulting in a natural birth control that is very specific to the pink boll worm and that has no effect on other species.

From Biology Today, 7E *by Eli C. Minkoff and Pamela J. Baker, 1996. Reprinted by permission of The McGraw-Hill Companies.*

IN YOUR OWN WORDS

1. Many Third World countries continue to use DDT to control crop pests and mosquitoes. Do you think the United Nations should impose a worldwide ban on the use of this insecticide?

2. The use of DDT was banned in the United States. Many farmers would like to be allowed to use DDT on a limited basis. Do you think this is a good idea? Why or why not?

3. Many scientists would like to increase crop yields by means of genetic engineering, which can make plants resistant to most pest species and so reduce the need for insecticide spraying. Where do you stand on this issue?

Skimming Exercises

The purpose of skimming is to gain a quick overview in order to identify the main points. When skimming, you will often skip words, sentences, and paragraphs. When you are satisfied that you have a general understanding of the author's key points, you put the reading material aside. Skimming, then, serves as a substitute for careful reading.

When you are skimming, be sure to move rapidly through the material, skipping the information you are already familiar with. You may wish to read the first and last sentences of each paragraph because that is often where main ideas are located. Read the introduction and the summary if one is provided. When examples are given, you may want to read a few of them until you understand the concepts they are meant to illustrate. When skimming a textbook chapter, glance quickly at the title, subheadings, italicized words, boldface print, and illustrations.

The article you are about to skim is from the textbook, *Anthropology: the Exploration of Human Diversity,* by Conrad Phillip Kottak.

1. Read the title and the introductory paragraph and answer the following questions based on them:

    a. What do you think the word "greening" means?

    _____

    b. What point of view do you think the author is going to be taking?

    _____

    c. Do you expect to read about a program that is a complete success? _____

    d. What words on the part of the author lead you to your conclusion?

    _____

2. Now read the last paragraph.

    a. Does this paragraph confirm your answers to question 1? _____
    b. Was the project a success? _____

3. Read just the first sentence of each paragraph and answer the following questions.

    a. Where is Java located? _____

    b. What political event led to problems during Java's green revolution?

    _____

    c. What group benefited most from the green revolution? _____

    _____

    d. Who launched an intervention program allowing students and villagers to work together? _____

"The Greening of Java"   *by Conrad Phillip Kottak*

READING

Anthropologist Richard Franke conducted an independent study of discrepancies between goals and results in a scheme to promote social and economic change in Java, Indonesia. Experts and planners of the 1960s and 1970s assumed that as small-scale farmers got modern technology and more productive crop varieties, their lives would improve. The media publicized new, high-yielding varieties of wheat, maize, and rice. These new crops, along with chemical fertilizers, pesticides, and new cultivation techniques, were hailed as the basis of a **green revolution.** This "revolution" was expected to increase the world's food supply and thus improve the diets and living conditions of victims of poverty, particularly in land-scarce, overcrowded regions.

The green revolution was an economic success. It did increase the global food supply. New strains of wheat and rice doubled or tripled farm supplies in many Third World countries. Thanks to the green revolution, world food prices declined by more than 20 percent during the 1980s. But its social effects were not what its advocates had intended, as we learn from Javanese experience.

Java received a genetic cross between rice strains from Taiwan and Indonesia —a high-yielding "miracle" rice known as IR-8. This hybrid could raise the productivity of a given plot by at least half. Governments throughout southern Asia, including Indonesia, encouraged the cultivation of IR-8, along with the use of chemical fertilizers and pesticides.

The Indonesian island of Java, one of the most densely populated places in the world, was a prime target for the green revolution. Java's total crop was insufficient to supply its people with minimal daily requirements of calories and protein. Could miracle rice, by increasing crop yields by 50 percent, reverse the trend?

5   Java shares with many underdeveloped nations a history of socioeconomic stratification and colonialism. Today, contrasts between the wealthy and the poor exist even in small farming communities. Stratification led to problems during Java's green revolution.

In 1963 the University of Indonesia's College of Agriculture launched a program in which students went to live in villages. They worked with peasants in the fields and shared their knowledge of new agricultural techniques while learning from the peasants. The program was a success. Yields in the affected villages increased by half. The program, directed by the Department of Agriculture, was expanded in 1964; nine universities and 400 students joined. These intervention programs succeeded where others had failed because the outside agents recognized that economic development rests not only on technological change but on political change as well. Students could observe firsthand how interest groups resisted attempts by peasants to improve their lot. Once, when local officials stole fertilizer destined for peasant fields, students got it back by threatening in a letter to turn evidence of the crime over to higher-level officials.

The combination of new work patterns and political action was achieving promising results when, in 1965–1966, there was an insurrection against the government. In the eventual military takeover, Indonesia's President Sukarno was ousted and replaced by President Suharto. Efforts to increase agricultural production resumed soon after Suharto took control. However, the new government assigned the task to multinational corporations based in Japan, West Germany, and Switzerland rather than to students and peasants. These industrial firms were to supply miracle rice and other high-yielding seeds, fertilizers, and pesticides. Peasants adopting the whole green revolution kit were eligible for loans that would allow them to buy food and other essentials in the lean period just before harvesting.

Java's green revolution soon encountered problems. One pesticide, which had never been tested in Java, killed the fish in the irrigation canals and thus destroyed an important protein resource. One development agency turned out to be a fraud, set up to benefit the military and government officials.

Java's green revolution also encountered problems at the village level because of entrenched interests. Traditionally, peasants had fed their families by taking temporary jobs, or borrowing from wealthier villagers before the harvest. However, having accepted loans, the peasants were obliged to work for wages lower than those paid on the open market. Low-interest loans would have made peasants less dependent on wealthy villagers, thus depriving local patrons of cheap labor.

10   Local officials were put in charge of spreading information about how the program worked. Instead they limited peasant participation by withholding information. Wealthy villagers also discouraged peasant participation more subtly: They raised doubts about the effectiveness of the new techniques and about the wisdom of taking government loans when familiar patrons were nearby. Faced with the thought that starvation might follow if innovation failed, peasants were reluctant to take risks—an understandable reaction.

Production increased, but wealthy villagers rather than small-scale farmers reaped the benefits of the green revolution. Just 20 percent of one village's 151 households participated in the program. However, because they were the wealthiest households, headed by people who owned the most land, 40 percent of the land was being cultivated by means of the new system. Some large-scale landowners used their green revolution profits at the peasants' expense. They bought up peasants' small plots and purchased labor-saving machinery, including rice-milling machines and tractors. As a result, the poorest peasants lost both their means of subsistence—land—and local work opportunities. Their only recourse was to move to cities, where a growing pool of unskilled laborers depressed already low wages.

These studies of the local effects of the green revolution reveal results different from those foreseen by policy makers, planners, and the media. Again we see the unintended and undesirable effects of development programs that ignore traditional social, political, and economic divisions. New technology, no matter how promising, does not inevitably help the intended beneficiaries. It may very well hurt them if vested interests interfere.

From Anthropology: The Exploration of Human Diversity, 7E *by Conrad Phillip Kottak, 1997. Reprinted by permission of The McGraw-Hill Companies.*

You have just skimmed the article to locate its main points. Now go back and carefully read the entire article so that you can answer the following questions:

1. The phrase "green revolution" means
   a. increasing the world's food supply by means of new crops and modern technology.
   b. schemes to promote social and economic change.
   c. methods to increase the class distinctions between wealthy and poor.
   d. the planting of trees.

2. Another good title for this selection would be
   a. "Increasing the World's Food Supply."
   b. "Colonialism in Java."
   c. "Unintended Effects of the Green Revolution in Java."
   d. "Political Turmoil in Java."

3. Which one of the following statements can you infer from the article?
   a. The program might have succeeded under the guidance of President Sukarno.
   b. Agricultural programs are likely to fail when they do not take into account the social and political structure of a region.
   c. Java is a crowded country in which poverty and hunger are serious problems.
   d. All of the above.

4. Which of the following statements are true based on the article? Read all of the statements before selecting your answer(s).
   a. Java is a densely populated region.
   b. Most peasants were ineligible for low-interest loans.
   c. Low-interest loans for peasants were not in the best interest of wealthy villagers.
   d. Both *a* and *c*.

Chapter 14 Test: "The Greening of Java"

Multiple Choice

1. The author of this article has created a tone that could be described as
   a. nostalgic.
   b. angry.
   c. cheerful.
   d. objective.

2. The author's primary purpose in writing this article is to
   a. explain how technological improvements can aid poor countries.
   b. describe to the reader the methods that can be used for better crop production.
   c. explain how new economic policies may produce unforeseen results.
   d. persuade developing nations to abandon the use of new technology.

3. In paragraph 2, the transition word *but* indicates a
   a. comparison.
   b. contrast.
   c. steps in a process.
   d. definition.

4. From this article, you could infer that
   a. the change in national leadership was the sole reason for the problems the program encountered.
   b. prior to the green revolution, Java's crop was sufficient to supply its populace with the minimum daily requirement of protein and calories.
   c. the peasants refused to consider the use of new technology.
   d. officials erred in not taking into account the social and cultural values of the local population.

5. A synonym for the word *insurrection* in paragraph 7 is
   a. rebellion.
   b. uprising.
   c. permanence.
   d. Both *a* and *b.*

6. Paragraph 11 is an example of
   a. satire.
   b. an extended metaphor.
   c. irony.
   d. personification.

True or False

_____   7. Java is a densely populated area.

_____   8. The green revolution was responsible for increasing the global food supply.

_____   9. Indonesia was the only country in southern Asia to encourage the use of IR-8.

_____ 10. Wealthy villagers encouraged peasants to take out government loans.

Vocabulary: Unit 7

aqueduct—The longest modern aqueduct is the California State Water Project, which is 826 miles long; 385 of these miles are canals.

Aquarius—

hydroelectric—At present, the largest hydroelectric producing plant in the world is the Grand Coulee Dam on the Columbia River in Washington. It was built in 1942 and today produces 6,480 megawatts of power each year.

Trivia Question #1

When were pneumatic tires discovered and patented? Answer at the end of this unit.

Trivia Question #2

Are horses native to our country? If not, how did they get here? Answer at the end of the unit.

This is the last vocabulary unit. The first group of words in this unit concerns water, air, and life. The second group concerns the "blood and guts" of your vocabulary study. The last group concerns the prefix *in*, but in several variant forms.

aqua—water   pneu—air; breathe; wind
hydro—water

aquarium	a tank or container filled with water in which collections of animals and plants live.
aqueduct	*Aqua* means "water" and *duc* means "to lead," so this word means literally "to lead water." An *aqueduct* can be a pipe for bringing water from a distant place, or it can resemble a canal or tunnel.
Aquarius	This is the constellation in the sky that looks like a man carrying water. If you were born from January 20 to February 18, your zodiac sign would be *Aquarius*.
hydrant	a large pipe with a valve for releasing water from a water main.
hydroelectric	*Hydroelectric* power is electricity generated by the energy of running water.
hydrologist	a person who studies water, including the cycle of evaporation and precipitation.
hydraulic	The literal meaning is a "water tube." Today, *hydraulic* is a term used to describe a system operated by a fluid, such as a *hydraulic* jack or *hydraulic* brakes.
pneumatic	containing wind, air, or gases; filled with or worked by compressed air. The tires on your car are *pneumatic* tires because they hold pressurized air.
pneumonia	an inflammation of the lungs creating difficulty in breathing. Our lungs work like an "air" pump, thus the origin of this word.

nat—birth   bio—life

nature	the essential character of something; what has always been there from birth.
native	There are a couple meanings here. First, your *native* state or country is where you were born. Second, *native* plants, animals, and people are the ones that originally came from an area. Eucalyptus trees are not *native* to the United States because they were brought here from Australia.
nativity	A *nativity* scene is a birth scene, such as you might see at Christmas when the birth of Jesus is celebrated.

innate	*In* here means "within," so your *innate* characteristics are those you were born with. Recently, there has been an ongoing debate over how much of our intelligence is inherited at birth (innate) and how much is determined by our environment. Psychologists refer to this as the "nature versus nurture" debate.
prenatal	before birth.
postnatal	after birth.
biography	an account of a person's life written by someone else.
autobiography	Because *auto* means "self," an *autobiography* is a story of one's own life written by oneself.
biochemistry	the study of the chemistry of life processes in both plants and animals.
biopsy	the removal of bits of living tissue for analysis.
biodegradable	matter that is capable of breaking down or decomposing so that it can return to the life cycle.
symbiotic	the living together of two different organisms for mutual benefit. Our large intestines are inhabited by "gut bacteria" that help us digest cellulose (fiber) and produce vitamin K. Because the gut bacteria derive nutrients from food absorbed by their human "host," the relationship between the bacteria and the person is considered *symbiotic,* or beneficial to both. By the way, antibiotics, which commonly kill off this "good" bacteria, can upset the *symbiotic* relationship.

Trivia Question #3

What element forms the basis for all living tissue? Answer found at the end of this lesson.

The next section discusses "blood" relations and the suffix *cide,* which means "killing."

mater, matri—mother	**cide—kill**
pater, patri—father	**homo—mankind**
soror, sori—sister	**genus—birth; begin; race**
frater, fratri—brother	

maternal	relating to a mother, such as *maternal* instincts.
maternity	the state of being a mother. The new mothers were on the *maternity* floor of the hospital.
matricide	The suffix *cide,* as in insecti*cide* and pesti*cide,* means "killing," so *matricide* is murdering one's mother.
paternal	relating to a father. Your father's father is your *paternal* grandfather.
paternity	the state of being a father. Some men are now taking *paternity* leaves so that they can stay home with their newborn babies.
patricide	murdering one's father.
fraternity	a brotherhood. College *fraternities* are groups of males who live together as brothers.

fratricide	murdering one's brother.
sorority	a sisterhood. College *sororities* are groups of females who live together as sisters.
sororicide	murdering one's sister.
homicide	the murder of one human being by another. We previously learned that *homo* means "same." But *homo* also has a second meaning of "man," which is the meaning that applies to the word *homicide* and other words. The *homo* meaning "same" has a different derivation than the *homo* meaning "man."
Homo sapiens	mankind; human beings. *Sapiens* means "wisdom," so *Homo sapiens* are humans with wisdom. This is the scientific term for all human beings.
genius	A *genius* is a person with very high intelligence. The word *genius* from *genus,* meaning "birth," has an interesting etymology. The ancient Romans believed that each person was assigned a guardian spirit at birth.
genocide	the systematic killing of a national or ethnic group. The word *genocide* was first applied to the attempted extermination of the Jews by Nazi Germany.
Genesis	the beginning, the origin. The first book of the Bible is called *Genesis* because it gives an account of the Creation.
genealogy	a history of a person's descent from ancestors. Your "family tree," or birth history shows your *genealogy*.

Another Meaning of *in*

As you learned in Vocabulary 3, the Latin prefix *in* has two distinct meanings: "not" as in the word *inactive,* and "within" and "into" as in the word *incarcerating* (meaning to put in jail or prison). In a few English words, *in* acts as an intensive, with the meaning "very" or "completely."

infamous	This word does not mean "not famous," but instead means "famous, but for the wrong reasons." The word *infamous* refers to people who have a bad reputation or are notorious, such as Jesse James, Bonnie and Clyde, and Charles Manson.
invaluable	*Invaluable* does not mean "not valuable," but instead means something so extremely valuable that it is priceless. Original copies of the Constitution, your mother's advice, and your grandmother's ring might all be considered *invaluable*.
inflammable	This word means "very flammable." IF SOMETHING IS INFLAMMABLE, IT WILL BURN EASILY. This word is related to the word *inflame*, which means "to catch fire." If something does *not* burn, it would be *non*flammable.

Answer to Trivia Question 1

Robert Thompson invented and patented the first pneumatic tire in 1845. John Dunlap patented his version in 1888 after producing a tire for his son's bicycle.

Answer to Trivia Question 2

Horses are not native to our country, but were brought here by the early Spanish explorers.

Answer to Trivia Question 3

Carbon forms the basis for all living tissue.

ingenious	*Ingenious* does not mean that a person is not smart. Instead, it means that a person is clever and creative. Its original meaning was possessing genius. Inventors such as Thomas Edison and Alexander Bell were very *ingenious* people.
ingenuous	being innocent about a subject; naïve. Spies cannot afford to be truly *ingenuous;* otherwise, they will be found out. But spies might want to pretend to be *ingenuous* so that no one will suspect them.

In the following exercise, match the names of people who have been previously mentioned in the seven units, to the vocabulary words that describe them. Some names have more than one "match."

Thomas Edison	extraterrestrial
Wright brothers	duel
Louis Pasteur	circumnavigate
David Letterman	infamous
John Glenn	ingenious
George Burns	homogenization
Red Barron	pasteurization
E.T.	centenarian
Adolf Hitler	triplane
Aaron Burr	biplane
Magellan	monologue

Vocabulary 7

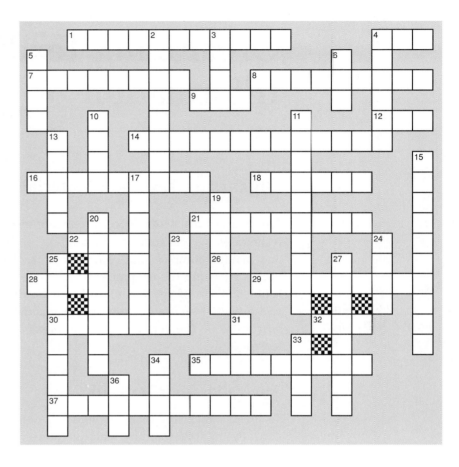

ACROSS CLUES

1. The little girl was badly burned because her nightgown was _____.
4. A word part meaning "life."
7. Jeffrey Dahmer, a serial killer, led an _____ life.
8. A study of your family's descent.
9. A word part meaning "around."
12. A word part meaning "below."
14. The story of your life written by you.
16. Air pressure.
18. Your *home* state.
21. Bill Gates, the founder of Microsoft, is considered to be _____.
22. A word part meaning "similar."
26. A word part meaning "toward."
28. A word part meaning "kill."
29. Water or liquid pressure.
30. The beginning.
32. Word part meaning "see."
35. A relationship of mutual dependency.
37. A person who studies water.

DOWN CLUES

2. A canal used to transport water.
3. A word part meaning water.
4. The removal of tissue for medical diagnosis.
5. A word part meaning "round."
6. A word part meaning "birth."
10. A word part meaning "air."
11. Killing your brother.
13. Word part meaning "birth."
15. Killing your sister.
17. The zodiac sign for "water bearer."
19. Characteristics you were born with.
20. Having the quality of motherly instincts.
23. A word part meaning "across."
24. A word part meaning "distance."
25. The story of your life written by someone else.
27. A birth scene.
31. A word part meaning "with."
33. A word part meaning "mankind."
34. A word part meaning "many."
36. A word part meaning "for."

Chapter 15

Organizing Textbook Information

Organizing Textbook Materials in Different Ways

This chapter discusses different ways of organizing your reading material. The techniques we will cover are annotating, outlining, mapping, making time lines, and making compare-and-contrast charts. We will illustrate each of these techniques by using the chapter entitled "Jazz" in *Music: An Appreciation* by Roger Kamien. Each of the techniques will be discussed individually, and then we will give you an opportunity to practice them and determine which ones work best for you. The chapter "Jazz" appears after our discussion of these various techniques.

Annotating Your Textbook

To *annotate* means to make explanatory notes. Because you own your textbooks, you can annotate them by making "notes" on the pages as you read and study them. The common ways of annotating a textbook are underlining, highlighting, and writing in the margin. Annotating is something you may want to begin doing the first time you read a selection. It is the simplest organizational technique, and one you may want to use before using one of the other techniques discussed below.

When annotating, keep in mind that less is often better. After skimming through the material, go back and carefully read it, underlining or highlighting key ideas or concepts, or ones that you have questions about or may want to refer back to later. If you underline or highlight too much, you're defeating your purpose, because then the important material you've marked no longer stands out.

One reason for annotating is that it gets you involved right away in the material you are reading by requiring you to think about what is important or difficult.

While writing in the margins is useful for marking important or difficult material, it also lets you comment on what you're reading. Do you strongly agree or disagree with something you've read? Say so in the margin. Do you have a specific question about something? Put your question in the margin. In this way, you're beginning to develop your thoughts and feelings about the material.

We have annotated part of the "Jazz" chapter that follows. Examine what we've done (see pages 379 and 380), and then you annotate the remainder of the section, which is entitled "Jazz Styles: 1900–1950."

374

Outlining

A more-formal way to organize material is with an outline. An outline should reflect an orderly arrangement of ideas going from the general to the specific. Outlines vary depending on how detailed and complete the information contained in them is. We are going to introduce you to two kinds of outlines: the *topical outline,* which is easier to construct because it is made up of single words or phrases, and the *descriptive outline,* which is more detailed and requires more explanation.

The reason outlining is called a *formal* way of organizing information is that it follows certain rules. These rules are described below.

Topical Outlines

The purpose of a topical outline is to organize material according to topics or subjects. It will show what topics are covered, the relationships between the topics, and the importance of the ideas in the order they were covered in the original material.

One rule for making a topical outline concerns how the topics are enumerated. Each additional division in an outline must contain information that is more specific than the division before it. Main headings are enumerated with Roman numerals (I, II, III, IV, etc.), the next level of subheadings is enumerated with capital letters (A, B, C, D, etc.), the next level of subheadings is enumerated with Arabic numbers (1, 2, 3, 4, etc.), and the next level of subheadings is enumerated with lowercase letters (a, b, c, d, etc.).

Another rule for making a topical outline is that you cannot have just one subtopic; there must be at least two. So, if there is a subtopic A, there has to be a subtopic B. If there is a subtopic 1, there must be a subtopic 2. The reason for this is that if a topic is divided, there must be at least two parts, though there could be three or four or more parts depending on how many times it is divided.

Here is a topical outline for the beginning of our chapter on jazz.

    I.   Jazz styles
        A.   Roots of jazz
        B.   Jazz in society
        C.   Elements in jazz
            1.   Tone color
            2.   Improvisation
            3.   Rhythm, melody, and harmony
   II.   Ragtime
        A.   What is ragtime?
        B.   Scott Joplin
  III.   Blues

Notice that in constructing this outline, we mainly used the author's headings. There's nothing wrong with this. The idea is to organize the information presented; a well-organized essay, article, or book should help us do this. Because the author had only one subtopic under Ragtime, we had to create another one to follow our rule that at least two subtopics are required. A good place to start in making a topical outline is often a book's table of contents.

Descriptive Outlines

A topical outline is good for obtaining an overview. But to fully organize your reading material, you need to place more information in your outline. When you take a topical outline and fill it in, making it more detailed and complete, what you end up with is a descriptive outline. Once you have put together a really good descriptive outline on your course material, that should be about all you need to study for a test. Below is the start of a descriptive outline that takes the beginning of our topical outline and develops it.

I.   Jazz styles
    A.   Roots of jazz
        1.   Started when European music was changing
        2.   Improvised, syncopated rhythm, steady beat, different tone colors, performance techniques
        3.   Not originally written down
        4.   West African, American, European background
        5.   West Africa—improvising, drumming, complex rhythm
        6.   Call and response
           a.   West Africa—originally chorus responding to solo
           b.   Jazz—responding with instruments
        7.   In America, work songs, spirituals, gospel hymns, dances
        8.   Influence of white America—hymns, popular songs, marches, piano pieces
    B.   Jazz in society—originally for dancing and controversial for sexuality, now for listening and well-respected

Now it's your turn. Starting with "Elements in jazz" at subtopic C, continue making our topical outline into a descriptive one.

Mapping

Recall our discussion on left-brain and right-brain orientations in Chapter 1. If you had trouble making a formal outline, or you found it an unpleasant task, it may be that you have a right-brain orientation. What you may find more useful is an organizing technique that is more visual and free-form. Mapping is just such a technique.

Like a formal outline, mapping seeks to organize topics to show the relationships among the topics. But it organizes in a way that is less restricted by rules and has more visual significance.

To get a sense of what mapping is all about, look at our example below. To begin mapping, write down a short description of the main idea or thesis, and put a circle around it. Next, find the material that directly supports the main idea. Organize this material into categories, write down a short description for each category, and put circles around your descriptions. Now use lines to connect your category circles to the circle for the main topic or thesis. If you want, you can create subcategories for your categories, write brief descriptions, circle them, and use lines to connect these circles to your category circles. Of course you can use boxes instead of circles. What you end up with is a logical, graphical summary of the material.

Now read sections 4 and 5 of our chapter on "Jazz." These sections discuss two types of jazz music and two famous jazz musicians, Louis Armstrong and Duke

Ellington. Below we have mapped the portion of this material discussing Louis Armstrong. Study how we did this, and then you prepare a map of the portion of the material discussing Duke Ellington.

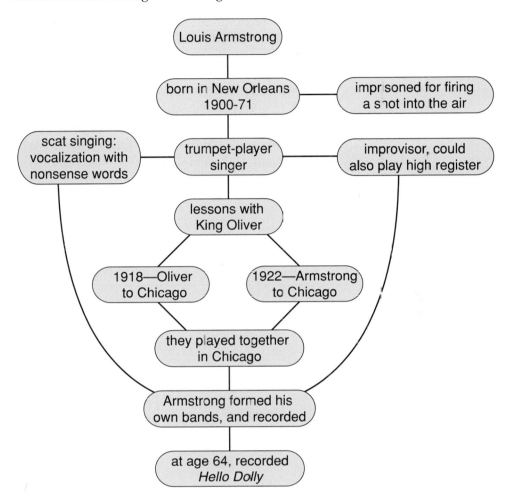

Time Lines

A time line is a specialized way of organizing information. Time lines are useful when material needs to be organized chronologically by dates, such as in a history class, though you could have a need to make one in almost any other class too.

All that a time line does is list dates in chronological order along a line and then assign information to the dates. You can make a time line vertically (up and down) or a time line horizontally (across). How specific you want to make a time line in terms of the number of dates and the amount of information you assign to each date depends on the reading material and your needs.

A sample time line from our essay on jazz appears below. Your assignment is to read section 4 of the essay, and make a more detailed time line organizing the information in that section.

1910–17	jazz begins, New Orleans
1917	Storyville closed
1920s	swing begins
1940s, 50s	cool jazz era

Compare-and-Contrast Chart

Another method of organizing information is the compare-and-contrast chart. As the name implies, this method of organizing is especially appropriate when the describing of similarities and differences is important. As a result, this is a more-specialized organizational technique than the others.

Below is a compare-and-contrast chart that you will use to show the differences and similarities among cool jazz, free jazz, and jazz rock. The first column (columns go up and down) is for the category in which you are making your comparison. The second column is for the information on cool jazz, the third column for the information on free jazz, and the fourth column for the information on jazz rock. We have filled in the first row (rows go across) for you. Your assignment is to fill in as many of the remaining rows as you can. Do not feel that you have to fill in all the rows.

TITLE: *COOL JAZZ, FREE JAZZ, AND JAZZ ROCK*

Category	Cool Jazz	Free Jazz	Jazz Rock
Time Period	1940s–1950s	1960s	1960s–present

JAZZ

VIII

[JAZZ **1**]

JAZZ STYLES: 1900–1950

New music style in Europe

New Orleans

At about the time when Schoenberg and Stravinsky were changing the language of music in Europe, a new musical style called *jazz* was being developed in the United States.* It was created by musicians—predominantly African Americans—performing in the streets, bars, brothels, and dance halls of New Orleans and other southern cities. ***Jazz*** can be described generally as music rooted in improvisation and characterized by syncopated rhythm, a steady beat, and distinctive tone colors and performance techniques. Although the term *jazz* became current in 1917, the music itself was probably heard as early as 1900. We do not know exactly when early jazz started or how it sounded, because this new music existed only in performance, not musical notation. Moreover, very little jazz was captured on recordings before 1923, and none at all before the Original Dixieland Jazz Band recorded in 1917.

check glossary for definition

Very little recorded before 1923

Various styles

Since its beginnings, jazz has developed a rich variety of substyles such as New Orleans style (or Dixieland), swing, bebop, cool jazz, free jazz, and jazz rock. It has produced such outstanding figures as Louis Armstrong, Duke Ellington, Benny Goodman, Charlie Parker, and Miles Davis. Its impact has been enormous and worldwide, affecting not only many kinds of popular music, but the music of such composers as Maurice Ravel, Darius Milhaud, and Aaron Copland.

ROOTS OF JAZZ

Blend of W. Africa, America, & Europe

Early jazz blended elements from many musical cultures, including west African, American, and European. Most American slaves originally came from west Africa, an area that today includes Ghana, Nigeria, and several other countries. West African elements that influenced jazz include its emphasis on improvisation, drumming, percussive sounds, and complex rhythms. Another feature of jazz that was probably derived from west Africa is known as *call and response*. In much west African vocal music, a soloist's phrases are repeatedly answered by a chorus. In jazz, ***call and response*** occurs when a voice is answered by an instrument, or when one instrument (or group of instruments) is answered by another instrument (or group). The call-and-response pattern of jazz was derived more directly from African American church services in which the congregation vocally responds to the preacher's "call." In America, blacks developed a rich body of music that became a vital source for jazz. This music included work songs, spirituals, gospel hymns, and such dances as the cakewalk. Much of this music was never written down and is now lost to us. But it was probably performed in a way that created sounds and rhythms similar to those of early jazz.

Call and response

vocal response to preacher

Most not written down

Black and white music influenced each other

Black music influenced and was influenced by the music of white America, which included hymns, popular songs, folk tunes, dances, marches, and piano pieces. In origin, this repertory was partly American and partly written or influenced by European composers. Nineteenth-century American and European musical traditions provided melodies, harmonies, and forms that became elements in the background of jazz.

Souza?

One major source of jazz was the American band tradition. Bands—both black and white—played an important role in American life during the late nineteenth and early twentieth centuries. Virtually every village had its band and bandstand; bands performed at picnics, parades, political rallies, dances, and carnivals. Many of the instruments used in marching bands—trumpet, cornet, trombone, tuba, clarinet, and drums—were also used in early jazz bands. Band music also influenced the forms and rhythms of early jazz.

Marching band instruments used in jazz

also ragtime & blues background

Along with band music, the immediate sources of jazz were ragtime and blues. *Ragtime* is a style of syncopated piano music that was popular from the 1890s to about 1915. The term *blues* refers to, among other things, a style of African American vocal music involving "bent" notes and slides of pitch. Ragtime and blues will be discussed more fully in Sections 2 and 3.

JAZZ IN SOCIETY

The world of jazz has witnessed many changes since its beginnings at the turn of the century. Geographically, its center has shifted from New Orleans to Chicago, Kansas City, and New York. Today, it is hard to speak of *a* jazz center, since good jazz is heard worldwide, from Paris to Tokyo. Jazz has changed in function, too. For a long time, it was basically music for dancing; but since the 1940s, many newer jazz styles have been intended for listening. Now we are as likely to hear jazz in a concert hall or college classroom as in a bar or nightclub. The image of jazz has also changed. It was originally condemned for its emphasis on sexuality, but it has long since become respectable. In recent years, jazz has been sponsored by major American cultural institutions. Both Lincoln Center and Carnegie Hall in New York City have regular jazz series, and a Jazz Masterworks Orchestra has been founded at the Smithsonian National Museum of American History in Washington, D.C.

Jazz Today
1) worldwide
2) many styles
3) concert halls
*   and bars*

ELEMENTS OF JAZZ

Like other music of the twentieth century, jazz is too diverse and complex to be defined by any single formula. We'll now consider some of the elements of jazz created before 1950. Jazz after 1950 is discussed in Section 7.

Tone Color

Jazz is generally played by a small group (or *combo*) of three to eight players, or by a "big band" of ten to fifteen. The backbone of a jazz ensemble is its rhythm section, which is comparable to the basso continuo in baroque music. The **rhythm section,** usually made up of piano, plucked double bass (bass), tuba, percussion, and—sometimes—banjo or guitar, maintains the beat, adds rhythmic interest, and provides supporting harmonies. Modern percussionists produce a variety of sounds from several drums and cymbals, using sticks, mallets, wire brushes, and bare hands.

The main solo instruments of jazz include the cornet, trumpet, saxophone (soprano, alto, tenor, baritone), piano, clarinet, vibraphone, and trombone. Jazz emphasizes brasses, woodwinds, and percussion rather than the bowed strings that dominate symphonic music. Brass players produce a wide variety of tone colors by using different mutes and muting techniques. A jazz performance usually involves both solo and ensemble sections. For example, a full ensemble might be followed by a trumpet solo and then by a clarinet solo or a duet for saxophone and trumpet.

Compared with "classical" musicians, who strive for an ideal sound, jazz performers aim for more individuality of sound and tone color. For example, it is usually easier to distinguish between two jazz trumpet players than between two "classical" trumpeters. Although jazz is basically instrumental music, its players try to match the personal quality of singing. In all, the distinctive sounds of jazz are easy to recognize but hard to describe. A jazz sound results from the particular way tones are attacked and released; from the type of vibrato used; and from a variety of pitch inflections that might be described as "smears," "scoops," "falloffs," and "shakes."

Improvisation

At the heart of jazz lies improvisation. Jazz musicians create a special electricity as they simultaneously create and perform, making decisions at lightning speed. The fertility of great improvisers is staggering. Their recorded performances represent only a tiny fraction of the music they create almost nightly.

Of course, not all jazz is improvised, and most contains both improvised and composed sections. Yet it is improvisation that contributes most to the freshness and spontaneity of jazz. The reputations of jazz performers rest mainly on the originality of their improvisations.

A jazz improvisation is usually in theme-and-variations form. The theme is often a popular song melody made up of 32 **bars,** or measures. The improviser varies this original melody by adding embellishments and changing its pitches and rhythms. Some improvised variations are similar to the original theme, but others are so different that the tune may be difficult to recognize. Often, jazz improvisations are based not on a melody but on a harmonic pattern, or series of chords. This harmonic pattern will be repeated over and over while the improviser creates melodies above it. In jazz, each statement of the basic harmonic pattern or melody is called a **chorus.** For example, a jazz performance that is based on a 32-bar melody might be outlined as follows:

Chorus 1 (32 bars)	Theme
Chorus 2 (32 bars)	Variation 1
Chorus 3 (32 bars)	Variation 2
Chorus 4 (32 bars)	Variation 3

A jazz performance usually includes improvised solos by various members of the ensemble. In addition, there may be sections of *collective* improvisation, during which several musicians make up different melodies simultaneously. Their music is held together by the underlying chords. Until the introduction of long-playing records in 1948, most recorded jazz performances were about 3 minutes in length, the duration of one side of a 78 rpm record.

Rhythm, Melody, and Harmony

Syncopation and rhythmic swing are two of the most distinctive features of jazz. We say that jazz performers *"swing"* when they combine a steady beat with a feeling of lilt, precision, and relaxed vitality. In most jazz styles, the beat is provided by the percussionist (on drums or cymbals) and by the bass player. There are usually four beats to the bar. Accents often come on the weak beats: 1-**2**-3-**4.** Many kinds of syncopated rhythms result when accented notes come *between* the beats. Jazz musicians also create a swing feeling by playing a series of notes slightly unevenly. For example, the second note of a pair of eighth notes will be shorter than the first:

But the rhythms of jazz are so irregular that it is difficult to notate them accurately. A performer must deviate from the notated rhythms to get a true jazz feeling. And as jazz has evolved, rhythms have become ever more irregular and complex.

Jazz melodies are as flexible in pitch as in rhythm. They use a major scale in which the third, fifth, and seventh notes are often lowered, or flatted. These "bent," or "blue," notes came into jazz through vocal blues, as you'll see in Section 3. Jazz uses chord progressions like those of the traditional tonal system. But over the years, the harmonic vocabulary of jazz—like its rhythm—has become increasingly complex and sophisticated.

RAGTIME $\begin{bmatrix} \text{JAZZ} \\ \mathbf{2} \end{bmatrix}$

Ragtime is a style of composed piano music that flourished from the 1890s to about 1915. It was developed primarily by African American pianists who traveled in the midwest and south playing in saloons and dance halls. Not long after it originated, ragtime became a nationally popular style that reached millions of people—both black and white—through sheet music, player pianos, ragtime songs, and arrangements for dance and marching bands.

Ragtime piano music is generally in duple meter ($\frac{2}{4}$) and is performed at a moderate march tempo. The pianist's right hand plays a highly syncopated melody, while the left hand steadily maintains the beat with an "oom-pah" accompaniment. A ragtime piece usually consists of several melodies that are similar in character. It takes such forms as AA BB A CC DD or introduction—AA BB CC DD EE. Although the forms of ragtime are derived from European marches and dances, its rhythms are rooted in African American folk music.

Early jazz musicians often used ragtime melodies as a springboard for their improvisations. The syncopations, steady beat, and piano style of ragtime were an important legacy for jazz.

SCOTT JOPLIN

The acknowledged "king of ragtime" was Scott Joplin (1868–1917), a composer and pianist whose father had been a slave. Joplin was trained in "classical" music and wrote a ballet and two operas, as well as many piano rags.

Joplin's most famous piano pieces include *Maple Leaf Rag* and *The Entertainer. Maple Leaf Rag* was named after the saloon in Sedalia, Missouri, where he worked as a pianist. After it was published in 1899, *Maple Leaf Rag* sold hundreds of thousands of copies. This success allowed Joplin to quit his saloon job and move to St. Louis, where he taught and composed.

In 1909, Joplin settled in New York City, where he spent the last years of his life. This was a bleak period for him: his health was poor, and he was unsuccessful in his desperate attempts to get a professional production of his opera *Treemonisha* (1911). Finally, in 1915, he mounted the opera himself in Harlem—without scenery, costumes, or orchestra. The failure of this endeavor led to a physical and mental breakdown. Joplin was confined to a hospital in 1916 and died the following year. Only recently has *Treemonisha* been revived, and with great success.

JAZZ 3 BLUES

Among the most important sources of jazz is a type of music known as **blues.** The term refers to a form of vocal and instrumental music and to a style of performance. Blues grew out of African American folk music, such as work songs, spirituals, and the field hollers of slaves. It is uncertain exactly when blues originated, but by around the 1890s it was sung in rural areas of the south. The original "country blues," usually performed with a guitar accompaniment, was unstandardized in form or style.

The poetic and musical form of blues crystallized around 1910 and gained popularity through the publication of *Memphis Blues* (1912) and *St. Louis Blues* (1914), by W. C. Handy (1873–1958). During the 1920s, blues became a national craze among African Americans. Records by such blues singers as Bessie Smith sold in the millions. The 1920s also saw blues become a musical form widely used by jazz instrumentalists as well as blues singers. Since then, jazz and blues have been intertwined. The continuing impact of blues is apparent in such popular styles as rhythm and blues, rock and roll, and soul.

Vocal blues is intensely personal, often containing sexual references and dealing with the pain of betrayal, desertion, and unrequited love. The lyrics consist of several 3-line stanzas, each in the same poetic and musical form. The first line is sung and then repeated to roughly the same melodic phrase (a a'); the third line has a different melodic phrase (b).

a : I'm going to leave baby, ain't going to say goodbye.
a': I'm going to leave baby, ain't going to say goodbye.
b : But I'll write you and tell you the reason why.

A blues stanza is set to a harmonic framework that is usually 12 bars in length. This harmonic pattern, known as **12-bar blues,** involves only three basic chords: tonic (I), subdominant (IV), and dominant (V). (The **subdominant** is the triad based on the fourth note—*fa*—of the scale.) The specific ordering of these chords can be outlined as follows: tonic (4 bars) —subdominant (2 bars)—tonic (2 bars)—dominant (2 bars)—tonic (2 bars). Here is how the 3-line stanza is set to this chord progression:

	Line 1 (a)				Line 2 (a')				Line 3 (b)			
Bars	1	2	3	4	5	6	7	8	9	10	11	12
Chords	I				IV		I		V		I	

Each stanza of the text is sung to the same series of chords, although other chords may be inserted between the basic ones of 12-bar blues. Singers either repeat the same basic melody for each stanza or improvise new melodies to reflect the changing moods of the lyrics. The music is in quadruple meter ($\frac{4}{4}$), and so each bar contains 4 beats.

Twelve-bar blues is divided into three phrases, each of which is 4 bars long. The soloist takes only about 2 bars to sing a line. This leaves the remainder of the 4-bar phrase to be filled in by the supporting instrument or instruments. In blues recordings of the 1920s and 1930s, instrumental responses to the singer's lines were often improvised by leading jazz musicians.

Blues singers have a special style of performance involving "bent" notes, microtonal shadings, and vocal scoops and slides. Their melodies contain many "blue" notes, which are produced by slightly lowering or flatting the third, fifth, and seventh tones of a major scale. Blues rhythm is also very flexible. Performers often sing "around" the beat, accenting notes either just before or after it.

Jazz instrumentalists imitate the performing style of blues singers and use the harmonic pattern of 12-bar blues as a basis for improvisation. This 12-bar pattern is repeated over and over while new melodies are improvised above it. As with the baroque ground bass, the repeated chord progression provides unity while the free flow of improvised melodic lines contributes variety. Music in this 12-bar form can be happy or sad, fast or slow, and in a wide range of styles. In Section 4, we'll consider an instrumental blues, *Dippermouth Blues,* which is an example of New Orleans jazz. Now we'll study a vocal blues by Bessie Smith.

NEW ORLEANS STYLE [JAZZ **4**]

From about 1900 to 1917, jazz developed in a number of American cities, but the major center was New Orleans—the home of such important jazz musicians as Ferdinand "Jelly Roll" Morton, Joseph "King" Oliver, and Louis Armstrong.

Around the turn of the century, New Orleans was a major port and a thriving cultural and commercial center with a cosmopolitan character. Its diverse population included people of African, French, Spanish, Portuguese, English, Italian, and Cuban ancestry. A particular group in New Orleans made up of people of mixed African, French, and Spanish descent maintained its own ethnic identity. This diversity of population was mirrored in the rich musical life of New Orleans. It included opera and chamber music as well as folk, popular, dance, and sacred music of all kinds. The tradition of marching bands and dance bands was particularly strong. There were frequent competitions between bands to see which could play more loudly or more brilliantly. Some band musicians were trained in classical music and could read musical notation; others played by ear and relied on improvisation. Many were only part-time performers who worked full time at other trades, such as bricklaying, carpentry, and cigar making.

Band music—including early jazz—was heard at picnics, parades, and political meetings and in dance halls. African American bands often played jazz during funeral processions. In the words of one New Orleans musician: "You'd march to the graveyard playing very solemn and very slow, then on the way back all hell would break loose! . . . We didn't know what a sheet of music was. Just six or seven pieces, half a dozen men pounding it out all together, each in his own way and yet somehow fitting in all right with the others."

But the main home of early jazz was Storyville, a red-light district of brothels, gambling joints, saloons, and dance halls. These establishments often employed a piano player or small band. Storyville provided not only employment but an atmosphere in which musicians felt free to improvise. When Storyville was closed down in 1917 on orders of the Navy Department, many jazz musicians left New Orleans. The center of jazz soon shifted to Chicago, Kansas City, and New York.

Jazz in **New Orleans style** (or **Dixieland**) was typically played by a small group of five to eight performers. The melodic instruments, or **front line,** included the cornet (or trumpet), clarinet, and trombone. The front-line players would improvise several contrasting melodic lines at once, producing a kind of polyphonic texture. This collective improvisation was the most distinctive feature of New Orleans jazz. Each instrument had a special role. The cornet was the leader, playing variations of the main melody. Above the cornet, the clarinet wove a countermelody, usually in a faster rhythm. The trombone played a bass line that was simpler than the upper lines, but melodically interesting nevertheless. The syncopations and rhythmic independence of the melodic instruments created a marvelous sense of excitement.

The front-line instruments were supported by a rhythm section that clearly marked the beat and provided a background of chords. This section usually included drums, chordal instruments (banjo, guitar, piano), and a single-line low instrument (plucked bass or tuba).

New Orleans jazz was usually based on a march or church melody, a ragtime piece, a popular song, or 12-bar blues. Some well-known tunes associated with this style are *When the Saints Go Marching In* and *Oh, Didn't He Ramble?* One or more choruses of collective improvisation generally occurred at the beginning and end of a piece. In between, individual players were featured in improvised solos, accompanied by the rhythm section or by the whole band. Sometimes there were brief unaccompanied solos, called **breaks.** The band's performance might begin with an introduction and end with a brief coda, or **tag.**

As New Orleans style evolved during the 1920s—mainly in Chicago— solo playing came to be emphasized more than collective improvisation. Soloists began to base their improvisations less on the original melody than on its harmonies. In addition, the trumpet gradually replaced the cornet, and the saxophone became a member of the band.

LOUIS ARMSTRONG

As both a trumpeter and a singer, Louis "Satchmo" Armstrong (1900–1971) had a worldwide impact on jazz. He was born on the Fourth of July in a poor black section of New Orleans, and he learned to play the cornet in a reformatory (where he was sent at the age of thirteen for shooting a gun into the air during a New Year's celebration). On his release after one year of confinement, Armstrong was soon playing in honky-tonks at night (he drove a coal wagon during the day). His musical ambitions were encouraged by the cornetist King Oliver, who took a fatherly interest in the boy and gave him some lessons. When Oliver left for Chicago in 1918—after Storyville was closed down—Armstrong took his place in the famous Kid Ory Band. Four years later, Armstrong himself went to Chicago to be second cornetist in King Oliver's Creole Jazz Band.

In 1925, he started to make a series of recordings with bands known as Louis Armstrong's Hot Five and Louis Armstrong's Hot Seven. The Hot Five included three New Orleans musicians—Johnny Dodds (clarinet), Kid Ory (trombone), and Johnny St. Cyr (banjo)—along with Lil Hardin (piano), whom Armstrong had married a year earlier. These recordings established Armstrong's reputation as the leading jazz trumpeter. After 1930 he appeared with a wide variety of groups, made many tours, and was featured in many films. In the 1950s and 1960s Armstrong served as a "goodwill ambassador" for the United States. And at age sixty-four, he had his greatest popular success, the hit recording *Hello, Dolly!*

Armstrong was one of the greatest jazz improvisers; he was able to invent extraordinary solos and to transform even ordinary tunes into swinging melodies through changes of rhythm and pitch. He revealed new dimensions of the trumpet, showing that it could be played in a higher register than had been thought possible. His playing style featured "rips" up to high pitches, along with a tone that was both beautiful and alive. One jazz expert has singled out the "subtly varied repertory of vibratos and shakes with which Armstrong colors and embellishes individual notes." Armstrong also introduced *scat singing,* vocalization of a melodic line with nonsense syllables. His gravel-throated voice was not conventionally "beautiful," but it conveyed the same jazz feeling as his trumpet playing.

SWING [JAZZ 5]

A new jazz style called *swing* developed in the 1920s and flourished from 1935 to 1945, a decade nicknamed the "swing era." (In this section, the term *swing* will refer to a specific style rather than to the rhythmic vitality characteristic of all jazz.)

Swing was played mainly by *big bands,* whose powerful sound could fill the large dance halls and ballrooms that mushroomed across the country, particularly after the repeal of prohibition in 1933. There were hundreds of "name" bands—both black and white—like those of Duke Ellington, Count Basie, Glenn Miller, Tommy Dorsey, and Benny Goodman (the "king of swing"). Some bands included such leading musicians as the saxophonists Coleman Hawkins and Lester Young and featured singers like Billie Holiday, Ella Fitzgerald, and Frank Sinatra. During the 1930s and 1940s, the big band was as important as the rock group has been since the 1950s. Swing became a truly popular music, reaching millions of people. Benny Goodman's band, for example, was heard coast to coast on a weekly radio show called *Let's Dance.* The kind of music once associated with honky-tonks and brothels had achieved a new respectability, symbolized by Benny Goodman's historic jazz concert at Carnegie Hall in 1938.

In Section 4, we noted that New Orleans jazz was performed by small groups of five to eight musicians and featured collective improvisation by several soloists. The typical *swing band* had about fourteen or fifteen musicians grouped into three sections: saxophones (three to five players, some doubling on clarinet), brasses (three or four each of trumpet and trombone), and rhythm (piano, percussion, guitar, and bass). A band of that size needed music which was more composed than improvised and was also *arranged,* or notated in written-out parts the musicians could read. With swing, the arranger became an important figure in jazz.

In a swing band, melodies were often performed by entire sections, either in unison or in harmony. Thus, in ensemble playing, it was usually necessary to rely on arrangements instead of improvising. What solo improvisations there were tended to be restricted in length. The main melody was frequently accompanied by saxophones playing sustained chords, or by saxophones and brasses playing short, repeated phrases called *riffs.* Arrangers often used a rapid alternation of brass and sax riffs to create tension and excitement. Each band took pride in the distinctiveness of its sound, which it owed to its arrangers as well as its players.

Not only was the swing band larger and more dependent on arrangements than the New Orleans-style band; it also had other distinctive features. For example, the saxophone became one of the most important solo instruments during the swing era. In addition, percussionists—such as Gene Krupa—had a more prominent role, often taking spectacular solos. They also kept the beat in a new way. While they continued to maintain the pulse on the bass drum, percussionists now used the cymbals to stress the second and fourth beats of the bar:

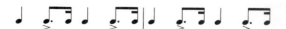

The harmonic vocabulary of swing was richer and more varied than that of earlier jazz, but its forms were essentially the same. As before, jazz performances were usually based on 12-bar blues or on a 32-bar popular song melody. Such melodies can usually be outlined A A B A. An 8-bar phrase is stated and then repeated (A A); a contrasting 8-bar phrase (B) follows; then there's a return to the opening phrase (A).

DUKE ELLINGTON

Edward Kennedy "Duke" Ellington (1899–1974) was perhaps the most important swing-band composer, arranger, and conductor; he certainly ranks among the leading figures in the history of jazz. Ellington's works, which span half a century, include hundreds of 3-minute band pieces, as well as music for film, television, ballet, theater, and church. He was among the first jazz composers to break the 3-minute "sound barrier" imposed by the 78 rpm record, creating extended jazz compositions such as *Black, Brown and Beige.* Ellington accomplished all this while playing the piano, touring the world, and writing such hit songs as *Satin Doll, Sophisticated Lady*, and *In a Sentimental Mood.*

Ellington's music—sometimes created in collaboration with his arranger Billy Strayhorn—is the product of constant experimentation and improvisation. "There is no set system," he once observed. "Most times I write it and arrange it. Sometimes I write it and the band and I collaborate on the arrangement. . . . When we're all working together, a guy may have an idea and he plays it on his horn. Another guy may add to it and make something out of it. Someone may play a riff and ask, "How do you like this?' "

"My band is my instrument," Ellington once remarked. His arrangements are outstanding for their rich variety of sensuous tone colors and for their exploitation of the distinctive sounds of individual musicians. "You've got to write with certain men in mind," he once explained. "I know what Tricky Sam can play on a trombone and I know what Lawrence Brown can play on the trombone, and it is not the same." With his respect for their talents, it's no wonder that many of Ellington's musicians remained in the band for long periods of time.

Ellington's works are richer in harmony and more varied in form than those of this contemporaries. Their variety of mood may be sampled in such works as *Ko-ko, Harlem Air Shaft, In a Mellotone*, and *Blue Serge* (all included in *The Smithsonian Collection of Classic Jazz*).

JAZZ

6

BEBOP

The early 1940s saw the development of *bebop* (or *bop*), a complex style of music usually for small jazz groups. In part, bebop was a rebellion by creative improvisers against the commercialism and written arrangements of swing bands. The new music was meant for attentive listening, not dancing, and its sophisticated harmonies and unpredictable rhythms bewildered many listeners. Bop performers were a special "in" group who sometimes drove other jazz musicians from the bandstand by using complex melodies and unusual chord progressions. "We knew that they couldn't make those chord changes," one bop drummer recalled. "We kept the riff-raff out and built our clique on new chords."

Bebop performers also differentiated themselves by their goatees, berets, and special "hip" language. The bebop center in the early 1940s was a Harlem club called Minton's Playhouse, where young innovators—like the alto saxophonist Charlie Parker, the trumpeter Dizzy Gillespie (1917–1993), and the pianist Thelonious Monk (1917–1982)—came to participate in jam sessions.

BEBOP STYLE

A typical bebop group might include a saxophone and a trumpet supported by a rhythm section of piano, bass, and percussion. The role of rhythm instruments in bebop was different from that in earlier jazz. For example, the bass drum no longer marked the beat but was reserved for occasional irregular accents called *"bombs."* Similarly, the pianist's left hand no longer helped emphasize the basic pulse but joined with the right hand to play complex chords at irregular intervals. Both hands were needed to perform bebop's dense chord structures. The beat, then, was marked mainly by the pizzicato bass.

Rhythms in bop melodies were more varied and unpredictable than those in earlier jazz. In an improvised solo by Charlie Parker, for example, accented notes might come on weak or strong beats, or at varying points within the beat. Bop melodies often had a stream of short notes with accents on the offbeats.

The new style may well have gotten its name from a vocalization of the two fast notes *(be-bop)* that often end phrases. The melodic phrases themselves were often varied and irregular in length. A two- or three-note fragment would be followed by a melodic unit lasting several bars. And the harmonies of bop were as complex as its rhythms. Performers often built melodies on chords consisting of six or seven notes rather than on the four- or five-note chords used in earlier jazz.

A bop performance generally began and ended with a statement of the main theme by one soloist, or by two soloists in unison. The remainder of the piece was made up of solo improvisations based on the melody or harmonic structure. As in earlier jazz, bebop musicians used popular songs and 12-bar blues as a springboard for improvisation. Often, however, they composed *new* tunes to fit the basic harmonies of familiar melodies. As an "in" joke, a bop musician might give a tune a new title so that only sophisticated listeners could guess its origin.

CHARLIE "BIRD" PARKER

The alto saxophonist Charlie Parker (1920–1955) was a towering figure among bebop musicians and one of the greatest of all jazz improvisers. His enormous influence was felt not only by other alto saxophonists but by many other instrumentalists.

Parker was born in Kansas City, Kansas, and grew up in Kansas City, Missouri. As a youngster, he roamed the streets listening outside nightclub doors to the jazz of Lester Young and the Count Basie Band. He was a professional musician by the age of fifteen, having dropped out of school. In his twenties, Parker lived in New York and participated in Harlem jam sessions. He made his first bebop recordings in 1944, and by the late 1940s he was a featured soloist in jazz clubs.

Parker became a prominent musician despite severe personal problems, including drug addiction, alcoholism, ulcers, and emotional illness. But after 1950, his playing declined along with his physical and emotional health. He died in 1955 at the age of thirty-four.

All the style characteristics of bebop were embodied in Parker's improvisations. He was able to control a rich flow of ideas at either slow or very rapid tempos. His amazing technique enabled him to create lightning-fast melodies that sound jagged and angular because of frequent changes of direction. Unlike earlier saxophonists, whose tone was lush and sweet, Parker produced a sound that was rather hard and dry. It perfectly matched the nervous intensity of his melodic lines.

7 JAZZ STYLES SINCE 1950

Since 1950, there have been many innovations and new directions in jazz. The range of styles is wider than ever. But as new styles proliferate, older jazz—from Dixieland to bebop—remains very much alive.

The introduction of long-playing records in 1948 inspired more extended jazz compositions and improvisations. Typically, a jazz performance on a long-playing record might last from 5 to 15 minutes, compared with the 3 minutes permitted by 78 rpm records before 1948. Also, more jazz now was meant for listening than for dancing. It was often heard at concerts on college campuses. Increasingly, jazz musicians studied at colleges and music schools and became familiar with much music other than jazz.

Since 1950, there has been an expansion in the musical resources used in jazz. New meters, rhythms, harmonies, forms, and tone colors have been explored. Orchestral instruments, such as the flute, French horn, and cello, have become a part of jazz. Since the 1960s, synthesizers and the electric piano and bass have come to be used more and more. Also, some musicians of the 1960s created *free jazz*, which discarded many of the forms and basic chord patterns of earlier jazz. Performers drew inspiration from a great variety of sources, including Bach, rock, and the music of Africa, Asia, and Latin America. The interaction between jazz and rock has led to a style known as *jazz rock*. Some musicians, such as Gunther Schuller (b. 1925), created a *third stream* style that is not quite jazz or "classical" but a blend of both. Among all these recent developments, we will consider three of the most important: cool jazz, free jazz, and jazz rock.

COOL JAZZ

During the late 1940s and early 1950s, a jazz style emerged that was related to bop but was far calmer and more relaxed in character. It was called *cool jazz* (in contrast to the "hot" jazz of an earlier era). The leaders of the cool jazz movement were Lester Young (1909–1959) and Stan Getz (b. 1927), tenor saxophonists; Lennie Tristano (1919–1978), a pianist; and Miles Davis (1926–1991), a trumpeter and bandleader who started out as a bebop musician and was also an important figure in jazz during the 1960s, 1970s, and 1980s. Performers of cool jazz played in a relatively subdued manner, with a gentle attack and little vibrato. Cool jazz pieces tended to be longer than bebop works and relied more heavily on arrangements. They sometimes used instruments that were new to jazz, including the French horn, flute, and cello.

One of the finest works in cool jazz style is *Boblicity* (1949), by Miles Davis and the arranger Gil Evans (included in *The Smithsonian Collection of Classic Jazz*). It is scored for an unusual ensemble of nine different instruments: trumpet, trombone, French horn, tuba, alto and baritone saxophones, piano, bass, and drums. The smooth, mellow, blended sound of this ensemble is typical of cool jazz.

Some cool jazz groups, such as the Modern Jazz Quartet, were influenced by the works of Bach and favored polyphonic textures and imitation. Another prominent group influenced by "classical" music was the Dave Brubeck Quartet. It pioneered in the use of meters that had been considered unusual in jazz, such as $\frac{3}{4}$, $\frac{5}{4}$ (in *Take Five*), and $\frac{7}{4}$ (in *Unsquare Dance*, studied in Part I, Section 3).

FREE JAZZ: ORNETTE COLEMAN AND JOHN COLTRANE

Until about 1960, jazz improvisations tended to be quite regular in form. That is, improvised variations kept the length and chord structure of the original theme, even if they abandoned the original melody. During the 1960s, some musicians broke from this tradition and created *free jazz,* a style that was not based on regular forms or established chord patterns.

"If I'm going to follow a preset chord sequence, I may as well write out my solo," commented Ornette Coleman (b. 1930), an alto saxophonist and a major composer of free jazz. In 1960 Coleman assembled eight musicians in a recording studio to improvise individually and collectively with almost no guidelines of melody, form, or harmony. The result was *Free Jazz,* a performance whose apparent randomness can be compared to the chance music created during the same period by John Cage and his followers. (An excerpt from *Free Jazz* is included in *The Smithsonian Collection of Classic Jazz.*) "I don't tell the members of my group what to do," Coleman has explained. "I let everyone express himself just as he wants to." Nevertheless, many performances by Coleman are more highly structured than *Free Jazz,* since they begin and end with a composed theme. (One example is *Lonely Woman,* also included in *The Smithsonian Collection of Classic Jazz.*) Like other free-jazz improvisers, Coleman develops melodic and rhythmic ideas from the theme. In many of his performances, a steady beat and tempo are emphasized much less than in earlier jazz, and his bass and percussion players are given more melodic and rhythmic freedom.

Another musician searching for rhythmic and harmonic freedom during the 1960s was John Coltrane (1926–1967), who was extremely influential as an improviser, tenor and soprano saxophonist, and composer. Coltrane's tone was large, intense, and equally powerful in all registers—an unusual trait. He could play higher than the normal top range of his instrument, and his arpeggios were flung at such lightning speed that they became "sheets of sound." The fury and passion of his improvisations sometimes led to sounds that might be described as "cries," "wails," and "shrieks."

Coltrane's style evolved steadily from the late 1950s, when he worked with Miles Davis, to his untimely death at the age of forty in 1967. His early performances—such as the pathbreaking *Giant Steps* of 1959—feature many complex chords that change very rapidly. His later works, on the other hand, are often based on a background of only two or three chords, each sustained in the accompaniment for many bars. Coltrane's pianist, McCoy Tyner, often sustained a single tone in the bass as a drone, or pedal point, while Coltrane improvised on modes (scales other than the conventional major or minor). Coltrane's growing use of drones and unusual scales may well have been influenced by his deep interest in Indian and Arabic music.

A drone accompaniment is used in Coltrane's meditative work *Alabama* (1963), for tenor saxophone, piano, bass, and drums (this too is in *The Smithsonian Collection of Classic Jazz.*) This short piece is in A B A' form. In the opening section, the saxophone melody is accompanied only by a sustained low broken chord in the piano. The contemplative melody conveys little sense of beat or meter. Only in the middle section is a definite beat heard. When the opening section returns (A'), there is a more active accompaniment as the bass and drums play complex rhythms.

JAZZ ROCK (FUSION)

Rock became a potent influence on jazz starting in the late 1960s. This influence led to *jazz rock,* or *fusion,* a new style combining the jazz musician's improvisatory approach with rock rhythms and tone colors. Jazz rock achieved a popularity unmatched by any other jazz style since the swing of the 1930s and 1940s.

A major figure in the development of jazz rock was the trumpeter Miles Davis, whose albums of 1969 *In a Silent Way* and *Bitches Brew* pointed the way to much of the music of the next decade. Many musicians who played with Davis on these recordings—including the pianists Herbie Hancock, Chick Corea, and Joe Zawinul and the saxophonist Wayne Shorter—became pacesetters of jazz rock during the 1970s, 1980s, and 1990s.

Jazz rock was only one of the substyles that could be heard during the 1970s, 1980s, and 1990s. Every kind of jazz we've studied—New Orleans, swing, bebop, cool jazz, and free jazz—had its fans and devoted performers. As they have done since the early days, jazz musicians continue to explore new resources to further the development of their art.

From Music: An Appreciation, 2E *by Roger Kamien, 1994. Reprinted by permission of The McGraw -Hill Companies.*

Multiple Choice

1. The general organization of this section is
    a. chronological.
    b. cause and effect.
    c. classification.
    d. both *a* and *c*

2. Which of the following could be said about "free jazz"?
    a. One of the major figures in its development was Miles Davis.
    b. It is played in a relatively subdued manner.
    c. It combines improvisation with rock rhythm.
    d. It discarded many forms and chord patterns of earlier jazz.

3. The second paragraph under the heading "Cool Jazz" is written to
    a. further define cool jazz.
    b. give an example of cool jazz.
    c. show the author's bias against cool jazz.
    d. set up a contrast to the previous paragraph.

4. As used in line 2 (of "Jazz Styles since 1950"), the word *proliferate* means
    a. to replace.
    b. to decrease.
    c. to multiply.
    d. to die out.

5. The author's primary purpose in writing section 7 is to
    a. show bias against older forms of jazz.
    b. discuss newer jazz styles.
    c. explain how to play newer styles of jazz.
    d. pinpoint why the new styles have died out.

True or False

_____   6. The interaction between jazz and rock led to a style known as "cool jazz."

_____   7. John Coltrane's style may have been influenced by his interest in Indian and Arabic music.

_____   8. The use of drones is characteristic of cool jazz.

_____   9. Jazz musicians continue to draw on new resources to further their art.

_____   10. The Dave Brubeck Quartet was influenced by classical music.

Vocabulary: Word Parts and Review

Vocabulary Word Parts

Following is a list of the word parts we have studied.

Word Parts	Meaning	Examples
ad	toward	advance
ambi	both	ambiguous, ambidextrous
amphi	both	amphibian
ann, enn	year	annual, biennial
ante(i)	before	anteroom, anticipate
anti	against	antiperspirant
aqua	water	aquarium, aqueduct
audio	hear	audience, auditory
auto	self	automobile, autograph
bi	two	bicycle, biathlon
biblio	book	Bible, bibliography
bio	life	biology, biography
centi	hundred, 1/100	century, centimeter
cide	death	homicide, insecticide
circ	around, ring	circle, circumference
co, com, con	with	coordinate, compare, connect
contra	against	contradict, contrast
cycle	circle, wheel	bicycle
dec	ten	December, decade
demi	half	demitasse
di	two	dioxide
duo	two	duet, duel
equi	half	equator, equinox
extra	over, above	extraordinary, extraterrestrial
frater, fratri	brother	fratricide, fraternity
gam	marriage	polygamy
genus	birth, beginning, race	genius, Genesis, genocide
graph	write	polygraph
hemi	half	hemisphere
hetero	different	heterosexual, heterogeneous
homo	same, man	homogenized, homicide
hydro	water	hydroelectric, hydraulic
hyper	over, above	hyperactive, hyperventilate
hypo	under, below	hypoactive, hypothermia
in	in, not	inside, invisible
infra	under	infrared, infrastructure

Word Parts	Meaning	Examples
inter	between, among	intercollegiate, interstate
intra	within	intravenous, intrastate
lat	side	lateral
macro	large	macroeconomics
magna	large	magnify, magnificent
mania	craving	pyromania
mater, matri	mother	maternal, matricide
mega	large, 1,000,000	megabucks, megabyte
micro	small, 1/1,000,000	microwave, micrometer
milli	thousand, 1/1000	millennium, millimeter
mono	one	monologue, monoxide
multi	many	multicultural
nat	life	natural, native
nov, non	nine	November, nonagenarian
oct	eight	October, octopus
ology	study of	sociology, psychology
omni	all	omnipotent, omnivorous
pan	around	panorama, Panasonic
para	beside, partial, similar	parallel, paralegal, paraphrase
pater, patri	father	paternal, patricide
ped, pod	foot	pedal, pedestrian
pent	five	pentagon, pentathlon
peri	around	periscope, perimeter
phobia	fear	claustrophobia, acrophobia
phono	sound	phonograph, phonics
pneu	air, breathe, wind	pneumatic, pneumonia
poly	many	polygon
post	after	postscript, postnatal
pre	before	pre-test, prenatal
pro	for	pro-democracy
pseudo	false	pseudoscience, pseudonym
quad, quar	four	quartet, quadrangle
quint	five	quintuplets, quintet
retro	backward	retroactive
scope	instrument for seeing	microscope, telescope
scrib, script	write	inscribe, scripture
semi	half	semicircle
sept, hept	seven	September, septuplet, heptathlon
sex	six	sextuplet
sorori	sister	sorority, sororicide
spect	see	spectator, spectrum

Word Parts	Meaning	Examples
sonar	sound	supersonic
sub	under, below	subtract, subscript
super	above, over	supersonic, superscript
syn	same	synonym, symphony
tele	distance	television
tetra	four	tetrahedron
trans	across	transportation
tri	three	tricycle, triangle
ultra	over, more, beyond	ultraconservative, ultrasonic
uni	one	unicycle, unison
vis	see	vision, visionary

Vocabulary Review Questions

Directions: Complete the following sentences with words from the vocabulary list on the preceding pages.

1. Your telephone bill may list _____ calls that you have made to other cities within your state.

2. If you eat a salad with your hamburger, you are eating both meat and plants, and so you are _____.

3. A jazz _____ would have five members.

4. The _____ occurs twice a year, once in March and once in September.

5. You now know that if you went to a nursery and bought some _____ flowers, they would not bloom again next year.

6. Dams on our large rivers provide us with _____ power.

7. Most whole milk that you purchase at the store is called _____ because the milk and the cream are mixed together.

8. In Chapter 1, you learned about _____, visual, and kinesthetic learning styles.

9. "Panorama" would be a _____ for "vista."

10. The chemical formula for water has a _____ in it.

11. People who believe in unidentified flying objects are likely also to believe that _____ have visited us.

12. Many of us are _____ to some extent because we use both our hands.

13. The _____ in Washington, D.C., houses the Defense Department.

14. The California _____ is a canal that moves water from the northern to the southern part of the state.

15. If you wrote a life history about Wynton Marsalis, a famous jazz musician, you would be writing his _____.

16. Present-day jazz music is recorded on compact discs. Jazz used to be recorded on 78 rpm _____ records that could hold only three minutes on a side.

Vocabulary Review

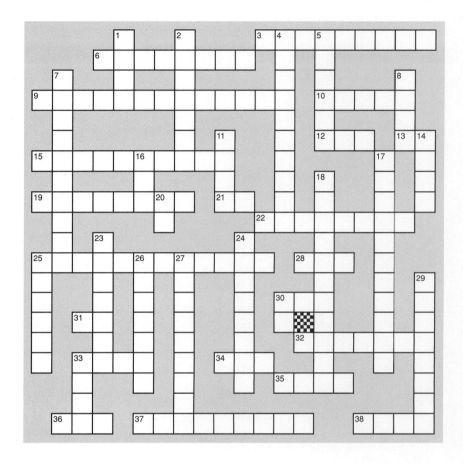

ACROSS CLUES

3. A story about a person's life.
6. Light waves that are too long to be seen by the human eye.
9. The perimeter of a circle is called a _____.
10. Word part meaning "within."
12. Word part meaning "six."
13. Word part meaning "toward."
15. Seven events, usually sporting.
19. To write, carve, or etch into.
21. Word part meaning "not."
22. The armed services have their headquarters in this building.
25. Ability to use both hands equally well.
28. Abbr. for what was originally the ninth month.
30. Abbr. for what was originally the 10th month.
31. Word part meaning "with."

32. Two oxygen atoms, as in carbon _____.
33. Word part meaning "below" or "under."
34. Word part meaning "for."
35. A fight between two people.
36. Word part meaning "see."
37. The tires of your car could be described as _____ because they have air in them.
38. Abbr. for what was originally the seventh month.

DOWN CLUES

1. Word part meaning "air."
2. To the side.
4. Between or among states.
5. Being very intelligent.
7. 1,000 years.
8. Word part meaning "beside," "partial," or "similar."
11. Word part meaning "against."

14. Word part meaning "half."
16. Word part meaning "three."
17. Being too cold.
18. Going back in time.
20. Word part meaning "two."
23. Study of life.
24. Your hearing skills.
25. Once a year.
26. When the sun crosses the equator making night and day of equal length.
27. An instrument for seeing from a distance.
29. Canal is a synonym for this word.
30. Word part meaning "two."
33. Word part meaning "half."

Appendices

We have chosen to place three sections in the Appendices: *Using the Dictionary, Visual Aids,* and *Test-Taking Techniques.* All three sections include an explanation of the topic as well as practice exercises. At the end of the Appendices, you will find copies of some of the forms that appear in the text.

As you learned in this book, you may need to use the dictionary to find a specific meaning for a word. For example, your textbook for a music appreciation class might contain the words "meter," "harmony," and "syncopation," and you would want to look up these words in the dictionary. This section will build your confidence in using dictionaries.

The section on visual aids will improve your skills in interpreting charts and graphs. Text is often supplemented by these materials, and the ability to work with them will help you in understanding what is being said. For example, a textbook for a music appreciation class might have a chart showing the percentage of CDs sold at mass-retail outlets, such as Kmart, versus those sold at smaller retail music shops.

Also included are some tips for improving your test-taking performance. The key to doing well on a test is adequate preparation, but at the very least these tips should help you keep your level of test anxiety under control.

Using the Dictionary

Introduction

The dictionary can be an invaluable tool for you, provided, of course, you have an appropriate one and know at least the fundamentals of using it. You now know that looking a word up in the dictionary is probably only useful if you already have a general idea what the unknown word means from the context of the sentence or article. The dictionary has tons of information, probably too much. You have to sort through it and find the information helpful to you.

Selecting a Dictionary

Rule 1—The dictionary needs to be up-to-date. Take a look at your dictionary. *Find the copyright date. If your dictionary is over 10 years old, you need a new one.* Our language changes. New words are added. Other words take on new meanings. Let's take the word "gay" and see how its meaning pertaining to homosexuality evolved through three different editions of what is now called the *American Heritage College Dictionary.* The writers of the first edition, originally published in 1969, considered the term "slang." By 1982, the word "gay" had become commonly accepted, thus calling it "slang" was no longer necessary. The authors of the third edition, copyrighted in 1993, felt that the term was not only commonly used, but that it needed further explanation. They, therefore, added a "usage note" to give the reader further information.

397

1969 edition   **gay** (gā) *adj.* **gayer, gayest. 1.** Showing or characterized by exuberance or mirthful excitement. **2.** Bright or lively, especially in color. **3.** Full of or given to social or other pleasures. **4.** Dissolute; licentious. **5.** *Slang.* Homosexual. [Middle English *gay, gai,* from Old French *gai,* from Old Provençal, probably from Gothic *gaheis* (unattested), akin to Old High German *gāhi*†, sudden, impetuous.] —**gay'ness** *n.*

1982 edition   **gay** (gā) *adj.* **-er, -est. 1.** Showing or characterized by exuberance or happy excitement; merry. **2.** Bright or lively, esp. in color. **3.** Full of or given to social pleasures. **4.** Dissolute; licentious. **5.** Homosexual. —*n.* A homosexual. [ME *gai* < OFr., of Germanic orig.] —**gay** *adv.* —**gay'ness** *n.*

1993 edition   **gay** (gā) *adj.* **gay·er, gay·est. 1.** Showing or characterized by cheerfulness and lighthearted excitement; merry. **2.** Bright or lively, esp. in color. **3.** Of, relating to, or sharing the lifestyle and concerns of the homosexual community. **4.** Homosexual. **5.** Given to social pleasures. **6.** Dissolute; licentious. —*n.* A gay person, esp. an openly gay person in contemporary society. [ME *gai* < OFr., poss. of Gmc. orig.] —**gay'ness** *n.*

       Usage Note: The word *gay* is now standard in its use to refer to the American homosexual community and its members; in this use it is generally lowercased. *Gay* is distinguished from *homosexual* in emphasizing the cultural and social aspects of homosexuality. Many writers reserve *gay* for male homosexuals, but the word is used to refer to both sexes; when the intended meaning is not clear in the context, the phrase *gay and lesbian* should be used. *Gay* may be regarded as offensive when used as a noun to refer to particular individuals, as in *There were two gays on the panel*; here a phrase such as *gay people* should be used instead. But there is no objection to the use of the noun in the plural to refer to the general gay community.

Note: Often discount department stores advertise dictionaries for a very cheap cost. Take off the cellophane wrapper and find the publication date. You may find it already a few years out-of-date. Remember that "you get what you pay for."

Rule 2—Have two dictionaries—one hardbound and one softbound. Preferably the two dictionaries should be written by two different publishing companies.

Hardbound dictionary—Hardbound dictionaries have hard covers. This dictionary should be kept at home on a shelf in your study area. Hardbound dictionaries include more words and information than their softbound editions. Contrast the two examples below, the first from the hardbound edition of the *Random House Webster's College Dictionary* and the second from its softbound counterpart, the *Random House Webster's School and Office Dictionary*. At first glance the two dictionaries look the same, but you simply cannot cram 1,500 pages of the hardbound version into 544 pages which is the length of the softbound book. The first example from the hardbound edition is, obviously, much more complete. The hardbound version of this dictionary has 160,000 entries while the softbound edition only has 60,000.

Hardbound edition

jazz (jaz), *n.* **1.** music originating in New Orleans around the beginning of the 20th century and subsequently developing through various increasingly complex styles, generally marked by intricate, propulsive rhythms, polyphonic ensemble playing, improvisatory, virtuosic solos, melodic freedom, and a harmonic idiom ranging from simple diatonicism through chromaticism to atonality. **2.** a style of dance music marked by some of the features of jazz. **3.** *Slang.* liveliness; spirit; excitement. **4.** *Slang.* insincere or pretentious talk. **5.** *Slang.* similar or related but unspecified things: *We like sightseeing, museums, and all that jazz.* —*v.t.* **6.** to play (music) in the manner of jazz. **7.** *Slang.* **a.** to excite or enliven. **b.** to accelerate. —*v.i.* **8.** *Slang.* to act or proceed with great energy or liveliness. **9. jazz up**, *Slang.* **a.** to enliven. **b.** to embellish. [1910–15, *Amer.*]

jazz•er•cise (jaz′ər sīz′), *n.* vigorous dancing done to jazz dance music as an exercise for physical fitness. [1985–90; JAZZ + (EX)ERCISE]

jazz•man (jaz′man′, -mən), *n., pl.* **-men** (-men′, -mən). a musician who plays jazz. [1925–30]

jazz′-rock′, *n.* music that combines elements of both jazz and rock and is usu. performed on amplified electric instruments. [1965–70]

jazz•y (jaz′ē), *adj.,* **jazz•i•er, jazz•i•est. 1.** pertaining to or suggestive of jazz music. **2.** *Slang.* active or lively. **3.** *Slang.* fancy or flashy: *a jazzy sweater.* [1915–20, *Amer.*] —**jazz′i•ly,** *adv.* —**jazz′i•ness,** *n.*

From *Random House Webster's College Dictionary* by Random House, Inc. Copyright © 1995, 1992, 1991 by Random House, Inc. Reprinted by permission of Random House, Inc.

Softbound edition

jazz (jaz), *n.* **1.** music originating in New Orleans, marked by propulsive rhythms, ensemble playing, and improvisation. **2.** *Slang.* insincere or pretentious talk. —*v.t.* **3. jazz up**, *Slang.* **a.** to enliven. **b.** to embellish.

jazz′y, *adj.,* **-i•er, -i•est 1.** of or suggestive of jazz music. **2.** *Slang.* fancy or flashy.

From *Random House School and Office Dictionary* by Random House, Inc. Copyright © 1997 by Random House, Inc. Reprinted by permission of Random House, Inc.

Softbound dictionary—These dictionaries have soft covers, similar to the ones on the outside of this book. Unless the football coach has told you to build up your shoulder muscles, you probably don't need the weight of that heavy hardbound dictionary in your backpack. We therefore suggest that you buy a softbound dictionary for quick and easy reference while you are in class or in the library.

Computer dictionary—Dictionaries are now beginning to be put on computer disks and CD-ROMS. If you are going to be using a computer to write your papers, you might also want to look into a good dictionary on a CD-ROM or a floppy disk. We highly recommend learning how to use a computer and writing all your papers on it. Buying a computer is well worth the money. You can decide whether or not it's worth the money to purchase one of these dictionaries on disk.

Unabridged dictionary—You don't need to buy an unabridged dictionary, but such a dictionary can be very useful. Unabridged dictionaries have all the words in our language. You can find these dictionaries in your college library. Many students find them useful to locate obscure words.

Note: Now why should you have a softbound dictionary written by one publishing company and a hardbound version written by another? Having two dictionaries gives you two different perspectives on a word. The definitions are written slightly differently. When you are having problems understanding the definition from one dictionary, then you can try the other one.

Dictionary Inventory

Take a look at your present dictionary and answer the questions below. Maybe this inventory will help you decide whether you need a new dictionary and/or what type of new dictionary would be best for you. Remember that dictionaries are like cars. There is no one best car or no one best dictionary. There are different companies making different models for different people.

Yes   No

_____ _____ 1. Is the publication date less than 10 years old?

_____ _____ 2. Are the definitions easy to understand? Does the dictionary help you?

_____ _____ 3. Does it have good biographical information, either in the main part of the dictionary or at the end? (Look up the name of a famous person, such as "Louis Armstrong.")

_____ _____ 4. Does it have geographical names, either in the main part of the dictionary or at the end? Look up a large city such as "New Orleans." Is the information given for this city suitable for your purposes?

_____ _____ 5. Does your dictionary give variations of words so you can spell them correctly? (For example, look up the word "consume." Does your dictionary also give the spelling for "consuming?" You might need to know that there is no "e" in the word "consuming.")

_____ _____ 6. Does it list word parts separately? Look up some of the word parts you have been studying:

_____ _____   retro

_____ _____   logy

_____ _____   audio

_____ _____ 7. Do some entries have the word in a sample phrase or sentence?

_____ _____ 8. Does the dictionary discuss the difference between words with similar meanings? (For example, look up the homonyms "affect" and "effect" and find out whether there is a discussion about the different uses of these two words.)

_____ _____ Does the explanation help you?

_____ _____ 9. Does your dictionary give subject labels for some definitions? (Look up the word "depression," for example.)

_____ _____ 10. Is the type large enough for easy reading? This is more important for some of us who are older.

Decide whether you need a new dictionary. Decide which one would be best for you. Go to a good bookstore, such as the one at your college, and buy yourself a dictionary. You won't regret your decision.

Organization

We have now found out about selecting an appropriate dictionary. Now let's see what's in this resource book. The discussion and examples below will often refer to the sample dictionary page found on the following page. We have taken an excerpt from pp. 1153–1154 of the _Random House Webster's College Dictionary_, 2nd ed., 1997, enlarged the print, and adapted the pages for your use.

1. Entry words
Dictionaries are organized like telephone books, in alphabetical order. Each entry word is usually in boldface type. Often dictionaries will also give common two- or three-word phrases as entry words.

What boldface entry comes after "sawbones"? _____

2. Guide words
As in a telephone book, there are guide words at the top of each page that indicate the first and last entries on that page.

What are the guide words for this page? _____

3. Entry word division versus pronunciation—syllabication division
For each entry, the word division and the pronunciation and syllabication division are usually the same.

How many syllables are there in the word "saxophone"? _____

You should realize that some dictionaries divide their entry words as you would for printers and typesetting, thus the entry word and pronunciation divisions may not be exactly the same. Take a look at the word "curious." Notice that the entry word is divided differently than its pronunciation.

cu•ri•ous (kyo͝or′ē əs), _adj._ **1.** eager to learn or know. **2.** taking an undue interest in others' affairs; prying. **3.** arousing attention or interest through being unusual or hard to explain; odd; strange; novel. **4.** _Archaic._ **a.** made or done skillfully or painstakingly. **b.** careful; fastidious. **c.** marked by intricacy or subtlety. [1275–1325; ME < L _cūriōsus_ careful, inquisitive, prob. back formation from _incūriōsus_ careless, der. of _incūria_ carelessness] —**cu′ri•ous•ly,** _adv._ —**cu′ri•ous•**

From _Random House Webster's College Dictionary_ by Random House, Inc. Copyright © 1995, 1992, 1991 by Random House, Inc. Reprinted by permission of Random House, Inc.

savvy to sb.

sav·vy (sav′ē), *n., adj.,* **-vi·er, -vi·est,** *v.,* **-vied, -vy·ing.** —*n.* **1.** Also, **sav′vi·ness.** practical understanding; shrewdness or intelligence; common sense: *political savvy.* —*adj.* **2.** shrewdly informed; experienced and well-informed; canny. —*v.t., v.i.* **3.** to know; understand. [1775–85; prob. orig. < *sábi* "know" in E creoles (< Pg *sabe,* pres. 3rd sing. of *saber* to know < L *sapere* to be wise; see SAPIENT)] — **sav′vi·ly,** *adv.*

saw[1] (sô), *n., v.,* **sawed, sawed** or **sawn, saw·ing.** —*n.* **1.** a tool or device for cutting, typically a thin blade of metal with a series of sharp teeth. **2.** any similar tool or device, as a rotating disk, in which a sharp continuous edge replaces the teeth. —*v.t.* **3.** to cut or divide with a saw. **4.** to form by cutting with a saw. **5.** to make cutting motions as if using a saw: *to saw the air with one's hands.* **6.** to work (something) from side to side like a saw. —*v.i.* **7.** to use a saw. **8.** to cut with or as if with a saw. —*Idiom.* **9. saw wood,** to snore loudly while sleeping. [bef. 1000; ME *sawe,* OE *saga,* c. MLG, MD *sage* (D *zaag*), OHG *saga,* ON *sǫg;*] —**saw′er,** *n.*

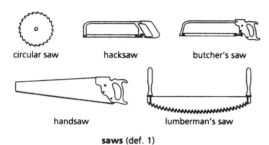

circular saw   hacksaw   butcher's saw

handsaw   lumberman's saw

saws (def. 1)

saw[2] (sô), *v.* pt. of SEE[1].

saw[3] (sô), *n.* a maxim; proverb; saying; *an old saw.* [bef. 950; ME; OE *sagu;* c. OFris *sege,* OHG, G *sage,* ON *saga* (cf. SAGA); akin to SAY]

Sa·watch (sə wäch′), *n.* a mountain range in central Colorado: part of the Rocky Mountains. Highest peak, Mt. Elbert, 14,431 ft. (4400 m).

saw·bones (sô′bōnz′), *n., pl.* **-bones, -bones·es.** (*used with a sing. v.*) *Slang.* a surgeon or physician. [1830–40]

saw·buck (sô′buk′), *n.* **1.** a sawhorse. **2.** *Slang.* a ten-dollar bill. [1860–65, *Amer.;* cf. D *zaagbok;* (def. 2) so called from the resemblance of the Roman numeral X to the crossbars of a sawhorse]

saw·dust (sô′dust′), *n.* fine particles of wood produced in sawing.

sawed′-off′, *adj.* **1.** cut off at the end, as a shotgun. **2.** *Slang.* smallish; of less than average size or stature. [1865–70, *Amer.*]

saw·fish (sô′fish′), *n., pl.* (*esp. collectively*) **-fish,** (*esp. for kinds or species*) **-fish·es.** any large, sharklike ray of the genus *Pristis,* living along tropical coasts and lowland rivers, with a bladelike snout edged with strong teeth. [1655–65]

saw·fly (sô′flī′), *n., pl.* **-flies.** any of numerous insects of the family Tenthredinidae, the female of which has a sawlike ovipositor for inserting the eggs in the tissues of a host plant. [1765–75]

saw·horse (sô′hôrs′), *n.* a movable frame or trestle for supporting wood while it is being sawed. [1770–80]

saw·mill (sô′mil′), *n.* a place or building in which timber is sawed into planks, boards, etc., by machinery. [1545–55]

sawn (sôn), *v.* a pp. of SAW[1].

saw′ palmet′to, *n.* a shrublike palmetto, *Serenoa repens,* native to the southern U.S., having green or blue leafstalks set with spiny teeth.

saw·tooth (sô′tōōth′), *n., pl.* **-teeth** (-tēth′), *adj.* —*n.* **1.** one of the cutting teeth of a saw. —*adj.* **2.** having a zigzag profile, like that of the cutting edge of a saw; serrate. [1595–1605]

saw′-toothed′, *adj.* having sawlike teeth; serrate. [1580–90]

saw′-whet′ owl′, *n.* a small North American owl, *Aegolius acadicus,* with a persistently repeated, mechanical sounding note. [1825–35, *Amer.;* from its cry being likened to a saw being whetted]

saw·yer (sô′yər, soi′ər), *n.* **1.** a person who saws wood, esp. as an occupation. **2.** any of several long-horned beetles, esp. one of the genus *Monochamus,* the larvae of which bore in the wood of coniferous trees. [1300–50; ME *sawier* = *sawe* SAW[1] + *-ier* -IER[1]]

sax (saks), *n.* a saxophone. [by shortening]

Sax., **1.** Saxon. **2.** Saxony.

sax·a·tile (sak′sə til), *adj.* living or growing on or among rocks; saxicoline. [1645–55; < L *saxātilis* frequenting rocks, der. of *sax(um)* rock]

Saxe (sAks), *n.* French name of SAXONY.

Saxe-Co·burg-Go·tha (saks′kō′bûrg gō′thə), *n.* **1.** a member of the present British royal family, from the establishment of the house in 1901 until 1917 when the family name was changed to Windsor. **2. Albert Francis Charles Augustus Emanuel, Prince of,** ALBERT, Prince.

sax·horn (saks′hôrn′), *n.* any of a family of brass instruments close to the cornets and tubas. [1835–45; after A. *Sax* (1814–94), a Belgian who invented such instruments]

sax·ic·o·line (sak sik′ə lin, -līn′) also **sax·ic·o·lous** (-ləs), *adj.* living or growing among rocks. [1895–1900; < NL *saxicol(a)* (L *saxi-,* comb. form of *saxum* rock + *-cola* dweller; see -COLOUS) + -INE[1]]

sax·i·frage (sak′sə frij), *n.* any of numerous plants of the genus *Saxifraga,* certain species of which grow wild in the clefts of rocks, other species of which are cultivated for their flowers. [1400–50; late ME < L *saxifraga* (*herba*) stone-breaking (herb) = *saxi-,* comb. form of *saxum* stone + *-fraga,* fem. of *-fragus* breaking; see FRAGILE]

sax·i·tox·in (sak′si tok′sin), *n.* a neurotoxin produced by the dinoflagellate *Gonyaulax catenella,* the causative agent of red tide. [1960–65; < NL *Saxi(domus),* a clam genus infected by the dinoflagellates (L *sax(um)* stone + *-i- -i- + domus* house) + TOXIN]

Sax·o Gram·mat·i·cus (sak′sō grə mat′i kəs), *n.* c1150–1206?, Danish historian and poet.

Sax·on (sak′sən), *n.* **1.** a member of a Germanic people or confederation of peoples, occupying parts of the North Sea littoral and adjacent hinterlands in the 3rd–4th centuries A.D.: later notorious as sea raiders, groups of whom invaded and settled in S Britain in the 5th–6th centuries. **2.** a native or inhabitant of Saxony. **3.** a native of England, or person of English descent, esp. as opposed to an inhabitant of the British Isles of Celtic descent. —*adj.* **4.** of or pertaining to the early Saxons. **5.** of or pertaining to Saxony or its inhabitants. [1250–1300; ME, prob. < LL *Saxō, Saxonēs* (pl.) < Gmc; r. OE *Seaxan* (pl.)]

sax·o·ny (sak′sə nē), *n.* **1.** a fine, three-ply woolen yarn. **2.** a soft-finish, compact fabric for coats. [1825–35; from SAXONY]

Sax·o·ny (sak′sə nē), *n.* **1.** a state in E central Germany, 4,900,000; 6561 sq. mi. (16,990 sq. km). *Cap.:* Dresden. **2.** a former state of the Weimar Republic in E central Germany. 5788 sq. mi. (14,990 sq. km). *Cap.:* Dresden. **3.** a medieval division of N Germany with varying boundaries: extended at its height from the Rhine to E of the Elbe. German, **Sachsen;** French, **Saxe.** —**Sax·o′ni·an** (-sō′nē ən), *n., adj.*

Sax′ony-An′halt, *n.* a state in central Germany. 3,000,000; 9515 sq. mi. (24,644 sq. km). *Cap.:* Magdeburg. German, **Sachsen-Anhalt.**

sax·o·phone (sak′sə fōn′), *n.* a musical wind instrument consisting of a conical, usu. brass tube with keys or valves and a mouthpiece with one reed. [1850–55; *Sax* (see SAXHORN) + -o- + -PHONE] —**sax′o·phon′ic** (-fon′ik), *adj.* —**sax′o·phon′ist,** *n.*

saxophone

say (sā), *v.,* **said, say·ing,** *adv., n., interj.* —*v.t.* **1.** to utter or pronounce; speak: *to say a word.* **2.** to express in words; state; declare: *Say what you think.* **3.** to state as an opinion or judgment: *I say we should wait here.* **4.** to recite or repeat. **5.** to report or allege; maintain. **6.** to express (a message, viewpoint, etc.), as through a literary or other artistic medium. **7.** to indicate or show: *What does your watch say?* —*v.i.* **8.** to speak; declare; express an opinion, idea, etc. —*adv.* **9.** approximately; about: *It's, say, 14 feet long.* **10.** for example. —*n.* **11.** what a person says or has to say. **12.** the right or opportunity to state an opinion or exercise influence: *to have one's say in a decision.* **13.** a turn to say something. —*interj.* **14.** (used to express surprise, get attention, etc.) —*Idiom.* **15. go without saying,** to be completely self-evident. [bef. 900; ME *seyen, seggen,* OE *secgan;* c. D *zeggen,* G *sagen,* ON *segja;* akin to SAW[3]] —**say′er,** *n.*

say·a·ble (sā′ə bəl), *adj.* **1.** of the sort that can be said or spoken. **2.** capable of being said or stated clearly, effectively, etc. [1855–60]

Sa·yan′ Moun′tains (sä yän′), *n.pl.* a mountain range in the S Russian Federation in central Asia. Highest peak, 11,447 ft. (3490 m).

say·est (sā′ist) also **sayst** (sāst), *v. Archaic.* 2nd pers. sing. of SAY.

say·ing (sā′ing), *n.* something said, esp. a proverb or maxim.

sa·yo·na·ra (sī′ə när′ə), *interj., n.* farewell. [1870–75; < Japn]

says (sez), *v.* 3rd pers. sing. pres. indic. of SAY.

say′-so′, *n., pl.* **say-sos. 1.** one's personal statement or assertion. **2.** right of final authority. **3.** an authoritative statement. [1630–40]

say·yid or say′yed or say·id (sā′yid, sā′id), *n.* **1.** a supposed descendant of Muhammad through his grandson Hussein. **2.** an Islamic title of respect, esp. for royal personages. [1780–90; < Ar: lord]

Sb, *Chem. Symbol.* antimony. [< LL *stibium*]

sb., substantive.

Look at the word "banana" and see how three different dictionaries divide the entry word.

American Heritage	ba•nan•a
Webster's New World	ba•nan|a
Merriam Webster	ba•nana

4. Pronunciation

Notice how most entries are followed by their pronunciations, but that the words are written quite differently. Dictionaries will use letters and symbols that represent sounds. Usually you will find a complete key to these sounds in the front part of the dictionary. Below is the Random House pronunciation key. Sometimes alternate pronunciations will also be given. For example, the word "sawyer" has two pronunciations (see previous page).

ENGLISH SOUNDS

a act, bat, marry
ā age, paid, say
âr air, Mary, dare
ä ah, balm, star
b back, cabin, cab
ch child, pitcher, beach
d do, madder, bed
e edge, set, merry
ē equal, bee, pretty
ēr earring, cheerful, appear
f fit, differ, puff
g give, trigger, beg
h hit, behave
hw which, nowhere
i if, big, mirror
ī ice, bite, deny
j just, tragic, fudge
k keep, token, make

l low, mellow, bottle (bot′l)
m my, summer, him
n now, sinner, button (but′n)
ng sing, Washington
o ox, bomb, wasp
ō over, boat, no
ô order, ball, raw
oi oil, joint, joy
o͝o oomph, book, tour
o͞o ooze, fool, too
ou out, loud, cow
p pot, supper, stop
r read, hurry, near
s see, passing, miss
sh shoe, fashion, push
t ten, matter, bit
th thin, ether, path

t͡h that, either, smooth
u up, sun
ûr urge, burn, cur
v voice, river, live
w witch, away
y yes, onion
z zoo, lazy, those
zh treasure, mirage
ə used in unaccented syllables to indicate the sound of the reduced vowel in alone, system, easily, gallop, circus
ᵊ used between i and r and between ou and r to show triphthongal quality, as in fire (iᵊr), hour (ouᵊr)

NON-ENGLISH SOUNDS

A as in French **ami** (A mē′)
KH as in Scottish **loch** (lôKH)
N as in French **bon** (bôN) [used to indicate that the preceding vowel is nasalized]

Œ as in French **feu** (fŒ)
R [a symbol for any non-english r sound, including a trill or flap in Italian and Spanish and a sound in French

and German similar to KH but pronounced with voice]
Y as in French **tu** (tY)
ᵊ as in French **bastogne** (ba stòn′yᵊ)

From *Random House Webster's College Dictionary* by Random House, Inc. Copyright © 1995, 1992, 1991 by Random House, Inc. Reprinted by permission of Random House, Inc.

What words show how "oi" is pronounced?_____

Write out the pronunciations for the following words:

sayable _____

sawyer (both pronunciations) _____

sawtooth _____

5. Parts of speech

Each word will also have its part or parts of speech listed: "n." would be for a noun; "v." would be a verb, and so forth. *Note:* "v.t." is for a transitive verb and "v.i." is for an intransitive verb. A transitive verb takes a direct object while an intransitive does not.

Find the parts of speech for the words below. Write out the whole word, such as "adjective" for "adj."

Saxe   _____

sayable   _____

sayyid   _____

6. Etymology

We have been studying word etymologies, or word histories, in the vocabulary units throughout this book. We will not list all the abbreviations used for different languages, but "L" is the abbreviation for Latin and "Gk" stands for Greek.

Find out the Latin meaning for

savvy _____

saxicoline_____

Many words in English come from other languages. From what language does the word "sayonara" come? _____

7. Words in phrases

Some dictionaries, such as the *Random House Webster's College Dictionary*, give some words in sample phrases. Take a look at the definitions for "say" and see how this word is used in sample phrases.

What are some of the phrases used for this word? _____

_____

8. Geographical and biographical information

Most dictionaries place this information in with the regular entries. Other dictionaries, such as the Merriam Webster dictionaries, give this information at the end of the dictionary.

Where is Saxony and what is its capital city? _____

Dictionary Practice Exercise #1   *Directions:* Answer the following questions using any available dictionary.

1. How many definitions are there for the word **empty?** _____

2. From what language does **macho** originate? _____

3. What is the difference between **appeal** and **appease?** _____

    _____

    _____

4. What is a synonym for **loiter?**_____

5. After liver transplant surgery, a patient needs many weeks to recuperate. What does the word **recuperate** mean in this sentence?

    _____

    What is the part of speech? _____

Use your dictionary pronunciation guide to identify these movies. Write the titles on the lines below.

6. brāv härt _____

7. grāt ek spek tā shəns _____

8. pəlp fik-shən _____

9. dī härd with a ven-jens _____

10. the brijiz əv mad-ə- sən kount-ē _____

    _____

11. What is the plural of the word **family?** _____

12. What part of speech is **compulsiveness?** _____

13. What part of speech is **conventional?** _____

14. What language does **gaiety** come from? _____

Dictionary Exercise #2   *Directions:* Use the dictionary page provided to answer the following questions:

1. How many syllables does each of the following entry words have?

   sawyer _____

   saxicoline _____

   sayable _____

2. Write the part(s) of speech for each of the following entry words:

   saw _____

   Saxon _____

3. Write the plural forms for the following words:

   sawbones _____

   sawfly _____

   sayso _____

   sawtooth _____

4. Find an entry word that is an example of each of the following:

   a place _____

   a person _____

   an animal _____

5. Name two entries that have pictures as aids to understand their meanings.

   _____

   _____

6. How many meanings are given for each of the following entry words.

   saw[1] _____

   sawyer _____

   Saxon _____

7. What suffixes are used to change "savvy" to different parts of speech?

    _____

8. What is the origin of the word "saxatile"? _____

    _____

9. Pronounce the following words. Then write each word using correct spelling.

    sak si tok sin _____

    sā ing _____

    sez _____

    saks _____

10. Refer to the dictionary page to answer the following questions. Use T for true and F for false.

    _____   a. **Sawbones** is slang for a surgeon or physician.

    _____   b. To **saw wood** means to sing loudly.

    _____   c. A **savvy** person is dull-witted.

    _____   d. The British royal family no longer uses the name **Saxe Coburg Gotha.**

Dictionary Exercise #3: Abbreviations   *Directions:* Most dictionaries use many abbreviations. Using the abbreviation key found on the next page, write what the following abbreviations and symbols mean.

1. ME _____   19. It. _____
2. pl. _____   20. L _____
3. n. _____   21. Gk. _____
4. v.t. _____   22. sing. _____
5. v.i. _____   23. obs. _____
6. adj. _____   24. orig. _____
7. adv. _____   25. poss. _____
8. prep. _____   26. pres. _____
9. conj. _____   27. Russ _____
10. pron. _____   28. Sp. _____
11. fem. _____   29. Syn. _____
12. masc. _____   30. Heb. _____
13. OE _____
14. < _____
15. E. _____
16. etym. _____
17. Fr. _____
18. Ger. _____

ABBREVIATION KEY

• unattested, reconstructed

< descended from, borrowed from

<< descended from, borrowed from through intermediate stages not shown

= equivalent to

> whence

ab. about

Abbr.,

abbr. abbreviation

abl. ablative

acc. accusative

adj. adjective, adjectival

adv. adverb, adverbial

AF Anglo-French

Afr. African

Afrik Afrikaans

AL Anglo-Latin

alter. alteration

Amer American

Amer. Americanism

AmerSp American Spanish

aph. aphetic

appar. apparently

Ar, Arab. Arabic

assoc. association

at. no. atomic number

at. wt. atomic weight

aug. augmentative

b. blend of, blended

bef. before

Bot. Botany

Brit. British

Bulg. Bulgarian

c about (Latin *circa*)

c. cognate with

CanF Canadian French

Cap. capital (of country or state)

cap.,

caps. capital, capitals

cent. century

Cf., cf. compare (Latin *confer*)

Ch. Church

Chin,

Chin. Chinese

cm. centimeter(s)

Com. Commerce

comb.

form combining form

comp.,

compar. comparative

conj. conjunction

contr. contraction

Cor. Corinthians

D Dutch

d. died

Dan, Dan. Danish

Dan. Daniel

dat. dative

def., defs. definition, definitions

der. derivative

Deut. Deuteronomy

diag. diagram

Dial., dial. dialect, dialectal

dim. diminutive

disting. distinguished

Du. Dutch

E English

e east, eastern

EGmc East Germanic

Eng. England, English

esp. especially

etym. etymology, etymological

Ex. Exodus

Ezek. Ezekiel

F French

fem. feminine

fig. figurative

Fin. Finnish

fl. flourished

fol. followed

Fr. French

freq. frequentative

Fris Frisian

ft. foot, feet

fut. future

G German

Gal. Galatians

Gallo-Rom Gallo-Romance

Gen. Genesis

gen. genitive

Ger. German

ger. gerund, gerundive

Gk, Gk. Greek

Gmc Germanic

Go Gothic

Heb, Heb. Hebrew

Hos. Hosea

Icel, Icel. Icelandic

IE Indo-European

illus. illustration

imit. imitative

imper. imperative

impv. imperative

in. inch(es)

ind., indic. indicative

inf. infinitive

interj. interjection

intransit. intransitive

Ir Irish

irreg. irregular, irregularly

Isa. Isaiah

It, It. Italian

Japn, Japn. Japanese

Jer. Jeremiah

km kilometer(s)

Kor. Korean

L Latin

LaF Louisiana French

Lat. Latin

l.c. lowercase

Lev. Leviticus

LG Low German

LGk Late Greek

Ling. Linguistics

lit. literally

Lith Lithuanian

LL Late Latin

m meter(s)

Mach. Machinery

masc. masculine

Matt. Matthew

MChin Middle Chinese

MD Middle Dutch

ME Middle English

Mech. Mechanics

MexSp Mexican Spanish

MF Middle French

MGk Medieval Greek

MHG Middle High German

mi. mile(s)

MIr Middle Irish

ML Medieval Latin

MLG Middle Low German

mm millimeter(s)

mod. modern

ModGk Modern Greek

ModHeb Modern Hebrew

MPers Middle Persian

N north, northern

n. noun, nominal

Neh. Nehemiah

neut. neuter

NL New Latin

nom. nominative

Norw, Norw. Norwegian

n.pl. plural noun

Num. Numbers

obj. objective

obl. oblique

Obs., obs. obsolete

Oc Occitan

OCS Old Church Slavonic

OE Old English

OF Old French

OFris Old Frisian

OHG Old High German

OIr Old Irish

OL Old Latin

ON Old Norse

ONF Old North French

OPers Old Persian

OPr Old Provençal

OPruss Old Prussian

orig. origin, originally

ORuss Old Russian

OS Old Saxon

OSp Old Spanish

PaG Pennsylvania German

pass. passive

past part. past participle

perh. perhaps

Pers, Pers. Persian

pers. person

Pg Portuguese

pl. plural

Pol, Pol. Polish

Port. Portuguese

poss. possessive

pp. past participle

prec. preceded

prep. preposition

pres. present, present tense

pres. part. present participle

prob. probably

Pron., pronunciation,

pron. pronounced

pron. pronoun

Pros. Prosody

prp. present participle

pt. preterit (past tense)

ptp. past participle

r. replacing

redupl. reduplication

repr. representing

resp. respelling, respelled

Rev. Revelations

Rom Romance

Rom. Roman, Romanian

Russ Russian

S south, southern

s. stem

Sam. Samuel

Scand Scandinavian

Scot. Scottish

ScotGael Scottish Gaelic

sing. singular

Skt, Skt. Sanskrit

Sp, Sp. Spanish

sp. spelling, spelled

SpAr Spanish Arabic

sp. gr. specific gravity

sq. square

subj. subjunctive

superl. superlative

Sw, Sw. Swedish

SwissF Swiss French

syll. syllable

Syn. Synonym (Study)

trans. translation

transit. transitive

Turk. Turkish

ult. ultimately

uncert. uncertain

usu. usually

v. verb, verbal

var. variant

var. s. variant stem

vi. intransitive verb

VL Vulgar Latin

voc. vocative

vt. transitive verb

W west, western

WGmc West Germanic

yd. yard(s)

From *Random House Webster's College Dictionary* by Random House, Inc. Copyright © 1995, 1992, 1991 by Random House, Inc. Reprinted by permission of Random House, Inc.

Visual Aids

How Do We Use and Interpret Graphs and Tables?

Visual aids are useful tools that help us to understand written material. Visual aids can be as simple as a street map or as complex as a statistical table. Because textbook authors frequently use visual aids to explain complicated information, it is very important to look closely at all illustrations and understand what they represent. Those of you who are strong in visual-spatial intelligence may find this section easier than those of you who have strengths in other areas. In this section, we are going to help you learn how to read and interpret graphs and tables found in various books, magazines, and newspapers.

Here are some steps to follow when looking at a visual aid:

1. Read the title and subtitle. It will tell you what the graph or table is about.

2. Read the key or legend. These will explain how to interpret the graph or table.

3. Determine the purpose of the graph or table. Why did the author include it? Is it there to provide objective information? Or to support the author's bias?

4. Determine the source of the information provided. A graph or table published by a government agency may be more objective than one published by a special-interest group.

5. Look at how the graph or table is set up. If there are horizontal or vertical scales, determine what they measure. What is the unit of measurement? Thousands? Millions?

6. Look for highs, lows, trends, and relationships. What conclusions can you reach?

TOP 15 REGULARLY SCHEDULED NETWORK PROGRAMS, 1995–96[1]

Rank	Program Name (network)	Total Percent of TV Households
1.	E.R. (NBC)	22.0
2.	Seinfeld (NBC)	21.2
3.	Friends (NBC)	18.7
4.	Caroline in the City (NBC)	17.9
5.	NFL Monday Night Football (ABC)	17.1
6.	Single Guy (NBC)	16.7
7.	Home Improvement (ABC)	16.2
8.	Boston Common (NBC)	15.6
9.	60 Minutes (CBS)	14.2
10.	NYPD Blue (ABC)	14.1
11.	Frasier (NBC)	13.6
11.	20/20 (ABC)	13.6
13.	Grace Under Fire (ABC)	13.2
14.	Coach (ABC)	12.9
14.	NBC Monday Night Movies (NBC)	12.9
Total U.S. TV households 95,900,000		

1. Sept. 8, 1995–May 22, 1996. Note: Percentages are calculated from average audience viewings, five minutes or longer and two or more telecasts.

Source: Copyright 1996, Nielsen Media Research. Reprinted by permission of Nielsen Media Research.

TOP 15 SYNDICATED TV PROGRAMS, 1995–96 SEASON

Rank	Program	Rating (% U.S.)[1]
1.	Wheel of Fortune	12.5
2.	Jeopardy	10.3
3.	Home Improvement	9.2
4.	Oprah Winfrey Show	8.0
5.	Seinfeld	7.3
6.	ESPN NFL—Regular Season	7.1
7.	National Geographic on Assignment	6.9
8.	Entertainment Tonight	6.7
9.	Star Trek: Deep Space Nine	6.3
9.	Wheel of Fortune (Weekend)	6.3
11.	Buena Vista I	6.2
12.	Simpsons	6.1
13.	Journeys of Hercules	5.9
13.	Inside Edition	5.9
15.	Home Improvement (Weekend)	5.7

1. Sept. 8–May 22, 1996.

Source: Nielsen Syndication Service National TV Ratings. Copyright 1996, Nielsen Media Research. Reprinted by permission of Nielsen Media Research.

PERSONS VIEWING PRIME TIME[1] (in millions)

	Total Persons
Monday	94.5
Tuesday	93.2
Wednesday	85.2
Thursday	88.8
Friday	79.2
Saturday	77.6
Sunday	92.8
Total average	**87.2**

1. Average minute audiences May 1996. Note: Prime time is 8–11 P.M. (EST) except Sun. 7–11 P.M.

Source: Copyright 1996, Nielsen Media Research. Reprinted by permission of Nielsen Media Research.

Exercise 1 Try working with these simple tables (see previous page) found in the *1997 Information Please Almanac*. A **table** is a list of facts and statistics in columns (up and down) and rows (left to right). The information given is usually labeled.

1. After reading the titles, describe what the tables are generally about. ____

   _____

2. What is the source of the information? _____

   Do you feel this information comes from an unbiased source? _____

   What is the ultimate use of this information? _____

   _____

3. How does the prime viewing time for Sundays differ from the one for other days? _____

   _____

4. What percentage of households watch Monday Night Football? _____

5. If you were an advertiser who wanted to sell beer, which show would give you the best audience for your purpose? Why? _____

   _____

   _____

Exercise 2 The organization Consumer Reports publishes findings on the reliability of various cars in the Spring issue of its magazine and summarizes this information in a yearly buying guide. The table found on the next page was taken from the *1996 Buying Guide*. Information given in this table might be helpful to someone interested in buying a car. The table looks at 16 "trouble spots" in Mercury, Mitsubishi, and Nissan vehicles. Study the key at the bottom of the table explaining the circle notations before attempting to answer the questions.

1. Draw the circle that indicates few problems. _____ Draw the circle that indicates many problems. _____

2. Which car has the better reliability record—the Mercury Topaz or the Mercury Sable? _____

3. If you were thinking of buying a friend's 1989 Mercury Sable, what might you want to investigate? _____

   _____

4. Do you see any changes in the Mercury Sable's reliability record over the years? _____ If so, what are these changes? _____

   _____

5. If you were buying either a 1988 Mercury Sable or a 1988 Mercury Tracer, which would you expect to be more reliable? _____

6. Overall, do the Mercury cars or the Mitsubishi cars appear to have the best reliability record? _____

Mitsubishi Galant 4

Mitsubishi Expo LRV

Mitsubishi Expo

Mitsubishi Eclipse Turbo (4WD)

Nissan 240SX

Mitsubishi Pickup 4

Mitsubishi Montero V6

Mitsubishi Mirage

TROUBLE SPOTS

Engine
Cooling
Fuel
Ignition
Auto. trans.
Man. trans.
Clutch
Electrical
A/C
Suspension
Brakes
Exhaust
Body rust
Paint/trim
Integrity
Hardware

Insufficient data

Mercury Tracer

Mercury Sable

Mercury Topaz

Mercury Grand Marquis

Mitsubishi Eclipse (2WD)

Mitsubishi Diamante

Mitsubishi 3000GT (2WD)

Mercury Villager Van

TROUBLE SPOTS

Engine
Cooling
Fuel
Ignition
Auto. trans.
Man. trans.
Clutch
Electrical
A/C
Suspension
Brakes
Exhaust
Body rust
Paint/trim
Integrity
Hardware

Insufficient data

Few — Many — Problems

★ Insufficient data

410

Exercise 3   A graph is a visual aid that shows how things compare at a particular time. Bar graphs use vertical (top to bottom) or horizontal (left to right) bars to show this information. The bar graph below comes from the textbook *Contemporary Nutrition*. Study the graph and then answer the questions that follow.

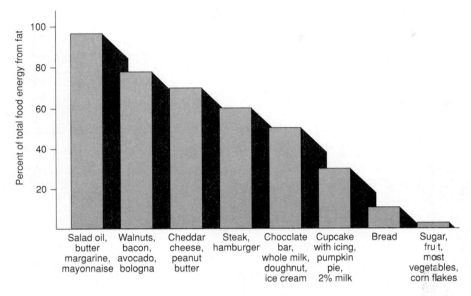

Percent of kcalories as fat in foods. Vegetable oils, butter, margarine, and mayonnaise provide almost all kcalories as fats.

From *Contemporary Nutrition: Issues and Insights* by Gordon M. Wardlaw, Paul M. Insel and Marcia F. Seyler, 1992. Reprinted by permission of The McGraw-Hill Companies

1. The scale on the left-hand side indicates _____ of total food energy from fat.

2. Does the graph actually tell us the number of kcalories in each of these food groups? _____

3. Which food group has the second-lowest percentage of kcalories from fat?

    _____

4. Approximately what percentage of kcalories in your favorite chocolate bar probably comes from fat? _____

5. Does the chart break down calories into different types, such as saturated versus polyunsaturated? _____

As you can see, graphs give only a limited amount of data. Often, as in this case, we would need to read the written material that goes along with the graph to fill in the gaps.

Exercise 4   The next visual aid is sometimes called an organization chart. When membership in a formal group grows beyond 10 or 12 people, the group tends to break into subgroups. Large organizations usually have a very formal bureaucratic structure. Most of those involved in the organization are grouped into a hierarchy, with each person directly responsible to the person above them in the chain of command. The organization chart on page 412 is taken from the *1996–1997 United States Government Manual*, p. 332. This chart shows the chain of command and structure for the Federal Department of Justice—who is responsible to whom.

DEPARTMENT OF JUSTICE

```
                              ATTORNEY GENERAL
                                     |
                             DEPUTY
                          ATTORNEY GENERAL
```

OFFICE OF PUBLIC AFFAIRS
OFFICE OF LEGAL COUNSEL
OFFICE OF POLICY DEVELOPMENT
OFFICE OF LEGISLATIVE AFFAIRS

ASSOCIATE ATTORNEY GENERAL

SOLICITOR GENERAL
OFFICE OF THE SOLICITOR GENERAL

OFFICE OF PROFESSIONAL RESPONSIBILITY
OFFICE OF THE PARDON ATTORNEY
UNITED STATES PAROLE COMMISSION

OFFICE OF THE INSPECTOR GENERAL
OFFICE OF INTELLIGENCE POLICY AND REVIEW
JUSTICE MANAGEMENT DIVISION
EXECUTIVE OFFICE FOR IMMIGRATION REVIEW

CRIMINAL DIVISION
BUREAU OF PRISONS
UNITED STATES MARSHALS SERVICE
U.S. NATIONAL CENTRAL BUREAU—INTERPOL

FEDERAL BUREAU OF INVESTIGATION
DRUG ENFORCEMENT ADMINISTRATION
EXECUTIVE OFFICE FOR UNITED STATES ATTORNEYS
IMMIGRATION AND NATURALIZATION SERVICE

UNITED STATES ATTORNEYS

CIVIL DIVISION
ENVIRONMENT AND NATURAL RESOURCES DIVISION
COMMUNITY RELATIONS SERVICE

CIVIL RIGHTS DIVISION
ANTITRUST DIVISION
TAX DIVISION

COMMUNITY ORIENTED POLICING SERVICES
OFFICE OF INFORMATION AND PRIVACY
FORIEGN CLAIMS SETTLEMENT COMMISSION

OFFICE OF JUSTICE PROGRAMS
EXECUTIVE OFFICE FOR UNITED STATES TRUSTEES

412

1. To whom is the head of the Drug Enforcement Agency (DEA) responsible?

   _____

2. To whom is the head of the Department of Immigration and Naturalization Service responsible? _____

3. To whom is the head of the Civil Rights Division responsible?

   _____

Test-Taking Techniques

The Multiple Choice Test

1. Read directions carefully.

2. Pay attention to oral directions.

3. Look through the entire test, and plan time accordingly.

4. Do not dwell on any question too long. Leave a difficult question blank, go on, and then come back.

5. If in doubt about two answers, go with your first gut-level reaction. Don't change an answer unless you are positive you are making the correct choice. You may only be changing a right answer to a wrong answer. Your time can probably be better used elsewhere on the test.

6. Have you ever become bored halfway through a long test? Most of us have at one point or another. So break the monotony by skipping around or going to the end and working backwards. However, and this is an important warning, if you are working on a Scantron, make sure you are marking your answers in the right places.

7. If you have to read short articles, you could read the ones you know something about first. Remember that all the answers count the same. Reading these articles first may build up your confidence.

8. If you think that you have more knowledge about the material than the author of the article or you think that the author is wrong, go with what the author says, not what you think.

9. Read through all the answers before picking one.

10. If one of your choices is a combination of two or more answers (such as "A and B"), remember that all parts of the answer must be correct (A must be a correct answer and B must also be a correct answer).

11. When in doubt and an answer includes language from the question in it, go with that answer. Also look for clues in the question that may help give away the answer.

12. Look at long answers first, especially if one answer is much longer than the others. A longer answer is more likely to be correct than a shorter answer. Why? It usually takes more words to write a correct answer because it needs to be written carefully. Also, right answers may need qualifying phrases to make them correct. Wrong answers are wrong anyway, so it doesn't matter how they are written.

13. When the question asks you to pick a missing word, use grammar clues such as *a* and *an*. An *a* goes with words beginning with consonants and *an* goes with words beginning with vowels.

14. Eliminate answers with all-inclusive words like *all, everyone, none, always, nobody*. Answers that include such words are quite likely wrong. Usually, the only time answers with such words are correct is when that is exactly what the author said. If there is one exception, the answer will be wrong.

15. When a question asks for the overall main idea of the selection or the best possible title, make sure your answer is broad enough to cover all parts of the selection.

16. Sometimes the last answer will be "all of the above." If you are pretty sure that two of the three answers are correct, but are unsure about the third answer, go with "all of the above."

17. Usually you should answer all of the questions including those you are unsure about. You may get some answers correct by chance. When there are four answers for each question, chances are that random guessing will give you a right answer for one out of every four questions. However, there is an important exception to this guessing rule for standardized tests such as the ACT or SAT, which penalize random guessing.

18. Two questions on the test may be similar. Use the correct answer for one question to help you find the correct answer for the other.

19. Allow at least a minute or two to check over your answer sheet. Is your name on it? Do you need to date it? Have you skipped any questions?

20. If you are putting your answers on a Scantron, make sure that your erasures are good. Scantrons will pick up incomplete erasures.

You can improve your chances for success on a multiple-choice exam by using these techniques. Remember, though, nothing beats studying.

Let's put our knowledge to work and take the following test. Louise Scott from Upper Iowa University in Fayette tells students to examine multiple-choice questions carefully because they may contain clues to the correct answers. She gives them this "nonsense" test to demonstrate her point. You know nothing about what is being tested, but you can answer all the questions correctly by going back to the techniques discussed above. Don't get discouraged. If you get stumped on question 1, go on to question 2. After you complete the test, check the correct answers below.

The Fribbled What?

1. Trassig normally occurs when the
   a. dissels frull.
   b. lups chasses the vom.
   c. belgo lisks easily.
   d. viskal flans, if the viskal is zortil.

2. The fribbled breg will snicker best with an
   a. Mors.
   b. Ignu.
   c. Derst.
   d. Sortar.

3. What probable causes are indicated when tristal doss occurs in a compots?
   a. The sabs foped and the doths tinzed.
   b. The kredges roted with the rots.
   c. Rakogs were not accepted in the sluth.
   d. Polats were thonced in the sluth.

4. The primary purpose of the cluss in frumpaling is to
   a. remove cluss-prangs.
   b. patch tremalls.
   c. lossen cloughs.
   d. repair plumots.

5. Why does the sigla frequently overfesk the trelsum?
   a. All siglas are mellious.
   b. Siglas are always votial.
   c. The trelsum is usually tarious.
   d. No tresla are directly feskable.

6. The snickering function of the ignu is most effectively performed in connection with which one of the following snicker snacks?
   a. Arazma tol.
   b. Fribbled breg.
   c. Groshed stantol.
   d. Frallied stantol.

Essay Tests

How To Improve Your Performance on Essay Tests

Before the Test   There is no substitute for simply knowing all of the course material well. But, that can be a big task, and realistically some parts of the material are probably more important, and more likely to appear on an essay test, than other parts.

One way to give your preparation some focus is to try to think of questions that might appear on the test. Because your teacher will likely be the one who writes the test, ask yourself what questions you think your teacher might ask. Review your class notes and any handouts to determine what the teacher emphasized in the course. What topics did the teacher spend the most time on? What topics did the teacher seem to care the most about?

Keep in mind that an essay question may ask for information on a specific topic or it may be directed at a general understanding of the course material. You need to prepare yourself for both kinds of questions.

Fribbled Answers

1. *d.*   The question uses the word "normally," and this is the only answer containing a qualifying phrase.
2. *b.*   This is the only answer beginning with a vowel. The word "an" at the end of the query phrase is the tip-off.
3. *a.*   The question asked for more than one cause.
4. *a.*   This answer contains the word "cluss," which was used in the question.
5. *c.*   The other answers are all absolutes.
6. *b.*   Fribbled breg was linked with ignu in question 2.

General or "big picture" essay questions often deal with relationships among topics or concepts. A good way to prepare for these questions is to make an outline or map of the course material. Look at your class notes, any handouts, and your textbook, and organize this material into an outline. If your teacher has closely followed a textbook, the book's table of contents should give you a good start on making your outline.

Once you have come up with a list of possible questions, use some of your studying time preparing answers to these questions. You may even want to practice writing out answers.

During the Test   Carefully read the question; you can't expect to write a good answer to a question you don't understand. In fact, you might write a wonderful essay, but if it doesn't answer the question, it will not do you much good. What is the question asking you to do? Does the question use any of the key words discussed below? If so, think about what that key word means.

Once you understand the question, begin thinking about how best to answer it. It's probably not a good idea to start writing immediately. Give yourself some time to think first. What material from the course will the answer involve? What do you remember about this material? At this point, you might want to start making some notes or jottings. If you prepared well for the test, the more you think about this material, the more of it you will remember.

Organizing Your Answer   Once you have recalled the material you need in order to answer the questions, you need to begin thinking about how to organize your answer. Knowing the information goes a long way toward writing a good essay, but how you organize the information also counts. This is especially true for a "big picture" essay question. Your organization will show the teacher how well you understand what is important and what the relationships are among ideas and concepts.

A traditional essay has an introduction, a conclusion, and three paragraphs of development. This does not mean that a good essay cannot have more or less than three paragraphs, but ordinarily an essay that is three paragraphs long will say what needs to be said without saying too much. Usually the three paragraphs of the traditional essay are developed in the same order in which their main ideas are mentioned in the introductory statement.

Example of an introductory statement:

An increase in state financial aid for public education will raise student scores on standardized tests because (1) teacher salaries can be increased, which will attract more-talented people into teaching, (2) more teachers can be hired, which will reduce class size, and (3) school districts will have more money available for learning resources and activities.

So, the first paragraph of this essay would discuss the need for more-talented teachers, and why the hiring of more-talented teachers should lead to an increase in the test scores. The second paragraph would discuss the need for smaller classes and how smaller classes should lead to increased scores. The third paragraph would discuss the need for more learning resources and activities and how improved resources and activities should boost test scores.

Often the secret to writing a good essay is constructing a good introductory statement, because once you have a good introductory statement, the rest of the essay just follows from it. This is one reason it makes sense to do some thinking and organizing before you start to write.

To write a good introductory statement, it sometimes helps to take the question and rearrange it into an introductory statement. For example, assume that the question says the following:

> Discuss whether an increase in state financial aid for public education will raise student scores on standardized tests.

Then you might use one of the following introductory statements:

> An increase in state financial aid for public education will raise student scores on standardized tests because . . .

> or

> An increase in state financial aid for public education will not raise student scores on standardized tests because . . .

Some Practical Pointers

1. Research shows that neatness counts, so write carefully and legibly. Try to avoid messy erasures, crossed-out words, and words written between lines and in the margins. You might want to consider using pens with erasable ink.

2. When a question has more than one part, make sure you answer all parts.

3. Remember that each paragraph should develop only one main idea.

4. Give specific examples to illustrate your points.

5. Answer in complete sentences.

6. Check to see if what you have written answers these questions: who? what? where? when? why? and how?

7. Save some time to proofread your essay for spelling and other errors that are likely to produce a bad impression.

8. If you find you have no time to answer questions at the end of the test, write some notes in summary form. These will often earn you at least partial credit.

9. Make use of your returned test papers. You can learn a lot by reading the instructor's comments and correcting the answers.

Key Words That Often Appear in Essay Questions

Following is a list of key words that often appear in essay questions. If you are going to write a good answer to an essay question that uses one of these terms, you need to know what the term means.

analyze	to break down the subject into parts and discuss each part. You will want to discuss how the parts relate to each other.
comment on	to discuss or explain.
compare	to show differences and similarities, but with the emphasis on similarities.

contrast — to show differences and similarities, but with the emphasis on differences.

criticize — The narrow meaning of *criticize* is to examine something for its weaknesses, limitations, or failings. Does the theory, article, or opinion make sense? If not, why not? In a more-general sense, criticize means to find both strengths and weaknesses. In this sense, the meaning of *criticize* is similar to the meaning of *evaluate*.

define — to state the meaning of a term, theory, or concept. You will want to place the subject in a category and explain what makes it different from other subjects in the category.

describe — to explain what something is or how it appears. What you need to do is draw a picture with words.

diagram — to make a chart, drawing, or graph. You will also want to label the categories or elements, and maybe give a brief explanation.

discuss — to fully go over something. You will want to cover the main points, give different perspectives, and relate strengths and weaknesses.

enumerate — to make a list of main ideas by numbering them.

evaluate — to examine for strengths and weaknesses. You will need to give specific evidence and may wish to cite authorities to support your position.

explain — to make clear, to give reasons. An explanation often involves showing cause-and-effect relationships or steps.

illustrate — to use a diagram, chart, or figure, or specific examples to further explain something.

interpret — to indicate what something means. A question that asks for an *interpretation* usually wants you to state what something means to you. What are your beliefs or feelings about the meaning of the material? Be sure to back up your position with specific examples and details.

justify — to give reasons in support of a conclusion, theory, or opinion.

list — to put down your points one by one. You may want to number each of the points in your list.

outline — to organize information into an outline, using headings and subheadings. Your outline should reflect the main ideas and supporting details.

prove — to demonstrate that something is true by means of factual evidence or logical reasoning.

relate — to discuss how two or more conclusions, theories, or opinions affect each other. Explain how one causes, limits, or develops the other.

review — usually means to summarize, but a narrower meaning of it is to analyze critically.

summarize   to put down the main points, to state briefly the key princi-
             ples, facts, or ideas while avoiding details and personal
             comments.

trace   to follow the course of development of something in a
             chronological or logical sequence. You will want to discuss
             each stage of development from the beginning to the end.

Test-Taking Skills Exercise   Read the explanations below. In the blank, write
a term that the instructor might use when posing the question to the students in
the class.

1. In class, the instructor has discussed the contributions of Auguste Comte,
    Herbert Spencer, and Max Weber to the field of sociology. On the essay
    exam, he wants the students to briefly go over the contribution of each of
    these persons while avoiding their own personal comments. What term
    will he use for this question?

    _____

2. In a child development class, the instructor has discussed the development
    of language from birth to 36 months. She now wants the students to present
    the course of language acquisition in chronological sequence. What term
    should she use?

    _____

3. In an art history class, the instructor wants the students to show the
    difference between engraving, drypoint, and etching. Which term would
    be used in the question?

    _____

4. In an American history class, the professor has discussed the Manhattan
    Project, which developed the atomic bomb during World War II. He now
    wants the students to examine the project for its weaknesses. What term
    will be used in the essay question?

    _____

5. In a biology class, the professor has explained the term "cloning." On a
    quiz, she wants to make sure her students understand the meaning of the
    concept. What term would she use in her question?

    _____

6. In an economics class, the professor wants the students to graph the
    1990–1991 recession, showing the rise and fall of the unemployment rate
    and consumer spending. What term should she use on her exam?

    _____

7. In a geography class, the teacher wants the students to make clear how
    pollution caused harm to the Costa Rican rain forest. What term will
    he use?

    _____

8. In a psychology class, the instructor wants her students to describe the ways in which long-term memory and short-term memory are alike and the ways in which they are different. What term will she use?

   _____

9. In a reading class, the teacher wants the students to write down the steps of SQ3R one by one, numbering each. What term will be used in her question?

   _____

ASSIGNMENTS

MONDAY

TUESDAY

WEDNESDAY

THURSDAY

FRIDAY

OTHER ASSIGNMENTS, TESTS, ETC.

MONTH_____

Sunday	Monday	Tuesday	Wednesday	Thursday	Friday	Saturday